GALLERY OF

OF

Best

COVER LETTERS

*A Collection of Quality Cover Letters
by Professional Resume Writers*

THIRD EDITION

DAVID F. NOBLE, Ph.D.

JIST Works
America's Career Publisher

Gallery of Best Cover Letters

A Collection of Quality Cover Letters by Professional Resume Writers

Third Edition

© 2007 by David F. Noble

Published by JIST Works, an imprint of JIST Publishing, Inc.
8902 Otis Avenue
Indianapolis, IN 46216-1033
Phone: 1-800-648-JIST   Fax: 1-800-JIST-FAX   E-mail: info@jist.com

Visit our Web site at **www.jist.com** for information on JIST, free job search tips, book chapters, and ordering instructions for our many products!

Other books by David F. Noble:

Gallery of Best Resumes
Gallery of Best Resumes for People Without a Four-Year Degree

See the back of this book for additional JIST titles and ordering information. Quantity discounts are available for JIST books. Have future editions of JIST books automatically delivered to you on publication through our convenient standing order program. Please call our Sales Department at 1-800-648-5478 for a free catalog and more information.

Trade Product Manager: Lori Cates Hand
Project Editor: Jill Mazurczyk
Proofreader: Jeanne Clark
Interior Designer: Debbie Berman
Page Layout: Toi Davis
Cover Designer: Amy Peppler Adams
Cover Photo: C Squared Studios/Photodisc Green/Getty Images
Indexer: Ginny Noble

Printed in the United States of America.

12 11 10 09 08 07   9 8 7 6 5 4 3 2 1

Library of Congress Cataloging-in-Publication data

Noble, David F. (David Franklin), 1935-
  Gallery of best cover letters : a collection of quality cover letters by professional resume writers / David F. Noble. -- 3rd ed.
      p. cm.
  Includes index.
  ISBN-13: 978-1-59357-425-3 (alk. paper)
1. Cover letters. I. Title.
  HF5383.N618 2007
  650.14'2--dc22

                        2007011235

We have been careful to provide accurate information in this book, but it is possible that errors and omissions have been introduced. Please consider this in making any career plans or other important decisions. Trust your own judgment above all else and in all things.

Trademarks: All brand names and product names used in this book are trade names, service marks, trademarks, or registered trademarks of their respective owners.

ISBN 978-1-59357-425-3

Contents

This useful "idea book" of best cover letters has three parts: Best Cover Letter Tips; a Gallery of 311 cover letters; and an Exhibit of 23 resumes, together with tips for improving resumes. These cover letters and resumes were written by 72 professional writers. With this book, you not only have a treasury of quality cover letters and resumes, but you'll also learn how to view them as superior models for your own cover letters and resumes.

This book is for *job searchers* who are applying for new positions, *career changers* who are looking for professional roles with other employers, *job changers* who are proactively climbing the corporate ladder, *graduate students* who are applying for higher levels of employment, and *new university graduates* who are seeking entry-level positions. The book is also for experienced workers who are scaling down their work, military personnel who are returning to civilian life, and women who are returning to the workforce after raising children. Because of the wealth and variety of quality cover letters in this new Gallery, this book is for *any job searcher* who wants examples of top-quality documents to create an outstanding cover letter for himself or herself.

This collection of professionally written cover letters shows you how to present yourself effectively through a cover letter to a prospective employer so that you can be more competitive as a job applicant.

Tips for Polishing Cover Letters........................13

A quality resume can make a great impression, but it can be ruined quickly by a poorly written cover letter. This section shows you how to eliminate common errors in cover letters. It amounts to a *crash writing course* that you won't find in any other job search book. After you read the following sections, you will be better able to write and polish any letters you create for your job search.

Part 2: The Gallery of Best Cover Letters..25

This Gallery has 34 categories of professional cover letters for a wide variety of occupations. Regardless of your career or occupation, you should check out all the letters throughout the Gallery for design tips, ways to express ideas, and impressive formats. At the bottom of each cover letter are comments that call your attention to noteworthy features or solutions to problems.

Part 3: Best Resume Tips

Best Resume Tips at a Glance

Dedication

*In memory of my mother,
Christena Brightwell Noble,
the letter writer*

Acknowledgments

This third edition of *Gallery of Best Cover Letters* was possible because of all the cover letter and resume submissions of the writers featured in this book. For their names, see the List of Contributors at the back of the book. When I compiled the first Gallery (*Gallery of Best Resumes,* JIST Works, Inc., 1994), I first became acquainted with professional resume writers only as names on a mailing list from the Professional Association of Résumé Writers, which I had joined. After the publication of that first Gallery and during the preparation of its early sequels (*Gallery of Best Resumes for Two-Year Degree Graduates,* JIST, 1996; *Professional Resumes for Executives, Managers, and Other Administrators,* JIST, 1998; and *Professional Resumes for Tax and Accounting Occupations,* CCH Incorporated and JIST, 1999), I joined a second organization—the National Résumé Writers' Association (NRWA)—and met many of the writers at annual meetings of their respective organizations.

For the third edition of the *Gallery of Best Resumes,* the second edition of the *Gallery of Best Cover Letters,* and the third edition of the *Gallery of Best Resumes for People Without a Four-Year Degree* (all published by JIST in 2004), I rejoined the Professional Association of Résumé Writers & Career Coaches and the National Résumé Writers' Association and joined for the first time Career Masters Institute. During work on these new editions, I learned of a fourth organization, the Professional Résumé Writing and Research Association, and received submissions from members of this group as well. In those new editions I was happy to showcase the latest work of members of all four of those professional organizations.

Currently I'm in the process of providing a new cycle of editions of those three books. The fourth edition of the *Gallery of Best Resumes* was completed in the spring of 2006, this third edition of the *Gallery of Best Cover Letters* will be a 2007 title, and the *Gallery of Best Resumes for People Without a Four-Year Degree* promises a new edition in the coming year. Professional writers from all four organizations have contributed to the first two of these three new titles. Most likely, the works of such contributors will appear in the upcoming edition of the third title. A difference is that the Professional Résumé Writing and Research Association is now named Career Directors International (CDI).

Originally, this cover letter book was possible also because of Mike Farr and Bob Grilliot of JIST Works. When I wrote the *Gallery of Best Resumes,* a *Gallery of Best Cover Letters* was the first title I thought of next, but other titles intervened. Bob Grilliot was the one who expressed a market need for the first edition of this book on cover letters, and Mike Farr approved it. I am grateful to JIST for showing interest in this third edition.

Continuing thanks to Lori Cates Hand for her guidance at JIST throughout this project. Special thanks are directed once again to my wife, Ginny, who managed and performed at home all of the many tasks necessary for creating yet another Gallery edition.

Introduction

Like the earlier Galleries in this series, *Gallery of Best Cover Letters* is a collection of quality cover letters from professional resume writers, each with individual views about cover letter writing. Unlike many cover letter books whose selections "look the same," this book contains cover letters that look different because they are *real* cover letters prepared by different professionals for actual job searchers throughout the country. (Certain information in the cover letters and companion resumes has been fictionalized by the writers to protect, where necessary, each client's privacy.) Even when several cover letters from the same writer appear in the book, most of these letters are different because the writer has customized each letter according to the background information and career goals of the client for whom the related resume was prepared.

Ninety-five of the 311 cover letters in this third edition are new to give you some of the latest examples of cover letters for contemporary job seekers. If you want to know what kinds of cover letters are helping job searchers find positions in today's job market under current economic conditions, this new edition will give you answers. A number of the captions at the bottom of each cover letter page indicate how a particular applicant was successful in focusing a job search, securing an interview, or eventually getting the targeted job.

Why a Gallery of Best Cover Letters?

One reason is that error-free cover letters are more difficult to write than most people imagine. When you put together a resume, you can work with just phrases, clauses, and lists. The common writing dangers are misspellings, errors with capital letters, wordy phrases, and faulty parallelism (for example, not having certain words in a series or list grammatically parallel). When you write a cover letter, however, you are somewhat obligated to write sentences that hang together in several paragraphs in a meaningful sequence. To write sentences and paragraphs is to enter a minefield of all of the potential errors and stylistic weaknesses that an individual with good communication skills can make. And many people who try to write a cover letter do make such errors—often unknowingly.

This *Gallery of Best Cover Letters* shows you, example by example, how to create cover letters that are free of errors and writing weaknesses that could ruin your chances for an interview. By studying the sentences and paragraphs in these letters, you can compare your writing with what you see and find new ways to express what you want to say to win that interview.

Another reason for having a *Gallery of Best Cover Letters* is that many of the cover letters in cover letter books on bookstore shelves are—there's no other way to say it truthfully—models of bad writing. Often they exhibit not just a stylistic weakness here and there, but grammatical errors that would sabotage your job search if you used those passages verbatim in your own cover letters. To browse through the letters in this book is to walk through a minefield free of mines.

Why Cover Letters by Professional Resume Writers?

Instead of assuming that "one cover letter style fits all," the writers featured in this book believe that a client's past experiences and next job target should determine the type, design, and content of each resume and its related cover letter. The writers interacted with clients to fashion resumes that seemed best for each client's situation at the time and to create one or more cover letters for the job(s) the clients were seeking.

This book features resumes from writers who share several important qualities: good listening skills, a sense of what details are appropriate for a particular resume and its cover letter, and flexibility in selecting and arranging the resume's sections and the cover letter's paragraphs. By "hearing between" a client's statements, the perceptive resume writer can detect what kind of job the client really wants. The writer then chooses the information that will best represent the client for the job being sought. Finally, the writer decides on the best arrangement of the information for that job. With this book, you can learn from these professional writers how to shape and improve your own job search documents. You can create such documents yourself, or, if you want, you can contact a professional writer who, for a fee, might create a custom resume and cover letter for you. See the Appendix, "List of Contributors," for contact information for the professional writers whose works are featured in this book.

Almost all of the writers of the cover letters in this Gallery are members of one or more of these organizations: Career Directors International (CDI), Career Masters Institute (CMI), the National Résumé Writers' Association (NRWA), and the Professional Association of Résumé Writers & Career Coaches (PARW/CC). Many of the writers are certified. For example, those who have CPRW certification, for Certified Professional Résumé Writer (again, see the Appendix, "List of Contributors"), received this designation from PARW/CC after they studied specified course materials and demonstrated proficiency in an examination. Those who have NCRW certification, for National Certified Résumé Writer, received this designation from NRWA after a different course of study and a different examination. A few contributors are not currently members of any organization but are past members of one or more professional organizations.

How This Book Is Organized

Part 1, "Best Cover Letter Tips," contains a discussion of some myths about cover letters, plus strategies for writing cover letters and tips for polishing them. Some of the advice offered here applies also to writing resumes.

Part 2 is the Gallery itself, containing 311 cover letters, which are grouped according to 34 occupational categories (for these, see the Table of Contents). Within each category, the cover letters are arranged alphabetically by occupational title. Note that the occupational title is usually, but not always, that of the *target position* the applicant is seeking, not the applicant's current or recent title. In resumes, job titles have to do with the individual's present and past positions. Cover letters, however, are concerned with a target position. You should keep this fundamental difference in mind as you use this book. (If the target position is not stated clearly in a cover letter, the applicant's current or most recent job is used to determine the occupational category of that letter.)

Even though most of the cover letters were written with a target position in mind, you can learn much by reading any or all of them. That is, to get the most from this book about writing cover letters, you should look at all of the cover letters in this collection and not just at those related to your particular profession or position of interest. All of the cover letters form a hunting ground for ideas that may prove useful to you for developing your own cover letters.

In the *Gallery of Best Cover Letters,* you will notice a few letters displayed in .txt format. This format is appropriate for the electronic submission of letters or resumes, which many employers now encourage because of timeliness and expediency in processing. Any of the letters in this book can be prepared for electronic transfer. If you intend to apply online for positions, be sure you follow the submission guidelines posted by the employer. If they are not clearly explained, phone or e-mail the company to inquire. You don't want to be disqualified for a job that suits you well because you did not follow the steps for successful submission.

Part 3 presents some resume-writing strategies, design and layout tips, and resume-writing style tips for making resumes visually impressive. These tips contain references to resumes in an Exhibit of 23 resumes at the end of Part 3. These references are to resumes that illustrate a strategy or a tip, but the references are not exhaustive. If you browse through this Exhibit, you may see other resumes that exhibit the same strategy or tip.

Even though the Exhibit contains only 23 resumes, it offers a wide range of resumes with features you can use in creating and improving your own resumes. Notice the plural. An important premise of an active job search is that you will not have just one "perfect" resume for all potential employers, but different versions of your resume for different interviews. The Exhibit of resumes, like the Gallery of cover letters, is therefore not a showroom where you say, "I'll take that one." It is a valuable resource of design ideas, expressions, and organizational patterns that can help make your own resume a "best resume" for your next interview.

The Appendix is the "List of Contributors," which contains the names, addresses, phone numbers, and other information of 73 professional resume writers from Australia, Canada, and the United States who contributed cover letters and resumes for this book. The list is arranged alphabetically by country, state or province, and city. Although most of these resume writers work with local clients, many of the writers work with clients by phone, e-mail, and the Internet.

You can use the Occupation Index to look up cover letters by the job being sought. This index, however, should not replace careful examination of all of the cover letters. Many cover letters for some other occupation may have features that are adaptable to your own occupation. Limiting your search to the Occupational Index may cause you to miss some valuable examples.

Who This Book Is For

Anyone who wants ideas for creating or improving a cover letter can benefit from this book. It is especially useful for active job seekers—those who understand the difference between active and passive job searching. A *passive* job seeker waits until jobs are advertised and then mails copies of the same resume, along with a standard cover letter, to a number of ads. An *active* job seeker believes that both the resume and the cover letter should be modified for a specific job target *after* having talked in person or by phone to a prospective interviewer *before* a job is announced. To schedule such an interview is to penetrate the "hidden job market." Active job seekers can find in the Exhibit's focused resumes a wealth of strategies for targeting a resume for a particular interview. The section "How to Use the Gallery" at the beginning of Part 2 shows you how to use the Gallery for improving your cover letters.

What This Book Can Do for You

Besides providing you with a treasury of quality cover letters and companion resumes whose features you can use in your own letters and resumes, this book can help transform your thinking about these job search documents. If you think that there is one "best" way to create a cover letter or resume, this book will help you learn how to design resumes and cover letters that are *best for you* as you try to get an interview with a particular person for a specific job.

1
P·A·R·T

Best Cover Letter Tips

Best Cover Letter Tips at a Glance

Best Cover Letter Tips

In an active job search, your cover letter and resume should complement one another. Both are tailored to a particular reader you have contacted or to a specific job target. To help you create the "best" cover letters for your resumes, this part of the book debunks some common myths about cover letters and presents tips for polishing the letters you write.

Myths About Cover Letters

1. **Resumes and cover letters are two separate documents that have little relation to each other.** Your resume and cover letter should work together in presenting you effectively to a prospective employer. The cover letter should draw attention to the most important information in the resume, the information you want the reader to be certain to see.

2. **The main purpose of the cover letter is to establish a friendly rapport with the reader.** Resumes show that you *can* do the work required. The main purpose of cover letters is to express that you *want* to do the work required. But it doesn't hurt to display enthusiasm in your resumes and refer to your abilities in your cover letters. The cover letter should demonstrate qualities and worker traits you want the prospective employee to see, such as good communication skills, motivation, clear thinking, good sense, thoughtfulness, interest in others, neatness, and so on.

3. **You can use the same cover letter for each reader of your resume.** Modify your cover letter for each reader so that it sounds fresh rather than canned. Chances are that in an active job search, you have already talked with the person who will interview you. Your cover letter should reflect that conversation and build on it.

4. **In a cover letter, you should mention any negative things about your life experience, work experience, health, or education in order to prepare the reader in advance of an interview.** This is not the purpose of the cover letter. You might bring up these topics in the first or second interview, but only after the interviewer has shown interest in you or offered you a job. Even then, if you feel that you must mention something negative about your past, present it in a positive way, perhaps by saying how that experience has strengthened your resolve to work hard at any new job.

5. **A resume is more important than its cover letter.** In a way, the cover letter can be more important. The cover letter is usually the first document a prospective employer sees. The first impression is often the most important one. If your cover letter has an embarrassing error in it, the chances are good that the reader may not bother to read your resume or may read it with less interest.

6.   **An error in a cover letter is not important.** The cost of a cover letter might be as much as a third to a half of a million dollars—even more—if you figure the amount of income and benefits you don't receive over, say, a 10-year period for a job you don't get because of the error that screened you out.

7.   **To make certain that your cover letter has no errors, you should proofread it or—better—ask a friend to "proof" it.** Trying to proofread your own cover letter is risky, even if you are good at grammar and writing. Once a document is printed, it has an aura about it that may make it seem better written than it is. For this reason, you are likely to miss typos or other kinds of errors.

   Relying on someone else is risky, too. If your friend is not good at grammar and writing, that person may not see any mistakes, either. Try to find a proofreader, a professional editor, an English teacher, a professional writer, or an experienced secretary who can point out any errors you may have missed.

8.   **After someone has proofread your letter, you can make a few changes to it and not have it looked at again.** More errors creep into a document this way than you would think possible. The reason is that such changes are often done hastily, and haste can waste an error-free document. If you make *any* change to a document, ask someone to proofread it a final time just to make sure that you haven't introduced an error during the last stage of composition.

9.   **It doesn't take long to write a cover letter.** You should allow plenty of time to write and revise…and revise…a cover letter to get it just right for a particular reader. Most people think that writing is 90 percent of the task of creating a cover letter, and revision is 10 percent. It's really the other way around: writing is closer to 10 percent of the task, and revision is 90 percent. That is true if you really care about the cover letter and want it to work hard for you.

10.   **It doesn't take long to print the cover letter.** To get the output of a printer looking just right, you may need to print the letter a number of times. Watch for extra spaces between words and sentences; unwanted spaces are usually easier to see in the printed letter than on-screen (if you are using word processing). Make sure your text is aligned correctly, such as indenting your bullets consistently or lining up all your text flush left. Finally, be sure that you leave enough vertical space for your signature between the complimentary close and your typed name.

Tips for Writing Cover Letters

To write well, you need to know why you are writing, the reader(s) to whom you are writing, what you want to say, how you want to organize what you say, and how you want to say it. Similarly, to write a good cover letter, you should clearly know its purpose, audience, content, organization, and style. The following tips, or strategies, should help you consider these aspects of cover letter writing. Consider using some of these strategies to ensure that your letters are impressive, even outstanding—and thus get the attention you deserve.

Purpose Strategies

1. **Make it clear in your letter that you really want the job.** See Cover Letters 15, 16, 161, and 276. An employer doesn't want to know that you just want a job. An employer wants to know that you *really* want a particular job. If you display a ho-hum attitude in a letter, the chances are that you will receive a ho-hum response, which usually means rejection.

2. **Consider putting a subject line near the beginning of the letter to indicate the target position you are seeking.** See Cover Letters 5, 42, 48, 54, 65, 69, 70, 77, 90, 99, 104, 106, 112, 121, 124, 129, 131, 139, 166, 168, 173, 175, 178, 188, 204, 213, 219, 241, 242, 251, 256, 258, 262, 265, 267, 275, 276, 279, 296, 299, 300, and 307.

Audience Strategies

3. **Make certain that the letter is addressed to a specific person and that you use this person's name in the salutation.** Avoid using such general salutations as Dear Sir or Madam, To Whom It May Concern, Dear Administrator, Dear Prospective Employer, or Dear Committee. (To ensure anonymity, however, some of the resume writers who have provided sample cover letters for this book have used general salutations. In the actual letters, these would be replaced with specific names.) In an active job search, you should do everything possible to send your cover letter and resume to a particular individual, preferably someone you've already talked with in person or by phone and with whom you have arranged an interview. If you have not been able to make a personal contact, at least do everything possible to find out the name of the person who will read your letter and resume, and then address the letter to that person.

4. **Don't let your opening statement or a sentence in your first paragraph give the reader a chance to think "No" and read no further.**

   > **Example:** "I am hoping that you are looking for a new auditor."

   > *The reader can think "I'm not" and stop reading.*

   > **Example:** "If you think your auditor should be as good at building teamwork as he is at building reports, we should talk."

   > *The reader can't disagree with this reasoning and will probably read further.*

5. **Play down experience that may threaten a prospective employer.** A senior applicant with much experience may have more skills, expertise, and administrative savvy than the hiring employer. Should the employer feel threatened by this disparity, it may be better to tone down some skills and expertise than to display all of one's strengths without restraint.

6. **Target your cover letter by researching the prospective company and showing in the letter that you know important information about that company.** See Cover Letters 25, 36, 253, and 278. Complimenting the employer in the first sentence is a nice touch in Cover Letter 56.

7. **For individuals leaving the military, avoid using military terms that may be unfamiliar to civilians.** Feel free, however, to play up military

responsibilities and achievements that a potential employer will understand and appreciate. See Cover Letters 124 and 197.

8. **If you don't want your present employer to know about your job search, explain clearly the need for confidentiality.** See Cover Letters 205 and 239.

9. **Toward the end of the cover letter, consider repeating the recipient's name to convey friendliness and to provide a personal touch.** See Cover Letters 47, 52, 169, 222, and 308.

Content Strategies

10. **If you are replying to an ad without a person's name and have no way to learn it, consider omitting the salutation and varying the subject line.** See Cover Letters 6 and 167.

11. **When you are short on professional work experience to qualify for a position, consider related voluntary experiences or an internship that may help you qualify.** See Cover Letters 280 and 290.

12. **If you are responding to a job that has been posted on an online database, include the reference number, if one has been provided.** See Cover Letter 188.

13. **Numbers that quantify accomplishments in dollar amounts or percentages are impressive.** See Cover Letters 1, 19, 23, 65, 72, 79, 134, 160, 178, 181, 192, 209, 226, 237, 240, 251, 257, 264, 272, and 302. Numbers in the opening sentence can be especially eye-catching. See Cover Letter 137.

14. **If you speak two or more languages fluently, say so in your cover letter.** Being bilingual is an important asset in today's job market. See Cover Letters 177, 212, and 288.

15. **Be sure to mention how your real-world experience in an unrelated field has helped qualify you for the current job target.** See Cover Letters 40, 41, 49, 252, 285, and 306. Likewise, if you are returning to a field, explain how your intervening job or additional education is relevant. See Cover Letters 151, 152, and 154.

16. **If you are responding to an ad placed in a newspaper, be sure to include the date of the ad.** See Cover Letters 93, 168, 214, 221, and 263.

17. **If you have been downsized and don't want to mention it in your cover letter, consider including the information but "downsizing" its impact by focusing instead on your strengths, abilities, and experiences.** See Cover Letter 182.

18. **Speak positively about a return to the workplace from retirement.** See Cover Letter 295.

Resume Connections

19. **If the intended reader of your resume suggested that you send it, or if you have recently spoken with the person, say this in the first sentence**

of the cover letter. Indicating that the resume was requested helps to get your resume past any "gatekeeper"—the person who opens the mail and makes preliminary routing decisions—and into the hands of the appropriate reader. See Cover Letters 58, 105, 199, 207, and 266.

20. **Similarly, if a third party has suggested that you submit your resume to the reader, mention that at or near the beginning of your cover letter.** See Cover Letters 28, 64, 86, 157, 185, 194, 201, 208, 212, 231, 253, and 286. Even mentioning the third party near the end of the letter may be beneficial. See Cover Letter 82.

21. **Include important information in your cover letter for which there is no room in the resume.** See Cover Letter 47, which describes the honor of being selected by National Geographic to participate in a summer institute. In Cover Letter 157, a candidate for criminal investigation links his survival skills to growing up in a tough neighborhood.

22. **Think of the cover letter as a hook for the resume.** A cover letter is not an end in itself but a means for getting the reader to read the resume. The letter might refer specifically to the most important part of the resume—the part that you want the reader to see for sure. See Cover Letters 24, which contains a boxed sentence referring to examples that are highlighted with borders in the resume, and 99. See also Cover Letter 102, which summarizes in a paragraph the candidate's experience with one company and thus echoes the corresponding information in the accompanying resume.

23. **Create a .txt or .pdf version of your cover letter and resume so that you can customize them as needed and e-mail them in response to online ads or post them to online job databases.** See Cover Letters 3, 26, 102, 271, and 305.

Testimonials

24. **Consider using one or more testimonials in a cover letter.** A testimonial is a quotation from a former or current boss, a co-worker, or someone else who knows the quality of your work or the strength of your character. Testimonials can be effective in setting your letter or resume apart from other "stock" submissions. If you use testimonials in your cover letters or resumes, be sure to get permission from the sources. See Cover Letters 1, 55, 82, 103, 125, 162, 229, 234, and 301.

Anecdotes

25. **If you have an impressive success story to tell about previous work experience, consider telling the story in your cover letter.** See Cover Letter 33. Similarly, Cover Letter 273 contains a humorous but fictitious story that illustrates the value of the candidate's expertise.

Follow-Up Plans

26. **At the end of the letter, consider keeping control of the follow-up by indicating that you will phone later.** See Cover Letters 11, 25, 27, 36, 44,

71, 77, 94, 112, 113, 127, 133, 138, 150, 175, 177, 181, 184, 186, 192, 220, 230, 233, 241, 247, 250, 252, 256, 264, 265, 266, 282, 286, 300, and 301.

27. **If you think that calling the prospective employer seems pushy, you can soften the tone of the statement about calling by asking permission.** See, for example, Cover Letters 63, 234, 243, 244, and 258.

Organization Strategies

28. **Consider presenting important information in two corresponding columns: the employer's needs (or requirements) and your qualifications.** See Cover Letters 38, 55, 58, 80, 81, 130, 152, 169, 187, 188, 212, 261, 262, 268, and 287. Compare these with Cover Letter 110.

29. **Try a change in format for a change of pace.** See Cover Letters 90, 125, 234, 264, and 269.

Style Strategies

Tone

30. **Try not to sound desperate, even a little bit.** The following examples may seem extreme, but try to avoid using any similar statements in your letter:

    "I'll take anything you have to offer."

    "It makes no difference what kind of job you have."

    "I can start immediately."

    "I am available for employment right away."

    "When's the first paycheck?"

31. **It's okay to be enthusiastic in a cover letter.** See Cover Letters 22, 48, 103, 212, 242, 255, and 256.

32. **Consider beginning or ending the letter with a quotation that sets the tone and provides insight for understanding your work, character, attitude, outlook, or whatever else you want to convey.** See Cover Letters 7, 19, 41, 51, 54, 101, 131, and 301.

Persuasiveness

33. **Consider making your cover letter not only informative but also persuasive.** See Cover Letters 17, 21, 46, 161, 243, and 244.

34. **Strive to make your cover letter hard to ignore.** Your task is easier, of course, if you are a great catch for any company. See Cover Letters 21, 100, 170, and 243.

35. **To grab attention, try making your first sentence a bold assertion or question.** See Cover Letters 1, 17, 21, 33, 77, 100, 120, 186, and 243. Cover Letter 293 begins with an excerpt from the mission statement of the Boys and Girls Clubs of America.

Font and Text Enhancement

36. **Consider using a combination of bullets and boldfacing to call attention to information you think the reader must see.** See Cover Letters 15, 23, 32, 57, 67, 79, 84, 100, 101, 119, 123, 124, 125, 128, 131, 142, 144, 158, 159, 162, 171, 173, 175, 177, 178, 179, 204, 210, 234, 242, 262, 268, 269, 274, 284, 301, and 307. It's hard to keep your eyes away from information that is bulleted and bold.

37. **For a change, consider putting key points in italic.** See Cover Letters 1, 73, 211, and 237.

38. **Consider using decorative bullets that relate to the kind of job you are seeking.** See the airplane bullets in Cover Letter 22.

39. **To catch the reader's attention, consider inserting a graphic that relates to the job you are seeking or that echoes a graphic appearing in your resume.** To add a bit of humor, a cartoon character is used in Cover Letter 212. A whimsical cartoon is included at the bottom of Cover Letter 236.

40. **To help the reader see your area of expertise, put a banner at the top of your letter.** See Cover Letters 89, 136, 137, 270, and 299. Think of other ways to make information visually stand out. Cover Letter 217 begins with three words in boldface. Cover Letter 232 uses a box and a second color (not shown) to explain what the candidate can do for the employer.

Language

41. **Try to make each paragraph fresh and free of well-worn expressions commonly found in cover letters.** See, for example, Cover Letters 46, 48, 170, and 218.

Tips for Polishing Cover Letters

You might spend several days working on your resume, getting it "just right" and free of errors. But if you send it with a cover letter that is written quickly and contains even one conspicuous error, all of your good effort may be wasted.

You can prevent this kind of tragedy by polishing your cover letter so that it is free of all errors. The following tips can help you avoid or eliminate common errors in cover letters. By becoming aware of these kinds of errors and knowing how to fix them, you can be more confident about the cover letters you send with your resumes.

Word-Processing Tips

1.   **Adjust the margins for a short letter.** If your cover letter is 300 words or longer, use left, right, top, and bottom margins of one inch. If the letter is shorter, you should increase the width of the margins. How much to increase them is a matter of personal taste. One way to take care of the width of the top and bottom margins is to center a shorter letter vertically on the page. A maximum width for a short cover letter of 100 words or fewer might be two-inch left and right margins. You might decrease the width of the left and right margins by two-tenths of an inch for every 50 words you add.

2.   **If you write your letter with word-processing or desktop-publishing software, use left-justification to ensure that the lines of text are readable and have fixed spacing between words.** The letter will have a "ragged" look along the right margin, but the words will be evenly spaced horizontally. Be wary of using full justification in an attempt to give a letter a printed look. You can make your letter look worse by giving it some extra-wide spaces between words. Resume writers who are experienced with certain typesetting procedures—such as "kerning," "tracking," and hyphenating words at the end of some lines—can sometimes use full justification effectively for variety in their documents. Note that if you use kerning and tight tracking to fit more words on a line, extra-narrow spaces can look unappealing as well.

Using Pronouns Correctly

3.   **Use *I* and *My* sparingly.** When most of the sentences in a cover letter begin with *I* or *My*, the writer may appear self-absorbed, self-centered, or egotistical. If the reader is turned off by this kind of impression (even if it's false), you could be screened out as someone who is not a team player without ever having an interview. Of course, you will need to use these first-person pronouns some of the time because most of the information you put in your cover letter will be personal. As a compromise, try to avoid using *I* and *My* at the beginning of most of the sentences and paragraphs.

     One strategy is to make some of your sentences "you-centered," where "you" means the reader. Sentences that begin with "You" or "Your" are friendlier than those that always begin with "I" and "My." Avoid referring to yourself in the third person, as in "this writer" or "this applicant." You avoid using "I," but the temperature of the letter drops considerably. Avoid also passive verbs (see upcoming Tip 8). They may help you avoid "I" at the beginning of a sentence, but the tempo of your letter slows down, and your language becomes indirect.

4.   **Refer to a business, company, corporation, or organization as "it" rather than "they."** Members of the Board may be referred to as "they," but a company is a singular subject that requires a singular verb. Note this example:

     New Products, Inc., was established in 1980. It grossed more than a million dollars in sales during its first year.

5.   **If you start a sentence with *This*, be sure that what *This* refers to is clear.** If the reference is not clear, insert some word or phrase to clarify what *This* means. Compare the following examples:

My revised application for the new position will arrive by noon on Friday. *This* should be acceptable to you.

My revised application for the new position will arrive by noon on Friday. *This revision* should be acceptable to you.

In the first example, a reader of the second sentence won't know what *This* refers to. Friday? Noon on Friday? The position? The revised application for the new position? The insertion of *revision* after *This* in the second sentence of the second example, however, tells the reader that *This* refers to the revised application.

6. **Use *as follows* after a singular subject.** Literally, *as follows* means *as it follows,* so the phrase is illogical after a plural subject. Compare the following lines:

Incorrect:	My plans for the day of the interview are as follows:
Fixed:	My plans for the day of the interview are these:
Correct:	My plan for the day of the interview is as follows:
Better:	Here is my plan for the day of the interview:

In the second set, the improved version avoids a hidden reference problem—the possible association of the silent "it" with *interview.* Whenever you want to use *as follows,* check to see whether the subject that precedes *as follows* is plural. If it is, don't use this phrase.

Using Verb Forms Correctly

7. **Make certain that subjects and verbs agree in number.** Plural subjects require plural forms of verbs. Singular subjects require singular verb forms. Most writers know these things, but problems arise when subject and verb agreement gets tricky. Compare the following lines:

Incorrect:	My education and experience has prepared me…
Correct:	My education and experience have prepared me…
Incorrect:	Making plans plus scheduling conferences were…
Correct:	Making plans plus scheduling conferences was…

In the first set, *education* and *experience* are two things (you can have one without the other) and require a plural verb. A hasty writer might lump them together and use a singular verb. When you reread what you have written, look out for this kind of improper agreement between a plural subject and a singular verb.

In the second set, *making plans* is the subject. It is singular, so the verb must be singular. The misleading part of this sentence is the phrase *plus scheduling conferences*. It may seem to make the subject plural, but it doesn't. Phrases that begin with such words as *plus, together with, in addition to, along with,* and *as well as* usually don't make a singular subject plural.

8.   **Whenever possible, use active forms of verbs rather than passive forms.** Compare these lines:

Passive:	My report will be sent by my assistant tomorrow.
Active:	My assistant will send my report tomorrow.
Passive:	Your interest is appreciated.
Active:	I appreciate your interest.
Passive:	Your letter was received yesterday.
Active:	I received your letter yesterday.

Sentences with passive verbs are usually longer and clumsier than sentences with active verbs. They often leave out the crucial information of who is performing the action of the verb. Spot passive verbs by looking for some form of the verb *to be* (such as *be, will be, have been, is, was,* and *were*) used with another verb.

A tradeoff in using active verbs is the frequent introduction of the pronouns *I* and *My.* To solve one problem, you might create another (see Tip 3 in this list). The task then becomes one of finding an active verb to replace the passive verb, as in the following:

   Active: Your letter arrived yesterday.

9.   **Be sure that present and past participles are grammatically parallel in a list.** See Tip 51 in Part 3. What is true about parallel forms in resumes is true also in cover letters. Present participles are action words that end in *-ing*, such as *creating, testing,* and *implementing.* Past participles are action words that usually end in *-ed*, such as *created, tested,* and *implemented.* These types of words are called *verbals* because they are derived from verbs but are not strong enough to function as verbs in a sentence. When you use a string of verbals, control them by keeping them parallel.

10.   **Use split infinitives only when *not* splitting them is misleading or awkward.** An *infinitive* is a verb preceded by the preposition *to,* as in *to create, to test,* and *to implement.* You split an infinitive when you insert an adverb between the preposition and the verb, as in *to quickly create, to repeatedly test,* and *to slowly implement.* About 50 years ago, split infinitives were considered grammatical errors; these days, however, opinion about them has changed. Many grammar handbooks now recommend that you split your infinitives to avoid awkward or misleading sentences. Compare the following lines:

Split infinitive:	I plan to periodically send updated reports on my progress in school.
Misleading:	I plan periodically to send updated reports on my progress in school.
Misleading:	I plan to send periodically updated reports on my progress in school.

The first example is clear enough, but the second and third examples may be misleading. If you are uncomfortable with split infinitives, one solution is to move *periodically* further into the sentence:

I plan to send updated reports periodically on my progress in school.

Most handbooks that allow split infinitives also recommend that they not be split by more than one word, as in *to quickly and easily write*. A gold medal for splitting an infinitive should go to Lowell Schmalz, an Archie Bunker prototype in "The Man Who Knew Coolidge" by Sinclair Lewis. Schmalz, who thought that Coolidge was one of America's greatest presidents, split an infinitive this way: *"to instantly and without the least loss of time or effort find...."*[1]

Using Punctuation Correctly

11. **Punctuate a compound sentence with a comma.** A compound sentence is one that contains two main clauses joined by one of seven conjunctions (*and, but, or, nor, for, yet,* and *so*). A comma is customarily put before the conjunction if the sentence isn't unusually short. Here is an example of a compound sentence punctuated correctly:

I plan to arrive at O'Hare at 9:35 a.m. on Thursday, and my trip by cab to your office should take no longer than 40 minutes.

The comma is important because it signals that a new grammatical subject (*trip,* the subject of the second main clause) is about to be expressed. If you use this kind of comma consistently, the reader will rely on your punctuation and be on the lookout for the next subject in a compound sentence.

12. **Be certain not to put a comma between compound verbs.** When a sentence has two verbs joined by the conjunction *and,* these verbs are called *compound verbs.* Usually, they should not be separated by a comma before the conjunction. Note the following examples:

I *started* the letter last night *and finished* it this morning.

I *am sending* my resume separately *and would like* you to keep the information confidential.

---

[1] Sinclair Lewis, *The Man Who Knew Coolidge* (New York: Books for Libraries Press, 1956), p. 29.

Both examples are simple sentences containing compound verbs. Therefore, no comma appears before *and.* In either case, a comma would send a wrong signal that a new subject in another main clause is coming, but no such subject exists.

Note: In a sentence with a series of three or more verbs, use commas between the verbs. The comma before the last verb is called the *serial comma.* The serial comma is optional; many writers of business documents and newspaper articles omit this comma. For more information on using the serial comma, see resume writing style Tip 66 in Part 3.

13. **Avoid using *as well as* for *and* in a series.** Compare the following lines:

Incorrect:	Your company is impressive because it has offices in Canada, Mexico, as well as the United States.
Correct:	Your company is impressive because it has offices in Canada and Mexico, as well as in the United States.

    Usually, what is considered exceptional precedes *as well as,* and what is considered customary follows it. Note this example:

    Your company is impressive because its managerial openings are filled by women as well as men.

14. **Put a comma after the year when it appears after the month and day.** Similarly, put a comma after the state when it appears after the city. Compare the following pairs of lines:

Incorrect:	On January 1, 1998 I was promoted to senior analyst.
Correct:	On January 1, 1998, I was promoted to senior analyst.
Incorrect:	I worked in Chicago, Illinois before moving to Dallas.
Correct:	I worked in Chicago, Illinois, before moving to Dallas.

15. **Put a comma after an opening dependent clause.** Compare the following lines:

Incorrect:	If you have any questions you may contact me by phone or fax.
Correct:	If you have any questions, you may contact me by phone or fax.

    Actually, many fiction and nonfiction writers don't use this kind of comma. The comma is useful, though, because it signals where the main clause begins. If you glance at the example with the comma, you can tell where the main clause is without even reading the opening clause. For a step up in clarity and readability, use this comma. It can give the reader a "feel" for a sentence even before he or she begins to read the words.

16. **Use semicolons when they are needed.** See resume writing style Tip 67 in Part 3 for the use of semicolons between items in a series. Semicolons are used also to separate main clauses when the second clause starts with a *conjunctive adverb* such as *however, moreover,* and *therefore.* Compare the following lines:

> **Incorrect:**   Your position in sales looks interesting, however, I would like more information about it.
>
> **Correct:**   Your position in sales looks interesting; however, I would like more information about it.

The first example is incorrect because the comma before *however* is a *comma splice,* which is a comma that joins two sentences. It's like putting a comma instead of a period at the end of the first sentence and then starting the second sentence. A comma may be a small punctuation mark, but a comma splice is a huge grammatical mistake. What are your chances for getting hired if your cover letter tells your reader that you don't recognize where a sentence ends, especially if a requirement for the job is good communication skills? Yes, you could be screened out because of one little comma!

Another use of the semicolon is to separate items of a series when an item has internal punctuation. Compare these sentences:

> **Incorrect:**   The committee consisted of a manager, three salespersons, and Beverley, who was hired yesterday.
>
> **Correct:**   The committee consisted of a manager; three salespersons; and Beverley, who was hired yesterday.

In the first sentence, commas separate the three items of the series, but visually the comma after Beverley can be confusing. Does it signify another series item to follow? In the revision, semicolons separating the series items make the items plain. There is no way to think that the comma after Beverley precedes another series item to follow.

17. **Avoid putting a colon after a verb or a preposition to introduce information.** The reason is that the colon interrupts a continuing clause. Compare the following lines:

> **Incorrect:**   My interests in your company *are:* its reputation, the review of salary after six months, and your personal desire to hire handicapped persons.
>
> **Correct:**   My interests in your company *are these:* its reputation, the review of salary after six months, and your personal desire to hire handicapped persons.

Incorrect:	In my interview with you, I would like *to:* learn how your company was started, get your reaction to my updated portfolio, and discuss your department's plans to move to a new building.
Correct:	In my interview with you, I would like to discuss *these issues:* how your company was started, what you think of my updated portfolio, and when your department may move to a new building.

Although some people may say that it is okay to put a colon after a verb such as *include* if the list of information is long, it is better to be consistent and avoid colons after verbs altogether.

18. **Understand colons clearly.** People often associate colons with semicolons because their names sound alike, but colons and semicolons have nothing to do with each other. Colons are the opposite of dashes. Dashes look backward (see resume writing style Tip 68 in Part 3), whereas colons usually look forward to information about to be delivered, as in the following sentence:

> Three items are on the table: a book, a pen, and a lamp.

One common use of the colon does look backward, however. Here are two examples:

> My experience with computers is limited: I have had only one course on programming, and I don't own a computer.
>
> I must make a decision by Monday: That is the deadline for renewing the lease for my apartment.

In each example, what follows the colon explains what was said before the colon. Using a colon this way in a cover letter can impress a knowledgeable reader who is looking for evidence of writing skills.

19. **Use slashes correctly.** Information about slashes is sometimes hard to find because *slash* often is listed in grammar reference books under a different name, such as *virgule* or *solidus*. If you are not familiar with these terms, your hunt for advice on slashes may lead to nothing.

At least know that one important meaning of a slash is *or.* For this reason, you often see a slash in an expression such as *ON/OFF.* This usage means that a condition or state, like that of electricity activated by a switch, is either ON or OFF but never ON and OFF at the same time. As you can see in resume writing style Tip 64 in Part 3, this condition may be one in which a change means going from the current state to the opposite (or alternate) state. If the current state is ON and there is a change, the next state will be OFF, and vice versa. With this understanding, you can recognize the logic behind the following examples:

Incorrect:	ON-OFF switch (on and off at the same time!)
Correct:	ON/OFF switch (on or off at any time)

Incorrect:	his-her clothes (unisex clothes, worn by both sexes)
Correct:	his/her clothes (each sex had different clothes)

20.   **Think twice about using *and/or*.** This stilted expression is commonly misunderstood to mean *two* alternatives, but it literally means *three*. Look at the following example:

> If you don't hear from me by Friday, please phone and/or fax me the information on Monday.

What is the person at the other end to do? The sentence really states three alternatives: just phone, just fax, or phone *and* fax the information by Monday. For better clarity, use the connectives *and* or *or* whenever possible.

21.   **Use punctuation correctly with quotation marks.** A common misconception is that commas and periods should be placed outside closing quotation marks, but the opposite is true. Compare the following lines:

Incorrect:	Your company certainly has the "leading edge", which means that its razor blades are the best on the market.
Correct:	Your company certainly has the "leading edge," which means that its razor blades are the best on the market.
Incorrect:	In the engineering department, my classmates referred to me as "the guru in pigtails". I was the youngest expert in programming languages on campus.
Correct:	In the engineering department, my classmates referred to me as "the guru in pigtails." I was the youngest expert in programming languages on campus.

Note this exception: Unlike commas and periods, colons and semicolons go *outside* double quotation marks.

Using Words Correctly

22.   **Avoid using lofty language in your cover letter.** A real turn-off in a cover letter is the use of elevated diction (high-sounding words and phrases) as an attempt to seem important. Note the following examples, along with their straight-talk translations:

Elevated:	My background has afforded me experience in…
Better:	In my previous jobs, I…
Elevated:	Prior to that term of employment…
Better:	Before I worked at…

Elevated:	I am someone with a results-driven profit orientation.
Better:	I want to make your company more profitable.
Elevated:	I hope to utilize my qualifications…
Better:	I want to use my skills…

In letter writing, the shortest distance between the writer and the reader is the most direct idea.

23. **Check your sentences for an excessive use of compounds joined by *and*.** A cheap way to make your letters longer is repeatedly to join words with *and*. Note the following wordy sentence:

> Because of my background and preparation for work and advancement with your company and new enterprise, I have a concern and commitment to implement and put into effect my skills and abilities for new solutions and achievements above and beyond your dreams and expectations. [44 words]

Just one inflated sentence such as that would drive a reader to say, "No way!" The writer of the inflated sentence has said only this:

> Because of my background and skills, I can contribute to your new venture. [13 words]

If, during rereading, you eliminate the wordiness caused by this common writing weakness, an employer is more likely to read your letter completely.

24. **Avoid using abstract nouns excessively.** Look again at the inflated sentence in the preceding tip, but this time with the abstract nouns in italic:

> Because of my *background* and *preparation* for *work* and *advancement* with your *company* and new *enterprise*, I have a *concern* and *commitment* to implement and put into *effect* my *skills* and *abilities* for new *solutions* and *achievements* above and beyond your *dreams* and *expectations*.

Try picturing in your mind any of the words in italic. You can't because they are *abstract nouns,* which means that they are ideas and not images of things you can see, taste, hear, smell, or touch. One certain way to turn off the reader is to load your cover letter with abstract nouns. The following sentence, containing some images, has a better chance of capturing the reader's attention:

> Having created seven multimedia tutorials with my videocamera and Dell Core 2 Duo computer, I now want to create some breakthrough adult-learning packages so that your company, New Century Instructional Technologies, will exceed $50,000,000 in contracts by 2008.

Compare this sentence with the one loaded with abstract nouns. The one with images is obviously the better attention grabber.

25. **Avoid wordy expressions in your cover letters.** Note the following examples and the shorter alternatives that follow them in parentheses:

at the location of (at)

for the reason that (because)

in a short time (soon)

in a timely manner (on time)

in spite of everything to the contrary (nevertheless)

in the event of (if)

in proximity to (near)

now and then (occasionally)

on a daily basis (daily)

on a regular basis (regularly)

on account of (because)

one day from now (tomorrow)

would you be so kind as to (please)

Trim the fat wherever you can, and your reader will appreciate your cover letter's leanness.

26. **At the end of your cover letter, don't make a statement that the reader can use to reject you.** For example, suppose that you close your letter with this statement:

> If you wish to discuss this matter further, please call me at (555) 555-5555.

This statement gives the reader a chance to think, "I don't wish it, so I don't have to call." Here is another example:

> If you know of the right opportunity for me, please call me at (555) 555-5555.

The reader may think, "I don't know of any such opportunity. How would I know what is right for you?" Avoid questions that prompt yes-or-no answers, such as, "Do you want to discuss this matter further?" If you ask this kind of question, you give the reader a chance to say no. Instead, make a closing statement that indicates your optimism about a positive response from the reader. Such a statement might begin with one of the following phrases:

> I am confident that…
>
> I look forward to…

In this way, you invite the reader to say yes to further considering your candidacy for the job.

The Gallery
of Best Cover
Letters

The Gallery
at a Glance

How to Use the Gallery

You can learn much from the Gallery just by browsing through it. To make the best use of this resource, however, read the following suggestions before you begin.

Look at the cover letters in the category that contains your field, related fields, or target occupation. Use the Occupation Index to help you find cover letters for certain fields. Notice what kinds of cover letters other people have used to find similar jobs. Always remember, though, that your cover letter should not be "canned." It should not look just like someone else's cover letter, but should reflect your own background, unique experiences, knowledge, areas of expertise, skills, motivation, and goals.

Use the Gallery primarily as an "idea book." Even if you don't find a cover letter for your specific position or job target, be sure to look at all the letters for ideas you can borrow or adapt. You may be able to find portions of a letter (the right word, a phrase, a strong sentence, maybe even a well-worded paragraph) that you can use in your own letter but modify with information that applies to your own situation or target field.

Compare some of the beginning paragraphs of the letters. Notice which ones capture your attention almost immediately. In your comparison, notice paragraph length, sentence length, clarity of thought, and the kinds of words that grab your attention. Are some statements better than others from your point of view? Do some paragraphs fit your situation better than others?

Compare some of the closing paragraphs of the letters. What trends do you notice? What differences? What endings are more effective than others? What are the different ways to say thank you? What are the best ways to ask for an interview? How are follow-up plans expressed? Which closing paragraphs seem to match your situation best? Continue to note differences in length, the kinds of words and phrases used, and the effectiveness of the content. Jot down any ideas that might be true for you.

If you find this kind of comparative study useful, compare the middle paragraphs across the letters of the Gallery. See how the person introduces herself or himself. Look for a paragraph that seems to be a short profile of an individual. Notice paragraphs devoted to experience, areas of expertise, qualifications, or skills. How does the person express motivation, enthusiasm, or interest in the target position? Which letters use bullets? Which letters seem more convincing than others? How are they more persuasive? Which letters have a better chance of securing an interview?

As you review the middle paragraphs, notice which words and phrases seem to be more convincing than other typical words or phrases. Look for words that you might use to put a certain "spin" on your own cover letter as you pitch it toward a particular interviewer or job target.

After comparing letters, examine the paragraphs of several letters to determine the design or arrangement of each one. For example, the first paragraph of a letter might indicate the individual's job goal, the second paragraph might say something about the person's background, the third paragraph might indicate qualifications, and the last paragraph might express interest in an interview. This letter would then have a Goal-Background-Qualifications-Interview design or pattern. If you review the letters in the Gallery this way, you will soon detect some common cover letter designs. The purpose of doing this is to discover which designs are more effective than others—all so that you can make your cover letter the most effective letter it can be.

By developing a sense of cover letter design, you will know better how to select and emphasize the most important information about yourself for the job you want to get.

Try comparing the cover letters also for their visual impact. Look for horizontal and vertical lines, borders, boxes, bullets, white space, and graphics. Which cover letters have more visual impact at first glance, and which ones make no initial impression? Do some of the letters seem more inviting to read than others? Which ones are less appealing because they have too much information, or too little? Which ones seem to have the right balance of information and white space? If visual impact is important, you will want to send a letter through the regular mail on fine paper or as an e-mail file attachment that can be read in Microsoft Word and printed without losing your letter's formatting. If sending a letter online quickly is more important than the letter's appearance, you may want to send your letter as a text (.txt) file with a minimum of formatting, or copy and paste it directly into an e-mail message.

After comparing the visual design features, choose the design ideas that might improve your own cover letter. Be selective here and don't try to work every design possibility into your letter. Generally, "less is more" in cover letter writing, especially when you integrate design features with content.

The Gallery contains sample cover letters that were prepared by professional resume writers to accompany resumes. (Some representative resumes are included in Part 3 of this book.) In most cases, the names, addresses, and facts have been changed to ensure the confidentiality of the original sender and receiver of the letter. For each letter, however, the essential substance of the original remains intact.

Use the Gallery of cover letters as a reference whenever you need to write a cover letter for your resume. As you examine the Gallery, consider the following questions:

1. **Does the writer show a genuine interest in the reader?** One way to tell is to count the number of times the pronouns *you* and *your* appear in the letter. Then count the number of times the pronouns *I, me,* and *my* occur in the letter. Although this method is simplistic, it nevertheless helps you see where the writer's interests lie. When you write a cover letter, make your first paragraph *you*-centered rather than *I*-centered.

2. **Where does the cover letter mention the resume specifically?** The purpose of a cover letter is to call attention to the resume. If the letter fails to mention the resume, the letter has not fulfilled its purpose. Besides mentioning the resume, the cover letter might direct the reader's attention to one or more parts of the resume, increasing the chances that the reader will see the most important part(s). It is not a good idea, however, to put a lot of resume facts in the cover letter. Let each document do its own job. The job of the cover letter is to point to the resume.

3. **Where and how does the letter express interest in an interview?** The immediate purpose of a cover letter is to call attention to the resume, but the *ultimate* purpose of both the cover letter and the resume is to help you get an interview with the person who can hire you. If the letter doesn't display your interest in getting an interview, the letter has not fulfilled its ultimate purpose.

4. **How decisive is the person's language?** This question is closely related to the preceding question. Is interest in an interview expressed directly or indirectly? Does the person specifically request an interview on a date when the writer will be in the reader's vicinity, or does the person only hint at a desire to "meet" the reader some day? Some of the letters in this book are more proactive and assertive than others in asking for an interview. When you write your own cover letters, be sure to be direct and convincing in expressing your interest for an interview.

5. **How does the person display self-confidence?** As you look through the Gallery, notice the cover letters in which the phrase "I am confident that…" (or a similar expression) appears. Self-confidence is a sign of management ability and essential job-worthiness. Many of the letters display self-confidence or self-assertiveness in various ways.

6. **Does the letter indicate whether the person is a team player?** From an employer's point of view, an employee who is self-assertive but not a team player can spell T-R-O-U-B-L-E. As you look at the cover letters in the Gallery, notice how the letters mention the word *team*.

7. **How does the letter make the person stand out?** Do some letters present the person more vividly than other letters? If so, what does the trick? The middle paragraphs or the opening and closing paragraphs? The paragraphs or the bulleted lists? Use what you learn here to help you write effective cover letters.

8. **How familiar is the person with the reader?** In a passive job search, the reader will most likely be a total stranger. In an active job search, the chances are good that the writer will have had at least one conversation with the reader by phone or in person. In that case, the letter can refer to any previous communication.

After you have examined the cover letters in the Gallery, you will be better able to write an attention-getting letter—one that leads the reader to your resume and to scheduling an interview with you.

An important note about style and consistency: The 311 cover letters and 23 resumes in this book represent 73 unique styles of writing—the exact number of professional resume writers who contributed to this book. For this reason, you may notice a number of differences in capitalization. To showcase important details, many of the writers prefer to capitalize job titles and other key terms that usually appear in lowercase. Furthermore, the use of jargon may vary considerably—again, reflecting the choices of individual writers and thus making each letter and resume truly "one of a kind."

Variations in the use (or *non*use) of hyphens may be noticeable. With the proliferation of industry jargon, hyphens seem like moving targets, and "rules" of hyphenation vary considerably from one handbook to another. In computer-related fields, some terms are evolving faster than the species. Thanks to America Online®, the term *on-line* is more often shown as *online,* but both forms are acceptable. And electronic mail comes in many varieties: *email, e-mail, Email,* and *E-Mail.* But the computer world is not the only one that has variety: both *healthcare* and *health care* appear in the cover letters and companion resumes in this book.

Although an attempt has been made to reduce some of the inconsistencies in capitalization and hyphenation, differences are still evident. Keep in mind that the consistent use of capitalization and hyphenation *within* a cover letter or resume is more important than adherence to any set of external conventions.

Note: To ensure the privacy of their clients, the professional resume writers whose work appears in this book have *fictionalized* the information about their clients. Omitting an address or salutation in a cover letter is another way of protecting a client's privacy. For this reason, some of the letters in this book include generic salutations such as "Dear Hiring Manager" or "Dear Sir/Madam." In an actual letter, such a salutation should be replaced with the name of an individual who works at the company to which you are applying.

Note: In some of the comments below the cover letters, the views of the resume writers themselves appear in quotation marks.

MARK FISHER, MBA, CPA

555-555-5555
jmf@email.com
5555 Kraft Lane, Knoxville, TN 55555

February 4, 2008

Barry Fox, President
National Bank
5555 George Street
Lincoln, NE 55555

Dear Mr. Fox:

"Your hard work positions our organization well for 2007."

General Manager

"During his tenure, Mark demonstrated a strong ability to drive for results for his team."

Director,
Consumer Ops

When was the last time you hired a **Senior Management** Executive who was able to hit the ground running and *generate expense reductions quickly?* Please allow me to introduce myself. As a Certified Public Accountant with extensive financial and auditing experience, I approach every situation from the perspective of operational efficiency.

Producing results requires leadership. Achieving fast results demands a new perspective, an ability to embrace and implement change, and buy-in from everyone involved. Results-driven highlights include

- Listening to front-line employees and responding to their concerns and suggestions. *Recommended that senior management eliminate customer online disconnect ability, yielding a $5 million annual savings.*

- Developing the incentive plan for sales reps that *drove market penetration to 35% on customer loyalty product sales.*

- Being *hand selected* by senior management for the Capstone Leadership Program, *a privilege afforded to the top 5 to 10%* of employees.

Controlling costs and reducing expenses are critical to an organization's profitability and viability. If you are looking for a results-driven leader holding a CPA and MBA who can *produce positive results quickly,* perhaps we should meet to discuss your needs and how I might help. I will call you next week and look forward to speaking with you.

Sincerely,

Mark Fisher

Enclosure

1

Certified Public Accountant. *Cindy Kraft, Valrico, Florida*

The first paragraph introduces the applicant, the second indicates bulleted achievements quantified in dollars and percentages, and the third proposes a meeting. Two testimonials sell the applicant.

PAUL KEENE, CPA, CMA

October 24, 2007

Hiring Agent, Title
Company Name
Address

Dear Hiring Manager:

As an accomplished financial professional with a solid background in both GAAP and managerial accounting, as well as experience as a controller, I believe I offer expertise that would be of benefit to your company. With a proven record in building solid financial infrastructures, improving accounting and reporting procedures, and providing sound financial analysis, I would like to explore the possibility of putting my talents to work for you.

As you can see from my enclosed resume, I was brought into my current position to integrate and upgrade the financial operations of four affiliated companies. For this challenging task, I successfully introduced a new financial reporting system, brought the books of all four companies into compliance with GAAP standards, instituted new procedures that standardized and improved operational reporting, and established new systems that simplified asset accounting. In addition, as a certified management accountant trained to use the EVA™ metric system, I am frequently called upon to provide the expert financial analysis that drives successful corporate decision making.

Equally skilled in closing the financial books and conducting analysis of financial results, I consider myself a team player willing and able to tackle any challenge in the financial arena. However, my true passion lies in cost analysis and the identification of cost-saving opportunities. Related to this, I pride myself on my ability to develop clear, cohesive financial reports that provide the basis and justification for change and improvement initiatives. Knowledgeable and forward thinking, I have proven to be a respected and valued financial leader in the past. With a record of success behind me, I am confident that I will be an asset to you as well.

I will be relocating to your area shortly and hope to find a rewarding position that provides the same diverse, fast-paced challenge that I currently enjoy. Therefore, I would be pleased to have the opportunity to meet with you to discuss your needs and how I might be able to meet them. I will contact you shortly to arrange an interview. I look forward to speaking with you soon.

Thank you for your consideration.

Sincerely,

Paul Keene, CPA, CMA

Enclosure

5 SIDNEY ROAD • BRIARCLIFF, NEW YORK 10001 • (333) 333-3333
pkeene@aol.com

Controller. *Carol A. Altomare, Three Bridges, New Jersey*

A cover letter for a resume should direct attention to the resume. The second paragraph mentions the resume and directs the reader's eyes to it and the notable accounting achievements it contains.

```
Re: Senior Tax Consultant

I have

~ 10+ years of tax and consulting experience working with industry leaders
Penney Waterhouse, Delloise & Tooshe, and Motorcola.

~ Level 3 CGA, a Master's degree in Accountancy, and a Master's degree in
Taxation.

~ Strong technical tax skills that include transfer pricing, corporate tax,
sales and use tax, customs duties, excise taxes, VAT, tax research,
international tax legislation, and tax reviews for contingent liabilities.

~ Gained a reputation for client service, commitment, knowledge, and creativity.

In my most recent position as Senior Associate with Penney Waterhouse, I
specialized in transfer pricing issues and planning for corporate clients both
in Canada and the U.S. In addition to demonstrating the strong tax research and
analysis skills required of the position, I demonstrated the critical ability to
understand and gain familiarity with the financial systems of large corporate
clients - a skill necessary for completing the financial analyses for complex
transfer pricing reports.

Throughout my career, I have developed the ability to thoroughly understand a
company's business and industry, analyze data, identify material tax issues, and
provide sound recommendations to the simplest and most complex tax issues.

I would welcome the chance to meet in person to learn more of this position and
to see if my expertise meets your needs. Please feel free to review my attached
resume and contact me at (555) 666-2222 to arrange an interview.

Thank you for your consideration.

Sincerely,
Julia Gaither
```

Senior Associate Tax Accountant. *Ross Macpherson, Whitby, Ontario, Canada*

This cover letter is in .txt (text) format for e-mailing. The letter begins with bullets so that the first 10 to 15 lines in the reader's e-mail window capture attention and display the applicant's qualifications.

William DeCoons, CPA

555 Seneca Ave., Waldwick, NJ 55555, (555) 555-5555 x555, wdecoons@aol.com

December 14, 2007

Mr. Robert B. Mishkoff
Mishkoff/Work Executive Search, Inc.
555 Madison Ave., Ste. 400
New York, NY 10022

Dear Mr. Mishkoff,

As an active partner in a CPA accounting firm who has developed the firm's consulting business, I am seeking to focus <u>all</u> my energies into management consulting.

My background includes 18 years of experience in accounting, auditing, finance and consulting. I am skilled in performing diverse financial analysis and developing business plans for various public- and private-sector enterprises and high-income individuals.

For each challenge, I have exceeded expectations and produced excellent results. Most notably, I

- Developed a business plan for a client that would expand his business while protecting his assets.
- Developed a consulting niche with municipal clientele that will net more than $100,000 in annual fees.
- Prepared a "Full Accounting of a Trust" by utilizing accounting software that would provide the format required by the New York State courts.
- Grew my private practice to more than $110,000 in revenues.

My goal is to join a progressive management consulting firm where I can help create value through innovative financing. I think and act "outside the box," and a company that values profitable problem solving will value me, for that is what I do best.

I prefer to stay in the metropolitan New York City area and anticipate an annual compensation package in excess of $100,000.

I look forward to speaking with you regarding any current search assignments appropriate for a candidate with my qualifications. Thank you in advance for your consideration.

Sincerely,

William DeCoons, CPA

Enclosure

4

Certified Public Accountant. *Igor Shpudejko, Mahwah, New Jersey*

This CPA wanted to transition to full-time management consulting. After doing some consulting, he discovered that he liked to find problems and fix them. The letter is addressed to a recruiter.

B r o o k e   C u m m i n g s

0000 Rock Cove • Parker, CO 80134
555.555.5555 • brooke@earthlink.com

November 7, 2007

Janis Dodge
Senior Vice President—Chief Financial Officer
New Era Mortgage Corporation
12345 Beverly Boulevard, Suite 100
Los Angeles, CA 92612

Re: Vice President—Controller

Dear Ms. Dodge,

Accounting can be a powerful resource to an organization. It is up to the controller to educate the organization on how to effectively use accounting resources to improve productivity and profitability.

I was delighted when Jane Doe informed me of the Vice President—Controller position at New Era Mortgage Corporation. I am currently the Controller at Colorado Funding, a mortgage lender in Lone Star, CO. My financial management expertise, leadership skills, and extensive experiences are an excellent fit with your position, and I am very interested in relocating to the area to be closer to family and friends.

As a top performer with 20+ years of experience in accounting, I have the knowledge and expertise it takes to bring about positive change. My enclosed resume highlights my contributions and accomplishments in the areas of general accounting, financial statements, audits, cash management, budgeting, profit performance, strategic planning, and regulatory compliance. I take great pride in my work and my abilities. I have made great strides in being recognized as a key player on the management team. My accomplishments will speak for themselves.

My success is due to a passion for quality and excellence, tenacity, and a willingness to confront and conquer tough challenges. I have exceptional organizational skills and a keen eye for detail. My strengths lie in building quality financial processes that meet and exceed expectations. I believe gaining a thorough understanding of all aspects of the business is required to financially guide the organization.

You will find that I am very skilled at developing sound action plans, as well as administering and following through on those plans. I strive to build and maintain a principle-centered environment that preserves the organization's core values while stimulating growth and profitability.

I am eager to begin contributing to the bottom line of New Era Mortgage Corporation. I welcome the opportunity to explore my potential with you.

Thank you for your consideration; I look forward to speaking with you soon.

Sincerely,

Brooke Cummings

Enclosure: Resume

5

Controller. *Roberta F. Gamza, Louisville, Colorado*

This letter names the source of a referral. The reference to the resume summarizes the applicant's areas of accomplishments, and the letter shows strongly that she can do the job and wants it.

KALLEN G. CASEY, CPA
000 GUST COURT ◆ COLUMBIA, MISSOURI 55555
RESIDENCE: 555-555-5555 ◆ WIRELESS: 555-555-5555
KGCCPA@EMAIL.COM

CORPORATE TAX CONSULTANT

LETTER OF INTRODUCTION

I am relocating to the Chicago area and am exploring new career opportunities as a **senior corporate tax consultant** and/or **business development strategist** in tax consulting. My goal is to affiliate with either a "Big Four" accounting and tax consulting firm or a major corporate entity where I can lead and/or co-manage a tax division. Tax consultants will be integral strategists in the profitable growth of complex corporate entities in today's environment. If you have need for a senior corporate tax consultant with expertise in new business development, we should meet.

Throughout my career, I have developed

- ✓ Expertise in corporate tax and compliance to enhance shareholder value through heightened profitability.

- ✓ Comprehensive tax solutions that impact corporate tax rates and reduce federal, state and local liabilities in an increasingly complex tax environment.

- ✓ Talent for new business development and relationship building with corporate executives, facilitating partnerships and opportunities never before attempted.

As Co-Chair of the Mid-America Tax Conference and frequent speaker on multistate tax matters, I am recognized nationally for my expertise in corporate tax solutions. I have been instrumental in the origination of a highly profitable business development program for tax consulting achieved through motivational leadership blended with sound corporate tax and strategic thinking. My challenge was to expand and strengthen the firm's presence through the introduction of new business initiatives to win competitive positioning and accelerate revenue growth. I spearheaded the implementation of such a program through the company nationwide. Throughout my career, I have brought absolute value to the firm's current and long-term business objectives.

With strong communication and presentation skills, I thrive in fast-paced, high-visibility environments that require innovative leadership and decisive action. I have the ability to capture the attention of a variety of audiences.

My resume is enclosed for your review. If you are looking for a senior corporate tax specialist who will make an immediate and positive impact on your revenue streams, I would welcome a personal interview to discuss how my qualifications would benefit your firm. I will call later this week to set up an interview. Thank you for your consideration.

Sincerely,

Kallen G. Casey

Enclosure

6

Senior Corporate Tax Consultant. *Gina Taylor, Kansas City, Missouri*

This applicant was moving to a new city. The writer highlights the individual's abilities as a business development strategist and his strengths in developing new revenue streams. He received two offers.

KATY SNOW
000 East Street • Charlottetown, NC 20000
(555) 555-5555

January 19, 2008

Mr. James Cathcart
Speedway Enterprises
5555 Racing Boulevard, Suite 555
Charlottetown, NC 55555

Dear Mr. Cathcart:

It is a long way we've come from those early race cars run in 1948 to the dynamic cars we have today, from the first NASCAR race in Daytona to the intricately engineered tracks of the present. Truly the exciting history of NASCAR is even more eventful today.

Those early days have disappeared, like the physician who made house calls, but they will never be forgotten. And neither will I forget my early years growing up in California, where my mother worked for an exhaust manifold manufacturer, Edelbrock, and my husband raced motorcycles. We attended NASCAR races at Riverside and Ontario Speedways in the early '70s.

Over the years, though, I built not race cars, but a career in accounting and finance, moving across the country (no longer by motorcycle but by car), eventually settling in Charlottetown in 1990. During this period I assumed responsible positions as a controller, operations manager, or finance manager, with wide-ranging challenges, from accounting and finance to operations, information and systems integration, and human resources.

With each opportunity came new challenges. With each advancement and move, I went through the same experience—a desire to grow and build value within each organization I joined. Along the way, I became even more enchanted with NASCAR events, frequently traveling on weekends to races in Charlotte, Bristol, Martinsville, and Atlanta. And two years ago, I took "NASCAR 101" (my name) at Central Community College to learn more about racing, its advertising and promotion strategies, and pre- and post-race driver activities. I even toured Lowe's Motor Speedway. The class, presented by NASCAR TV commentator Tony Raines, was enlightening, engaging, and exhilarating.

Over the last few years, I've been preparing myself for the next step: to apply these skills to an organization within the NASCAR industry. My children are grown, and, with fewer familial obligations, my life has changed. Now I would like to join a winning NASCAR team. During this period of change, I view my situation much as Napoleon did when asked how he intended to combat seemingly insurmountable circumstances. His reply: "Circumstances? . . . I *make* circumstances."

If you are interested and have a need for someone with my skills, a desire to work hard, and enthusiasm for NASCAR, then give me the green flag. To quote William D. Smith, Vice President of the Jewel Tea Company back in 1948 (and it still makes sense today): "Take your job seriously—but don't take yourself too seriously. Believe that HOW you work is more important than WHERE you work [unless it's NASCAR] . . . To keep young you must play and you must have fun; make your job and your life a game—and play the game to win."

If you need a capable, devoted, and hardworking professional, I may be able to help. Can we talk? I will call to explore the possibility of an in-person meeting.

Sincerely,

Katy Snow

Controller. *Doug Morrison, Charlotte, North Carolina*

Having always worked in accounting and finance, this applicant wanted to combine her skills with her avocation—being an avid, lifelong NASCAR fan—and change her work environment completely.

Margaret V. Baxter

000 Anoka Drive   555-555-5555
Waterford, Michigan 55555   mbaxter@network.net

March 15, 2008

Dear Practice Manager:

My previous five-year-long position as a Medical Receptionist/Biller was the best job of my life! I enjoyed the patients and my coworkers. I loved the challenges it presented and that each day was different. My most recent job took me away from the medical field, and I have really missed it. That's why I am contacting you—to learn about employment opportunities for an experienced, effective, and, most important, motivated receptionist/biller/administrative support provider. My resume describes my experience.

When you review my resume, I hope you will notice that, although I have been working with engineers and automobiles instead of patients and charts, the same skills are important. For example, in my current position I must be highly accurate when working with vehicle part numbers. That isn't much different from coding patient charts with the precise ICD-9 numbers. Among my responsibilities is keeping track of vehicles, keys, and projects. That ability to multitask is equally valuable in a medical office. Also, people are people, and I believe I possess strong communication and interpersonal skills.

Bottom line, I am eager to get back into the medical field to share my enthusiasm and commitment to patients. I am confident that I would be an enhancement to your practice. I am prepared to work hard to get back up to speed with the billing side of the office as quickly as I can. I will give you a call to arrange an interview. Thank you for your time and attention.

Sincerely,

Margaret V. Baxter

Enclosure

8

Medical Receptionist/Biller. *Janet L. Beckstrom, Flint, Michigan*

This applicant wanted to move from a position that was too analytical and had little interaction with people and to return to a position in a field she truly enjoyed (medical office administration).

Katherine Sullivan
555 County Lane, Newton, MA 05050

505-555-0505   ksullivan@xyz.com

March 5, 2008

William Lodge
Dexter & Lodge Recruiters
555 Commonwealth Ave.
Boston, MA 05550

Dear Mr. Lodge,

For 15 years I have been providing administrative support to senior managers and busy departments. With a corporate reorganization pending, I am currently looking for an opportunity to apply my skills in a new setting. Perhaps one of your clients is looking for the experience and expertise I have to offer.

As the enclosed resume indicates, I thrive in a high-pressure environment and welcome the challenge of performing multiple tasks. My background includes introducing a wide variety of procedures that improve office efficiency and free managers to attend to other tasks. Given a high degree of autonomy, I have made key purchasing recommendations and decisions; coordinated a wide variety of conferences, meetings, and special events; and performed day-to-day administrative functions. In particular, I have developed a high level of expertise with a variety of software applications, most notably creating PowerPoint presentations, and have been called upon by secretaries and managers for computer training and technical assistance. My dedication, hard work, and excellent performance throughout my career are a source of pride for me, and they have been recognized over the years through numerous promotions and achievement/excellence awards.

I am very interested in talking with you about the contribution I can make in a new position. You can reach me at 505-555-0505. I look forward to hearing from you. Thank you for your consideration.

Sincerely,

Katherine Sullivan

Enclosure

Administrative Assistant. *Wendy Gelberg, Needham, Massachusetts*

This letter, sent to a recruiter, plays up the applicant's value in a role that often does not have quantifiable results. The writer calls attention to background, efficiency, and scope of operations.

GIMMIE A. SAMPLE
234 Typist Street
Somewhere, IL 60654
555-232-3241
admin@adminit23.com

Dear Hiring Manager:

I would like to join your team in a position where I may utilize my customer service skills, and I'm attaching my resume for your review. Specifically, I would like to expand my experience in sales support, reception, customer service, and personnel administration.

✓ My most recent positions at Tectura, the Signature Group, and Dominick's required extensive customer communications and problem-solving skills, and I've been recognized for my ability to expedite inquiries tactfully, promptly, and accurately.

✓ I am very dependable and self-motivated, and have proven my ability to bring out these qualities in the people I supervise. I'm also very time sensitive, efficient, and quality minded, and this helps me work well with all types of customers.

These are among the skills I can now bring to your company. I am available for an interview and will contact you next week to set up a convenient time.

Thank you for your time and consideration.

Sincerely,

Gimmie A. Sample

Enclosure

10

Administrative Assistant. *Steven Provenzano, Schaumburg, Illinois*

The first paragraph indicates interest in a position, and the two statements show that the person has the skills to be effective in that position. The second paragraph looks for an interview.

AMANDA PIERCE

55555 Road 19
Hollings, NC 00000

Cell: 555-555-5555
amanda245@msn.com

Date

Hiring Manager
Company
Address
City, State ZIP

Re: [Job Title] advertised [where and when]

Dear [person or title],

As a hardworking individual with excellent administration and communication skills, I would like to explore the possibility of putting my skills and experience to work for you as a [job title]. Highlights of my background and abilities include the following:

- Extensive experience in providing efficient office support in a variety of environments.

- Proven ability to implement new processes in order to realize increased efficiency and cost savings.

- Expertise with written and verbal communications, including relating well to a wide range of people and writing contracts, letters, and minutes.

- Excellent ability to coordinate small and large special events and meetings, as well as organize travel arrangements.

The accompanying resume will provide you with additional details of my accomplishments and skills. I would welcome the opportunity to meet with you and learn how I can make a positive contribution to your company. I will call next week to inquire about the possibility of a meeting.

Thank you for your time and consideration.

Sincerely,

Amanda Pierce

11

Administrative Assistant. *Michele Angello, Aurora, Colorado*

The applicant was applying to many job postings, so the writer created a letter template that could be personalized for each job. The bullets highlight administrative abilities crucial to employers.

MARSHA NEWBERG

1212 Lake Lane – Minneapolis, MN 88888
999.888.7777 (C) – marsha.newberg@tfl.net

ADMINISTRATIVE ASSISTANT ~ PROJECT MANAGER

December 12, 20XX

John Brown
CEO
ABC Corporation
1122 9th Street
Madison, WI 99999

Dear Mr. Brown:

As an effective administrative assistant / project manager, I can identify problems and provide solutions. I also have the unique ability to translate concept into accomplishment as well as possess the vision to capture opportunities that will contribute to the long-term profitability of an organization.

Throughout my career, I have leveraged my leadership, planning, organizational, and financial skills to streamline processes, optimize efficiencies, reduce costs, and increase customer satisfaction. As my resume demonstrates, I have

- Improved project processes through identification of best practices and the creation of resolutions. Increased productivity by maximizing organizational skills and capabilities. Been an integral part in the seamless integration of two organizations by unifying processes and procedures—as Executive Assistant to the Chairman.
- Saved 50% in man-hours by designing more efficient office forms—as Executive Assistant to the Chairman.
- Expedited the merger of the company as Lead Support Administrator for one of 16 integration teams—as Executive Secretary to the Division VP.
- Consistently met deadlines and budget goals and was an essential player in the formulation of training manuals, materials, and presentations—as Administrative Assistant.

My success is due, in part, to an inherent ability to communicate effectively with others. It has enabled me to motivate and lead cross-functional teams. Likewise, it also has assisted me in the mentoring and retention of exceptional personnel committed to professional excellence.

Due to the relocation of my husband's position, I am seeking new career challenges and look forward to the opportunity to discuss your needs and my potential contributions. I will contact you by e-mail in a few days to set up a time we can meet.

Sincerely,

Marsha Newberg

Enclosure

12

Administrative Assistant. *Sally McIntosh, St. Louis, Missouri*

This letter for a high-level administrative assistant includes a bulleted list of accomplishments mentioned in the resume. A spouse's relocation is the occasion for her job change.

Susan E. Williams

0000 Indianwood Road
Clarkston, Michigan 55555

555-555-3333
sueew@network.net

[Date]

[Name]
[Company]
[Address]
[City, State ZIP]

Dear Director of Employment:

A BBA degree, 20+ years of experience in the banking industry, and a background in administrative support—that's what I have to offer your organization. After a rewarding career at Michigan National Bank, I find myself in the position of seeking new career opportunities. My resume is enclosed for your review.

My career at the bank encompassed diverse areas that required skills valuable to any industry. For example:

❖ Thorough understanding of administrative/office operations
❖ Event-planning and management experience
❖ Customer-focused attitude
❖ Attention to detail and strong organizational skills
❖ Ability to oversee multiple responsibilities simultaneously
❖ Computer fluency

In combination with my financial responsibilities, I took a personal interest in every client. There were cases that necessitated my intervention to arbitrate differences between feuding beneficiaries. Sometimes I was called upon to schedule doctor appointments or arrange for home repair on a client's behalf. But serving the client (or the client's estate, as the case may be) was always my top priority.

Thank you for taking the time to review my credentials. I hope you feel a personal meeting would be beneficial; I am available at your convenience. If you have any questions—or when you are ready to schedule an interview—please give me a call at 555-555-3333.

Sincerely,

Susan E. Williams

Enclosure

13

Administrative Assistant. *Janet L. Beckstrom, Flint, Michigan*

This applicant was downsized by a bank after 30 years. The writer prepared this general cover letter. The applicant was hired as an Administrative Assistant for a large medical center.

AMBER CHILDS
P.O. Box 000   Los Gatos, CA 00000   000-000-0000   amchilds@msn.com

August 29, 2007

Ms. Helen Tipton
Human Resources Manager
Arrow Furniture Distribution
0000 Tarman Road
Los Gatos, CA 00000

Subject: Position as an Office Administrator / Executive Assistant

Dear Ms. Tipton:

Your requirement for an experienced Office Administrator / Executive Assistant attracted my attention because of my extensive background in administrative-office management and support of senior-level management. The enclosed resume highlights my relevant strengths and accomplishments.

It is important to me to make a difference in the organization I work for, and I have been recognized by management for doing that in my current and previous employment situations. I am also dedicated to finding and making improvements in the efficiency of the office wherever possible. My present supervisor, who is the CEO of Alver International, has described me as "a very conscientious, able employee [who] has what it takes to smoothly run a business."

Throughout my career, I have established a pattern of delivering results that benefit the organization by identifying opportunities for cost reduction and other operating enhancements and then taking the necessary steps to obtain the desired results. In some cases, I have exercised initiative and acted independently, but I also understand the importance of teamwork and have maintained positive working relationships with others in order to achieve common goals.

In view of my commitment to producing excellent results and my extensive administrative experience, I believe I can add substantial value to your organization as an Office Administrator / Executive Assistant, and I would like to arrange an interview. My employer is aware of my job search because the organization is preparing to close its operations, so I can be available for a meeting during regular business hours. I will contact you to set up a time that is convenient for you.

Sincerely,

Amber Childs

Enclosure

14

Office Administrator/Executive Assistant. *Georgia Adamson, Campbell, California*

The current employer was shutting down, so this applicant could search openly for a new position. The quotation in the second paragraph attests to the quality of her work.

PURDEEP MEHTA

000 Elizabeth Street
Augusta, Ontario A1A 1A1
555-555-5555

February 17, 2008

Joseph Camarra
Director of Administration
Fieldway Automotive Partners
440 Torris Boulevard
Augusta, Ontario
B2C 3D4

Dear Mr. Camarra,

I understand you are looking for a "Girl Friday"—someone to take control of the critical administrative and customer service functions at your location in Pinehurst, Ontario. If you're looking for a motivated and hardworking professional with an above-average performance record, outstanding interpersonal skills, and a "get it done" attitude, I think you've found the best person for the job.

Over the past few years, while working for Group Six Security, I have routinely met with your company's representatives. From this contact, I have gained an understanding of the work that you do and an appreciation for your need for strong administrative support. In my current role with TGO Consulting, I do just that: managing all critical administration for the company and supporting the activities of 30 consultants and project managers.

I invite you to review my attached resume, which details the skills and experience I offer. Highlights include

- ✓ **Strong communications and interpersonal skills**—personable and friendly, with the ability to work well with colleagues, superiors, clients, and vendors
- ✓ **Extensive administrative and office support skills**—includes invoices, billing, scheduling, A/P and A/R, file management, and data entry
- ✓ **Outstanding customer service**—award-winning performance providing friendly and effective customer service in both corporate and retail environments
- ✓ **Self-motivated and hardworking**—personally love challenges, extremely quick learner, and motivated to exceed expectations

I believe that my strong skills and solid work ethic would make a significant contribution to your team, and I would welcome the opportunity to meet in person to discuss this position and why I believe I am the strongest candidate you will see.

Thank you for your consideration. I will contact you soon to arrange a personal interview.

Sincerely,

Purdeep Mehta
Encl.

15

Administrative Support Position. *Ross Macpherson, Pickering, Ontario, Canada*

The applicant had heard about an unposted job through contacts in the industry. This cover letter was a bid for that position. Bullets point to her skills and traits. The entire letter displays confidence.

Angela Granato

1234 Pinewood Street   (000) 000-0000
Charleston, SC 00000   agranato@fastmail.com

January 14, 2008

Natasha Henderson
Human Resources Director
Comprehensive Insurance Associates
Belvista Corporate Park, Building II
Charleston, SC 00000

Dear Ms. Henderson:

In my daily walks through your corporate campus, I often thought how great it would be to work here in these beautiful surroundings so close to my home. Then, as luck would have it, while looking through the classifieds this Sunday, I became very excited when I saw your large ad, which listed an available Administrative Support position. Having a solid background of 7 years performing administrative functions for insurance companies, I knew this opportunity was ideally suited for me. I am extremely interested in learning more about this position or any other related vacancy that may currently be open or anticipated.

As you review my resume, you will see that I handled many aspects of internal and external customer service for a domestic and international clientele. In my daily activities, I developed my organizational and communications skills to the high level your company demands. I am also proficient in managing data on a computer, which involved the balancing of monetary transactions to reflect accurately in client accounts as well as the general ledger. Because I quickly learned new computer applications, management depended on me to train other department members who were less skilled.

You will also note that I am a state-licensed insurance producer for property and casualty, and health insurance. Although your open position does not require licensing, perhaps there will be a need at some future date.

I was very happy at my last position with Liberty Insurance, but unfortunately, in the process of restructuring its organization, my department was recently eliminated. I believe the diversity of my experience and problem-solving abilities will enable me to be productive in your business almost immediately. My salary requirements are negotiable, depending on the demands of the position and the total compensation package.

If you feel as I do that I am the perfect candidate, I will be glad to meet with you at your convenience to discuss in more detail how I can contribute as a member of your team. I will call early next week to set up a time for us to meet.

Sincerely,

Angela Granato

Enclosure

16

Administrative Support Position. *Melanie Noonan, West Paterson, New Jersey*

The first paragraph makes known the applicant's extreme interest in the advertised position. The letter then indicates her experience, licensing, and reason for applying. See the corresponding Resume 3 in Part 3.

One Concentric Circle
Nobleton, Virginia 12345
June 1, 2008

Dear Sir or Madam:

How does one make an office run smoothly, like a well-oiled machine?

- By understanding its components and their interrelationships, for example, the different kinds of equipment necessary to run a modern office, how they are used, and how they interact and interface.

- By understanding not only modern equipment, such as computers, scanners, and fax machines, but also older kinds of equipment, such as typewriters. By understanding not only when to use computers, but also when typewriters work faster and better and when the human hand works faster and better than the typewriter.

- By understanding not only the machinery, but the people who use it. By understanding how they feel about the technology they use. By understanding the conditions under which they use the machinery best.

I have been making things run smoothly at Brite Industries for more than ten years. I understand machines, and I like machines. But it's my understanding of people that has made possible the kinds of success documented in the attached resume, detailing my progressively responsible administrative career at Brite and elsewhere. Many listen. I listen and acknowledge. It's one thing to be heard, but another to know you're being heard. I think, and then determine better and faster ways of doing things. When something goes wrong, I discover the misunderstanding that caused the problem and clarify it.

This is how I saved $100,000 and increased productivity 40% at Brite. This is how I upgraded five positions, significantly improving morale. This is how I anticipated a question from our president, ensuring it was answered *before* it was asked. This is how I recommended, for an incident center, a new location that was subsequently approved by management, saving both time and money. This is how I significantly reduced absenteeism through informal and formal counseling to departmental staff.

And this is how I can help you. Please take a look at the attached document. I am confident that, on reviewing it, you will agree I have the potential to become a worthy member of your team. Kindly phone or e-mail me to set a convenient time to meet, so that we could discuss how I might best serve your organization.

Sincerely yours,

Anna Marie Di Magenta

P.S. Please call me at (777) 654-3210 or e-mail me at dimagenta@aol.com.

17

Office Equipment Support Position. *Howard Earle Halpern, Toronto, Ontario, Canada*

Cover letters that resemble other cover letters can be boring. This letter is different in *offering* the reader original ideas to be helpful in the selection process, instead of *asking* for something.

BRENDA BELLOWS

000 Morris Street • Bronx, NY 00000

Home: (555) 555-5555   Brenda456@mail.com   Mobile: (555) 655-5555

November 13, 2007

[Name]
[Title]
[Employer]
[Address]
[City, State ZIP]

Dear [Mr. or Ms. Name]:

A high-performing marketing organization staffed with individuals demonstrating a successful track record is an essential part of your company's continued growth.

I believe you will agree that my qualifications, highlighted in the enclosed resume, confirm that I have the creativity, marketing savvy and management experience that can contribute to your company's success.

Specifically, what do I offer?

- Fashion, beauty, fragrance and cosmetics industry background
- Developing marketing programs, promotions and events
- Coordinating national print and broadcast advertising
- Leading the creation and production of marketing materials
- Nurturing strategic partnerships with clients and trade publications
- Managing and delivering multiple projects/budgets in deadline-driven environments

Examples of my accomplishments:

- Restructured entire co-op advertising program at Estée Lauder, improving budget controls, tracking system and forecasting.
- Orchestrated successful marketing programs for an outdoor advertising association, including the annual award show and gallery that increased participation 50% each year.
- Initiated sales/marketing tool that contributed to new business development at a start-up media company.
- Saved more than $100,000 just in production/tagging costs through effective negotiation skills.

I welcome the opportunity to meet with you and discuss the value I would add to your team as a Marketing Coordinator. May I call next week to set an appointment?

Sincerely,

Brenda Bellows

18

Marketing Coordinator. *Louise Garver, Enfield, Connecticut*

With print, broadcast, and outdoor advertising experience, this applicant wanted to move to the next level in marketing. This letter enabled her to win interviews that led to an excellent offer.

Chase Williams

SENIOR-LEVEL MARKETING EXECUTIVE

ADVERTISING · BRANDING · PUBLIC RELATIONS

[Insert Date]

[Insert Contact Name]
[Insert Contact Title]
[Insert Company Name]
[Insert Contact Address]
[Insert Contact Address]

An entrepreneur at heart, I get the job done. "There is always a better way" is my mantra and the force that drives me to consistently achieve seemingly impossible results and ROI.

Dear [Insert Contact Name]:

As a seasoned senior-level marketing professional with client-side, agency, and consulting experience, as well as a background building a spectrum of major organic and natural brands—including Tom's of Maine, Burt's Bees, and Nature's Bounty—I can help [Insert Company Name] meet the rapid challenges in today's marketplace.

With a thorough understanding of marketing, business, and global trends, coupled with a deep knowledge of consumer wants, needs, and buying behaviors, I will leverage the strengths of your organization. I know how to drive spirited strategy development and implementation, construct solid organizational and product-line plans, optimize the use of funds, and keep the business and tech sides on the same page. I typically get it right the first time, no matter the challenge!

You will find me to be a low-risk hire who will deliver needed ROI. I determine ways to execute campaigns correctly without compromising their effectiveness due to internal constraints, and I use all technology (internal and external) to the company's advantage. Significant accomplishments predictive of contributions I can make to [Insert Company Name] include

- Successful launch of a new Green Mountain brand, seamlessly and without disruption to other core businesses.
- Reduction of acquisition costs by up to 75% in key segments—35% on average—through remarketing targeted to nonpurchasing Green Mountain prospects.
- Launch of Hannaford's most successful new North American product in 25+ years.
- Leadership of a group that delivered a 42% year-over-year increase in fee revenues for Stonyfield, Inc.

Strategy is hard-wired into my thinking—I play chess three to five moves out and plot a marketing or business plan the same way. Everywhere I have worked I have anticipated and solved likely problems before they happened. I am known to quickly learn from mistakes and redirect energies. A strong team player, I play to win the prize for the company. I operate as an agent to deliver change and lead by example.

Marketing today is not as simple as it used to be. Time to market is crucial, and it is no longer acceptable to progress at a comfortable pace with internal capabilities when these resources are lacking. I maximize profitability of customer segments through the entire customer life cycle to grow ROI and sustain competitive strength. As an entrepreneurial and strategic leader, I squeeze the most possible out of internal expertise and capabilities and then supplement and draw on external solutions as needed to buttress internal capabilities.

[Insert Contact Name], I'd like to discuss with you my ability to 1) continue to cost-effectively drive leads that convert into customers in the increasingly complex organics space, 2) overcome the infrastructure weaknesses specific to growing companies, 3) build a brand while reducing customer acquisition costs, and 4) use segmentation and modeling to maximize ROI. May we schedule a meeting?

Sincerely,

Chase Williams

4573 Cliff Drive, Denver, CO 55555 · 000-000-0000 · organicmktng@aol.com

19

Senior Marketing Executive. *Deborah Wile Dib, Medford, New York*

Resumes for senior executives with much experience are often longer and more detailed. The same is true for their cover letters. The bulleted items list notable, quantified achievements.

Frederick Charleston

55 NE Resnold Drive   •   Vancouver, Washington 99999

e-mail: fc333@hotmail.com   555-555-5555

December 1, 2007

Attention: Hiring Professional
Ginger's Airline Products
555 NW Pioneer Street
Vancouver, WA 99999

Dear Hiring Professional:

Enclosed is my resume for your review. As you will note, the United States Navy has provided me 19.5 years of experience in aviation. I am experienced in all aspects of aviation maintenance—proficient in providing maintenance on a variety of aircraft and able to effectively manage and train a maintenance crew, provide quality assurance, and maintain aircrafts at 100% for readiness and safety.

My management skills are well proven, and I enjoy working with each individual. If a particular position and individual are not working out, I take the time to review the individual's personality, looking for strengths and then using that person in a more suitable position. I find that taking strengths and fitting them to requirements result in much higher production with less manpower turnover.

The position you have available appears to be one that closely matches my skills. I would like the opportunity to meet with you personally to see where my strengths and your company requirements may blend. I will call you soon to set up an interview.

Thank you for your time.

Sincerely,

Frederick Charleston

20

Aircraft Maintenance Manager. *Rosie Bixel, Portland, Oregon*

Employers want to hear at least two statements from an applicant: "I can" and "I want to." The first two paragraphs deliver "I can" information; the last paragraph indicates the applicant's interest.

CONFIDENTIAL   *Ready to relocate to the Clovis area*

Charles Henry Kraft
0000 Sledgeway Street — Anchorage, Alaska 55555
☎ 907.555.5555 (Cell) — apmaster@whiz.att.net

Thursday, February 26, 2008

Mr. Joe North
Director of Maintenance
TopLine Airlines, Inc.
555 Northridge Parkway
Suite 555
Clovis, New Mexico 55555

Dear Mr. North:

I want to make it easy for TopLine Airlines to add me to your team as your newest aircraft maintenance supervisor.

As a first step, I thought you deserved to see more than the usual tired lists of jobs held and training completed. In their place you'll find a half dozen examples of maintenance teams motivated, productivity boosted, liability reduced—in short, problems solved. And, while a resume format tailored to your needs is good at documenting results, it cannot tell you *how* I contribute to our leadership's peace of mind.

Therefore, as you read, I hope the following ideas stand out:

❑ I am only as good as the last job I signed off—conditions in the remote parts of Alaska leave little room for maintenance errors.

❑ I am only as good as my last quarter's MX statistics. If I don't spot and correct trends, we'll lose time and money.

❑ I am only as good as the teams I attract, recruit, train, and retain. Our labor market is among the tightest in the nation.

I'm employed now and my company likes my work. However, I want to relocate to be closer to my family. That's why I am testing the waters with this confidential application.

When it comes to something as important as finding TopLine Airlines's next aircraft maintenance supervisor, words on paper are no substitute for people speaking with people. So let me suggest a next step. I'd like to get on your calendar in a few days so that we can explore how I might serve your special maintenance needs. I will call to set up a time to meet.

Sincerely,

Charles Henry Kraft

Encl.: Resume

CONFIDENTIAL

21

Aircraft Maintenance Supervisor. *Don Orlando, Montgomery, Alabama*

This writer is a master at avoiding clichés and whatever else is trite, timeworn, and customary. Study this and his other cover letters in this book for his fresh ideas.

ALICIA DWYER

47 Bedford Road, Carindale, QLD 4444
(b) **(07) 7777 7777** • **(h)** **(07) 5555 5555**
aliciad@powerup.net

27 March 2008

Stewart McAdam
Vestal Airlines
Level 62, Riverview Place
Park Road
Brisbane Qld 4444

Dear Mr. McAdam:

Fasten your seatbelt… as I navigate you through the career profile of a highly accomplished, dynamic professional, who just happens to have a great sense of humour and your vital prerequisite: a passion for people and for life.

Throughout my career, working predominantly within the **airline industry**, I have demonstrated an exceptional record of accomplishment, continuously setting myself high standards and achieving *outstanding quantifiable results*.

My attached resume emphasises numerous achievements and expounds upon my proven record of excellence within human resource management; my proactive formulation of benchmark interview and recruitment procedures; and my outstanding leadership, communication and interpersonal expertise.

I submit the following highlights for your perusal:
- → Spearheaded development of high-volume recruitment and selection procedures and personally conducted more than 2,000 interviews. Accountable for annual wages expenditure in excess of $15 million.
- → Directed and motivated more than 400 management and staff, consistently employing dynamic leadership and team-building skills in combination with excellent coaching and training expertise. Facilitated delivery of Corporate Culture Program to 16,000 staff over two-year period.
- → Key ability to build strong, respectful business and corporate relations across all levels of management. Achieved minimal customer disruption and maximum level of efficiency in servicing corporate clientele during 10-month pilot dispute.
- → Excellent educational qualifications and accreditations, including Graduate Diploma of Counselling, Accredited "Target Selection" Certificate, Accredited OH&S Certificate, International Interpersonal Management Skills and Certificate IV Workplace Training and Assessment.

What is more challenging to put down on paper is my genuine love of people—my love of drawing out the very best that is within and motivating individuals to achieve results beyond their personal expectations.

I am proud to state that during my 11 years in the aviation industry, I have seen individuals, without exception, work harder than they have ever worked before and rise to levels above those to which they would normally aspire.

Vestal Airlines enjoys an excellent reputation throughout the industry. I am eager to share my expertise within your organisation as a vital catalyst for growth and the achievement of personal and corporate excellence. So…

…before we reach cruising altitude, I invite you to read the attached. No, not safety instructions, although it could be just as lifesaving…

Yours sincerely,

Alicia Dwyer
Enc.

22

Airline Position. *Beverley Neil, Victoria Point West, Queensland, Australia*

This applicant's experience was in the aviation industry but not related specifically to airlines, which was her target. The writer devised this letter to show how the experience was relevant. The applicant got an interview.

TOM CARTER

555 Maple Drive   555-555-5555
Pittsburgh, PA 55555   tcarter@aol.com

August 30, 2007

Mr. James Ryan
Cooper and Associates
5555 Peachtree Lane
Atlanta, GA 55555

Dear Mr. Ryan:

A fresh perspective, new strategies, and an objective viewpoint are just a few of the distinguishing characteristics I can bring to your company. As an executive, my focus has always been on growth and improving the company's bottom-line performance through progressive, customer-driven strategies. I welcome the opportunity to do the same at your company.

No business can progress and grow without leadership. In the final analysis, leadership and effective management are the only real advantages one organization has over another, especially in today's competitive marketplace. As both a career training and development executive with Fortune 500 companies and a leader/manager of small businesses focusing on delivering training and professional education, here is a snapshot of recent accomplishments:

- **Turnaround experience**—transitioned underperforming company with $40 million in revenue and 4% profit to $70 million and 13% profit within 18 months.

- **Successful P&L experience**—range of $1 million to $70 million.

- **Challenging environments**—manage successfully in a very complex international environment, as a service provider to the federal government, as President and CEO of the largest subsidiary of a publicly traded company.

- **New program development and execution**—direct market research; course design; delivery infrastructure; product positioning; marketing; sales; and finally profitable, recurring revenue streams.

- **Strategic partnerships and business alliances**—initiate, negotiate, and implement domestic and international alliances that benefit all parties.

As you review the enclosed resume, I am confident you will determine that my background and management skills match or exceed those required by your company. I would be delighted to meet with you to expand on my achievements and discuss how I can apply my strengths to positively impact your company's bottom line. I will call to schedule a meeting. Thank you for your time and professional consideration.

Sincerely,

Tom Carter

Enclosure: resume

23

Training and Development Executive. *Jane Roqueplot, Sharon, Pennsylvania*

Bullets and boldface highlight accomplishments to meet the job description of a prospective position. The second paragraph presents the applicant's views on company competitiveness.

CONFIDENTIAL

JOHN HARMAN
1111 Greenberry Court
Montgomery, Alabama 00000
jharman2@capitol.net
☎ [334] 555-5555 (Home) — [334] 555-6666 (Cell)

Friday, January 20, 2008

Ms. Sandy Reisman
Industrial Training Program Developer & Technical Writer
Alabama Industrial Development Training
One Technology Court
Montgomery, Alabama 00000

Dear Ms. Reisman:

As soon as I saw your announcement for a Training Program Developer and Technical Writer, I thought my experience in manufacturing in Alabama might make me a perfect match for you. Said another way, I wish I had the benefit of AIDT-trained employees in my plants. Thinking about AIDT's immediate future, I wanted to meet your needs, our employers' needs, and the needs of people seeking to enter the workforce. I have covered the details in the attached resume.

My resume documents function, performance, and results—not just lists of job titles and responsibilities. There are 15 examples of payoffs I've gotten for employers just like the ones AIDT serves. The six training examples are highlighted with borders. As you read, I hope this central idea stands out: All my job titles have a manufacturing aspect. However, I was always evaluated on how well I recruited, trained, and retained my workforce. I was measured on productivity. Even so, there is essential information no resume can transmit well.

I think of myself as a trainer with a subject matter expert's point of view. That has always been necessary because my bosses didn't grade my work based on lesson plans, test question ease indexes, or strict compliance with standardized terminology in writing objectives and samples of behavior. They demanded what your customers demand: increased productivity, reduced costs, and lowered liability. So I did much more than skills training. For me, skills without a solid work ethic didn't count for much. All my "students" got both the skills and attitude to underwrite their success in the workplace.

I know you'll soon make a decision about whom to interview. Nevertheless, I would like to hear about AIDT's "needs analysis" in your own words. If I am fortunate enough to be hired, that's the best way I know to be productive right from the start. I will call in a few days to explore opportunities for a meeting.

Sincerely,

John Harman

Encl.: Resume

CONFIDENTIAL

24

Training Program Developer and Technical Writer. *Don Orlando, Montgomery, Alabama*

To make this letter different from the average letter, the writer placed "CONFIDENTIAL" in a header and a footer, used a graphic for "phone," and put a border around the sentence about borders.

Nancy T. Ditillio
000 Raven's Way ▪ Martinsburg, WV 21775 ▪ 555-000-0732 ▪ nditillio@hotmail.com

October 4, 2007

AB&C Group
Robert Vance, Human Resources
One Executive Way
Ranson, WV 25438

Dear Mr. Vance:

Finding and retaining good employees are reported to be two of the biggest challenges faced today by businesses large and small. Retention data suggests that employees target and remain faithful to companies that are committed to their personal and professional development.

A recent visit to the AB&C Group Web site confirmed for me that yours is a company dedicated to employee development and training. Your acknowledgement in the *Wall Street Journal,* the Ranson Learning Center, and the Elaine Looney Achievement Center are testimonies to your commitment. I share in that commitment and have a proven record of achievement to that end. For these reasons, it is with great interest and enthusiasm that I am submitting my resume for consideration in filling your current opening for a **Director of Corporate Training.**

With more than 18 years in the education, employment, and training arena, I am confident I have much to offer:

► **Experience designing, developing, and delivering training.** I have written curricula covering everything from life skills and career management to computer software applications and the Internet. I have trained college students, corporate professionals, customer service representatives, professional peers, and factory workers, to name a few.

► **A proven record of delivering projects on time,** best exemplified by my experience in successfully writing and coordinating the submission of numerous federal grants.

► **Strong platform skills** and ongoing recognition as a high-energy, entertaining, and motivational trainer and workshop facilitator.

► **Supervisory and leadership experience,** whether serving on a board of directors for a community organization or coaching and mentoring individuals to define and take charge of their own success.

► **Creativity** and an innate ability to identify areas in need of improvement and the vision to develop and implement successful action plans.

Since this correspondence can only provide you with a brief overview of my skills and accomplishments, I would welcome the opportunity to talk with you about AB&C Group and your vision for developing your corporate training programs. I will phone early next week to follow up on this correspondence and explore the possibility of scheduling some time with you. I look forward to talking with you then.

Sincerely,

Nancy T. Ditillio

Director of Corporate Training. *Norine Dagliano, Hagerstown, Maryland*

This letter was a response to a newspaper ad. Bulleted items incorporate both the actual requirements listed in the ad and the candidate's experience that matches each requirement.

MARIANNE M. CLARK
0000 Berkeley Lane
Frederick, MD 21701
marck@aol.com
301.555.5555 (home)
301.000.0000 (cell)

Dear Hiring Manager:

Could you use a high-energy, creative salon professional who appreciates the vital link between well-trained, motivated personnel and increased company profits? If so, I would enjoy speaking with you to discuss how my skills and experience might strengthen your organization.

With more than 20 years in the cosmetology industry, I recently made a short-term move from "behind the chair" to a training and management position at Hair Club for Men. As has always been my nature, I met this new challenge head-on. I am proud to say that, through expert training and motivational team building, my contributions have proven instrumental in positioning the Falls Church, Virginia, center as a leader in the corporation for sales and service.

I discovered that I not only love personnel training but also am good at it! My current manager credits me with being "an integral part of changing the way the HCM seasoned stylist thinks when it comes to what is best for the client."

I feel I have taken advantage of all that my current position has to offer and am ready to push my career to the next level as a full-time Trainer or Manager. I am very open to a geographic move and amenable to travel.

My resume is pasted below. I have also attached, for your convenience, a copy in Word 2000 format. This will provide you with some additional information about my background.

Please phone or email me at the address or numbers printed above. I look forward to talking with you!

Sincerely,
Marianne M. Clark

Trainer/Manager. *Norine Dagliano, Hagerstown, Maryland*

This electronic cover letter in .txt (text) format was used by the candidate for online posting and for sending the letter with an electronic resume by e-mail to a hiring manager (in that case including an actual name).

AEVAH B. JONES

0000 Summers Court • Anywhere, Michigan 55555 • (555) 222-2222
aevah@email.com

December 8, 2007

Tomas Smith, Director
ABC Incorporated
555 Main Street
Anywhere, Michigan 55555

Dear Mr. Smith,

As a successful and established recruiting professional, I bring more than eight years of experience and knowledge in locating highly qualified candidates pursuing mid-management to executive-level positions for various employers in diverse industries. I have the drive for developing business relationships and enjoy working one-on-one with employers and candidates. I find networking is key to professional and personal growth.

Through my efforts and success as a recruiter, I have received two prestigious awards from my last employer and have built a reputation for providing genuine leadership and working effectively with others. My talents and expertise in creative sourcing, networking, interviewing techniques and presentations have allowed me to make significant contributions to my employers, as noted in my resume.

Because I have been very successful in recruiting and enjoy the everyday challenges of my profession, I have decided to launch my career as an independent recruiter. I would appreciate the opportunity to speak with you personally to provide more details on my background and the expertise I can offer your firm.

Your time and consideration in reviewing my credentials are appreciated. I will contact you next week to see if we can schedule a day that we can meet to answer any questions you may have regarding my qualifications. I look forward to speaking with you soon.

Sincerely,

Aevah Jones

Enclosure

27

Independent Recruiter. *Maria E. Hebda, Trenton, Michigan*

The letter indicates in four paragraphs the applicant's experience and motivation, awards and areas of expertise, new direction and interest in an interview, and plans for following up the letter.

ANGELA PUPPALA

45 Oak Avenue • Springfield, MA 00000 • puppalaang@xxxxx.com • 413.555.0000

January 11, 2008

Ms. Greer Gaston
Vice President, Human Resources
Ace Company
100 State Street
Hartford, CT 00000

Dear Ms. Gaston:

John Batten, Ace's Comptroller, suggested I contact you regarding your opening for a Manager for Training and Development. With my solid and diversified experience in process improvement, organizational development, and training for a merged company of 13,000 employees in an industry similar to yours, I can design and coordinate an extensive training plan and facilitate the trainings within weeks.

I hold certifications in Tennessee Associates Continuous Improvement, Zenger-Miller, Franklyn Covey—What Matters Most, Career Systems International Franklin Quest Time Management, and the Myers-Briggs Type Indicator.

I will contact you so that we may discuss your needs and how I can fulfill them.

Sincerely,

Angela Puppala

Enclosure

28

Training and Development Manager. *Ellen Mulqueen, Springfield, Massachusetts*

Reference to a third party may lead a reader to pay more attention to a cover letter, particularly if the third party is well known and respected. The second paragraph lists certifications held.

James Howard

0000 Tracer Downs ♦ Perry, GA 00000 ♦ (H) 000-000-0000 ♦ (C) 000-000-0000

[Date]

Mr. (Ms.) _____
[Company]
[Address 1]
[Address 2]

Dear Mr. _____

[Insert 2-line paragraph about how you heard of the position and why you are applying for it. For example: "If the information in the *Times Courier* is still accurate, you are currently seeking to fill the position of Customer Service Manager. This letter is to introduce myself as a candidate for just such a position."]

I am an experienced and highly qualified management professional. My areas of expertise lie in operations management, facilities management, transportation and embarkation, inventory and logistics, purchasing and procurement, personnel and human resources, materials management, public and motivational speaking, written and oral communications, information gathering, data analysis, team coordination, and budget administration. I accepted my current position with the Air Logistics Center at Robins AFB, GA, in an attempt to gain meaningful employment within the infrastructure of civil service. Because opportunities for advancement from this position are quite limited, I am seeking a position within the community at large where my wealth of knowledge and expertise can be fully utilized to the benefit of both my employer and myself.

The enclosed resume briefly outlines my experience and accomplishments. If my qualifications appear to meet your current needs, I would be happy to discuss my background in a meeting with you. I will contact you next week to explore the possibility of an interview.

Sincerely,

James Howard

Enclosure

Customer Service Manager. *Lea J. Clark, Macon, Georgia*

This letter, based on a template, is in progress. Some information is not yet supplied. The first paragraph still has directions for the paragraph. In effect, you are looking over the writer's shoulder.

"¿Hola, como está usted?"

> **Bilingue con 6 años de experiencia de gerente en servicio al consumidor las 24 horas.**
>
> **Bilingual Call Center Manager with 6 years of experience in a 24/7 customer care environment.**

David Gutierrez

0000 Hirsch Rd., Houston, Texas 00000   PH: 555-555-5555   e-mail: dbgtr2@attbi.com   pager: 000-000-0000

December 12, 2007

Thomas Richardson
Vice President—Operations
Triumph Satellite Systems, Inc.
0000 West 18th St.
Houston, Texas 00000

Dear Mr. Richardson:

The implementation of your newly acquired Panama call center will profit from the leadership of an experienced *bilingual* **CALL CENTER MANAGER.** Fluent in Spanish with an extensive customer care background in the versatile setting of a 24/7, 250-seat center, my qualifications offer you the reality of a seamless transition into the world of international customer service.

My professional experience spanning six years of multilevel responsibility has been dominated by the implementation and use of cutting-edge call center technology such as *Witness* (call quality and monitoring), *CMS* (call statistics), *Emvolve* (performance management), *IEX* (workforce scheduling) and *People-Trak* (human resource information). I possess the confidence needed to face the toughest leadership challenges and have a proven track record as a solid achiever. Notable career accomplishments include the following:

- Achieved a $4 million annual gross profit for 2007.
- Improved agent retention by 47% with a workforce defined by 200 Customer Service Representatives, 25 Customer Care Experts, 60 Order Fulfillment Agents, 15 Quality Assurance Agents, 50 Administrative Operations Agents and 22 Manager/Support Staff.
- Attained service-level goals of 80 / 20 on a consistent basis with a variety of client programs and products for a major telecommunications firm producing a volume of 10,000 calls per day.
- Demonstrated a strong ability to strengthen cost-profit ratios by creating financial models with forecasted revenues of $1 million per month with a year-to-date 5% accuracy for budget variance.
- Recognized as the lowest charge-back percentage producer among all client call centers at a rate of .5% by developing and implementing effective fraud-prevention procedures.

With great enthusiasm I submit my resume for your serious consideration as the Operations Manager for your customer-care call center in Panama. Please allow me to share my enthusiasm, flexibility and availability in a personal interview at your earliest convenience. I will call to make an appointment.

Sincerely,

David Gutierrez

Enclosure

> ***Gracias!***

30

Call Center Manager. *MeLisa Rogers, Victoria, Texas*

The writer wanted to convey the candidate's bilingual ability. This letter is a fictionalized version of an entry that was named "Most Eye-Catching Cover Letter" at the 2002 PARW Annual Convention.

Darlene L. Matheson

0000 Emerald Forest • Austin, Texas 78745 • 555-555-5555 • darlene@internet.com

March 21, 2008

Star Communications
Attn: Daniel Rawlings
Human Resource Director
5555 7th Street, Suite Y
Dallas, Texas 75228

Dear Mr. Rawlings:

The Star Communications call center operation will not only reach but also **exceed** the 2008 goals and objectives under the leadership of an experienced and seasoned **CALL CENTER DIRECTOR**. With an extensive customer-care background in the fast-paced, demanding setting of a 24/7 environment—*servicing customers of the nation's premier companies*—my qualifications offer you the reality of a seamless transition into the world of a results-oriented, quality-focused operation.

My professional experience, spanning 14 years of multilevel responsibility, has been dominated by repeated successes in

- Enhancing client satisfaction and relations
- Increasing profits
- Exceeding client quality expectations
- Implementing process development strategies

I possess the confidence needed to face the toughest leadership challenges and have a proven track record as a solid achiever. In my current position, I administer internal *consultation to foreign and domestic call center operations* for Micro Systems Outsourcing Contact Center Solutions division.

With great enthusiasm I submit my resume for your serious consideration as the Call Center Director for Star Communications. Please allow me to share my enthusiasm, flexibility and availability in a personal interview at your earliest convenience. I will call in a few days to set a time.

Sincerely,

Darlene Matheson

"Darlene has the keen ability to leverage her extensive call center operations expertise with creating master processes that are understood and followed by all levels of the operation...agent to Vice President...to achieve high-level success."
Senior Human Resource Manager—Micro Systems Contact Center Solutions

---

31

Call Center Director. *MeLisa Rogers, Victoria, Texas*

The applicant's current assignment as a National Process Manager needed to be downplayed, and her extensive previous experience as a Call Center Manager needed to be emphasized.

— LYNN MATHEWS —

5 Spring Road • Riverside, Pennsylvania • (555) 555-5555 • lynnmat@aol.com

[Date]

[Name]
[Title]
[Company]
[Address]

Dear _____:

Perhaps your graphics department needs a professional with demonstrated creativity and technical skills along with a strong desire to continue learning and to succeed. If so, the qualifications I can offer to your department include the following:

- **Design/illustration experience.** Earned a Bachelor's degree in Illustration from the University of Hartford and acquired extensive training in illustration and design/graphics, utilizing computer software programs such as Aldus FreeHand, QuarkXPress, and PageMaker with a Macintosh system.

- **Award-winning talent.** Recipient of several awards/honors for my artistic talent and academic achievements: the Faith Ferguson Art Award, first place winner in the Honors Art class, and membership in the National Art Honor Society. Many of my illustrations were selected and displayed in the Senior Illustration Show.

- **Technical skills.** Proficient in using various media, including oils, acrylics, gouache, scratchboard, pen and ink, cut paper, color pencils, watercolors, image processing, and etching. Credited for my innovative approach, a great eye for color, excellent technique, and an ability to generate clever ideas.

In both educational and employment settings, I have proven myself to be a dependable, hardworking individual who is always prepared, well organized, and able to manage multiple projects/assignments. I take great pride in the quality of my work, never having missed a single deadline. Additionally, I possess excellent interpersonal skills, am team-oriented, and am willing to "go the extra mile" as needed.

I would welcome a conversation to discuss the contributions I can make to your department, even if you do not have a position available now. I am eager to begin a career in my chosen profession and look forward to speaking with you soon. Thank you for your consideration of my qualifications.

Very truly yours,

Lynn Mathews

Enclosure

32

Graphic Designer. *Louise Garver, Enfield, Connecticut*

The applicant was a recent college graduate in the field of art. Bullets point to strong experience, talent, and skills. She secured a position as a graphic designer at a consumer products company.

CATHERINE T. LEBO

555 SW Morrison Street
Portland, OR 55555

ctlebo@yahoo.com

(000) 000-0000 Residence
(000) 000-0000 Mobile

October 28, 2007

Ms. Jill Horvath
Operations Manager
Starbucks Corporate
1000 Second Avenue
Seattle, WA 55555

Dear Ms. Horvath:

You will want to interview me for the Creative Director position with Starbucks because I have outstanding design/creative skills, am a perfectionist who always strives to improve what I do, and thrive on challenges.

In my current position, as creative director for a start-up beverage company, the president of my firm came to me and asked if I could add an animation piece to the presentation that he was to give at a conference a couple of days from then. **He wanted an animated graphic of himself jumping up and down.** At that time, I didn't have any experience in creating animated graphics, but the request intrigued me. I found the application to design it in and was able to create an animated graphic of my boss jumping up and down while waving a white flag! It was very funny, and **my boss was very impressed that I was able to pull it off, especially in such a short timeframe.** He thought he was giving me an impossible request, but **I made it possible.** Most people would just say no when asked to do things they've never done before, but I see it as a personal challenge and an opportunity to learn something new.

After you review the enclosed resume and visit with me, I think you'll agree that I'm the missing piece to your team. My experience in the creative field is solid, from developing a strong corporate image from the ground up to developing quirky traditions with a lasting impression. I have enclosed a puzzle (one of the traditions I have instituted in my current position) to challenge you and to remind you to give me a call.

I will follow up with you in the next few days and look forward to meeting you. Thank you for your time and consideration.

Sincerely,

Catherine Lebo

Enclosure

33

Creative Director. *Jennifer Rydell, Portland, Oregon*

The writer includes a funny story in the second paragraph to illustrate the applicant's skills. Boldfacing in that paragraph focuses attention on the applicant's accomplishment and its impact.

JENNIFER GEORGE

78 Holland Brook Road • Mooresville, NJ 22222 • (333) 333-3333 • jngrge@earthlink.net

January 10, 2008

[Hiring Agent, Title]
[Company Name]
[Address]

Dear Hiring Manager:

Your posting for a [position title] caught my attention as it seems an ideal match for my experience and talents. As an accomplished graphic designer with a broad range of industry experience, I believe I am someone who will be an asset to your company. With strong creative instincts and a proven record in producing visual designs and written copy that sell products, I would like to explore the possibility of putting my skills and experience to work for you.

As you can see from my enclosed resume, my career encompasses roles in marketing, advertising, sales, and management. An award-winning graphic designer, I am also well-versed in managing all aspects of client projects to successful completion. Key to my success, the depth of my creative talents is fully matched by a disciplined focus on achieving outstanding results. Therefore, I am someone who consistently delivers top-quality projects no matter what the challenge.

Among my other strengths, I have solid sales instincts and have been successful in cultivating long-term relationships with key clients. With a strong customer focus, I often earn the repeat business of clients. Persuasive, self-confident, and effective, I have proven to be a respected and valued employee in the past. With a record of success behind me, I am confident that I will be an asset to you as well.

I would be pleased to have the opportunity to discuss future employment and look forward to speaking with you. I will contact you to set a mutually convenient time.

Thank you for your consideration.

Sincerely,

Jennifer George

Enclosure

34

Graphic Designer. *Carol A. Altomare, Three Bridges, New Jersey*

This letter is for an applicant who had both creative and administrative/relationship management skills. Each of the first three paragraphs shows that she is a designer with extra talent.

SAMUEL LAFITTE

555555 Rio Grande
Valencia, California 91355
email: lafitte@earthlink.net

Voice mail: 555-555-5555
Residence: 000-000-0000

January 13, 2008

Goldcrest Graphics, Inc.
25517 16th Street
Santa Clarita, California 91321

Ensuring Quality Control requires an experienced staff with the expertise to analyze an independent contractor's or employee's ability to do the job correctly for the best price. I possess an innate ability to assess employees' work, equipment, and quality standards. My commitment is to quality while remaining price conscious.

As a Senior Graphic Designer for Adexa earlier this year, I acted as liaison for the director, writer, and printers and edited the full project. Through my supervision of others, I was able to develop a cohesive unit that worked toward a common goal. My management skills led to **greater efficiency** and **cost reduction** while easily meeting deadlines.

Others have pointed out my unparalleled imagination, which allows me to properly evaluate designs, whether for catalogs, Web sites, or software. My diverse background encompasses

- Work for the Los Angeles County Arts Commission
- Murals for Transamerica Insurance, Inc., toy stores, restaurants
- Fascias for Michael Jackson Enterprises
- 3-D animation for Mad TV
- Character design and model creation for a television pilot
- Animation, direction, and production of a short claymation film
- Logo creation

Additional strengths include

- Capability to handle many tasks at one time and meet every deadline, even when those deadlines occur hourly
- Motivation and desire to complete all projects in a timely manner
- Ability to remain respectful, patient, and level-headed under pressure

Artists are famous for being perfectionists, and it is a reputation that is well earned. Although I design on a Mac, I also use a real-world, hands-on approach to business and am confident I can make a significant contribution to Goldcrest Graphics. I can serve both your creative and post-production needs. I am available for any shift, for contract work, for travel, on any basis—you name it. I have no ego, only a desire to do my job to perfection and an ability to use technical skills with creativity to achieve an artistic end.

Eager to hear your ideas, I would appreciate a moment of your time. Could you spare a few minutes to discuss this with me in person? I will call next week to set a time for a personal interview.

Sincerely,

Samuel Lafitte

Enclosure

35

Senior Graphic Designer. *Myriam-Rose Kohn, Valencia, California*

Short paragraphs make a long letter easier to read. Bullets introduced by one or two sentences help to break up a page of short paragraphs. Both techniques are used effectively in this cover letter.

215 Crestview Avenue
Indianapolis, IN 46220
555.555.5555
PhOstbg@earthlink.com

November 15, 2007

Mr. Douglas Shuck
Human Resources Manager
WTW Architects
609 Candlewood Street
Pittsburgh, PA 15212-5801

Dear Mr. Shuck:

Each architect holds his/her own unique paradigm. It has *always* been my dream to be an architect. As an elementary student, I remember drawing projects from my own perspective—viewing the world through different eyes than those of my classmates. Because I enjoy my work and know that success and fulfillment stem directly from working in one's passion, I submit my resume and portfolio to you for consideration.

My resume clearly shows that I have a variety of qualifying skills and abilities. Briefly, they are as follows:

(1) A Bachelor of Arts School of Architecture degree from Miami University with a respectable GPA achieved through hard work and attention to detail,

(2) A very strong background in computer-oriented design as evidenced by keen realistic imaging and detail-oriented visualization to provide innovative, practical design solutions while utilizing a consistent application of the fundamentals, and

(3) A sincere desire to apply these artistic and technical skills in a creative, fulfilling position in a firm such as yours.

I recently saw on the cover of *Buildings* magazine that WTW Architects was awarded "Best New Construction" for the Hetzel Union Building/Paul Robeson Cultural Center at Pennsylvania State University. The article caught my attention because I visited Penn State with my cousin in the spring and saw the "HUB." The building's oval interior commands a unique presence through the use of natural light and open spaces—a concept developed and perfected by Frank Lloyd Wright. One of your senior principals, Paul Williams, stated in the article, "The circle is symbolic of mankind—a symbol of civilization; a symbol of the town, the village, and the individual." The influence of Frank Lloyd Wright's design and expression is clearly evident through your firm's architecture—the same design and expression woven throughout my portfolio.

As you can see from my portfolio, I take pride in my work, too. It would be an honor to be a contributing member of your team and to work hard toward achieving WTW's goals and objectives. Because "proven skills" are best explained in person, I welcome the opportunity to introduce myself in an interview to discuss the value I offer WTW Architects. I will follow up with a phone call the week of November 21. Thank you for reviewing my portfolio, and I look forward to our meeting.

Sincerely,

Phillip Ostberg
Enclosures

36

Architect. *Sharon Pierce-Williams, Findlay, Ohio*

The writer used the AIDA style of business writing for persuasive sales letters, where Attention, Interest, Desire, and Action paragraphs sell the product—in this instance, the candidate.

Susan D. Chambers

100 Windy Way
Madison, CT 00000
(800) 555-1212
schambers@email.com

[Date]

[Mr./Ms. _____]
[Company]
[Address 1]
[Address 2]

Dear Hiring Professional,

As a qualified educator with a strong background in Special and Early Childhood education, I am writing to introduce myself as a candidate for the position of Special Education Administrator that was advertised in the *Daily News* on September 7, 20XX.

I am a skilled and qualified professional with extensive experience in Special Education and Early Childhood Education Administration. I have exceptional skills as an educator, as well as the ability to analyze, coordinate, and implement special-needs and early-childhood curriculum based on the individual needs of the classroom and the child.

My background includes managing personnel and administrating activities related to maintaining federal grants. Based on previous successes in the educational field, and recognition by state and local agencies as an expert in my field, I believe I would be an immediate asset to your organization's management team.

The enclosed resume briefly outlines my experience and accomplishments. If it appears that my qualifications meet your current needs, I would be happy to further discuss my background in a meeting with you. Please feel free to contact me at the above telephone number or e-mail address.

Sincerely,

Susan D. Chambers

Enclosure

37

Special Education Administrator. *Lea J. Clark, Macon, Georgia*

A cover letter concentrating on experience wasn't working. The writer wrote this letter to highlight accomplishments and administrative abilities. The applicant got four interviews within a few weeks.

Wendy R. McClean

0000 Potter Street
Saginaw, MI 55555

555-555-5555

February 19, 2008

Discovery Center
Attention: Search Committee
9874 E. Maple Road
Troy, MI 48084

Dear Search Committee Members:

I was excited to read your advertisement in the *Oakland Press* for Director of the Discovery Center. It seems as if the ad could have been written for me! Most of my adult life has been spent working with or for children, culminating in an Associate degree in Early Childhood Education. I am enclosing my resume for your review.

As I said, I match the qualifications you are seeking. Let me elaborate:

Your Requirements	*My Qualifications*
♥ CDA	♥ I have applied for my CDA and expect approval soon.
♥ At least 12 credits in child development, child psychology, or early childhood education	♥ I recently earned an Associate degree with High Honors in Early Childhood Education.
♥ Strong leadership skills	♥ In addition to operating my own day care center for four years, I have been instrumental in planning and implementing several fund-raising events for the Easter Seals Society.

When you take a look at my resume, you will see that my quest to improve my knowledge hasn't stopped in the classroom. I regularly attend conferences, professional association activities and continuing education opportunities so that I can remain current in the field. The fact that I worked full time (operating my own day care center) while attending college exemplifies my motivation and commitment.

In conclusion, I am confident I have the training and experience to excel in this position. I hope you will contact me to arrange an interview at your convenience. Thank you for your time and consideration.

Sincerely,

Wendy R. McClean

Enclosure

38

Child Care Center Director. *Janet L. Beckstrom, Flint, Michigan*

The applicant had just earned her associate degree and wanted to head a child care center. The Your Requirements… My Qualifications scheme calls attention to the applicant's relevant credentials.

SUKI OSAKA

15 Longwood Avenue
Northampton, Massachusetts 55555
Cell: (555) 555-5555
Home: (555) 500-5000
sukiosaka@aol.com

September 25, 2007

Nadine Phillips
Principal
Hadley School System
3 Rindge Road
Hadley, MA 50000

Dear Ms. Phillips:

What I love most about teaching students with moderate special needs is the children themselves. They know that I am interested in them by my enthusiastic approach and my ability to help them learn in the areas in which they are experiencing the most difficulty. I am confident that I would be a strong asset to your special-needs program as a Learning Center Teacher.

I am skilled at developing modifications to curricula and lessons to ensure that each individual's learning style is addressed with appropriate instructional plans. My students are highly motivated by the creative, multisensory lessons I develop. Seeing students grow academically, socially, and emotionally using these approaches is very satisfying.

In order to be the best teacher I can be, I worked hard to develop my skills and knowledge base in my Master's program at Clark University (4.0 GPA). I gained top-notch experience as an Inclusion Assistant in the highly regarded Amherst Public Schools for the past two school years. Also, I have had extensive practicum experience in neighboring school systems. I feel equipped now to assume the responsibilities of the top teaching role in a learning center.

I am certified in elementary education and moderate special needs (K–9). My experience encompasses teaching the full curriculum to general education classes containing some inclusion students, as well as adapting instruction to specific children in small-group and individual contexts. I collaborate well with other teachers in a team-teaching setting and as part of a multidisciplinary team focused on enhancing the learning experience for each child. This range of experience prepares me well for teaching students in a learning center.

I would appreciate an opportunity to meet with you. I will contact you to set a convenient time. Thank you for considering my sincere interest in the position.

Best regards,

Suki Osaka

39

Learning Center Teacher. *Jean Cummings, Concord, Massachusetts*

The applicant was in an assistant position. The challenge was to persuade the school system to give her a full teaching position by highlighting her personality as a sensitive, caring individual.

David R. Chance

103 N 3rd Street
Sunshine, PA 00000-0000
(800) 555-1212 • david@someisp.org

[date]

[contact name]
[facility]
[address]
[address]

Dear Hiring Professional [or contact name]:

As an experienced Christian educator with a 9-year background in youth ministries, I am writing to explore teaching opportunities with your university. I believe you will find my qualifications suitable to a position where I may share knowledge with those who desire to serve students and young adults by proclaiming the Gospel message and drawing people to Jesus Christ.

I earned my Bachelor's and Master's degrees from ABC Seminary and have recently applied for candidacy in a Ph.D. Organizational Leadership program with Biblical University. My career focus has been placed on reaching youth through the creation and implementation of education, missions, and study programs with today's young people in mind. I believe my experience in this area has positioned me to serve the students of your school in enhancing their individual knowledge and ability to go forth and practice the evangelism of our faith.

My accomplishments and qualifications are outlined in the enclosed Curriculum Vitae. I will call you next week to discuss whether my education and experience meet the needs of your organization.

Thank you for your time and consideration.

Sincerely,

David R. Chance
Pastor of Student Ministries, Community Church

40

University Instructor. *Lea J. Clark, Macon, Georgia*

This Christian educator completed a master's degree and wanted to teach at a Christian college. This cover letter with a curriculum vitae helped him get two part-time positions. One became full-time.

Susan Wiley

Permanent Address:
1111 Clinton Avenue
Houston, TX 00000
(281) 000-0000

swiley2222@msn.com
cell: (000) 000-0000

Current Address:
2102 Indiana Street #222
Lubbock, TX 00000
(806) 000-0000

January 30, 2008

Jan Pearson, Principal
Hart Elementary School
2323 Middleton Street
Houston, TX 00000

"One hundred years from now it will not matter what my bank account was, the sort of house I lived in, or the kind of car I drove, but the world may be different because I was important in the life of a child."
—Anonymous

Dear Mrs. Pearson:

I love the preceding quote! Although it may be seen as too "sentimental" by some, I truly believe that being able to make a positive difference in children's lives is a worthwhile endeavor—and the *true* reward in life. I am excited about the opportunity to launch my teaching career and influence student growth, and I am certain that my enthusiasm and ability to motivate would be a welcome addition to your faculty.

My educational experiences have convinced me that being a teacher is a wonderful career choice. While taking upper-level courses in secondary education and completing observation hours at local junior high and high schools, I studied educational theory and, more importantly, realized the value of consistent discipline enforcement, student-centered learning, and classroom/lesson organization, among many other educator functions. Through my Cum Laude G.P.A. and performance on major grade projects, I demonstrated a strong background knowledge in these areas, and although theory does not always translate into practice, I am confident that my knowledge will transfer effectively in an educational setting.

I have had two very different, yet interesting experiences in my employment history that indirectly prepared me for some of the challenges I will face as an educator. As a server at The Olive Garden restaurant, I was recognized by management for providing excellent, prompt service in an environment that could best be described as fast-paced and highly stressful. As an intern reporter for the *Moore County News Press*, I developed a keen appreciation for the richness and value of small-town living through firsthand observations and interviewing local residents for human-interest stories. Although both experiences are quite different from working day-to-day in an educational setting, I do feel that these positions prepared me for handling difficult situations and relating to diverse individuals on a one-to-one basis.

My resume is enclosed to provide details about my background and qualifications. If permissible, I will contact you to follow up on this letter of inquiry, or you may contact me at the number of my current residence. I look forward to meeting with you and discussing how I can contribute to the success of your school.

In addition, I have a particular interest in sponsoring extracurricular activities and would like to discuss with you how I could contribute to your school in this regard.

Thank you for your time and consideration.

Sincerely,

Susan Wiley

Enclosure

41

Entry-Level Teacher. *Daniel J. Dorotik, Jr., Lubbock, Texas*

The anonymous quotation amounts to the applicant's philosophy of teaching and enables her to express in the first paragraph her excitement and enthusiasm at the beginning of her teaching career.

JENNIFER DEAN

555 Bracebridge Road   jennie_dean@yahoo.com
Memphis, TN 55555   555-555-5555 (cell)

September 15, 2007

Dr. Edward Tallant
Mathematics Department Chair
Winningham College
5555 Aloe Street
Santa Clara, CA 55555

Subject: Mathematics Instructor Position

Dear Dr. Tallant:

Your requirement for a Mathematics Instructor interests me greatly because of my longstanding commitment to advancing the skills of students in this subject area, as well as my desire to return to California. My resume is enclosed for your consideration.

My teaching career encompasses substantial student diversity, including high school and college students from different cultural backgrounds, both one-on-one and in classroom settings. In several instances, students were in my class only because they were required to take it. In spite of this, I succeeded in instilling in many of them a respect for the subject and a grasp of the fundamental principles.

Because of my technical experience, I am comfortable using a combination of technology and traditional teaching methods to communicate mathematical concepts to students and have successfully done so throughout the past few years.

As an experienced, dedicated educator, I believe I can provide significant value to your institution and its students. I would like to arrange an interview to discuss the specific needs of Winningham College and its Mathematics Department, as well as my ability to make a worthwhile contribution to the growth of your students. I will contact you in the coming week to set a mutually convenient time to meet.

Sincerely,

Jennifer Dean

42

Mathematics Instructor. *Georgia Adamson, Campbell, California*

The individual was teaching in a southern state and wanted to return to California. The key second paragraph highlights her experience with diversity and skill in making math popular.

Julia Scully

20 Angela Street ◆ Colonie, NY 00000 ◆ (555) 555-5555 ◆ sclly@sage.edu

[Date]

[Hiring Agent Name]
[Title]
[School Name]
[Address]
[City, State ZIP]

Dear Mr. / Ms. _____:

As a dedicated, highly knowledgeable Teacher with certification to teach pre-Kindergarten through grade 6, I believe my skills and talents can make an immediate and long-term contribution to [name of school].

During my intensive teaching assignments with Russell Sage College, I have enjoyed teaching elementary and preschool students in a variety of jobs and educational settings. I am skilled at developing and implementing stimulating lesson plans, administering and evaluating standardized tests, writing profiles, and conducting parent-teacher conferences. I am a team player capable of working well and building strong rapport with students, professionals, parents, and staff members. My educational background includes a Bachelor's degree in Elementary Education with a minor in Psychology from Russell Sage College. My proven ability to help children achieve their highest levels through positive motivation will be an asset to your team.

The accompanying resume provides further details of my accomplishments and what I have to offer. I believe it would be mutually beneficial for us to meet and discuss your current or anticipated teaching positions. I will call next week to inquire about such a meeting.

Thank you for your time and consideration.

Sincerely,

Julia Scully

Enc. resume

43

Pre-Kindergarten Teacher. *John Femia, Altamont, New York*

This letter is for a recent graduate. The opening paragraph indicates her occupational goal, the middle paragraph sells the candidate, and the third paragraph looks for an interview.

Mari Madison

10180 Springton Road • Mechanicsville, VA 23116 • Home: 804-730-1575 • madison@college.edu

EDUCATION ADMINISTRATOR / DISTANCE LEARNING DIRECTOR
Top Expert in Distance Learning and Educational Technology

Goal: Driving the advancement of distance learning via cutting-edge technology, leadership, vision, and collaboration.

October 10, 2007

David H. Gill, Assistant Vice Chancellor
Educational Programs & Instructional Effectiveness
Virginia Community College System
James Monroe Building 16th Floor, 101 North 14th St.
Richmond, Virginia 23219

Dear Sir:

Your college advertised for an educational technologist… someone who can help you build anytime, anyplace education to parallel today's anytime, anyplace workplace… someone with both technical vision and collaborative skills… a real leader in education administration and distance learning— whether for on-campus, between campuses, or even international audiences. I am such a person!

I have more than 15 years of hands-on experience in developing online advanced-degree programs and distance-learning programs—*from scratch*. I also have direct experience in faculty-training programs, technical training, and education technologies.

My Value to a Learning Institution

- Development and delivery of online advanced-degree programs
- Creation and administration of distance-learning courses
- Optimization of educational technology for online and on-campus programs
- Establishment of cutting-edge labs for learning and courseware development
- Successful design of Web sites, learning matrices, and learning portals
- Effective Web-based systems for accreditation management
- Technical direction and advice for administrators, faculty, and technologists
- Intercollegiate collaboration for implementation of programs

If you are looking for someone who can truly build—and administer—anytime, anyplace education, I am confident that I can bring the perfect marriage of distance learning, education technologies, experience, and vision to your school.

Accordingly, my resume is enclosed. I will call you in a few days to follow up and hopefully to schedule an interview. I look forward to talking more about your goals and what I may do for you as your Director of Education Technology.

Sincerely,

Mari Madison, Ph.D.

Enclosure: Resume

44

Educational Technologist. *Helen Oliff, Reston, Virginia*

Most resume writers make resumes eye-catching. Here's an eye-catching cover letter. The two bold lines, centered "heading," italicized goal, bold paragraph, and bulleted values all get attention.

LORRAINE SIMMONS

899 Forest Lane
Southland, PA 00000

(555) 555-5555
lorsim@aol.com

[Date]

[Name]
[Company]
[Address]
[City, State ZIP]

Dear [Name]:

My interest in contributing to your school system as an elementary teacher has prompted me to forward my resume for your consideration. With several years of service in different grade levels and all curriculum areas, my qualifications are a match for the position.

Specifically, I offer the following:

Education	♦ Master of Arts in Teaching from the College of Our Lady of the Elms.
Experience	♦ I have 8 years of experience in elementary school environments, including the past 5 years as a classroom teacher instructing fourth-grade students. ♦ I have taught diverse student populations representing various cultural and socioeconomic backgrounds as well as different emotional/learning needs. ♦ My experience includes curriculum design and using a variety of creative teaching techniques to engage students with different learning styles and needs.
Leadership	♦ Extensive planning, program development, organizational and coordination skills combine with leadership strengths, including serving on a committee to develop and implement a performance-evaluation program for the faculty.
Philosophy and Attributes	♦ A skilled and dedicated teacher, I have excellent classroom-management, conflict-resolution, communication and interpersonal abilities. ♦ Monitoring, evaluating and actualizing teaching practices to facilitate the academic, social and personal needs of all learners are among my strengths.

If you are seeking a teaching professional who can stimulate elementary students' interests and focus their intensity and curiosity, then I may be the candidate you need. I enjoy challenges, and I work diligently and cooperatively to achieve common goals. Equally important, I am committed to the students, parents and community whom I serve. In addition, I strive to build effective relationships in my interactions with other educators and administrators.

I appreciate your serious consideration and will call in the near future to arrange a meeting to discuss the position further.

Sincerely,

Lorraine Simmons

45

Elementary Teacher. *Louise Garver, Enfield, Connecticut*

This letter helped the applicant secure an elementary teaching position. Bulleted items are clustered according to four criteria as bold side headings, making the items easier to comprehend.

Jennie S. Donaldson

000 Sheridan Place • Saginaw, MI 48601 • 555-555-5555 • jennied@comcast.net

[Date]

[Name]
[Company]
[Address]
[City, State ZIP]

Dear Administrator:

The education field is in a predicament right now, isn't it? Many districts are faced with a need for teachers but may not have the funds to hire experienced educators, especially those with advanced degrees. I am one of those "seasoned" teachers, and I would like to explain why I believe my experience is valuable to your district.

This is my eleventh year of teaching at the early elementary level. Over time I have learned what works and what doesn't, what motivates children and what turns them off. Since I know what to expect from students at the beginning of each year, we can get right down to the business of learning. Given the importance of standardized test scores such as MEAP, it is important to start covering relevant material as soon and as often as possible. I don't have to teach by trial and error—I've been there, done that.

My ability to earn the trust and respect of my students is a key point as well. Getting parents involved in their children's education is important, too. My classroom is high energy and creative, and I'm not afraid to try new techniques. Completing a master's degree in teaching and curriculum has certainly helped round out *my* education.

I hope you'll give me an opportunity for an interview so that I can give you additional information about my teaching style, capabilities, and enthusiasm for the job. I'll contact you next week to explore a convenient time to meet. Thank you for your time and attention.

Sincerely,

Jennie S. Donaldson

Enclosure

46

Elementary Teacher. *Janet L. Beckstrom, Flint, Michigan*

Many teacher layoffs had created a huge applicant pool. Districts were hiring less-experienced teachers for less money. This letter explains why this experienced elementary teacher is "worth it."

CHRISTINE L. BERNARDO
000 ATTAWA ROAD
NEW VISTA, NM 88888

March 22, 2008

Dr. Stephanie Stasos, Assistant Superintendent
Human Resources Department
New Vista Public Schools
New Vista, NM 88888

Dear Dr. Stasos:

Recently, my neighbor, who teaches at New Vista High School, informed me that there may be several elementary and middle school teaching positions available for the coming school year. Since my last correspondence with you, I have received my middle school endorsement, in addition to my certification to teach in elementary grades. I am now certified to teach social studies at the middle school level through grade eight.

May I add that I feel quite honored to have been chosen from among more than 200 applicants to participate—along with mainly seasoned teachers—in a fully paid summer institute sponsored by the National Geographic Society. I am confident that this unique experience will add much interest to my own classes in project development and general class discussions.

As a substitute teacher in the New Vista schools this past year, I found administrators, supervisors, and faculty exceptionally helpful and pleasant. Such welcoming support from them is particularly assuring to entry-level teachers like me. I felt like one of the family!

Thank you, Dr. Stasos, for taking time from your busy schedule to see me last spring, and I look forward to another meeting with you soon to discuss in more depth my goals and long-range ambitions in the teaching profession. I would appreciate your scheduling me for a formal interview as I apply for a teaching position in the New Vista Public School District.

Sincerely,

Christine L. Bernardo

Enclosures: resume; employment application packet

---

(555) 555-5555   ◊   Cell: (000) 000-0000   ◊   chrsbrnrdo@earthlink.com

47

Middle School Teacher. *Edward Turilli, North Kingstown, Rhode Island*

Networking breaks the ice in the first paragraph. The applicant strengthens her candidacy by informing the superintendent of her recent accomplishments and complimenting his school system.

Ethan Breines
86 Pinegrove Avenue, Mapleshade, NJ 55555
555-555-5555 (h) | 000-000-0000 (c) | etbreines@tru.net

January 5, 2008

Jillian Holmes
Superintendent of Schools
Mapleshade School District
76-23 Third Street
Mapleshade, NJ 55555

RE: Middle school or high school Social Studies teaching position.

Dear Ms. Holmes:

Recent deep school-budget cuts mean that there are many candidates for a very limited number of positions in the Mapleshade School District. Why should you hire me?

Here's the difference I believe I bring to Mapleshade's students—dedication, motivation, and fun. I can make students work hard, I can make them laugh, and I can make them want to come to class. And I'll do it with all students, not just the top of the class.

But that's not the whole picture. I am absolutely committed to helping students see the world as a whole, not as a town in New Jersey. I want them to know that they are important to this country and to the world—that as citizens they have an obligation to be informed, to make considered choices, to vote, and to participate in the democratic process. I want them to be excited about the past and about how the lessons of the past impact the future.

I want them to love to come to Social Studies class and to groan if they have a substitute teacher because I make Social Studies the best part of their school day. I want them to love to learn, to be excited about what every class brings, to be inspired critical thinkers and writers, and to do well on tests so they will have a better future. I want them to see me walking the halls, chatting with students, attending school events, and coaching sports. I want them to know that I care enough to be there off-hours.

Maybe that's how all new teachers think, but I am sincere and believe I can make it happen—or at least I can try, and never give up. In fact I know it can happen because I've had teachers like that— and that is why I'm writing you today.

Thank you very much for your attention; I look forward to meeting with you and the school board.

Sincerely,

Ethan Breines

Enclosure

48

Social Studies Teacher. *Deborah Wile Dib, Medford, New York*

The question at the end of the first paragraph hooks the reader for the next paragraph. The repetition of "I can make" and "I want them" keeps interest in the middle three paragraphs.

Donald R. Jones

206 Hawkins Lane • Columbus, Ohio 43200 • 614.456.0000 • drjones@juno.com

April 17, 2008

Mr. Scott Trobough
Superintendent
Columbus City Schools
1234 Morse Road
Columbus, Ohio 43200

Dear Mr. Trobough:

After a successful career in government, I recently fulfilled a lifelong desire to become an educator at the secondary level. I have completed my education and licensure requirements and am excited to begin my teaching career. This letter is sent to inquire about possible teaching opportunities within the Columbus City Schools. The enclosed resume will provide detailed information regarding my background and experience in support of my candidacy.

To briefly highlight my qualifications, I offer you the following:

- Social Studies Comprehensive Certification (7–12) complemented by a Bachelor of Arts degree in Political Science

- Successful classroom teaching experience as a substitute and student teacher in diverse classroom settings—experienced in developing and implementing integrated lesson plans for cooperative learning

- More than 10 years of professional involvement in government at the local, state and federal levels providing invaluable insight and knowledge to bring into the classroom

In short, I bring a unique combination of education and "real world" experience not often found in today's classroom teachers. I believe the time I spent in government can only enhance my social studies teaching. Should you have a teaching position available, I would appreciate being considered a serious candidate. You should also know that I would be interested in serving as an advisor for extracurricular clubs and/or activities. Feel free to contact me to set up an interview or to answer any questions you may have regarding my background and experience.

Thank you for your time and consideration. I look forward to hearing from you.

Sincerely,

Donald R. Jones

Enclosure

49

Social Studies Teacher. *Melissa L. Kasler, Athens, Ohio*

The applicant was transitioning from government employment to teaching. Because of his background in real-world government and politics, he wanted to be a social studies teacher.

MICHAEL STACK
000 Lexington Drive / Albany, NY 00000 / (555) 555-5555 / stackm@email.com

February 10, 2008

Dr. Taylor Raine Coleman
Putnam Valley Central School District
111 Peekskill Hollow Road
Putnam Valley, NY 10579

Dear Dr. Coleman:

Please accept this letter and enclosed resume for the social studies position that is currently available within your district. As an experienced social studies teacher, I offer vast classroom exposure, a great deal of energy, and a commitment to the students.

Over the course of my career, I have taught both middle-school and high-school students in a variety of subjects, including U.S. History and Global History. Two years ago, my wife and I relocated to the Mohawk Valley from Albany, NY. Currently, I teach 8th-grade social studies in Herkimer Central School District. Prior to this, I taught for 14 years at Schenectady Central School District.

As a professional educator, my efforts extend beyond academics. I work hard at instilling a sense of school pride, building community awareness, and motivating students to set higher standards. In addition to general education, my teaching experience encompasses inclusion classes. With all my students, I take the time to connect with each one, demonstrating genuine sensitivity when working with those who have special needs. Through an ongoing process of planning, delivering, reflecting, and refining lessons, I am consistently successful at balancing individual needs with the NYS Standards & Assessments. I also have a proven record of success (98% passing rate) with the 8th-Grade Social Studies Assessment.

Most significant to my teaching ability is my enthusiasm for the material and appropriate sense of humor. Through these, I am able to engage students and facilitate the learning process. Daily lessons include classroom discussion of current events while activities focus on creating and using information for knowledge and understanding. I also highlight the modes of communication within the community and integrate technology and media into lessons. Whatever the topic, my goal is to emphasize the fact that knowledge and access to information are essential to responsible citizenship and participation in a democracy.

Thank you in advance for your time. I look forward to speaking with you to further discuss my qualifications and will call to schedule an appropriate time.

Sincerely,

Michael Stack

Enclosure

50

Social Studies Teacher. *Kristin M. Coleman, Poughkeepsie, New York*

In this well-designed letter, the last sentence of the first paragraph indicates the key topics of the second, third, and fourth paragraphs, respectively. The letter gives the impression that the applicant has an orderly mind.

Wanda Ortiz

2 Fir Lane   (555) 555-5555
Smithtown, NY 11787   w_ortiz@aol.com

There is no more beautiful life than that of a student.
~ F. Albrecht

During my years as a bilingual educator, I have developed a keen understanding of the importance of student assimilation and respect for their native upbringing. These key principles make teaching bilingual students a rewarding and challenging career path.

As an educator, I wear many different hats: those of teacher, motivator, and leader. I am confident in my ability to create a "love of learning" environment for bilingual students that will enrich their academic growth.

I adhere to new procedures and commissioner regulations for LEP and have hands-on knowledge of the following academic standards: Language for Information and Understanding, Language for Literacy Response and Expression, Language for Critical Analysis and Evaluation, and Language for Social Interaction.

If your school district is looking for an enthusiastic and engaging educator who enjoys building brighter futures, I would love to speak with you. I will contact you next week to set up a personal interview.

Sincerely,

Wanda Ortiz

Enclosure

51

Bilingual Educator. *Linda Matias, Smithtown, New York*

The applicant was going to use the cover letter at a teachers' job fair. Therefore, she could not personalize each letter. Instead of a salutation, the writer put first an inspirational quotation.

JAMES L. HAMMARLUND
63 Bay Vista Street, Westerly, WA 00000
(555) 333-4444
jlhamm@aol.com

February 22, 2008

Dr. Frank Kessler, Superintendent
Westerly School District
788 Whitman Road
Westerly, WA 00000

Dear Dr. Kessler:

Please accept this letter in response to your advertisements in *The Westerly Weekly Press*, February 20, 2008, and *The Westerly Sunday Journal*, February 22, 2008, for a Physical Education / Health teacher at Westerly High School. I have enclosed my resume and a completed application for employment.

As a Washington State–certified, experienced, and successful teacher of Physical Education / Health and an athletic coach for nine years, I have consistently demonstrated my ability to motivate and handle youngsters, both in the classroom and on the playing field. Equally important, I possess a sincere caring for teenagers and extend myself to help ensure their success.

My strengths as a teacher include patience, dedication, and a strong sense of organization. Although I enjoy working within a rather structured curriculum, I am quite able to adapt to most working environments. Finally, of utmost importance to me is that my students receive physical education instruction of the highest quality. I strive to inculcate integrity in all that they do as students and future citizens and leaders of our city and country.

Thank you, Dr. Kessler, for considering my application for employment in the Westerly School District. I look forward to meeting with you to reveal and discuss my objectives during professional development. May I call next week to set up an appointment to meet?

Sincerely,

James L. Hammarlund

Enclosures: resume / application

52

Physical Education/Health Teacher. *Edward Turilli, North Kingstown, Rhode Island*

This physical education teacher makes the point that he teaches the whole student instead of promoting only the student's physical well-being. This approach makes him appear unique.

Arthur Hampton, M.Ed.

1111 Parker Street
Brunswick, New Jersey 07777   ahteach@aol.com

Home: 222-999-5555
Office: 222-666-6600

January 16, 2008

Worthington Area School District
ATT: James Drury, Superintendent
14 Atherton Street
Worthington, New Jersey 06666

Dear Superintendent Drury:

Allow me to introduce myself.

For the past 19 years I have been involved in the educational leadership of two highly respected private schools. Two of my key responsibilities have been to introduce competitive and demanding instructional programs and to hire and develop the appropriate staff to meet those challenges. I'm happy to say that I have been successful in both areas, as reflected in the enclosed resume. Best of all, I have enjoyed making learning an exciting and enjoyable process for the students!

I am at a point in my professional career where I am ready for a new challenge. Key areas where I can make a contribution to your district are the following:

- Planning and developing curriculum
- Achieving accreditation
- Building teamwork and cohesive work groups
- Setting goals and high academic standards
- Managing budgets and fund-raising activities

It would be my pleasure to meet with you to discuss the ways in which I can make an immediate and positive impact on your fine district.

Thank you for your consideration and professional courtesy in reviewing my resume. I will call you soon to explore the possibility of an interview.

Sincerely,

Arthur Hampton

Enclosure

53

Administrative Position. *Karen Conway, Media, Pennsylvania*

At a pivotal point in his long career, this educational leader wanted an administrative position in which he could further apply his leadership skills. Bullets point to his possible key contributions.

KATHERINE KNOCKWOOD

5555 7th Street ~ Cotton, Texas 79000 ~ (000) 000-0000
(000) 000-0000, Ext. 000 (Work) ~ (000) 000-0000 (Cell)
katherineknockwood@yahoo.com

February 17, 2008

Human Resources Coordinator
Cotton Independent School District
#10 Module Avenue
Cotton, Texas 00000

RE: QUADRANT LEADER POSITION

To excel is to reach your own highest dream. But you must also help others, where and when you can, to reach theirs. Personal gain is empty if you do not feel you have positively touched another's life.
~~ Barbara Walters

Dear Human Resources Coordinator:

Years of perseverance in striving to become school principal have brought me to this place in my professional career. After recently gaining a certification in Mid-management/Principal from Cotton University, I am eager to apply my college education and teaching/diagnostician experience in the capacity of school principal. The enclosed resume reflects credentials that meet the requirements of a Quadrant Leader position at Cotton Independent School District (CISD).

In addition to a relevant academic and career background, I possess several personal traits that will surely benefit a position of this caliber. A personable demeanor and sense of humor allow instant rapport with others; passionate diligence toward improving the educational system adds distinction to our industry; flexibility promotes adaptation to change; and focused listening and perceptiveness ensure met needs.

Following are the philosophies that I incorporate daily into personal and work environments:

- Each day is a new beginning to make positive contributions to work, colleagues, community, and family.
- Goals that embrace the highest ethical and service standards can only promote personal and professional growth.
- A school official must reflect integrity, accountability, and professionalism in all situations.
- The key to successful interaction with peers, parents, and students is a friendly, understanding, accepting, and diplomatic attitude that respects the dignity of every human.
- Effective programs are those that empower parents, students, and staff through interactive participation, collaboration, and shared decision making.
- A proactive approach to problem prevention saves energy, time, and money.
- Follow up, follow up, follow up!
- Strong leadership skills include the ability to motivate, mediate, facilitate, and delegate.
- A good leader has insight into and consideration for the feelings, concerns, and aspirations of others.

These skills and values could contribute greatly to the contributions of a CISD school principal. An opportunity to talk with you in person will be mutually beneficial. Please expect a phone call within the week to set up an appointment at your convenience. In the meantime, thank you for your time and consideration.

Sincerely,

Katherine Knockwood

Enclosure: Resume

54

Quadrant Leader. *Edith A. Rische, Lubbock, Texas*

This teacher wanted to become the principal in her own school. Her letter had to be strong because she would be a superior to her previous peers. The writer therefore stressed strengths.

SARA ANNE STEEL

(999) 999.9999

May 3, 2007

Mr. Roger MacAfee, Dean of Fine Arts
RIO GRANDE UNIVERSITY
900 W. Casa Ave.
Yellow Creek, New Mexico 99999

"I am interested in ideas, not merely visual products."

~ Marcel Duchamp

Dear Mr. MacAfee:

An instructor in good standing at Rio Grande University, I am very interested in transitioning from painting, design, and art appreciation instructor to your recently posted **Jewelry Repair and Design Faculty position.** I was thrilled to discover an **exceptional match between your requirements for this opening and my skills and qualifications.** The enclosed curriculum vita reflects a progressive career path and a credible candidate for this position. Qualifications follow:

Your Requirements:	My Qualifications:
MFA in Metals	MFA in Jewelry / Metalsmithing from Freemont Art University of New York, 1997.
Bench work / experience with jewelry repair practices	Jewelry repair and bench work for local retail jeweler. Experience includes stone setting, soldering, pearl bead stringing, ring sizing, jewelry designing, and riveting. Consider value and safekeeping.
Teaching, jewelry design education, and curriculum development	Two years of teaching experience. Comprehensive knowledge of casting gained through education, freelance, and contract work includes wax carving, wax chasing, and mold making.
Excellent communication skills	Excellent oral and written self-expression. Deliver clear instructions and relate well to students. Relaxed communication style fosters encouragement and support. Subscribe to open-door policy.
Commitment to working with a diverse population	Successfully teach and interact with physically and mentally challenged individuals, as well as people of all ages from varied backgrounds and cultures.
Ability to manage projects and set specific objectives	Extremely goal-oriented, giving particular attention to planning and follow-up for positive results. Day planner and "to-do" lists spark productivity. Experience coordinating special events such as art shows, parties, and dinners.

Photography, gemology, and sculpture round out my talents. Personal qualities include a cheerful, energetic demeanor; positive attitude; dedication; self-sufficiency; and creative / innovative idea generation. I am passionate about art, teaching, and mentoring, and enjoy the two-fold return of the enthusiasm I bring to class.

Additionally, positive feedback from both peers and students precedes me:

- "I have never seen painting so strong from the art department," and "you are raising the bar."
- "I got more from this class (Painting I) than most others I've had."
- "This was the most exciting / stimulating class I've taken in 1½ years."
- "It was nice to see your work and know that it came from someone as normal as the rest of the world."
- "Your help contributed most to my learning. You were not afraid to help in any way you could."

Comments like these are especially fulfilling. Other job satisfaction comes from observing facial expressions when students finally comprehend a theory or concept and helping students discover and expand their creativity.

The safety issues involved in running a jewelry / metals lab and properly taught techniques and procedures are of vital importance. The prospect of teaching in my field and being on the ground floor of a future jewelry department energizes me. A fresh perspective to course and curriculum development at Rio Grande University is guaranteed. I will call to schedule a personal interview to further discuss your needs. Thank you for your time and consideration.

Sincerely,

Sara Anne Steel

Enclosure: Resume

9999 Old Mill Road, Paintbrush, MO 99999

sasteel55@mindspring.com

55

University Instructor. *Edith A. Rische, Lubbock, Texas*

The applicant wanted to become part of a new department. This letter positions Requirements and Qualifications each in two side-by-side columns bounded by vertical lines.

MICHAEL R. KELLEY

4567 Ridgeway Avenue • Lewiston, KY 44444 • 606.123.4567 • mrk@aol.com

July 22, 2007

Ms. Nancy Spires
Human Resources
Kenyon College
1234 Meadowbrook Avenue
Racine, Ohio 45771

Dear Ms. Spires:

First off, belated congratulations to everyone at Kenyon College for being listed in the *Kaplan/Newsweek* "How to Get into College" issue as one of the year's "hottest colleges." To that end, it would be an honor for me to join the Kenyon staff as the Head Men's Basketball Coach and strive to uphold the high standards of your institution. Please accept the enclosed resume as my sincere interest in this position.

With 18 years of coaching (14 of those at the collegiate level), extensive experience in Division III athletics and broad knowledge of the North Coast Athletic Conference, I have much to offer as the Head Coach of the Kenyon Lords.

In addition, my background as a Division III player and coach have greatly helped shape my coaching and administration philosophies regarding intercollegiate athletics. Those philosophies begin and end with academics and the true meaning of being a student-athlete.

I am eager to discuss with you my background and the position of Head Men's Basketball Coach. Feel free to contact me if you have any questions concerning my resume and references. I look forward to the opportunity of meeting with you to discuss my candidacy and will contact you soon to set an appointment. Thank you for your time and consideration.

Sincerely,

Michael R. Kelley

Enclosure

56

Head Men's Basketball Coach. *Melissa L. Kasler, Athens, Ohio*

This coach wanted to convey his knowledge of the school/athletic program to which he was applying. To set a positive tone, the writer first congratulates the college on a recent achievement.

LAWRENCE CHIN, Ph.D.
0000 East State Street
Ithaca, NY 55555

(000) 000-0000 Home   lchn75@attbi.com   (000) 000-0000 Mobile

January 4, 2008

Professor Stephen Shinseki
Director, Laboratory of Solid State Physics
Harvard University
Cambridge, MA 55555

Attention: Experimental Physics Search

Dear Professor Shinseki:

I am responding to your advertisement for an assistant professor in experimental condensed matter physics and have enclosed my CV, publication list, and statement of research interests for your review.

Some highlights of my research achievements include the following:

- Resolved a long-standing controversy about the nature of wide bands in rare earth-based, inter-metallic compounds by incorporating high-resolution photoemission, which **was cited in multiple papers in professional journals, including *Nature* and *Science*.**

- Mapped electronic and magnetic nature in Fe/Cr nanowedges by conducting depth-resolved hard X-ray standing wave spectroscopy with bright elliptically polarized light. **This work decorated the front page of *Science* as the work of the year for 2007.**

- Obtained the world record tunneling magnetoresistance and excellent thermal stabilities in metallic tunnel junctions by introducing a new type of deposition process and materials. **This work is patented and appeared in *Science* and *Physics* magazines.**

In my present position as a research associate professor at Cornell University, I have made several scientific and technological breakthroughs in the development of magnetic random-access memory devices. My work has not only made substantial contributions to the development of high-speed, high-density, low-power, and non-volatile magnetic devices, but also provided a fundamental understanding of the microscopic underlying mechanisms in the transport properties and the electronic structure of state-of-the-art magnetic nanostructures.

Thank you very much for your time and consideration. I look forward to discussing how my experience, credentials, and achievements meet your departmental needs. I will call to schedule an interview at your convenience.

Sincerely,

Lawrence Chin

Enclosures

Assistant Physics Professor. *Jennifer Rydell, Portland, Oregon*

The writer wanted to place the applicant's impressive achievements front and center "while still maintaining an understated feel for the academic world." Note the boldfacing of impressive information.

YVETTE SEITLIN

555 Andrews Road, Apt. 4   Pasadena, California 91030   555-555-5555   YvetteS@history.tulane.edu

March 6, 2008

Mr. James Goldberg
Cataloguing Operations Manager
Survivors of the Shoah Visual History Foundation
P.O. Box 3129
Los Angeles, California 90078-3168

Dear Mr. Goldberg:

It was a pleasure meeting you on Friday. I would like to join the Survivors of the Shoah Visual History Foundation project. My position at UCLA ends in December, and I am eager to win one of the research positions you mentioned at the tour's end. My experience in historical research, teaching, publishing and study qualify me for the position.

Your Needs	My Qualifications
M.A. degree in history	◆ Ph.D. Candidate in History, Tulane University, expected in 2008. Coursework focused on war and nationalism in the United States and in modern Europe.
	◆ Doctoral research focuses on civilians who faced enemy soldiers during the Civil War, much like the Holocaust survivors themselves.
	◆ M.A. in History, plus B.A. in History and English.
Superior research skills	◆ Doctoral research has taken me to more than 15 archives in 9 states. In addition, I have used countless other published, online and microfilm sources.
	◆ Awarded national and university funds to conduct research in field of study.
Ability to prioritize many tasks under deadline while displaying excellent attention to detail	◆ Selected as a research assistant for 2 noted professional historians. Completed many tasks while balancing my own coursework.
	◆ Conducted independent research for thesis, dissertation, conference presentations and research assistant projects.
	◆ Met all self- and institution-imposed deadlines for all research, coursework and publications.

58

Historical Researcher. *Gail Frank, Tampa, Florida*

The applicant found out about a "hidden" job by taking a tour of the Shoah Foundation. The tour-giver mentioned open research positions for which the applicant was a perfect fit. This letter highlights her eagerness and interest in the position. She was so confident in her ability that

YVETTE SEITLIN PAGE 2

<u>Your Needs</u>	<u>My Qualifications</u>
Strong interpersonal skills and excellent communication ability	♦ Taught as an adjunct instructor at UCLA for an upper-level history course.
	♦ Taught as a Teaching Assistant for an undergraduate history course at the University of Cincinnati.
	♦ Successfully presented 2 papers at History conferences with 2 more papers proposed for 2008.
	♦ Copy edited 2 books, one of which was a historical atlas with geographical terminology.
	♦ B.A. degree in both History and English demanded ability to write well.
Team player willing to make a commitment to the Foundation	♦ Strong, lifelong interest in Holocaust and its causes and significance. Belief in importance of this project.
	♦ Jewish ancestry makes this project even more significant to me.
	♦ Demonstrated ability to make long-term commitment to research and writing through achievement of thesis and pending dissertation.
Computer skills	♦ Strong skills in Microsoft Word and Excel, the Internet and database programs.

My resume/CV provides further details of my accomplishments. I have also attached a sheet of my references for your convenience. I will contact you next week to arrange a meeting so that we may discuss the Foundation's needs in greater detail.

Sincerely,

Yvette Seitlin

Enclosures

cc: Professor T. Smythe, Tulane University
    Professor G. Ryder, Tulane University
    Professor A. Roberts, UCLA

she included a set of references with her letter. Although this is not usually done, she wanted to provide all of the needed information right away (and she alerted her references to possible inquiries about her).

JOAN SMITH

6 Honeyberry Court • Frankston • Vic 3333 Australia
Ph: (613) 000 0000 (W) • (613) 000 0000 (H) • email: j.smith@hotmail.com

Date

Mr. De Kretzer
Head Dean
Melbourne University—Deakin Campus
65-150 Richmond Road
Melbourne, Vic 3000

Dear Mr. De Kretzer:

With the pending conferral of my Doctor of Philosophy, I am seeking a position as **Researcher / Educator** with your university and believe my academic accomplishments, extensive research and teaching expertise would certainly be transferable to this role.

My enclosed resume demonstrates my

☑ Distinguished record in teaching and technical innovation achieved through conceptualisation, development and implementation of flexible delivery style learning techniques. I have lectured to several campuses simultaneously through ISL (Distance) Education and through self-developed Online Course Web pages, and I am proficient in the operation of numerous popular software applications.

☑ Expertise in applying sophisticated quantative and qualitative research methodologies demonstrated in working towards successful completion of Ph.D.; numerous self-researched/published writings; continued professional development and conference attendance; and extensive research assistant work, utilising SPSS, N*VIVO and NUD*IST.

☑ Exceptional interpersonal, communication and presentation skills. Able to build and maintain strategic relationships with students and colleagues from diverse backgrounds. Recognised as a positive role model, teacher, lecturer, tutor and mentor.

☑ Facilitation of proactive classroom environments, encouraging active student participation to further enhance learning outcomes. Committed to holistic student development and learning experiences.

☑ Visionary, goal-driven work ethic, combined with solid team collaboration competencies and individual strengths utilising sound follow-through and detail orientation to plan and achieve projects from concept to successful conclusion.

Given the combination of these competencies, I am confident that I have developed a professional resourcefulness and personal diversity that will enable me to become a productive member of your faculty. Your consideration of my qualifications and academic and professional accomplishments will be appreciated.

Sincerely,

Joan Smith

Enclosure

59

Researcher/Educator. *Annemarie Cross, Hallam, Victoria, Australia*

This applicant was nearing the completion of her Ph.D. She had gained extensive experience throughout her short career. This letter sums up her experience and what she has to offer.

PATRICIA GREEN

444 Circle Drive • Brentwood, NY 55555 • (555) 444-2222 • Trainer@ITclass.net

---

[Date]

[Name]
[Company]
[City, State ZIP]

Dear [Name]:

Perhaps your organization is seeking to recruit a talented instructor to teach the complexities of advanced networking infrastructures to broad student populations. If this is the case, then please find the accompanying resume, highlighting my career as an MCSE instructor, Systems Administrator, and Consultant, for your review and consideration for a position teaching advanced MCSE curriculums/Windows with your facility.

Currently, I maintain tenure as an MCSE instructor with InfoTech Training Solutions, a leading provider of high-end networking certifications in Microsoft, Novell, and Cisco; and as an innovator of the industry's first Hands-on–Technical Training Lab (HOTT™). In this capacity, I continue to effectively teach classes throughout InfoTech's headquarters and university-based satellite locations. I oversee the instruction of other trainers as part of the organization's Train-the-Trainer program, which I initiated, developed, and continue to implement.

My ability to teach curricula based on both theory and realistic business models not only has prepared students for today's competitive workplace, but also has resulted in an unprecedented 100% student passing rate on A+, MCP, and all MCSE core exams. I am confident that my verifiable track record, coupled with my personal and professional dedication to quality teaching, would greatly benefit your organization.

Although the accompanying resume illustrates my background well, I feel that a personal interview would better demonstrate my knowledge and abilities. Therefore, I would appreciate an opportunity to meet with you for an in-depth interview to discuss the possible merging of my strengths with your organization's training objectives. Thank you for your review and consideration. You will hear from me soon regarding the possibility of an interview.

Sincerely,

Patricia Green

Enclosure

60

MCSE Instructor. *Ann Baehr, Brentwood, New York*

The first paragraph is a probe to learn of any interest in an instructor, and the second indicates the applicant's current position and areas of expertise. The third attests to her effectiveness.

RICHARD BOULDER

55 Forest Drive • Dayton, OH 00000

Home: 555-555-5555 • Mobile: 555-555-5555 • boulderr5005@hotmail.com

[Date]

[Person's Name]
[Title]
[Company Name]
[Street Address]
[Town, State, ZIP]

Dear [Person's Name]

As a Senior Software Engineer, I would bring to your organization over ten years of experience in software design and development within the telecommunications and defense-related industries and expertise in all phases of the software development life cycle. In addition, I have substantial experience analyzing, troubleshooting, and resolving complex software issues. Further highlights of my background include

- An extensive background developing and debugging software systems and solutions in C, C++, Perl, and Java in UNIX, Linux, and Windows NT environments.
- Proficiency as technical lead or individual contributor on cross-functional product development teams challenged with ensuring on-time, on-budget, and on-target results.
- A Bachelor of Science Degree in Electrical Engineering with a concentration in VLSI design and microwave engineering.

For the past ten years I have provided engineering expertise for multiuser telecommunications systems at Cummings Networks, where I have been called upon to investigate and resolve complex software issues, troubleshoot and repair bugs, design new functionality and software enhancements, and deliver technical product training to peers and field engineers. I've earned a sound reputation as THE person to call on when critical customer acceptance issues have eluded resolution by others.

If your organization is seeking a dependable, results-driven team player with a solid-performance track record and outstanding technical capabilities, you need look no further. The accomplishments noted within the accompanying resume will illustrate the valuable contributions I can make to your team. I would be very interested in learning more about your open position and discussing my qualifications more fully. I will take the initiative to contact you next week to see if we can arrange for a mutually convenient meeting.

Thank you for your time and consideration. I look forward to speaking with you.

Sincerely,

Richard Boulder

61

Senior Software Engineer. *Jeanne Knight, Melrose, Massachusetts*

The applicant wanted to move from product support to software development. The writer highlighted experience in software design and development. He got an immediate interview.

RYAN G. SMITH

555-555-5555
ryansmith@email.com

0000 Snowfall Drive
Colorado Springs, CO 80903

March 30, 2008

Mr. Robert Johnson
Lockheed Martin Corporation
6801 Rockledge Drive
Bethesda, MD 20817-1877

Dear Mr. Johnson:

➢ More than 13 years of professional experience in engineering sophisticated avionic systems, with a Bachelor of Science in Mechanical and Manufacturing Technology;

➢ Keen analytical and problem-solving skills;

➢ Proven ability to deliver quantifiable cost savings, whether leading the project, working independently, or operating as part of a cross-functional team;

➢ Experience in authoring ISO, process control writings, and training syllabi, as well as delivering the associated training; and

➢ A verifiable record of improving workflow and manufacturing processes that positively impact budgetary goals.

I would like to bring my expertise and experience as a **process engineer** to Lockheed Martin. My technical knowledge, drive, determination, and solid communication skills will allow me to make an immediate contribution to your organization.

Thank you for your consideration. I look forward to speaking with you and will call you next week to set up an interview.

Sincerely,

Ryan G. Smith
Enclosure

62

Process Engineer. *Cindy Kraft, Valrico, Florida*

Creating a simple vertical line and positioning the letter in the second "column" can make a letter stand out from a host of other letters. Starting the letter with bulleted items also is unique.

AVAILABLE FOR RELOCATION

Benito Hoover
maintenance reliability engineer

90 Carleton Drive
Macon, Georgia 00000
000.000.0000 — bh1@smartx.net

Thursday, June 17, 2008

Mr. Charles W. Moran
Crest, Inc.
2130 Interstate Parkway
Suite 400
Atlanta, Georgia 00000

Dear Mr. Moran:

If you think Crest's maintenance reliability engineer should go beyond the important functions of asset protection and regulatory compliance, we should explore adding me to your team.

To start, you'll find five solid, profit-building capabilities I can offer your company on the next pages. Backing them up are a half dozen examples of problems solved, thousands of dollars saved, durable measures taken to ensure compliance, and new corporate standards set to boost productivity.

I am employed by one of the largest companies in the world. I love what I do and GE has promoted me four times in the last seven years. And, although there are always contributions to be made, the challenges I handle every day aren't as interesting as I would like them to be. Hence, I'm testing the waters with this confidential application.

I thrive when I can help management uncover and fix the problems so that firms like Crest get all the benefits of maintenance reliability. So let me suggest a next step: May I call in a few days to explore your special requirements? I'll do my best to make that time very well spent.

Sincerely,

Benito Hoover

Encl.: Resume

63

Maintenance Reliability Engineer. *Don Orlando, Montgomery, Alabama*

Too often in the past, this applicant found jobs that turned out to be far below his abilities. This letter was designed to position the applicant as a key advisor to the management team.

EVERETT C. DANIELS

505 Trevor Lane • Dover, DE 50005
505.500.0505 • evcdan5@aol.com

December 16, 2007

Mr. Jacob B. Smythe
Unit Director
Department of Transportation
State of Delaware
Dover, DE 50005

Dear Mr. Smythe:

Donald Hurley suggested it could prove valuable for us to talk. I am presently exploring opportunities toward which my extensive background managing successful civil, environmental, and heavy construction projects would be an asset. Specifically, I am interested in being considered as a candidate for the position of Senior Project Manager.

As my background demonstrates, I have had the opportunity to leverage business development opportunities for each of my employer companies through well-executed expansion into related industries. I have broad expertise in all aspects of civil, engineering, and heavy construction and a proven ability to effectively manage a profitable operation. My background is complemented by a degree in Surveying/Civil Engineering as well as a very high level of customer service orientation. My projects are consistently characterized by the professional manner in which objectives are achieved—and all parties are satisfied, even when working through sometimes extensive change order processes.

My managers describe me as a self-motivated, ambitious, and hardworking team player with a strong sense of working collaboratively. My track record of performance in all areas reflects my ability to learn quickly and competently, and I always give 110% to any job I undertake. I have a reputation for doing whatever it takes to give exceptional quality and value. I am able to effectively team with individuals at all levels—from superintendents and general contractors, project owners, and municipal leaders to laborers and tradesmen in the field … skills that will prove invaluable to the DOT.

In addition to these strengths, I have key skills in the area of business development and management and possess expert relationship management skills. I am known for my tact and diplomacy and an ability to effectively troubleshoot and successfully resolve any situation. I look forward to meeting with you to discuss the DOT's hiring needs for a Senior Project Manager and how I might contribute to your operations. I will contact you next week to set an appointment.

Sincerely,

Everett C. Daniels

64

Senior Project Manager. *Jan Melnik, Durham, Connecticut*

The applicant used a mutual contact to seek an opportunity with the state DOT. The writer highlighted a background in civil and environmental engineering and heavy construction.

RANDY TAYLOR

000 Tollhouse Road   Menlo Park, CA 00000   000-000-0000   rantay1@hotmail.com

September 12, 2007

Mr. Peter Grace
Executive Vice President of Engineering
Ridgewood Electronics
0000 Forster Avenue
San Jose, CA 00000

Subject: Position as Director of Hardware Engineering

Dear Mr. Grace:

Few companies can thrive in today's hotly competitive, global business environment unless they apply innovation and cost-effective approaches to develop industry-leading products that raise them above their competitors in customers' minds.

Throughout my career, I have consistently driven the development of products that offer standout benefits to customers and employers. For example, an enterprise-class, chassis-switch project that I led increased revenues 40% and reduced costs 30%, while achieving high-performance product capabilities.

The strengths and expertise I offer include the proven and well-documented ability to
- Attract, motivate, and retain highly skilled technical talent.
- Act as an objective and persuasive influencer to obtain cooperation among cross-functional teams.
- Present and discuss product issues and strategies with senior management, manufacturing, and other internal groups, as well as with third-party organizations.
- Effectively manage the performance of multicultural and multilingual engineering-development groups at sites located in multiple time zones.
- Communicate overall engineering direction to internal groups and to external customers and partners.

For the past several months I have enjoyed the challenge of launching a startup company in Nevada. Recently, however, I relocated to California and have begun investigating situations there that will allow me to use my skills and talents to increase the success of a new employer.

I am confident my qualifications will enable me to add significant value to your company as Director of Hardware Engineering. I will call you to arrange an interview to discuss the challenges and opportunities your company faces and the contribution I can make to its ongoing success.

Sincerely,

Randy Taylor

65

Director of Hardware Engineering. *Georgia Adamson, Campbell, California*

The individual had spent several months out of his career field to help friends launch a startup company. He wanted to return to California. The writer highlighted strengths and accomplishments.

CHRISTOPHER CASHTON
BSc, PEng
One Concentric Circle • Suite 000 • Toronto M5M 5M5

September 1, 2007

Mr. Hy Ringo Thorty
Director of Engineering
Galactic Enterprises, Inc.
555 Milky Way, 5th Floor
Toronto, ON M5M 5M5

Dear Mr. Thorty:

I want to be your next **Systems Engineer.**

As the attached resume indicates, I have had more than 12 years of progressively responsible related employment.

I demonstrated the ability to work efficiently as *Systems Engineer/Coordinator* at Universal Electronics, Inc., where I installed 15 television distribution systems in only three months. Normally, it takes two-and-a-half days to install such a system in an open area. I can do it in under five hours. I am efficient because I am well organized.

If I had to name one characteristic that I believe makes me a good employee, it would be flexibility. This quality helped me greatly as a supervisor at Universal. I got along well with staff because I paid attention to them. I made a point of finding out the strengths of each employee. I motivated them by showing confidence in them when I knew they had the capacity to do a particular task well.

I gave them leeway, so that they would have a sense of ownership in their work. When they proved themselves worthy, I gave them more leeway. I also maximized my own productivity by delegating liberally.

My flexibility was instrumental in enabling me to work well on teams. I observed that people typically withheld information, motivated by a competitive spirit. I made a point of sharing information with my colleagues. In so doing, I was able to help them do their job better, and this was appreciated. I recognize individual differences. I understand there is more than one way of doing something well and, by avoiding a judgmental attitude, engender good will not only among those I supervise, but also peers.

Please have a look at the attached resume. I am confident that, on reviewing it, you will agree I have the potential to become a worthy member of your team. I will phone to set a convenient time to meet, so that we can discuss how I might best serve Galactic Enterprises.

Yours truly,

Christopher Cashton

P.S. I can be reached at (555) 000-0000.

Attachment: resume

66

Systems Engineer. *Howard Earle Halpern, Toronto, Ontario, Canada*

The letter explains how the applicant worked efficiently, elaborates on his supervisory style, highlights attributes recruiters typically seek, and shows how he is a flexible team player.

HARRY STRONG

900 Starling Lane
Indianapolis, IN 00000

harrystrong@yahoo.com

Cell: (555) 555-6555
Office: (555) 555-5555

January 25, 2008

[Name]
[Title]
[Employer]
[Address]
[City, State ZIP]

Dear Mr. or Ms. _____:

Like many other recent graduates, I am searching for an opportunity to apply my skills while contributing to a company's growth. Unlike others, though, I don't believe that a new bachelor's degree is enough to qualify in today's highly competitive market.

As a result, I have worked diligently to supplement my college education with hands-on experience in financial environments, equipping me with a wide range of skills as a Financial or Business Analyst. Through my employment and educational training, I have developed the qualifications that will make me an asset to your company:

- **Financial Skills and Experience:** More than 2 years of experience in a corporate environment as a financial advisor, along with a solid background in financial analysis, reporting, budgeting, negotiating and business/financial planning. Apply financial tools to identify, manage and maximize investment funds.

- **Keen Research, Analytical and Quantitative Skills:** Adept at reviewing, analyzing and synthesizing financial data, as well as viewing challenges from different perspectives to arrive at creative solutions.

- **Computer Software Tools:** Demonstrated proficiency in learning new applications quickly. Skilled in using Microsoft Word, Excel and Access database software. I also use Morningstar extensively to research data on mutual funds.

- **Proven Communications, Organizational and Interpersonal Skills:** My collective experiences have enabled me to hone my interpersonal, written and verbal communications skills, which include developing financial reports, interfacing with internal and external customers and delivering presentations. Cultivating and maintaining positive relationships with a wide range of personalities has resulted in a large referral network from satisfied clients. Another strength is my ability to efficiently organize and manage my day-to-day responsibilities for maximum productivity.

Based on my talents and dedicated efforts, I have been recognized for my contributions to business growth and success. If you need a highly motivated professional who grasps new concepts quickly; loves to learn; and offers the personal drive, skills and confidence to succeed, I would welcome an interview. I'll contact you in a few days to explore the possibility. Thank you.

Sincerely,

Harry Strong

Enclosure

67

Financial or Business Analyst. *Louise Garver, Enfield, Connecticut*

This letter is for a new graduate who found an opportunity as a Financial Analyst. Bullets and boldfacing draw attention to the applicant's qualifications, which he gained from experience and education.

Angela T. Ingram

0000 Merritt Highway
Orlando, Florida 32821

555-555-5555
atingram@network.com

Director of Employment
Company
Address
City, State ZIP

Dear Director of Employment:

After a successful and satisfying career with Iowa's largest independently owned financial institution, I recently moved to Florida and am looking forward to embarking on a new career here. I am taking the liberty of enclosing a resume describing my background. When you review it, you may notice that I am experienced in and capable of stepping into a variety of areas. Let me elaborate.

Project Management. A consistent thread through my career at the bank was that I was often given the responsibility to oversee projects ranging from implementing new software to managing a major consolidation of branches. I have proven that I have the expertise to manage people and processes, resulting in minimal disruption to clients and/or staff.

Administration. I believe I have succeeded in providing administrative and technical support to management and users at all levels within the corporation. I am skilled in assessing others' needs and developing strategies to meet those needs. My communication skills are well developed, which facilitates my efforts.

Training and Supervision. My experience encompasses both. Because I had no formal technical training, I had to constantly self-teach and update my own skills. That gave me a unique perspective and helped me to become an effective trainer. As my resume indicates, I supervised a high-volume second-shift processing department.

In addition to the traits listed above, my performance reflects a dedication to my employer and a high degree of self-motivation. Performing beyond expectations is the norm for me. After you have examined my material, I hope you will contact me to arrange an interview. I am confident I can make significant contributions to your organization. I can be reached at home (555-555-5555) or on my cell phone (000-000-0000). Thank you for your time and consideration.

Sincerely,

Angela T. Ingram

Enclosure

68

Bank Supervisor. *Janet L. Beckstrom, Flint, Michigan*

The applicant was moving across the country and was qualified to work in diverse capacities. The writer capitalized on the applicant's broad experience and drew attention to it with bold-facing.

GREGORY JOHN GARSON

5555 59th Street, Flatland, Texas 55555   *gjg95@hotmail.com*   **(555) 555-0000**
P.O. Box 555, Green River, Texas 55555   **(555) 500-5555**

September 7, 2007

Karen M. Black
DAVID WELLS, INC.
P.O. Box 55555
Border Town, Texas 55555

RE: **Summer 2007 Internship**

Dear Ms. Black:

I am very interested in an **internship with David Wells, Inc.,** and have enclosed my resume for your review and consideration. Having interned several summers for financial organizations and worked for my father (John G. Garson), a representative and role model at David Wells, Inc., in Green River, I am no stranger to the arena. Plus, this firsthand observation of the financial industry has solidified my choice of careers, making me a sincere candidate for this internship.

I am concurrently working on a **master of science in family financial planning** while completing coursework for a **bachelor of business administration in finance** from Superior University. My goal is to earn a master's degree so that I may sit for the Certified Financial Planner (CFP) exam in the spring of 2008.

Through exposure to the daily business operations of my father's David Wells office, I have learned

- That David Wells is paramount in providing individuals with the investments, services, and information they need to achieve their financial goals.

- That meeting customer needs in a professional manner through personal contact is primary to success in the financial industry, and supports your efforts to keep contacts face-to-face as opposed to utilizing impersonal Internet services.

- That David Wells rewards representatives who are self-motivated, profit-oriented achievers, decisive, and able to implement actions to benefit both the organization and its clients.

I am confident that I will be able to surpass expectations and make substantial contributions to your organization, and I hope to begin my career as a member of a team such as that at David Wells.

A drive to succeed, combined with my knowledge and previous experience, makes me a strong candidate for an internship at David Wells, Inc. Please do not hesitate to contact me should you desire additional information. I will be available for this internship from mid-May through mid-August of this year. I would welcome an interview at your convenience to further discuss my qualifications and prospects for serving your company.

Thank you for your time and consideration.

Sincerely,

Gregory John Garson

Enclosure: Resume

69

Summer Intern. *Edith A. Rische, Lubbock, Texas*

The letter is employer-oriented in that it lists admirable aspects of the company, highlights the company's culture, and addresses the applicant's "service" to the company.

MARIAN R. SMITH, CFA

555 Grove Street, St. Louis, MO 55555
Home: 555-555-5555
Cell: 500-500-5000
smithm265@verizon.net

BUILDING BEST-OF-BREED TREASURY FUNCTIONS
BALANCE SHEET AND LIQUIDITY MANAGEMENT
GLOBAL BANKING RELATIONSHIP MANAGEMENT
CORPORATE FINANCE DEAL EXECUTION
BUILDING & LEADING HIGH-PERFORMANCE TEAMS
ADVANCED PENSION AND RISK MANAGEMENT

September 25, 2007

Victor Hellman
President
CRB Limited
555 Conant Ave.
St. Louis, MO 55555

Re: Treasurer Position—Reference Code 55555

Dear Mr. Hellman:

My specialty is bringing cost-conscious leadership to the treasury function of a global corporation. Using my broad, 17-year experience in corporate finance and treasury operations, I am able to envision and implement company-wide solutions that reduce costs, add to the bottom line, and minimize risk.

I have demonstrated an ability to optimize the balance sheet and effectively maintain liquidity within multinational corporations. My notable strengths in communication and relationship-building have resulted in fruitful relationships with both internal clients and external members of the financial and regulatory communities. These skills have also enabled me to build strong international corporate treasury teams.

I am a skilled negotiator with an expert grasp of financial instruments, business opportunities, and the competitive financial landscape. I have been able to close major deals that have been critical to the financial health of the organizations for which I have worked. Some examples of my achievements include the following:

- Closed bond deals valued at $400 million in the tight credit environment of 2000 and 2001.
- Developed an interest rate strategy that yielded $65 million in new revenue from strategic interest-rate swapping activities.
- Instituted a Global Enterprise Risk Management System to protect the corporation from poor governance practices going forward.

My most recent titles have been Assistant Treasurer at two multinational companies with $3 billion and $6 billion in annual revenues, respectively. These roles offered me unusual opportunities to participate at the highest levels of the corporate treasury function. As the #2 treasury professional in such large global corporations, I was frequently in the position of executing the responsibilities of Treasurer. Although my recent titles read "Assistant Treasurer," I am ready to "hit the ground running" in the top treasury position.

I anticipate with pleasure an opportunity to learn about the challenges CRB Limited is facing and to discuss with you the contributions I could make as Treasurer to the prosperity of your organization. I will call next week to set an appointment.

Sincerely,

Marian R. Smith, CFA

70

Treasurer. *Jean Cummings, Concord, Massachusetts*

The applicant wanted to work for a multinational company and wanted her new title to be Treasurer, not Assistant Treasurer. The writer explained the person's qualifications for the top job.

CHARLES BEST

1568 Brownsville Drive
Herndon, VA 20170

E-mail: CBest@aol.com

Home: 703-264-1171
Cell: 703-346-8888

SR. FINANCIAL ANALYST / DIRECTOR OF FINANCE
Operations ~ Growth & Development Strategy ~ Decision Support & Reporting ~ Market Entry

Goal: A strategic position in financial advisement and decision analysis.

October 10, 2007

Paul Blalock
Sprint Nextel
Investor Relations
2001 Edmund Haley Drive
Reston, VA 20191

Dear Mr. Blalock:

Does your company need someone with experience in entrepreneurial investment, acquisition, P&L, and startup? Someone who can leverage technology and co-sourcing and lead you through fast growth? Someone who can look at the numbers, but still draw a conclusion based on the big picture?

If you do, I am a 3-time board member and angel investor with 15 years of experience in financial analysis and business management. And as a fast-growth company—in a service/delivery sector—I am very interested in your company!

Here's what I can do for your company from day one:

- Business planning, budgeting, forecasting, variance analysis, and internal controls
- Operational metrics, profit management, and decision support
- Competitive analysis and due diligence for mergers and acquisitions
- Investment and capital planning
- Creation of finance, HR, accounting, and reporting systems to support fast growth

And here are my best soft skills:

- Outstanding analysis and communication
- Strong accuracy and sense of urgency
- Mentoring teams to high performance
- Quick study for any industry

I will call you within a few days to follow up and determine any goals or challenges you might have that I can help you optimize. In the meantime, a copy of my career portfolio is enclosed.

Sincerely,

Charles Best

Enclosure: Financial Analyst Portfolio

71

Senior Financial Analyst. *Helen Oliff, Reston, Virginia*

The opening paragraph of questions in boldface attempts to connect with the reader's needs. The two sets of bulleted items call attention to the applicant's abilities and "soft skills."

RICHARD KIMBLE
rkimble@aol.com

12 Norwood Avenue
Oakland, NJ 07420

(555) 555-5555 (H)
(000) 000-0000 (W)

November 18, 2007

Hiring Authority
Company
Address
City, State ZIP

Dear Hiring Authority,

After 20 years as a successful small-business owner, I'm changing career directions to follow my longtime desire to be a financial planner. To that end, I am currently enrolled in a CFP program.

Although I have no professional experience as a financial planner, I have frequently advised others on investment strategies. In my own case, I developed an investment strategy for my portfolio that yielded an annual return of 10.5% for a 10-year period ending 12/31/06. I also managed the disbursement of assets for 2 estates.

I can be characterized as an entrepreneur with sound business judgment, maturity, good sales skills, and high integrity. I enjoy challenges that require learning new skills and interacting with the public. I am steady and patient, having built my own business from the ground up to more than $500,000 in annual revenues.

My goal is an exciting and rewarding position with a company facing new prospects. I am eager to participate in any training process that will build on my skills and provide the knowledge I need to be successful.

I prefer to stay in the metropolitan New York City area, but will consider attractive opportunities in the tri-state region. I would prefer to travel no more than 50% of the time.

I will contact you in the coming weeks to explore the possibility of an in-person meeting. Thank you for your consideration.

Sincerely,

Richard Kimble

Enclosure

72

Financial Planner. *Igor Shpudejko, Mahwah, New Jersey*

This professional photographer wanted to transition to being a financial planner without related experience. The writer emphasized the applicant's maturity and sound business judgment, which are needed by FPs.

BRITTANY LYONS

000-000-0000

lyons@email.com

0000 S. Front Street, Tulsa, OK 74107

March 12, 2008

Ms. Lisa Hart
First Bank of Columbus
1383 Main Street
Columbus, OH 43204

Dear Ms. Hart:

Numbers drive good business decisions … collecting and analyzing data is critical to sound decision making.

My career experience within the banking industry has been broad-based, but it has always involved generating the necessary data to foster decisions that positively impact an organization's bottom line. My ability in this area is well documented in my resume. I have

➤ Held full decision-making authority for *deploying, expanding, and optimizing the banking delivery network* within the Florida region for the past three years.

➤ Ensured the *successful transition of employee incentive plans* following Barnett Bank's merger with Bank of America.

➤ Developed *uniform reporting mechanisms* to promote efficient line-management activities.

➤ *Reengineered and standardized* national sales incentive programs.

➤ Taught *staffing needs calculations and employee utilization* to branch offices to ensure delivery of top-notch customer service while controlling costs.

➤ Created a *cost analysis system* to effectively track internal profitability.

I will be relocating to the Columbus, Ohio, area within the next few months and would appreciate the opportunity to discuss how I might deliver similar results for your organization. May we talk? I will be in town the week of March 24 and will call to set up an appointment with you.

Sincerely,

Brittany Lyons

Enclosure

Ability is what you're capable of doing. **Motivation** *determines what you do.*
Attitude determines how well you do it. — Lou Holtz

73

Bank Executive. *Cindy Kraft, Valrico, Florida*

A number of features make this letter distinctive: the partial line in the contact information, the business axiom in boldface, the bulleted items enhanced with italic, and the Lou Holtz quote.

KIMBERLY A. CARTER

888 West Road • Anywhere, Michigan 55555 • 555.222.2222 • kac@email.com

January 8, 2008

Marcy Johnson
ABC Accounting Company
333 Capital Avenue
Anywhere, Michigan 55555

Dear Ms. Johnson,

As a well-qualified credit account specialist, I demonstrate my ability to effectively communicate with clients, resolve payment issues, and collect past-due payments. I bring more than 18 years of accounts receivable experience in addition to being involved in all processing stages of collections. The scope of my experience includes, but is not limited to, commercial, automotive, and manufacturing environments.

My focus is to deliver results and provide superior service by quickly identifying problem areas in accounts receivable and developing a solution strategy to ensure that issues are resolved. My expertise lies in my strong ability to build rapport with clients, analyze accounts, and manage all aspects related to my appointed position and areas of responsibility. I find these qualities to be my greatest assets to offer employers.

Because of an unforeseen circumstance, I was unable to continue my employment as a cash applications analyst with a well-known automotive industry leader. Since my employment with A-1 Corporation, I have accepted a temporary position as a billing assistant with a local company. My objective is to secure a position in accounts receivable and credit collections with an established company. As you will note, my resume exhibits a brief review of contributions I have made to my employers, and I enjoy challenges.

A complete picture of my expertise and experience is very important. Therefore, I will follow up with you next week. I look forward to speaking with you soon to answer any questions you may have regarding my background.

Regards,

Kimberly Carter

Enclosure

74

Credit Account Specialist. *Maria E. Hebda, Trenton, Michigan*

This letter is strong because of four carefully crafted paragraphs. These indicate in turn the applicant's experience, areas of expertise, career objective, and follow-up plans.

Regina Openhence
125 S.E. Stanley Court • Palance, Utah 99999
regop@insightbb.com

555-555-5555 *cell*   *home* **555-555-5555**

December 16, 2007

Attention: Lindsey Harold
Codder County Bank
P.O. Box 9229
Palance, UT 99999

Dear Ms. Harold:

In response to your recent advertisement for an experienced Commercial Loan Officer, I have enclosed a copy of my resume for your review. As you will note, I have spent more than 20 years in the banking industry in a variety of positions. My expertise is in working in the commercial loan department and one-on-one with the customers, walking them through the loan process, educating them, and making sure they are receiving the fullest benefits possible.

I have achieved numerous accomplishments and have a record for developing a strong bottom line for the bank. My personal passion as a "people person" shines through in the successes I've achieved. I am computer literate, analytical, thorough, and well experienced in the complete loan process.

I would like the opportunity to meet with you personally where we may further discuss your bank's requirements and my qualifications. It appears from your advertisement that our needs may be a very close match. I will call to schedule a time when we may meet and review how we may mutually benefit each other. Thank you for taking the time to review my resume, and I look forward to meeting you personally.

Sincerely,

Regina Openhence

Enclosure

75

Commercial Loan Officer. *Rosie Bixel, Portland, Oregon*

This letter contains just three strong paragraphs. The first directs attention to the resume and the applicant's expertise, the second mentions worker traits, and the third asks for a meeting.

HARRY STRONG

900 Starling Lane
Indianapolis, IN 55555

harrystrong@yahoo.com

Cell: (555) 555-5555
Office: (555) 555-5555

January 25, 2008

[Name]
[Title]
[Employer]
[Address]
[City, State ZIP]

Dear Mr. or Ms. _____:

Like many recent graduates, I am eager to begin my career in finance. Unlike others, I realize that a new bachelor's degree is not enough to qualify in today's highly competitive market. As a result, I have worked diligently to supplement my college education with hands-on experience in financial environments, equipping me with a wide range of skills as a Financial Analyst. Through my employment and educational training, I have developed the qualifications that will make me an asset to your company.

Financial Skills and Experience:

More than 2 years of experience in a corporate environment as a financial advisor, along with a solid background in financial analysis, reporting, budgeting, negotiating, and business/financial planning. Apply financial tools to identify, manage, and maximize investment funds.

Keen Research, Analytical, and Quantitative Skills:

Adept in reviewing, analyzing, and synthesizing financial data as well as viewing challenges from different perspectives to arrive at creative solutions.

Computer Software Tools:

Demonstrated proficiency in learning new applications quickly, I am skilled in using Microsoft Word, Excel, and Access database software. I also utilize Morningstar extensively to research data on mutual funds.

Proven Communications, Organization, and Interpersonal Skills:

My collective experiences have enabled me to hone my interpersonal, written, and oral communications skills, which include developing financial reports, interfacing with internal and external customers, and delivering presentations. Cultivating and maintaining positive relationships with a wide range of personalities has resulted in a large referral network from satisfied clients. Another strength is my ability to efficiently organize and manage my day-to-day responsibilities for maximum productivity.

Based on my talents and dedicated efforts, I have been recognized for my contributions to business growth and success. If you need a highly motivated professional who grasps new concepts quickly, loves to learn, and offers the personal drive, skills, and confidence to succeed, I would welcome an interview. I will call you in a few days to set a convenient time.

Sincerely,

Harry Strong

76

Financial Analyst. *Louise Garver, Enfield, Connecticut*

The applicant, a recent graduate, was seeking a position as a financial analyst. This letter gave him an edge on the competition by showing that he had goal-oriented skills beyond his degree.

MR. GAHRAM MEESHAN

0000 Central Avenue
Glendale, California 91208

555-555-5555
g_meeshan@earthlink.net

March 10, 2008

HORIZON MORTGAGE LENDERS, INC.
522 N. Purdham Avenue
Glendale, California 91203

Attention: Robert Vesag, Sales Manager

RE: **Loan Officer**—Monstertrak no. 1039888

Dear Mr. Vesag:

Once in a while, someone wakes up to find himself living in the wrong life.

As a forensic biomechanics assistant and a personal trainer, I have extensive experience in dealing with people, difficult or otherwise, as well as in research and data collection. These are skills that would be easily transferable to the loan industry because I would also have to deal with people and data, albeit in a different environment.

My current goal is to explore new career options that fit better with my personality. I like numbers but would rather deal with them in a financial environment.

In your ad under qualifications, it states "No experience necessary." As my resume indicates, I am a quick learner and problem solver while dealing with new concepts, systems, and procedures; therefore, a good fit exists between your requirements and my abilities. I do have a bachelor's degree, although not in the discipline you prefer. Again, this should not be an obstacle as I have a strong desire to learn and to succeed.

I will call you on Thursday to set up an appointment and further explore the possibilities of our working together.

Thank you for your time and consideration.

Sincerely,

Gahram Meeshan

Enclosure

77

Loan Officer.   *Myriam-Rose Kohn, Valencia, California*

This applicant was a forensic biomechanic's assistant and wanted to become either a broker or a loan officer. The letter, therefore, mentions transferable skills, the reason for a switch, and motivation.

Susan E. Williams

0000 Indianwood Road
Clarkston, Michigan 48348

555-555-3333
susiew@network.net

August 11, 2007

Dear Director of Employment:

A BBA degree, 20+ years of experience in the banking industry, and a comprehensive understanding of probate law—that's what I have to offer your organization. After a rewarding career at Michigan National Bank, I find myself in the position of seeking new career opportunities. My resume is enclosed for your review.

My recent experience at the bank has been in the Personal Trust/Probate department. In my capacity as Trust Officer, I was responsible for personal trust, estate, and investment accounts. I settled estates, coordinated the administration of legal documents, and directed the disbursement of funds according to the trust and/or applicable laws (among many other things). This comprehensive background would be a distinct asset to your firm.

In addition to my fiduciary responsibilities, I took a personal interest in every client. There were cases that necessitated my intervention to arbitrate differences between feuding beneficiaries. Sometimes I was called on to schedule doctor appointments or arrange for home repair. But serving the client (or the client's estate as the case may be) was always my top priority.

When you review my resume, you will see that I also managed the corporate trust division and provided administrative support in the employee benefit area. This experience adds to my versatility.

Thank you for taking the time to review my credentials. I hope you feel a personal meeting would be beneficial; I am available at your convenience. If you have any questions—or when you are ready to schedule an interview—please give me a call at 555-555-3333.

Sincerely,

Susan E. Williams

Enclosure

78

Trust Officer. *Janet L. Beckstrom, Flint, Michigan*

The applicant had extensive experience in a bank's trust/probate department. She was looking for a position with a law firm that could benefit from her experience and transferable skills.

RAYMOND MARLIN

12 Main Street
New York, New York 00000
(555) 555-5555 • raymon44@cox.net

February 8, 2008

Mr. Fred Johnson
President/CEO
Reynolds Corporation
666 Mason Road
New York, New York 00000

Dear Mr. Johnson:

Perhaps your company could benefit from a strong chief financial officer with a record of major contributions to business and profit growth.

The scope of my expertise is extensive and includes the full complement of corporate finance, accounting, budgeting, banking, tax, treasury, internal controls, and reporting functions. Equally important are my qualifications in business planning, operations, MIS technology, administration, and general management.

A business partner to management, I have been effective in working with all departments, linking finance with operations to improve productivity, efficiency, and bottom-line results. Recruited at The Southington Company to provide finance and systems technology expertise, I created a solid infrastructure to support corporate growth as the company transitioned from a wholesale-retail distributor to a retail operator. Recent accomplishments include the following:

- **Significant contributor to the increase in operating profits from less than $400,000 to more than $4 million.**
- **Key member of due diligence team in the acquisition of 25 operating units that increased market penetration 27% and gross sales 32%.**
- **Spearheaded leading-edge MIS design and implementation, streamlining systems and procedures that dramatically enhanced productivity while cutting costs.**

A "hands-on" manager effective in building teamwork and cultivating strong internal/external relationships, I am flexible and responsive to the quickly changing demands of the business, industry, and marketplace. If you are seeking a proactive finance executive to complement your management team, I would welcome a personal interview. I will call to explore the possibility of a personal interview. Thank you for your consideration.

Very truly yours,

Raymond Marlin

Enclosure

79

Chief Financial Officer. *Louise Garver, Enfield, Connecticut*

This senior-level applicant wanted a finance executive position that encompassed all areas of finance and not just treasury operations (his most recent position). He was successful in reaching his goal.

DAVID JOHNSON
5 Mulberry Street
Simsbury, CT 00000
(555) 555-5555
davidj@compusa.com

February 3, 2008

Mr. George Meadows
Chief Executive Officer
Danaher Corporation
678 City Center
Hartford, CT 00000

Dear Mr. Meadows:

As a manufacturing executive, I have consistently delivered strong performance results through my contributions in cost reductions, internal controls and technology solutions. The comparison below outlines some of my accomplishments as a Chief Financial Officer in relationship to the position requirements.

Your Requirements	My Qualifications
Full range of finance, accounting and treasury experience; operational focus; strong internal controls.	Built and led strong finance organizations, creating solid infrastructures and strengthening internal controls. Instituted formal budgeting, forecasting, cash management and other management processes. Proven record for designing growth strategies and financial consolidations to achieve business objectives.
	Recruited by Halstead Company to provide expertise in acquisitions, financing and MIS and to orchestrate an IPO. Comprehensive background in all areas of finance, accounting and treasury. Recognized for strengths as a consensus/team builder and effective arbitrator/negotiator.
Mergers and acquisitions experience.	Acquired extensive experience in the analysis of new business opportunities and with mergers and acquisitions throughout career history. Effectively merged and streamlined two divisions, which resulted in substantial savings and positioned company for future growth.
	Spearheaded acquisition of several operating businesses with sales ranging from $1 million to $220 million, which included personally handling all negotiations, performing due diligence, developing tax structure and coordinating legal and accounting activities.
MIS background.	Led installation of state-of-the-art MIS technology in different companies. Improved inventory management, boosted sales and cut annual operating expenses through MIS technology implementation.

I would welcome a personal interview to discuss how my experience would contribute to the achievement of your company's objectives for growth and success. I will contact you next week to set up an interview.

Very truly yours,

David Johnson

Enclosure

80

Chief Financial Officer. *Louise Garver, Enfield, Connecticut*

Some resumes and cover letters for executives have smaller type to fit in more information. This letter is an example. This two-column format was successful in generating interviews and offers.

Beverly Armstrong, C.P.A.

0000 Harbour Walk Road
Weston, CT 06883

555-555-5555 • Cell: 000-000-0000
bevarmstrong@yahoo.com

January 17, 2008

The Azure Group
P.O. Box 21648
Weston, CT 06883

Dear Hiring Professional:

The position of **Director of Finance** advertised online accurately describes my skills and abilities. I may be the ideal candidate for you—I not only have the experience you request but also additional perspective from other fields and positions to draw on.

Your Needs	My Qualifications
Minimum of a B.A. in Accounting or Finance	◆ Certified Public Accountant
	◆ Bachelor of Business Administration from Colby with a concentration in Accounting and Finance
5–7+ years of progressively responsible experience providing high-level financial analyses	◆ More than 14 years in a variety of financial positions of escalating responsibility for large and small companies in different fields
	◆ VP of Finance and Controller for $250 million public company, managing monthly financial close, daily cash flow analysis, overall financial and profitability analysis, acquisition and systems integration, coordinating audits, health and property & casualty insurance, and human resources
	◆ Results include negotiating competitive contracts to reduce expenses from $250K–$400K annually, reducing cash outlay by $1.25 million due to creative financing deals, and achieving post-merger synergies of $3–$4 million annually
A strong insurance background	◆ More than 4 years at Commercial Insurance company, promoted to Director of Reinsurance, reported directly to CFO
Ability to create and implement new procedures and systems	◆ At Director and VP levels, implemented new processes to improve cash management, credit card processing, staffing, cost reduction, automated reporting systems, and many others
Experience in reviewing contracts and agreements	◆ As Director of Acquisitions, reviewed and revised documents, including all confidentiality/nondisclosure agreements, letters of intent, and stock/asset purchase agreements
	◆ In VP of Finance and Controller positions, reviewed and improved cash management procedures, health insurance agreements, reinsurance contracts, and fronting agreements

81

Director of Finance. *Gail Frank, Tampa, Florida*

This similar two-column format extends to a second page. The size of type would be too small if you tried to fit all of this letter's information on one page. The visible "weight" of the second column gives the impression that this candidate's qualifications more than adequately meet the

Beverly Armstrong, C.P.A.   page 2

555-555-5555 • Cell: 000-000-0000
bevarmstrong@yahoo.com

Your Needs	**My Qualifications**
High degree of personal integrity and effective interaction skills with executives, clients, vendors, and other internal/external parties at all levels	♦ Excellent relationship-development, problem-solving, negotiation, and presentation skills; manage sensitive relationships with executive management, directors, employees, clients, bankers, insurance regulators, venture capitalists, investment bankers, joint-venture partners, and acquisition targets

My resume provides further details of my accomplishments. I look forward to discussing yet another career opportunity with you. I will e-mail you to set a time we can sit down for an interview.

Sincerely,

Beverly Armstrong

Enclosure

prospective employer's needs. If you feel that long paragraphs slow down the reading of a letter, you can see that the tempo of reading across columns from left to right is quicker, which makes the format successful.

LISA HILLIARD

555 N. Windset Avenue   Chicago, IL 60605   555-555-5555   lhillrd@worldnet.att.net

February 21, 2008

The Community Foundation
P.O. Box 569
Chicago, IL 60605

Dear Hiring Professional:

In response to your search for a **Vice President of Finance and Administration,** I bring more than 20 years of extensive experience in all areas of Finance and Administration, as well as Information Technology and Human Resources.

I am an extremely high-energy and innovative manager who leads by example. I consistently produce strong results with a high degree of integrity, dedication and organized communication skills. My track record speaks for itself; I have been involved in virtually every area of an organization, and have made substantial contributions wherever I have been. One of my former bosses had this to say about me in a review:

> *Lisa is at the high end of the exceptional scale. She has exceptional management skills, intelligence and people skills. She has done an exceptional job in a wide variety of areas. She is extremely capable as an individual and as a manager and leader. Her entire group exudes a "can-do" enthusiasm.*

I spoke with Sam Barlow, a Board Member Emeritus of The Community Foundation, about the position and my interest and excitement about it. I know Sam from my volunteer work at the Unity Church, as he is President of the Church Board. He too was enthusiastic about my potential fit with your organization and thought that I could help you reach your goals.

My interest in moving to the nonprofit world is genuine; I have spent years in corporate environments, and since I went back to school have had a chance to better define where and how I want to contribute my talents. I have become very involved both in my church and as a volunteer in the bookstore, technology and fundraising committees and on the technology and finance task forces of the organizing/steering committee for the Illinois Institute of Noetic Sciences.

My resume provides further details of my accomplishments. You will note that I have progressed in responsibility levels throughout my career. I look forward to discussing yet another career opportunity with you, and will contact you next week to arrange a meeting so that we may discuss the organization's needs in greater detail.

Sincerely,

Lisa Hilliard

Enclosure

cc: Sam Barlow

82

Vice President of Finance and Administration. *Gail Frank, Tampa, Florida*

To indicate the applicant's breadth of experience and high standards, the writer provided in the center of the letter a quotation in italic from one of her performance reviews. The reader's eye goes right to it.

Aniyah Alexander
19 Lawnside Dr
Balmain NSW 2040

Mobile: 0414 981 062
Home: (02) 9999 9999
E-mail: aniyah@optusnet.com.au

[Date]

[Company Personnel]
[Company Department]
[Company Name]
[Address]
[Suburb, State, Postal Code]

Dear _____,

When I joined the International Society of Logistics Trading (ISLT) in 1990, it was in bankruptcy with only 152 members. Today it is a $2M international organisation with a membership base of 1,600 members. I transformed ISLT into a strong organisation, with a positive cash flow and outstanding member retention. This success was mainly due to leading the establishment of a 501c3 for the organisation and in the planning and execution of events and programs that generated more than $1.5M in annual revenue and increased asset position from zero to $1.3M.

Prior to working for ISLT, I provided business perspective, strategic visioning, and events management to the ASA Underwriter Association that led to the business becoming a successful and viable organisation through increased membership and community visibility. Through my leadership of the Award Committee, the organisation repeatedly won awards in the annual award recognition programs for Achievement, Public Service, Public Relations, Education, and Members, which were granted to local and state groups by the National Association of Life Underwriters. Prior to my appointment, they had won only two awards in 80 years.

These two examples clearly demonstrate the value I can bring to your organisation. My strengths are in the planning and execution of fund-raising and special events, and in managing the administration of an organisation or event to meet business goals and objectives. I am a creative visionary with a strong team spirit that has an innate ability to take charge, interpret complex issues, and identify opportunities, while still focusing on the actual raising of revenues and membership.

As such, I would welcome an interview to discuss your current needs and my potential contributions. Thank you for your time and consideration of my application. I look forward to speaking with you soon.

Yours sincerely,

Aniyah Alexander
Encl.

83

Executive Director. *Jennifer Rushton, Sydney, New South Wales, Australia*

The applicant wanted a position in fund-raising/events management. The letter shows her ability to turn around poorly performing organizations and increase membership, participation, and revenue.

Cindy Springs
2016 Warm Avenue
Seattle, WA 88888
(555) 555-5555
cindysprings@msn.com

April 16, 2008

Steve Franklin
Canyon Sheriff's Youth Foundation
1632 Barley Drive
Seattle, WA 88888

Dear Mr. Franklin,

As a highly organized professional with experience in coordinating fundraising events and office management, I invite you to consider the enclosed resume in support of my application to secure a position with Canyon Sheriff's Youth Foundation.

I have successfully implemented and monitored strategic objectives and projects to meet the diverse needs of the Seattle Chamber of Commerce as the Manager, consistently completing projects within or under budget. My experience and knowledge will bring immediate improvements to your current and future projects. Please consider the following in addition to my enclosed resume:

- **In-depth project management,** planning, organizing, and evaluating programs for effectiveness and efficiency. Held presentations with officials and community leaders addressing all concerns and showcasing solutions.
- **Decisive, innovative, and dedicated team leader,** inspiring strong team morale as shown by building a team of professionals, coupled with promoting high-quality work supported by a community-oriented attitude.
- **Developed strong relationships with customers,** subordinates, senior management, volunteers, council officials, and community representatives through outstanding communication skills and business etiquette.

It is with great interest that I encourage you to consider my resume, as I am confident that your organization will benefit from my focus on achieving company objectives as a dedicated leader and team member. I am certain that a personal interview would more fully reveal my skills and desire to join your team, and I will call next week to set a mutually convenient time.

Sincerely,

Cindy Springs

Enclosure

84

Fund-Raiser and Office Manager. *Denette D. Jones, Boise, Idaho*

This three-paragraph letter is enhanced with bulleted statements after the second paragraph. Boldfacing enhances the key topic of each bulleted statement, making the topics readily visible.

Benjamin Hall

56 Sunny Dr. ♦ Poughkeepsie, NY 12601 ♦ 555–555–5555 ♦ ben@aol.com

February 20, 2008

Ms. Taylor Coleman, Director
The American Heart Society
12 Tucker Drive
Wappingers Falls, NY 12590

Dear Ms. Coleman:

I am a beauty industry professional who is writing to express interest in employment opportunities within your organization. My goal is a promotional position where I can use my marketing expertise and industry contacts in the area of events planning. With my commitment to social advocacy and enthusiasm for cause-related marketing, I believe that I could positively contribute to your endeavors.

For more than six years I have been working as an events planner for various social causes and issues. Currently, I am responsible for leading the marketing and fund-raising efforts for b•cause—a foundation that I established. Throughout my career I have served in a volunteer capacity in an effort to generate philanthropic support and galvanize industry professionals to embrace issues affecting our community.

My career accelerated after Revlon recognized my ability to spot trends and deliver results. Revlon signed me as its National Fund-raising Director. In only a few years, I conceptualized and brought to fruition countless fund-raisers and events, raising more than $500,000. I was successful in planning and executing these programs through a substantial knowledge of the beauty industry (its business, leaders and experts) and a broad understanding of fund-raising.

While I have an innate ability to take charge of and interpret complex issues, my skills focus on the actual raising of revenues through donor acquisition, corporate giving and personal solicitation. Equally notable has been my ability to identify opportunities, gain high-profile support and negotiate corporate sponsorship. More specifically, I have consistently demonstrated an ability to establish credibility and confidence with individuals or large groups. Further, I am experienced and comfortable in dealing with top public and private community leaders.

Enclosed is a copy of my resume for your review. I look forward to the opportunity to provide you with further details of my professional value and personal commitment during an interview. I will call to determine a mutually convenient time to meet. Thank you for your time.

Sincerely,

Benjamin Hall

Enclosure

85

Events Planner. *Kristin M. Coleman, Poughkeepsie, New York*

Striking in this letter is the amount of white space in relation to the great amount of information it supplies. The writer accomplished this feat through smaller-than-average type and narrower left and right margins.

35–12 Cottonboll Drive
Selma, AL 00000

Yasheika Ojimobi

Banquet Management Specialist

yasheika@partytime.com

Phone: (000) 000-0000
Pager: (000) 000-0000

January 14, 2008

Victor Gibson
Director of Human Resources
Sheridan Corporation
1674 Eldridge Avenue
Montgomery, AL 00000

Dear Mr. Gibson:

In speaking recently with Maxine Ray, who works for Jake Levitz, your Convention Services Manager, I learned that there may be several positions open for persons who are skilled in setting up banquets or managing on-site activities for convention services and trade shows. Because I was intrigued by these opportunities, I am acting on Maxine's suggestion to send you my resume and this letter of interest.

Having spent the past 15 years performing every imaginable task associated with putting together successful banquets and events attended by hundreds of people, I know I have the essential qualifications to be an asset to your organization. As you review my resume, you will see the scope of my involvement and the versatility I can offer. I take great pride in my work, and I am totally dedicated to meeting and even exceeding the expectations of a demanding clientele for their social or corporate functions.

Throughout my career, I have been most effective in orchestrating a team effort while recognizing individual talents to accomplish project goals. The key to my success has been my ability to efficiently manage multiple and varied activities, all taking place simultaneously. Given the opportunity, I can demonstrate this in any project situation calling for broad cooperation.

In addition, I am receptive to new learning experiences; welcome challenges; and have no objection to travel, late hours, or weekend work.

I would appreciate meeting with you personally to discuss your organization's plans and how I may be able to contribute to their accomplishment. I will call you within the next week to determine your interest and perhaps arrange a time when we can meet. Thank you for any consideration.

Sincerely,

Yasheika Ojimobi

Enclosure: Resume

86

Banquets and Events Planner. *Melanie Noonan, West Paterson, New Jersey*

Extra-wide left and right margins provide satisfying white space in this letter. The first paragraph mentions a referral, and the next three paragraphs play up the applicant's merits. See corresponding Resume 8 in Part 3.

Ashina Hartnett
555 55th Avenue, Rochester MN 55555
(555) 555-5555

January 24, 2008

Mr. Samuel Gleason
James T. Conference Coordinators
555 Salome Boulevard
Chicago IL 66666

Dear Mr. Gleason:

Banquet and Conference Coordinator

My work with a highly diverse clientele has been very rewarding, and the experience has reinforced my need to work in an independent capacity that draws together decision-making, problem-solving, and superior people skills.

Staff and the general public respond positively to my managerial, leadership and communication style. I would like to continue working in a business or people-related position with public visibility, and have enclosed a resume for your review. Some of the other qualities I offer are

- Ability to listen closely and react to what people actually say or mean
- Diplomacy, discretion, and consistent style
- Positive attitude
- Flexible nature attuned to changing markets and needs
- Attention to details and concerns
- Efficient multitasking and performance under pressure
- Professional manner, with strict adherence to confidentiality
- Awareness of the importance of professional networking—willingness to attend Chamber of Commerce and other relevant meetings

I've enjoyed assisting in the sales department of a major hotel the last two years and have been called on to fill in when the Conference Coordinator needed additional help with the multitude of details for an unusually large conference. I have not only done some of the "grunt" work but also conferred with various clients, set up the technical logistics, handled last-minute changes, and coordinated with the banquet department. Testimonials from the Conference Coordinator and General Manager will back up my skills and abilities and will verify their opinion that I would be a good fit for a full-time banquet and conference coordinator.

I am highly responsible and trustworthy, and clients and employees alike feel comfortable that I'll do what I say and that promises won't "fall between the cracks." My genuine concern for quality customer service and improved worker motivation is readily apparent, as is interest in professional development and ongoing learning.

It is difficult to determine from resumes career potential and in which areas a person can make a difference to a company. I am looking forward to meeting with you to discuss your needs, to exchange information, and to address any questions.

Sincerely,

Ashina Hartnett

87

Banquet and Conference Coordinator. *Beverley Drake, Rochester, Minnesota*

The applicant was moving from sales to conference work. Unique "multisheet" bullets suggest that each bulleted quality is multifaceted. The third paragraph refers to relevant experience.

Beverly Chase Ryan

0000 Big Horn Road
Bldg. 12, Apt. C
Vail, Colorado 89898

(555) 666-8888   beverlyryan4@aol.com   Cell: (555) 666-7777

January 12, 2008

Leonard R. Victors, Human Resources Manager
AAA Giant Events, Inc.
222 Johansen Boulevard
Vail, Colorado 89898

Dear Mr. Victors:

I was thrilled to find your firm's advertisement in the *Vail Sunday Times*, January 12, 2008, for a Senior Winter Events Consultant. My broad management experience in events planning, coupled with my enthusiasm for working in the skiing industry, clearly matches your stated requirements for the ideal candidate to fill this position.

Most of my professional adult life has been occupied with sports, sports marketing, public relations, successful promotional endeavors, and executing all operations within a high-end catering business in Newport, Rhode Island. My athletic achievements and participation in numerous activities in college point to my early accomplishments in building a solid foundation for the intensive responsibilities of planning and successfully executing such events as AAA regularly engages in.

In addition, my experiences as advertising account executive for North American Skiing Companies, director of retail marketing for a radio station, and director of public relations for a baseball team have strengthened my abilities to meet any challenges that may lie ahead in my focused ambition to go further in this growing field of sports events planning.

I would appreciate meeting with you to discuss my candidacy for the position as Senior Winter Events Consultant with AAA Giant Events, Inc. I will call your office to request a meeting date convenient to you.

Thank you for considering my application. I eagerly look forward to our meeting and the opportunity to discuss my credentials and career aspirations for this position.

Sincerely,

Beverly Chase Ryan

Enclosure: resume

88

Senior Winter Events Consultant. *Edward Turilli, North Kingstown, Rhode Island*

This letter displays the applicant's enthusiasm toward the advertised opening and the prospect of pursuing further her field of athletics. She mentions key experiences for sports events planning.

CATHRYN LYLE

20 Reynolds Place
Mt Waverley Qld 4555   **cathrynl@ozemail.com**   **Phone: (00) 5555 5555**
                                                                                        Mobile: 5555 555 555

CORPORATE SPECIAL EVENT & STAGE MANAGER PRESENTING WITH VERIFIABLE HISTORY
OF OUTSTANDING ACHIEVEMENTS IN CHALLENGING ENVIRONMENTS

---

7 May 2007

Ms S Naylor
Managing Director
Events on Ice
14 Sampson Avenue
Ringwood South Qld 4000

Dear Ms Naylor

Understanding the event management industry as intimately as I do, I appreciate the seasonal changes and the dramatic fluctuations tossing a company between "a few jobs on" to "absolutely insanely busy". It is during these times of maximum capacity that I offer to you my expert contractual services, confident in my ability to always hit the ground running to achieve outstanding results.

Here I offer a very brief overview of my expertise and invite you to peruse my attached resume, which provides more in-depth information:

✏ History of undertaking challenging stage and event management assignments, including two seven-day international family conferences consisting of 600 adults and 600 children/teens and an outdoor rock concert with six bands in a remote regional town. I have repeatedly been sought out to undertake these and numerous other events due to my methods of operation, which remove all stress from the client, my ability to guide and instruct in a fun environment, and my intrinsic ability to "make the company look good".

✏ Instinctive knowledge and ability to "read the room" and to implement rapid changes when required. Excellent ability to prioritise, then re-prioritise, combined with skilful assessment of personalities to delegate and formulate the most effective teams and partnerships.

✏ Vital ability to communicate in an easy-to-understand and confident manner to brief all participants, including actors, waitpersons, managing directors, and others, to train personnel in all elements of the event industry and to address, instruct, motivate, and inspire large groups.

✏ Excellent academic qualifications include Bachelor of Arts: Major in Drama & Design gained through the New South Wales University of Arts and Drama, where I was accepted as one of only 33 students out of a total of 1,200 applicants and was chosen as joint lead set designer for the final-year productions; Certificate in Priority Management, which I have found invaluable when combined with my natural organisational expertise and career experience.

In event and stage management I have found my niche and in this arena I excel. If you are looking for an original, flexible, and diverse professional able to infuse creative and innovative ideas into cohesive strategies within time-critical goals and within budget, I would like to explore this opportunity with you. Thank you for your time.

Yours sincerely

Cathryn Lyle
Att: resume

89

Corporate Special Event & Stage Manager. *Beverley Neil, Victoria Point West, Queensland, Australia*

The applicant was returning to the industry after a year and wanted to work by contract. The letter highlights her expertise and accomplishments. Within weeks she achieved a six-month contract.

March 21, 2008

Mr. William Babinski
Staffing Director
Chambers Medical Clinic
Duluth, Minnesota

RE: MEDICAL TRANSCRIPTIONIST

Dear Mr. Babinski:

Enclosed is a resume for the posted position.

Graduating with honors in 2007 from the medical transcription certification program at Manchester Community and Technical College, I am ready to begin the career for which I have worked so hard.

My medical records experience will be especially helpful in this position. Not only am I highly familiar with patient record management, but also I bring the following:

- Positive collaboration with physicians and other medical personnel
- Understanding of team concepts, legalities, confidentiality, hospital code and patient rights
- Experience working with pneumatic record transport systems
- Multicultural experience

General business skills complement my experience. This includes data entry, word processing, strong communication skills and accuracy, as well as the ability to monitor my own work. I've established a good track record for a positive attitude, initiative, organizational skills, pride in my work, confidence and team spirit.

I very much look forward to hearing from you regarding this position.

Sincerely,

Nina Altonson

NINA ALTONSON

Chauncey Court #16
Rochester MN 55555

(555) 555-5555

ninaa@minnonline.com

**MEDICAL OFFICE
PROFESSIONAL**

◆ ◆ ◆

BUSINESS SKILLS

Data Entry 12,500 KPH
Telephone Skills
Pneumatic Record Transport System
Facilitation
Problem Solving
Customer Service
Filing (Numeric & Alpha)
Training of Staff

CULTURAL DIVERSITY & LANGUAGE

Four Years of Spanish
Extensive Travel–Western U.S.
Multicultural Experience

90

Medical Transcriptionist. *Beverley Drake, Rochester, Minnesota*

Making a cover letter look different from others is a challenge. Using a multicolumn format can produce good results. The vertical line can be in a narrow, separate column or as a side border of a text column.

Ariel Adams
111 Washington St.
Hunterville, IL 60030
(111) 222-2222
aadams@email.com

October 27, 2007

Human Resource Manager
Lucas County Health Department
Human Resources Office
111 Greenich Rd.
Lucasville, IL 00000

Dear Human Resource Manager:

When I read your advertisement for a ***Patient Care Representative*** on Lucas County's Web site, I thought that you had written the job description with me in mind. As you require, I am fluent in both English and Spanish and have excellent interpersonal skills. Additionally, I have experience in handling cash and performing inventory.

For the past 3 years, I have been caring for an elderly relative who is now deceased. During that time, I gained a considerable amount of experience scheduling appointments and communicating with medical staff and patients. I can be very empathetic and patient with sick individuals who may be confused or upset.

As soon as I complete my GED next month, I will be available to start work. As you will see on my attached resume, I am actively working to improve myself. For 10 hours each week, I have been practicing typing and am confident that I can meet your expectations in this area.

I am eager to make a difference at the Lucas County Health Department. I will contact your office at the end of the week to verify that you have received my letter and resume and to talk to you further about this opportunity. In the meantime, feel free to contact me at (111) 222-2222.

Thank you for your time and consideration,

Ariel Adams

Enclosure: Resume

91

Patient Care Representative. *Eva Locke, Waukegan, Illinois*

The writer cast as strengths the skills this applicant used in caring for a sick relative. Because the applicant lacked GED and typing requirements, these are mentioned as being met in the near future.

JENNIFER E. EMERSON, LPN

000 PEABODY AVENUE
MELROSE, MA 00000
(444) 888-2222

CELL: (444) 888-0000
E-MAIL: JEMERSON@AOL.COM

February 5, 2008

Madeline Detweiler, Practical Nurse Administrator
Lowden Family Health Centers
4444 South Main Road
Pohasset, MA 00000

Dear Ms. Detweiler:

I am writing in response to your advertisement in *The Melrose Daily News* for a full-time Licensed Practical Nurse. I believe that I can fill that position well due to my education, health care experience, and professional sincerity.

A recent LPN graduate of the Pohasset Regional Technical School in Taunton, MA, I currently hold a license in Massachusetts and have also applied for a New Hampshire license.

My demonstrated strong organizational and communication skills derive from my successful employment experiences in business offices, as my enclosed resume confirms. These skills, coupled with my LPN education and training, should prove to be of great benefit to your family health center.

I am confident that you will agree that my qualifications match your requirements for this position. Therefore, I would greatly appreciate an opportunity to meet with you to fully reveal my keen interest in the health care field and to determine how I may fit your staff profile. I can be reached by e-mail, home phone, or cell phone days or evenings to arrange for an appointment. If I do not hear from you by Monday, February 15, I will call your office to request a meeting at a time convenient to you or another member of your staff.

Thank you for considering my application for employment at Lowden Family Health Centers.

Sincerely,

Jennifer E. Emerson, LPN

Enclosure: resume

92

Licensed Practical Nurse. *Edward Turilli, North Kingstown, Rhode Island*

The challenge was to convince a recruiter that the entry-level applicant's proactive manner in obtaining her degree and another state license outweighed her minimal nursing experience.

Frances C. MacSorley

1212 Juniper Circle
North Kingman, CT 66666
francesmac@earthlink.com

(000) 222-1111   Cell: (000) 222-3333

January 27, 2008

Philippe J. Desjardin
Director of Human Resources
New Haven Memorial Hospital
111 Brently Street
New Haven, CT 00000

Dear Mr. Desjardin:

This letter is in response to your advertisement in *The New Haven Sunday Times*, January 27, 2008, for a Licensed Practical Nurse to be employed at the Leone Mathieu Life Care Center.

I believe that my qualifications are strong for this position, for my 15 years in practical nursing have given me excellent professional experience in addition to my personal career objective of providing and maintaining the highest level of nursing care and quality of life to patients under my charge. My total nursing experience has been, and continues to be, full-time, direct patient care.

Always deeply committed to the nursing profession, I have striven to keep abreast of the latest data through in-service learning and reading various journals and selected publications. Courses taken in the liberal arts are in direct preparation for my Associate degree as a Registered Nurse. Moreover, they have broadened my capacity to deal with humanitarian issues that are so much a part of healing.

If you agree with me that my credentials are sound for this position at the Leone Mathieu Life Care Center, I would very much appreciate an opportunity to meet with you to discuss my candidacy for this opening at Memorial Hospital. I can be reached by e-mail, at my home after 5 p.m., or at any time by my cell phone to schedule an appointment at a time that is convenient to you.

Thank you for considering me for this position. I look forward to meeting with you soon and will contact you to schedule an interview.

Sincerely,

Frances C. MacSorley

Enclosures: resume / application

93

Licensed Practical Nurse. *Edward Turilli, North Kingstown, Rhode Island*

After 15 years in practical nursing, the applicant wanted another LPN position while she worked on her registered nursing degree. The letter shows her commitment to nursing and humanitarian issues.

Grace Messenger, R.N.

000 Oak Grove Place ▪ Canandaigua, NY 14424 ▪ 585-555-0000 ▪ nurse@aol.com

March 19, 2008

Dr. David Mansfield
Superintendent of Schools
Canandaigua City School District
99 North Street
Canandaigua, NY 14424

Dear Dr. Mansfield:

As a Licensed Registered Nurse with five years of related experience, including public school nursing, I have great interest in your opening for a School Nurse.

For the past two school years, I have been employed at Phelps Central School, providing routine and emergency health services to the staff and school population of 1000+ students. In addition, I gained experience in school nursing on a substitute basis with your district as well as Manchester-Shortsville. In these roles, I have been able to apply and hone my generalist skills, most notably in assessment, emergency care, and health counseling. Notable accomplishments in my current position include

- Completion of School Nurses Orientation Program.
- Training in Section 504 regulations.
- Automated External Defibrillator Training and Certification, as well as involvement in school policy development for defibrillator use and placement selection; I also manage the equipment maintenance program.
- Management of student attendance using a custom software application.

As a lifelong resident of Canandaigua and parent of school-aged children, I have been actively involved in the community and the school for more than a decade. I believe this offers me a unique perspective and understanding—of the environment in which I would work, of the individuals receiving care and their families, and of the impact to our community.

A collaborative professional, I am both dedicated and visionary. I will use my clinical and personal skills in partnership with the administration to support the school's mandate to provide and maintain a healthy and safe environment for its students and employees.

It is my hope that we can meet to discuss your School Nurse opening and my background in greater detail. I will follow up this letter and resume with a call to your office but invite you to contact me anytime at 555-0000.

Thank you for your consideration and time.

Sincerely,

Grace Messenger

Enclosure

94

School Nurse. *Salome A. Farraro, Mount Morris, New York*

The applicant earned her credentials after seeing her three children through elementary school. The second paragraph and the bulleted items show that she had solid experience in school nursing.

Stephanie Tusston
111 S. Lake St.
Garthville, IL 00000
(111) 111-1234
stusston@someemail.com

August 2, 2007

Dr. Polack
Polack Care Clinic
123 West St.
Garthville, IL 00000

Dear Dr. Polack:

In response to your recent advertisement, please accept this letter in application for the Billing position currently available within your office. I am seeking to transition back into the medical field after the birth of my children. My husband is now the full-time childcare provider for our family, so I am eagerly seeking to advance my career.

As you can see from my enclosed resume, I was employed as a Lead Cashier at a local hospital for almost 1 year. My supervisor was so impressed with my communication style with insurance companies that he promoted me to Medical Claims Processor. I have up-to-date training in billing and coding and am proficient with a variety of software.

I would appreciate the opportunity to discuss my credentials with you at a mutually convenient time. I will contact you next week to set a time. Thank you for your consideration.

Respectfully yours,

Stephanie Tusston

Enclosure: Resume

95

Billing Specialist. *Eva Locke, Waukegan, Illinois*

The letter explains a gap in the applicant's recent work history. The second paragraph calls attention to her former success as a Lead Cashier and promotion to Medical Claims Processor.

CAMILLE DEROSA

35 Flower Trail Lane ◆ North Babylon, New York 11703 ◆ (555) 555-5555
cderosa@optonline.net

Name
Company
Address
City, State ZIP

Date

Dear Sir or Madam:

In May, I will graduate from the State University of Stony Brook with a **Bachelor of Science in Cytotechnology, with a minor in Biology.** I am seeking to pursue my long-term personal and professional goal of a challenging career as a **Cytotechnologist** *within a hospital environment for the variety of specimens and the opportunity to participate in fine needle aspiration procedures.* Let me briefly highlight the skills, values and contributions I will bring to your healthcare facility:

- Dedicated commitment to a long and successful career as a **Cytotechnologist.**

- Excellent patient relations/evaluation, time-management, troubleshooting, interpersonal and communication skills, developed through experience at **Good Samaritan Hospital as a Cytology Prep Assistant.**

- Ability to perform independently or as part of a team, building cooperative working relationships among management and support staff in order to meet goals and achieve successful results.

- Aptitude to collaborate with physicians to implement protocol; provide new product evaluations and procurement.

- Proven success in prioritizing time and completing intense workloads under severe pressure to attain goals and meet project deadlines, achieving desired results.

- An energetic, hardworking and self-motivated work ethic, coupled with a flexible approach to assignments.

Because a resume can neither fully detail all my skills and accomplishments nor convey my potential to your **Cytology Department,** I would welcome a personal interview to further explore the merging of my *education, experience, ambition* and *enthusiasm* with your facility's objectives. I will call next week to inquire about a mutually convenient time.

Very truly yours,

CAMILLE DEROSA

Enclosure

96

Cytotechnologist. *Donna M. Farrise, Hauppauge, New York*

The two-line page border, boldfacing and italicizing of key information and keywords, and bulleting of skills and worker traits make this letter attractive, strong, and easy to grasp at a glance.

Elizabeth Santiago

11 Riverside Drive
New York, NY 10023

(555) 555-5555
esantiago@xyz.com

April 23, 2008

Michael Kahn
Director of Human Resources
St. Luke's–Roosevelt Hospital Center
Roosevelt Division
1000 Tenth Avenue at 58th Street
New York, NY 10019

Dear Mr. Kahn:

After reading about your organization's new health care initiatives, as described on the hospital's Web site, I was excited to learn of an opening for a Clinical Laboratory Scientist. My background in developing and implementing testing and instrumentation procedures can bring an immediate benefit to the hospital as it strives to improve patient care. I am enclosing my resume for your review.

With 15 years of experience in the hematology and pathology departments of two major teaching hospitals, I am able to prioritize workflow and resolve problems to ensure the efficiency and accuracy of department operations. In particular, I have reviewed and revised operating procedures to achieve regulatory compliance. Among my key accomplishments are the following:

- Managed installation and implementation of new coagulation system, including writing procedures and training staff. Coordinated with multiple departments for successful completion within a one-month time line.

- Integrated a standardized coagulation system across two hospital campuses to ensure better patient care and quality assurance.

- Established, wrote, and set up a preventative maintenance schedule for hematology instrumentation to ensure the quality of performance.

I look forward to the opportunity to talk with you in person about the contribution I can make to your hospital. I will contact you in the near future to schedule an interview.

Thank you for your consideration.

Sincerely,

Elizabeth Santiago

Enclosure

97

Clinical Laboratory Scientist. *Wendy Gelberg, Needham, Massachusetts*

The applicant did background research on the prospective employer's Web site and links her accomplishments directly to the mission of the company. Bullets point to the accomplishments.

KATHERINE TEOJEN
555 Caswell Avenue
Charlotte, NC 28888
(000) 000-0000
katherinet@ncnet.com

March 27, 2008

Dr. John Irving
Director of Clinical Recruitment
Carolinas Medical Center
Charlotte, NC 28888

Dear Dr. Irving:

On the high seas, navigation is very important. In fact, few persons could play a more significant role than the captain of a large cargo vessel.

When the cargo vessel approaches the mainland or nears port, a towering beacon of golden light flashes and revolves to guide ships and warn of obstacles. Here, the lighthouse and its keeper bring the ship through the maze of rocks, atolls and barnacled debris, to safe harbor.

The speech-language pathologist is comparable to the lighthouse keeper; she is the beacon, the guiding light, with the training to show the way to those less fortunate. I understand, intimately, the importance of such training. At age six, to correct the mispronunciation of the letter "r," I went to a speech therapist. This was a pivotal moment, for I realized that *I* could be helped and that speech-language problems were correctable.

Over the years, this interest has grown and taken on a new meaning. Two years ago, I volunteered for Operation Smile, a project in which local physicians travel to Third-World countries and perform reconstructive surgery (usually pro bono) to correct cleft palates of children.

Since then, I have worked as a volunteer at Lake Forest School for the Deaf, teaching basic life skills using sign language. And at Mercy Speech & Hearing Center, a clinic sponsored by the United Way, I currently volunteer, observing and evaluating children with articulation and audiology problems.

Since August 2007, while completing requirements for a master's degree, I have been employed at The Center for Speech Excellence in Charlotte, administering tests and tutoring children in the Fast-Forward Program, an intensive six-week interactive program, with emphasis in receptive language skills, auditory processing and central processing disorders. Working under the auspices of Pamela Wright, a speech pathologist, I have shadowed her while working with children with cochlear implants. The Center treats hearing-impaired children and also works with adults (e.g., accent reduction, voice pitch alteration, and stuttering).

My goal is to provide diagnostic, therapeutic and associated counseling services within a hospital or other clinical setting. I am particularly interested in working with children with articulation, fluency, language, voice and neurological deficits. If your hospital needs a speech pathologist—to be that "guiding light"—I would appreciate the opportunity to discuss your needs in a personal interview. I look forward to meeting with you. A brief resume of my background is enclosed.

Sincerely,

Katherine Teojen

Enclosure

98

Speech Pathologist. *Doug Morrison, Charlotte, North Carolina*

The ambition of this young speech-language pathologist to help others overcome obstacles (because of her own early problems with speech) is embodied in the opening and closing analogy.

RACHEL WINSLOW
55 W. Parker Street   Campbell, CA 55555   555-555-5555   rachel_wins@yahoo.com

August 31, 2007

Ms. Edna Farnsworth
Human Resources Department
Arroyo Healthcare Corporate Office
5555 15th Street
Mesa, CO 55555

Subject: Healthcare Employment Opportunities

Dear Ms. Farnsworth:

News regarding your construction of the Arroyo Medical Center, scheduled to open in November, prompted me to contact you because of my long-term involvement in the healthcare field and because I admire Arroyo's commitment to providing future-oriented, quality healthcare for its patients. Although I currently live in California, I plan to relocate to Colorado once I obtain suitable employment. I am enclosing my current resume for your consideration.

As my resume indicates, I have gained diverse experience in a hospital environment over the past several years. This has included frequent patient interaction and support, ranging from registration and appointment-setting to arrangements for critical care transport. I have also consistently established and maintained positive work relationships with a variety of individuals at the medical centers, including physicians and nurses.

Because of my experience, dedication to providing excellent service, and enthusiasm for the healthcare field, I am confident I can make a worthwhile contribution to your organization. I would like to arrange an interview to discuss possible openings you might have where my experience would be an asset. I will call you next Thursday.

Sincerely,

Rachel Winslow

Enc.

99

Healthcare Worker. *Georgia Adamson, Campbell, California*

The applicant wanted to relocate out of state, heard about a new medical center, and wanted to explore possible positions before they were advertised—hence, no mention of a specific position.

Winthrop "Lee" Kent
0000 Carlton Circle — Memphis, Tennessee 00000
winlee@extra.com — ✆ 000.000.0000 – 555.555.5555 (Cellular)

Friday, January 30, 2008

Dr. Charles Fleming, MD
Medical Associates of Crofton, P.C.
500 Elm Street
Suite 400
Crofton, Alabama 36100

Dear Dr. Fleming:

If you could "design" the best practice manager for Medical Associates, would the following meet your needs?

- ❏ A **cash-flow expert** who combines the realistic outlook of an auditor with the profit-building drive of an entrepreneur,

- ❏ A **productivity multiplier** with a proven track record of leading diverse employees to greater productivity and loyalty,

- ❏ A manager with a gift for **freeing decision makers** for the tasks only they can do, and

- ❏ A dedicated administrator who can replace the distractions of business with **peace of mind** that comes from lessened liability and greater profits.

You have just read the 76-word version of my resume. You'll find the complete document on the next pages. What you won't find are the usual "summary of qualifications" and lists of responsibilities. In their places are more than a half dozen documented contributions that helped move organizations forward.

I enjoyed working for the state. And I was promoted twice in just eight months because the state valued my contributions. But my real calling is working in the private sector.

Because I have a natural desire to fill people's needs, I would like to hear about Medical Associates' special requirements in your own words. I will call in a few days to find a few minutes to do that.

Sincerely,

Winthrop Kent

Encl.: Resume

100

Medical Practice Manager. *Don Orlando, Montgomery, Alabama*

This letter helped a state employee transition to a medical practice manager. The letter opens with an engaging question, and the answers—as bulleted items—appeal to the needs of the reader.

REBA WOODWARD

9999 Oracal Ave.
Sunny, Texas 79000
(999) 999-9999 (H)
(999) 999-0000 (C)
rwood586@hotmail.com

February 15, 2008

Human Resources Coordinator
Sunny Home Nursing Service
9999 Hospital Ave.
Sunny, Texas 79000

Re: ADMINISTRATOR OF HEALTHCARE SERVICES

"We make a living by what we get,
but we make a life by what we give."
~ Winston Churchill

Dear Human Resources Coordinator:

Your recent classified ad in the *City-Wide Journal* caught my eye. As an experienced registered nurse, I am currently investigating career opportunities in the field of management in the healthcare industry where my highly developed skills will transfer nicely. The enclosed resume reflects an exceptionally viable candidate for the above-named position.

I am a well-established native of this area with a background as program director; school nurse; operating room circulator; and charge nurse in clinic, ER, OR, and hospital floor environments. The following skills and characteristics are reason to take a closer look at my credentials. I am

- *Strong in handling multiple tasks and multifaceted situations while maintaining satisfactory interpersonal relationships with staff, physicians, patients, students, and families.*

- *An expert at ensuring compliance with regulations while keeping costs within budget.*

- *Talented in prioritizing issues and tasks and visualizing the "big" picture when considering the long-term effects of my decisions.*

- *An outcome-oriented self-starter with superior organizational and administrative skills.*

After reviewing my resume, you will discover that my qualifications are a good match for this position. The opportunity for a personal interview to further discuss employment possibilities would be mutually beneficial. I will call you to schedule an appointment at your convenience. In the meantime, thank you for your time and consideration.

Sincerely,

Reba Woodward

Enclosure: Resume

101

Administrator of Healthcare Services. *Edith A. Rische, Lubbock, Texas*

The applicant wanted a career change from a registered nurse to a healthcare administrator. The letter highlights her transferable skills through a list of bulleted statements in boldface.

Julie Windham
1111 Madison Avenue
Boise, ID 00000
(000) 000-0000
jwindham@earthlink.net

January 30, 2008

Human Resources Department
Access Health Care
2323 Woodhaven Street
Boise, ID 00000

Dear Human Resources Representative:

It is with great interest that I forward my resume for consideration as Program
Director. Currently, as Admissions Coordinator for the ABC Rehabilitation and
Care Center, I spearhead marketing efforts for this health care service
provider, ranked #1 in a heavily competitive market, drawing clients from all
parts of Idaho. My results have been significant and include the following:

* Occupancy rate increase from 90% to 98% (highest rate among facilities in
Idaho);

* Patient increase from 6-7 to 18-19 through strategic marketing communications;

* Cost-effective service rate wins through tactical negotiations with insurance
companies.

My resume is attached to provide you with specific details concerning my
background and qualifications. Thank you for your time.

Sincerely,

Julie Windham

102

Program Director. *Daniel J. Dorotik, Jr., Lubbock, Texas*

This e-mail letter in text (.txt) format shows that online letters (and resumes) are preferably
shorter than those in traditional format. Readers like window-size documents that require little
scrolling.

KRISTEN MARTELL

555.555.5555

555 West Haven Ave., #7 • New Wilmington, PA 55555

August 30, 2007

Mr. Rob Tyler
University of Washington Medical Center
555 Union Street
Seattle, WA 55555

Dear Mr. Tyler:

With my upcoming graduation from Sharon Regional Health System School of Nursing, I am excited about using my nursing skills to provide patient care at your facility.

As you review my resume, you will note that this is a second career for me. I spent several years as a stylist, where I gained much experience in interacting with the public and providing excellent customer service. These interpersonal skills, combined with my acquired clinical skills, will enable me to make positive contributions to the healthcare team at your facility. I am confident you will determine that my clinical skills meet those established by you. Let me share what Thomas Pepper, RN, MSN, Nursing Instructor, had to say about my performance:

> *Kristen performed head-to-toe assessments [and] is a very active learner. [She] demonstrates … a good knowledge base of disease process for each client … critical-thinking and problem-solving skills in caring for clients … [and] a caring attitude for all her clients.*

> *Kristen is knowledgeable of the patients' medical diagnosis. She is able to discuss and make connections to the patients' past medical history and the current diagnosis. Kristen is able to perform nursing skills from previous classes [and] is also organized and communicates well with staff, patients, and families.*

In anticipation that you would like to meet with me, I would be delighted to make myself available. I will call to determine a mutually convenient time. Thank you for your time and consideration.

Sincerely,

Kristen Martell

Enclosure: resume

103

Clinic Worker. *Jane Roqueplot, Sharon, Pennsylvania*

With only an education and no actual career-field experience, this applicant wanted to work in a clinic. The writer indicated the applicant's transferable skills and instructors' recommendations.

FOSTER M. CLAYTON
9 Cranberry Lane ■ Oxford Hills, PA 19666
Home: (555) 888-9999 ■ Mobile: (555) 555-6666 ■ E-mail: Clay212@aol.com

December 16, 2007

Ms. Liz Carter
MHS Recruiters
999 Old Nathan Road
Suite 333
Eagleville, PA 19777

RE: Orthopedic/Musculoskeletal Product Line Director
Main Health Systems

Dear Ms. Carter:

It is with great interest that I submit my resume and collateral materials for consideration as Orthopedic/Musculoskeletal Product Line Director at Main Health Systems. It is my understanding that the successful candidate will possess qualifications and experience that closely match those detailed in my resume, and it would be my pleasure to meet with you to discuss this exciting opportunity.

Highlights of my professional career include

- More than 20 years of top-flight management experience in the healthcare services and products industries.

- Expertise in the start-up of new healthcare ventures and accelerated growth within existing provider organizations.

- Delivery of strong revenue and profit growth within extremely competitive healthcare markets.

- Strong qualifications in new business development, strategic planning, marketing, risk management, program development, and teaching.

- Broad-based general management skills in human resource affairs, training, financial planning and analysis, and presentations to various boards and professional groups.

- Extensive network of professional, technical, and medical contacts throughout the healthcare community.

My leadership style is direct and decisive, yet I am flexible in responding to the constantly changing demands of the industry, customers, and the market. I am familiar with most regulations governing healthcare practice and have been actively involved in several professional organizations within the field.

I look forward to speaking with you to discuss this opportunity and will call next week to request a meeting. I would be pleased to provide professional references, additional biographical information, and work samples in preparation for an interview. Thank you for your consideration.

Sincerely,

Foster M. Clayton

Enclosure

104

Orthopedic/Musculoskeletal Product Line Director. *Karen Conway, Media, Pennsylvania*

This letter's first paragraph directs the reader to the resume, and the bullets draw the reader's attention to the applicant's most relevant experience, expertise, qualifications, and skills.

JANE BARTLETT, PA-C
PHYSICIAN ASSISTANT

88 Murray Road
Atlanta, GA 55555
555.555.5555
e-mail: bartlett@aol.com

May 20, 2007

Fred Martin, M.D.
Chief of Staff
Atlanta Medical Center
44 Hospital Drive
Atlanta, GA 55555

Dear Dr. Martin:

As a follow-up to our conversation, I am forwarding my CV in consideration for a Physician Assistant position at Atlanta Medical Center. Graduating next month from Southland College's PA Program, I am eager to begin my career. I would bring to your department solid experience acquired through my education, training, and clinical rotations.

My practical experience includes serving a 3-month clinical rotation in general medicine at Georgia Memorial Hospital under the direction of Elizabeth Jones, PA-C, and Dr. Thomas Gillan. Along with the medical experience I acquired, I also rotated on various psychiatric units on a weekly basis. In addition, I completed a clinical rotation in psychiatry at Malvern Psychiatric Associates.

Through my extensive training, I have developed solid clinical skills and competency in performing various procedures. Along with my technical capabilities—as my evaluators will confirm—I have a talent for quickly gaining patients' trust and working effectively with all members of the health care team. My interpersonal, communications, organizational, and decision-making skills are among my strong suits.

If your department could utilize a professional with my technical competencies, maturity, and passion for medicine, I would welcome an interview and will call to set a convenient time. I am confident in my ability to add value to your department. Thank you for your serious consideration.

Sincerely,

Jane Bartlett, PA-C

105

Physician Assistant. *Louise Garver, Enfield, Connecticut*

This recently graduated physician assistant submitted this letter and a curriculum vitae to get an interview and won an offer for a PA position. The letter mentions two friends of the Chief of Staff.

PAUL JOHNSON

14 Westlake Drive
Framingham, MA 01702

Email: paul@johnson.com

Cell: 000 000 0000
Residence: 555 555 5555

11 February 2008

Mr. David Paul
ATCT Hospital
18 Saddleback Road
Framingham, MA 01702

Re: Chief Executive Officer

Dear Mr. Paul:

For almost 20 years, I have been at the forefront of initiatives that have positioned organizations to support significant growth, and have turned around floundering and problematic divisions to regain the respect of the people they serve. I have conceived new ideas to strengthen core services to customers, project-managed new infrastructure initiatives, and maintained the morale of "the troops" despite periods of instability and change.

Considered a senior executive with a combination of vision and corporate realism, I have been acknowledged for my capacity to harness the enthusiasm and talents of others, identify core issues, and exploit the necessary resources available to stretch funds and achieve management objectives in healthcare and medical environments.

Experience of this magnitude hasn't been developed overnight; successes have been hard won, and commitment has been tireless. Yet the rewards of seeing an idea take hold of people's imaginations for better and more responsive service delivery remains to this day one of my greatest motivators, and it is a skill I'm keen to demonstrate for my next employer as I meet the next challenge of my professional life.

Eager to tackle new opportunities, my last major role as Vice President, Business Delivery, consulting primarily to medical, healthcare, and education sectors, has now concluded. I have transformed what was a new business unit into a vital, responsive operation that delivered strong productivity increases and growth in just two years.

And now the time is ripe for a new challenge. Broad-based knowledge across diverse sectors and specialist executive consultancy experience in healthcare and medical sectors position me well for joining your leadership team.

Experienced in hospital operations; case management; and all the economic, procedural, and staff issues inherent in such environments, I believe I can bring a unique skill set to the role of hospital CEO. Having worked closely with senior executives in major healthcare facilities and hospitals, I know and understand the complexities of the healthcare system, the infrastructure, and how to position the organization for genuine growth. I see significant opportunities in aligning myself with ATCT Hospital, opportunities I'm keen to tackle and achieve measurable successes in, for our mutual benefit.

Naturally I would be delighted to explore your needs in detail at an interview and can arrange to meet at a mutually convenient time. In the meantime, my resume is attached for your review, and I can be contacted at the numbers provided. Thank you for your time and consideration, and I look forward to speaking with you soon.

Sincerely,

Paul Johnson

106

Chief Executive Officer. *Gayle Howard, Chirnside Park, Melbourne, Australia*

The challenge of this cover letter was to convince the reader that this senior consultant, who had worked in healthcare for many years, was qualified to assume the role of a hospital CEO.

CATHERINE SITTON
555 N. Johnson Avenue, Apt. 5
Brookhaven, Pennsylvania 19333
(555) 555-8888
cate_sitton@penn.net

December 16, 2007

Sodexo Marriott Corporation
ATT: Franklin Hunt, Director of Personnel
5 Landon Way
Princeton, NJ 08888

Dear Mr. Hunt:

I would like to express my interest in joining Sodexo Marriott in a management capacity. I am particularly interested in a senior-level position involving corporate dining, catering, and banquet events. Enclosed is my resume, reviewing my extensive background and accomplishments in staff and operations management, for your consideration.

As an effective manager and chef, I have a proven track record in all facets of the food service industry. My greatest strength would have to be my ability to generate employee loyalty and create a team environment. Equally strong is my ability to control labor and food costs. I am especially proud of the fact that former staff members often request to join me when I accept a new assignment. I provide extensive training, direction, and feedback; they are clearly aware of my expectations and interest in their welfare.

Other key attributes include attention to detail, the ability to work effectively in high-pressure situations, a high level of motivation, and emphasis on sanitation. Here are several career highlights that may be of interest:

- Significantly reduced Workers' Compensation costs in all locations through close attention to safety.
- Acquired an excellent reputation as a chef, skilled in the areas of menu planning, timing, presentation, and food quality.
- Hired as a consultant to assist a new center-city restaurant during its start-up phase.
- Developed training manuals and completed staff training for all positions.

On a final note, it goes without saying that guest satisfaction is key to a successful operation. I consistently stress to my staff the importance of communicating effectively with guests. Not only does the guest feel unique and special, but also it demonstrates confidence on the part of the employee. That equates to a successful dining experience and repeat business, which has been the norm in each of my operations.

I believe my education and background have provided the tools and experience necessary to manage a large-scale operation, and I would welcome the opportunity to discuss employment prospects at Sodexo Marriott in a personal interview. I believe your organization would be an ideal work setting for someone with my skills and personality.

I'll look forward to meeting with you and will contact you to set a mutually convenient time for an interview.

Sincerely,

Catherine Sitton

Enclosure

Hotel Manager. *Karen Conway, Media, Pennsylvania*

A series of equally short paragraphs makes this longer-than-average cover letter relatively easy to read. The bulleted items provide relief from the series and draw attention to career highlights.

Michael J. Fisher, C.M.C.

56 Madison Avenue
Summit, New Jersey 07901
(555) 555-5555
mjfcmc@earthlink.net

[Date]

[Name]
[Title]
[Address]
[City, State ZIP]

Dear Sir/Madam:

Enclosed is my resume for your review. I am confident that my extensive experience as an executive chef and hotel/restaurant manager would serve as an asset to a position in your organization. My career began 23 years ago as an apprentice training under several notable, internationally known chefs. Since that time I have been involved extensively in the area of food services management and marketing.

I am currently General Manager and Corporate Executive Chef of Hague Nieuw-York. In 1999, I was hired to start up this 225-seat restaurant. The casual dining establishment is part of Avanti Brands, Inc., USA. I am responsible for all financial reporting and instituted key control systems to meet the standards of the parent company. Additional achievements include gaining excellent media publicity, creative menu development, and directing on- and off-site catering for many New York City premieres. I was asked to coordinate all aspects of our new construction and assist in the design aspects of the kitchen.

As Director of Operations for Town Square Katering and Times Square Restaurant in Hoboken, New Jersey, my staff and I expanded the business to accommodate parties ranging from 10 to 4,000 people and grossed more than $1.5 million in sales.

Working as Vice President of Operations and Executive Chef for Pine Ridge Country Club, I oversaw all profit-and-loss functions for a 165-seat, a la carte restaurant and a 1,000-seat banquet facility. The club had an 18-hole championship golf course that I managed, with an active membership of 1,000 members.

I gained extensive international experience working as Executive Chef for Ordini's, a five-star-rated restaurant in New Zealand, preparing food for the Prime Minister, various heads of state, and visiting dignitaries. I obtained my New Zealand Master Chef's Certification. In addition, I served as an Executive Pastry Chef and Chef for a Hawaiian hotel owned and operated by the Sheraton Corporation.

Thank you for your consideration. I look forward to speaking with you personally regarding my qualifications and how I can contribute positively as a member of your management staff. I will contact you next week to inquire about the possibility of a personal interview.

Sincerely Yours,

Michael J. Fisher, C.M.C.

Enclosure

108

Executive Chef and Hotel/Restaurant Manager. *Beverley and Mitchell I. Baskin, Marlboro, New Jersey*

Inferior cover letters wallow in generalities and abstraction. This letter is unusually interesting because of its many references to restaurants in specific locations around the world.

KRISTEN MOORE

5555 Winter Road • Hermitage, Pennsylvania 55555 • 555-555-5555
kmoore@aol.com

August 31, 2007

Mary Brenner
Five Star Restaurant
5555 Michigan Avenue
Chicago, IL 55555

Dear Ms. Brenner:

I have been fortunate throughout my career in hospitality to work in positions that challenged me and benefited from my passion for management and inventive solutions. I delivered programs that captured market share, accelerated revenue growth, and won dominant competitive positioning. While secure in my current position, I am confidentially seeking a new career opportunity.

By combining my expertise in strategic planning, team building, leadership, and time management with my expertise in budgeting and cost control in the restaurant business, I have significantly contributed to boosting my employer's performance. The strength of my character, my commitment to quality, and my endless ideas and enthusiasm will be an invaluable asset to your establishment.

As a service-oriented professional who focuses on people, let me highlight some of my specific skills relative to a restaurant environment:

➢ Recruit a nucleus of staff to effectively and efficiently support the needs of the restaurant. Established reputation for a motivational, hands-on management style that inspires teamwork and builds confidence in others.

➢ Emphasize training of all personnel in food preparation, front/back house operations, and problem solving for peak customer satisfaction.

➢ Adept at controlling food and beverage costs while maintaining the highest level of customer service.

➢ Skilled at marketing and advertising. Identify demographics of target clientele. Recognize need for changes to menu and facility to capitalize on current as well as upcoming trends.

In reviewing the enclosed resume, I am confident you will determine that my qualifications match those established by your restaurant for your next Manager.

I would be delighted to meet with you to expand on the snapshot of my experiences noted in this resume. I will call you next week to set an appointment. Until we speak, I thank you for your time and consideration. I look forward to our conversation.

Sincerely,

Kristen Moore

Enclosure: resume

109

Restaurant Manager. *Jane Roqueplot, Sharon, Pennsylvania*

The goal for this letter was to focus on four main areas of need (see the bulleted statements) at the target organization, as identified through the applicant's market research.

ERIC A. PRYOR, CCM

45 Ellenger Street ▪▪ Hartford, CT 55555
Home: 555.555.5555 ▪▪ Mobile: 555.555.5555 ▪▪ ericapryor@aol.com

[Date]

[Name]
[Title]
[Organization]
[Address]
[City, State ZIP]

Dear _____:

A general manager with an impeccable record of performance in all areas of operations, service, and financial management is essential to your club's continued growth and success.

As a club management professional with a career history rich in achievements at prominent clubs, you will find on my resume more than a dozen documented examples of my success in **driving membership and revenue growth** while **reducing costs, ensuring efficiency and productivity,** and **promoting unparalleled member service.**

Here's what your club needs … Here's what I offer …

➢ Designation as a Certified Club Manager with extensive and consistent results in ensuring peak standards of operations, efficiency, productivity, quality, and service.

➢ Delivering bottom-line results throughout my career in club management: $10 million in total revenues, $2.9 million in annual membership dues, and $3.4 million in food and beverage.

➢ Demonstrated strengths in financial management and budgeting as evidenced by my ability to reduce/control costs without sacrificing member satisfaction or quality and ensure fiscally sound operations.

➢ Recognition as a natural leader/team builder with managerial strengths combined with the ability to attract, motivate, develop, and retain quality talent who are dedicated to achieving common business goals.

➢ Leadership that earned Region Club of the Year awards and #1 ranking in member satisfaction.

➢ Selection by the Club Management Association as the training club for the North Region.

My success stories arise from my core business beliefs: fostering a positive, productive working environment through hands-on leadership *and* creating an exceptional membership experience to drive bottom-line results. As a result, my efforts have been recognized with multiple awards during my club management career, including "Club of the Year," "Manager of the Year," and "Creativity in Management."

If your client's club could benefit from my talents, I would welcome the opportunity to discuss my potential contributions. I will call to explore the possibility of a face-to-face meeting.

Sincerely,

Eric A. Pryor, CCM

110

Certified Club Manager. *Louise Garver, Enfield, Connecticut*

The person was between assignments. The letter highlights the credentials that set him apart from the competition. He seemed a perfect match and landed an interview out of 150 applicants.

Cliff Stanton

February 1, 2008

John Smith
Hyatt Hotel
1234 Larimer Street
Denver, CO 80000

Re: Position HY123456

Dear Employment Director:

It's all about heads and beds and customer satisfaction in the hospitality industry. It takes an innovative and tenacious manager to face successfully the tremendous challenges confronting today's leading hotels. I have made a career out of turning around faltering properties, raising service standards, increasing organizational efficiency, and significantly improving bottom-line profits.

I am currently the General Manager of the Executive Hotel, Denver. The owners have decided to convert the property into an assisted-living facility, and while they have asked me to stay with the property, my passion for the hotel business necessitates that I move on. I am seeking a management position with an upscale hotel such as yours.

My resume speaks to my history of decisive leadership as well as strong financial and operating results. Most notably I have

- Turned unprofitable properties into consistently performing, multimillion-dollar organizations.
- Streamlined operations and eliminated duplicate functions to reduce costs and increase productivity and revenue.
- Integrated finance and operations, creating proactive business units focused on the bottom line and positioned for long-term growth and profitability.

The value I bring to Hyatt Hotels is broad experience spanning all core business functions with a primary focus on operations and finance. My success is directly attributable to my ability to unify organizations, initiate action, and deliver results.

I welcome the chance to explore any current assignments commensurate with my management skills. I am willing to relocate for the right opportunity.

Thank you for your time and consideration, and I look forward to hearing from you.

Sincerely,

Cliff Stanton

Enclosure

P.O. Box 1234 · Denver, CO 00000 · Home (555) 555-5555 · Mobile/Pager (555) 555-5550 · cliffs@yahoo.net

111

Hotel General Manager. *Roberta Gamza, Louisville, Colorado*

The applicant wanted to move to a luxury, full-service hotel chain. To get the reader's attention, the writer began by getting to the point about what is important in the hospitality industry.

Shanna Collins
000 Sharps Boulevard NE
Norfolk, Virginia 55555

☏ (555) 555-5555

December 20, 2007

Mrs. Linda Thorndyke
Director of Human Resources
Heritage Companies
PO Box 555
Houston, Texas 55555

RE: Human Resources Assistant

Dear Mrs. Thorndyke:

I am very interested in re-careering to the Human Resources field and have enclosed a resume for your review. Originally an accountant, I am now returning to the paid workforce after a period of extensive community and volunteer work.

Balancing a number of general business skills, I also have a valuable complement of human-service-related strengths, including the following:

facilitation, interviewing and assessment   training and tutoring
patient and customer service   client research and analysis
client data gathering and consultation   listening and communicating

One of the main things I missed in accounting work was direct interaction with people and the opportunity to feel as if my work would make a difference in the lives of others. My nature is one of compassion, patience and responsibility. Solution-oriented, I believe that all problems can be worked out. Research and assessment skills, time management, decision making and multitasking add to the value of my people skills. Adding more flexibility, my working style is one that easily lends itself to either an independent or a group work environment.

Others describe me as highly professional, sensitive to the needs of others, a positive thinker, detail-oriented and dependable. I feel that my maturity and combination of business and people skills are assets and would like to meet with you to discuss your needs, including how I might contribute to those goals.

I will contact your office to see whether additional information is needed and to determine a suitable time to meet with you.

Sincerely,

SHANNA COLLINS

Enclosure

112

Human Resources Assistant. *Beverley Drake, Rochester, Minnesota*

After a period of volunteer work, this accountant wanted to return to the workforce but in the field of human resources. The letter identifies her transferable strengths, skills, and worker traits.

Hank R. Johnson

123 Main Street • Annapolis, Maryland 21403 • (410) 555-1234 • E-mail: **hank@protypeld.com**

April 1, 2008

Any Company USA
Attn: John Doe, Human Resources Director
123 Main Street
Any Town, MD 21032

Dear Mr. Doe,

With my background and experience in Human Resources and Operations Management, I am all too aware of the changes that have influenced the industry over the past few years. Never before have we experienced such a phenomenon or so many challenges at such a rapid pace. Today we are expected to accomplish more, often with less, and generally in a shorter time frame. As an experienced professional in these fields, I have routinely been faced with such challenges. I have a proven track record of success because I face every challenge with passion and energy.

My special talents and skills are supported by some outstanding core strengths:

> **Outstanding corporate team contributor—a solutions specialist**
> **Human Resources generalist and recruiting/training professional**
> **Extensive experience with large and complicated payrolls and compensation**
> **Management operations and consulting expertise in competitive environment**

During my employment history, and with every assignment I have accepted, I have devoted my energies toward being a good steward of available resources. I attribute my ability to improve the operational performance of my employer almost immediately to my resourcefulness and creativity.

You will find that I am a decisive, proactive, and result-driven professional, offering a unique blend of academic achievement, technological expertise, practical experience, organizational and motivational leadership, creativity, resourcefulness, and the flexibility for change.

I would like to meet with you so that we can discuss the special needs of Company USA. We should discuss exactly how my experience and qualifications would best contribute to your success. I will contact you by April 15 to confirm that you received my resume and discuss how I can fit into your organization. Thank you for your time and consideration.

Sincerely,

Hank R. Johnson

Enclosure: Resume

113

Human Resources Generalist. *Beth Colley, Crownsville, Maryland*

The first paragraph indicates that the applicant is aware of the current state of the HR field. A list of outstanding core strengths in boldface focuses on what the individual can bring to the company.

MARIGOLD TRUMAN

555 Windy Way East • Brentwood, NY 11717 • (555) 555-3333 • HR@TheBranch.net

June 25, 2007

Ms. Mary Smith
Recruitment Administrator
Human Resources Department
THE BRANCH BANK
One Branch Plaza
Brentwood, New York 55555

Dear Ms. Smith:

The enclosed resume and supporting documentation are presented for your review and consideration for acceptance into The Branch Bank's Human Resources Associates Program. Ideally, this opportunity will develop and strengthen my skills and knowledge while exposing me to a broad spectrum of areas and challenges conducive to professional growth in the field of Human Resources.

I offer a Bachelor of Arts degree in Psychology and tenure with The Branch Bank since June 2000 in the position of Senior File Clerk, Pre-Arbitration/In-Coming Collections Department. Initially, I joined this department as a temporary employee and proved myself as a team player capable of handling a heavy caseload while significantly improving the quality of office procedures. As a result, my current position was created for me on a permanent basis.

Further, to ensure the continuity of positive changes that I have brought to the department, I provide ongoing training to employees, a role I greatly enjoy. To date, I have been recognized and rewarded for my drive to go above and beyond what is expected of me, with recent contributions that include an interim position as a fully trained Auto Call Directory representative. I am confident that my education, record of excellence (including perfect attendance), and personal attributes (strong organizational, overall communication, and computer skills), combined with a firm aspiration to further my career in Human Resources, qualify me as a suitable candidate.

Although this application, along with my personnel file, illustrates my background well, I feel that a personal interview would better demonstrate my knowledge and abilities. Therefore, I would appreciate an opportunity to interview with you at a convenient time. Thank you for your review and consideration. I will contact you soon regarding the next step in the process.

Sincerely,

Marigold Truman

114

Bank Human Resources Position. *Ann Baehr, Brentwood, New York*

The unusual horizontal lines are eye-catching. With its filled circle on the left, the top line balances the contact information. With a filled circle on the right, the bottom line balances the top line.

KIMBERLY BLAKELY

000 Romeo Drive
Commack, New York 11725
(555) 555-5555
kimberlyblakely@yahoo.com

[Date]

[Name]
[Title]
[Address]
[City, State ZIP]

Dear Sir or Madam:

Reflecting on my professional experience within the insurance industry, it is at this point in my career that I am seeking to pursue my long-term personal and professional goal of a challenging career within **Human Resources.** Let me briefly highlight the skills, values, and contributions I will bring to your organization:

- Dedicated commitment to a long and successful career within **Human Resources.**

- Excellent customer service/relations, time-management, troubleshooting, and communications skills, developed through many years in the insurance industry as a **Claims Specialist.**

- Ability to perform independently or as part of a team, building cooperative working relationships among management and support staff in order to meet goals and achieve successful results.

- An energetic, enthusiastic approach with proven success in prioritizing time and resources to attain goals and meet project deadlines.

My personal and professional education, work experiences, interests, and strengths have all contributed to outstanding business achievements. I am accountable for diverse responsibilities, including serving clients and the general public. My acquired knowledge and experience as a contributing individual in the business world will prove to be a quality that will enhance the goals and standards of any Human Resources department.

Please take the time to review the aforementioned credentials. I firmly believe you will find them to meet the needs of your company, and I am confident my contributions to your organization will prove to be lasting, if given the opportunity. Thank you for your time and consideration.

Very truly yours,

KIMBERLY BLAKELY

Enclosure

115

Human Resources Position. *Donna M. Farrise, Hauppauge, New York*

This insurance claim specialist wanted a position in any human resources department. Boldfacing highlights Human Resources as a goal. Bullets point to values, transferable skills, and worker-trait contributions.

Available for relocation

Sue Allard

000 Roberts Road, Martinville, Alabama 00000
☎ 334.555.5555 (home) — 334.555.6666 (cell)
suealla@clark.com

November 2, 2007

Ms. Deborah Montiel
States Bank
44 Charleston Street
Montgomery, Alabama 00000

Dear Ms. Montiel:

I want to make it as easy as possible for States Bank to add me to its team as a Human Resources Assistant. Moving toward that goal starts with my resume.

I wanted to give you something more valuable than the usual job titles, responsibilities, and college course work. That's why I've included examples of HR-related problems solved. At school, my problem-solving skills were reviewed by senior HR professionals who were paid to evaluate my work against tough industry standards. At work, everyone saw my workforce management abilities—from supervisors to coworkers to customers. In fact, it was my work experience that motivated me to get a degree in Human Resources while I continued learning on the job.

My development program is almost finished. I have just obtained my BS in Human Resources. But I want to start putting my energies and skills to work in that field as soon as I can.

So, as a next step, I would like to hear about States Bank's specific HR needs in your own words. I will call in a few days to set up time to do that.

Sincerely,

Sue Allard

Encl.: Resume

116

Human Resources Assistant. *Don Orlando, Montgomery, Alabama*

The applicant had a recent HR degree but never had held an HR position. The third sentence in the second paragraph counters any view that college instruction is out of touch with the real world.

Randi Madden

107 W. HAMMOND RD, APT. 3 ● DAYSTOWN, IL 00000
888-555-1212 ● SOMEONE@ANYISP.NET

Dental and Medical Office Management
Human Resources & Personnel Management

[date]

Mr. (Ms.) _____
[Company]
[Address 1]
[Address 2]

Dear Hiring Professional [or insert contact name]:

As a proactive, detail-oriented, and achievement-driven team player with more than 18 years of combined experience, I am writing to apply for the Regional Office Manager opening with your organization. I am quite interested in joining your team in a position where I can apply my proven abilities in management and administration of people and resources across multiple facilities, with a strong background in the healthcare industry.

I possess effective communication skills with excellent leadership and management abilities. Achievement-driven, analytical, and multitasking, I have a proven ability to organize time and execute tasks in a way that allows for consistent achievement of milestones and corporate goals.

As a proven team leader, I am able to foster a workplace environment that results in cohesive, communicative teams that achieve desired results. I possess the knowledge, skills, and abilities necessary to fulfill the role of Regional Office Manager and believe I would be greatly beneficial to your enterprise and management team.

The resume I have enclosed will provide you with an overview of my skills and present you with a positive reason to allow me the opportunity to meet with you personally so you can assess how well my abilities will meet the needs of your organization. If you have any questions, or would like to schedule an interview, please do not hesitate to contact me, at your convenience. I look forward to meeting with you.

Thank you for your time and consideration.

Sincerely,

Randi Madden

Enclosure

117

Regional Office Manager. *Lea J. Clark, Macon, Georgia*

This individual wanted to move from the medical/dental field to another sector of healthcare. The writer highlighted transferable skills. The applicant got three good offers in just under six weeks.

RACHEL SWATHMORE

HUMAN RESOURCES SENIOR EXECUTIVE

[Insert Date]

[Insert Contact Name]
[Insert Contact Title]
[Insert Company Name]
[Insert Contact Address]
[Insert Contact Address]

Dear [Insert Contact Name]:

Are you looking for an innovative and multidimensional senior manager who understands and leverages Human Resources strategy and operations management to meet corporate goals?

With more than 15 years of experience as a Human Resources executive with world-class entertainment and hospitality companies including STC Corporation, Trump World, and Wynn Entertainment, I have been directly involved in the formation of corporate vision and strategy, the management of rapid growth from acquisitions, and the direction of daily operations from a human capital perspective. Abilities that I bring to the table include the following:

Corporate leadership and change management impacting thousands of employees:
As the senior HR executive for STC Corporation / Gaming Division, I strategized and integrated distinctly different business cultures, instilling a "one company mentality" throughout the organization.

Identification of business challenges and development of action plans to address those challenges:
As senior HR executive at Trump World, I developed a winning HR strategy for an underperforming operating unit. I also assumed a new regional role to consolidate HR functions for multiple properties.

Provision of counsel and advice to senior corporate executives:
While at Trump World and Wynn Entertainment, I reported to the Chairman / CEO. My independent counsel and perceptions of people and issues were highly respected and carried weight in final evaluations.

Development and management of HR strategies on a global basis:
As Senior Vice President of Human Resources for STC Corporation, I managed HR systems / processes impacting thousands of employees on four continents. I am experienced in multicultural business practices including executive recruitment, management development, succession planning, compensation / benefits, and cultural integration.

Management of difficult business situations involving complex people issues:
As a senior manager, I have tackled many complex, high-value projects. At STC Corporation and Trump World, Inc., I managed the HR-related aspects of the company's dynamic growth through acquisitions where I produced organization-wide support for management's new vision.

[Insert Contact's Name], may we set up an exploratory meeting?

Sincerely,

Rachel Swathmore

---

25 Grove Avenue, Atlantic City, NJ 55555 | 000-000-0000 | E-mail: rachswath@aol.com

118

Human Resources Senior Executive. *Deborah Wile Dib, Medford, New York*

This letter template for an HR Senior Executive was ready to send to different addressees. The applicant just provided different information where indicated for each new contact.

Peter Hamilton

50 Chestnut St.
Needham, MA 05550

555-555-5555
phamilton@xyz.com

September 1, 2007

Maria Constantine
Vice President of Finance
Massachusetts Medical Manufacturing
189 Lexington Ave.
Waltham, MA 02454

Dear Ms. Constantine:

Your description of the Director of Human Resources position at Massachusetts Medical Manufacturing closely matches my background, and I am enthusiastically submitting my resume for your review.

With extensive experience in human resources management, I have the vision and the solid track record of results that can help Massachusetts Medical Manufacturing as it prepares to acquire California Medical Instruments and develop new lines of medical products. In my current role as Director of Human Resources at Boston Medical Devices, I provide the full spectrum of human resources support for our worldwide patient monitoring division. After an acquisition of a German company in 2003, my mission—which I accomplished—was to blend the cultures, operations, and procedures smoothly to enable our division to meet production deadlines and achieve sales goals.

Specific areas of accomplishment include the following:

➢ **Acquisitions:** Provided leadership in two acquisitions to develop procedures that identified and implemented best practices, reduced redundancies, and achieved several million dollars in cost savings.
➢ **Strategic Planning:** Consulted with senior management to design and implement programs and policies concerning recruitment, employee development, diversity, regulatory compliance, conflict resolution, and performance management.
➢ **Organizational Development:** Integrated teams from Purchasing, Manufacturing, and Engineering to change corporate culture and define common vision of success, resulting in on-time product delivery.

I am confident my background and experience can benefit Massachusetts Medical Manufacturing, and I would like to talk with you to learn more about the company and to explore how I can contribute to its future success. I will contact you next week to set a time to do so. I look forward to meeting with you.

Thank you for your consideration.

Sincerely,

Peter Hamilton

Enclosure

119

Director of Human Resources. *Wendy Gelberg, Needham, Massachusetts*

In researching a prospective company, the applicant learned that it was acquiring another company. The writer highlighted the applicant's experience that was relevant to an acquisition.

REBECCA B. STILLS
0000 Prosperity Road • Monroe, NC 28888 • (555) 555-5555 • rbstills@gmail.com

April 20, 2008

Ms. D. Finnegan
TICS Corporation
P.O. Box 7488
Charlotte, NC 28241

Dear Ms. Finnegan:

Why did Abraham Lincoln win log-splitting contests so easily?

You've heard the reason: He knew exactly where to place his wedge to give his blows the most power. When Lincoln won these contests, he was the same age as I am now; and I, too, want to enter a log-splitting contest.

I have a good, strong wedge and a sturdy hammer, but I need a log: a company whose growth I can contribute to and build a career with.

In the first place, I want to get into the field of human resources—as a generalist—starting as a *human resource assistant*. I have strong computer skills (Word, Excel) and the ability to master new things. In addition, I possess strong communication skills, honed through four years as a waitress and as a customer service representative within a fast-paced, quality-minded call center environment.

In May, I will receive my baccalaureate degree in Psychology; I lack only one three-hour course, which is offered at UNCC in the evening this summer. During my college years, I worked to provide 75% of all expenses, so I have grown accustomed to long hours and hard work. And during this time I have been molding my wedge: working as an HR intern (please see enclosed resume) and learning about employee benefits plans and procedures.

This, then, is my wedge into the field of human resources: to be a human resource assistant, acquire experience and advance to more responsible positions. Your company and its opportunities can be my log.

Will you let me enter the contest?

I look forward to meeting with you and will call to set up an appointment.

Sincerely,

Rebecca B. Stills

Enclosure

120

Human Resources Assistant. *Doug Morrison, Charlotte, North Carolina*

This recent graduate was keenly interested in entering the field of human resources. The letter displays her motivation, strong interest, enthusiasm, youthful vitality, and career goals.

PHYLLIS MARTIN, PHR   **(555) 555-5555**
5555 Maxwell, Clearview, Texas 79000

February 12, 2008

Sid Critefelder
Vice President of Human Resources
NATURAL GAS COMPANY
P.O. Box 5555
Panhandle, Texas 79408

RE: HUMAN RESOURCES GENERALIST

Dear Mr. Critefelder:

Your recent HR generalist vacancy has prompted me to send you my resume for review. As you will discover, I offer the depth of experience necessary to successfully administer safety, benefits, and compensation programs; recruit, train, develop, and retain staff; build community relations; assess and fulfill staffing needs; and evaluate / revise policies and procedures. **Thirteen years of collective HR experience** also enforce comprehensive knowledge of state and federal personnel regulations. Additionally, my history reflects a loyal, stable employee who thrives on increasing responsibility and progressive learning. It would be an honor to contribute to a corporate culture such as yours, which values people and appreciates differences.

The following attributes and well-developed skills are additional reasons to take a close look at my credentials:

HUMAN RESOURCES ADMINISTRATION
- Integrity, loyalty, and diligence earn respect and reflect distinction.
- Ownership of responsibility and accountability demonstrate leadership and character.
- Time management and organization skills help streamline tasks and cultivate efficiency.
- Investigation and decrement foster effective problem resolution.
- Analysis and interpretation skills assist in understanding guidelines, policies, and procedures.

COMMUNICATION / INTERPERSONAL SKILLS
- Direct communication and appropriate interpersonal style enhance understanding.
- Enthusiastic presentation stimulates interest in and retention of material.
- Attentive listening enhances interviewing, counseling, and mediating.
- Professional / personal security reflect a genuine person who easily integrates into teams.
- Ability to build rapport strengthens community ties and maintains valuable resources.
- Persuasiveness sells ideas and promotes acceptance of change.

PERSONAL CHARACTERISTICS
- Friendly, personable, helpful attitude contributes to an accommodating environment.
- Attention to details and focus on excellence inspire others to excel.
- Capacity to easily learn and retain procedural information suggests decreased training time.
- Willingness to embrace challenging, changing situations indicates flexibility and adaptation.
- A sense of humor and positive outlook help ease stress in the workplace.

Experience, confidence, and drive will enable me to make significant contributions to your HR goals. Because a personal interview would benefit us both, I will contact you within the week to schedule an appointment at your convenience. In the meantime, thank you for your consideration.

Sincerely,

Phyllis Martin, PHR

Enclosure: Resume

121

Human Resources Generalist. *Edith A. Rische, Lubbock, Texas*

This letter is full of keywords relevant to the field of human resources. The clustering of the bulleted items according to three categories breaks up a long list and makes the items easier to grasp.

RUBY SLATER
RubySlater@email.com

5555 Arguello Avenue
Los Angeles, California 55555

Residence (310) 555-5555
Mobile (310) 555-0000

[Date]

[Name]
[Title]
[Company]
[Address]
[City, State ZIP]

Dear [Ms./Mr. Name]:

Strong human resources leadership can have a tremendous impact on operating results. By building and managing an effective HR infrastructure, developing successful productivity, efficiency, quality and performance management, I have consistently made a direct contribution to corporate goals. Highlights of my professional career include

- 15 years of senior-level experience as an HR Generalist, providing HR planning and leadership in union and nonunion environments across diverse industries

- Implementation of HRIS technology and applications to improve information flow and use in strategic planning initiatives

- Strong qualifications in employee relations with ability to build confidence and trust between employees and management

- Introduction of loss control, safety and Workers' Compensation fraud programs

- Authoring employee manuals to provide employee guidelines in compliance with changing regulatory environments

Most significantly, I have positioned myself and the HR function as a partner to senior management in working together toward producing top-performing workforces able to meet operating challenges. Currently I am looking for a new opportunity as a senior-level HR professional with an organization seeking talent, drive, enthusiasm and leadership expertise. I would welcome a personal interview to explore such positions with your organization and will contact you to arrange a time to meet. Thank you.

Sincerely,

Ruby Slater

Enclosure: Resume

122

Human Resources Generalist. *Vivian VanLier, Valley Glen, California*

The applicant was seeking a position as a senior-level HR professional. Bullets point to highlights of her 15-year career. In the last paragraph, she places her HR role on a par with senior management.

BILL HESS
11100 Sherman Street, Denver, CO 80111 – **303-111-5555**

March 19, 2008

Parker Hospital
10235 Parker Way
Parker, CO 80111

Attention: Hiring Committee for Human Resources Director

Dear Hiring Committee:

Recently I learned about your search for a Human Resources Director via the Society of Human Resources Management. I would love to be an integral part of your leadership team, ensuring that Parker Hospital continues to attract, motivate, and retain the best and brightest performers while meeting performance and fiscal objectives.

As the Human Resources Director for the last 10 years for a nonprofit healthcare organization with 230 employees, I am confident that that I meet all your advertised criteria for knowledge, skills, and educational qualifications. A detailed resume follows this letter and provides further information my qualifications. Here are a few highlights:

- **As a member of SHRM,** I offer current knowledge of HR best practices. Additionally, I offer a Master of Arts in Organizational Management and 10+ years of progressive experience in HR leadership in highly regulated, customer-focused environments in which I gained strong understanding of risk management and safety programs.

- **As an executive team member,** I am considered a strategic business partner who provides counsel and problem solving across multiple departments. I have contributed to the development and implementation of numerous long- and short-range organizational change initiatives.

- **As an HR Executive,** I have proven skills in guiding, developing, and implementing smart operational policies across all facets of HR, including labor relations, recruitment and employment processes, and comprehensive benefit programs. Additionally, I offer strong results in program administration, project management, and business process improvement. I am well versed in all aspects of reporting, budget administration, documentation, and employee record management.

- **Additionally, I am a diplomatic and influential communicator** with a strong ability to build consensus, drive decision-making processes, and communicate key concepts to individuals of all backgrounds.

- **And finally, I am results-focused, energetic, and perseverant,** ensuring timely, quality achievement of multiple projects, programs, and tasks. I offer advanced computer skills that enable me to fully leverage existing information systems as well as contribute to system upgrades.

Thank you for considering me one of your most qualified, enthusiastic candidates for this exciting role with Parker Hospital. I look forward to talking with you soon!

Best regards,

Bill Hess

123

Human Resources Director.   *Tracy Laswell Williams, Arvada, Colorado*

This letter uses bullets and boldface to highlight qualifications mentioned in the resume. Bullets and boldface capture attention to ensure that the reader sees this information.

4/23 Cuttingway Street
Rocklin, CA 95677
(407) 555-6666 (Cell)
smithkarl@hotmail.com

KARL SMITH

September 2, 2007

Ms. Sarah Lancer
HR Director
Leading Technologies, Inc.
155 Crystal Road
HILLTOP, NY 11787

Dear Ms. Lancer:

Re: HUMAN RESOURCE PROFESSIONAL

Building and sustaining a professional, committed, and top-performing staff to support the demands of a multinational corporation working within constantly changing and demanding environments requires a unique blend of operational planning/management expertise and decisive human resource leadership. Possessing these skills and more, I have managed diverse teams being solely responsible for staff ranging from 100 to 25,000 personnel, demanding expertise across all facets of leadership, training, communications, performance monitoring, policies, procedures, and change management in order to successfully achieve performance goals.

As a talented HR professional I offer strong qualifications and experience across all core generalist functions, organisational change, and productivity/performance advancements, combined with strong cross-cultural communication and interpersonal skills.

My enclosed resume highlights my professionalism, commitment, and proven competencies, to which I add the following achievements:

- **HR System & Policies Development:** Employed as subject-matter expert revolutionizing an existing lengthy and costly employment review process into a robust and transparent system that fast-tracked staff reviews. This initiative realized a **saving of $5.75M in the first year** of implementation and **increased savings by 47% to $8.5M in the second and subsequent years in salaries alone.**

- **Staff training and knowledge expansion:** Campaigned and amplified part-time staff's participation and completion of career development courses, expanding number of competent staff, thus increasing operational capability and staff suitability for national/international assignments.

- **Staff Recruitment & Retention:** Acknowledged for the development of innovative and proactive recruitment programs, currently exceeding all other divisions in their recruitment campaigns to secure high-quality staff despite candidate shortages across the board. Successfully increased staff retention and minimized personnel changeover.

- **Leadership and team building:** Headed all staffing functions involving 350 full- and part-time staff achieving all corporate performance objectives despite lack of staffing resources, which were overcome by empowering junior managers and adopting supportive leadership approach to successfully lift team morale and collaboration.

I thank you for your consideration and welcome the opportunity to discuss my application in further detail and how I may be able to contribute to the ongoing success of your company. I will contact you by September 15 to set a time when we can talk further.

Sincerely,

Karl Smith

124

Human Resources Professional. *Annemarie Cross, Hallam, Victoria, Australia*

This applicant was transitioning from the military and had few achievements in his first resume and cover letter. The writer pinpointed many achievements and showed areas of competence.

Denise Herman

000 Peacock, Amarillo, Texas 79105   C: 000-000-0000   H: 000-000-0000   e-mail: dherman3@email.com

Will you ever find time for that career path project? How about those first-quarter goals...are they still incomplete on the white board?
Then please call...together we can do it all!

HUMAN RESOURCE PROFESSIONAL
Available Immediately for:

Temporary or Permanent
❖
Short-term or Long-term
❖
Full-time or Part-time

Dear Mr. Coleman,

It is with great enthusiasm that I respond to your posting for a Human Resource Director for Shady Oak Center. My professional employment history is a great match for the qualifications you have listed, and...I am available immediately!

Six years of increasing human resource responsibility in a 24x7 environment defines my flexible work ethic and supports your requirement of holidays and weekends. My professional background relative to your position is highlighted as follows:

- **Human Resource Management**—state / federal employment law; unemployment compensation; organizational policies / procedures; safety / health; benefits administration; departmental budget; job descriptions
- **Training and Development**—agent / management training programs; organizational development strategies; quality improvement programs
- **Employee Climate Survey**—employee feedback for improved workforce solutions
- **HRIMS Utilization**—records management; employee database reports

Additionally, I am available to relocate, travel or assume special assignments at your request. I can also offer you a variety of employment status options to meet your budget.

Your satisfaction is guaranteed with this win-win opportunity!

The downsizing of my previous Human Resource Manager position coupled with my desire to return to the Houston area makes this offer possible. A personal meeting at your earliest convenience to discuss our mutual employment goals would be greatly appreciated. I will call to arrange a meeting place and time.

I look forward to meeting you soon.

Sincerely,

Denise Herman

> "Denise has a great attitude and will do everything from data entry and filing to flying across the country to assist in interviewing and hiring."
> —Quote from a fellow HR Professional who utilized Denise on a contract assignment

125

Human Resources Director. *MeLisa Rogers, Victoria, Texas*

This HR Manager candidate was downsized and needed an immediate assignment, preferably in Texas. The writer marketed the person's flexibility and sold her availability into a contract assignment.

JACK BARRY

000 Drummond Boulevard
Campbell, CA 95008

jbarryweb@yahoo.com
555-555-0000

February 15, 2008

Ms. Harriet Tallant
Director of Corporate Web Development
Reaching Out, Inc.
444 Dublin Avenue
San Jose, CA 95100

Dear Ms. Tallant:

Your requirement for an Interactive Web Designer interested me because of my enthusiasm for Web development/design and my strong desire to continue working and building a career in that field. My resume is enclosed for your consideration.

In recent years, I have utilized my creative, analytical and problem-solving skills to complete several Web-related projects, both independently and as a project team member. These include the following:

- Building, programming, testing and refining an enrollment-tracking application with an intuitive user interface
- Designing and developing one module for the successful, timely release of a new product
- Designing and implementing a Web user interface
- Creating a process and templates for production of JPEG images for hotel Web sites

Prior to that time, I gained solid experience as a programmer/analyst, a software architect and a software /support engineer. Key activities included database development and troubleshooting, small-business application development and interactive product testing. My ability to understand and analyze complex problems; communicate with clients to assess their needs; and develop innovative, practical solutions enabled me to make a worthwhile contribution to each of my employers during that period.

As I prepare to close out my work on the software application I developed for A Higher Experience, I am beginning to search for an employment situation that will allow me to use my existing experience and skills in Web development/design while also offering potential opportunities to expand and enhance my professional strengths.

I am definitely interested in being considered for the position of Interactive Web Designer with Reaching Out and would like to arrange an interview at your earliest convenience to discuss how I can contribute to your team. I will call you soon.

Sincerely,

Jack Barry

Encl.

126

Interactive Web Designer. *Georgia Adamson, Campbell, California*

This letter is easy to read because of its chronological organization: In recent years.... Prior to that time.... As I prepare.... Bullets point to completed projects. The last paragraph shows interest in the job.

Sami Sosa
5941 Glendower Lane
Plano, TX 75093
Res: (555) 555-5555
Cell: (555) 000-0000
s.sosa@iee.org

[Date]

[Name]
[Company]
[Address]

Dear Hiring Executive:

I am exploring leadership opportunities with your company. With a strong background in the launch of software applications and services such as Intelligent Networks, as well as operational support systems in North and South America, Europe, Asia, Africa and the Middle East, I maintain excellent customer relationships and deliver on commitments. As a hands-on team builder with solid management, operation and product development skills, I am certain I could make a valuable contribution to your goals. Areas of expertise and transferable skills include

P&L Responsibility	Strategic Planning	Problem Analysis & Resolution
Budget Planning & Forecasting	Project Management	Team Leadership
Product Management	Product Development	Business Development
Training & Development	Network Applications	Systems Integration
Technology Management		

Throughout my career I have

→ Combined in-depth technical knowledge with operational business knowledge.
→ Managed P&Ls of more than $400 million and staff of 1,500 throughout the world.
→ Developed an exceptional ability to build strong, long-term customer relationships.

My peers can confirm that I thrive in an atmosphere of challenge. An in-depth knowledge of all phases of business activity, along with specialized abilities that set my performance apart, enables me to offer a truly unique talent. I'm confident I can bring to the table a package of skills, experience and abilities that will provide you with an invaluable resource.

I will follow up with you in a few days to answer any questions you may have. In the meantime, you may reach me at (555) 555-5555 home, (555) 000-0000 cell or through email at s.sosa@iee.org. I look forward to our conversation and thank you for your time and consideration.

Sincerely,

Sami Sosa

Enclosure

127

Information Systems/Technology Position. *Steven Provenzano, Schaumburg, Illinois*

The opening paragraph is impressive because of its global connections. The three-column list of areas of expertise and transferable skills is useful because it can be modified for each targeted employer.

ROBERT J. LITTLEFIELD
0000 Indiana Avenue ◆ St. Paul, MN 00000 ◆ (000) 000-0000 ◆ name@aol.com

January 30, 2008

Mr. Ted Morrison, IT Director
ABC Computers
3434 Smith Street
St. Paul, MN 00000

Dear Mr. Morrison:

I read your advertisement for a Software Developer with considerable interest, as my background and skills meet your requirements for this position. Therefore, please accept my resume for your review and allow me to explain briefly the positive qualities I can bring to your company.

Because my resume contains the specifics regarding my BBA degree, educational awards, and technical competencies in areas such as object-oriented programming, I will not need to go into detail here about these particular items. Instead, I'd like to point out a few of my qualities not covered on the resume that I would contribute to help your organization meet its development project objectives:

- **Highly focused work ethic**—I maintain a strong focus on "getting the job done right" in a field where the back-and-forth nature of the project cycle can lead to getting sidetracked and committing errors.
- **Ability to modify communications**—I am skilled in altering my communications to gain understanding from end users with minimal IT knowledge and team members with limited English skills.
- **Enthusiastic attitude**—I truly enjoy software engineering and the challenges inherent in an ever-changing, leading-edge field. To this end, I always enjoy learning about emerging industry trends.

Companies today need more than "technologists" to ensure the success of high-priority goals; they need individuals who can also master the teamwork, the communications, and the relationship-building side of projects. I am the type of person who would bring this balance of technical and nontechnical skills to help your firm achieve success.

I am available immediately for a personal interview and offer you competence, dedication, and a strong work ethic. Thank you for your time and consideration, and I look forward to the opportunity to meet with you. I will call you to set an appointment.

Sincerely,

Robert J. Littlefield

Enclosure

128

Software Developer. *Daniel J. Dorotik, Jr., Lubbock, Texas*

A resume typically presents details not found in a cover letter. This cover letter is different in indicating qualities not covered in the resume. Bullets and boldfacing call attention to these qualities.

Leonard Curtis

123 Circle River Drive · Littleton, CO 00000
555.555.5555 · Lencurt@msno.com

January 21, 2008

John Jones
Vice President, Software Development
Axis Technologies
Table Mesa Drive
Boulder, CO 00000

Re: Position 1234, Software Development Manager

Dear Mr. Jones:

I am passionate about developing products that provide real-world solutions and have an impact on customers' business. Understanding the challenges our customers face, combined with practical implementations of product concepts and technologies, is key to successfully designing and delivering value-rich, profitable products.

I noted with great interest your advertisement in the *Denver Post* for a Software Development Manager. My technical management expertise, leadership skills, and extensive experience in VC++ are an excellent fit with your position.

My strengths are in creatively applying or modifying industry products to job requirements and incorporating new technologies quickly and proficiently. My track record as outlined in the enclosed resume demonstrates that I can

- Manage programs from initial concept through deployment at customer sites.
- Supervise/mentor cross-functional teams as well as software and hardware engineering teams.
- Serve marketing with my technical expertise, influencing product development, client presentations, and contract negotiations.

I admire the corporate culture and core beliefs that Axis Technologies exemplifies. I am eager to apply my knowledge and expertise, and I welcome the opportunity to explore my potential contributions with you.

Thank you for your consideration; I look forward to speaking with you soon.

Sincerely,

Leonard Curtis

Enclosure

129

Software Development Manager. *Roberta F. Gamza, Louisville, Colorado*

The person was applying to a company known for its friendly and laid-back corporate culture and wanted to refer to the company's culture in the letter. Short paragraphs help to make it easy to read.

WILLIAM SHINDLEY

783 NE Fremont Drive
Lake Oswego, OR 55555
wil.shindley@hotmail.com

(000) 000-0000 Residence   (000) 000-0000 Cell

March 14, 2008

Mr. Edward Hosack
Human Resources Manager
PacifiCorp
1843 SW First Avenue, Suite 200
Portland, OR 55555

Dear Mr. Hosack:

I read your recent ad for a Software Program Manager on Monster.com with interest, as it seems a perfect match to my background and experience. As a software program manager with expertise in managing successful software projects in the $10K to $5M range, **I bring the kind of experience needed to get the job done, on time and at or under budget.** Allow me to highlight my skills as they relate to your stated requirements and interests:

YOUR REQUIREMENTS	MY QUALIFICATIONS
Bachelor's degree in related area or 3+ years of project management experience in a software development environment.	Bachelor's degree in computers and 3+ years of project management experience in a software development environment. **Strong record of delivering project results.**
Demonstrated knowledge of development processes, metrics, project planning, and project management.	Significant background as a programmer/software developer, 3+ years of project management experience, and **project management certification (PMP).**
Good working knowledge of MS Word and Excel. Experience with MS Project a plus.	**Strong skills in MS Word, Excel, and Project.**

As an additional plus, I possess an **understanding of user interface design and usability** through my experience as both a programmer and a project/program manager.

I look forward to an interview with you so that we can discuss specific examples where I have used these skills to positively influence my employer's bottom line. I will follow up with you in the next week.

Thank you for your time and consideration.

Sincerely,

William Shindley

Enclosure

130

Software Program Manager. *Jennifer Rydell, Portland, Oregon*

The Your Requirements… My Qualifications format was used because the applicant was a perfect match to the job ad he was responding to. This format and boldfacing show off the applicant's skills.

PAUL M. GUTIERREZ

5555 9th Street, Lubbock, Texas 55555 ▪ pmgutierrez@sbcglobal.net
555-555-5555

September 30, 2007

[Name]
[Title]
[Company]
[Address]
[Street, City ZIP]

"I regard network downtimes as unacceptable, yet realize they sometimes happen due to powers beyond my control. I always have contingency plans." —Paul M. Gutierrez

RE: SENIOR NETWORK CONTROL TECHNICIAN / ADMINISTRATOR, Lubbock, Texas, Area

Dear Personnel Recruiter:

As I consider career options that offer new and challenging opportunities to expand my growth, I am excited by your Internet job posting for Senior Network Control Technician / Administrator. My qualifications and technical background, as well as fieldwork, marketing, and customer service experience, match your requirements for this position. The enclosed resume reflects the experience and technical training / expertise necessary to provide customized network and hardware / software solutions to meet remote customer needs.

The following *key strengths* also exemplify highly marketable skills and characteristics. Your company will gain

- *Deadlines met on time and within budget enforced by an accommodating attitude and willingness to work hard at any level to accomplish tasks.*

- *Effectively prioritized responsibilities and job assignments to balance customer needs with company goals.*

- *Less computer downtime through strategic planning to restructure company systems to realize major improvement and head off problems.*

- *A customer-friendly reputation developed by a pleasant technician who respects the dignity of his clients while explaining problems / solutions in simple, illustrative language.*

- *New business through consultative, straightforward communication techniques that promote development of lasting rapport and trust.*

- *Company distinction from a work ethic that honors integrity and excellence.*

- *Increased productivity from an innate psychological insight and a talent for motivating others to work at a higher level.*

An interview to further investigate your needs and my qualifications would be mutually beneficial. I'll call next week to schedule one. In the meantime, thank you for your valued time and consideration.

Sincerely,

Paul M. Gutierrez

Enclosure: Resume

131

Senior Network Control Technician/Administrator. *Edith A. Rische, Lubbock, Texas*

This cover letter lists potential benefits to the company that hires this IT professional. The applicant wrote his own quotation for this letter. Note the effective use of boldface.

Bruce Barnes
000 Ichabod Crane Lane
Montgomery, New Jersey 08502
000-000-0000
E-mail: Bruce_Barnes45@email.com

Date

Name
Company
Address
City, State ZIP

Dear Sir/Madam:

As a senior **Operations and Systems Professional,** I understand that success depends on the ability to merge the strategic with the practical, to understand needs and expectations in the corporate environment, and to communicate those needs to appropriate managers. I believe that my background and accomplishments reflect a commitment and an ability to find solutions to these challenges.

My career includes 15 years with Merrill Lynch, four of those years as First Vice President of Fund Operations, Systems, and Infrastructure. More recently, I served as President of GovXcel, a specialty software firm; and as Chief Information Officer / Senior Vice President of VerticalNet, an Internet company that acquired and maintained 59 virtual scientific and engineering communities. In all positions, I was responsible for streamlining their operations.

One of my greatest strengths is hiring and developing motivated, long-term employees and building strategic teams. I have developed contacts in several industries, enabling me to work with people on all levels. Among the people I have managed are Ph.D. scientists and engineers, systems and technical professionals, and accounting personnel.

Many of my assignments have been with start-up operations. I approach my work with a strong sense of urgency, working well under pressure and change. I am a forward thinker and a team player who has a strong commitment to my people and the organizations I work for.

Thank you for your consideration. I look forward to meeting with you personally so that we may discuss how I can make a positive contribution to your corporation. I will call next week to inquire about a convenient time to meet.

Sincerely yours,

Bruce Barnes

Enclosure

132

Operations and Systems Professional. *Beverley and Mitchell I. Baskin, Marlboro, New Jersey*

In five short paragraphs, the applicant indicates his views on success, the shape of his 15-year career, his people skills, his worker traits, and his anticipation of a positive interview with the reader.

JEN JAMIE

407 E. Minnesota Street
Rapid City, SD 57701

Phone: (605) 343-1010
jamie@yahoo.com

STRATEGIC RELATIONSHIP MANAGER: ALLIANCES & PARTNERSHIPS
Objective: Strategic relationship management, preferably in a federal or Fortune market.

Expertise in Database, Content, Security, and Web and SOA Middleware.

October 10, 2007

Michael Kovacs
Director, Corporate Marketing
Sanmina SCI Systems, Inc.
755 E. Disk Drive
Rapid City, SD 57701

Dear Mr. Kovacs:

If one word describes me, it is Relationships.
Another word is Networked.

My value to a potential employer is my strong blend of engineering and people skills.
I have the critical skills to lead critical relationships—and the critical thinking to meet customer IT requirements. I also have a strong track record for starting and retaining key relations that work. By that, I mean they produce multimillion-dollar contracts and last years after the original contract is over—even in the federal government.

I am looking for a company where true teamwork is the norm and where I can be a catalyst for collaboration. And based on what I know about SCI, you might want someone like me—especially if you need someone who understands the current business drivers... someone with current relationships in federal, system integrator, and third-party communities... and someone who can catalyze all those teams for profitable results.

Therefore, I am sending you a courtesy copy of my resume, along with a few case studies that highlight my skills. I have nearly 5 years of experience working directly with federal and military customers, 15 years working with federal system integrators and solutions providers, about 5 years in pure business development, and almost 20 years managing key relationships.

I will call you within a few days to learn more about your goals and business needs and to hopefully schedule an interview. I know you make excellent technologies!

Sincerely,

Jen Jamie

Enclosure: Management Portfolio

133

Strategic Relationship Manager. *Helen Oliff, Reston, Virginia*

Notice the use of small caps (in the person's name); a centered profile and expertise statement, and use of boldface. Line spaces throughout the letter ensure adequate white space.

STEVE BRODY

999 Royal Augusta Road, #234
Pinehurst, Ontario A1A 1A1

stevebrody@email.com

Home: 555.222.8888
Cell: 444.777.6666

February 2, 2008

Ronald Kleinberg
Senior VP, Technology Management
IBC Technology
600 Century Place
Pinehurst, Ontario
B2C 3D4

Dear Mr. Kleinberg,

Stan Morrisey of Suntech and Ellis Cantasi of Levinson Solutions both suggested that I contact you, as they believe that my skills, expertise, and leadership in technology development are a perfect match for IBC. Having reviewed your Web site, I am very impressed with your successes and aggressive plans for the future and would like to draw your attention to the value I can offer.

Put simply, my expertise lies in delivering high-performance, enterprise-class technology solutions, and throughout my career, I have leveraged the following skills and experience to exceed expectations in service bureau, government, and national retail environments:

- ➢ More than 15 years of experience in leading and developing enterprise data centres, voice and data communications, and information-storage technologies
- ➢ Shrewd business skills with a solid grasp of the "business" of technology
- ➢ Full-cycle project management, including strategic planning, design, implementation, and maintenance
- ➢ Superior leadership capabilities with outstanding people skills and a customer-centric focus

Results have been consistent and significant, and include the following:

- ➢ **Recently negotiated $12 million annual savings** in strategic print-sourcing initiative
- ➢ Spearheaded consolidation of two corporate print shops, realizing an **annual savings of $600,000**
- ➢ **Under-cost critical UNIX and Data Warehousing acquisition** project by $2.5 million
- ➢ Introduced and supported new **debit and POS technologies across 8,000 retail registers nationally**
- ➢ Successfully proposed innovative Y2K solution, **saving more than $2.5 million in application upgrades**

I invite you to review the attached resume, which further outlines the value I can offer your technology team, and would welcome the opportunity to discuss how I could contribute to IBC's future growth and success. If you are interested in a dedicated professional with a reputation for generating real results, then I believe we would have much to discuss.

I thank you for your time and look forward to the opportunity to meet in person. I will contact you in the near future to set a time for an interview.

Sincerely,

Steve Brody

Encl.

134

Technology Development Position. *Ross Macpherson, Whitby, Ontario, Canada*

The letter first refers to some mutual acquaintances and then indicates the applicant's expertise and achievements. The company had no opening, but he got an interview to discuss another position.

BRAD LAWRENCE

776 Ellington Drive
San Diego, CA 55555

555.555.5555

E-mail: lawrence@comcast.net

June 10, 2007

[Name]
[Title]
[Employer]
[Address]
[City, State ZIP]

Dear Mr. or Ms. _____:

Providing strategic planning, design innovation, and cost-effective technology solutions that improve performance and achieve business objectives are among the qualifications that I would bring to your company as Information Systems Manager.

As a business-focused technology management professional with more than 10 years of progressive experience in rapidly growing environments including the pharmaceutical industry, I have successfully

- Built and directed the IT function from start-up, forging strong relationships with business units and leading large-scale projects such as Accelerated SAP/R3 implementation at 2 sites—on schedule and well under budget.

- Pioneered the design and leveraged existing technology and knowledge base with internal resources to implement Baan ERP system that enabled company to retain a $40 million account and provide the foundation for rapid Baan implementation methodology while gaining a competitive market advantage.

- Rescued a failed e-commerce project, resulting in restored customer confidence and retention of a $350-million-a-year account. Solution is now utilized as an enterprise standard to provide cost-effective Web access for all customers.

My success thus far results from an ability to see the "big picture" and deliver the greatest value out of IT solutions quickly. As a result of my unique accomplishments with SAP and Oracle software, I was invited to deliver customer-success-story presentations for both organizations.

Although secure in my present position, I am confidentially exploring new challenges in information systems management. May we meet to discuss the value I would add to your company's IT organization? I will call to set a mutually convenient time.

Sincerely,

Brad Lawrence

Enc.

135

Information Systems Manager. *Louise Garver, Enfield, Connecticut*

The individual wanted to transition from a manufacturing environment to a pharmaceutical company. The writer mentioned pharmaceutical industry experience and relevant projects.

Vicker T. Seed

0000 N. Lincoln Avenue
Altadena, CA 91001
Home: (555) 555-5555
Cell: (000) 000-0000
VTSeed@msn.com

VENTURE CAPITAL ■ FUNDRAISING ■ IT ACQUISITION

February 15, 2008

Bill Gates, CEO
Microsoft Corporation
One Microsoft Way, Ste. 303
Redmond, WA 98052-8303

Dear Mr. Gates:

An IT expert, I have 20 years of real-world experience in fundraising and acquisitions. I have a track record for raising seed and venture capital and originating and closing IT acquisitions—of both products and businesses.

My potential value to an employer includes the following:

➤ Seasoned fundraising, acquisition, and negotiation for multimillion-dollar IPOs and technology investments.

➤ Multiyear relationships with technology markets. Expertise in venture capital, seed and growth companies, and IT acquisitions.

➤ Exceptional "brand" loyalty from IT institutions and investors—based on multiple business investments and joint ventures.

I am seeking opportunities to perform capital fundraising and acquisition services for a growing technology firm and its investors. I will contact you within the next week to discuss any needs you may have and to schedule an interview.

Sincerely,

Vicker T. Seed

Enclosure: Resume

136

IT Fundraising and Acquisitions Position. *Helen Oliff, Reston, Virginia*

The applicant was older and lacked the blue-chip credentials typical among investors. The challenge was to demonstrate—through bullets and boldfacing—the candidate's potential value to an employer.

MARY LAWSON, 84 Swan Lane, Blaine, MN 55555
(555) 555-5555   Email: mllaw@network.com

February 5, 2008

Mr. Charles Phillip
Gantry Communications
303 Mountain Pass
Denver, CO 55555

INFORMATION TECHNOLOGY IN EDUCATIONAL AND NONPROFIT SECTORS
MARKETING ▶ ANALYSIS ▶ DATA ▶ APPLICATIONS

Dear Mr. Phillip:

Promoted 11 times in 21 years by Nelson International Technologies, I have an extensive background in information systems and project-based work. Since leaving traditional employment in 2003, I've been challenged by entrepreneurial ventures, career exploration, and civic work.

Enclosed is a resume detailing my strengths and abilities, with particular emphasis on marketing and technical skills. Other relevant areas of knowledge and expertise include the following:

- ▶ Leadership, consulting, and relationship building
- ▶ Strategic analysis and creativity
- ▶ Speech writing, presentations, instruction, and training
- ▶ Data synthesis and research
- ▶ Applications for academic learning approaches
- ▶ Marketing programs and client relations

Achievements, awards, and recognition attest to my ability to think "out of the box," apply theory, test concepts, and contribute to breakthrough ideas. Leading edge ... change-oriented technology ... resourceful ... self-motivated—these are qualities describing my style and approach to whatever I do.

An interview would provide the opportunity to exchange information, address issues, answer questions, and determine applicant suitability. I am most interested in discussing your company's goals and needs and will call within the next week to schedule a time to meet. I look forward to speaking with you.

Sincerely,

Mary Lawson

Enclosure

137

Information Technology Position. *Beverley Drake, Rochester, Minnesota*

A banner between the reader's address and the salutation indicates the applicant's target fields and areas of expertise. After the second paragraph, bullets point to additional areas of knowledge and expertise.

Florence Finch
1234 W. Berkley St.
Round Lake, IL 60000
(222) 222-2222
ffinch123@email.com

[Date]

Ms. Sylvia Smith
Jimpsom Corporation
4321 E. 176th
Deerfield, IL 60000

Dear Ms. Smith:

I recently graduated from Comp Technical Institute with a Computer Programming Certificate representing 350 hours of IT studies. Jason White, who also graduated from this course and is currently employed with your company, tells me that Jimpsom is seeking IT professionals with up-to-date programming skills. I believe I am just the person you are seeking!

With advanced training in Java and C++, I possess the communication and problem-solving skills to design and troubleshoot virtually any software. As you will see on my enclosed resume, I have more than 10 years of experience in office positions that required extensive computer use and have a firsthand knowledge of the needs of the end user. Previous supervisors have described me as patient and logical.

I would appreciate the opportunity to speak with you further about a future role at Jimpsom. I will call you at the end of this week to ensure that you received this letter and to answer any questions that you may have. In the meantime, feel free to contact me at (222) 222-2222. I look forward to speaking with you soon.

Many thanks,

Florence Finch

Enclosure

138

Information Technology Professional. *Eva Locke, Waukegan, Illinois*

This recent graduate had a certificate in computer programming but did not have formal experience in that field. The letter emphasizes her training, transferable skills, and useful experience.

Kate Dobson

0000 Autumnbrook Drive ▪ Atlanta, GA 00000 ▪ (000) 000-0000 ▪ name@aol.com

January 30, 2008

Human Resources Department
ABC Solutions
3434 Pinetree Avenue
Atlanta, GA 00000

RE: Position as Systems Administrator

Dear Staffing Representative:

It was with great interest that I noted your advertisement for the position of Systems Administrator. I believe I am the ideal candidate for your consideration, with qualifications correlated to your requirements. Thus, please allow me to explain briefly how I might contribute to your firm's operational performance.

Throughout my career, my expertise has been in providing systems integration solutions for multimillion-dollar clients. As a Senior Systems Integrator for IBM, I have instituted technology assimilations and changes for our clients that produced cost savings and positioned them for success in their respective markets. I would now like to use my systems management and integration skills to help your company maintain a strong customer base and improve productivity.

Additionally, my background in help desk administration, project management, and IT applications could benefit your firm in specific need areas. I enjoy being a diverse "team player" within an organization and contributing to my employer's success in various capacities.

To provide you with details concerning my qualifications and accomplishments, my resume is enclosed. I will contact you next week to follow up on this letter of inquiry; perhaps we could arrange a meeting to discuss our mutual interests.

Thank you for your time and consideration. Please do not hesitate to contact me if I can answer any questions.

Sincerely,

Kate Dobson

Enclosure

139

Systems Administrator. *Daniel J. Dorotik, Jr., Lubbock, Texas*

This letter is a response to an ad. Short paragraphs mention in turn the applicant's qualifications; areas of expertise and skills; background and worker traits; and resume, providing details.

Victoria A. Future

0000 Woolery Lane, Dayton, OH 45415
Phone: (555) 555-5555 | E-mail: vfuture@jitaweb.com

Date

Contact
Company
Address
City, State ZIP

Re: Network Administrator position

Dear Mr(s). _____:

In desktop support and as a network administrator, I handled a number of technical, maintenance, and support issues for the corporate and branch computers at S^3 Business Techs. I configured and installed hardware, software, and peripherals—and diagnosed and troubleshot complications pertaining to the local area network (LAN). I worked with virus-protection software and utility programs, ensuring that company policies and procedures were followed and that each new feature addressed technological advancements.

Stepping up to the plate, you'll discover that I've applied key performance by installing the LAN system at S^3 Business Techs in only 7 months, saving $1.5 million in fines by integrating an EDI system and Ordernet mailboxes. I saved up to $256,000 the first year by implementing a self-help process for end users that eliminated the need for costly technical support on small problems.

Skills recap includes the following:

- Managed LAN network life cycles on a Windows platform, from software and hardware applications to equipment layout and technical support

- Have in-depth knowledge of LAN maintenance and troubleshooting, including desktop support, configuration, and workstation issues, from initial problem analysis to final end resolution

- Integrate amongst technical support, ensuring that multiple tasks and parallel deadlines are met and in line with technological advancements and company growth

Contact me at (555) 555-5555 should you require clarification of my skills or would like to schedule a meeting time for us to discuss this position.

Sincerely,

Victoria A. Future

Attachment

140

Network Administrator. *Teena Rose, Huber Heights, Ohio*

This direct letter indicates immediately the applicant's experience and quantified accomplishments. Bullets point to network experience, network knowledge, and technical-support expertise.

James Madison, CCNA, MCSE
00000 Autumnwind Drive ◆ Houston, TX 00000 ◆ (000) 000-0000 ◆ name@ev1.net

January 24, 2008

ABC Systems
2323 Smith Avenue
Houston, TX 00000

RE: Senior WAN Engineer position, ID #6970

Dear Hiring Authority:

It was with great interest that I read about your opening for a Senior WAN Engineer, as my background and abilities meet your requirements for this position. Please allow me to explain briefly what I can offer your organization.

With several years of experience as a Network Engineer, Manager, and Administrator, I have demonstrated the ability to fulfill business goals through network solutions, maintain excellent client relationships, and make bold decisions to achieve corporate and client objectives on critical projects. The following accomplishments illustrate these skills:

- As a Network Engineer and Director of Engineering Services with Cisprint, I completed a complex VPN installation project involving 20 bank locations within an aggressive one-week deadline.
- As a Network Engineer and Special Projects Manager with IED Communications, I received commendations for my work on implementing Cisco VPN networks using PIX and 1720 VPN routers.
- As a Network Administrator for Top Networks, I built loyal client relationships through constructing, installing, and configuring desktops, workstations, servers, and all network-essential equipment.

I have found that the most effective skills for a network engineering position lie in an understanding of both the technological and business goals within an organization. What I would bring to ABC Systems is a combination of technical expertise and business intelligence to help fulfill your company's ongoing and future objectives.

I have enclosed my resume to provide additional details regarding my background and qualifications, and I welcome the opportunity to interview for this position.

Thank you for your time and consideration.

Sincerely,

James Madison

Enclosure

141

Senior WAN Engineer. *Daniel J. Dorotik, Jr., Lubbock, Texas*

This well-organized letter displays the ABC, A+B+C thematic structure. Three roles indicated in the second paragraph (Network Engineer, Manager, and Administrator) appear again as bulleted items.

AMANDA LEE JANSEN   555 Olde Floppy Drive • Suite 000 • Montréal H5H 5H5

January 5, 2008

Mr. Jean-François Hébert
Director, Web Development
Technova Corporation
555 Compu Techway
Silicon Valley North
Ottawa, Ontario K0K 0K0

Dear Mr. Hébert:

I want to be your next **Software Developer/Programmer,** a position I saw advertised on your "Job Opportunities" Web page. As the attached resume indicates, I am presently working as a *Senior Java Programmer Analyst* with Best Bullion Bank. I am involved in a $6 million project, migrating web applications from Netdynamics to Websphere. My resume details a wide range of programming and related projects in which I have participated during the last 15 years.

Throughout my career, I have

- Undertaken projects critical to the success of my employers and their clients.
- Adopted a team-oriented approach toward problem solving.
- Proactively shared relevant knowledge and findings with fellow developers, who frequently approached me for guidance.
- Developed clean code that has been virtually bug-free.
- Demonstrated passion for learning new technologies and finding better ways to use old ones.

Having written software for users extensively, I now wish to focus on scripting tools for other developers. I have done what these developers do, and I know what they need. I have the knowledge and experience to devise methods whereby they will be able to do their job faster and better. In particular, I like working with Java. I especially like the fact that the source code is open.

Since entering the IT field, I have taken an interest in examining source codes for software at all levels, including operating systems (e.g., MS-DOS, UNIX) and development tools (e.g., JDK). Writing for an O/S without examining source code is analogous to completing a jigsaw puzzle, start to finish, with one's eyes closed.

Another analogy involves a comparison between recent editions of MS Word and WordPerfect. Although Word now makes it easier to view codes than did prior versions, it lacks the advantage that WordPerfect has in permitting a high degree of user control. In Word, you never know exactly which codes are embedded in your document or where they are. In WordPerfect, not only do you know their syntax, but you can delete and replace them at will, making for a cleaner, tighter document. Just as serious word processors prefer WordPerfect, serious developers check source codes for components of the environments in which they work.

My qualifications and experience are documented in the attached resume. I am confident that, on reviewing it, you will agree I have the potential to become a worthy member of your team. I will call to set a convenient time to meet, so that we could discuss how I might best serve Technova Corporation.

Sincerely yours,

Amanda Lee Jansen

142

Software Developer/Programmer. *Howard Earle Halpern, Toronto, Ontario, Canada*

The applicant knew exactly what she wanted and indicated her technical preferences and biases, screening out incompatible employers. This letter resulted in two successive contracts.

Steven Brooks

1111 Lawrenceville Road ◆ Haven, CT 00000 ◆ 000-000-0000 ◆ user@adelphia.net

(Date)

(contact name)
(company name)
(street address)
(city, state ZIP code)

Dear Hiring Professional (or insert contact name):

As a goal-oriented, progressive individual with more than 20 years of combined experience in positions that allowed for the development of diverse skills and proactive management in the areas of Recruiting and Information Technology, I feel my skills and qualifications are ideal to fill the position of (insert job title) in your (insert department), as listed with (insert source) on (insert date).

My background has positioned me to accept employment where I can use a wide range of skill sets within a small- to mid-range organization. The ideal position will allow me to provide a wealth of experience to employ a combination of strategic marketing, budget administration, technological and sourcing skills to grow revenues and increase bottom-line profitability.

I have enclosed a copy of my resume for your review. Please feel free to contact me, at your convenience, if you have any questions or would like to schedule an interview. I look forward to discussing the mutual benefit of our association.

Thank you for your time and consideration.

Sincerely,

Steven Brooks

Encl.

143

Information Technology Recruiter. *Lea J. Clark, Macon, Georgia*

This letter template with fill-in fields is adaptable to different kinds of job targets. You can make the changes necessary to reflect your own experience, qualifications, skills, and follow-up plans.

TIMOTHY L. MICHAELS

000 King Street • Fairport, New York 14450 • 555-555-5555 • timm2@localnet.net

January 25, 2008

Mr. I. M. Important, CIO
Important Industries, Inc.
1234 Industrial Parkway
Rochester, New York 14699

Dear Mr. Important:

Capitalizing on a 12-year career with Eastman Kodak Company that has encompassed Systems Administration, IT Project Management, and Business Analysis experiences, I am seeking to use my broad-based IT knowledge in a challenging position with your firm. In pursuit of that goal, I have enclosed for your review a resume that outlines my professional background.

Some of the key capabilities that I can bring to a position with your firm include the following:

- **Supporting precision manufacturing operations, including clean room environments. During the start-up and launch of Kodak's thin film manufacturing facility, I was accountable for setting up and maintaining process control, inventory management, and resource planning applications that contributed to the efficient and profitable operation of that plant.**

- **Managing database tools that allow sales and marketing teams to capture customer information, track market trends, and plan sales/marketing strategies. In my current assignment, I maintain applications that are utilized by 100 managers in the field, plus close to 100 marketing and headquarters staff, to manage relationships with a customer base exceeding one million total accounts.**

- **Implementing and maintaining HR applications and e-mail utilities to serve up to 500 end users. As a Senior Systems Analyst with the team that launched the Office Imaging Group, I had responsibilities in these areas, including controlling user access and establishing accounts.**

- **Serving in Business Analyst roles that have included using innovative IT solutions to streamline and optimize various materials-forecasting functions.**

I believe that the knowledge and expertise developed over the course of my career can be a valuable asset to a smaller firm on the rise. I would enjoy meeting with you to explore how I can best serve your current and future needs, and I encourage you to contact me to arrange an initial interview.

Thank you for your time and consideration. I will call you soon to explore the possibility of an interview.

Sincerely,

Timothy L. Michaels

Enclosure

144

IT Project Manager/Systems Administrator. *Arnold G. Boldt, Rochester, New York*

To avoid a bland list of technical proficiencies, the writer presented this applicant in the context of his project-management and customer-relation skills. Bullets and boldfacing make these skills stand out.

FRANK D. ZAZZARA, MCP
0000 Ocean Avenue • Huntington, New York 11740 • (555) 555-5555
frankzazz@optonline.net

Dear Sir or Madam:

As an **IT / Systems Engineer / Network Specialist,** I am routinely faced with the challenges to evaluate specific technologies and their ability to meet operating requirements. I am seeking an **MIS** opportunity where I can continue to contribute to company growth and technological expansion through change, refinement and improvement. Highlights of the experience, qualifications and contributions I would bring to your organization include the following:

- Design, lead and supervise the development and delivery of cost-effective, high-performance technology solutions to meet challenging business demands—developed through IT support efforts with Fortune 500, marketing, graphic arts, litigation and insurance companies.

- Offer extensive experience in business process reengineering and workflow analysis techniques.

- Provide the flexibility to expand technical support services systems competency through internal development and external acquisition initiatives.

- Have extensive qualifications in all facets of project lifecycle development, from initial feasibility analysis and conceptual design, through documentation, implementation, user training and enhancement.

- Provide contributions to the vision, strategy and long-range development of technical support services infrastructures through organizational, leadership, team building and project management qualifications.

Because a resume can neither fully detail all my skills and accomplishments, nor predict my potential to your organization, I welcome the opportunity to meet, discuss and explore the possible merging of my talent, experience and qualifications with your organizational **MIS** system needs. I will call you to set a time we can meet.

Very truly yours,

FRANK D. ZAZZARA, MCP

Enclosure

145

IT Systems Engineer/Network Specialist. *Donna M. Farrise, Hauppauge, New York*

Boldfacing and bullets help to focus this applicant's multifaceted letter. The letter relies especially on the bulleted items to highlight the applicant's experience, qualifications, and possible contributions.

Lydia Cunningham
4444 Alapaha Drive
Golden, Maryland 00000
[000] 555-5555 — [000] 555-6666 (Mobile) — lcunningham4012@propser.net

Wednesday, 07 March 2008

Drayton Nabers
Director of Finance
c/o State of Maryland Personnel Department
Post Office Box 00000
Annapolis, Maryland 00000-0000

Dear Mr. Nabers:

As soon as I saw your announcement for Chief Information Officer, I made writing this application my first priority. Because my natural inclination is to anticipate and try to fill needs, I thought you deserved a good deal more than the standard application and resume.

I designed my resume in a new way. Gone are the usual "summary of qualifications" and sterile lists of responsibilities. In their places, starting right at the top, are eight capabilities I want to offer the Governor and the people of Maryland. Backing them up are 14 sample contributions made to organizations of all kinds—from large public-sector agencies to small businesses to nationally known IT leaders. Finally, I wanted you to have a detailed list of my technical skills. Nevertheless, there is important information no resume format or application form can transmit well.

I've already begun a personal, professional development program. I designed it to make me productive right from the start. I am studying the National Association of State Chief Information Officers' Transition Handbook, Governor's Transition Team IT Assessment Template, and the Chief Information Officer Transition Handbook. And I've begun to form professional relationships with CIOs in several states. They've given me invaluable insights into tough problems they are dealing with right now—problems that are similar to ones we face in Maryland today.

Normally, I would take the next logical step and ask for a little time on your schedule so that I could hear about your specific IT needs and goals in your own words. However, I am sensitive to the instructions that accompanied the announcement. If a personal meeting isn't possible now, I encourage you to test me for yourself in an interview soon.

Sincerely,

Lydia Cunningham

Enclosures:
1. Application for Examination
2. Resume
3. IT Capabilities the State of Maryland Can Use at Once
4. College-Level Course Work Applicable to CIO Performance

146

Chief Information Officer. *Don Orlando, Montgomery, Alabama*

The challenge was to find a way to get the hiring decision maker's attention. The letter shows that the applicant was already learning about state government and could be effective at once.

ROBERT P. BARNES, CBCP
Certified Business Continuity Professional

1434 Madison Boulevard
Orlando, FL 38917
Residence: 555-555-5555
Mobile: 000-000-0000
RobertPBarnes@earthlink.net

April 8, 2008

Samuel Ryan, CIO
Global Financial Services, Inc.
495 Central Avenue
Orlando, FL 38917

Dear Mr. Ryan:

Development of a comprehensive, state-of-the-industry business-continuity program is critical to a company's ability to achieve its core mission. Employee safety, shareholder value, corporate reputation, revenues and profits, data integrity and IT systems—these are some of the corporate interests that an effective business-continuity program is designed to protect. My expertise is the ability to deliver, within a complex multinational organization, innovative business-continuity plans that are integrated with overall corporate strategy and aligned with corporate goals.

In my work as Business Recovery Manager at Morgan Summers Financial Services, I established just such a program. My groundbreaking thinking and writing promoted business-continuity planning as a strategic, business-driven process in which IT played a supporting role. My contributions helped ensure that the company would mitigate risk, survive potential disruptions and recover in a timely manner. Achievements included the following:

— Developed and executed business-continuity plans for an organization with $176 billion in assets under management, 40 business units, 800 employees and 19 different IT systems running 200 applications.

— Promoted my visionary concept of the role of business-continuity planning throughout the organization and achieved buy-in for plan initiatives from 40 business units (including six IT business units) and two disaster-recovery vendors.

— Implemented a multifaceted employee-awareness program to help ensure that employees knew how to implement plans in the event of a business disruption.

I came up through the ranks as an IT professional and earned both my M.B.A. degree and my Bachelor's degree in Business Computer Information Systems. As an experienced BCP manager who is a Certified Business Continuity Professional, I am well credentialed for assuming a leadership position in business-continuity planning.

Please contact me if you are interested in my demonstrated ability to help a company mitigate risk and protect critical assets. I look forward to an opportunity to speak with you in person about your business requirements and will call in two weeks. Thank you.

Sincerely,

Robert P. Barnes

Enclosure

147

Business Recovery Manager. *Jean Cummings, Concord, Massachusetts*

This cover letter is for a position in an increasingly important field: business continuity planning. Dashes serve as bullets to indicate the applicant's achievements with "heavy numbers."

Danielle Quinones

danielleq@homenet.com

Current Residence:
515 Abernathy Court
Richland, NJ 00000
(000) 000-0000

After March 1, 2008:
70 Turtleback Trail
San Jose, CA 00000
(000) 000-0000

January 3, 2008

Stevenson, Pellegrino & Delacruz, P.C.
Attorneys at Law
194 Morse Avenue
San Jose, CA 00000

Attention: Law Office Administrator

Please accept this letter and resume in application for the position of Legal Administrative Assistant you posted recently on the Internet.

Although I presently reside in New Jersey, I will be relocating to California in the near future. I am extremely interested in the position you describe and precisely meet your qualification requirements. As I plan to complete my undergraduate education at Los Gatos University and then continue on to pursue a law degree, this position seems like an ideal opportunity to expand my knowledge in the various aspects of a legal practice.

In my current position as a legal secretary for an attorney specializing in personal-injury litigation, I have had extensive experience in organizing workflow and meeting multiple deadlines. I can assess what needs to be done and take appropriate action with minimal direction. Having no prior legal experience, I quickly learned on my own initiative how to open and keep track of a large number of case files varying in complexity. Managing a variety of responsibilities in an environment with deadline pressures is a challenge that I truly enjoy.

I hope you will give me the opportunity to prove my ability to make a significant contribution to your organization. If you are interested in speaking with me further, I will gladly fly to California to interview for this position. Please contact me by leaving a message with Joe or Katy Ventura at (000) 000-0000. They will also serve as my personal references.

Sincerely,

Danielle Quinones

Enclosure: Resume

148

Legal Administrative Assistant. *Melanie Noonan, West Paterson, New Jersey*

The opening paragraph identifies the position, and the second paragraph tells of the applicant's relocation plans. The third mentions crucial experience and skills. See corresponding Resume 12 in Part 3.

CHRYSTAL SCOTLAND

55 Horrace Drive
Brentwood, New York 55555
(555) 555-5555
CS@LawandOrder.net

Date

Name
Company
Address

As a second-year law student at The Long Island University School of Law, I look forward to realizing my long-held dream of practicing law. As I move toward receiving my Juris Doctor in May 2008, my career focus has remained steadfast with a strong interest in the emotionally charged world of Family Law. After careful research, I have chosen to seek a summer position with your law firm that will allow me the opportunity to further develop myself professionally. Ideally, this position will build upon recent undergraduate internship experience working within a progressive Domestic Violence Clinic headed by the Long Island Law Service Committee.

In this position, my oral advocacy skills, technique for conducting witness examinations, and ability to effectively negotiate on behalf of clients played a vital role in achieving a favorable outcome for my client when given the opportunity to try a case in Family Court. This achievement, coupled with my experience as a Student Editor on Long Island University's *Family Court Review*, solidified my interest in Family Law.

Prior experience includes three years as an Administrative Assistant with The Law Offices of McLaughlin & Meyers, P.C., a position held while attending school full-time. In this capacity, I exercised strong research, communication, and problem-resolution skills, along with the ability to handle pressing assignments in the office and at the courthouse. It is with your firm that I hope to continue in this vein as I strive to further my education and develop myself professionally.

The accompanying resume illustrates well my experience, academic achievements, and community service. However, I feel a personal meeting would better convey the value I could bring to the appropriate position. I welcome the opportunity to participate in a confidential interview to discuss in person the possibility of my joining your law firm.

Thank you in advance for your consideration. I will contact you soon.

Sincerely,

Chrystal Scotland

149

Legal Administrative Assistant. *Ann Baehr, Brentwood, New York*

This law student was looking for a summer position to continue her professional development. The letter shows that she is already an effective worker who could help a law firm significantly.

JULIE R. MICHAELS

555 S. Global Trail ♦ Broomfield, CO 80455 ♦ Home 303.000.5555 ♦ jm999@comcast.net

[Date]

[Manager]
[Company]
[Street Address]
[City, State ZIP]

Re: [name of position] advertised on [date]

Dear [person or title],

Through my studies for certification as a Paralegal, I have gained strong skills in conducting legal research and a broad knowledge of the legal system. My professional goal is to apply this knowledge in order to provide quick and efficient research and administrative assistance for my next employer. Highlights of my background include the following:

> ➤ Completed courses in Business Law; Contracts; Criminal Law; Constitutional Law; Real Property; Legal Research; Civil Litigation; Wills, Trusts & Estates; and Domestic Relations through the Paralegal Technical Institute. I maintained a 4.0 G.P.A. throughout this coursework.

> ➤ Repeatedly recognized as a quick learner with strong analytic and problem-solving skills. Possess excellent skills in technology and a variety of computer applications.

> ➤ Gained excellent feedback regarding timeliness and quality of completed projects throughout work history.

> ➤ Broad exposure to variety of cultures and races gained from military experience and worldwide travels. Strong ability to relate to persons with diverse backgrounds and on different levels.

The accompanying resume will provide you with the additional details of my accomplishments and skills. I would welcome the opportunity to meet with you and learn how I can make a positive contribution to your firm. I will call next week to inquire about the possibility of a meeting.

Thank you for your time and consideration.

Sincerely,

Julie R. Michaels

150

Paralegal. *Michele Angello, Aurora, Colorado*

The applicant had just finished school, wanted a law position, but lacked practical experience. The writer emphasized completed course work, a high GPA, and skills desirable to a law office.

THOMAS QUARTER

490 Apple Lane   Villa, Indiana 11111   222-222-2222   tomquarter@letter.com

Date

Address Block

Dear XXXX,

In 2004, an unexpected opportunity presented itself, and I left the practice of law to found a niche confectionary company specializing in Swiss chocolate. Although I have enjoyed running my own business and met with success, I feel that my entrepreneurial curiosity has been satisfied and I am now in a position to step away from my company. Consequently, I am ready to return to the challenges of a legal career and am interested in joining your firm as an associate.

My experiences as an entrepreneur have allowed me to look at the business of law from a fresh perspective. I can better appreciate the pressures that the partners of a law firm feel and understand why they expect so much of their associates and other employees. I have no doubt that my work ethic, motivation, and recent experiences will allow me to quickly become a valued member of your legal team.

A brief and partial listing of my qualifications includes the following:

- Extensive experience in marketing and business generation and outstanding customer/client relations skills.
- Proven abilities in negotiating and drafting high-dollar power purchase and sales agreements as well as mediation experience.
- Exemplary educational background that includes a BA from New York University and a JD from Columbia University School of Law.

My main desire is to resume the practice of law; therefore, I am flexible with regard to graduation-year classification. I will call you in the near future to further discuss how I can benefit your practice. Thank you for your time and consideration.

Regards,

Thomas Quarter

151

Lawyer. *Alyssa Pera, Los Angeles, California*

This individual had taken a break from the legal profession to open his own business and now wanted to return to the practice of law. His entrepreneurial experiences are cast as positive.

Arthur J. Norton, Esquire
555 Donaldson Lane   **555.555.5555**
Hermitage, PA 55555

The Family Center, Inc.   August 31, 2007
Box CAD
55 Reade Street, 5th Floor
New York, NY 55555

Dear Personnel Manager:

After practicing law in the Commonwealth of Pennsylvania for more than three years, I am hoping to return to the State of New York. Please accept the enclosed resume for consideration for your advertised full-time position of Staff Attorney.

I am confident you will find that my qualifications meet those established by The Family Center, Inc., for this position:

• Interest in public-interest law, family law, or HIV/AIDS law	✓ Knowledgeable regarding custody, protection from abuse, landlord-tenant issues, supplemental security income, welfare, unemployment compensation, bankruptcy, and debt collection.
• Strong commitment to public service	✓ Through varied internships in New York and currently at Northwestern Legal Services, I have developed a passion for assisting people to ensure their rights.
• Strong organizational and writing skills	✓ Inherent ability for meticulous organization resulting in concise, analytical communication and presentations /arguments in written and oral format.
• Strong interpersonal skills	✓ Consistently demonstrated my ability to put clients at ease and gain their trust by employing skills to develop rapport for effective representation.
• Juris Doctor degree from accredited law school	✓ Awarded Juris Doctor by City University of New York School of Law.
• License to practice in New York State	✓ Admitted to New York State Bar in August 1997.

I am eager and enthusiastic to assist individuals and families with serious illnesses, such as AIDS, in protecting their rights within the legal system.

I welcome the opportunity to meet with you to further relate how I can quickly become a contributing member of the legal team at The Family Center, Inc. I will call you September 5 to set a time.

Sincerely,

Arthur J. Norton, Esq.

Enclosure: Resume

152

Staff Attorney. *Jane Roqueplot, Sharon, Pennsylvania*

A family center solicitation indicating qualifications for a position enabled the writer to set up a two-column match between the job's requirements and the applicant's abilities and experience.

Kevin Finn

000 Horseback Lane • Stamford, CT 33333 • (111) 111-1111 • Kevin@finn.com

Postdate

Address Block

Dear _____:

My ambition to become an attorney has always been synonymous with my desire to practice labor and employment law. In pursuit of this goal, I recently earned both a Juris Doctor with a Labor and Employment Law Certificate and a master's degree in Human Resources from Antioch University. Presently, I am planning to relocate to the Washington, D.C., area to be at the forefront of this rapidly evolving field. As such, I wish to apply for a position as a first-year associate at your firm.

My graduate studies in both law and human resources have enabled me to gain valuable insight into the most current legal issues affecting the workplace. I conducted classroom presentations on many of these issues, such as employment discrimination, sexual harassment, union disputes, and Workers' Compensation. As employment law is an expansive discipline, I have also gained experience in areas such as administrative and criminal law in order to understand this area from diverse perspectives.

Throughout law school, I have taken advantage of every opportunity to apply what I learned in the classroom to real-world situations. Through internships and numerous community-service activities, I have assisted people from diverse backgrounds with a variety of concerns. As a result, I have developed excellent communication skills and a keen ability to assess individual clients' needs. Each experience, both academic and work related, also afforded me the opportunity to develop the necessary research, writing, and analytical skills required of a first-class attorney.

I would appreciate the opportunity to meet with you and further discuss my qualifications. I will contact you to set a time that is convenient for you. Thank you for your time and consideration.

Very truly yours,

Kevin Finn

153

Labor and Employment Lawyer. *Alyssa Pera, Los Angeles, California*

This graduate was enthusiastic about practicing labor and employment law. His enthusiasm is evident in all three main paragraphs. His master's degree in Human Resources shows his commitment.

SIMON D. HARRIS
89 Fledgling Plaza ▪ Columbus, OH 33333
(111) 111-1111 ▪ simon@harris.com

[Date]

[Address]

Dear [Name]:

I am an experienced legal professional with an LL.M. in Taxation, interested in joining your firm as an associate. Although my desire to practice tax law represents a career change for me, it is a change made with a great deal of planning and resolve. As outlined below, I have spent the past few years preparing myself for this shift, and I am eager and feel well prepared to begin this new stage of my career.

For 13 years, my practice focused on the litigation of large and complex personal-injury cases. Seeking a more transactional practice, I left private practice in 2000 to work for JRO—an insurance industry leader. My work with JRO somewhat satisfied my interest in transactional work; however, I desired a more significant change. After evaluating my strengths and interests, I eventually settled on taxation as the area that would best fulfill me as a professional.

Understanding that such a transition could not be made without the proper educational background, I enrolled in the University of Ohio's six-course program in business finance while still employed with JRO, earning a certificate in 2005. This program reinforced my desire to move into taxation, and I consequently entered the University of Ohio's LL.M. program in that area of concentration.

Now I am ready to put my academic training into action. I offer highly transferable skills that will be assets as I enter this practice area. As a result of my background, I have developed excellent drafting skills and an acute attention to detail. Additionally, I have experience providing effective counsel and engaging in frequent client contact.

I am confident that I can be of value to your practice and hope to further explore how I might benefit your firm. If you would like to set up a meeting or speak with me in more detail about my qualifications, please contact me at your earliest convenience. I look forward to hearing from you.

Sincerely,

Simon D. Harris

Enclosure

154

Estate Planning Lawyer. *Alyssa Pera, Los Angeles, California*

The applicant wanted to transition to a new legal practice area, and the letter explains his reasons and qualifications for doing so. The change is not hasty but based on years of preparation.

Dennis L. Richards

1234 Oak Tree Drive • Bloomington, IL 61704 • 309.555.5555 • dlrichards@aol.com

CORPORATE COUNSEL

Litigation Management ~ Attorney Management

[Date]

[Name]
[Title]
[Company]
[Address]

Dear Sir/Madam:

I am an accomplished corporate attorney with a successful career and have enclosed my resume for your review. Throughout my positions at State Farm Insurance, I have been praised for my ability to direct multiple legal cases and manage a large staff of lawyers.

I believe I have mastered the art of contact management, corporate networking, and personal relationship building. In doing so, I developed a thorough knowledge of all aspects of business law. Listed below are some accomplishments of which I am proud:

- Promoted twice over a five-year period to my present position as Legal Counsel after demonstrating exceptional legal and managerial expertise.

- Acknowledged for leadership skills in corporate and governmental affairs. Serve as an advocate and liaison between clients and corporations.

- Experienced in the areas of litigation, arbitration, mediation, and budgetary management.

Thank you for your consideration. I believe my success as a professional reflects my personal integrity, extensive communication skills, and willingness to work hard. I look forward to speaking with you to discuss how I may make a positive contribution to your executive team.

Sincerely yours,

Dennis L. Richards

Enclosure

155

Corporate Counsel. *Beverley and Mitchell I. Baskin, Marlboro, New Jersey*

This applicant was a successful lawyer with management skills. Managerial expertise is a theme that appears repeatedly in this letter: in the first two paragraphs and in the first and third bulleted items.

ROGER LEVY

48 Green Grove Lane
Greenville, SC 33333

(333) 333-3333   rlevy@green.com

Date

Address

Dear Salutation:

I am a widely experienced professional seeking an opportunity to combine my skills in law and technology in a position with your company. Since graduating from law school, my career has followed a dual trajectory in technology and law—I have provided counsel to numerous companies regarding software development and contracts, and, as an associate with Wolf & Green, represented individuals and entities in complex litigation. At this juncture, I desire to move into an in-house role where I can employ my ability to evaluate and understand technology in the protection of the company's interests.

My background well prepares me to counsel on strategic direction as well as how to protect developed intellectual assets once that direction has been solidified. With extensive experience as a computer programmer, I possess an exceptional capacity to advise on highly specific issues that impact agreements and intellectual property matters. I can also present complex technical issues to others in a way that is easy to comprehend.

In addition to technical expertise, I am an effective mediator who can see all sides of an issue and patiently work out agreements between parties. Further, my skills in analysis and presentation allow me to successfully present my position with regard to intellectual property disputes. I believe this combination of traits and professional history will serve me well in a corporate environment, and I look forward to beginning this next stage of my career.

I welcome the opportunity to further discuss my potential to benefit your company. I will contact you next Tuesday to arrange an interview.

Sincerely,

Roger Levy

Enclosure

156

Corporate Counsel. *Alyssa Pera, Los Angeles, California*

The individual had two backgrounds: one in computer technology and the other in law. After graduating from law school, he integrated both areas of expertise in software-development contracts.

Luis Colón

000 East 19th Avenue, Allentown, PA 00000 ■ ■ ■ ■ ■ ■ ■ ■ ■ ■ (000) 000-0000

February 17, 2008

Mr. Eugene Zontag
Lehigh County Prosecutor
1015 Malcolm Street
Allentown, PA 00000

Dear Mr. Zontag:

I am writing to you and sending my resume at the suggestion of Dr. William Jarvis, who recently spoke to you regarding my potential for a field position with the County Prosecutor's Office. I would be interested in exploring the possibilities for employment in a criminal investigative unit such as narcotics, homicide, robbery, arson, or fraud.

In 2004 I was honorably discharged from active duty, having served for three years in the U.S. Army. I am currently in the Army Reserves and also have four years of experience as an Emergency Medical Technician. As you will see from my resume, these experiences as well as my volunteer work with urban youth have trained and prepared me for any challenge requiring a physically fit and highly disciplined individual. Because I grew up in a tough neighborhood, I learned street survival skills early in life. I am not intimidated by anyone, and have mastered the art of unarmed self-defense in addition to the proficient use of firearms and other weapons.

I feel I could contribute significantly to the law enforcement efforts in your district by taking an active part in the thorough investigation of alleged criminal offenses. I would appreciate the chance to meet with you personally to discuss how my skills and experience could best be utilized to meet your needs.

Thank you for your consideration, and I look forward to meeting you soon.

Sincerely,

Luis Colón

157

Criminal Investigator. *Melanie Noonan, West Paterson, New Jersey*

The referral in the opening paragraph establishes a connection immediately with the reader of the letter. The second paragraph explains why the applicant's background makes him fit for a position.

BRYAN K. BOWLES

24684 County Highway P   bryankbowles@yahoo.com   Residence: (262) 845-7634
Oconomowoc, WI 53066   Mobile: (262) 313-4058   Office: (262) 845-1753

November 6, 2007

City of Oconomowoc
Attn: Human Resources
174 East Wisconsin Avenue
Oconomowoc, Wisconsin 53066

To the Human Resources Director and the Search Committee:

As your advertisement indicated, the position of Public Safety Director/Chief of Police requires an individual with a strong law enforcement leadership background, as well as a complete understanding of the many unique challenges facing the City of Oconomowoc. A life-long resident of Oconomowoc with more than 20 years as a certified law enforcement professional, I am the best-qualified candidate to continue the effective police leadership the city has received.

◆ **You require 10 years of law enforcement experience with at least 5 years at the administrative and command level. Additionally, you require a proven record of leadership, including successful labor management experience.** I have a 16-year record of effective leadership and management that has included (1) command-level planning and organizing; (2) supervision of 40 employees and delegation of authority; (3) efficient administration of resources; (4) communication and successful relations with union-represented and nonrepresented employees, staff, and constituents; and (5) the involvement of others in consensus building and decision making. My experience covers several functional and specialty areas including patrol, detective bureau/investigation, court services, tactical enforcement, school/police liaison efforts, and search/rescue.

◆ **You require a demonstration of community-oriented policing experience.** Throughout my tenure with the Jefferson County Sheriff's Department, I have directed and/or served in community policing initiatives including command of the school/police liaison program; direction of law enforcement service contracts, direction of the police honor guard unit, and command of the search-and-rescue dive team.

◆ **You require a demonstration of budgeting experience.** Over the last 15 years, I have assisted with the development of operational and capital budgets, as well as examining and reallocating resources to achieve higher return on investment.

I would appreciate the opportunity to interview for this position. As you begin the screening process, should you have any additional questions, please feel free to contact me at any of the numbers listed above. Thank you.

Sincerely,

Bryan K. Bowles

Enclosure:
    Resume
    Letter of Recommendation

158

Public Safety Director/Chief of Police. *Michele J. Haffner, Glendale, Wisconsin*

A series of indented, bulleted paragraphs indicate how the applicant is the best-qualified candidate for the position. Diamond bullets are stronger than circular bullets for getting attention.

GAIL C. SMITH

55 Hill Street ■ Brooklyn, NY 00000 ■ 555.555.5555 ■ gails@yahoo.com

March 15, 2008

Mark Wright
Delta Town Hall
555 Commerce Lane
Delta, GA 00000-0000

Dear Mr. Wright:

With 15 years of New York City Police Department experience, currently as a Senior Law Enforcement Official, it is with great interest and enthusiasm that I submit my resume to be considered for the **Police Chief** position with the Delta Police Department. I will be relocating to the state of Georgia within the next few months and believe my experience and background would be an excellent match for this position.

Throughout my career with the New York City Police Department, I've had the opportunity to enhance the quality of life and provide a safe and secure environment for the residents of New York City by partnering with various city, state and federal agencies, collaborating with social service and youth organizations and participating in ongoing trainings and professional development. Highlights of my background and experience include

- **COORDINATING** 100 Supervisors, 500 Detectives and Police Officers, and 25 civilian staff from various units and departments.

- **MANAGING** a $5.3 million budget and obtaining outside funding through grant awards and other sources (approx. $350,000).

- **SUPERVISING** and planning various emergency response efforts including 9/11 World Trade Center Disaster, 2003 Blackout, and American Airlines Flight 587 crash.

- **INVESTIGATING** high-profile cases and analyzing data and statistics to identify crime patterns and trends.

- **ATTENDING** trainings and continuous professional development courses to enhance skills and abilities.

I have visited the town of Delta a number of times in the past and found it to be a very charming and progressive community, one in which I have a strong desire to serve. I will call to schedule a personal interview to discuss your current needs and my strong law enforcement qualifications. I look forward to speaking with you soon. Thank you for your time and consideration.

Sincerely,

Gail C. Smith

Enclosure

159

Police Chief.   *La-Dana R. Jenkins, Staten Island, New York*

The letter's objective was to showcase the applicant's ability to be the chief of a police department after years of being a lieutenant and sergeant. She was also willing to move to a small town.

BILL STEADMAN, CPP

CORPORATE EXECUTIVE ● CHIEF SECURITY OFFICER

"Security is always too much...until it's not enough."
—Daniel Webster

«Date»

«First_Name» «Last_Name»
«Title»
«Company»
«Postal_Address»

Dear «Courtesy_Title» «Last_Name»:

Within minutes, the disastrous events of September 11, 2001, transformed our conceptualization of corporate security—changed its significance, scope, and strategy—from an optional "diligence" to an absolute requirement. Undoubtedly, the 15,000+ companies that were directly affected that day have since created, expanded, and / or upgraded corporate security.

In these perilous times, today's socially and financially conscientious enterprise is obligated to take a serious, urgent, and comprehensive approach to protecting infrastructure, property, and people from internal and external threats. Globally, companies are reprioritizing corporate security in their plans and actions, despite the soft economy.

Today's conundrum? Do more with less—again! This is where I come in! Through 20+ years of experience in the planning, deployment, and management of full-scale corporate security programs, I can provide <Name of Company> with the capacity to efficiently and cost-effectively avoid / mitigate risk and loss. In addition, I bring the added value of senior-level executive achievement, advanced academics, and an understanding of technology.

The following are highlights of my successes:

- Served as Head of Security for all of Your Cable's corporate entities and assets and managed related strategies, projects, inventories for corporate headquarters, and two operating divisions. Controlled $7 million capital and expense budget.

- Assisted SVP of Security (solid line to CEO) with enterprise-wide budget and team oversight ($24+ million / 800+ employees).

- Contributed to $1+ million in annual cost savings related to corporate security.

- Formed and managed an internal organization—Intelligence Services Group—as a solution to employee and vendor security issues.

- Planned and managed technology-based security—personnel, proprietary, and intellectual property protection—systems projects representing investments, some in excess of $1 million.

- Contributed to post-9/11 strategic plans and actions for high-profile venues and events (e.g., West Side Arena, Lyman Recital House, and Senior GMA Tournament). Consulted on Metropolis Plaza security issues after the '93 bombing.

<Name of Contact>, if you see value in the breadth of my experience, scope of my knowledge, and caliber of my management qualifications, please get in touch so we can set up a meeting. I look forward to discussing your needs and my solutions, and you can expect to hear from me soon. I can guarantee you a substantial ROI.

Sincerely,

Bill Steadman

Enclosure

vulnerability assessment ● access security ● event security ● workplace / employee security
executive protection ● electronic surveillance / countermeasures ● competitive intelligence / countermeasures
emergency preparedness ● crisis response ● intellectual / proprietary property protection

25 Bristol Road, Smallville, New Jersey 33333 ● Home: 444-444-4444 ● Cell: 777-777-7777 ● E-mail: bstead@verizon.net

160

Corporate Security Officer. *Deborah Wile Dib, Medford, New York*

Contact information is put at the foot of the page so that the Webster quotation can go at the top. This quote sells the need for security right upfront. The bulleted successes and the keywords near the foot are strong.

JONATHAN A. EAGEN
4444 Martin Road • Allentown, PA 19222 • (666) 888-0000

March 17, 2008

Michael Chertoff, Secretary of Homeland Security
White House
ATT: Office of Homeland Security
1600 Pennsylvania Avenue
Washington, DC 20502

Dear Secretary Chertoff:

As you build your Homeland Security team, it is my hope that you are looking for individuals like me—people who have been in the trenches and who are willing to "do what it takes" to accomplish a task. If you spoke to Jack Long in Lt. Governor Justine's office, he would tell you that I *am* that person and that I would be a strong contributor to this uncharted and unprecedented challenge you face.

Until August, I was a Research Analyst and Campaign Coordinator for Senator Don Thornton. Following Senator Thornton's retirement, I served as a Campaign Coordinator for Representative Lisa Carpenter, working closely with the Republican State Committee. At this point, I am ready for a new challenge, and I can envision no other personal or professional opportunity more fulfilling and rewarding than being a member of the Homeland Security team.

From the time I was a young man, I have had an interest in public service. You will note in my resume that I have served as a Councilman and Committeeman in my home borough. Although I didn't realize it at the time, I was taking the first steps toward a career serving the public and my country. When I envision the perfect job and work environment, there are three things that rank high on my list of priorities:

- I work best on a team...particularly one that is targeting a meaningful goal such as homeland security;

- I *must* be aligned with a leader who is known for his/her integrity, character and strength of purpose...an individual who leads by personal example; and

- I want to be given the opportunity to tackle any challenging, responsible assignments that I'm deemed capable of handling. I make it my business to learn all I can about my organization's mission, strategies and functions so that I can work from a standpoint of knowledge.

On a personal level, you should be aware that I am single, available for travel and open to working extra hours to accomplish the team's objective. To say I am organized and work well under pressure would be an understatement. I've had to be in order to balance full-time employment with my educational requirements. And whether large projects or small—you can count on me to get the job done. I have a "can-do" attitude and plenty of persistence, and I enjoy doing the footwork.

I would be proud to join this top-flight team concerned with protecting our nation and its citizens. I have enclosed my resume, outlining my experience and credentials, for your consideration. I realize that a resume is only a brief overview, so I can be available to meet with you for a personal interview at your convenience. Please note that I have submitted my resume online as well. I look forward to talking with you in the near future.

Respectfully,

Jonathan A. Eagen

Enclosure

161

Homeland Security Position. *Karen Conway, Media, Pennsylvania*

Referrals in the first two paragraphs help to catch the reader's attention. The letter then turns to building a case for regarding this applicant as a worthy candidate for a Homeland Security position.

CST. DANIEL TURCOTT #544

000 King Street, Apt. #212
Augusta, Ontario A1A 1A1

Phone: (555) 444-8888
Pager: (905) 444-5555

January 12, 2008

RE: PROMOTIONAL REVIEW BOARD

Dear Sir/Madam,

It is with great interest that I submit my qualifications for the Promotional Review Board. I am a highly skilled and highly regarded police officer with recent experience working as an Acting Sergeant and considerable international leadership experience. In all capacities, I have consistently distinguished myself as a dedicated, well-organized, and highly capable leader.

In addition to the experience and expertise outlined in the attached resume, I offer strengths in the following specific areas:

➤ **Leadership**—Through my current role as Acting Sergeant with the Augusta and Pinehurst Community Police Services, and additionally from my experience in Kosovo as the Chief of Border Police Unit, I have demonstrated strengths in leading officers through example, coaching, and the clear communication of expected performance standards. In delegating responsibilities and specific tasks to subordinate officers, I am mindful of developing officers and ensure that they are part of the team. I provide leadership by example, showing compassion and respect for fellow officers while maintaining good guidance and direction.

➤ **Communications Skills**—My communication is clear and concise, and I have excellent listening skills. In Kosovo, I was responsible for representing our United Nations Border Policing efforts in politically tense meetings with Yugoslav, Macedonian, NATO, and UN representatives. These meetings were extremely volatile at times and required the highest levels of diplomacy, clarity, and interpersonal expertise.

"Mr. Turcott enjoys a natural ability to interact and converse well with people of all walks of life. His interpersonal skill is the trait that is far superior and the envy of many."
> Everson W. Summerset, Inspector
> Chief of Training for United Nations Mission in Kosovo

➤ **Organizational Skills**—I have consistently been commended for my organizational and logistical skills. While in Kosovo, I effectively managed all resources and coordinated the activities of 130 officers and 60 police vehicles across five international border crossings. Most recently, I reviewed and updated 433 ARPS files on outlaw motorcycle gang members and their associates.

"There were always logistical problems and bureaucratic issues to be handled. These circumstances never deterred Turcott from accomplishing his mission, even under difficult circumstances."
> Willis B. Redfield, Senior Case Agent, Narcotics Division
> New York Police Department

➤ **Above-Standard Proven Work Record**—As a Uniform Officer, I maintain one of the highest levels of statistics with regards to drug and criminal investigations within my division. Additionally, I am consistently identified for special projects and investigative work within my division, the Intelligence Unit, and other police services.

Page 1 of 2

162

Police Constable. *Ross Macpherson, Pickering, Ontario, Canada*

This Police Constable had to "apply" for a promotion to Sergeant. Because hundreds of officers applied for the promotion and the letter and resume carried so much weight, the standard one-page length was replaced with a powerful two-page letter that included achievements and

CST. DANIEL TURCOTT #544

000 King Street, Apt. #212
Augusta, Ontario A1A 1A1

Phone: (555) 444-8888
Pager: (905) 444-5555

continued...

➢ **Dedication**—Extremely self-motivated and driven to succeed, I have a consistent desire to improve skills and exceed expectations. Proven flexibility and adaptability.

➢ **Self-Discipline**—I was personally selected by Division Inspector to develop, coordinate, and implement a 6-week Street Level Drug Investigation within the Pinehurst community. As Officer in Charge, I successfully managed budget allocation, vehicle rentals, and undercover buys, and directed junior and senior officers in the execution of all search warrants.

➢ **Conflict Resolution**—I successfully created a 130-officer Border Police Unit in Kosovo, requiring advanced conflict-resolution skills in a post-war restoration scenario. Given that no such police unit existed in the region when I arrived, our presence in such a volatile region created considerable conflict among residents and the international police officers I was responsible for training and supervising. In spite of these obstacles, I was able to create an effective Border Police Unit covering five international border locations between two sovereign countries.

[Officer Turcott's] sensitive, honest, and positive team approach garnishes the mutual respect between himself and others that permit effective conflict resolution."

Everson W. Summerset, Inspector
Chief of Training for United Nations Mission in Kosovo

I am confident that my work experience, reputation, and dedicated work ethic will exemplify the type of officer you require. Thank you for your consideration.

Sincerely,

Constable Daniel Turcott #544

testimonials in seven top functional areas. Boldfacing and underlining make these areas stand out. Italic is used for the important testimonials. This candidate got the promotion over more than 200 other officers.

BRUCE T. THOMASON

98 Ben Franklin Drive ● Austin, TX 78734
Home: (555) 222-2222 ● ThomasonB@aol.com ● Work: (555) 333-3333

<Date>

[Company Name]
[Department]
[Address]
[City, State, ZIP]

Dear [Name],

It is with great interest that I am forwarding my resume for consideration as Major within your agency. As a highly motivated Director of Informational Systems within your law enforcement agency, and having served in many capacities within this agency, I am confident that I possess the skills, the knowledge, and—most important—the dedication and commitment to ensure that citizens are provided with safe, efficient, quality protection.

My desire to make a difference in the community and in the lives of the people in that community led me to a career in law enforcement. The teamwork, dedication, and commitment involved in serving the community make this work extremely rewarding, as does the continual effort to be the "Best of the Best." Law enforcement is a physically demanding and dangerous occupation, requiring physical fitness, discipline, and teamwork. My team-building, leadership, and motivational skills will be an asset to the position, as will my stamina and capacity to act decisively in emergency situations.

With more than 25 years of law enforcement experience, I will bring to this position extensive expertise and departmental knowledge. With a vision of a progressive Sheriff's Office with a continuing tradition of exemplary service, I believe my values of honesty, embraced diversity, respect, commitment, and full accountability, combined with knowledge gained from extensive experience, will guarantee my ability to do this important work.

Throughout my career, I have demonstrated my ability to handle full responsibility and leadership. My responsibilities have been diverse and have included departmental management, strategic planning, project management, and financial analysis. Having successfully executed tactics to cut costs and improve efficiency, I possess the ability to conceive and implement business solutions to problems while working closely with personnel and projects, building a reputation for quality and overall results. My mission is for a Sheriff's Office by and for the people, committed to justice by serving and protecting our community.

Thank you for your time and consideration of my application. I look forward to discussing in detail with you the ways in which I can make a significant contribution to your agency, and I invite you to contact me, at your convenience, at either of the above numbers.

Sincerely,

Bruce Thomason

Enclosure

163

Police Officer, Major. *Jennifer Rushton, N. Richmond, New South Wales, Australia*

The individual was applying for an internal position as Major within his agency. He wanted to show both his commitment to law enforcement and his ability to lead and implement changes.

DARWIN E. TOHALT

637 Lazy L Road ● Ginsville, Missouri 64730
Office: 555-555-5555 ● Wireless: 000-000-0000 ● Fax: 000-000-0000
Email: darwintohalt@ctcis.net

LETTER OF INTRODUCTION

This letter is to introduce Darwin E. Tohalt, Accredited Traffic Accident Reconstructionist. As a retired highway patrolman and a member of the Major Crash Investigation Unit, I possess the knowledge, specialization, training, and experience to investigate and analyze traffic accidents beyond the normal investigation performed by the police.

Attached is a professional profile that highlights my qualifications. I have investigated and reconstructed hundreds of accidents involving passenger and commercial vehicles, pedestrians, and bicycles. These credentials will render my opinion in court as an "expert" in traffic accident reconstruction. My experience extends to consulting with attorneys and insurance companies in any accident case, for the prosecution and defense, along with civil cases representing both the plaintiff and the defendant. Also, I have performed extensive research and evidence documentation.

There are many areas of an accident that can be analyzed. Vehicle speed is the most common issue, and there are several methods, including speed from skid marks, conservation of energy, crush damage, and conservation of linear momentum, that can be applied. There can be questions of collision avoidance or the ability of a driver to see a hazard. Most accident cases require that several issues be analyzed and correlated so that an overall picture of the situation can be presented. Computer programs are used to assist in reconstruction of accidents. These programs are very complex and require considerable training to use correctly. Various types of scale diagrams, photos, animations, and scale models are prepared.

There is no set fee for the reconstruction or analysis of a traffic accident. My services are provided on an hourly fee basis. A simple situation may take very little time, while a complex situation may take several days just to collect the required information. Then there is the time required for trial or deposition appearances. There is no charge or obligation for the initial review and consultation on any traffic accident case. With this review, a cost estimate can be provided.

From responding to an accident scene, to documentation and preservation of the evidence, to determination of vehicle speeds or avoidability, to courtroom presentations and exhibits, I can assist you in all of your needs for traffic accident reconstruction.

Sincerely,

Darwin E. Tohalt

Attachment

164

Traffic Accident Reconstructionist. *Gina Taylor, Kansas City, Missouri*

The applicant was a retired highway patrolman who wanted to go into accident investigation for insurance and law firms. The writer developed this letter of introduction for the new company.

DAVID MARTINEZ
45 Hillside Lane
Wilmington, MA 55555
(w) 555-555-5555 (h) 555-500-5000
e-mail: dm45@verizon.net

EXECUTIVE/VIP PROTECTION
TEAM & TASK FORCE LEADERSHIP
SECURITY OPERATIONS MANAGEMENT
NATIONAL & INTERNATIONAL INVESTIGATIONS
TRAINING PROGRAM DEVELOPMENT/DELIVERY
SECURITY POLICY/PRACTICE DEVELOPMENT

September 25, 2007

Thomas Jones, Secretary of Public Safety
State of Connecticut
Executive Office of Public Safety
3 State Street, Suite 5555
Hartford, CT 55555

Dear Secretary Jones:

I understand that your office will shortly be seeking a Director of the Office of Commonwealth Security. I would bring to the position key competencies in the areas of terrorism-prevention strategy development, security operations management, and interagency cooperation.

My expertise is protecting large and small groups against terrorist attack. For more than 25 years, I have worked for the United States Secret Service in a range of capacities. Currently I am Assistant to the Special Agent in Charge of Hartford's Protection and Intelligence Squad. During my career, I served on multiple task forces where communication and cooperation were critical to achieving results. Earlier, I conducted high-profile fraud and forgery investigations. Highlights of my achievements include the following:

- Contributed as a member of the U.S. Secret Service Airport Security Review to the analysis of security breaches and the development of remediation plans.
- Resurrected and reenergized a financial organized crime task force that had lost the support of key stakeholders. With my skills in leadership, communication, negotiation, and collaboration, I was able to bring back to the table three federal agencies and the Hartford Police Department, among others.
- Developed a strategy for protecting the 2004 Presidential Debate in Hartford from disruption. Executed security operations in a large, coordinated effort. Deployed agents from several public agencies to secure an environment in which media, celebrities, and political staff numbered in the thousands.
- Protected a former U.S. president as leader of a protective detail. Managed operations, scheduling, and training for agents. Developed a plan for relocating the former president in the event of a national crisis.

I understand that developing a coordinated strategy to protect the state from terrorism will be a key mission for the new Director. With my intimate understanding of issues surrounding protective security operations and my expertise in strategizing and executing large protective operations, I am well equipped to take on the task.

I would also be able to make important contributions in another critical area: promoting communication and collaboration between agencies to obtain proper intelligence and then acting expeditiously and collaboratively to develop seamless security solutions. I have a strong track record of coordinating efforts with multiple stakeholders to get work done.

I look forward with interest to speaking with you in person and will call to set an appointment. Thank you for considering my strong interest in the position.

Sincerely,

David Martinez

165

Director of the Office of Commonwealth Security. *Jean Cummings, Concord, Massachusetts*

The individual wanted to move up to the top security job in the state. The writer brought together all the pieces of his experience that qualify him for this position. Note the bulleted highlights.

TED PELLETIERE

Home:
000 Mullen Road
Peekskill, NY 00000

E-mail: pellted@cox.net
(555) 555-5555

Mailing Address:
P.O. Box 445
Peekskill, NY 00000

March 23, 2008

New York Times
Box 990
New York, NY 00000

RE: INVESTIGATIONS MANAGER

As a professional with extensive hands-on and supervisory experience in law enforcement, private industry, and the military, I believe that my expertise is a match for this position. Accordingly, I have enclosed for your review a resume that summarizes my skills and accomplishments in investigations management.

I have achieved a successful record as an investigator and supervisor in delivering results to corporate clients as well as in community and executive protection. My skills encompass undercover criminal investigations • background checks • fraud investigations • arrests and extradition • fugitive location and apprehension • electronic surveillance and detection • employee dishonesty.

Currently as Chief Inspector at the State's Attorney's Office, I direct a team in security, safety, and investigation operations. As a supervisor, I am accountable for the development, training, and supervision of a diverse workforce. I also am well versed in security program planning and critical incident/crisis management based on my experience as a member of the Federal Anti-Terrorism Task Force.

Previously employed with the New York Police Department, I progressed through increasingly responsible law enforcement positions that included development of the training division, establishing and overseeing the department's narcotics unit, and training new staff. In addition, my diverse experience includes providing successful investigative services for corporate clients in the insurance industry, as well as conducting criminal/counterintelligence investigations during my military reserves tenure.

I am confident that my expertise and professionalism would allow me to meet the challenges of this managerial role and protect your clients' interests. Thank you for your consideration. I will contact you later this month to explore the possibility of a personal interview.

Sincerely,

Ted Pelletiere

Enclosure

166

Investigations Manager. *Louise Garver, Enfield, Connecticut*

This applicant wanted an investigations management position in a corporate setting. The letter refers to the individual's experience, skills, current position, and previous NYPD employment.

ALLEN JURGENS

0000 Red Barn Road
Agua Dulce, California 91350

555-555-5555
ajurgens@netzero.net

January 5, 2008

Benson Security
35000 Sierra Highway
Agua Dulce, California 91350

**Proficient Loss-Prevention Expert
Committed to Helping You
Achieve a Healthier Bottom Line!**

Each year, retailers lose an estimated $26 billion in merchandise to shrinkage, primarily through theft and employee error. This means 1 to 2 percent of total sales are lost, and for larger companies, this loss totals in the millions. Some companies find themselves in this predicament because of an ineffective loss-prevention program or lack of one.

Here's how I can help…

- Draw on practical experience to identify and solve loss-related problems.
- Develop and implement sound strategies to arrive at effective solutions.
- Use effective management techniques to train loss-prevention staff.
- Collaborate with team members to address current problems and anticipate future challenges.

I believe in the Golden Rule and have always applied it; it was one of the first things I instilled in my staff. Throughout my law enforcement career, I have focused on empowering my subordinates to succeed by encouraging them to develop their strengths and grow professionally. In many cases where individuals were dissatisfied, I resolved the underlying problems and turned their attitude around. This approach consistently produced highly effective, supportive teams under my command.

Qualifications I bring to your company [use name of company if you have it] include

- Proven performance in fast-paced and high-stress working environments.
- Strong analytical skills with exceptional attention to detail.
- High motivation and ability to aggressively take on great responsibility.
- Hands-on experience with classified documentation.
- Experience in intelligence report writing, including in-depth reports on high-interest areas of operation.

Based on my experience, strong work ethic, and commitment (no one will "outwork" me), I am confident that I can add significant value to your security function. If appropriate, I would like to schedule a meeting to discuss your needs and the contribution I can make to the success of your organization. Should any questions arise regarding the information on my résumé, please contact me; otherwise, I will call you next week [if you have or can look up contact number] to set up an appointment. I look forward to speaking with you soon.

Sincerely,

Allen Jurgens

Enclosure

167

Loss Prevention Expert. *Myriam-Rose Kohn, Valencia, California*

This letter's pattern includes these items in turn for the reader: your problem, how I can help, my work with subordinates, my qualifications, and my confidence in being useful to your organization.

Thomas J. Sonner

333 West Boulevard
Hansing, WA 98888-8888
(777) 777-7777
email: TJS777@email.com

March 18, 2008

General Manager
Senior Gardens
77 Mystery Drive
Hansing, WA 98888

RE: Community Relations Director

I enclose my resume in response to your March 8 ad in *The Hansing Bee* for a Community Relations Director. It seems a surprisingly good match for my background, and I would welcome an opportunity to discuss it with you personally.

My considerable experience as a highly successful, respected, and beloved pastor / counselor / teacher, briefly summarized on the enclosed resume, testifies to my relationship-building expertise—I am confident in my ability to represent Senior Gardens to prospective residents and their families. My work with diverse populations has honed my innate ability to recognize needs and present workable solutions—I can easily relate to your customers. Of course, successful networking with civic and religious leaders in local and state communities, office personnel, administrators, executives, children, and adults is one of my fortes.

With my experience in recruiting volunteers, public speaking, presentations, and training, I have well-developed powers of persuasion—easily translated to sales and marketing skills— and certainly ministry and teaching can be considered long-term-care industries.

I hope you can see the potential here for my making a significant contribution to your business. I will give you a call in two weeks to schedule a time we can meet to discuss the opportunity further. Thank you for your consideration.

Sincerely,

Thomas J. Sonner

enc: resume

168

Community Relations Director. *Janice M. Shepherd, Bellingham, Washington*

The applicant was a Roman Catholic priest who had decided to transition to secular work. This letter was successful in getting an interview for him, and he was successful in landing the job.

Paul Patton

15711 Clinton Avenue
Houston, TX 00000

Home: (000) 000-0000
Email: name@aol.com

January 14, 2008

Dr. Ken Woolforth
Vice President for Enrollment Management
University of Houston
P.O. Box 00000
Houston, TX 00000-0000

Dear Dr. Woolforth:

It was with great interest that I learned about the opening for a Director of Professional Services, as my qualifications match your requirements for this position. Please allow me to explain briefly how my skills and abilities can contribute to the success of the University of Houston.

In reviewing the requisition for this position, I noted that you are seeking a candidate with the ability to "apply universal business principles to a variety of environments"; as the Director for my advertising firm and a General Manager in several other capacities, I have held full responsibility for a broad range of business disciplines and functions, including marketing, accounting, budgeting, sales, production, customer service, staffing, and general administration. In addition, I meet the following specific requirements:

Your Requirements:

- 7 years of management experience
- Bachelor's degree from accredited university
- Knowledge of printing, copying, and mailing processes
- High level of financial and administrative management skills

My Qualifications:

- 15+ years of experience in various management positions
- BS from the University of Houston
- Experience in printing, mailing, and copying functions as Director of XYZ Advertising
- Track record of meeting tight budgets, streamlining processes, and ensuring workplace efficiency

My resume is enclosed to provide you with additional details regarding my background and achievements, but I am certain that a personal interview would more fully reveal the diversity of my management experience and the unique contribution I can make to your university. Thank you, Dr. Woolforth, for your time and consideration.

Sincerely,

Paul Patton

Enclosure

169

Director of Professional Services, University. *Daniel J. Dorotik, Jr., Lubbock, Texas*

This letter was a response to an ad. The writer used a Your Requirements... My Qualifications format to draw attention to the excellent match between the applicant and specific ad requirements.

Shemaka Drew
414 Chapel Hill Road Morraine, Georgia 30000 ☎ [678] 555-5555 (Home) sd200@charge.com

Friday, April 9, 2008

Mr. Charles W. Moran
Chairman, Board of Directors
The Wentworth Foundation
2230 Corona Boulevard
Suite 100
Atlanta, Georgia 30000

Dear Mr. Moran:

I want to be the one who translates your vision for The Wentworth Foundation into results as your Executive Director. Over the years, I've done just that for not-for-profit entities that range from a large university to a humane society to a minority arts festival to a science museum to a family and career services provider.

How well did I do? On the next pages, you'll read about some two dozen documented contributions. But I thought you deserved more than a typical resume, with its sterile lists of job titles and responsibilities.

In their place are examples of donors found and retained, funds raised, staff and volunteers inspired, services expanded — in short, everything The Wentworth Foundation should have to be the center of excellence in the field. However, even a specially tailored resume format can't show *how* I've built my track record.

Behind the results is this professional code that guides all I do:

❑ Building financial support is good; keeping financial support growing is better.
❑ Making your organization more visible is good; having it synonymous with its function is better.
❑ Recruiting volunteers is good; keeping them is not only better, it's more fun.

Now I am ready to put all my energy to work for The Wentworth Foundation. However, when it comes to your special needs, words on paper are no substitute for personal conversations. I will call around the middle of next week to hear about your organization's special needs.

Sincerely,

Shemaka Drew

Encl.: Resume

170

Executive Director, Foundation. *Don Orlando, Montgomery, Alabama*

The applicant had many positions during the last few years. The letter refocuses attention away from the applicant's job history and to the benefits the person can bring to the foundation.

JOHN D. HALL

57 Elbe Drive ▪ Crestwood, NY 00000 ▪ (555) 555-5555 ▪ johnhall@msn.com

Case Management/Investigations/Employment/Training/Counseling
Evaluation/Assessment/Field Visits/Reporting/Community Outreach

June 1, 2007

Dear Human Resources Professional:

With a successful 12-year career in the social services and educational fields providing outstanding and dedicated service to youth and adults, it is with great pleasure that I submit my resume to be considered for your **Manager of Family Services** position.

Highlights of my professional qualifications and experience include the following:

- **Managing** a caseload of more than 60 clients in the areas of family services and employment and job-readiness development.

- **Evaluating** and assessing the progress and development of clients through counseling, observation, and employment placement.

- **Conducting** orientations, trainings, and professional development for clients on job readiness and placement, healthcare, family relationships, and finances.

- **Investigating** various types of domestic issues and cases including child and substance abuse, neglect, and residential placement and housing.

- **Developing** ongoing relationships with health institutions, schools, and government agencies to gather and document information for legal proceedings and client progress reports.

I am currently exploring new opportunities within the human services field and welcome the possibility of an interview with you to discuss your current needs and my strong qualifications. I will call next week to schedule an appointment. I look forward to speaking with you and thank you for your time and consideration.

Sincerely,

John D. Hall

Enclosure

171

Manager of Family Services. *La-Dana R. Jenkins, Staten Island, New York*

The writer called attention to this applicant's diverse background in human services to show that he was able to manage a department. Highlights are bulleted and enhanced with boldface.

GEORGE CARRIZALES, EIT

800 Indiana Avenue
Austin, TX 79423

Home: (000) 000-0000
name@msn.com

January 30, 2008

ENERGY Corporation
200 Apple Center
Houston, TX 00000

Dear Hiring Manager:

Please accept the enclosed resume in application for current openings the ENERGY Corporation has available. After researching your company's Web site, I recognized the dedication you have for your clients' best interests and I fully agree with your mission statement in that ***"management of environmental and public health risk is integral to the successful operation of a business."*** I am confident that I could contribute to your organization's and clients' future needs.

My graduate and undergraduate studies at the University of Texas provided me the opportunity to study and analyze key concepts, principles, and practices in environmental engineering. Subsequently, I demonstrated in-depth knowledge of environmental issues and problem-solving strategies through my work in upper-level class assignments and projects. Because I am a strong advocate of continuing education and intend to maintain professional development throughout my career, you can be assured that I will stay on top of emerging, critical environmental matters.

Of course, there is a notable difference between academic studies and practical field experience. While I completed my Bachelor's and Master's degrees, I worked as a Research Associate and Assistant for the University of Texas. In this environment, I learned the importance of precise analysis and attention to detail in field research. Also, I gained experience in examining and solving problems with environmental concerns such as wastewater treatment and brush control. Both my experience and education demonstrate the level of performance I would bring to your organization.

My resume is enclosed to provide additional details concerning my background and achievements. I will call next week to further discuss how I can help your organization achieve its goals. Thank you for your time and consideration.

Sincerely,

George Carrizales

Enclosure

172

Environmental Engineer. *Daniel J. Dorotik, Jr., Lubbock, Texas*

This letter was written in response to an ad. The student conveys convincingly that he should be interviewed despite a lack of strong experience. Boldfacing highlights his agreement with the company's mission.

John J. Doe

333 222nd Place, Seattle, WA 98100
206.333.3333 home // 206.444.4444 cell // JohnDoe@hotmail.com

January 13, 2008

Mr./Ms. _____
Recruiting
Nordstrom Direct
One Union Square
Seattle, WA 98101

RE: Assistant Inventory Manager, Job Code 3333

Dear _____,

I'm writing because I share Nordstrom's core values and genuinely want to work for your company. I value the company's commitment to service and quality, its dedication to its employees, and the exemplary way it conducts business. Wishing to leave a successful career in hospitality, I offer a sound sense of customer service, often-commended initiative, and a track record of teamwork and meeting stated objectives. I'm enclosing my resume for your current position, Assistant Inventory Manager.

In the Nordstom family tradition, my family owned a well-known retail store in Spokane, WA. I was raised to value hard work. Starting at age five, I stocked shelves, moving to managing books and inventories, monitoring profits, making sales, and keeping customers happy, day in and day out. I sincerely want to advance this mutual family tradition, growing customer relationships and profits for Nordstrom. Per my resume, skills matching those listed in the posted job include the following:

➤ **Teamwork and Leadership:** Advanced within current restaurant position to oversee all areas of operations, working cohesively as part of an 8-person team.
➤ **Sales, Goal Achievement and Time Management:** Received numerous bonuses, exceeding sales quotas for an auto-glass installer while attending college.
➤ **Inventory, Delivery Assurance, and Project Management:** Accurately handled ordering, tracking, and delivery assurance for 30 custom jobs simultaneously.
➤ **Management, Initiative and Business Expertise:** Owned a profitable catering company while simultaneously attending school and manning a busy bartending position.

I am confident that my values and personality will fit within your team and meld well with your mission. While I may not have every skill listed in your ad, I'm one who learns quickly, asks pertinent questions, and works efficiently to help my next employer advance competitively. I am commended by supervisors for managing my time well, working positively with the public, and meeting any target put before me. I can offer very positive references, upon request.

I look forward to talking with you to discuss how I can become a contributor to Nordstrom's continued success. Sincere in my wish to join a quality company, I plan to e-mail you next week to check on the status of your hiring process and discuss opportunities.

Thank you for your consideration. I truly feel we have something to talk about and look forward to meeting you soon.

Sincerely,

JOHN J. DOE

173

Assistant Inventory Manager. *Alice Hanson, Seattle, Washington*

The letter did not get an interview for the posted job but did get an interview with a Nordstrom recruiting manager to explore other opportunities. Boldfacing highlights important skills.

SENTA WEIL

555 Hammel Drive Beverly Hills, CA 90210	www.sentaweil.com	Office/Cell: 310/555-5555 senta@weil.com

John Jacob Jingleheimer
555 Michael Drive
Beverly Hills, California 55555
September 7, 2007

Dear Mr. Jingleheimer,

I am a skilled supervisor, trainer, and motivator combining Ph.D., MBA, and JD degrees with extensive service in public, private, and nonprofit venues. I offer an outstanding history of successfully managing projects from conception, through development, to implementation. I am especially skilled at negotiations and strategic planning and am an inveterate problem solver and decision maker with an unexcelled record of reducing operating costs, increasing productivity, and bringing mission-critical projects in on schedule and within budget.

While most people are either dreamers or doers, I am both. I am a compassionate and visionary leader who tirelessly works on many projects to benefit our community by combining a lifelong and heartfelt commitment and dedication to helping others with exceptional communication talents, outstanding interpersonal skills, and a proven ability to convey complex concepts in understandable terms.

Generally recognized as an "idea/strategy" person, I also possess the know-how and wherewithal to implement my ideas. In fact, my entire history is one of creating something where it did not exist before. While I can follow the lead of others, my main value is in creating new and pioneering methods to achieve goals by working the "big picture" and effectively managing staff to assist me. I combine exposure to many experiences, an excellent education, and a self-starting personality to get done what needs to be done.

If you are searching for an innovative leader who will generate growth and profit, please contact me to arrange an interview. I am eager to learn more about the challenges facing your organization and to discuss how I can make a difference.

Sincerely,

Senta Weil

Enclosure

174

Corporate Director. *Janice Worthington, Columbus, Ohio (with Jason and Jeremy Worthington)*

The writing challenge was to provide an all-purpose letter for a position in either a public sector or a corporate environment. The applicant wanted the letter to be generic but also remain powerful.

MARTIN JEWEL

5555 55th Street • Spirit Wind, Oklahoma 55555 • mjewel99@aol.com
(555) 555-5555 (Cell)

....

March 30, 2008

Melissa Brown
Human Resources Coordinator
ACCESSORIES OFFICE SOLUTIONS
7777 55th Street, Suite 99
Oklahoma City, Oklahoma 99999

RE: STORE MANAGER—CENTRAL

Dear Ms. Brown:

As I return to the Oklahoma area, I am considering new career opportunities that would utilize my *management expertise*. A background as owner/operator in competitive customer service markets offers many transferable skills that would *add distinction to any management position*, such as the *ability to recruit and train leaders; motivate others to higher levels; build long-term peer, team, and client relationships; affect superior customer service; and make sound decisions.* The enclosed resume not only demonstrates these skills, but it reflects several major career achievements.

The following **key strengths** also exemplify *highly marketable skills and characteristics.* I possess

- *Functional experience in operations turnaround, marketing and new business development, budgeting and financing, strategic planning and forecasting, and personnel staffing.*

- *Strategic-planning skills that have enabled major improvements through restructuring of company personnel, processes, and goals.*

- *An aptitude for defining problems, pitching and selling ideas, setting timelines, initiating steps, and facilitating positive change.*

- *A talent for selecting, recruiting, training, and retaining top producers.*

- *A management style that promotes integrity, unity, teamwork, shared decision making, support, and recognition.*

- *Honest, straightforward communication techniques that promote development of strong and lasting rapport and trust.*

- *The ability to recognize and develop the potential in every person.*

- *A positive attitude that fosters growth in others.*

An interview to further investigate your needs and my qualifications would be mutually beneficial. I will contact your office within the week to confirm receipt of my resume and to explore convenient appointment times. In the meantime, thank you for your time and consideration.

Sincerely,

Martin Jewel

Enclosure: Resume

....

175

Store Manager. *Edith A. Rische, Lubbock, Texas*

The applicant did not want to display quantitative figures, so the writer focused on the applicant's management expertise and successes. Bullets and boldface highlight key strengths.

VICTORIA L. WILLIAMS

555 Hillcrest Circle • Anywhere, Michigan 55555
(555) 555-5555 • vic_wil@upnet.net

April 8, 2008

Dale Peterson
ABC Corporation
555 Logan Street
Anywhere, Michigan 55555

Dear Mr. Peterson,

My career experience in retail operations management along with working for one of the largest housewares manufacturing companies has provided me great opportunities to demonstrate my strengths in operations management and merchandising while undertaking full P&L responsibilities.

Equally notable are my strengths in developing effective programs and finding creative solutions to meet or exceed corporate objectives. The achievements noted in my resume reflect the most recent contributions I have made to my employer. I am a proactive business leader and manager with a reputation for developing innovative programs, enhancing productivity and efficiency while developing teams that provide bottom-line results.

I am currently exploring new professional challenges and am willing to relocate. I would welcome the opportunity to discuss my background with you further so that I may provide you more detail on the organizational leadership I can offer your company.

Next week I will contact you to see if we can schedule a meeting at your convenience. I look forward to speaking with you soon.

Regards,

Victoria L. Williams

Enclosure

176

Retail Operations Manager. *Maria E. Hebda, Trenton, Michigan*

The four brief paragraphs indicate in turn the applicant's experience and career field, strengths and achievements, willingness to relocate and interest in an interview, and follow-up plans.

CRYSTAL M. DAVIS

2721 Terra Firma Drive, Lawrenceville, NJ 08640
Tel: 609.771.5555 ▪ Email: crystaldavis@bellnet.com

September 2, 2007

Mr. Tom O'Kane
Human Resources Manager
Firmenich Incorporated
P.O. Box 5880
Princeton, NJ 08543

Dear Mr. O'Kane,

Kirsten Alexander of Human Resources suggested that I contact you regarding the open position of **Administrative Manager.** If you have need of a well-qualified professional with **German and French language skills** and experience in office administration, customer service, sales, training, and marketing, then we should meet. My resume is enclosed for your review. Highlights include the following:

☑ More than **eight years of experience** in organization, coordination, communication, and customer service with Devoneaux, an international exporter of consumer goods. Consistent focus on creating and maintaining profitable client relationships. Supervised and trained 15 administrative assistants and customer service reps in stellar client communications.

☑ A resourceful **problem-solver** with a track record of getting positive results, including a record-setting 75% collection rate on accounts 90 days past due.

☑ Ability to **build confidence and trust** at all levels with domestic and international customers, and demonstrated experience in promoting results-oriented environments. Achieved lowest turnover rate for administrative assistants and customer service reps in company's history.

☑ **Proven communication skills,** including fluency in French and German. Up-to-date technology skills in MS Office Suite (Word, Excel, Access, PowerPoint, and Outlook), Internet, e-mail, and multiple peripherals (fax machines, scanners, digital cameras, and printers).

My career success has been due in large part to building supportive relationships and tackling persistent problem areas with creative approaches. I am seeking the opportunity to transition my experience, skills, and enthusiasm into a new organization where I can have an impact on company growth.

I will call your office next week to answer any initial questions you may have and to set up a mutually convenient appointment. Thank you for your consideration.

Sincerely,

Crystal M. Davis

177

Administrative Manager. *Susan Guarneri, Three Lakes, Wisconsin*

The job had been posted for some time before the applicant learned of it. The writer used a third-party reference, bullets, and a testimonial to capture attention. The applicant got the job.

RON BATTISTA

999 Augusta Crescent
Pinestone, Ontario L1N 8G7

Home: (555) 666-4444
Cell: (555) 777-9999

March 3, 2008

Salvatore Bosso
Bosso Associates Inc.
333 Bayfield Avenue
Suite 1550, P.O. Box 16
Pinestone, ON A1A 2B2

<u>**Re: Manager, Technical Services**</u>

Dear Mr. Bosso,

To be a truly effective manager, you have to get your hands dirty.

Throughout my management career, this has a been a major key to my success—getting in the trenches, spotting opportunities for improvement and cost savings, leading the team by example, and knowing firsthand that things are running at optimum levels. If this is the type of manager you're looking for, then I'd welcome the opportunity to speak with you about the contribution I can make.

In recent management positions, I have been responsible for overseeing and optimizing the logistics and operations of expansive, high-volume environments. In every position, I have considered my mandate not only to manage activities, but to find opportunities to improve processes, eliminate redundancies, cut costs, increase revenues, and improve service. The results have been dramatic:

- **Slashed distribution costs by $500,000 for National Review**
- **Inherited district with lowest customer satisfaction rating and turned it around to first place in less than one year**
- **Increased dealers from 600 to 1,150 in less than 7 months**
- **Reduced inventory costs by $16,000 within one year**

I believe I can offer you the very same level of expertise, and I am confident that the results would speak for themselves. I would welcome the opportunity to meet in person to discuss the value I can bring, and I am available for a personal interview at your convenience.

Thank you for your consideration. I will contact you soon to set an appointment for a personal interview.

Sincerely,

Ron Battista

Enclosure

178

Technical Services Manager. *Ross Macpherson, Whitby, Ontario, Canada*

The candidate wanted to convey in the opening paragraphs his hands-on management style. The bullets then communicate strong quantified achievements he has provided for previous employers.

Kerry Green

2307 Freetown Court
Reston, VA 20191

Phone: 703-716-0077
E-mail: kgreen@msn.com

MANAGING DIRECTOR / EXECUTIVE VP
Cross-collaboration ~ Center for the New Workforce ~ Startup & Strategy

*Goal: Leading a startup or de novo in a financial holding company, to facilitate
cross-collaboration across departments, affiliates, and subsidiaries.*

October 10, 2007

M. Evans, President & CEO
Evans Bancshares, Inc.
3600 Lafayette Rd.
Evansdale, IA 50707

Dear Ms. Evans:

*Is your holding company looking for a front-line leader and visionary? Someone who is a profitable personnel and
relationship builder? Someone who can bring Fortune 50 consulting experience to your business challenges and startup?
I am such a person, and I am looking for a company I can help lead to the next level.*

If you hire me as the Managing Director for your newest de novo bank in DC, your business can benefit from all of these skills—
day one:

- **Leadership**—Executive coaching, strategic research, and vision for financial services businesses
- **Strategy**—Track record for niche acquisition strategies and value propositions that grow businesses
- **Operations**—Re-maximize productivity, quality, and service delivery for niche companies
- **Finance**—Ensure retention of employees and customers, and optimal allocation of the corporate resource
- **New Workforce**—Balance people and performance to achieve maximum performance

I can also bring big-company consulting to your small business. I am a trusted advisor and workforce evaluator for the following:

- **Top banks**—Cole Taylor, Barclay's, First Indiana, Sterling Financial, First Rand, Standard Bank of South Africa, the Bank
  of Ireland, the Commonwealth Bank of Australia, and West Pacific
- **Top DC employers**—Discovery Communications, Marriott, Calvert Group, Gazette, Lockheed Martin, and NIH
  (National Institute of Health)

Since your holding company is so in alignment with my skills and experience, I am enclosing a copy of my Executive Portfolio.
It only takes 2 seconds to start a conversation, and 2 minutes to potentially add value. So I will call you within a few days
to discuss any needs you may have for your DC de novo and to hopefully schedule an interview.

Sincerely,

Ms. Kerry Green

Enclosure: Executive Portfolio

179

Managing Director. *Helen Oliff, Reston, Virginia*

In the first paragraph the questions in boldface capture attention for the answer at the end of
the paragraph. Bullets and boldface lead the eye to skills and potential business targets.

Michael Fisher

555 Melody Lane
Hubbard, Ohio 55555
(555) 555-5555

August 30, 2007

Mr. Mark Johnson
Duferco Manufacturing
5555 Youngstown Road SE
Warren, OH 55555

Dear Mr. Johnson:

Throughout my career in manufacturing, I have demonstrated exceptional knowledge of a variety of processes and kept current on changes in technology. Combining technical with management expertise, I am confident I can deliver positive contributions to your company as its next Vice President.

As a manager, I capably direct, motivate, coach, facilitate, train, and coordinate the efforts of multifunctional teams performing multiple assignments and ensuring optimum performance, while keeping an eye on the bottom line. I have strong expertise in managing capital and operating budgets, inventory, cost results, service results, safety issues, customer satisfaction, and labor relations.

I work to identify and implement methods to enhance optimization of production yields and finished product while minimizing downtime and improving scrap management. As a direct result of these efforts, notable results were achieved for several major accounts, leading to increased productivity for numerous parts production per month. Let me share some of these:

1. General Electric *Locomotive Mainframe Casting and Electric Motor Housings*
   - Reduced costs
   - Improved timely deliveries
   - Modified production process
   - Dramatically reduced scrap
   - Visited customer and identified areas where they could use help

2. Siemens *Electric Motor Housing*
   - Slashed costs and scrap
   - Developed new business
   - Designated as contact person for any questions or concerns from the customer

3. Ingersoll-Rand *Air Compressor Castings*
   - Worked on their team to manufacture product to tighter tolerance, allowing them to reduce their machine times while reducing scrap

4. Energy Industries *Gas Booster Compressor Castings*
   - Collaborated with their engineers to reduce leakage problems

At this point in my career, I seek new challenges and look forward to meeting with you to discuss how I can contribute to your company and make a positive impact on your bottom line. In response to your request for salary history, my compensation has been within industry norms for each position, ranging from mid 50s to low 60s, and I assume you will offer a competitive compensation package. Thank you for your time and consideration in reviewing my qualifications in the enclosed resume. I will call you next week to explore the possibility of an interview.

Sincerely,

Michael Fisher

Enclosure: resume

180

Vice President. *Jane Roqueplot, Sharon, Pennsylvania*

The writer showcases the applicant's accomplishments to demonstrate his ability to meet the company's standards and goals. Results are grouped by company and category of parts.

Jon W. Nederstein
0000 Winchester Court, #2B
Alexandria, Virginia 22314-5780
(555) 555-5555

March 22, 2008

Todd Norling
Human Resource Director
Artesia Drilling Equipment Company
14502 Highway 14 East
Stafford, Texas 77700

Dear Mr. Norling:

Over the years, I have seen many examples of great leadership. What separates the truly successful from the rest is a higher level of contribution toward the organization's most important goals. Are you looking for a vice president of operations who can motivate a team to implement plans that not only meet but also exceed growth and financial goals? If so, I am the person who can deliver these contributions.

As you will note on the enclosed resume, the breadth of my expertise covers a wide area of responsibilities. I am a hardworking, ambitious leader and motivator. I am consistently recognized for team building, creative problem solving and a high degree of expertise in the manufacturing field. Would you like to see some of these events take place in your facility?

- Turnover rate of 12% per month brought to 3% per month
- Scrap rate cut 50%
- Increased output threefold
- Profits raised 200% in 2 years

These accomplishments demonstrate what I have done in the past for other manufacturing facilities and can do in the future for you. At your convenience, I would like to meet with you and explore the possibility of using my experience and knowledge to benefit Artesia Drilling Equipment Company. I will call later this week to see if we can arrange an appointment. Thank you for your time and consideration.

Sincerely,

Jon W. Nederstein

Enclosure: Resume

181

Vice President of Operations. *Michele Angello, Aurora, Colorado*

Bullets in the body of the letter emphasize accomplishments that are commented upon in the resume. The text refers to the applicant making the same type of improvements for the next employer.

Brad Atkins

00000 Pinehill Drive
Harrisburg, PA 17101

Office: 555.000.2334
brad@aol.com
Cell: 555.000.0191

[Date]

[Name]
[Title]
[Company]
[Address]

Dear Hiring Manager,

I had an early start to my management career in the trucking services/logistics industry when I launched a truck repair facility in Harrisburg, PA. I grew the shop from a one-man operation to a successful business, serving 100 carrier accounts nationwide. RUAN Leasing Company liked my style, recruited me after I sold the business, and provided me with an avenue to use my talents in managing their Northeast region. Unfortunately, companies reorganize and, in doing so, let go of good people. I have had the misfortune of being one of those "good people" and find myself among the "chosen" to be "RIFed."

If your organization is in need of an Operations Manager with a proven track record in building and leading effective teams that set the standard for preventative maintenance currency, employee commitment to the job, creative approaches to quality improvement, and controlling operational costs, then you should give me a call or email me.

For the last 10 years I have worked remotely from a home-based office and traveled extensively throughout my region to ensure face-to-face, personal attention. With this arrangement in mind, I see no need to confine my search to any particular geographic area. For the right opportunity, I would consider expanding my reach beyond my Western Pennsylvania home base and relocating to a new area.

My resume follows. I will follow up with you next week to further discuss opportunities within your company.

Sincerely,

Brad Atkins

182

Operations Manager. *Norine Dagliano, Hagerstown, Maryland*

This letter was created for posting to online job banks in the logistics industry. The opening paragraph explains why the candidate is a job seeker. The second tells of his worth as a manager.

Richard B. Silverman

3434 Smith Avenue
Newark, NJ 00000
Home (000) 000-0000
Work (000) 000-0000 x0000
name@yahoo.com

January 30, 2008

Ms. Renee Wilson, Human Resources Director
AFA Manufacturing
1111 Lafayette Lane
Trenton, NJ 00000

ATTN: Job Number A-5846

Dear Ms. Wilson:

It was with great interest that I learned of your opening for the position of Operations Manager. I believe I am a worthy candidate for your consideration, with qualifications matching your requirements. Thus, please allow me to explain briefly how I might contribute to your firm's operational and financial performance.

Throughout my career, my expertise has been in leading production operations to profit growth through continual improvement and efficiency. For the past six years, I have built a track record with Builders Depot that demonstrates my ability to lead dramatic profit and organizational growth, indicated through the following sample of highlights:

* Coordinated and executed both improvement and relocation projects, completed on time and on budget, that produced savings ranging from $575,000 to $9 million;
* Forged strategic relationships with vendors and external business partners that enabled quick resolution of problems and positioned Builders Depot for business development and expansion;
* Led departments consistently to multimillion-dollar sales and profit increases through strategic cost-slashing initiatives, workforce performance improvements, and quality-control management.

To provide you with details concerning my qualifications and accomplishments, my resume is enclosed. Thank you for your time and consideration, and please do not hesitate to contact me if I can answer any questions.

Sincerely,

Richard B. Silverman

Enclosure

183

Operations Manager. *Daniel J. Dorotik, Jr., Lubbock, Texas*

Almost all formatting features have been removed from this letter to make it scannable for job search databases. Bullets point to accomplishments. The first is quantified with dollar amounts.

Mark Forbart, Operations Manager

555 Frank Road, Winthrop, MA 02152 ◆ (555) 555-5555
forbartm@yahoo.com

February 15, 2008

ATTN: HR DEPT.
GENCO MANUFACTURING
451 Andover Street
Lowell, MA 01852

Dear Hiring Professional:

In response to your search for a quality Manufacturing Management professional, I bring 8 years of extensive, hands-on experience in Operations. This includes project and facility management, people development, quality procedures and new product development.

I am an extremely high-energy and innovative engineer who leads by example. I consistently produce strong results with a high degree of integrity, dedication and problem-solving skills.

Many of my achievements are due to my ability to create and maintain rapport with individuals within the organization. This quality, coupled with a drive to think analytically and manage deadlines, has given me a track record of success. Some highlights include the following:

- Promoted from Process Engineer to Manufacturing Supervisor to Productions Engineer to Manufacturing Manager to current Operations Manager position within an 8-year time frame
- Succeeded with both ISO 9001 and ISO 9002 programs
- Led new product introduction, pilot plant production and national expansion
- Set up new facilities in record time
- Made several process improvements, inventory-level improvements and reductions in stand product costs
- Hired, trained and developed team of 38 employees with 21 direct reports

My resume and a summary page provide further details of my accomplishments. You will note that I have progressed in responsibility levels throughout my career. I look forward to discussing yet another career opportunity with you. I will contact you next week to arrange a meeting so that we may discuss your company's needs in greater detail.

Sincerely,

Mark Forbart

Enclosure

184

Operations Manager.   *Gail Frank, Tampa, Florida*

The applicant's plant was closing. The writer points out his top accomplishments and emphasizes that he is a "people person" who builds strong relationships and values teamwork and integrity.

Daniel E. Parsons

0000 Shoreham Drive   Charlotte, NC 28211
(H) 555-555-5555 (C) 000-000-0000 e-mail: dparsons@carolina.rr.com

January 6, 2008

Mr. Robert McCaine
Production Manager
BF Goodrich Tire Company
8925 Springsteen Blvd.
Windsor, NY 13865

Dear Mr. McCaine:

Throughout my 19 years of professional employment, I have always been recognized as someone who could *"get the job done."* Being a multitasker who thrives on responsibility and achievement, I excel in a fast-paced, production-oriented environment. Jon Peterson, a mutual friend and colleague, suggested that I contact you to discuss the contribution that I could make to BF Goodrich Tire Company in potential positions at your facility. Your review of my résumé in consideration of my qualifications with regard to these opportunities would be greatly appreciated.

In review of my background, you will note a comprehensive career that spans eight years in the tire industry. Six of those eight years are associated with *Michelin Tire and Rubber.* While my management background is defined by successes in *safety, team building, logistics management, quality and communication,* my operations knowledge is extremely strong in the *curing and final finish* operations. I have directed 100% of operations in curing and final finish, including but not limited to

- Manpower Planning
- Team Building
- Quality Control
- Inspection and Classification
- Warehousing
- Defect Management

As an operations manager and department leader, I believe strongly in giving employees ownership of their work while motivating them to achieve success. *This empowerment model results in an increase in employee retention, loyalty, production, efficiency and safety awareness.*

At this juncture in my career I am seeking the opportunity to transition my qualifications into a high-growth corporation in need of strong leadership. BF Goodrich Tire Company is the corporation I am interested in. An opportunity to personally meet to discuss my qualifications in consideration of the following positions would be greatly appreciated:

- Department Manager
- Shift Coordinator
- Supervisor (willing to enter at this level to prove my potential for growth opportunities)

I am extremely enthusiastic about the possibility of joining the team at BF Goodrich Tire Company, and I can be reached at 555-555-5555 or 000-000-0000 at your convenience. Thank you again for your professional consideration, and I will contact you soon.

Sincerely,

Daniel E. Parsons

Enclosure

185

Operations Manager. *MeLisa Rogers, Victoria, Texas*

This candidate was eager to get his foot in the door and was therefore willing to accept a position of lesser responsibility to prove himself. The writer emphasizes his abilities and proven track record.

STAN MARLEN

Now: 887 Atlantic Ave., Saint Paul, MN 55106
Phone: 651-555-1212 • stanmarlen@gmail.com

After Oct 30: 2307 Freetown Court, Reston, VA 20191
Phone: 703-264-1171 • smarlen@comcast.net

SENIOR DIRECTOR / PROGRAM DIRECTOR
Public Affairs ~ Customer Strategy ~ Government Affairs ~ Marketing

*Goal: A management position involving end-to-end strategy and development,
preferably in a pharmaceutical, healthcare, or education setting.*

October 10, 2007

B. R. McConnon, III
President & CEO
Democracy Data & Communications, LLC
1029 North Royal St., Suite 200
Alexandria, VA 22314

Dear Mr. McConnon:

The true measure of strategists and consultants is their ability to help clients solve difficult problems. Success happens mostly because consultants bring the right ideas to the table— understand the factors for success in a given industry and work closely with their clients to implement positive change. I have a strong track record for doing this.

Could your company use a consultant with a combination of government and business skills—skills developed in the consulting industry while solving problems for public affairs and PAC customers? I am such a candidate. That's why your ad for a Strategic Consultant (on YohConsultant.com) grabbed my attention.

I am looking for an opportunity that will let me leverage my background in healthcare with my experience in strategy, technology, and communication. If you hire me, your company will immediately gain these benefits:

- Critical thinking and directive consultation
- Results-oriented team leadership
- Initiative and perspective from the agency and client side
- Maximum service and satisfaction on $100K+ accounts
- Retention of key customers and relationships year over year
- The ability to sell $25K add-on products—while increasing customer loyalty

From what I know of your business, we should have a lot to talk about. I have done much for coalitions, grassroots organizations, government and public affairs offices, and PACs. I should be relocated to Reston, Virginia, by the end of October… but I will call you next week to follow up and to hopefully schedule an interview. In the meantime, a courtesy copy of my resume is enclosed for you.

Sincerely,

Stan Marlen

Enclosure: Resume

186

Strategic Consultant. *Helen Oliff, Reston, Virginia*

The opening paragraph in boldface indicates the applicant's views about strategists, consultants, and their success. Bullets highlight benefits the applicant can bring to the company.

BETH SMITHEY

000 Reynolds Court	Valrico, Florida 33594	(555) 555-5555	bethsmithey@aol.com

April 9, 2008

Cargill Animal Nutrition
ATTN: Florida Position
P.O. BOX 8250
Montgomery, AL 36108

Dear Hiring Professional:

The Cargill Animal Nutrition management position you advertised recently accurately describes my skills and abilities. I am a professional with a strong track record of success who would love to join your company!

Your Needs	**Examples of My Qualifications**
Team player	◆ Currently a case manager for a juvenile offender release program after completion of boot camp. Have to create a team environment with the juvenile, drill instructor, psychologists, teachers and parents to ensure post-release success. Our program has the highest success rate in Florida.
Adaptability	◆ Ran a retail store and performed any and all functions that had to be completed, from sales to administration to customer service. ◆ Set up and ran a new branch of a company that provided auto financing. Had to adapt rules and procedures to accommodate car dealers and customer needs.
Communication skills	◆ Have developed and given numerous presentations and classes to groups and organizations. ◆ In Human Resources position, gave new-employee orientations, completed and filed paperwork and answered employee questions.
Decision-making skills	◆ All my jobs have required exceptional decision-making ability: from developing case-management and release plans to running a store or managing human resource benefits for employees.
Manage multiple tasks simultaneously	◆ Currently supervise and oversee the cases of up to 30 juveniles who are in different phases of release, simultaneously managing their needs, program plans and paperwork. ◆ Background in Human Resources, where conflict management and multitasking were essential to successful performance.
Conflict-resolution skills	◆ As case manager for a youth offender program, am constantly resolving and mediating conflicts among the juveniles, their parents, the system, teachers and other authority figures.

My resume provides further details of my accomplishments. I look forward to discussing a new career opportunity with you. I will contact you next week to arrange a meeting to discuss your company's needs in greater detail.

Sincerely,

Beth Smithey

187

Project Manager. *Gail Frank, Tampa, Florida*

A poorly worded, "loose" want ad asked for a lot of generic skills. The applicant had little experience in the field. The writer played up the applicant's communication skills and team-player achievements.

David Lee Thompson
6798 Broad Street West, Milwaukee, WI 53202
414-291-5555 Home ▪ 414-220-3333 Cell ▪ dleethompson2@comcast.net

October 11, 2007

Hiring Manager
Carrington Ice Cream Products Company
Dubuque, IA 52001

Re: Regional Licensed Manager
Licensed Stores—Dubuque, IA
Ref ID: 00007311RLM

Dear Hiring Manager,

Your job posting for a **Regional Licensed Manager—Licensed Stores, Dubuque (IA)** on Monster.com demonstrates that your company's values match mine and piqued my interest in contacting you.

As an experienced multiunit retail store operations manager, I am most interested in joining an organization where increasing sales does not take a back seat to quality and customer service. Carrington's reputation for brand standards and integrity, as evidenced in the Carrington "Quality Customer Experience," is renowned. I'd like to be associated with your winning team!

My resume is enclosed for your review. With 10 years of experience in the retail sales industry, my background includes direct sales, sales management, operations management, strategic planning, P&L management, merchandising, buying, team building, marketing and promotions, human resources, and customer-relationship management. I have outlined below how my qualifications match your requirements:

Your Requirements	My Qualifications
1. Progressive sales management experience within a retail environment, merchandising, and influencing others to achieve sales and profitability results—10 years.	1. Ten years of progressive sales management experience in consumer retail industry. Currently on target to achieve **double-digit million-dollar gross margin profits** for 2007. Motivated teams to win district, division, and regional awards and rank in top five (out of 190 stores) in earnings.
2. Progressive experience managing multiunit retail operations—minimum of 3 years.	2. Three years of multiunit retail operations experience, combined with one year of category management experience for **2000 stores and 5 distribution centers**. Track record of gaining trust and buy-in from store directors that contributed to award-winning performances for store sales.
3. Supervision—8 years.	3. Ten years of supervisory experience, including positive team-building and effective change management. Participatory management style has led to **increases in morale, productivity and sales,** while **reducing shrinkage to record lows.**
4. Analysis of financial performance—minimum of 2 years.	4. Full P&L management experience for nine years, overseeing multimillion-dollar operating budgets. Closely monitored cost controls and **captured millions of dollars in cost savings** through careful vendor and product negotiations.

My sales management and retail operations experience has equipped me to drive consumer sales—I would like to do the same for you. May we talk soon? I will call to set an appointment. Thank you for your time.

Sincerely,

David Lee Thompson

188

Regional Licensed Manager. *Susan Guarneri, Three Lakes, Wisconsin*

The numbered, side-by-side comparison chart makes it easy to check off each requirement as met. Phrases in boldface allow for quick scanning of key points and results.

FRANKLIN HARRIS

0000 Park Boulevard • East Syracuse NY 13900
555-555-5555 • fharris@myemail.com

February 10, 2008

Reverend Henry Richmond
President
Onondaga County Coalition of Churches
P.O. Box 857
Syracuse, NY 13909

RE: **Projects Coordinator**

Dear Reverend Richmond:

Your posting from the *Syracuse Daily News* is of great interest to me. In the next month, I will be retiring from the State of New York and am seeking a challenging, rewarding, and flexible opportunity. My resume is enclosed for your review.

Project and program coordination/management have been a staple of my career with the state, beginning in Social Services (Foster Care and Child Protection Services) and concluding in the Division of Parole. Beyond tenure in these departments, I have been an instructor, trainer, and curriculum developer … director of two nonprofit organizations … and the designer and first coordinator of a public school's home/school program. Contributing to my community has always been important, and notable current involvement includes President of the East Syracuse–Minoa Central School Board, Uniform Instructor for the Sea Cadets, and Councilman for the Town of East Syracuse.

Educational credentials earned include a BS in Criminal Science with graduate studies in Social Work as well as Psychology. I am a Certified Peace Officer in line with my Parole Division experience. I have completed diverse professional development as well as training necessary to serve responsibly in several volunteer capacities.

In addition to my well-honed interpersonal and communication skills, positive attitude, and dedication, my familiarity with your service area and established contacts in it would be beneficial. I am very comfortable having accountability for an organization's effective use of its resources and am confident in my ability to contribute positively as your Projects Coordinator.

It would be a pleasure to discuss this opportunity with you in greater detail, and I will contact you later this week to explore the possibility of meeting. I look forward to talking with you soon.

Thank you for your time and consideration.

Sincerely,

Franklin Harris

189

Projects Coordinator. *Salome A. Farraro, Mount Morris, New York*

This applicant wanted to move from a position as state parole officer to a position as projects coordinator for a county coalition of churches. The letter focuses on chief transferable skills.

BART SAVARD

April 10, 2008

Expertise Technology Consultants
ATT: V.P. of Development
565 West Highlands Street
Chicago, IL 60605

Dear Hiring Professional:

In response to your search for a strong technical team member, I bring more than 15 years of experience at IBM. As a Senior Development Manager, I provided the technical, planning and operational management on several key projects for the company. Developing and launching complex computer systems is my expertise.

I am an extremely creative and innovative leader who is always looking for new ways to approach a project. Many of my achievements are due to my ability to create and maintain rapport with individuals—peers, subordinates and management. These qualities, coupled with a drive to think strategically and excellent technical ability, have given me a track record of success. Some areas I can help you with include the following:

- Project management: setting objectives, critical path planning and allocation of resources
- Planning and coordinating test strategies and release analysis
- Problem resolution and creative solutions
- Hiring, interviewing and training
- Budget development, administration and tracking
- Creation and presentations to management regarding project status

I am eager to relocate to your city within the next year and plan to be in town next month interviewing for positions at several companies. I would love to meet with you then and discuss your company's needs and my relevant experience in greater detail. I will e-mail you next week to set a time that we could meet.

Sincerely,

Bart Savard

Enclosure

555 Benoit Circle   Rochester, MN 55901   555-555-5555   savard55@yahoo.com

190

Senior Development Manager. *Gail Frank, Tampa, Florida*

This technical applicant's three-page resume listed his many accomplishments. The letter is purposely nontechnical to emphasize the areas in which he can help a future company at a new location.

PETER SAMUELS

67 Downey Street ■ West Milton, CT 55555 ■ 555.555.5555 ■ petersam@aol.com

[Date]

[Name]
[Title]
[Organization]
[Address]
[City, State ZIP Code]

Dear Mr. or Ms. _____:

During my 10-year career as a public official, I have acquired broad experience and honed diverse skills that I believe will be of interest to the Town of West Milton. My background, highlighted in the enclosed resume, demonstrates that I possess the necessary strategic planning, financial, project, and people management capabilities that would qualify me to serve as your community's Town Administrator.

What do I offer?

- More than 10 years of municipal government experience as a Selectman and Chair governing the Town of Southington, which is complemented by concurrent private-sector management experience.
- Proactive leadership with proven ability to inspire cooperation, communication, and consensus among personnel and other groups.
- Development and administration of $10 million budget as well as planning and overseeing multiple projects to meet community needs.
- Contributing to economic development by building strong public/private partnerships and negotiating agreements.

Examples of my accomplishments:

- Leadership of several town revitalization projects providing key services.
- Negotiating Tax Incentive Financing Agreements for retaining and attracting employers.
- Sound fiscal management that includes improved benefit programs without cost increases.
- Fostering a work environment that builds team spirit and energizes employees to perform at their best. As a result, our staff is recognized for exceptional responsiveness and positive community relations.

This position as Town Administrator is particularly exciting to me for several reasons. As a native of the community, I am familiar with the area's demographics and general issues facing West Milton. In addition, I still consider the community my "home" as I have an extended family living in the area, am a property owner, and would love to be a resident of the community once again.

I have always had a passion for municipal government service and would enjoy making it my full-time career. Therefore, I welcome the opportunity to discuss my qualifications and the contributions I would make as your community's Town Administrator. Thank you for your consideration.

Sincerely,

Peter Samuels

191

Town Administrator. *Louise Garver, Enfield, Connecticut*

The applicant was changing careers from daytime sales management to after-hours town management. The letter focused successfully on accomplishments in municipal government.

CLYDE T. PHELPS

0000 SE Melrose Drive
Lake Oswego, OR 55555
(000) 000-0000
ctphelps@msn.com

April 10, 2008

Mr. David Lawson
Operations Manager
Turner Construction Company
563 NW Pettygrove Street
Portland, OR 55555

Dear Mr. Lawson:

Could your company use a results-oriented problem solver with a thirst for new challenges? As a seasoned **Construction Project Manager/Owner's Representative** experienced in successfully completing diverse commercial construction projects ranging in value from $250K to $40M, I bring

- 10+ years of experience managing successful projects from initiation to completion
- B.S. in Architecture
- Strong commitment to customer service and quality in everything I do
- Exceptional skills in fostering team rapport through direct communication
- Proven ability to develop, monitor, and meet construction deadlines, finishing at or under budget

Here's a sampling of some of my successes:

- Completed construction of $8.5M hotel project three weeks ahead of schedule and $250K under budget, while exporting and replacing 50,000 cubic yards of contaminated soil.
- Maintained a nearly 100% within-budget and on-schedule success rate in completing construction of 12 fast-food restaurants within a 12-month period.
- Reduced time required creating punch lists by 50%. Created and facilitated efficient hotel-room construction inspection process.
- Decreased time required to track and expedite units to jobsite by 50% through development of unique estimating spreadsheet that categorized custom door and window unit types and prices.

Could you use someone like me on your team? If so, I look forward to discussing how my skills and experience could benefit your organization. I will follow up with you by phone in the next week and look forward to speaking with you soon.

Sincerely,

Clyde Phelps

Enclosure

192

Construction Project Manager. *Jennifer Rydell, Portland, Oregon*

The writer developed this "cold" inquiry letter for an applicant with strong experience and accomplishments. Bullets point first to an experience list and then to quantified accomplishments.

FRANK CREESHER
000 South Stewart Way · Sacramento, CA 99999 · (555) 555-5555 · fcreesher@aol.com

March 28, 2008

Thomas Lindsay
Projects Manager
Evinco Metus
1632 Artic Avenue
Sacramento, CA 99999

Dear Mr. Lindsay,

Leading construction management projects for high-growth companies within the microelectronics industry is my area of expertise. I am currently exploring opportunities where I can contribute significant experience in project management—hence, my interest in Evinco Metus.

As you will note on the enclosed resume, the breadth of my expertise covers a wide area of responsibilities, thereby providing me with insights into the total operation. My experience includes microelectronics cleanroom facilities, hazardous occupancies, laboratories and workspaces to support integrated micro systems research and development, as well as production. Allow me to highlight several key projects of particular relevance to Evinco Metus:

- Project Manager for **Command Semiconductor project** (Manassas, VA) through Marrow Contractors, Inc.;
- Senior Project Manager for **Hysteria E-4 Wafer Fab project** (Eugene, OR) through M+W/Marrow joint venture;
- Pre-Construction Manager for **Miasma Technologies Fab 6 project** (Boise, ID) through Morose.

You will find me to be a dedicated project manager who leads by example and is accustomed to a fast-paced environment where deadlines are priority and handling multiple jobs simultaneously is the norm. I have more than 15 years of experience and throughout my career have built a reputation as an individual who takes charge and responsibility for planning and executing challenging projects and for being a talented and determined manager who accomplishes results.

I am confident that the mixture of my work experiences, along with my strong communication skills, would benefit your company. I welcome the opportunity to meet with you to explore how my expertise and talents could best meet the facilities and construction project needs of Evinco Metus.

I appreciate your time and consideration and look forward to speaking with you soon. I will follow up in a few days to explore the possibility of a personal interview.

Sincerely,

Frank Creesher

Enclosure

193

Construction Project Manager. *Denette D. Jones, Boise, Idaho*

The applicant wanted to move from construction management to project management. Bullets and boldfacing highlight key projects relevant to the targeted company, which is mentioned three times.

Lynn Struck   0000 Eagle Drive   555-555-5555
                   Sterling Heights, MI 48310   lynnst@network.net

April 12, 2008

DaimlerChrysler
Employment Division
1000 Chrysler Drive
Auburn Hills, MI 48326

I am contacting you to apply for a production position with Daimler-Chrysler. I have eight years of valuable production experience. My husband, Adam Struck, is a current DaimlerChrysler employee at Warren Assembly. He suggested I send my resume for consideration.

My first production position was with Plastics Research in its Brighton, Michigan, plant. I learned a lot about assembling parts and operating machinery. Since 1998 I have held a seasonal position with Conrad Foods on a packaging line. To say that I'm a hard worker is an understatement. For example, my first summer on the job I packed an average of 3,000–4,000 jars a day (the standard is about 1,200 jars/day). Because of my performance, the next year I was promoted to Crew Leader, the only seasonal employee to hold that position. I get along well with my coworkers and am constantly on the lookout for ways to improve my performance.

I really enjoy the fast-paced production environment, and it would be great to work for DaimlerChrysler. Once you've read my material, I hope you will forward my resume to the specific units that need production workers. I am available for an interview and will call you to find a mutually convenient time. Thank you for your time and consideration.

Sincerely,

Lynn Struck

Enclosure

194

Automotive Production Position. *Janet L. Beckstrom, Flint, Michigan*

The applicant wanted a production position in an automotive plant. She mentioned her husband's name because the company offers hiring preference to those recommended by current employees.

SHANNON HEWLETT

| 0000 Fourth Street | New York, NY 10012 | 555.555.5555 | SHewlett@hotmail.com |

April 3, 2008

Mr. John Wyle
Director of Human Resources
Broadcasting Company USA
30 Madison Avenue
New York, NY 10017

Dear Mr. Wyle:

As an experienced Associate Producer with a steadfast career that reflects several years in responsible positions for major clients across new media production, including HBO and Hewlett-Packard, I am enthusiastic about my decision to move my career in the direction of broadcasting.

I bring an accomplished background that encapsulates my ability to conceive, create, and manage the production of independent and high-profile projects with a sense of purpose and a record of achievement. As a renaissance professional who continues to push the envelope of creativity while meeting the demands of workflow and people-management requirements, I continue to prove my ability to cut through red tape and confusion by providing clarity and direction with a demonstrated combination of intellect, artistic talent, and business savvy.

Whether working on proposals, negotiating with vendors, consulting clients, or traveling cross-country to conduct large group training seminars, I deliver results and secure the respect of senior management based on my high performance level. Through hands-on leadership of cross-functional teams, I maintain a cohesive synergy between clients and production teams from point of planning to market launch of multimillion-dollar projects. My ability to work in the present and anticipate what's ahead continuously ensures that deadlines are met on time and within budget with superior results. It is with your organization that I hope to continue in this vein while taking on new challenges in the field of broadcasting.

If, on reviewing my accompanying resume, you feel there is a mutual interest, I would welcome the chance to meet with you to discuss the possibility of my joining your production team as Associate Producer. Thank you for your time. I look forward to speaking with you soon and will call to set an appointment.

Sincerely,

Shannon Hewlett

195

Associate Producer, Broadcasting. *Ann Baehr, Brentwood, New York*

The applicant sought to move as Associate Producer from one career (in media production) to another (broadcasting). The letter refers to the many areas in which her experience is relevant to the new field.

Jacqueline S. LeFevre

50 Daytona Street
South Palm Beach, FL 50555
(505) 505-5555
jacquil@yahoo.com

December 6, 2007

Mr. Dean S. Arnold
Executive Producer
PBC Studios
5000 Ocean Boulevard
Los Angeles, CA 50005

Dear Mr. Arnold:

- Presenting the images and text that optimally tell the story
- Creatively managing to successful fruition multiple projects with overlapping deadlines
- Achieving a vision that is authentic, innovative, and compelling

These are all key strengths that I can bring to PBC Studios in the role of a media strategist. Meld with this my talent for working with high-level decision makers, including celebrities—and an unwavering commitment to producing work of exceptional quality—and I think you'll find me to be a very well-qualified candidate. In addition to highlights presented on my resume, you'll find me to be

- Skilled in developing a powerful media image (or enhancing one to ensure it is totally on-point). I combine strong visual skills with a creative variety of media formats and applications to develop a compelling media image.
- Talented in capturing the right tone and look of a piece that best conveys the desired message.
- An effective communicator and collaborator. I am able to work at all organizational levels while maintaining confidentiality and sensitivity. I have earned a reputation for successfully garnering project approval by all stakeholders.
- A capable researcher and storyteller. I am skilled in defining the project, succinctly telling the story through impactful visuals, and selecting footage and all creative elements that most effectively present the complete picture.

From 1999 through spring of this year, I worked with Streamline Productions, exclusively handling projects for NBC and serving as the editor and, frequently, series editor for a number of high-profile projects. Since then, I have provided freelance production talent to a number of exciting independent projects. Consistent throughout my career has been an ability to keep a project on time and under budget—while delivering outstanding quality. I'd like to bring this same level of talent to PBC. I believe I can provide a degree of innovation and skill that will augment your existing production capabilities in a very complementary manner. Let's speak later in the week.

Sincerely,

Jacqueline S. LeFevre

Enclosure

196

Media Strategist/Editor. *Jan Melnik, Durham, Connecticut*

With years of experience with a prominent production company that supported a big-three network, this person wanted a key media position with another big studio. Bullets highlight skills.

Jillian K. Young
000 Hawkeye Court   Iowa City, IA 52242   *jkyoung@network.net*
                                                                           555-555-7777

Date

Name
Company
Address

Dear Hiring Manager:

How many times do resumes cross your desk from individuals who have extensive warehouse experience *plus* mail-handling experience? I imagine not a lot. So I hope you will review my material and consider my interest in an appropriate position with your organization.

I gained the bulk of my experience during seven years of service in the military, much of which was as a Supply/Warehouse Manager. Not only did I keep track of 10,000 parts in a 10,000-square-foot depot, but I also coordinated repair requests for equipment and vehicles, processing about 300 work orders per day. Additionally, I have been trained in hazardous materials handling, manual and computerized inventory control, and overall warehouse management. Since I left the military in 1999, I have been a Mail Carrier. One of my periodic assignments is to reduce the accumulation of mail that has been designated *nondeliverable*. It takes research and perseverance, but eventually I whittle down the pile.

My experience in the military cultivated a strong work ethic and helped me develop many personal skills, not the least of which are organization and communication. In fact, my superior officer commended me for my efficient and accurate methods. I have no problems delegating and supervising others.

I will soon be joining my husband in our new home in Cedar Rapids, and I am eager to begin working in the area. I will give you a telephone call to discuss employment opportunities. Of course I can make arrangements to be available for an in-person interview as well. Thank you for your time and consideration.

Sincerely,

Jillian K. Young

Enclosure

197

Warehouse Manager. *Janet Beckstrom, Flint, Michigan*

The applicant had warehousing experience in the Army and worked for the U.S. Postal Service. She could not transfer to a Post Office in her area, so she sought a warehouse management position.

PATRICK M. FINLEY

21 Madison Avenue
New York, NY 10000
Phone: 555-555-5555
Finley1243@msn.com

March 22, 2008

Attention: Mr. Green
ABC Company
15 Green Street
New York, NY 10011

Dear Mr. Green:

Managing and motivating large groups of personnel under high-pressure circumstances while maintaining 100% accuracy is what I do best. I have coordinated and directed groups in excess of 5,000 during complex operations with responsibility for multimillion-dollar equipment, and have consistently received commendation from superiors for outstanding performance.

I chose not to reenlist after 10 successful years with the United States Marine Corps in favor of a civilian career. I am seeking the opportunity to transition my experience into a corporate organization where I can continue to plan, strategize, and direct projects.

The energy, professionalism, and discipline I will bring to ABC Company, paired with my responsiveness to ever-changing business conditions, will streamline operations, improve morale, and ensure continued success. This will positively impact your company's productivity and bottom line.

Although my resume is detailed, it cannot convey the full level of my team-mentality and communication skills. My desire to intensively interact with others has sharpened my ability to quickly build rapport and gain trust from superiors and subordinates. You will find that I am a fast learner who knows both how to give and how to take direction.

I would welcome the opportunity to meet with you to discuss your challenges and my qualifications. I will call in a few days to arrange a time that is convenient for you. In the meantime, if you need more information, please feel free to call me at 555-555-5555.

Sincerely,

Patrick M. Finley

Enclosure

198

Corporate Manager. *Ilona Vanderwoude, Riverdale, New York*

After 10 years in the Marine Corps, this individual wanted to transition to a corporate position. The first paragraph indicates what he did; the third suggests what he might do for the company.

Deputy Director Resource Development

Timothy Cavanaugh
0000 Muroc Drive, Burleson Air Force Base, Texas 00000
☎ 000.000.0000 (Office) — 000.555.5555 (Home) — 999.0000 (DSN)
tim.cavanaugh@burleson.af.mil

Monday, 12 July 2007

Colonel Jordan Cliff
Director of Staff
Headquarters Resource Command
1100 Operations Drive
Burleson Air Force Base, Texas 00000-0000

Dear Colonel Cliff:

Just as you suggested, I have nominated myself for the upcoming GS-14 position that will convert the Deputy DS to a civilian slot. But as I focused on filling out the required resume builder, I became convinced that you deserved a great deal more than just data constrained by character limits of that online form. This package is the result.

Because the next deputy will likely have long-lasting impact on Resource Command, it seemed that two vital pieces of information had to be documented. As a baseline, I had to show my understanding of the kinds of problems I'll be asked to solve. And supporting that baseline had to be vivid examples of my ability to solve similar problems very well.

For the baseline to be valuable, I went beyond the usual consideration of traits or staff skills. I focused on capabilities I must provide to make enduring contributions to the RC mission. You'll find nine of them right at the top of my resume. For proof of capabilities, I had to go beyond just summarizing past problems solved. And so I selected 16 contributions to my organizations that illustrated those capabilities in action.

However, there is some vital information no format, no matter how tailored, can provide. As you read, I hope this central idea stands out clearly: All my efforts are aimed at maximizing long-term returns on every resource investment RC and the Air Force make. I want every tasking, every initiative, to be an opportunity to motivate, lead, and educate others to that same point of view. For me, that vision stands behind every duty, every standard, every KSA, and every classification criterion that might appear in the job announcement.

It's difficult for me to be distracted from the daily business of Resource Command, particularly when that distraction requires me to focus on myself. Therefore, if I have overlooked any information you need, I know you will not hesitate to call on me.

V/R,

Timothy Cavanaugh, Colonel, USAF

Atch: Resume

199

Deputy Director, Resource Development. *Don Orlando, Montgomery, Alabama*

This retiring senior Air Force officer wanted to stay on in his position as his own civilian replacement. Some Air Force jargon is evident in the letter. For example, "V/R" means "Very respectfully."

Marissa Hagan

509 Simmons Avenue
Parkersburg, WV 26101

(304) 555-2222
marissahagan@wahoo.com

August 4, 2007

Roberta Vickers, Director
Ritchie County Center for the Developmentally Disabled
475 Brookview Terrace
Parkersburg, WV 26101

Dear Ms. Vickers:

My dream of becoming an occupational therapist began while I was still in high school as a volunteer at the Ritchie County Center for the Developmentally Disabled. My older sister, Claire, who was born with Down syndrome, is a resident at one of your group homes. I am amazed at what she has been able to accomplish because of the patience and guidance of your wonderful staff. From seeing her progress, I was convinced that occupational therapy was the right career for me.

Having recently received my associate's degree and COTA certification, I am now qualified as an occupational therapy assistant. As you will note from my resume, my training included internships at a nursing home, a rehabilitation facility for brain injuries, and a school for special-needs children. However, my most rewarding experience was at the County Center, where I observed how the therapists assist patients in learning how to lead independent, productive lives. The aspect that is most appealing to me is working with high-functioning adults, such as my sister, who today is able to take public transportation, hold a job, and balance a checkbook. While these are ordinary things we all take for granted, for someone so challenged, they were major achievements.

During my training, I helped various patients increase their strength, manual dexterity, and coordination. Also, through the use of games, puzzles, and computer activities, my patients learned to improve mentally in the areas of memory, perception, decision making, abstract reasoning, and sequencing. Noticing even their slightest gains was extremely gratifying to me.

Besides a genuine desire to help people, I possess additional attributes for success, which include patience, compassion, enthusiasm, creativity, and abundant physical stamina. Nothing could give me greater career satisfaction than to further develop my occupational therapy skills at the County Center. I am available for an interview at your convenience and will call to set up an appointment.

Sincerely,

Marissa Hagan

Enclosure

200

Occupational Therapist. *Melanie Noonan, West Paterson, New Jersey*

After getting an associate degree and certification, the applicant wanted a position at the center where she had been an intern and her sister is a resident. The letter displays concern.

Keith Robinson

73 Meadows Lane
Milwaukee, WI 53203
Residence (414) 555-1111
Mobile (414) 555-1010

April 16, 2008

Mr. Albert Gordon
President
Gordon Chemical Company
2060 Route 93
Milwaukee, WI 53203

Dear Mr. Gordon:

Because I understand your concern for the safety of your employees as well as the preservation of the environment, I am writing to you at the suggestion of your plant manager, Mr. John Baynes. You may recall I was the OSHA inspector who visited your workplace on March 27 and was escorted around the building and grounds by Mr. Baynes. As you have probably seen from my report, there are several violations that need to be abated.

When I asked about your safety policies, Mr. Baynes told me that it has been almost two years since they were updated and enforced. He mentioned at one time you had an environmental health and safety manager on your staff, who attended to these matters. However, his position had not been replaced since he left your company, which is my real reason for this letter and enclosed resume. Since your plant manager cannot be everywhere at once, it is obvious that you need someone to fill this vacancy, and I'd like you to know I am a very interested candidate.

My assignments with OSHA have concentrated on the operations of chemical and biomedical facilities, which produce a significant amount of hazardous waste. In addition to business acumen, I have the required knowledge of EPA laws, chemistry, natural sciences, human anatomy, physiology, and math to be effective on the job. Coming from a government agency that most employers regard with trepidation, I have a keen awareness of what needs to be done to bring your workplace up to regulatory standards.

From my tour of your facility, courtesy of Mr. Baynes, I noticed quite a few ways I could make some immediate improvements as well as initiate programs to avoid fines, control accidents, and ultimately reduce your insurance premiums in the future. With your best interests in mind, I will contact you as to when we could get together to discuss my ideas.

Sincerely,

Keith Robinson

Enclosure

201

Environmental Health and Safety Manager. *Melanie Noonan, West Paterson, New Jersey*

Reference to a third party and a previous visit by the applicant helps to gain the reader's attention. The applicant presents his possible services as a solution to unresolved problems.

Patrick D. Wilder

11 Monroe Street, Salt Lake City, UT 55555
(555) 555-5555 home   patrickw@prodigy.net   (555) 555-5555 cell

March 25, 2008

Todd Hazeltine
Safety and Health Management
St. Jude's Hospital
16 Rock Lane
Salt Lake City, UT 55555

Dear Mr. Hazeltine:

The purpose of this letter is to introduce myself and then to meet with you about the opportunity for me to provide my expertise in managing safety and health programs to your organization. My confidential resume is enclosed for your review, and I am certain that you will find me very well qualified. Highlights of my resume include

- More than 20 years of experience in Occupational Health and Nursing
- Significant expertise working with OSHA regulations and regulatory compliance
- Ability to develop, conduct and oversee safety and health programs
- Effective communication, preparing technically sound reports, including recommendations for correction of hazards

My professional background, along with my sincere interest in helping others, has enhanced my desire to excel. As a highly motivated professional, I enjoy the challenge of complex, demanding projects.

I am available to meet with you to discuss my qualifications at your convenience and will call to schedule a meeting. I would like to thank you in advance for your time and any consideration you may give me. I look forward to hearing from you.

Sincerely,

Patrick D. Wilder

Enclosure

202

Occupational Health and Safety Professional. *Denette D. Jones, Boise, Idaho*

Bullets point to resume highlights concerning the applicant's experience, areas of expertise, field-related skills, and communication skills. The rest of the letter shows his motivation and interest.

Cathy Carter
321 Maple Way
Big Lake, IL 00000
555-555-5555 cellular
ccarter@hotmail.com

Date

Mr. George Pappas
Manager
Extreme Workout World
555 Central Avenue
Chicago, IL 00000

Dear Mr. Pappas:

In response to the opening you posted for Fitness Instructor, I have enclosed my resume for your review. I understand that this position requires customer service skills and experience in leading fitness programs, and I believe I have the qualifications you seek.

Having spent the past year learning how to develop sales in the business technology industry, I am now ready to return to the field of fitness—an area I have been passionate about for a long time. In my search, I am targeting positions that will use my knowledge of fitness products and training techniques and my skills in business writing, customer service, and group leadership. I would appreciate the opportunity to discuss how my skills can help you meet the challenges you face in 2007 and beyond.

I will contact you soon to explore the possibility of an interview. Thank you for your time and consideration.

Sincerely,

Cathy Carter

Enc.

203

Fitness Instructor. *Christine L. Dennison, Lincolnshire, Illinois*

The applicant wanted to move to the fitness industry—her real passion—after unsatisfying work in business technology sales after college. The letter stresses skills. See corresponding Resume 7 in Part 3.

BRIE MCALLISTER

42 Southbury Road, Sandgate Qld 5555
M: 5555 555 555 • **E: bmca@intercon.com**

14 March 2008

Ms T Mason
Fitness Works
1/14 Groves Avenue
South Brisbane Qld 4001

RE: OPPORTUNITY AS PERSONAL TRAINER

Dear Ms Mason

<u>Consistently Achieve Top Ten Out of 350 Nationwide</u>

<u>2005 Training Coach of the Year Nominee</u>

To achieve these results there can be only one reason—a consuming passion for personal training!
Working within the health industry and with individuals to sell, promote, and educate on a product or program that is beneficial—this has been my lifeblood.

Throughout my career, building outstanding customer rapport and securing the sale has been a major source of challenge and achievement for me. My enclosed resume details my career thus far, but I am keen to draw your attention to the following highlights that meet with your criteria:

☆ **Built my own territory within the club from zero to 150 clients within 12 months.** As you would know, this is regarded as an outstanding achievement in our challenging, competitive industry.

☆ **Approach rejection with a proactive attitude,** reassessing, asking for feedback, and formulating a new angle of approach. This philosophy, combined with my ability to interact with individuals on all levels within a team environment or autonomously, and the adrenalin I draw from challenging environments, has ensured my ongoing success and the club's bottom line.

☆ **Utilise motivational and management aptitude** to work with new trainers to advance their communication and selling skills and build a strong client base. When one succeeds, we all succeed!

I believe in really listening and showing the customer respect, finding that this always brings its own rewards in trust, open communication, and increased sales. I have also always believed in hard work, loyalty, and consistently working to the highest standard of professionalism. I am confident that these innate belief systems, in conjunction with my ability to rapidly assimilate new information and techniques, position me as an ideal candidate for your advertised role of Personal Trainer.

Thank you for your time and consideration. I earnestly hope that we can meet soon to discuss this exciting opportunity.

Yours sincerely

Brie McAllister
Encl: resume

204

Personal Trainer. *Beverley Neil, Victoria Point West, Queensland, Australia*

Energy and motivation are paramount in personal training, so the writer showcased these attributes of the applicant, as well as her professional expertise and outstanding success rate.

ANGELA S. FAGAN
333 South Street ▪ Philadelphia, PA 19111
Home: (555) 999-3333 ▪ Mobile: (555) 444-1111 ▪ e-mail: afagan@aol.com

January 29, 2008

Ms. Rose Mayer, Director
Celebrity Associates, Inc.
44 Lake Road
Malvern, PA 19484

Dear Ms. Mayer:

I was excited to discover fabjob.com. I've known for some time that a 9 to 5 job wasn't the right fit for someone with my background and personality, and I would like to explore the possibility of becoming a Celebrity Personal Assistant.

The Guide certainly clarified the unique skills and expectations of a Celebrity Personal Assistant. Many of the qualifications mirrored my responsibilities as Entertainment/Promotions Coordinator for Harrah's Entertainment. On any given day, I had multiple balls in the air—from coordinating arrangements for celebrities (lodging, transportation, meals) to selecting costumes and overseeing myriad administrative duties associated with a popular entertainment site. I had an excellent reputation for putting out fires and going the extra steps to achieve success. Flexibility and the ability to remain calm were the key elements that allowed me to function effectively in such a high-pressure environment.

On an administrative level, I am very organized and meticulous. Careful follow-up is important when coordinating special events and projects, particularly when you are involved with senior-level executives and celebrities. Of course, it goes without saying that I am familiar with various technology and equipment, including a Blackberry, since my background has always involved administrative duties.

Wearing multiple "hats" keeps my daily calendar at maximum capacity, an environment in which I tend to flourish. Overall, I feel my organizational skills and my ability to handle different personalities with varying degrees of understanding and maintenance, regardless of the time element involved, would serve me well as a Celebrity Personal Assistant.

Would you allow me to formally introduce myself? I am very interested in expanding my professional horizons and eager to discuss a future association.

I can be available at your convenience with somewhat minimal notice. My employer is not aware I am contacting you, however, so I would appreciate your confidentiality. A complete resume is enclosed for your review.

Thank you in advance for your consideration.

Sincerely,

Angela S. Fagan

Enclosure

205

Celebrity Personal Assistant. *Karen Conway, Media, Pennsylvania*

Each paragraph conveys the applicant's enthusiasm toward becoming a Celebrity Personal Assistant. Her organizational skills, technological expertise, and evident maturity temper well her excitement.

Kathryn Tamburro

0000 66th Avenue North ✦ Frankfort, NY 00000 ✦ 555.555.5555

April 2, 2008

The Ritz-Carlton
3000 Central Florida Parkway
Orlando, FL 32837

Dear Employment Specialist:

I am writing to express my interest in the esthetician position that is posted on your Web site. I was very interested to see this opportunity as my background and qualifications match the requirements outlined in the posting. My goal is to relocate to the Orlando area and secure a position where I can utilize my esthetic training and sales experience.

As you will see from the enclosed resume, I am a newly licensed esthetician (New York State). Since earning my certificate, I have been working in an upscale salon in Millbrook, NY—an affluent town outside New York City. Working in this salon has helped develop my business competency and enhanced my knowledge of service delivery for high-end clientele. In addition to my certification and licensure, I hold a bachelor's degree from Vassar College in Poughkeepsie, NY.

The value I bring to the Ritz-Carlton is not only a broad-based background, but a strong business sense and creative flair. More importantly, I know how to comport myself with high-profile clientele and understand the level of service required from clients seeking world-class spa treatment.

While my esthetic training emphasized specialized techniques and provided exposure to the most up-to-date methods (influenced by Manhattan's progressive market), I also gained valuable product sales experience through the school's operational storefront. Working in the store sharpened my sales, marketing and general business skills. It also contributed to my understanding of the financial impact of daily decisions as well as an awareness of the importance of maintaining positive customer relations.

I am confident that these qualifications will enable me to make immediate contributions toward your overall service goals. I would be happy to make myself available for a personal interview at any time and will call to inquire about a mutually convenient time. Thank you in advance for your time and attention. I look forward to meeting with you.

Sincerely,

Kathryn Tamburro

Enclosure

206

Esthetician. *Kristin M. Coleman, Poughkeepsie, New York*

A task of this letter is to show an upscale employer that the applicant is suitable for the employer's clientele. Every paragraph indicates that she is more than a match for high-profile clients.

Richard Chisholm

15 Clubhouse Drive
Stony Point, NE 00000

(000) 000-0000
richpix@verizon.com

March 10, 2008

Mr. John Ambrose
News/Picture Assignment Editor
Seward Daily Journal
229 West Rugby Street
Seward, NE 00000

Dear Mr. Ambrose:

As a follow-up to our phone conversation, I am very interested in joining your photo department in a part-time photography position, eventually leading to full-time employment. As you review my resume, please note that I have thorough technical knowledge of shooting and editing as well as a creative personal style to envision and tell a story through the lens.

In the photo-intensive environment of a newsroom, I know the importance of teamwork and the ability to adapt to different formats. I am also accustomed to the pressures of constant deadlines and dealing with temperamental personalities. When problems arise, I remain calm, think clearly, and resolve the issues as quickly as possible. In addition, my flexible schedule will allow me to be available on holidays or at other times you may be shorthanded.

If you are seeking candidates who have a strong passion for photojournalism and subscribe to high NPPA standards, I would appreciate your consideration of my qualifications. I am confident that I can make a significant contribution to your photo department and look forward to discussing potential employment.

Sincerely,

Richard Chisholm

Encl. Resume

207

Photographer. *Melanie Noonan, West Paterson, New Jersey*

This applicant wanted to give the impression of being someone with creative talent. The writer chose a nonconventional font to convey the idea that his photographer had aesthetic taste and was flexible.

HAROLD VEETER
000 Tidewater Road
Springfield, MA 00000

(555) 555-5555

HARVT@home.com

February 4, 2008

Mr. Fred Jones
Director of Procurement
Technologies Corporation
3229 Polumba Drive
Springfield, MA 01087

Dear Mr. Jones:

During a recent conversation with Paul Browning, he suggested that I contact you about my interest in a procurement position in your department. Although you may not have an opening at this time, I would welcome the opportunity to learn more about your procurement function and industry.

As you may know from Paul, I recently sold my business and am enthusiastic about the prospect of new challenges. In anticipation of the business closure, I have taken the time to evaluate my career interests, skills and strengths to determine my options.

Procurement was one of my primary responsibilities and a function I enjoyed tremendously. As a result, I have decided to pursue a search in this field. Briefly, my qualifications include a bachelor's degree plus 10 years of experience in supplier/broker relations, cost-effective contract negotiations and managing a multimillion-dollar purchasing volume.

Well-organized with excellent communication and interpersonal skills, I am confident in my ability to add value to an organization. My conversation with Paul reaffirmed my interest in your company, and I look forward to meeting with you to explore the possibilities in relationship to your department's needs. I will call next week to further discuss opportunities with your company.

Sincerely,

Harold Veeter

Enclosure

208

Procurement Position. *Louise Garver, Enfield, Connecticut*

The individual wanted to make a career change and used this letter to obtain a networking meeting that ultimately led to a job offer. The purpose of networking is made clear in the first paragraph.

ELIZABETH GREEN

5555 Oak Tree Lane • Northridge, CA 55555
(555) 555-5555 • egreen@email.com

[Date]

[Name]
[Address]
[City, State ZIP]

Dear _____:

If you are seeking a motivated and detail-oriented Purchasing Professional with a proven ability to streamline operations, motivate teams and achieve significant cost savings in a multimillion-dollar environment, then my enclosed resume should be of interest to you.

Common themes that have run throughout my professional career have been outstanding team-building and leadership strengths as well as my ability to see the "big picture"—integrating the purchasing function into corporate goals. Representative of my past accomplishments are the following:

- Directed $200 million purchasing unit for West Coast Entertainment Company...
- Hired, trained and motivated top-performing team members...
- Consistently identified and developed talent in others...
- Employed technology to streamline procedures, including automating the download of purchasing orders to the Letter of Credit system, improving on-time issuance from 20% to 75% within two years...
- Consolidated supplier base from 1,200 to 650 within one year...
- Sourced and developed excellent working relationships with outside and internal vendors...
- Participated in key negotiations...

I am currently seeking a new professional challenge where I can make a positive contribution to future goals and success. I possess a high level of energy and motivation, learn quickly, adapt well to new environments and enjoy challenges. I look forward to a personal meeting, at which time we can discuss your needs and my qualifications in detail. I will call you to set up a meeting. Thank you in advance for your time and consideration.

Sincerely,

Elizabeth Green

Enclosure

209

Purchasing Professional. *Vivian VanLier, Valley Glen, California*

The middle paragraph with bulleted accomplishments is the key paragraph in this letter. Quantified representative achievements sell the reader on the superior worth of this candidate.

GARRY FUNG

1234 Augusta Crescent
Pinehurst, Ontario A1A 1A1

Phone: (555) 333-7777
Email: gfung@email.com

January 24, 2008

Joseph Neiman
Chief Technology Officer
Sandoz Investments
123 Young Boulevard, Suite 2305
Pinehurst, Ontario

Dear Mr. Neiman,

- **Is your organization fully prepared to safeguard its technology services, information, and facilities in the event of a disaster?**

- **Are you taking full advantage of high-value and cost-effective vendor agreements?**

- **Do you benefit from high team performance and low turnover?**

If you answered "No" to any of the above questions, then allow me to introduce myself and the expertise I can offer your organization. With a proven and award-winning track record of achievement, I offer a unique combination of expertise in disaster recovery/business continuity planning, vendor management/negotiations, and team leadership. I am currently offering my services to organizations within the Durham region and would like to draw your attention to the value I offer.

Put simply, my expertise is delivering results. In previous positions, I have designed, implemented, and optimized comprehensive enterprise-class disaster recovery and information security procedures, saved millions in vendor negotiations and third-party service agreements, and led a variety of cross-functional teams to consistently achieve and exceed organizational mandates.

If the following interests you, I invite you to review the attached resume, which further illustrates my experience, achievements, and expertise:

- **Expert in disaster recovery, information security, and business continuity**—expertise includes planning, protection, and off-site recovery of technology services, databases, and facilities

- **Superior contract procurement, negotiation, and vendor-management capabilities**—proven record for negotiating agreements that improve service quality and save millions in vendor costs

- **Strong, decisive, and motivating leader**—reputation for building and leading high-performance teams to breakthrough achievement

- Available for **full-time, part-time, contract, and consulting opportunities**

If you believe that you could benefit from a highly motivated and talented professional with a reputation for generating results, I would welcome the opportunity to meet and discuss the specific value I can offer your organization.

I thank you for your consideration, and I look forward to speaking with you soon. I will call you to set an appointment.

Sincerely,

Garry Fung
Enclosure: Resume

210

Vendor Contract Negotiator. *Ross Macpherson, Whitby, Ontario, Canada*

This candidate offered a variety of expertise, so this broadcast letter opens with a few questions to get the reader thinking. The candidate landed five interviews and a lucrative contract in six weeks.

WALTER E. ELLIS
75 Clover Street
Rochester, New York 14610-4261
555-555-5555 (Home) / 000-000-0000 (Cellular)
walteree@rochester.rr.com

February 27, 2008

Mr. B. Thomas Golisano
President & CEO
Paychex, Inc.
911 Panorama Trail, South
Rochester, New York 14625

Dear Mr. Golisano:

Capitalizing on a career that encompasses broad-based experience in brand marketing, public relations, and customer relations, I am seeking an opportunity to apply these skills in a marketing communications position that will offer the potential for advancement based on performance. I believe that I possess knowledge and expertise that can be an asset to your firm and have, therefore, enclosed for your review a résumé that outlines my professional background.

Some key points that you may find relevant to a marketing communications role with your organization include the following:

- *Identifying target audiences and developing marketing messages that reach those audiences. In both business-to-business and consumer products settings, I have been successful in researching potential market segments and creating strategies that effectively communicate product features and promote brand awareness.*

- *Implementing innovative, technology-based approaches to marketing, including championing e-commerce initiatives that both augment product sales and afford opportunities to gather information about customers.*

- *Spearheading public relations efforts that coordinate with marketing strategies and advance overall business goals. These have included placement of features in both electronic and print media, participation in high-profile public events, and implementation of "strategic philanthropy" initiatives.*

- *Directing an array of brand management activities, which have encompassed graphic design; copy writing; and production of collaterals, point-of-sale materials, and product packaging.*

I am confident that my experience, education, and enthusiasm will allow me to make a meaningful contribution to your ongoing business success. I would enjoy meeting with you to discuss in detail how my capabilities can best serve your marketing communications needs. Please contact me to arrange a mutually convenient date and time when we might initiate a dialogue.

Thank you for your time and consideration. I will contact you soon to set up an interview.

Sincerely,

Walter E. Ellis

Enclosure

211

Marketing Communications Position. *Arnold G. Boldt, Rochester, New York*

The applicant was transitioning from a marketing position with a small firm to a corporate setting. The challenge was to show that his marketing skills were transportable to a corporate environment.

Tina Nestavez

| 0000 W. Inman Ave. | Tampa, FL 33609 | (555) 555-5555 | t.nestavez@juno.com |

March 20, 2004

Mr. Gary Frank
Director of Marketing
Nike, Inc.
One Nike Drive
Seattle, Washington 98744

We hope Tina joins our team!

Dear Mr. Frank:

"Just Do It." That is what I said to myself after hanging up the phone with my friend Jim Heald. He had just described his conversation with you—about needing a new public relations person in Brazil. I had to write after hearing your requirements! Jim said they are the following:

YOUR NEEDS	MY EXPERIENCE
Communicate in Portuguese and Spanish	✓ Fluent in reading, speaking and writing Portuguese, Spanish and English ✓ Translated an entire book from Portuguese to English ✓ Lived, worked and studied in Brazil
International Experience	✓ B.A. in International Relations ✓ Currently have 100% travel job with extensive foreign travel ✓ U.S. citizen who has lived in Brazil, Japan, Australia and Africa
Public Relations/Liaison/ Communications/Sports Experience	✓ Completed Sporting Goods Analysis on Brazil's economy for U.S. Department of Commerce ✓ Effective multiorganizational liaison as a relief worker in Africa ✓ Resolve ongoing public relations and communications challenges as the "flight attendant in charge," American Airlines

My enclosed resume provides further details of my accomplishments and experience. I look forward to reviewing them with you. I will call you in a few days to see if we can meet next week to discuss how I can help you meet the goals for "Brasil futebol." I'm ready to go!

Sincerely,

Tina Nestavez

Enclosure

212

International Publicist. *Gail Frank, Tampa, Florida*

This letter is an update of the version that appeared in the first edition of this book. The applicant needed a letter that made her stand out. The check marks under My Experience serve as a "YES!" for each qualification.

Emily Everly

1 N. Jackson St.
Racine, WI 22222
(333) 333-3333
(444) 444-4444
eeverly@someemail.com

Re: Marketing & Communications Associate

November 23, 2007

Dear Hiring Manager:

I am interested in the <u>Marketing and Communications Associate</u> position available within Hephert International, Inc. As you can see in my attached resume, I have almost 8 years of experience in a social service position where I am intensively involved with training, volunteerism, and marketing/ public relations. I have been seeking to transition into a corporate environment but wanted to locate an organization with a "heart." After reading the *Comfort stories* and *Being magazine* on your website, I'm intrigued. I would love to talk with you further about how I may fit in at your organization.

I understand that you are looking for someone who can promote, coordinate, and document the volunteer activities of your staff members. I believe my position as a Resource Specialist at Lake County Workforce Development has perfectly equipped me to do that! I serve as an interagency and community liaison for our organization and promote the organization via the website and a biannual newsletter. I also regularly attend and assist with the coordination of community events. The position requires meticulous documentation of confidential information and an ability to clearly communicate with diverse individuals.

Thank you for reviewing my resume. I would love to speak with you personally and will contact you next week.

Sincerely,

Emily Everly

213

Marketing and Communications Associate. *Eva Locke, Waukegan, Illinois*

The applicant had no specific experience in the position for which she was applying. The letter addresses her reason for transitioning and describes her transferable skills.

Katherine Lacey Elliot

999 Kettlepond Circle
Salesbury, CO 22222

(000) 999-6666
Cell: (000) 999-9898
kathy5@earthlink.net

February 12, 2008

Susan Mary Anthony, Human Resources Manager
ABC Advertising Corporation
000 Weybosset Street, Suite 1000
Whitehead, CO 55555

Dear Ms. Anthony:

Your advertisement in the *Whitehead Sunday Globe,* February 11, 2008, for a copywriter to work in ABC's media relations department excited me, for this position would fulfill my ideal goal. Although a recent college graduate, I believe that my experience and academic training may be just what you are seeking in a candidate to fill this post. Please note that my enclosed resume illuminates my practical field experiences in written communication.

As an English major at Newberg State College, with a concentration in writing, I have worked beyond traditional courses of study by planning and completing independent study projects that took place here and abroad. My cross-cultural studies in Ireland have given me not only a better understanding of education and business in Europe, but also a more global vision of the world marketplace and the tremendous influence that America exercises there. In addition, I would like to share my research article on psychology and the media.

Another independent-study project that has strengthened my base of preparedness for employment in communications was in journalism at *The Salesbury Citizen News.* You may be interested in looking over my portfolio of samples as evidence of substance and style in written communication. I believe that I have excelled in working independently to plan and execute programs on my campus radio show, although I learned that cooperating in teams often brought about stimulating ideas and results.

If you agree that my qualifications meet your standards for this position in the media department, please contact me to make an appointment for an interview at a time convenient to you. I can be reached at my telephone or cell phone, both equipped with voice mail. Thank you for considering my application; I look forward to meeting with you soon.

Sincerely,

Katherine Lacey Elliot

Enclosure: resume

214

Copywriter, Advertising. *Edward Turilli, North Kingstown, Rhode Island*

This entry-level job seeker indicates her wide experience in communications and zeal to enter this field. Her time in Ireland points to her global awareness as an edge over traditional competitors.

Tim K. Petersen

0000 Groveland Avenue ♦ Kalamazoo, MI 49004 ♦ 555-555-2222 ♦ tkpetes@network.net

March 5, 2008

Mr. Roger Sanderson
National City Bank
3291 Westnedge Avenue S.
Kalamazoo, MI 49008

Dear Mr. Sanderson:

Marjorie McCarthy suggested I contact you regarding the Public Relations Manager and Communications Specialist positions that were recently posted on your Web site. When you have a chance to review the enclosed resume, you will see that I meet or exceed the qualifications for both positions.

You will notice that over the last 15+ years I have worn many hats. Because the organizations with which I was associated were small, I was responsible for everything from writing press releases to community outreach, grant writing to marketing, and fundraising to budget management. The common thread among these responsibilities: **communication.** Putting the organization's best foot forward was always the priority. I believe my accomplishments (described on my resume) reflect my ability.

My personal assets lend themselves to your positions. For example, you will find that I am

- ♦ Highly organized (I had to be to wear all those hats!)
- ♦ An accomplished writer (newsletters, marketing material, scripts)
- ♦ A strategic thinker (erased red ink and turned a significant profit in 3 years)
- ♦ Versatile (all those hats, remember?)

That's why I am confident I can become a successful team member of National City's Communications/Marketing Department. I hope you'll give me an opportunity to speak with you personally so I can elaborate on my qualifications and motivation. I will call you next week to set up a meeting at your convenience. Thank you for your consideration and I'll look forward to hearing from you.

Sincerely,

Tim K. Petersen

Enclosure

215

Public Relations Manager/Communications Specialist. *Janet L. Beckstrom, Flint, Michigan*

The applicant was transitioning from work primarily in a nonprofit arena to work for a for-profit organization. The second paragraph displays a variety of experience from which he could draw.

Jonathan Crosswilt

0000 S.E. Mountain Road
Milwaukie, Oregon 99999

(555) 555-5555

January 28, 2008

Trailblazers, Inc.
555 NE MLK Blvd.
Portland, Oregon 99999

Dear Hiring Executive:

I appreciate this opportunity to apply for the position of *Executive Director of Communications* for the Blazers. Enclosed is a copy of my résumé, which shows that I have obtained outstanding experience in a variety of areas, including expertise in communications and public relations.

With more than 26 years of business experience, I have developed strong communication techniques and a unique ability to work effectively with the media. As a successful business owner, I have had the direct responsibility for planning and directing all aspects of the business, developing policies and procedures, and detailing strategic plans. I also have a strong background in promoting concepts while at the same time securing a strong position in the market. While working with Tim Owen's Autogroup, I was responsible for the organization and public relations relating to sponsored auto races at Portland International Raceways, including working with celebrity guests such as Paul Newman.

In working with various basketball teams over the years, I have had the privilege of developing teams from scratch, promoting the team concept to various school districts, and marketing the sport to the public. You will find me to be highly energetic, diplomatic, and results-oriented with a history of success that will support my achievements.

Needless to say, submitting a brief review on paper does not give you a complete picture of my abilities. I would very much like the opportunity to meet with you personally to detail more in depth the qualifications I can share with your organization. I believe that your requirements and my skills are a close match. I will call to set up an interview time.

Sincerely,

Jonathan Crosswilt
Enclosure

216

Executive Director of Communications. *Rosie Bixel, Portland, Oregon*

The opening paragraph indicates the targeted position and focuses the applicant's expertise. Experience is the topic of the second and third paragraphs. The fourth is an interview request.

Diane C. Cartwright

0000 Main Street
West Nyack, NY 00000

000.000.0000
dcc41@mydomain.com

April 20, 2008

Ms. Allison Campbell
The ACME Agency
151 West Third Street
Somerset, NJ 00000

Dear Ms. Campbell:

Creativity. Power. Results.

With more than 10 years of experience in writing business-to-business and direct-mail copy, I have a diversified agency background that has exposed me to several different industries, including health care, financial services, insurance, medical, retail, real estate, and pharmaceuticals. As a seasoned professional, I have consistently created captivating and powerful copy that captures target-market attention and gets the desired results.

Looking for someone who can multitask?

Multitasking has become second nature for me. On average, I balance anywhere from 15 to 20 assignments at any given time. What's more, many of my assignments consist of multiple parts (letters, reply cards, brochures, etc.) and require not only creativity but refined editing skills to ensure that the copy is polished and sharp.

As you required, I have enclosed three representative samples from my portfolio along with my resume. I am confident that, if chosen for this position, I will be able to take The ACME Agency's copy assignments and produce attention-grabbing results.

I welcome the opportunity to discuss with you The ACME Agency's objectives and share how I believe I can contribute to the desired end results. I will contact you to arrange an appointment. I look forward to speaking with you.

Sincerely,

Diane C. Cartwright

Enclosures

217

Business Communications, Writer. *Patricia Traina-Duckers, Edison, New Jersey*

The line between this occupational group and the preceding one is thin. Besides writing ad copy, however, this applicant wrote different documents for different industries.

Brittany K. Torres

5-A Riverside Towers
Hackensack, NJ 07602
(201) 555-5555
bkt999@net.net

January 6, 2008

Sarah Weinstein
Editor-in-Chief
Fashionista Magazine
1500 Seventh Avenue
New York, NY 10000

Dear Ms. Weinstein:

My friends tell me I have a passion for fashion, and I entirely agree. In my spare time, I'm usually found checking out the latest in hairdos to footwear and everything in between. If I'm not at the malls, I'm tuned in to the fashion shows on TV, and of course, I can hardly wait for the latest issue of *Fashionista* magazine to arrive in my mailbox!

As a journalism major, I had exposure to news story reporting, script editing, and press release writing before I landed my first real job as lifestyle editor for my small-town weekly. The pay was minimal, but I had the chance to travel and write freelance articles on topics that interested me, such as wardrobe accessorizing. Most of them were published in various national magazines, including *Fashionista*. Eventually, I relocated to the metropolitan area and am currently employed as a copywriter at an advertising agency with clients in the apparel industry. However, it was always in the back of my mind that someday I'd love to join the editorial staff of a major fashion publication. You can imagine my excitement at seeing your ad in *Women's Wear Daily* for just such a position!

Realizing that I'm up against some serious competition, I am, nevertheless, throwing my hat in the ring and submitting my resume along with a few samples of my freelance articles. If I am considered for the features editor position, an acquaintance of mine, who is a big name in the fashion world, will serve as one of my references. She and I have collaborated closely on advertising campaigns, and I am certain she will vouch favorably for my character, abilities, and work habits.

Thank you for taking the time to review my materials, and I look forward to your further consideration of me. May we meet soon? I will call to determine a mutually convenient time.

Sincerely,

Brittany K. Torres

Enclosure

218

Fashion Magazine Features Editor. *Melanie Noonan, West Paterson, New Jersey*

The first paragraph indicates specifically the applicant's "passion for fashion." The second paragraph states that the target magazine has already published some of her articles.

Audra Sessoms
5555 Pulaski-Mercer Road · Mercer, Pennsylvania 55555 · 555.555.5555

August 28, 2007

Human Resources
American Museum of Natural History
Central Park West at 55th Street
New York, NY 55555

Re: Technical Writer (Information Systems) position

To Whom It May Concern:

Having recently completed my undergraduate studies, combining my passion for Marine Biology and English/Communications, the time has come to apply these interests and aptitudes. I am extremely versatile, and an employer can expect more of me than just what I am hired for. After reviewing my resume, I am confident you will agree that your advertised position for a **Technical Writer (Information Systems)** is a good match for my qualifications.

My proficiency in the use of desktop publishing applications is an immense aid in preparing presentations and reports. Honing my skills in writing by being involved in the university's newspaper (4 years on staff and one as editor-in-chief) and literary journal has also contributed to an improvement in my writing skills, which will be an asset to the American Museum of Natural History. I managed all aspects of the *Troubadour*'s biweekly production from scheduling, distribution, circulation, interviewing, copy writing, editing per Associated Press standards, layout and advertising. This was a daunting challenge that I mastered repeatedly.

In anticipation that you will want to meet with me, I would be delighted to make myself available to discuss how I can contribute to the continued success of the American Museum of Natural History. Thank you for your time and consideration. I will call next week to set up an interview.

Sincerely,

Audra Sessoms

Enclosure: resume

219

IS Technical Writer. *Jane Roqueplot, Sharon, Pennsylvania*

The applicant had no actual work history. The writer's goal was to demonstrate specific notable accomplishments while the individual was in school. All three paragraphs display self-confidence.

JANET EBERHART

192 CAVENDER TRAIL
MEDFORD, OR 97501

HOME: (541) 555-7777
CELL: (541) 555-8888

FAX: (541) 555-9999
E-MAIL: JEBERHART@BEACONREALTY.COM

September 29, 2007

William Fennimore
Managing Partner
Solid Gold Properties, LLC
6336 Hawthorne Parkway
Portland, OR 97208

Dear Mr. Fennimore:

I recently learned of your expansion plans to open new offices in southern Oregon, and thought you might be interested in my proven track record of substantial business increases in start-up and rapid-growth situations in the residential real estate marketplace.

By way of background, I founded and have been broker of record for a multi-operational real estate company that has grown since 1998 from a 4-person office into a $28 million operation. With my dedicated team of 17 associates and 3 support staff, we handle property management, sales and leasing, and appraisal services. Through intensive marketing, high gross commission sales, and financial stability, I established the company's presence to qualify for prestigious affiliation with one of the nation's largest franchise networks.

I personally list an average of 30 properties per year. In addition, I oversee 30 to 40 ongoing transactions under contract, intervening to resolve problems that may impact closings. Over 75% of our listings result in sales. In the capacity of officer, I:

 — Manage all aspects of daily operations, create operating budgets, design expansion plans, and designate funds for company investments;

 — Develop and implement programs for lead generation through community involvement;

 — Coordinate advertising efforts, including development of collateral materials, direct-mail campaigns, and newspaper ads; and

 — Facilitate numerous sales closings by establishing beneficial relationships with executives at financing organizations known to provide alternative lending strategies.

Owing my success to teamwork, I developed a sales training program, capitalizing on each individual's strengths and utilizing appropriate incentives, which has promoted high levels of motivation and productivity and 90% workforce retention. My top producer has shown the potential to follow in my footsteps, so I plan to turn over the reins to her upon finding another challenging opportunity where I could repeat my past accomplishments. Hopefully, it will be with your dynamic organization.

As I am sure you are aware, running a profitable real estate sales office depends heavily on client satisfaction, achieved through building relationships of trust and negotiating win/win outcomes, as well as astute planning and forecasting. I know I have what it takes, and would welcome the opportunity to discuss how my professional skills can contribute to penetrating your new market and positioning Solid Gold Properties for future growth. I will call your office next week to arrange a mutually convenient time to meet.

Sincerely,

Janet Eberhart

Enclosure: Resume

220

Real Estate Broker/Office Manager. *Melanie Noonan, West Paterson, New Jersey*

The applicant wanted to head a new real estate office in her state. The letter indicates in turn her interest, background and experience, success, managerial ability, and self-confidence.

PHILLIP MILES PORTER, JR.
9 CINDYANNE PLACE
WESTPORT, MA 00000

(222) 555-6666   PORTERPM@PROPERTY.NET   CELL: (222) 555-7777

March 28, 2008

R. Bruce Billings, Human Resources Manager
Markham Management Corporation
287 Chadworth Street
Boston, MA 02222

Dear Mr. Billings:

Your advertised position for a property manager at a prestigious condominium development in Watertown, published in the Sunday *Boston Globe*, March 21, 2008, captured my attention. I firmly believe, and hope you agree, that my long, embedded, and rich experience in residential and commercial property management meet the standards, drawn from your profile of the ideal candidate, to fill this position.

My background and foundation in real estate and property management are well documented in the enclosed resume, which highlights my notable competence and wide experience in rentals, leasing practices, inspections, financing, maintenance, and budgeting. Having successfully managed and advertised rental properties for M.P. Valois Real Estate, Ltd., during the past five years has given me a solid footing in this field.

In addition, I am very familiar with all the Boston real estate developments over the past 17 years, having worked extensively with the J. Varnum Corporation as Project Manager for such impressive developments as Windham Heights and Patriot Towers. At the latter development, I leased 19,000 square feet of condominium space and capably negotiated leasing contracts to tenants for commercial space that totaled 40,000 feet at the concourse.

Mr. Billings, if you agree with me that my qualifications match your specific employment requirements for this position, I would appreciate an opportunity to meet with you or another representative to review my candidacy in more depth. I look forward to hearing from you and thank you for your consideration of my application for this employment opportunity.

Sincerely,

Phillip Miles Porter, Jr.

Enclosure: resume

221

Condominium Property Manager. *Edward Turilli, North Kingstown, Rhode Island*

In this ad response, the first paragraph identifies the target position and begins to indicate the person's experience. The next two paragraphs elaborate on his experience and suitability for the job.

DAN FARRON

1111 Autumnbrook Drive
Houston, Texas 00000

home: 713.000.0000
name@aol.com

January 19, 2008

Mr. Jonathan Trammel, President
XYZ Corporation
3434 Main Street, Suite 100
Houston, TX 00000

Dear Mr. Trammel:

I noted your advertisement for a Vice President of Operations in *The Houston Chronicle* with a great deal of interest. Your candidate description and position requirements appear to be an excellent match with my background and qualifications.

As Senior Vice President of a diversified Texas real estate firm, I have more than 18 years of expertise in all property types and all facets of commercial real estate investments, including acquisitions, dispositions, development, management, renovation, reuse, finance, and asset management. Some of my skills and experiences that indicate the value I can bring to your company are the following:

- Handled more than 150 commercial transactions nationally, examining every angle and determining appropriate resolutions. I have been successful in acquiring and marketing underdeveloped or mismanaged properties and repositioning them into profitable real estate.
- Built extensive relationships, networks, and alliances with brokers, lenders, and third-party consultants, allowing me to obtain one of the most important value-driven components in real estate: information.
- Developed experience in commercial real estate and demonstrated ability to structure financial loans, venture equity, and troubled debt restructuring, as well as market commercial property.

With commercial foreclosures up, bankruptcies increasing, and long-term interest rates at a 40-year low, opportunity is "knocking at the door" again to recognize and take advantage of these significant market changes and acquire distressed or underperforming properties.

I believe that my experience and qualifications, along with my drive and enthusiasm, make me an excellent candidate for your opening. Perhaps we could arrange a meeting to discuss your current needs and the strategies I could contribute toward their fulfillment. Thank you, Mr. Trammel, for your time and consideration.

Sincerely,

Dan Farron

Enclosure

222

Vice President of Operations. *Daniel J. Dorotik, Jr., Lubbock, Texas*

The opening paragraph claims a match between the applicant and the advertised position. The next two paragraphs, together with the bulleted items, give evidence of expertise and achievements.

Melinda H. Jacobson

0000 Westwood Drive NE   Grand Rapids, MI 49505   555-555-4444
melindajacobson@yahoo.com

Date

Name
Company
Address
City, State ZIP

Dear Employment Director:

What does it take to be an excellent appraiser? Accuracy. Thoroughness. Attention to detail. Understanding of the process. I believe you will find that I have these assets and more. That's why I am contacting you—to learn about opportunities in commercial appraising, appraisal review, appraiser management or other related positions with your organization. My resume is enclosed for your review.

You will see that I have been appraising commercial properties for several years. I have found that my skills are particularly geared toward commercial lines in that I am very analytical and I understand how the process actually works. The challenges that commercial appraising present are also exciting.

The breadth of my experience is described on my resume. I have generated many complex files and appraised diverse properties, from vacant land to manufacturing plants and strip malls. In addition to my commercial and residential experience, I have been training appraisers and reviewing/releasing their work. This has presented its own challenges, which have solidified my knowledge of the field.

I sincerely hope you will agree that I have the potential to join your team as a great commercial appraiser. A personal interview would give me a chance to expand on my qualifications and give you an opportunity to see firsthand how motivated I am. I will call you to make arrangements. Thank you for your consideration.

Sincerely,

Melinda H. Jacobson

Enclosure

223

Commercial Appraiser. *Janet L. Beckstrom, Flint, Michigan*

The applicant's experience was mostly in residential appraising, but she wanted to transition to the more profitable realm of commercial appraising. The focus is on previous commercial experience.

William R. Rudd
55 North Drive
Atlanta, GA 55555
(555) 555-5555
wrr253@verizon.net

September 25, 2007

James Salvatori, President
Salvatori Venture Partners
5055 Mass. Ave.
Atlanta, GA 55555

Dear Mr. Salvatori:

As you are in a position to strengthen your portfolio companies' growth by influencing their strategic hires, you may be interested in my background. My area of expertise is Internet marketing. As a member of the pioneering Ewire.com team during its rapid rise to a dominant position in e-commerce, I was involved in almost every aspect of Internet marketing and customer acquisition. If you are aware of a company that would benefit from expertise in these areas, please let me know.

At Ewire, I made contributions in the areas of identifying new marketing channels, developing online marketing programs, project management, industry report writing, metrics analysis, relationship building with affiliate partners, advising companies on online media buys, and vendor management. Contributions I made to the company's fast growth include the following:

- Built corporate marketing value in the travel industry to #1.
- Developed creative affiliate programs with Reuters and CNBC.
- Evolved and managed a leads generation / account acquisition program adopted by leading online brokers such as E*Trade.
- Advised top companies such as Southwest Airlines and Expedia.com on how to enhance their websites as customer acquisition tools and use Doubleclick and ModemMedia in their multilevel marketing and media buys.

Following Ewire, I held executive positions with a strong marketing focus and pursued a second Master's degree—a Master of Science in Management of Technology from the Sloan School of Management at MIT. These experiences give me the agility and breadth of understanding of technology, marketing, and business management to play a valuable role in a creative, quickly evolving company.

My advanced level of exposure at one of the frontiers of web technology development gives me a level of technology sophistication that can only enhance my ability to deliver competitive results as an Internet marketing manager. If you could connect me to corporate executives who might be interested in the value I could bring in this role, I would be greatly obliged. Thank you.

Sincerely,

William R. Rudd

224

New Venture Marketing Manager. *Jean Cummings, Concord, Massachusetts*

This letter targets a venture capital firm for networking purposes. The individual is hoping to hear about early-stage technology ventures that need someone with his experience and skills.

Tom Mitchell

111 Pacific Drive, Gridlake, IN 00000   222-222-2222   tmitchell@someemail.com

December 5, 2007

Blue Diamond Parts
125 North Ave.
Melrose Park, IL 60099

Dear Hiring Manager:

I saw on the International Truck and Engine Corporation's website that you are seeking a **Technical Sales Manager.** When reviewing my attached resume, you will see I have 8 years of experience in the sale of automotive parts and services. In my previous position with NAPA, I led a team of four members who won national awards in 2004 and 2005 for customer satisfaction.

Throughout my career, I have demonstrated the ability to remain abreast of current industry trends and developments. In fact, I was asked in 2005 to conduct a training session for Chicagoland representatives regarding a new line of products for ignitions and brakes.

I would enjoy speaking with you personally about this opportunity. May I contact you next week to set a time for us to speak?

Sincerely,

Tom Mitchell

Enclosure

225

Technical Sales. *Eva Locke, Waukegan, Illinois*

The applicant was responding to a position posted on the Web. The first paragraph refers to his years of experience and award-winning leadership. The second paragraph highlights other skills.

Eric Hamlin

0000 North Way ◆ Atlanta, GA 00000
Phone: (770) 000-0000 ◆ E-mail: name@yahoo.com

January 30, 2008

Todd Worthington, Director
XYZ Company
1111 Stenson Avenue
Atlanta, GA 00000

Dear Mr. Worthington:

Perhaps you are in need of a dependable, skilled Account Director who can help you manage accounts and contribute to performance and revenue increases. Please allow me to explain briefly how my ability to manage operations, staff development, and client relationships can contribute to your organization.

Through my ten years of experience in sales, data, and project management, I have built a track record of increasing assets, revenues, and productivity for each of my employers. Some of my achievements include the following:

➢ Equifax: Awarded recognition by executive management for surpassing production goals.
➢ Prudential: Boosted number of assets by 30% within first year with firm.
➢ Progressive: Increased sales by 15% through strategic marketing plans.

Above all, I have demonstrated the ability to lead others both by example and direct instruction/mentoring. My teams maintain excellent performance and productivity gains, and I earned the respect and trust of numerous representatives and associates whom I trained and coached. You can be assured that I would add value to your operations as well through my leadership and staff-development initiatives.

I have enclosed my resume to furnish you with additional details concerning my background and achievements, but I am certain that a personal interview would more fully reveal my strengths and what I have to offer your organization. I will call next week to arrange a time we can meet. Thank you for your time and consideration.

Sincerely,

Eric Hamlin

Enclosure

226

Account Director. *Daniel J. Dorotik, Jr., Lubbock, Texas*

In this broadcast probe for an unadvertised need, the letter indicates the individual's job goal, experience, and record. Bullets highlight achievements. The third paragraph stresses leadership.

DEREK McADAMS

dmcadams12@sbcglobal.net

9625 South 124th Street
Oak Creek, WI 53132
414.545.9076

November 8, 2007

James Hoffmann, President
Hoffmann Howe & Associates, Inc.
1200 Southside Boulevard
Chicago, IL 60101

Dear Mr. Hoffmann:

For the past five years as a Sales Manager, I have planned, rolled out, and directed value-added technical sales and service programs targeted to Tier 1 and mid-market organizations within the Chicago/Northern Illinois, Wisconsin, and Iowa marketplaces. In addition, I have more than 10 years of business operations management experience.

Overall, my success stems from the ability to translate strategic marketing plans into tactical sales actions, while driving sustainable revenue growth, improving earnings, and outperforming the competition through my development and leadership of top-producing sales teams. Please note my sales and business development accomplishments from the attached resume. These selected achievements are indicative of the quality and caliber of my entire professional career.

If you are working with a client company seeking a well-qualified sales management executive, I would welcome the opportunity to speak with you. I am open for relocation and currently earn more than $150,000 in annual compensation.

Regards,

Derek McAdams

Enclosure: Resume

227

Sales Manager. *Michele J. Haffner, Glendale, Wisconsin*

The first paragraph indicates the applicant's experience. The second paragraph refers to his abilities and to the selected achievements mentioned in the applicant's resume.

Tim Slater

555 Lincoln Avenue
Grove City, Pennsylvania 55555
555.555.5555 tslater2@hotmail.com

August 30, 2007

E.M. Tully & Associates
Management Consultants
555 Chestnut Street
Pittsburgh, PA 55555

Dear Mr. Tully:

As you will note in my resume, I have considerable management, leadership, and organizational skills. I have consistently spearheaded changes that favorably impacted the bottom line through procedural and process innovations, inventory controls, and creative product presentation programs. I am confident in my ability to make significant contributions to Pittsburgh Custom Metal Forming by becoming a member of the management team as the Marketing/Sales Manager, contributing to the corporate culture essential to further growth and profitability.

My past accomplishments serve as an excellent indicator of what I can do for your client. I will share some of these here:

- Initiated cost savings programs, continuous improvement projects, and quality improvements to boost profits from break-even to $1.2 million within 3 years.
- Spearheaded new plant start-up and consolidated 5 plants. Increased revenue from $18 million to $27 million within 4 years.
- Directed scrap reduction team, reducing scrap from 5% to 2.5% within 3 years and realizing a savings of 450,000 lbs. of material ($270K) per year.
- Negotiated materials contracts, securing 10% savings in materials costs over a 2-year period.
- Tightened standard operating procedures to reduce tooling damage caused by poor installation, saving $250K in tooling costs in 1 year.
- Significantly reduced product waste, operating costs, and maintenance by upgrading production lines.
- Key contributor to driving dealership to all-time sales high during 2-year tenure with firm.

I look forward to what I anticipate will be the first of many positive communications to discuss how my qualifications match the requirements needed for the Marketing/Sales Manager. Additionally, I would be interested in demonstrating how my diversity and qualifications can contribute to the continued success of Pittsburgh Custom Metal Forming in any other appropriate position. I will call next week to set a time that is convenient for you. Thank you for your time and consideration.

Sincerely,

Tim Slater

Enclosure: resume

228

Marketing/Sales Manager. *Jane Roqueplot, Sharon, Pennsylvania*

This letter was addressed to a consultant who was negotiating on the applicant's behalf. The writer makes notable achievements clearly evident so that the consultant would see them.

DONALD VINCENT

5555 State Route 111, Parker, PA 55555   Home: 555-555-5555   dvincent@aol.com

August 30, 2007

Michael Johnson
JCPenney
Shenango Valley Mall
5555 State Street
Hermitage, PA 55555

Dear Mr. Johnson:

Please take a moment to review my resume for the position of Sales Associate with your organization. As a recent high school graduate, I am eager to begin my career with a reputable firm such as yours. In order to shorten the "learning curve" and enable you to "predict" my behavior on the job, I took the liberty of completing a professional behavioral assessment. I am prepared to offer you a copy of this assessment, which further details my behavioral strengths as they relate to employment. Please note the four key environmental factors listed below and the assessment's description of my natural response. I am pleased to fully endorse the accuracy of the assessment.

Problem Solving—Challenges

"Donald will be quite cooperative by nature and attempt to avoid confrontation as he wants to be seen as a person who is 'easy' to work with."

People—Contacts

"Donald is enthusiastic about his ability to influence others. He prefers an environment in which he has the opportunity to deal with different types of individuals. Donald is trusting and wants to be trusted."

Pace—Consistency

"Donald is appreciative of the team concept and feels quite secure in an environment where the need to move from one activity to another quite quickly is held to a minimum."

Procedures—Constraints

"Donald is independent in nature and feels comfortable in situations where the constraints are few and far between."

Thank you again for your consideration for this opportunity. I would appreciate an interview, and I am available at your convenience. You may reach me anytime at the following number: 555-555-5555.

Sincerely,

Donald Vincent

Enclosure: resume

229

Sales Associate. *Jane Roqueplot, Sharon, Pennsylvania*

This letter was for a high school graduate with no work experience. The writer composed the letter by using information directly from the graduate's behavioral assessment.

SHEILA BEST   555-555-5555

sheilabest@email.com
0000 Rabbit Road, Birmingham, AL 35210

January 21, 2008

Chairman, Search Committee
Birmingham Chamber of Commerce
106 N. Starline
Birmingham, AL 35210

Dear Chairman:

    With strong family roots in Birmingham County and 10 years of broad-based Chamber experience, I feel my qualifications make me an ideal candidate for the president position with the Birmingham Chamber.

    Born and raised in Mountain Brook and a graduate of Central High School, I know the Birmingham community very well. As Senior Vice President of the Mountain Brook Chamber of Commerce, I have full P&L responsibility for a $1.6 million budget encompassing production and sales, membership, and operations. While Vice President of Publications and Directory, I directed a staff of 11 in successfully meeting or exceeding annual financial objectives for five consecutive years.

My chamber experience includes

- ➤ implementation of innovative programs and benefits to expand and retain membership;
- ➤ sales and production of the only chamber-produced directory in the United States;
- ➤ documented success in establishing long-term, mutually beneficial, and profitable corporate liaisons and alliances; and
- ➤ the establishment of a network of contacts to maintain the strong community tie.

    I would appreciate the opportunity to discuss in more detail how my experience might benefit the Birmingham Chamber and will give you a call early next week to make sure you have received my resume and to answer any questions you may have. I look forward to speaking with you.

Sincerely,

Sheila Best

Enclosure

230

President, Chamber of Commerce. *Cindy Kraft, Valrico, Florida*

Knowledge of an area and promotional abilities are two key requirements for a chamber of commerce leader. The second paragraph and the bulleted items show the applicant's suitability.

Bob Madden
1645 Franklin Avenue
Phoenix, AZ 99999
(555) 555-5555
bobmadden@javelina.net

April 16, 2008

Frank Armstrong
Search Committee Chair
Sun Devil Athletic Association, Inc.
Arizona State University
1910 University Drive
Tempe, AZ 99999

Dear Mr. Armstrong,

I am writing to express my interest in the Assistant Director position with the Sun Devil Athletic Association, Incorporated. I offer a distinguished record of achievements in directing process improvements and designing action plans to achieve organizational goals.

Your organization has been highly recommended to me by Robert Franklin. He has appreciated your friendship over the years and has advised me to forward my resume. I am accustomed to a fast-paced environment where deadlines are priority and handling multiple jobs simultaneously is the norm. I enjoy a challenge and work hard to attain my goals, and I believe that if I had the opportunity to interview with you, it would be apparent that my skills are far-reaching.

I believe the combination of my education and business experience offers me the unique opportunity to make a positive contribution to your organization. My skills and experience include the following:

- Extensive background in all areas of staff management, budget development, strategic planning, public relations, and marketing
- Excellent communication skills
- Demonstrated ability to approach management from a broad base of management experience in a number of areas, particularly the development and implementation of new programs
- Career experience complemented by a Bachelor's degree in Marketing

Although the accompanying resume illustrates my strengths well, I am certain of my abilities to make a significant contribution early on and that a personal interview would better demonstrate how I could meet the needs of the Sun Devil Athletic Association. I look forward to the opportunity of discussing in person how my expertise could best fit your needs. In the interim, thank you for your consideration, attention, and forthcoming response.

Sincerely,

Bob Madden

Enclosure

231

Assistant Director, Athletic Association. *Denette D. Jones, Boise, Idaho*

The opening paragraph indicates the targeted position, and the second paragraph begins with a referral to build rapport with the reader. Bullets point to significant skills and experience.

DAVID SMITH
12000 Jefferson Avenue, Newport News, VA 23606
Home: 555-555-5555 ■ Mobile: 000-000-0000 ■ DSmith@leader.com

STRATEGIC MANAGER ■ SENIOR BUSINESS DEVELOPER ■ MARKETING TEAM LEADER

January 30, 2008

E. Ransom, CEO
Newport News Life
One Chesapeake Way
Newport News, VA 23606

Hello, my name is David Smith.

I specialize in bringing strategic vision, integrity, and energized team leadership to growth companies that are looking for high-impact results.

I've spent the past 20 years leading a wide range of growth organizations and projects. Now I'm looking for the next opportunity to join a committed, enthusiastic, and creative team environment that wants proven senior leaders and repeatable results.

> If I work for your company, you can count on me to excel at driving new revenue sources and exceeding sales projections. My thorough understanding of direct marketing principles and consumer "hot buttons" will directly drive quantitative results. You will get a leader who wants the responsibility to develop passionate, motivated, and powerful teams that embrace change, while seeding the next generation of business leaders for your company. You can expect formalized programs in "new idea" creation and implementation, to ensure that business development is a dynamic, ongoing process. You will also gain an unmatched commitment to people, both inside your business and outside with your valuable customers.

My resume is attached for your consideration. I would love to meet with you to discuss my fit with your company and any needs or goals that I can help you meet.

If you take the time to meet with me, I guarantee you will walk away from our meeting with at least one great idea for your business—whether or not we end up working together! I will call you next week to schedule a meeting.

Sincerely,

David Smith

Enclosure: Resume

232

Business Developer. *Helen Oliff, Reston, Virginia*

The target company wanted a match with its existing leadership team. The writer embedded a "vision statement" to demonstrate the applicant's leadership philosophy and management style.

CHRIS PRENTICE

000 Cranberry Street
Salt Lake City, UT 84117

Email: cprentice@hotmail.com

Mobile: (555) 555-5555
Residence: (000) 000-5511

5 February 2008

Mr. Fred Hall
Director of Sales & Marketing
TechIT, Inc.
4024 South 2100 Street
Salt Lake City, UT 84117

Re: Senior Business Development Manager

Dear Mr. Hall:

As I read your advertisement, it becomes evident that the candidate you seek needs proficiency in many areas. A clear resolve for quality, revenue growth, and profits, coupled with continuous improvement and firm leadership, will be essential to ride the turbulence of the market as we enter these troubled times.

At the same time, consultation, communication, and teamwork will underpin trust, cooperation, and the development of a shared vision, so that your company's long-term growth can be achieved.

In short, the market today is not for the faint-hearted, yet the current crop of challenges to the IT industry are not insurmountable if an individual with my experience, capability, and tenacity takes on the role.

Commercially, I am the seasoned manager you seek. I have extensive national experience in introducing products to market and winning prominence against established competitors. I have built distribution networks, fought hard-won battles to win market share and brand acceptance, and demonstrated the type of maturity that can win consensus in the most highly charged of atmospheres.

Team-focused, I am a strong proponent of the power of people, believing in the "all hands on deck" philosophy to achieve common goals.

Fresh from my last assignment as the Director of New Business for a provider of information systems to the SME market, I have a renewed sense of confidence toward tackling new challenges.

Naturally, I would be delighted to meet with you to review your needs in detail, and I have enclosed a copy of my resume to provide a basis for future discussions. I will call you in the next couple of days to see if our schedules can permit a brief meeting.

I look forward to speaking with you soon.

Sincerely,

Chris Prentice

233

Senior Business Development Manager. *Gayle Howard, Chirnside Park, Melbourne, Australia*

Eight short paragraphs quicken the reading tempo of this letter and make it seem shorter than it is. Five of the paragraphs are only one sentence. The impression is that this person does not waste time.

Jane A. Simmons

9007 Rainor Road ▪ Chapel Hill, NC 00000 ▪ Home: 555.555.5555 ▪ Mobile: 555.555.5555 ▪ janeasimmons@aol.com

"Having worked with Jane in a very dynamic and fast-paced environment, I was always impressed with her ability to look straight at the goal and help guide the team to the objectives that were set out to achieve. This ability was invaluable to the group when working with various organizations, people, and processes, to build cohesive business and marketing plans spanning the entire worldwide organization. Jane has the leadership to build a common understanding of the customers and the marketing organization we were working with, as well as to assist the organization in defining strategies and programs to address this market."

Fred Jones, VP-Marketing, Center Technology, Inc.

"Jane could be counted on to take an assignment, project, complex problem and pull the right resources together (people and funding) to drive to success. She works to understand the customer needs, requirements, and pain points and then addresses those in creative new ways. She drives her team and her projects with great independence and with an eye for quality, ultimately delivering exceptional results on behalf of the end user customer and our company. She is an extraordinary team player and one of the most talented individuals I have had the pleasure to work with in my 18 years."

Ellen Lawrence, Worldwide VP-Marketing, Center Technology, Inc.

Date

Name
Title
Company Name
Address
City, State, ZIP

Dear Mr. or Ms. _____:

As a business and marketing leader in program management and process improvements that result in increased revenues and reduced costs, I can offer a wealth of knowledge and skill sets to your company. My expertise in leading companies through periods of growth and change have prepared me for any number of challenges that your company may be facing.

Highlights of my achievements during my rapid growth at Center Technology, Inc., include the following:

As Marketing Manager for the global business unit:

- Led a global team of marketing and product managers to redefine the program scope, which increased storage revenue by more than $50 million incrementally in 6 months.

As Marketing Manager for the hardware program:

- Directed the reduction of more than 120 marketing programs with a $13 million quarterly budget down to 8 marketing programs with an $8 million budget.
- Implemented promotions and extensive training programs to increase cross-sell of PCs and support services by more than 25%.

As Business Planning Manager:

- Leveraged the company's global account organization and sales force to increase global accounts revenue by more than 12%.
- Improved relationships between the Americas' regional business and marketing teams through the implementation of best practices.

If you need a strategic marketing executive with strong business acumen and out-of-the-box problem-solving talent blended with extraordinary team leadership and the ability to execute tactically, then I am your candidate. I would welcome the opportunity to discuss how my vision, creativity, and skill sets could benefit your organization. May we meet?

Sincerely,

Jane A. Simmons

Enclosure

234

Strategic Marketing Executive. *Louise Garver, Enfield, Connecticut*

This individual wanted to move up to the next level in her career path in technology. The letter emphasizes her leadership skills and results, supported by two testimonials from company VPs.

THOMAS LEONE CORDEIRO
000 Eighth Avenue West
Manhattan, NY 77777
(000) 333-9999

February 6, 2008

Rodney Spurrier, Director of Human Resources
Avery Missile Design Systems, Inc.
000 Washington Highway, Suite 000
New London, CT 00000

Dear Mr. Spurrier:

I am writing to you in response to your need for a Sales Manager, as advertised in *The New York Times*, February 5, 2008. I fully believe my qualifications will meet or exceed your ideal candidate standards.

With 17 successful years of experience in business sales, management, and customer service to my credit, I welcome the opportunity to discuss my qualifications for this opening in sales management with Avery Missile Design Systems. My positions as sales manager and supervisor have shown positive results in vastly increased sales volumes through reorganizing and rebuilding of staff, instituting powerful incentive programs, and implementing improved marketing procedures.

Experienced in—and undaunted by—challenging work environments, I am capable of assuming concurrent tasking responsibilities while effectively managing a staff with $6M in annual sales volume. Additionally, during my seven years in customer service—the last five as supervisor—I have become adept at dealing with client concerns, resulting in higher sales figures and improved customer satisfaction.

My training, experience, and rapid learning curve in using computers and various applications are borne out in my employment environments during my entire career. My technical background includes positions in operations support, software technical services, software manufacturing, programming, and technical writing. I hope you agree with me that this knowledge strengthens my candidacy for any sales management position requiring fast-paced storage and retrieval of information.

I would appreciate your contacting me to make an appointment at your earliest convenience to review my qualifications for this position, or another for which you may find me suitable. If I do not hear from you by February 15, I will contact your office to request an appointment suitable to your schedule.

Thank you for your consideration of my application for the position of Sales Manager with your firm.

Sincerely,

Thomas Leone Cordeiro

Enclosure: resume

235

Sales Manager. *Edward Turilli, North Kingstown, Rhode Island*

The applicant, in all paragraphs, confidently proves his strong experience in sales management. His intention to request an appointment if not contacted by a certain date shows his proactive manner.

KATHY CHISHOLM

555 Maynard Street, Providence, Rhode Island 01976, (555) 555-2645, kat3434@island.net

SalesFinders, Inc.
453 Ashland Court, Suite 285
Providence, RI 01976

I am writing to you for help in locating a new job in sales. Your name was in a directory of recruiters.

Currently I am employed as an Assistant National Accounts Manager for Revlon Corporation. My account responsibility is for CVS Pharmacy drugstores, located in Woonsocket, RI. CVS is Revlon's #4 account.

I've been in Providence for almost five years now—and I love it! I want to stay in New England but want to work in an organization where I can better use my creativity and skills to build a top-notch sales department. I'd like to do that as a Regional Manager.

My experience is broad in all areas of sales. Through my development of promotional campaigns and business analysis, I also have marketing experience. People enjoy working with me because of my fun, outgoing personality.

My attached resume and summary sheet describe what I am seeking in my next career move. My current compensation is more than $70K, with a base salary of $65K and a 10% bonus.

I would be happy to answer any questions or provide any clarification you may need. Thank you for your consideration as you review your clients' requests for new employees.

Sincerely,

Kathy Chisholm

Attachments

236

Regional Manager. *Gail Frank, Tampa, Florida*

Because this letter was sent to a sales recruiter, the writer used a cartoon and an informal font for the applicant's name to make the letter stand out from all the others recruiters get.

JOHN CORBIN
0000 Monroe Avenue
Cleveland, Ohio 00000
(555) 555-5555
corbin@cox.net

December 12, 2007

Dear _____:

Could I help you as a sales management executive or general manager?

I have created strong sales and marketing organizations, driving forward consistent revenue growth through the following areas of expertise:

strategic sales planning and management
team building, training and development
identifying and capitalizing on market opportunities
building and managing multichannel distribution networks
developing and managing key account relationships
consultative selling, negotiating and closing skills

At Harmon Company, I designed and implemented sales strategies that **generated a pipeline of more than $45 million** in the first 5 months of employment. At Technology Systems, I rebuilt a new sales team in just 4 months and **grew sales from $2.5 million to $7.5 million** in the first year. At the Benton Company, I delivered **38% cumulative sales growth** over a 3-year period and developed an effective multidistribution network producing more than 40% of overall revenue.

If you have the need, I am confident that I can accomplish profitable results for your company. Regarding salary requirements, I understand that flexibility is important in this market and am willing to discuss your organization's target salary range for an executive with my experience.

May we talk?

Sincerely,

John Corbin

Enclosure

237

Sales Executive/General Manager. *Louise Garver, Enfield, Connecticut*

This sales executive had lost his position in a merger, and this letter helped him gain multiple interviews that led to offers. Highlighting items with boldface, italic, and center-justification is effective.

ADAM JULIENE

123 Glen Street • Denver, CO 00000 • 555.555.5555 • adjul@msnaol.com

January 30, 2008

John Jones
Sales Manager
StorageTek Corporation
1 Tape Drive
Louisville, CO 00000

Dear Mr. Jones:

In today's intensely competitive marketplace, efficient and effective sales operations are critical to a company's success. The ultimate success of any sales operation requires a manager who can develop, implement, and optimize sales processes designed to achieve strategic corporate goals by enabling and empowering the sales teams.

My strengths lie in building quality processes that get the job done and building consensus within cross-functional teams. My track record as outlined in the enclosed resume demonstrates that I can

- Streamline existing processes and design new processes aligned with corporate infrastructure and existing organizations.
- Build a shared vision and consensus between cross-functional organizations and vested parties.
- Develop business models, market and sales strategies, policies, and organizational structure.
- Clarify and strengthen the organization's core values and principles to facilitate growth, profitability, and employee performance and satisfaction.

I attribute my success to my ability to assume leadership and turn around underperforming organizations by developing/sharing best practices that increase quality, effectiveness, and productivity. Equally important is my talent for developing effective cross-functional relationships. You will find that I am very skilled at developing sound action plans, as well as administering and following through on those plans. I strive to build and maintain a principle-centered environment that preserves the company's core values while stimulating growth and profitability.

I am eager to make an immediate and enduring contribution to StorageTek. I welcome the opportunity to explore my potential contributions.

Thank you for your consideration; I look forward to speaking with you soon and will contact you to set a time we can meet.

Sincerely,

Adam Juliene

Enclosure: Resume

238

Sales Manager. *Roberta F. Gamza, Louisville, Colorado*

The applicant was pursuing an opportunity at a well-respected local employer but did not have any contacts in the organization. Bulleted abilities and a paragraph on skills make the person stand out.

TERRA A. CARR

0000 Tomahawk Road • Shawnee Mission, Kansas 66802
Residence: 555-555-5555 • Wireless: 000-000-0000
Email: terracarr@email.com

CONFIDENTIAL

Your confidentiality and consideration of the accompanying information is requested.

CAREER OVERVIEW

Building corporate value is my expertise... value measured in aggressive strategic marketing in existing and new market sectors. Whether challenged to launch the start-up of a new business unit or product or to introduce innovative marketing programs for repositioning or branding purposes, I have achieved results.

My strengths lie in my ability to conceive and implement the strategic marketing plans to identify new market opportunities, initiate product and service introductions, and negotiate strategic alliances to drive domestic and global market expansion and revenue/profit growth. My challenge has been to expand and strengthen market presence through the introduction of a diversified portfolio of new business development, advertising, and public relations initiatives. I have instilled a sense of entrepreneurial vision and creativity to drive forward innovative strategies to win competitive positioning and accelerated revenue growth.

Although enjoying my current position, *I am exploring opportunities as a senior marketing executive with a progressive organization active in international expansion* where I may continue to provide strong and decisive marketing leadership. I would welcome a personal interview to discuss how my qualifications would benefit your organization and will call to set an appointment. Thank you for your consideration.

Cordially,

Terra A. Carr

Enclosure

239

Senior Marketing Executive. *Gina Taylor, Kansas City, Missouri*

This individual wanted to relocate to the West Coast. Italic draws attention to the centered heading and statement requesting confidentiality. Italic in the last paragraph makes the position evident.

PAUL D. LEWIS

555 Clare Street • Melville, New York 44444 • (333) 222-4444 • salespro@soldout.net

Date

Name
Company
Address

Dear Name:

Success is broadly founded in hands-on leadership with a firm belief in performance ownership and accountability. With a career track in senior sales management positions with System-Tel, Virtual-Communication, and Global Wireless, my well-honed consultative sales style and drive to succeed have proven effective in building and sustaining C-level relationships and revenue gains across highly competitive vertical markets.

Perhaps your organization is seeking to recruit a sales executive with these talents to develop and lead its sales organization to success in the face of emerging competition and uncertain economical climates. If this is the case, you will want to consider me as a viable candidate. But first, let me briefly highlight my 13-year sales career with the aforementioned leading organizations to give you a better idea of who I am and the value I would bring to the appropriate executive sales position.

- Over-quota Annual Sales Track Record with System-Tel

  | 2006 | **173%** | 2004 | **142%** | 2002 | **129%** | 2000 | **120%** |
  | 2005 | **166%** | 2003 | **135%** | 2001 | **131%** | 1999 | **133%** |

- Develop and execute sales solution strategies for mid-tier and large-scale corporations.
- Train, coach, mentor, and lead more than 30 top-gun sales professionals.
- Cultivate alliance relationships with industry partners.
- Conceptual, technical knowledge of enterprise-wide, technology-based software solutions.

I realize you must be inundated with resumes—some good, some not—and find it increasingly difficult to decide on top talent. As such, I strongly encourage a meeting—either in person or preliminarily by telephone following your review of my accompanying resume, to discuss how I can contribute to the growth of your organization's bottom line.

I will call you next week to explore the possibility of an interview. Thank you in advance for your time and consideration. I look forward to meeting with you soon.

Sincerely,

Paul D. Lewis

Sales Executive.   *Ann Baehr, Brentwood, New York*

The applicant was a sales executive looking for a senior sales management position. His success at sales is a recurrent theme in the first two paragraphs. Boldfacing of percentages highlights growth.

ERIC J. MANSON
Cascade Towers, 0000 76 Avenue, Bloomington, MN 55555
Cell / Voice Mail 555 555 5555 • Home 555 555 5555 • E-mail: ejmn@concord.net

February 2, 2008

Mr. Roberto Oltone
Telecommunications Department
Superior Networks
82 Jason Street
Kansas City, Missouri 55555

MARKETING AND SALES MANAGEMENT

Dear Mr. Oltone:

I am most interested in the position advertised recently in the *Sun-Times* and have accordingly attached a professional resume for your review.

With more than 20 years of executive-level experience in marketing electronics and communication equipment and service, I've negotiated numerous contracts; achieved solid revenue growth; and bought, sold, and merged companies. My major strengths fall into the following arenas:

- Marketing and Sales
- Business Development
- Finance
- Training and Development
- Management and Leadership

Personal skills enhance my expertise in marketing management. I am known for having tenacity, a tremendous work ethic, an aggressive solution-oriented focus, and a team-oriented manner. My aversion to micromanaging has generated loyalty from others, as has the ability to listen to suggestions and concerns of customers, managers, and staff. With an intuitive nature and vision for the future, problem solving and decision making come easily to me.

I will be calling your office to determine your interview schedule for this position, and look forward to discussing the company's needs and in what ways I might contribute to those plans. Please let me know if you need further information before then.

Sincerely,

Eric J. Manson

241

Marketing and Sales Manager. *Beverley Drake, Rochester, Minnesota*

In this response to a newspaper ad, bullets point to major strengths. The third paragraph tells about the applicant's managerial abilities, people skills, and additional strengths.

Lisa A. Santos

555 Victoria Avenue
Augusta, Ontario A1A 1A1
lisasantos@email.com
Home: 555.666.9999
Cell: 555.999.7777

March 3, 2008

Terrance Flaherty, CEO
Consultronix
345 Pine Valley Road, Suite 4460
Augusta, Ontario
B2C 3D4

<u>**Re: Director of Marketing**</u>

Dear Mr. Flaherty,

I love a challenge!

Whether leading the marketing and promotional initiatives for the Canadian arm of one of the world's largest management consulting firms, spearheading the corporate development efforts of a $25 million fundraising campaign to fight polio, or coordinating high-profile executive luncheons and promotional events with the "who's who" of Canadian business, I approach each challenge with the same "get it done" attitude.

It is exactly this determination—combined with exceptional skills in marketing, promotions, business development, and executive relationship management—that has enabled my successes to date, and that in turn I can offer to your firm. From what I have read in the industry journals of your plans to enter new technology and telecom markets, you need someone who can step in now and create a singular market presence—and with the IT-Com Conference coming to Augusta this September, it needs to be done quickly.

In short, as my attached resume attests, here's what I can offer you:

- **Expertise in creating high corporate visibility and brand recognition**—proven ability to create the appropriate marketing vehicle or event, secure widespread media attention, and stimulate excitement around a product or service

- **A creative mind for promotional opportunities and marketing campaigns**—solid track record for conceiving and organizing high-profile executive luncheons, industry roundtables, and special events

- **Exceptional market research and analysis skills**—critical for appropriate market segmentation and targeted marketing/promotional campaigns

- **Strong project management and leadership capabilities**—organized, focused, and able to pull teams together around a common goal

Please feel free to contact me at your earliest convenience to arrange a personal meeting, and I would be glad to discuss why I'm the person for the job. I already have a number of ideas that should interest you.

I thank you for your consideration and look forward to speaking with you soon.

Sincerely,

Lisa A. Santos

Encl. Resume

242

Director of Marketing. *Ross Macpherson, Whitby, Ontario, Canada*

The unique first paragraph grabs the reader's attention. Bullets and boldfacing highlight what the applicant can do for the company. This letter stood above the rest; in the end she got the job.

Available for relocation to the Dallas area   C O N F I D E N T I A L

Lily Duart   1200 Westie Circle, Montgomery, Alabama 00000
[000] 000-0000 (home) — [000] 000-5555 (cell) — [000] 555-5555 (fax) — 001@scratch.com

Monday, 15 March 2008

Mr. Norman French, CEO
Carley Products, Inc.
625 Express Highway
Building 333
Dallas, Texas 00000

Dear Mr. French,

In a few seconds, you are going to see a half dozen capabilities I would like to put under Carley's control, followed by three indicators that reflect my success as a Director of Sales and Marketing in nationwide competition. Finally, I thought you deserved to see a half dozen documented contributions to the bottom line. But the story behind the results is as important as the numbers themselves.

I believe that most people—even your sales and marketing staff—can probably do much more than they think they can. And I believe the personal rewards they earn at those new levels will keep them producing at very high rates. I found my philosophy works wonders, regardless of the product being sold or the market being worked or the competitors' actions. Now that I've reached near the top in one industry, I'm ready for the fun of applying what I've learned in new fields.

It all starts with building mutual, beneficial relationships. Therefore, let me suggest this: May we talk soon so that I can learn more about Carley's special needs? I'll call in a few days to find a time when our schedules align.

Sincerely,

Lily Duart

Encl.: Resume

C O N F I D E N T I A L

243

Director of Sales and Marketing. *Don Orlando, Montgomery, Alabama*

The applicant had very strong ideas about her philosophy of sales and marketing. By setting these out boldly, the writer appealed to companies that shared the applicant's outlook.

CONFIDENTIAL   *AVAILABLE FOR RELOCATION*

Alex McLean

0000 Duart Drive   Montgomery, Alabama 00000   topdog0000@west.com   000.000.0000

Thursday, April 8, 2008

Ms. Laura Worth
Sales Manager
Blue Sky, Inc.
1227 Amelia Island Parkway
Suite 200
Jacksonville, Florida 00000

Dear Ms. Worth:

For years, I've been making sales happen in the immediate future. But there's another reason why I have met or exceeded significantly rising sales goals every year for the last decade: I now generate add-on sales for products I championed from an idea to reduce an inventory. Results? I built my district from scratch and led us from $0 sales to $75M in sales annually.

My company obviously likes what I do. And maybe it's because I love sales so much that now, frankly, I am bored. That's why I am "testing the waters" with this application.

Because I thrive on anticipating requirements, I was thinking about Blue Sky's needs as I considered the form of my resume. Gone are the tiring recitations of job titles and responsibilities. In their places are a half-dozen examples of contributions measured in millions of dollars.

As you read, I hope some central ideas stand out clearly. First, I make it my business to get competitive intelligence faster than our competitors. Second, I make it my business to know my customers' operations almost as well as they do. Third, I make it my business to lead our customers to choose us through clear and compelling evidence that they think is their own good idea.

If Blue Sky can use someone with my track record, I'd like to explore how I can meet your specific sales needs. May I call in a few days to arrange a time to do that?

Sincerely,

Alex McLean

Encl.: Resume

244

District Salesperson.   *Don Orlando, Montgomery, Alabama*

The goal of this letter was to show that the applicant sold at many levels and used what he learned in the market to help his company beat the competition. Note the strong next-to-last paragraph.

TERRY NARBOW
0000 Jasmine Drive
Agoura Hills, California 91301
(555) 555-5555 (000) 000-0000
tnarbow@aol.com

January 23, 2008

M&R Associates
23457 Abelia Road
Calabasas, California 91304

Attention: Ms. Carolyn Hatten

Dear Ms. Hatten:

Achieving sales and marketing success in today's competitive marketplace requires a creative and strategic thinker who has the ability to establish profitable relationships, accelerate revenue growth, and maintain value-added service.

The company I left in 2007 was quite healthy, but despite record sales and profitability, there were few challenges on the horizon. I could have drawn a fine salary while serving secure accounts, but I was motivated to seek greater challenges. So I resigned in order to complete my B.A. in Business with an emphasis in Marketing as quickly as possible because this was my new chosen path.

Let me assure you, however, that I can make a compelling presentation of my candidacy whether I am selected for a position or not. My background encompasses research, development of categories of questions, creation of forms, merchandising, and displays. My innate ability to know what to ask allows for finding the most efficient way to improve procedures. Whatever the task—research, brand management/recognition, sales—it is my constant focus until completed.

Highlights that may be of particular interest include the following:

- Integration of diverse business practices, systems, and infrastructures to create top-performing organizations.
- Success in leveraging advanced technologies with core business operations.
- Cross-functional expertise in sales, new business development, and general management.
- Introduction of innovative marketing, business development, and promotional strategies that accelerated growth within existing business units and delivered revenues beyond projections.
- Realignment and expansion of third-party distribution network, capturing 20% revenue growth and strengthening competitive market position.

I understand that I may not be able to enter the marketing or brand field at a managerial level. All I am asking for is an introduction to one of your clients. Communication skills are one of my strengths (I continually take public speaking courses at various colleges), and I possess the will to succeed.

At this point in my career, I am interested in exploring new opportunities where my creative drive and energy can be further utilized and where I can continue to grow professionally.

Thank you for your consideration.

Sincerely,

Terry Narbow

Enclosure

245

Sales and Marketing Position. *Myriam-Rose Kohn, Valencia, California*

The opening paragraph is a miniprofile, and the second paragraph indicates the value this applicant placed on a bachelor's degree and career growth. Bullets point to areas of experience and success.

Rachel Fehren

name@hotmail.com

Current Address:
0000 Clinton Ave., Lubbock, TX 00000
(806) 000-0000

Permanent Address:
00000 Red Dr., Houston, TX 00000
(713) 000-0000

January 30, 2008

Human Resources Department
Office Max
1111 Durango Street
Houston, TX 00000

Dear Human Resources Representative:

It was with great interest and enthusiasm that I read your advertisement for a Marketing Assistant, as my background and abilities match your requirements for this position. Please allow me to explain briefly how my combination of sales, marketing, and customer service knowledge/experience can contribute to your organization's growth and success.

I will receive my B.B.A. degree in Marketing in August of this year; therefore, I have focused the majority of my professional development on marketing studies. However, my work history consists mainly of sales and customer-service positions. I see this as a strength because sales, marketing, and customer service are linked through their many similarities; they all share a common focus on consumer patterns, customer needs fulfillment, and business growth as the ultimate goal.

As a member of your team, I could use my knowledge of marketing and business-development strategies, ability to increase sales, and skills in customer satisfaction/retention to contribute to your organization's growth and success. Additionally, I can add value to your operations through my willingness to put forth an extra effort in all activities and perform tasks beyond those that fall under my job requirements. My former and current supervisors will attest that I am a dependable employee whom they trust implicitly.

My resume is enclosed to provide you with additional details concerning my background. Thank you for your time and consideration. I will call you next week to discuss the position further and look forward to speaking with you then.

Respectfully,

Rachel Fehren

Enclosure

246

Marketing Assistant. *Daniel J. Dorotik, Jr., Lubbock, Texas*

This candidate explains well the connections between her college major in marketing and work experience in customer service. She views both marketing and customer service as her skill areas.

FRANCES VESSEY

555 Q Street • Boston, MA 00000 • 555.555.5555 • vesfra@isp.com

George Grow, President
APEX, Inc.
555 S Street
New York, New York 00000

Dear Mr. Grow:

I read in *BusinessWeek* that your company will be introducing four cutting-edge products in the next 18 months, and I would be proud to be part of an organization with this kind of growth.

As a marketing specialist, I have solid experience in planning, implementing, and marketing product images, leading to significant increase in sales and product recognition. I have built strategic alliances with key marketing partners and vendors and have overseen sales teams, providing lead generation and marketing support.

I was the key manager of an integrated corporate image campaign featuring baseball star David Ortiz, which increased distributor sell-in and overall brand awareness. The campaign was awarded the Boston Advertising Association's 2005 "Advertising Campaign of the Year."

I welcome the opportunity to meet with you and discuss ideas I have for launching your new products. I will call you next week to set up an appointment.

Sincerely,

Frances Vessey

Encl. (Resume)

247

Marketing Specialist. *Ellen Mulqueen, Springfield, Massachusetts*

The applicant detected a job opportunity for marketing future products mentioned in a magazine. The letter indicates the person's interest, experience, and award-winning campaign management.

SAMUEL KRAMER

555 East End Street, Deer Park, New York 11729 • (555) 555-5555 • Salesman@topproducer.net

November 21, 2007

Dear Human Resources Administrator:

Perhaps your company is seeking to recruit the talent of someone who can grasp complex concepts, roll with the punches, and contribute to the success of a product's performance. If this is the case, then please accept the accompanying resume for your review and consideration for a position in which these strengths and diverse experience will be of value.

During my Internship as a Sales and Marketing Associate with Claire Rose, I effectively managed broad areas of the sales and marketing process from building and maintaining key accounts to product promotions. With a background in office management and field sales, I bring an ability to view situations from multiple perspectives and to maximize opportunities. As an effective problem solver, I see my role as one of cutting through red tape and confusion by providing clarity and practical business solutions for the company I represent and its clients.

Creatively, I enjoy brainstorming about innovative ideas that take into consideration demographics, target markets, advertising strategies, and shifts in the economy that have a direct impact on consumer buying trends and the influences that drive those changes. With these combined abilities, I am confident that I would make a significant contribution to the continued success of your company.

Although the accompanying resume illustrates my background well, I feel that a personal interview would better demonstrate my knowledge and abilities. Therefore, I would appreciate an opportunity to interview with you at a convenient time. Thank you for your review and consideration. I will contact you soon to request a personal interview.

Sincerely,

Samuel Kramer

248

Sales and Marketing Position. *Ann Baehr, Brentwood, New York*

Phrases such as "complex concepts," "multiple perspectives," and "innovative ideas" point to uncommon thoughtfulness and suggest that this applicant will bring valuable insight to a company.

Gene W. Mandren

19 S.E. Weldrum Avenue • Everett, Washington 99999

555-555-5555 *cell*   *home* 555-555-5555

April 14, 2008

Attn: Human Resources
Shelconney Products, Inc.
P.O. Box 421
Everett, WA 99999

Dear Name:

I have taken the opportunity to enclose a copy of my resume in application for the position you have advertised under *Sales* in *The Guard*. You will note from my resume that I have cultivated an outstanding background in sales over the last few years. I have managed million-dollar accounts and have been highly successful in developing strong relationships.

Over the past six years, while I was at General Steel (a nonretail business), I developed accounts from cold calls to ongoing repeat-customer relationships with high-profile customers. I am professional and meet people well. You will find me to be highly disciplined and adaptable with the ability to tenaciously and tactfully "court" customers to their satisfaction, ultimately giving me and my company excellent success. I learn quickly, thoroughly enjoy a challenge, am self-motivated with strong common sense, and do enjoy making money. I work well as a team member as well as independently.

It appears from your advertisement that your requirements and my qualifications may be a close match. I would like the opportunity to meet with you personally where we can discuss how we may further benefit each other. You may reach me easiest at my cell number, 555-555-5555. Thank you for your time in reviewing my resume, and I look forward to your call.

Sincerely,

Gene W. Mandren

Enclosure

249

Sales Position. *Rosie Bixel, Portland, Oregon*

Two successful activities (development and management) directed to two targets (accounts and customer relationships) are of continuing interest, making this candidate appealing to a company.

REDI DAVIS

1608 Thomas Avenue, Saint Paul, MN 55104 • Phone: 651-204-0665 • rd@aol.com

SENIOR ACCOUNT EXECUTIVE: INTERNET & ENTERPRISE SALES
C-Level Sales • Consultative Selling • Customer Account Management
Goal: To develop and penetrate customer accounts and fuel business growth in hot technologies
— preferably for an energized, entrepreneurial company.

October 10, 2007

Marissa Ross, VP
Sales & Investor Relations
Symantec Corporation
20330 Stevens Creek Blvd.
Cupertino, CA 95014

Hello, Marissa:

If you really want to grow your business, penetrate existing customer accounts, and retain your current customers, we should talk. I have a strong track record for doing this.

I am essentially a strong leader—targeting other strong leaders in Fortune and Federal markets and closing C-level sales. In a single company with the growing pains of 50 acquisitions, 9 layoffs, and 1 merger, I still excelled because I consistently deliver what I say I will and embrace your goal as if it were mine.

I am looking for a way to leverage my background in IT and Enterprise solutions with my skills in selling, partnering, and revenue growth—experience all gained while solving customers' problems. If you hire me, your company will gain these benefits—day one:

- Critical thinking and consultation for C-level customers
- Results-driven sales leadership and sales strategies
- Long-term customer retention and account development
- Year-over-year revenue growth—even in shrinking markets
- A multiyear network of IT and Enterprise customers and solutions partners

From what I know of your business, you might find I am a good fit. I will call you within a few days to discuss your needs and to hopefully schedule an interview with you and your colleagues.

Regards,

Redi Davis

Enclosure: Resume

250

IT Senior Sales Executive. *Helen Oliff, Reston, Virginia*

This individual wanted to bring his IT expertise to a major player in computer technology. The second paragraph is a profile, and the third indicates possible benefits from hiring him.

Lesley Mitchell

555 Mass. Ave.
Stamford, CT 55555
(555) 500-0000
Lesley52Mitchell@aol.com

September 25, 2007

Samuel Jones
Pharmaceutical Sales Recruiter
Jones Solutions
555 Williams Road
Stamford, CT 55555

Re: Position as Pharmaceutical Sales Representative

Dear Mr. Jones:

If you are working with a company seeking an entry-level pharmaceutical sales representative, you may find my achievements interesting. The most important qualification I have for the role is my record as a top sales performer. I combine skills in executing the sales cycle with a passion for building strong customer relationships. Also, I recently earned my Bachelor of Arts in Communication. I believe that these qualifications together are a good predictor of my future success in pharmaceutical sales.

To date, I have five part- and full-time years of experience at high-quality retailers. During that time, I produced top sales numbers while concurrently serving as sales manager. Here are some highlights of my career to date:

- Earned the #1 ranking out of 30 sales reps while also achieving the highest numbers for units and dollars per transaction. These results attest to my sincere interest in conveying the unique selling points of my products and in helping the customer through the whole sales cycle from initial inquiry to post-sales customer service.
- Ranked #3 out of 20 in a part-time sales role *while* managing the entire sales staff, earning praise for high-level customer service, and planning two sales events targeting professional and academic markets.
- Achieved 200% of the full-time staff target for opening new accounts while working only part-time.

Customers respond to me and are interested in what I have to say. They quickly realize that I am very well-informed about my products and know how to counter any concerns or objections they may have. I have also found that I am able to gain access to decision-makers because of my relationship-building strengths, professionalism, assertiveness, and persistence.

I am known for my leadership; proactive, self-directed style; and collaborative team skills. At this time, I am poised to begin a pharmaceutical sales career with an already honed professional image and professional-level sales skills. I am confident that I would prove to be an excellent hire for a pharmaceutical company. I will contact you to find out whether you are aware of any opportunities for which I would be an excellent, low-risk choice. Thank you for your kind consideration.

Sincerely,

Lesley Mitchell

251

Pharmaceutical Sales Representative. *Jean Cummings, Concord, Massachusetts*

The letter was to a recruiter from someone seeking to break into pharmaceutical sales. The writer's strategy was to explain the value of the applicant and to counter any doubts.

Judy Smith
123 Main Street
Annapolis, MD 21403

410-555-1234; cell 443-555-1234
E-mail: sales@aol.com

Drug Company USA
Mr. John Smith, Regional Sales Manager
1234 Main Street
Any town, MD 21032

Dear Mr. Smith,

As the Regional Sales Manager with Drug Company USA, I'm sure that you receive numerous inquiries daily from applicants hoping to land a sales representative position with your company. What sets me apart from other applicants is that I already have experience speaking with physicians and other health care providers about effects of certain medications from a clinical perspective.

As a teacher with seven years of experience teaching special education students, I have tracked and charted many students' progress as they adjust to various central nervous system stimulants (CNS) in treating conditions related to childhood/adolescent learning difficulties and behavioral disorders. I am already familiar with interpreting and studying various charts/graphs and data related to these medications, and I am confident that I could quickly grasp an understanding of any medication that I would be responsible for promoting.

Communication is a key factor in helping people to understand concepts and ideas, and as a teacher, I have communicated to both individuals and groups of people daily for a number of years. I have solid presentation skills and can quickly adapt my presentation style and methods to reach any audience. An example of my versatility in this area might include conducting a presentation to a group of teachers on how to implement a particular reading program, applying that particular program to a classroom of sixth graders, speaking to a parent about a child's progress in my class, and then tutoring a student privately after school hours. In the period of one day, I have had to adapt my presentation method communication style to a minimum of four different audiences.

I am looking for a new and challenging career outside of classroom teaching and believe that I have the skills and background that your company is seeking. I am self-motivated, creative, flexible, and organized. I am further qualified for this position by my Master's Degree in Special Education and a Bachelor's Degree in Psychology and Neuroscience. I already possess a basic scientific understanding of the biological effects different medications can have on the human body.

Mr. Smith, thank you for your time and consideration for the sales representative position. I will follow up with you by April 1 to confirm that you received my information and to answer any questions you may have at that time. Should you need to contact me before then, it's easiest to reach me at 443-555-1234 or e-mail me at sales@aol.com. I look forward to speaking with you soon.

Sincerely,

Judy Smith

Enclosure

252

Sales Representative. *Beth Colley, Crownsville, Maryland*

This special education teacher wanted to transition to pharmaceutical sales. The letter highlights the applicant's ability to communicate to a broad audience, including parents and physicians.

Carlos C. Serito
555 Main Street
Parker, IL 00000
555-555-5555
ccs321@aol.com

March 15, 2008

Mr. James Cohen
Vice President, Sales and Marketing
Technology Division
XYZ Solutions, Inc.
555 Corporate Street
New York, NY 00000

Dear Mr. Cohen:

At the suggestion of Julia Corrado, I have enclosed my resume for your review. My consistent success in creating and establishing profitable sales and marketing strategies for business technology consulting would be an asset to XYZ Solutions. I understand that one of your priorities for this year is to improve the sales results in the Chicago market, and I would appreciate the opportunity to talk with you about how my Chicago experience can help you achieve that goal.

The primary focus of my experience has been in successful turnarounds of weak or unprofitable territories and product lines. I enjoy the prospect of researching problem areas and developing the relationships and resources needed. In my search I am targeting companies that would benefit from my ability to . . .

- Identify market opportunities in the Midwest and develop new territories for intangible services.
- Build and maintain relationships with corporate and institutional clients, from Fortune 50 to small- and medium-sized businesses.
- Consistently exceed sales quotas, winning sales and sales management competitions; establish effective business plans and budgets; and control expenses.
- Provide in-depth knowledge acquired in a variety of business environments.

You can reach me at the phone number or e-mail listed above. I look forward to discussing the challenges you face in 2008 and beyond. Thank you for your time and attention.

Sincerely,

Carlos C. Serito

Resume enclosed

253

Sales and Marketing Position. *Christine L. Dennison, Lincolnshire, Illinois*

This applicant with managerial experience was not looking explicitly for a managerial position but wanted to make use of his Chicago experience to help a company develop its Chicago market.

ANTOINETTE JOUVENAUX

213 Michigan Avenue North
Fox Point, WI 53217
ajouven@wi.rr.com

Residence: (414) 352-5241
Office: (262) 545-9000
Mobile: (414) 333-1432

Personal and Confidential

November 8, 2007

Alex McGovern, Managing Partner
Midwest Consultants, Inc.
2229 North Broadway Avenue
Chicago, IL 60601

Dear Mr. McGovern:

The advent of multiple electronic technologies in tandem with existing sales/marketing channels creates almost unlimited options for business development. At the same time, it can also create tremendous confusion for executives in evaluating and determining their most appropriate strategic solutions. My success lies in the ability to lead the entire organization through this process, resulting in brand enhancement, market share increases, and top-/bottom-line revenue improvements.

Throughout my professional career, I have facilitated the planning, development, and implementation of marketing and sales programs to strengthen and accelerate base business while launching the introduction of numerous new products, services, and technologies. My ability to build and lead cross-functional teams of analysts, creative design, marketing, sales, technology, operations, and management personnel has been critical to our performance.

In my current position, I was recruited to lead the marketing and communications organization through a period of rapid growth and expansion. To date, our results have been significant and include revenue increases of 31% and net income increases of 23%. As a member of the senior leadership team, I have had direct influence on these results.

Now, at this point in my career, I am seeking new professional challenges where I can continue to provide strategic, tactical, and creative leadership. As such, I am interested in meeting with you to explore opportunities with Midwest Consultants, Inc. I will contact you to determine an appropriate time. Thank you.

Sincerely,

Antoinette Jouvenaux

Enclosure: Resume

254

Senior Sales Executive. *Michele J. Haffner, Glendale, Wisconsin*

The letter indicates the applicant's abilities, broad experience, and achievements quantified in percentages. She has no specific position in mind but wants to bring expertise to the company.

0000 Marley Avenue, Denver, CO 00000
(000) 000-0000

bandaide@waycool.com

Deirdre Janovic

January 4, 2008

Mr. Brian Paxton
Chief Engineer
Niteglo Productions
900 Blackrock Turnpike
Denver, CO 00000

Dear Mr. Paxton:

I know that you are busy and must receive hundreds of unsolicited resumes from hopeful communications majors looking for work in the music recording industry. To be honest with you, I'm no exception. But before you discard or file away my request, I'd appreciate your attention for just a moment so that I can tell you a little about myself.

First of all, I have an immense, profound love for popular music, whether it be rock, rap or R&B. Since the age of 7, I've been reading liner notes and have amassed quite a thorough knowledge of who's who in the recording business. It's love such as this that breeds dedication. Despite the tremendous competition that I'm up against, nothing will discourage me from pursuing my dreams of a career in the music industry. This is my calling!

Briefly, I offer

- ◆ Boundless creative energy with an imaginative way of dealing with problems.
- ◆ Articulate verbal skills and the ability to deliver messages with impact.
- ◆ Personal assertiveness, especially in face-to-face or phone contact with high-profile clients.
- ◆ A strong sensitivity to the needs of others, enabling the development of solid business relationships.
- ◆ Excellent planning, organizing and numerical skills, as well as a familiarity with computers.

Some examples of my abilities are illustrated in the enclosed resume. Up to now, my work experience has been limited, but my high degree of motivation has been recognized by my employers, who have quickly promoted me to positions of increased responsibility.

My enthusiasm and potential are there, waiting to be unleashed and molded as you see fit. Ultimately, my goal is a position as an artist relations or marketing rep, but all I want at this point is to get my foot in the door of an organization associated with the music recording industry. It doesn't matter if I'm assigned to the mailroom or some other clerical area. Salary is also not my primary concern. I would even be interested in an unpaid internship if it presented an opportunity to learn the industry from the ground up.

If any situations exist where you think I could be of value, or if you have any suggestions as to others with whom it might be beneficial to speak, I'd like to hear from you. I'm looking forward to the chance of meeting with you to discuss these possibilities. Thank you in advance for your time and consideration.

Sincerely,

Deirdre Janovic

Enclosure: Resume

255

Marketing Representative, Music Industry. *Melanie Noonan, West Paterson, New Jersey*

This communications major was looking for an entry-level position in the music recording industry. With little work experience, she was willing to be an unpaid intern just to get her foot in the door.

JAMES DUFFY

555 Interval Street #55
Long Beach, CA 55555

james-duffy@pacbell.net

555-555-5555 (H)
000-000-0000 (C)

September 9, 2007

Mr. Howard Pepper
Vice President of Sales
Top Level Products
555 Percival Street
Mountain View, CA 55555

Subject: Sales Manager Position

Dear Mr. Pepper:

Ongoing successful results depend not only on what a sales manager has done recently but also on what he has achieved throughout his career that serves as a strong foundation for future growth and profitability. Among other things, an astute manager knows the value of building an enthusiastic team and surrounding himself with effective people who are committed to surpassing expectations. The enclosed resume highlights my strengths and accomplishments in these and other, related areas.

My enthusiasm for building and leading a high-performing team matches closely with my commitment to discerning the critical needs of customers and presenting them with solutions tailored to meet those needs. I also strive to instill this sense of enthusiasm and commitment in my team, with encouragement and support provided to help them achieve their goals.

A large part of my success rests on my ability to take a unique look at existing challenges and develop ideas and plans to obtain the maximum results in those situations. For example, when I led the campaign to establish a presence in Alaska for Lehman Industries, success in that region had previously eluded the company. However, I felt convinced that opportunities existed there, and I proceeded to gain the support needed to prove it. In addition to subsequently generating exceptional sales results in Alaska, I also displaced a formidable competitor by establishing relationships with several influential individuals.

Having recently evaluated my current situation and career goals, I decided that it was time to pursue new opportunities in the sales/management area. Because of my successful track record, I am confident I can add to the success of your organization as a sales manager, and I would like to arrange a personal interview to discuss possibilities in greater detail. I will call you shortly to follow up on this letter.

Sincerely,

James Duffy

256

Sales Manager. *Georgia Adamson, Campbell, California*

The applicant had been laid off two years ago and had been doing only out-of-field assignments. The writer focused on the individual's overall stellar record rather than recent weaker experience.

292 Gallery of Best Cover Letters

Jayne Smyth
101 Main Street
Friendship, CT 06000
555-555-5555
JSmyth@123.zzz

February 10, 2008

Hallmark Cards, Inc.
ATTN: Human Resources Director
P.O. Box 100000001
Kansas City, MO 64141

Re: Positions for **Sales Professionals**

Dear Human Resources Director:

When you care enough to send the very best...send me!

The opportunity to represent Hallmark Cards, the perennial industry leader, would be a dream come true. Because I share your philosophy that only my best is good enough to offer, I have consistently been a top-producing sales representative for my current employer, constantly exceeding sales quotas and earning recognition from clients, peers and supervisors. Accomplishments have included the following:

- Among 50 sales representatives, rank in the top three for the past two years, supporting the achievement of departmental sales goals averaging $500,000 per month.
- Regularly produce 30% or more over daily sales goals.
- Selected to manage key national accounts.
- Commended by peers for providing sales assistance/support with accounts in a competitive environment.
- Chosen to mentor new hires.

I offer you solid sales experience, a strong customer focus and effective leadership skills, in combination with an "only the best will do" work ethic. I eagerly anticipate the opportunity to discuss your goals for your new territory and the ways in which I might help Hallmark achieve and exceed them. I will call next week to explore the possibility of an interview. Thank you for considering my qualifications.

Sincerely,

Jayne Smyth

Enclosure

257

Sales Representative. *Debra O'Reilly, Bristol, Connecticut*

The targeted company required outside sales experience, which the applicant lacked. The letter emphasized her sales success and good match for the company. Within a week, she got the job.

JOHNNIE JUNDLAND

555 Riverside Drive Houston, TX 50505 555-505-5555
johnniej@juno.com

August 31, 2007

Mr. William White
Regional Vice President
Newsome Medical
Five Dallas Drive
Fort Worth, TX 55055

Re: Medical Sales—Reference Job Med555

Dear Mr. White:

FACT: *A recent study by XLMED Group of San Antonio, Texas, found that 41% of medical sales reps never made it past the gatekeeper; and only 12% of rep visits with a key decision maker lasted longer than three minutes.*

FACT: *Market leaders demand results-driven relationship builders to open doors and sustain business. Simply stated…I can do that for Newsome Medical!*

Jules Pattern, a mutual contact, apprised me of a pending vacancy in your Southwest Division based in Fort Worth. Given that your company distributes a product I know and have used for 12 years as an R.N., coupled with my deep desire for a marketing and sales career, I am eager to visit with you. Please know that I am fully prepared to represent your company in offering state-of-the art medical technology to support the health and well-being of others.

As a Nursing Manager and Registered Nurse, I am cognizant of both the clinical and administrative aspects of achieving the optimal health of patients. I've had numerous opportunities to collaborate with physicians and, in so doing, have become both confident and comfortable in these meetings. That, however, is not the primary reason I believe I would be a most valuable addition to Newsome Medical—what I have discovered is a passion and talent for marketing and sales through my work as a Nursing Manager and Administrator. Colleagues will attest that my self-directed, competitive, and results-driven spirit has been a true asset in producing desired results in a demanding, challenging, and ever-changing health care industry.

Enclosed please find a professional resume to delineate my qualifications to join your company in a sales role. I look forward to continued conversation with members of your team and am optimistic that the outcome of this communication will be the first step toward a mutually beneficial affiliation with Newsome Medical. May I meet with you soon to explore this outstanding opportunity? I will call to set an appropriate time.

Best regards,

Johnnie Jundland

Enc.

258

Medical Sales Representative. *Billie Ruth Sucher, Urbandale, Iowa*

The individual had no prior experience in medical sales but wanted to secure a position in this highly competitive field. This sale-driven letter helped to secure an interview.

GABE CONNOR

1219 Wall Street Heights, New York, NY 10005
Home: (917) 333-9999 ▪ gconnor@gmail.com ▪ Cell: (917) 222-1111

Date

Company Personnel
Company Department
Company Name
Address
City, State, Postal Code

Dear _____,

When I was promoted to the Senior Sales Manager position at IBM, the company was fraught with major client communication and business challenges. I was personally selected to rebuild account loyalty with key clients Corbro and AMMO and drive hardware sales. I strengthened relationships to the point where I achieved more than $25 million in sales and gained the trust and confidence of AMMO into new initiatives and opportunities that will account for an additional 35% in revenue.

In my previous role at IBM, I turned around a major product suffering a 5-year decline in sales to regain product value recognition that increased sales by 35% and brand awareness by 40%. The product catapulted from one of the lowest-profile brands within IBM with customers looking to move off the platform to one where client representatives were asking to implement non-iSeries workload on iSeries, a notion that previously would not have been considered with representatives.

Prior to this I was recognized for improving operational areas by developing new approaches to finding and attracting new business within target markets, implementing appropriate marketing and sales strategies to achieve growth in sales revenue and improve market share, and proactively developing and building customer relationships by delivering customer solutions.

These examples clearly demonstrate the value I can bring to your organization. My strengths are in devising creative solutions to overcome obstacles, adapting to circumstances, and achieving business growth. I have earned a reputation as an intuitive business strategist who has consistently left each division in an infinitely improved position. I bring to your organization more than 20 years of IT managerial experience, outstanding analytical and strategic thinking, and a ruthless focus on achievement of revenue and profit goals.

My resume is enclosed to provide you with details of my skills and accomplishments, but I am certain that a personal interview would more fully reveal my desire and ability to contribute to your organization. I will call in the coming week to set up an appointment. Thank you for your time and consideration of my application, and do not hesitate to contact me if you have any questions. I look forward to speaking with you soon.

Sincerely,

Gabe Connor
Encl.

259

Director of IT Sales. *Jennifer Rushton, Sydney, New South Wales, Australia*

The person was a senior manager who could turn around declining IT product areas, deliver results, and strengthen client relationships that generated revenue. The letter makes this clear.

Sandy Wexler
777 Vantage Drive, Chalfont, Pennsylvania 19333
Home (666) 888B9999 • Mobile (666) 666-5555

February 22, 2008

Bader Associates
3 Wadsworth Drive
Buckingham, PA 19222

Dear Hiring Manager:

Success in sales is about people, persistence, and performance!

As a sales representative with proven skills and strong sales accomplishments, I am confident my qualifications and experience will be of interest to you. Characteristics that have contributed to my success are...

- Meticulous attention to customer service and follow-up
- Energy, enthusiasm, and motivation
- Excellent planning, time-management, and organizational skills
- Ability to perform effectively in a fast-paced atmosphere

The enclosed resume summarizes more than 17 years of experience in both business and consumer environments. In each of my previous positions, I have quickly attained sales results and established a loyal customer base. I am very proficient in all stages of the sales process—from the cold call to a signature on the contract. The process begins with building rapport with my clients and continues by delivering the extra effort necessary to achieve the goals of all concerned...a "win-win" situation.

My selling skills are complemented by equally strong creative abilities. I am able to work with people to generate ideas that work. My goal is to become a key contributor on your professional sales team and help you meet your overall objectives in any way I can.

Although secure in my present position, I am interested in a more challenging opportunity. It will be a pleasure to meet with you in a confidential interview to discuss my credentials in detail. I am available for a personal interview at your earliest convenience. I will contact you in the coming days to set a mutually convenient time we can meet.

Thank you for your consideration.

Sincerely,

Sandy Wexler

Enclosure

260

Sales Representative.   *Karen Conway, Media, Pennsylvania*

This letter, calling for confidentiality, is for a person who is successful in her current position but wants a change for a more challenging opportunity. The whole letter displays her confidence.

CONFIDENTIAL   Job #100-12   *Ready to relocate*

Robert Savage

000 Martin Terrace   Starkley, Alabama 00000   robert_savage@zipx.com   ☎ 334.555.5555

Monday February 16, 2008

Ms. Laura Worth
District Sales Manager
TopLine Pharmaceuticals, Inc.
500 Northridge Parkway
Suite 400
Montgomery, Alabama 36100

Dear Ms. Worth:

I would like to join the TopLine Pharmaceuticals team as your newest pharmaceutical sales representative. To give you confidence that I am the right person to interview, this letter anticipates your needs in the following areas:

Your likely requirements:	My capabilities:
• **Strong sales experience.**	• Proven record in closing the most difficult kind of "sales": persuading all my customers to give up their property at a reasonable price and avoid costly legal battles.
• Ability to **master steep learning curves** in new fields.	• Three years of handling rapidly increasing responsibility with absolutely no formalized training.
• Dedication to **reach tough goals independently.**	• Embarked upon a personal, professional development program to learn about your industry from pharmaceutical reps, professional organizations, and trade magazines.

My resume has the details. It may not look like others you have seen. I thought you deserved a good deal more than the usual unsupported summary of "professional qualifications," standard job titles, and unfamiliar responsibilities. In their places are a half dozen profit-building capabilities I am ready to offer now, backed up by selected examples of performance.

If my approach and track record will benefit TopLine, I'd like to hear about your specific sales requirements. May I call in a few days to arrange a time to do just that?

Sincerely,

Robert Savage

Encl.: Resume

CONFIDENTIAL

261

Pharmaceutical Sales Representative. *Don Orlando, Montgomery, Alabama*

This applicant never had the word "sales" in any of his job titles. To compensate, the writer introduced a table that matched the individual's abilities with likely corporate needs.

TINA B. STEWART

5555 55th Street ▪ Lakeview, Texas 79000 ▪ *(555) 555-5555*

April 12, 2008

TROY PHARMACEUTICALS
5555 Magnum Street
Ft. Cloud, Mississippi 55555

Re: West Texas Pharmaceutical Sales Specialist, Code SPMDT

Dear Human Resources Coordinator:

I am committed to improved patient care, a quality that characterizes value to medical professionals. As an *established pharmaceutical sales representative* covering West Texas and Eastern New Mexico territories, I offer *beneficial industry knowledge* from *six years of experience.* It would be an honor to represent TROY, a highly regarded pharmaceutical company whose mission to enhance and preserve quality of life coincides so closely with mine.

The enclosed resume reflects a *match between my credentials and your requirements for a pharmaceutical sales specialist.* A qualification summary follows:

JOB REQUIREMENTS	PERSONAL QUALIFICATIONS
Five years of sales experience, preferably pharmaceutical	▪ *Six years of proven success* in pharmaceutical / medical sales industry. ▪ *Established rapport with 200+ West Texas physicians* specializing in a spectrum of healthcare disciplines.
Bachelor's degree	▪ *Bachelor of science* in political science with minor in public relations.
Project and account management experience	▪ Exclusively *acquired six-figure surgical center account,* orchestrated *total equipment installation,* and *troubleshot logistical problems.* ▪ Employ *continuous customer contact, needs assessment, and strategic planning* to manage and grow 180+ accounts.
Sales / persuasion skills	▪ Consistently rank in *top 10% of regional sales* representatives for exceeding 100% of annual sales goals. ▪ Use *scientific / consultative sales approach* to gain customer acceptance of products and services.
Communication and presentation skills	▪ Relate to physicians through *lighthearted yet authoritative communication style* to create enjoyable sales environment. ▪ Incorporate analogies, illustrations, sales / detail aids, and humor into presentations and training seminars to *engage audiences, retain interest, and improve comprehension.*

Given a *preestablished client network, technical knowledge, and personal values,* I am confident I would well serve TROY PHARMACEUTICALS's goals and objectives. I hope to *share business development ideas* during a personal interview and will contact your office within the week to schedule an appointment at your convenience. In the meantime, thank you for your consideration.

Sincerely,

Tina B. Stewart

Enclosure: Resume

262

Pharmaceutical Sales Specialist. *Edith A. Rische, Lubbock, Texas*

In going beyond the resume, this Job Requirements… Personal Qualifications format focuses on the candidate's relevant strengths. The style is simple because the individual's achievements speak for themselves.

SANDRA A. PEACE, D.C.
10000 Pleasant Drive, Asheville, NC 28888
Home: (704) 555-1212   *Cell:* (704) 444-7777
sap@mindspring.com

February 1, 2008

Pfizer, Inc.
555 Medical Drive
Bldg. 2, Suite 200
Cateret, NJ 08000

Re: *The Richmond Times Dispatch* advertisement, October 28, 2008: Pharmaceutical Sales (Code K007)

If there were a recurring theme in my life, it would have to be "Nothing is certain but change." Of course, not everyone may see this as a driving force, but for me it has always served as a great motivator.

In my opinion, success boils down to three things:

- Establishing structured goals and creating/implementing a master plan to achieve those goals
- Developing the skills, knowledge and expertise—in short, the tools—to be successful
- Providing top-quality service to customers

As you will see from my enclosed resume, this strategy has also served me well in business development over the last 12 years. For example, after working as a medical laboratory technician for eight years, I changed career paths—investing four years of professional and academic training to become a chiropractic physician. As a self-starting, focused professional, I achieved this goal, eventually establishing my own practice, which I operated quite profitably for more than eight years. Last year, I sold the practice (at a profit) and moved to Asheville (from Charlotte), where I have managed (very hands-on) a satellite office of another physician.

During the business development phase of my practice—which I always treated as a business—I sought additional training in sales and marketing, receiving ideas and inspiration from the best "gurus" in the business, such as Jay Conrad Levinson (*Guerilla Marketing*); Jay Abraham (*How to Get from Where You Are to Where You Want to Be*); Chet Holmes (*The Seven Steps to Every Sale* and *The 10 Follow-up Steps for Bonding with Clients*); Kenneth Blanchard (*The One-Minute Manager* and *The Heart of a Leader*); Napoleon Hill (*Think and Grow Rich*); and Dale Carnegie (*How to Win Friends and Influence People*), among many others. With Holmes, Abraham and Levinson, I participated in a 90-minute, monthly interactive seminar. I implemented these ideas in my practice, applying sales and marketing strategies to grow the business.

My point in telling you all of this is twofold: (1) to provide some substantive evidence of self-motivation and (2) to demonstrate, as my resume attests, personal sales, marketing and business success. Seeking professional growth, and no stranger to change, I now want to change the course of my life once again.

What do I want to do now? Apply my sales, marketing and business development, relationship-building and medical experience to a career in pharmaceutical sales. I have extensive medical knowledge, an understanding of the physician's mind-set and a desire to succeed.

I would welcome an opportunity to speak with you regarding this—or another related—position with Pfizer, and would appreciate your time and consideration of my qualifications. I will call next week to set an appointment.

Sincerely,

Sharon A. Wright

Enclosure

263

Pharmaceutical Sales Representative. *Doug Morrison, Charlotte, North Carolina*

After four years of chiropractic school and eight years in private practice, this applicant wanted to become a sales rep for a pharmaceutical company. This letter shows her personality and motivation.

LEONARD
CURTIS
GELI

0000 E. 75th Street/6B ⚔ New York, NY 10123 ⚔ leonardcgeli@hotmail.com
Home: (555) 555-5555 ⚔ Cell: (555) 555-5555

March 26, 2008

Michael F. Paisley
VP of Sales
Merkx, Inc.
25 Sixth Avenue
New York, NY 10011

INTRODUCTION ▶ Dear Mr. Paisley:

Sandra Smith recommended that I forward my resume to you concerning a **Sales Representative** position with your company. Although currently employed as Director of Sales at Home Market, Inc., I am pursuing my long-time goal: a career in the pharmaceutical industry.

FEATURES ▶ I offer Merkx a unique background of successful experience in sales and science, with natural relationship-building and selling skills and an innate fascination for science as related to health care. My 13-year track record is characterized by consistent bottom-line contributions through exceeding sales quotas, and proactive problem-solving initiatives.

BENEFITS ▶ I am familiar with and impressed by your company's selling and marketing strategies, and I would welcome the opportunity to join your team and increase sales by leveraging the following:

- Communication, negotiation, and closing skills—generated $4 million in sales for Home Market's merchants in a year.
- Ability to build trust and rapport instantly—penetrated challenging territory to sign 25 merchants in three months, exceeding quota of 10.
- Customer service and client-retention skills—96% customer satisfaction rate. Handle full sales and customer service cycle.
- Tenacity, determination, and follow-through—commended by vendors/partners for persistence, leading to contracts.
- Entrepreneurial, self-motivated mentality—launched direct marketing initiatives. Pursued clients through networking presentations, cold calling, and account-management efforts.
- Energy and enthusiasm about product benefits to clients.

BONUS ▶ Please note that I am fluent in Spanish and willing to travel or relocate.

ACTION ▶ A personal meeting would be a great way for us to discuss your sales challenges and the benefits I can bring to Merkx. I can make myself available at your convenience and will call you next week to schedule an appointment.

Sincerely,

Leonard C. Geli

264

Pharmaceutical Sales Representative. *Ilona Vanderwoude, Riverdale, New York*

With a background in science teaching, premed coursework, and sales, this applicant wanted to go into pharmaceutical sales. The unique headings with bullets match the applicant's aggressiveness.

REBECCA HOLLOWAY

555 Candelabra Drive ▪ San Jose, CA 55555 ▪ 555-555-5555 ▪ hollowaybecca@mindspring.com

August 31, 2007

Ms. Paula Edgar
Employment Manager
Roseland Pharmaceuticals
55 E. Main Street
San Rafael, CA 55555

Subject: Employment Opportunity—Pharmaceutical Sales Representative

Dear Ms. Edgar:

If you could use a sales rep who has established a successful track record in a highly competitive industry and has contributed to achieving company objectives through sales expansion, profitability improvement, and high-level customer relationship management, I believe you will find the enclosed resume worth a close look.

My record reflects an intense desire to exceed the expectations of my employer and its customers. I enjoy the exhilaration of negotiating and closing business deals in a competitive environment, and I am committed to taking whatever steps are necessary to accomplish this result. Although able to work independently, I frequently utilize my relationship-building skills to obtain cooperation from internal support staff and others in order to meet customers' needs.

Effective customer interaction has been one of my strongest points throughout my career, including the establishment of trust-based relationships with customers at the senior executive level. But I don't stop there—I target and pursue contacts that enable me to generate substantial business expansion within each customer organization.

Although I appreciate the challenges I have encountered in my present company and the growth I have gained through those challenges, I am currently looking for a new opportunity that will allow me to use my strengths more fully. Among the qualifications I can offer you is my ability to relate to individuals from diverse cultures and understand the differences in how they conduct business. In particular, I am targeting positions in Southeast Asia that will allow me to utilize both my strong sales skills and my cultural background, including language skills, to pursue and secure business internationally.

With my extensive sales experience and my dedication to delivering exceptional results, I am confident I can produce measurable results for your organization as a Pharmaceutical Sales Representative. I will contact you within the next few days to follow up and see whether an interview can be arranged.

Sincerely,

Rebecca Holloway

265

Pharmaceutical Sales Representative. *Georgia Adamson, Campbell, California*

This individual wanted to move to a different company. She was a high-energy salesperson, and the writer emphasized this throughout the letter, avoiding criticism of the current company.

Agnes Smith-Bucci

95 Huling Lane
Providence, RI 02222

(555) 555-5555
E-mail: sbucci2@aol.com
Cell: (000) 000-0000

March 7, 2008

Mr. Arthur Spellman, Sr.
888 Harris Avenue South
Newport, RI 00000

Dear Mr. Spellman:

Please accept this letter and my application for a pharmaceutical sales position with Pfizer, Inc. I appreciate your invitation to contact you for your assistance in my attempt to receive an interview for employment. If hired, I firmly believe that I will make a solid contribution to Pfizer as a salesperson.

As you may know, my extensive employment experience with sales negotiations in travel and real estate, coupled with an excellent education and training in becoming a Licensed Practical Nurse, provide me with ideal credentials for a position in sales of pharmaceuticals. In addition, my LPN training has served to refocus my own professional objective toward sales in this important, rapidly expanding, and fascinating arena of the health field.

Perceptive to the needs of clients and resolute in securing all potential sales, I have built a solid reputation with employers and customers for being trustworthy, dependable, and dedicated in my responsibilities. I am a proven self-starter willing to take on significant responsibilities, as I have worked competently on independent projects and as a contributing team member.

I genuinely look forward to discussing my qualifications with a Pfizer representative for a position in pharmaceutical sales. I would appreciate a company representative contacting me at my home number, e-mail, or cell phone to set up an interview and an opportunity to tour the facility. If I do not hear from Pfizer by April 7, I will contact the human resources office to request an appointment.

Thank you kindly for your offer to assist me in my application for employment at Pfizer.

Sincerely,

Agnes Smith-Bucci, LPN

Enclosures: resume / application

266

Pharmaceutical Sales Representative. *Edward Turilli, North Kingstown, Rhode Island*

The applicant coupled her LPN status with her sales experience to break into pharmaceutical sales. The letter stresses her independent work—an excellent foundation for salespeople on the road.

Richard A. Gonzales

0000 Clinton Avenue ▪ Houston, TX 00000 ▪ (281) 000-0000 ▪ name@yahoo.com

January 30, 2008

Human Resources Department
Pfizer Pharmaceuticals
1111 Grant Drive
Houston, TX 00000

RE: Position as Pharmaceutical Sales Representative

Dear Staffing Representative:

I am submitting my resume in application for the position of Pharmaceutical Sales Representative. I believe I am the ideal candidate for your consideration, not only because my qualifications match your requirements, but also because my strong network of contacts in the local/regional healthcare industry and ability to build strong relationships will enable me to increase sales growth and market share for your company.

My combination of healthcare experience, pharmaceutical product knowledge, and relationship-selling skills has provided me the opportunity to deliver substantial revenue gains for the ABC Medical Center in Houston and develop solid, sustainable relationships with a broad cross-section of healthcare professionals throughout the Greater Houston area. Accomplishments that may be of interest to you include the following:

- I spearheaded a revenue increase of **$600,000** within the first month and **$7.6 million** in my first year as Director of the Cardiac Cath Lab at the ABC Medical Center.
- I created a new computer program that ensured proper matches between physician and lab billing, producing significant savings and demonstrating my ability to pinpoint opportunities for profit growth.
- I maintained an excellent record in pharmaceutical purchasing, serving as the sole point of contact for pharmaceutical sales representatives and playing a pivotal role in physician decisions.

My resume is enclosed to provide you with specific details concerning my qualifications and accomplishments, but perhaps a personal interview would more fully reveal my ability to contribute to your market share growth. I look forward to the possibility of such a meeting.

Thank you for your time and consideration. Please do not hesitate to contact me if I can answer any questions. If I don't hear from you in two weeks, I will call to explore the possibility of an interview.

Sincerely,

Richard A. Gonzales

Enclosure

267

Pharmaceutical Sales Representative. *Daniel J. Dorotik, Jr., Lubbock, Texas*

The writer emphasizes specific accomplishments for this applicant, who was seeking to transition to a new position within the same industry. Boldfacing highlights key quantified achievements.

DORIS C. KITTERING

7721 Templeton Street
Milwaukee, WI 53202

Mobile: (414) 291-2222
E-mail: dorisckitt@mynet.com

October 22, 2007

Mary Theresa Wright
Social Technology, Inc.
5050 Wacker Dr.
Chicago, IL 60601
E-mail: mary@socialtech.com

Dear Ms. Wright,

Your online job posting at CareerBuilder.com for a **Regional Sales Director** is such a good fit with my background, you might be skeptical that I could really exist! Let me assure you, I am most interested in this challenging position (I thrive on challenges) and have just what you require…and more.

My resume is enclosed for your review. You will notice that my experience, training, and personal attributes meet all of your stated requirements and preferences, and even surpass them.

Your Requirements & Needs	**My Qualifications**
▪ Paid nonprofit experience in direct service environment	▪ Five years of experience in **paid nonprofit social services agency** and 10 years of experience with government-funded human services agency in direct service delivery. Increasing the effectiveness of nonprofits resonates with my values and life mission.
▪ Bachelor's Degree in Social Sciences	▪ **Bachelor's Degree** in Psychology.
▪ Sales experience—minimum 5 years	▪ 12 years (part-time and full-time) in inside sales, retail sales, membership sales, and sales management. **Top-performing producer** in all sales environments.
▪ Working knowledge of software programs	▪ Experienced using **The Clinical Manager** (database software for Case Managers), as well as **MS Office** (Word, PowerPoint, and **Outlook**). Quick study in new software programs and applications.
▪ Industry knowledge	▪ 15-year background in social services industry, both nonprofit and government-funded positions.

As a former human services Program Director and current Case Manager, I am thoroughly familiar with the software needs, expectations, and unspoken "pain" of your prospective customers. Because of my background in social services, my credibility and trust-building capacity would be enhanced with your target audience. Couple that with a well-established track record in needs assessment and consultative sales, and I believe you have a winning combination.

May I have the opportunity to make my case? Since I plan to relocate to the Chicago area soon, I would be available for an appointment at your convenience. I will be in town next week and will call to schedule an appointment. Thank you for your consideration.

Sincerely,

Doris C. Kittering

268

Regional Sales Director. *Susan Guarneri, Three Lakes, Wisconsin*

This applicant had a former history in sales and a recent history in social services. The target position integrated technology sales and social services. The letter shows her combination of both.

AVERY M. COSGROVE

5555 28th Street, Lubbock, Texas 55555 ▪ amcosgrove33@isprovider.com   **(555) 555-5555**

December 12, 2007

Name
Title
Company
Address
City, State ZIP

Ability is what you're capable of doing. Motivation determines what you do. Attitude determines how well you do it. —Lou Holtz

Dear Mr. (Name):

A senior at Texas Tech University, I anticipate a **B.A. in Marketing** in May 2008 and am eager to put my education and experience to work in a professional career. A major in marketing affords a highly motivated and creative student the opportunity to create promotions and use effective sales strategies to increase revenues. Energy and a competitive spirit will also boost my potential for achieving company goals. I am confident that after reviewing the enclosed resume, you will find me an excellent choice for a marketing or sales representative position in your company.

As you will discover, I provided 100% of college tuition and living expenses while maintaining grades and participating daily in the cheerleading program. This achievement demonstrates an ability to manage time and balance priorities. Furthermore, an employment check will reflect a conscientious, capable, and responsible leader.

In addition to education, training, and work experience, your company will benefit from the following character and personality traits:

- **Quality of service and steady profitability derived from goal setting, motivation, and high standards**
- **Savings of time and money from a constant quest to "get it right the first time"**
- **A superior work ethic modeled by diligence, ownership of responsibility, and giving more than expected**
- **Positive outcomes attained from effective problem analysis and direct solutions**
- **Rapport and trust with others gained from a personable demeanor and respect for differences, as well as good listening and communication skills**
- **Credible presentations using excellent English and grammar**

If given a chance, I can contribute greatly to any effort. That being said, an opportunity to further discuss your needs and my qualifications in a personal interview will be mutually beneficial. Please expect a phone call in the immediate future to answer your questions and schedule an appointment at your convenience.

In the meantime, thank you for your time and consideration.

Sincerely,

Avery M. Cosgrove

Enclosure: Resume

269

Marketing/Sales Representative. *Edith A. Rische, Lubbock, Texas*

This is a networking letter for a newly graduated college student seeking an entry-level marketing position. The applicant can easily adjust the first paragraph to target a particular company.

DAVID VAN ALDEN

10 Azure Court, Rosevale SA 5555
(H) 05 5555 5555 • (M) 5555 555 555 • (E) david@hotmail.com.au

INCREASED SALES REVENUE • TERRITORY GROWTH • PERSUASION

21 June 2007

Mr Alan Johnston
Human Resource Manager
Pharmaceutical Suppliers Pty Ltd
33 Dunnart Boulevard
Adelaide SA 5555

**International Pharmaceutical Sales Representative
moves to Australia seeking new challenges.**

Dear Mr Johnston

Yes! That's me. I have relocated from South Africa, bringing with me an 8-year sales history rich in growing territory; identifying and maximising opportunities; exceeding targets; and establishing friendly, respected client and peer relationships. I am now keen to move into the pharmaceutical industry here in South Australia and enthusiastically submit my resume for your perusal.

First, let me draw your attention to just these two points, which may be of interest to you:

☑ Captured additional 12 pharmacies and grew revenue by $75,000 in just two quarters.
☑ Conducted presentations that consistently resulted in strong orders. Utilised ability to break down cost per tablet/per day as powerful, effective selling point to revenue growth.

My current goal is to establish myself here in Australia with the same degree of success—more—to be able to develop as far as I can within the industry by exercising my passion for exceeding sales targets, which in turn spurs me on to greater sales success. Due partly to my love of being with people and going out of my way to assist them, I am considered a 'likeable person' who is easy to talk to and who always puts people at ease. Through this I find that others enthusiastically endorse the products I am marketing.

Not long after my arrival in Australia I gained employment as a Despatch Operator with Dickson Food Enterprises, in order to be employed while I examined the local market and my options. While the role is way outside my field, I have nonetheless managed to advance client relations, boost company image, increase efficiency, and earn a reputation, and receive appropriate recognition as a highly valued employee.

I am proud to say that this seems to be the natural flow on wherever I work and means that these abilities and outcomes are intrinsic to me and can be focused to be of immeasurable advantage to your company.

Though my resume gives a strong outline to my career history, I am confident that a personal interview would reveal my level of commitment and drive, and I would welcome the opportunity to prove that I would make an outstanding addition to your sales team. I thank you for your time.

Yours sincerely

David Van Alden
Enclosure: resume

270

Pharmaceutical Sales Representative. *Beverley Neil, Victoria Point West, Queensland, Australia*

The applicant had moved to Australia and took the first job he could find. To help him return to his field of pharmaceutical sales, the letter highlights his best accomplishments and worker traits.

Charles A. Robertson
Regional Sales Manager
Norton & Company
charles_robertson@norton.com

Dear Mr. Robertson:

Your posting for a College Sales Representative in Western and Central New York is of great interest to me. My resume is attached in Word format for your review.

I have a diverse background, both academically and through employment. In 2001, I earned a Master's in Library Science and have held related positions since 1999. Currently I am Special Services Consultant for 18 public libraries and 9 other libraries housed in correctional facilities. Additionally, I hold a BA in Psychology (Magna cum Laude) and have more than 10 years of experience with developmentally disabled adults as a program manager, teacher and residential supervisor. I believe that my professional experience parallels the sales/client relationship in that I seek out, identify and meet the needs of those I serve.

My passions for reading, lifelong learning and computer technology were motivators to return to the classroom for my master's degree. I possess an intrinsic ability to set and meet both personal and professional goals, evident in pursuit of both degrees while raising a family.

My well-honed interpersonal, organizational and communication abilities will also be valuable as a College Sales Representative. I offer Norton enthusiasm, a high comfort factor with the targeted market and the skill and desire necessary to achieve and succeed.

It would be a pleasure to discuss your College Sales Representative opening and my background in greater detail. You may reach me at 555-555-5555 or through e-mail at k_emory@myemail.com.

Thank you for your time and consideration.

Kelly Emory

271

College Sales Representative. *Salome A. Farraro, Mount Morris, New York*

This text-only letter was an e-mail submission. The applicant wanted a position closer to her children. She hoped that her diverse background and strong interpersonal abilities would earn an interview.

AMANDA JONES

000 Cedar Lane • Old Towne, NJ 00000 • mandy000@aol.com • mobile: 000-000-0000 • home: 000-000-0000

Date

Name
Title
Company Name
Company Street Address
Town, State, ZIP

RE: Position title _____ OR Job #_____

Dear Mr. / Ms. _____:

As a Sales Professional with 10+ years of experience in the real estate, retail and service industries, I have consistently met or exceeded aggressive sales targets through my expertise in initiating and developing productive business relationships. Thus, I am an ideal candidate for the position of Pharmaceutical Sales Representative.

Coming from a family of physicians, I am very familiar with the medical environment and am confident that I could add value. My ability to communicate well with highly educated professionals is outstanding. In addition, my organizational skills are superb, and I have been well-liked by all of my employers throughout my career.

The following are some of my career highlights:

- Consistently attained top 10% in rankings of 500+ sales associates.
- Recognized by industry professional association as a top revenue generator.
- Achieved membership in prestigious Million Dollar Sales Club every year in full-time sales.

My interpersonal and communication skills are outstanding and have significantly contributed to my success.

Attached is my resume for your review. I am confident that my demonstrated expertise would add value to your firm and contribute to your continuing success.

I will contact you in the near future and can, of course, be available for an interview at your convenience.

Very truly yours,

Amanda Jones

Attachment: resume

272

Pharmaceutical Sales Representative. *Fran Kelley, Waldwick, New Jersey*

The applicant had successes in sales and wanted to move to pharmaceutical sales. The letter emphasizes her sales skills and physicians in her background. See corresponding Resume 18 in Part 3.

WILLIAM H. HARRINGTON
1888 Shangri-La Drive · Pleasantville, NC 28888
Home: (555) 555-5555   *Fax:* (000) 000-0000
E-mail: willyh@argus.net

March 27, 2008

James L. Starnes
President
Leathercraft Furniture
3030 Haywood Road
Hickory Grove, NC 28601

Dear Mr. Starnes:

I grew up in the furniture business. My grandfather was an executive with Drexel Heritage; my father, a board member of several firms. In spite of my early background, I swore I'd *never* get into the furniture business. But I did. And in the 15 years since I entered the industry (initially as a salesman for Simmons U.S.A. and for the past 14 years as a sales representative for Hickory House), I've discovered that selling quality products excites me. Furniture is simply in my blood!

I think you will know from your own experience that it takes years to develop and cultivate extensive contacts, understand the complexities of fabric applications, and become creative in developing marketing strategies.

This is how I fit in: I have just established a sales company, representing leather and fabrics, in North and South Carolina. I am knowledgeable about the residential side of the business, but to expand my outreach I plan to pursue contract opportunities and alternative distribution routes, including auto manufacturers and the garment industry.

I really want to be of help to you—by representing your line in the Carolinas or other areas in the Southeast. I'll call on present and prospective users to tell them about new and existing products. I can provide expert advice without prejudice. It's my job to do just that.

To illustrate my point, let me tell you the story about the firm that installed a large piece of machinery, but after it was set up, no one could start it. Experts were called in from near and far, each fiddling and adjusting, but to no avail. Finally, as a last resort, the company president called a two-for-cent mechanic (or so they thought). In he strolled with his small sledgehammer and walked over to the machine. He studied the unit for several moments and then set his eyes on one spot. He struck three blows with the hammer and, much to the surprise of the onlookers, off she went!

> "Just how much do we owe you?" asked the president.
> "One thousand three dollars," replied the mechanic.
> "What's the thousand three dollars for?" asked the president.
> "Three dollars for three blows, and a thousand for knowing where to hit," the mechanic retorted.

So, in the long run, if a fellow knows his business, it's easy; if not, it's too bad for him <u>and</u> his customer. With 15 years of experience, I know "where to hit" when it comes to marketing and selling furniture and fabric. You are taking no chances when you let me help you.

I am enclosing a resume and list of references. If you think you may be interested in talking about a mutually beneficial relationship, I would be glad to meet with you. I will call in a few days to set a time we can talk.

Sincerely,

William H. Harrington

273

Sales Representative. *Doug Morrison, Charlotte, North Carolina*

A sales rep for 15 years, this applicant wanted to strike out on his own. He formed his own company to represent a manufacturer. The letter conveys his knowledge. (Be sure to read the story in the fifth paragraph.)

Sandra Day

17 BROUGHAM TERRACE, #3 ● COSTA DEL ROMA, CA 00000
888-555-1212 ● 888-866-0000 ● SANDRA@HOTMAIL.COM

Marketing Communications Professional

(Date)

(Contact Person)
(Company)
(Address 1)
(Address 2)

Dear Hiring Professional (or contact name):

I am writing to explore employment opportunities within your organization. As a proven and recognized marketing communications professional, with more than 15 years of combined experience and a solid background as a top performer, I believe I possess the qualifications and experience necessary to become an active and beneficial member of your executive management team.

As a qualified and experienced professional, I have a proven record of accomplishment in new business development, product launch, market penetration, new hire training, and team building and leadership. A highly motivated self-starter with multitasking and follow-through abilities, I consistently achieve both personal and organizational goals, meet timelines, and ensure highest quality/quantity cost per item on deliverables.

A few of my most notable accomplishments include the following:
> Planning and executing a successful introduction of **Intro Sports™ High Profile™ FOOTBALL** that debuted on *The Sports Show.*
> Developed and maintained high-level media communications, created story proposals, organized conference calls, and wrote article text for U.S. and global publications, gaining international exposure that increased Web traffic by more than 150%.
> Spearheaded and executed e-campaign projects for magazines, software, books, and recordings, generating new subscribers, promoting new releases, and achieving a 23% increase in subscriptions.

The enclosed resume briefly outlines my experience and accomplishments. If you have any questions, or would like to contact me to schedule an interview, please feel free to do so, at your convenience.

Thank you for your time and consideration. I look forward to meeting with you soon and will contact you to schedule a time.

Sincerely,

Sandra Day

274

Marketing Communications Professional. *Lea J. Clark, Macon, Georgia*

This singer/songwriter had an artistic background that kept potential employers from seeing her as a marketer. She soon got a job in the marketing department of a fine arts training center.

ANNE HILL

3200 Main Street, Urban, IA 50300 – 717-111-5555

May 19, 2007

Eddie Bauer
P.O. Box 97000
Redmond, WA 98000

Attention: Jane Smith, Human Resources Director

Cc: John White, Human Resources Manager

Re: Merchandise Manager (PTC 000) or Merchandiser (PTC 131) opportunities

Dear Ms. Smith:

I'm persistently pursuing a career with Eddie Bauer. In recent months, I have been in contact with several insiders, discussing various career opportunities with Eddie Bauer. And now I see that you have posted ads for merchandising professionals on the corporate Web site. Fantastic!

Why am I so persistent? Eddie Bauer is one of the retail industry's most reputable and successful companies. Everyone knows Eddie Bauer is a great place to work—I hear it's an energetic environment in which business gets done with integrity and an unparalleled commitment to developing employees and communities. Your product line is always impressive, diverse yet focused, and consistently of the highest quality. And the company's commitment to quality, value, and service is surely the reason the company is approaching its 82nd anniversary! Who wouldn't want to work for a company like Eddie Bauer?

Following this letter you'll find my resume, which outlines my 10+ years as a Buyer and Manager in the retail industry. My qualifications include

- Five years as a buyer for multi-location retail operations
- Exceptional skills in vendor negotiations and assortment planning
- Direct experience creating and presenting seasonal plans and merchandise assortment strategies to executives
- A Bachelor of Science in Merchandising, Textiles, Apparel, and Furnishings, with a minor in Business

Of course, I have excellent interpersonal and communication skills. I can serve as a team lead and trainer, and can effectively articulate and sell an idea with team members to ensure project success. I am also proficient in all of the computer skills required of these positions. My managers and colleagues will tell you that I consistently demonstrate initiative and innovation, not to mention a high level of professional integrity, productivity, and leadership skills.

Thank you for your time! I look forward to speaking with you soon to get your impressions of my qualifications. I will follow up with you (persistently!) to determine when we might set up an appointment to interview soon.

Best regards,

Anne Hill

275

Merchandise Manager. *Tracy Laswell Williams, Arvada, Colorado*

The applicant's enthusiasm for the target company is evident everywhere in this letter. A recurrent theme is persistence. Bullets highlight significant experience and skills.

BUFFY LASWELL

*1122 Apple Lane, Denver, CO 80122—**720-111-5555***

December 16, 2007

Qwest
1801 California Street
19th Floor
Denver, CO 80202

Attention: Blaine Smithers, Senior National Account Manager

Re: National Account Manager position

Dear Mr. Smithers:

Recently our mutual colleague, Sam Summers, contacted me to tell me about the National Account Manager position currently open within Qwest. You may recall that we met a few months ago to discuss another opportunity within your department that was filled from within.

My interest in Qwest remains as strong as ever—the new spirit of service is not just a clever marketing concept. I truly believe that the company is reorganizing and revitalizing itself around this customer service statement. And the company's renewed efforts in new product development are sure to get market attention, because I'm already seeing the change…I know quite a few business owners who are switching back to Qwest because they like the products, see the value, and have faith that they'll receive excellent service.

So yes, count me in! I'd love to be considered a top contender for the National Account Manager position. I enjoy working with a variety of products, but I have always had great success studying new products and then introducing them and generating strong sales. I think that Qwest should hire me because I am passionate about new product development and customer service excellence. I am working hard at becoming an expert in Voice Over IP (VoIP) products and would enjoy helping Qwest become a major provider of this "next-step" technology.

My approach to sales is all about building strong, consultative relationships with my customers, understanding their business goals and technology requirements, and then delivering an unbeatable solution. I have direct experience in all the major roles and responsibilities listed in your ad, including

- The ability to manage and optimize numerous national accounts, effectively servicing the customer with the right combination of products and services.

- The ability to orchestrate strategic business planning initiatives as well as service delivery projects among internal and external customer groups to ensure total customer satisfaction.

- A demonstrated track record of meeting and exceeding revenue targets through a comprehensive, proactive approach to account development.

- A strong thirst for knowledge as well as an ability to rapidly acquire and share product knowledge through independent and structured learning opportunities.

My resume follows this letter and offers specific examples of the qualifications I've outlined above. **I look forward to the opportunity of meeting with you again, so I will follow up with you soon.**

Best regards,

Buffy Laswell

276

National Account Manager. *Tracy Laswell Williams, Arvada, Colorado*

Reference to a third party as a mutual colleague establishes rapport between the applicant and the reader. Boldface for the lead idea in three paragraphs helps to keep the reader's attention.

Monique Almondry

| 134 Mt. Veil Avenue | Chicago, Illinois 99999 | monique@yahoo.com | 555-555-5555 |

April 1, 2008

Hiring Professional
Gap, Inc.
Chicago, Illinois
Fax # 555-555-5555

I appreciate this opportunity to apply for the Assistant Buyer position you have available at Gap, Inc. Enclosed is a copy of my resume for your review.

As you will note, I have recently been working as an Assistant Buyer in Jefferson, Illinois, where I had the privilege of working in-depth with the Olympic vendors and strategizing to merchandise top-selling trends. This was, indeed, an exciting adventure. I thoroughly enjoy working together with others to produce a winning outcome. I have strong analytical skills with a keen sense for upcoming design and fashion. With the experience of working in the background in office management and the processing of paperwork required to operate a successful fashion business, I have gained invaluable knowledge about attractive layouts, store design, and the complete process of the fashion industry.

You will find I work well with others and am a strong motivator. I also work efficiently with business planning and predicting trends. I am professional and look forward to developing a long-term career in the fashion and design industry.

I would like to meet with you personally to discuss further where your requirements and my qualifications may blend. I will call you to set up an interview time. Thank you for your time. I look forward to meeting with you soon.

Sincerely,

Monique Almondry

Enclosure

277

Assistant Buyer. *Rosie Bixel, Portland, Oregon*

The second paragraph summarizes the applicant's relevant experience, interest in working with vendors and identifying fashion trends, analytical skills, and knowledge of the fashion industry.

James Bader

00000 Stone River Drive ▪ Houston, TX 00000 ▪ name@hotmail.com
residence: (713) 000-0000 ▪ mobile: (281) 000-0000

February 14, 2008

Steve Johnson, Program Director
The Home Depot
5515 1-59
Houston, TX 00000

Dear Mr. Johnson:

It is with great interest and enthusiasm that I am submitting my resume in application for The Home Depot Store Leadership Program. As the current industry leader in home improvement products and services with more than $45 billion in annual revenues (**ranked #9 in *Fortune*'s Global Most Admired Companies** list), The Home Depot has certainly established itself as a company poised for even greater success in the future, and I feel that my skills and abilities make me a worthy candidate for the Associate position within this program.

Throughout my career in marketing and HR management, I have maintained a consistent record of meeting and exceeding goals for business growth, organizational leadership, and service delivery. Allow me to briefly call your attention to some of my accomplishments:

➢ Initiated recruiting process for start-up operations that led to the hiring of **150** customer service representatives in **two months,** despite the fact that I had no prior experience as an HR Manager.

➢ Selected as my company's representative for the **Leadership Houston** program based on my leadership potential, gaining valuable knowledge and insight into team building and leadership.

➢ Increased **Alumni and Family Relations network and support** for the University of Houston through special events coordination, training of volunteer networks, and marketing campaigns.

In an August 2007 article from CBS.MarketWatch.com, Home Depot CEO Robert Nardelli emphasized that "…in this environment you can't wait for the customer," and I agree that a proactive, results-oriented approach to business growth is the key to success and profitability in the current market. That The Home Depot has continued to succeed and expand despite the struggling economy further attests to its staying power as a leader in the field, and I am confident that I would contribute to The Home Depot's growth and success in a future position.

My resume is enclosed to provide additional details concerning my background and achievements, but I am certain that a personal interview would more fully reveal my capabilities and desire to join The Home Depot team. Thank you, Mr. Johnson, for your time and consideration of my candidacy.

Sincerely,

James Bader

Enclosure

278

Retail Manager.   *Daniel J. Dorotik, Jr., Lubbock, Texas*

For this ad response, the applicant has done his research and mentions company information and a quotation from the CEO. The goal is admission to a leadership program rather than a specific job.

Lisa A. Guerrero

1111 Martin Lane ▪ Philadelphia, PA 00000 ▪ (000) 000-0000 ▪ name@yahoo.com

Barnes & Noble College Bookstores
3434 Smith Street
Philadelphia, PA 00000

RE: Position as General Merchandise Manager, Job ID 000-000

Dear Human Resources Representative:

It was with great interest that I learned about your opening for a General Merchandise Manager, as my qualifications match your requirements for this position. I am confident I can contribute to the success of Barnes & Noble College Bookstores; therefore, please accept my resume in application for this position and allow me to explain briefly how I meet your requirements and how I can add value to your organization.

As I read your company's advertisement, I noted several connections between what you seek and my background:

Your Requirements:	My Qualifications:
▪ College degree preferred	▪ Bachelor of Arts degree from Temple University
▪ Strong commitment to customer service	▪ Exceeded service delivery goals as Customer Care Manager for Verizon Wireless
▪ 3 years of retail management experience	▪ 4 years as Senior Assistant Manager for retail outlet Shoppers Galore
▪ Team-leadership skills	▪ As manager with Verizon, led team to improved QA scores and 3× sales increase within 3 months of hire
▪ Excellent communication skills	▪ Superb communicator with customers, team members, and upper management
▪ Flexibility is required	▪ Worked varying hours and weekend shifts frequently as manager with Shoppers

Beyond my qualifications, what I can contribute most significantly to your company's future success is my ability to develop great relationships. Whether resolving a customer concern, addressing an issue with upper management, or mentoring a fellow team member, I consistently use a "positive communication" approach that leads to resolved problems and happy customers. In addition, my dedication and work ethic are strong, as my former supervisors will readily verify.

Thank you for your time and review of my qualifications. Please do not hesitate to contact me if you have any questions, and I wish you the best in your candidate search for this position.

Sincerely,

Lisa A. Guerrero

Enclosure

279

General Merchandise Manager. *Daniel J. Dorotik, Jr., Lubbock, Texas*

In this ad response, the writer links the job seeker's qualifications to company requirements line by line. Bullets in both columns help the reader read matching items from column to column.

Kendall Rose Coleman

76 Columbia Street
Poughkeepsie, NY 12601
555.555.5555

000 West 57th Street, Apt. E
New York, NY 10021
000.000.0000

January 27, 2008

Ms. Grace Amere, Fashion Director
Paisley Park Designs
123 Prince Street
New York, NY 10025

Dear Ms. Amere:

Please accept this letter of introduction and enclosed resume for consideration for a merchandising position within your firm. As a graduate of F.I.T. (Fashion Institute of Technology) with a B.B.A. in Fashion Marketing, my training is current, and I have a solid understanding of textiles and apparel in the global economy.

My academics have been supplemented with real-world experience through F.I.T.'s internship program, which provides advanced experience through employment. Working in various capacities throughout college helped develop my business competency and enhanced my knowledge of contemporary processes, fashion concepts and merchandising strategy. As an intern, I demonstrated a strong commitment to appropriate business practices and excelled at creative plans and trend analysis.

Throughout college, I consistently demonstrated initiative and disciplined work habits. In addition to earning my degree and internship participation, I worked full-time with major retail chains in order to pay for school. Working full-time while being a full-time student in New York City sharpened my time-management skills. It also contributed to my understanding of the commercial impact of decisions, as well as my awareness of the importance of positive customer relations.

With exposure to various retail markets and experience in the development of marketing/merchandising strategies, I feel that my ability to provide vision and access new ideas is abundant. This, combined with my powerful work ethic, will enable me to make immediate contributions toward your company's goals.

Thank you in advance for your time and attention. I will contact you soon to set up a time we can meet to discuss the position further.

Sincerely,

Kendall Rose Coleman

Enclosure

280

Merchandising Position. *Kristin M. Coleman, Poughkeepsie, New York*

Unlike many recent graduates without much work experience, this applicant worked full-time in major retail chains to pay for school. The letter makes much of this relevant full-time experience.

Jenny Johansen

0000 S.E. Highway 313, Unit F-7 • Deschutes, Oregon 99999

Email: jjjj3953@aol.com   555-555-5555   *Cell* 555-555-5555

April 9, 2008

Gene Reserve
Store Manager
Starbucks
1900 S.E. Miller Road
Deschutes, Oregon 99999

Dear Mr. Reserve:

Your name has been given to me as one who could introduce me to your District Manager. I would like the opportunity to apply for a position as ***Store Manager*** for a Starbucks store. I've taken the liberty to enclose a copy of my resume. Please feel free to pass this letter and my resume on to your District Manager.

As you will note, I have spent 12 years working in the fast-food industry. I am now eager to transfer to working for Starbucks. This is an area that has fascinated me over the last few years, and I am now ready for a change. I have experience managing a crew, empowering them to be the best they can be, and providing excellent customer service for McDonald's. I have created a strong cash flow for the stores I have been involved with by making sure the customer is well taken care of, monitoring inventory, and maintaining control of labor costs. The successful daily operations have also been an important portion of my duties, as well as the implementation and maintenance of all company policies.

Your requirements for a ***Store Manager*** appear to match my qualifications very closely. I am highly "service" focused and understand the inner workings, financial requirements, and team spirit required to operate a successful store. My resume only briefly describes my skills. I would appreciate the opportunity to meet with your District Manager directly to further discuss where my qualifications and Starbucks requirements may blend. Please have your District Manager give me a call at her earliest convenience to set up a time when we may meet.

Thank you for your time and assistance.

Sincerely,

Jenny Johansen

281

Store Manager. *Rosie Bixel, Portland, Oregon*

In this networking letter, the applicant asks the reader to pass the letter and a resume on to the hiring manager. The second paragraph tells of relevant experience; the third indicates strengths.

Jeremiah Josephs

555 Any Street, Millersville, MD 21108 ● 410-555-5555 ● jj55555@media.net

May 15, 2008

Company USA
Mr. John Doe, Lab Manager
123 Main Street
Baltimore, MD 12345

Dear Mr. Doe,

As an experienced senior-level lab technician in a gas chromatograph lab, I will bring the needed skills and expertise to your lab that your company is seeking. After more than 20 years with Lab Testing, Inc., I've decided that it's time to seek new challenges and responsibilities.

Throughout my career, I have supervised and conducted thousands of tests, drafted and presented hundreds of reports, and trained numerous personnel on the proper use and maintenance of gas chromatographs, X-ray diffraction units, carbon sulfur analyzers, a microactivities unit, and a mercury porsimeter, along with other lab equipment. With careful planning and attention to detail, we have maintained a very high level of safety, expedited testing procedures to meet deadlines, and improved the accuracy of tests performed. I also have a thorough knowledge of chemistry and assisted with the compilation and editing of a procedures manual for two commonly performed lab tests.

In addition to my lab management responsibilities, I have held leadership and management-level positions in a volunteer capacity with many local nonprofit organizations and institutions. I am ready to take my skills and experience to the next level and believe that Company USA is just the place to take that step.

I will follow up with you by June 1 to confirm that you received my information and also to answer any questions you may have at that time. Should you wish to contact me sooner, it's best to reach me either at home, 410-555-5555, or work, 410-555-6555, or through e-mail at jj55555@media.net. Thank you for your time and consideration for this position.

Sincerely,

Jeremiah Josephs

Enclosure

282

Senior Lab Technician. *Beth Colley, Crownsville, Maryland*

The letter calls attention to this applicant's experience, supervisory roles, familiarity with different procedures, volunteer work, and interest in seeking new challenges and responsibilities.

VICTOR A. WILLIAMS

447 North Diamond Back Road • Bethpage, New York 11714 • (555) 555-5555
vaw555@hotmail.com

Dear Sir or Madam:

As a **Supervising Chemist,** I am seeking the opportunity to apply my skills within a challenging **biotechnology environment.**

My background closely parallels the mechanics involved in biotechnology. I supervise the research, proficiency testing, chemical analysis instrumentation, and related software application to analyze the components and physical properties of community drinking water. Highlights of the qualifications and contributions I would bring to your organization include the following:

- Excellent administration, public relations, and communications skills, developed through experience as a **Supervisory Chemist for the largest, most advanced drinking water laboratory in the U.S.**

- Aptitude to conceptualize and coordinate procedures to meet the changing dynamics of assignments, organizational needs, or specific projects. Proficient analytical, planning, and advisory techniques.

- Ability to prioritize time and resources to meet company objectives while reducing operating budget expenses.

Within the course of my work, I have been extensively involved with technical problem-solving and the handling of multiple projects, effectively communicating my findings to management and interdisciplinary professionals. I am eager to continue to use my knowledge and skills where I can provide the direction to support your organization's plans, strategies, and objectives.

I appreciate your time in reviewing my qualifications and look forward to a personal interview. I will call next week to set a time for an interview. Thank you.

Very truly yours,

VICTOR A. WILLIAMS

Enclosure

283

Supervising Chemist. *Donna M. Farrise, Hauppauge, New York*

This letter uses boldface to call attention to the most important information about the applicant: his name at the top, his occupation, his targeted field of activity, and his current position.

TAMMY D. MILLER
17 Old Willets Path
Hauppauge, New York 11788
(555) 555-5555
tammydmiller@yahoo.com

Dear Sir or Madam:

I have recently relocated to New York with the intention of pursuing a position in the field of *scientific research.* My goal is to obtain an opportunity within a **Biotech/Bioengineering company.** I genuinely desire to be an integral part of a team research effort and the clinical trial process. Highlights of my academic achievement and employment experience include the following:

> ➤ **Exceptional Academic Record…B.S. in Microbiology** with a concentration in **Molecular Biology…**consistently maintained superior grades with **honors in Virology, Immunology, Advanced Bacteriology, and Microbial Genetics.**

> ➤ **Analytical and Organizational Skills…**practical employment allowed me to demonstrate my **strength in data research, analysis, and documentation.**

> ➤ **Strong Project Management Skills…**with extensive experience working as a Structured Finance Coordinator, Center Director, Area Supervisor, and R.O.T.C. Cadet. I have been **involved in the planning, data research, written communication, and public service** that resulted in significant accomplishments in leadership, organization, and self-discipline.

> ➤ **Communication and Public Relations Skills…**in each of my positions, I have dealt cooperatively with the general public, colleagues, and superiors. My skills at interpersonal relations and cross-cultural communications are considerable.

Throughout my academic background and employment history, I have consistently driven myself to meet challenges and achieve goals. It is within this type of challenging and results-oriented environment that I thrive.

I would appreciate the opportunity to meet and further share with you my qualifications and enthusiasm for joining your company research team. I will call soon to find a mutually convenient time.

Sincerely,

TAMMY D. MILLER

Enclosure

284

Researcher. *Donna M. Farrise, Hauppauge, New York*

This letter by the same writer as Cover Letter 283 shows the same technique of using boldface to direct attention to key information. Bold italic is an additional attention-getting enhancement to show the field.

JOHN H. CLARKE, LCPC
0000 N. Buffalo Grove Road
Arlington Heights, Illinois 60004
Telephone: (555) 555-5555

April 8, 2008

James Morgenstern, Ph.D.
Director of Adult Services
Alexian Brothers Northwest Mental Health Center
1606 Colonial Parkway
Palatine, Illinois 60067

Dear Dr. Morgenstern:

I am a Licensed Clinical Professional Counselor and a Master of Arts–Psychology graduate from UIC and am presently conducting a search for a position in an accredited mental health agency or psychotherapy practice. Please review the attached curriculum vitae as it may relate to potential opportunities that might exist within your organization.

My CV indicates that I have 10+ years of experience working in the business world prior to my enrollment at UIC, as well as my current position as a Psychotherapist and previous counseling internship. In my business career, I interacted with many different personality types and developed a keen interest in general psychological issues of adults. I frequently dealt with difficult customers and felt limited in my ability to assist them beyond the boundaries of my employers' products or services. I finally concluded that I could best serve people if I had more knowledge of human behavior, which is why I chose to enter the field of professional psychology. Because your agency provides services for adult populations, I feel that my current experience, academic coursework and business background represent a good fit.

I would welcome the opportunity to further discuss my educational and professional background in relation to the needs of your agency's clientele. I will contact you to determine a time that is convenient to meet. Thank you for your time and consideration.

Sincerely,

John H. Clarke, LCPC

Curriculum Vitae enclosed.

285

Licensed Clinical Professional Counselor. *Joellyn Wittenstein-Schwerdlin, Elk Grove Village, Illinois*

This candidate mentions to potential employers how he transitioned from the business world to the status of Licensed Clinical Professional Counselor (LCPC) while working his way through school.

ROY NASH

4900 Boulevard, Carson City, NV 00000   (000) 000-0000

January 15, 2008

Ms. Sadie Brown, M.S.W.
Director
Hope Rehabilitation Center
860 Truckee River Parkway
Reno, NV 00000

Dear Ms. Brown:

As a follow-up to a recent phone conversation with your associate, I learned that there may be opportunities for employment within your organization, and I am writing to express my interest. I have not only a clear understanding of the problems leading to addictive behavior but also the prerequisite education to work in alcohol and drug counseling. I sincerely want to help others who are experiencing the same horrors I went through as an alcoholic and cocaine addict. My ultimate goal is to become a Certified Alcohol and Drug Counselor, for which I need to accumulate 6,000 hours of practical experience under the direction of certified counselors.

Currently, I am a counselor assistant at Straight and Narrow, a psycho-social rehabilitative agency, where I have begun to develop my professional and clinical skills through work with groups of substance abusers in recovery. I am considered by others to be self-determined, enthusiastic, and reliable, with the ability to adjust well in a new environment.

My resume is enclosed for your review. If your rehabilitative staff requirements allow for continued training with a certified counselor, I would like to learn more about the opportunity. I will be calling you within a week to determine your interest and perhaps arrange for a time when we can meet.

Very truly yours,

Roy Nash

Enclosure

286

Alcohol and Drug Counselor (in Training). *Melanie Noonan, West Paterson, New Jersey*

As a follow-up to a recent phone call, this letter expresses interest in a possible position and tells of the applicant's relevant experience and current extensive work for certification. See corresponding Resume 21 in Part 3.

JASMINE HIGHLANDER

555 Harrison Avenue   Brentwood, NY 55555   (333) 444-5555   advocate@4campuslife.net

Date

Name
Company
Address

Dear Name:

The accompanying resume is presented for your review and consideration for the position of Assistant Director of College Housing. To further illustrate my qualifications, the following outlines the scope of my experience as it pertains to this position's specific requirements.

Your requirements	**My qualifications**
• Bachelor's degree, or	• Master's degree in Clinical Counseling.
• Four years of experience in lieu of degree.	• Eight years of combined experience in residence hall administration and counseling capacities.
• Promote and develop educational programming and maintain extensive budget.	• Plan, develop, and implement educational programs, and manage an operational budget.
• Administration of three to five residence halls housing approximately 1,000 students.	• Administration of residence halls housing up to 500 students.
• Supervise, develop, and evaluate three to five full-time residence hall directors.	• Supervise, develop, and evaluate 26 Resident Advisors with direct responsibility for four RAs and a Head Resident Advisor (HRA).
• Develop departmental policies and procedures, manage area office including billing, occupancy, and facilities records.	• Direct all aspects of front desk management and facilities maintenance operations.
• Assist in the development and leadership of departmental committees, and serve as manager for student conduct cases.	• Held a one-year position as Vice President of Committees for the Student Government with the State University of New York.

Thank you for your review and consideration. I will call you next week to set a time we can meet. I look forward to speaking with you then.

Sincerely,

Jasmine Highlander

287

Assistant Director of College Housing. *Ann Baehr, Brentwood, New York*

A two-column format is useful for showing how an applicant's qualifications match a company's requirements. This letter shows further that some of the qualifications can exceed requirements.

ANNA M. SANCHEZ

123 Fort Avenue • Anywhere, Michigan 55555 • (555) 555-0000 • Cellular (555) 888-2222

February 8, 2008

John Gomez, Director
Family Community Center
555 Main Street
Anywhere, Michigan 55555

Dear Mr. Gomez,

After serving the Family Community Center for more than 17 years, I have had the opportunity to grow in my profession as an office assistant while helping others in time of need. It gives me pleasure to know I am able to provide much-needed assistance to individuals who turn to our center for support.

My experience has allowed me to work with a large number of adults and children from different ethnic backgrounds, providing assistance to individuals assigned to community service, as well as the elderly. I speak and read Spanish fluently, which is a must because our center serves a great number of Hispanics in the local area.

At this time, I feel my experience and commitment to the Family Community Center have positioned me to take on increased responsibilities. My objective is to secure the Direct Assistance Coordinator position upon its availability, and I welcome the opportunity to discuss my qualifications further. I have enclosed my resume to give you a brief review of my background and experience.

I will follow up with you next week to answer any questions you may have regarding my application. If you would like to speak sooner, please contact me anytime. Thank you in advance for your consideration.

Regards,

Anna M. Sanchez

Enclosure

288

Direct Assistance Coordinator. *Maria E. Hebda, Trenton, Michigan*

This future position was the person's goal after 17 years of service to the organization. She believed that she could take on additional responsibilities and built a case for being considered seriously.

Heather C. Bjorn

999-B Stetson Boulevard
Cranston, SC 55555
(111) 222-3333
heatherb@earthlink.com

March 16, 2008

Ms. Rebecca Phipps, Director of Human Resources
South Carolina State Department of Social Services
1111 Baltimore Street, 2nd Floor
Cranston, SC 55555

Dear Ms. Phipps:

Please accept this letter of application for employment in the South Carolina Social Services Division for Children and Their Families. My education, training, and experience have built a solid, relevant foundation for employment in this division, as I believe my current enclosed resume proves.

Working with children in multicultural and diverse socioeconomic strata is a challenge in which I am eager to engage as a professional social worker. Although I am content and qualified to continue in my current position with the Easter Seals–SC, Cranston ARC, I feel that my greater strength and enthusiasm lie in assisting youth, as evidenced in my volunteer work with the Children's Crusade. Developing and promoting proper independent living skills is a goal and dream of mine that I shall pursue until I am in such a position to assist youngsters during their crucial, formative time of cultural and behavioral development.

If you feel that my credentials, along with my genuine enthusiasm to work with children, are sufficient to meet your criteria for employment in this field, please contact me when an opening occurs. I can be reached at heatherb@earthlink.com or (111) 222-3333 during the day or evening. I look forward eagerly to meeting with you to discuss my professional qualifications.

Thank you for your time in consideration of my application.

Sincerely,

Heather C. Bjorn

Enclosure: resume

289

Social Services Counselor. *Edward Turilli, North Kingstown, Rhode Island*

The challenge of this letter was to prove to the recruiter that the applicant, having performed well for Easter Seals in social services, would thrive in a career directly assisting needy, disadvantaged youth.

EVELYN MORRIS

0000 Summit Drive • Englewood, NJ 00000 • (555) 555-5555 • Morris30@aol.com

January 6, 2008

Ms. Suzanne Reynolds
Director, Social Services
Borrin Correctional Institution
2299 Central Avenue
Englewood, NJ 00000

Dear Ms. Reynolds:

Becoming a social worker has been a lifelong dream of mine, and I have taken the first step toward fulfilling this dream. In May, I will graduate with a bachelor's degree. As part of my educational training, I am seeking an internship at the Borrin Correctional Institution to further develop my clinical social work skills while applying my training to benefit others.

Currently, I am completing a clinical internship at the Borrin Families in Crisis Center. This experience has not only taught me valuable lessons about human life, but has also reinforced my interest in employment in a correctional environment following graduation. My future plans include pursuing a master's degree in clinical social work.

Complementing my education in social work are both employment and volunteer experiences that relate to my career interests while adding to my skill development in this profession. Such experiences over the past several years have included employment as a medical assistant at a physician practice, providing support services to families of children with cancer at a community hospital and volunteering at a crisis-counseling center. In addition, my professors and supervisor at the Borrin Families in Crisis Center have frequently commented on my natural aptitude for a career in social work.

Highly self-motivated with an energetic style, I am eager to learn new skills and enhance my education while contributing to your organization. My strengths also include communications, maturity and the ability to relate effectively with individuals at all levels and cultural backgrounds as demonstrated throughout my prior career in business.

I look forward to discussing an internship opportunity at your institution and appreciate your consideration.

Sincerely,

Evelyn Morris

Enclosure

290

Social Worker. *Louise Garver, Enfield, Connecticut*

This prospective graduate was seeking an internship at a correctional facility to develop her clinical social work skills. The letter indicates her experience and strengths. She secured the internship.

Marie C. Bedford

0000 West 81ˢᵗ Avenue
St. Louis, MO 00000

home: (000) 000-0000
name@msn.com

January 15, 2008

Human Resources Department
United Way
155 Toulouse Street
St. Louis, MO 00000

Dear Human Resources Representative:

It was with great interest that I read your advertisement for the position of Program Manager. I believe that my qualifications and experience match your requirements, and I am confident that I can add to your continued success and growth.

My 10 years of experience as a Director of Social Services, Care Plan Coordinator, Case Manager, and Social Worker have provided me the opportunity to build a strong track record of success in program leadership, service delivery, and community relations development. Thus, I could benefit your firm's sales growth in several ways:

- I have met and exceeded objectives in providing the highest level of service for patients in facilities ranging from **120** to **176** beds, earning the respect and trust of residents and family members;
- I have demonstrated the ability to maintain **100%** compliance with state and federal regulations, with personal commendations from state auditors and several "zero violations" scores on state audits;
- I keep up-to-date about changes and developments in all aspects of the human/social services industry, and my current plans include re-obtaining my **LSW** license;
- I am a results-driven program management and community relations professional who builds strong networks and develops win-win relationships with program participants, team members, and community leaders.

My positive attitude and dedication to both personal and professional growth are traits I held when I initially entered into the field of social services, and they remain an integral part of my work ethic today. You can be assured that I will demonstrate an uncompromising focus on service delivery, quality assurance, and the achievement of organizational objectives and goals as a member of your team.

My resume is enclosed to provide you with additional details concerning my background and qualifications. I will contact you within the week to follow up on this inquiry; perhaps we could arrange a meeting to discuss how I could contribute to your organization.

Thank you for your time and consideration. Please do not hesitate to contact me if I can answer any questions.

Sincerely,

Marie C. Bedford

Enclosure

291

United Way Program Manager. *Daniel J. Dorotik, Jr., Lubbock, Texas*

The writer called this a "resume letter" because it has specific details and bulleted statements. Specific numbers illustrate accomplishments. Boldfacing calls attention to the numbers and the applicant's LSW license.

FRANKLIN HARRIS

84 Park Boulevard · East Syracuse, NY 13900
555-555-5555 · fharris@myemail.com

February 10, 2008

Reverend Henry Richmond
President
Onondaga County Coalition of Churches
PO Box 857
Syracuse, NY 13909

RE: Projects Coordinator

Dear Reverend Richmond:

Your posting from the *Syracuse Daily News* is of great interest to me. In the next month, I will be retiring from the State of New York and am seeking a challenging, rewarding and flexible opportunity. My resume is enclosed for your review.

Project and program coordination and management have been a staple of my career with the state, beginning in Social Services (Foster Care and Child Protection Services) and concluding in the Division of Parole. Beyond tenure in these departments, I have been an instructor, trainer and curriculum developer … director of two nonprofit organizations … and the designer and first coordinator of a public school's home/school program. Contributing to my community has always been important; notable current involvement includes President of the East Syracuse–Minoa Central School Board, Uniform Instructor for the Sea Cadets and Councilman for the Town of East Syracuse.

Educational credentials earned include a BS in Criminal Science with graduate studies in Social Work as well as Psychology. I am a Certified Peace Officer in line with my Parole Division experience. I have completed diverse professional development as well as training necessary to serve responsibly in several volunteer capacities.

In addition to my well-honed interpersonal and communication skills, positive attitude and dedication, my familiarity with your service area and established contacts in it would be beneficial. I am very comfortable having accountability for an organization's effective use of its resources and am confident in my ability to contribute positively as your Projects Coordinator.

It would be a pleasure to discuss this opportunity with you in greater detail, and I will contact you soon to discuss the possibility. I look forward to talking with you soon.

Thank you for your time and consideration.

Sincerely,

Franklin Harris

292

Projects Coordinator. *Salome A. Farraro, Mount Morris, New York*

Retiring from the New York State Division of Parole, this individual applied for the Projects Coordinator position. This letter, together with his resume, helped him get an interview and an offer.

Carmen M. Kennedy

carmkenn@hotmail.com
642 Riverview Drive ▼ Parkersburg, WV 26000 ▼ 304.224.0000

April 2, 2008

Kristi Vanderpool
PO Box 1278
Vienna, WV 26111

Dear Ms. Vanderpool:

To inspire and enable all young people, especially those from disadvantaged circumstances, to realize their full potential as productive, responsible and caring citizens.

The mission of the Boys & Girls Clubs of America is something that I strongly believe in. That is why I read with great interest your recent ad in the *St. Mary's Oracle* for a Teen Outreach Coordinator with the Boys and Girls Clubs of Wirt County. As a native of Wirt County with a lifelong desire to work with children and excellent leadership skills, I believe I have much to offer in this capacity.

A music education major at Marietta College, I prepared for a future career of educating children. I've spent more than 100 hours in the classroom working with, teaching and observing students and have realized that this is where I want to focus my career: working to prepare the youth of today for tomorrow's world. In addition, I have been actively involved in various youth activities throughout my life. It would be an honor for me to be able to contribute to the Boys & Girls Clubs' mission of providing

- *A safe place to learn and grow*
- *Ongoing relationships with caring adult professionals*
- *Life-enhancing programs and character-development experiences*
- *Hope and opportunity*

An interview would allow me to share my qualifications in greater detail and learn more about this exciting opportunity. I will call you next week to follow up. Thank you for your time and consideration. I look forward to speaking with you soon.

Sincerely,

Carmen M. Kennedy

Enclosure

293

Teen Outreach Coordinator. *Melissa L. Kasler, Athens, Ohio*

The writer used information from the mission statements of the Boys and Girls Clubs of America to convey this applicant's dedication. He was called for an interview immediately and given the job.

George Lease

3333 Falcon Drive • Fairfield, ND 99999
555-555-5555
georgel@fairfield.com

Date

Name
Company
Address

Dear Hiring Professional:

In response to your recent advertisement, I've enclosed a copy of my resume. I have recently moved to the Northwest from Texas, where I owned an automotive repair shop. I still have quite a bit of equipment but am not interested in owning or starting a business again.

I have very strong diagnostic and repair skills with the belief that no job is too difficult. While building a strong business, I developed the reputation of complete honesty with the ability to perform accurate and lasting repairs. I also had a strong reputation among the dealers, with them often calling me for advice. My work was honored by a company that provided rebuilt motors by warranting any motor supplied by them that I installed. As you can see, I developed a positive and strong business reputation for high quality and honest work. I would like to assist another company in their success by providing top-notch technician work for them.

The position you have available appears to be one that matches my skills very closely. I would like the opportunity to meet with you personally where we may further discuss your requirements and my abilities. You may contact me at 555-555-5555 to set up a mutually convenient time. Thank you for taking the time to review my resume, and I look forward to your call.

Sincerely,

George Lease

Enclosure

294

Automotive Repair Position. *Rosie Bixel, Portland, Oregon*

Having moved to a new location, this applicant wanted only to work for another firm. The task of the letter is to convey the impressive reputation he had earned as the owner of his own repair shop.

ALLEN T. RANDOLPH

8001 Satchel Drive
Greenfield, MA 55555
Home: (555) 555-5555 • Cell: (555) 555-5555
E-mail: allentr@aol.com

July 24, 2007

Mr. John Deering
Director of Facility Maintenance
Marietta Manufacturing
Marietta Plaza
Greenfield, MA 98554

Dear Mr. Deering:

Although I opted for retirement at a young age, I have come to realize that I have too much energy and many skills that I still enjoy using. Retirement is definitely not for me. Therefore, your ad for a maintenance specialist caught my attention as I offer the key qualifications your company needs.

Specifically, I have an excellent performance record in the operation and maintenance of building systems and equipment, including electrical, HVAC, telecommunications, pneumatic, electromechanical, and hydraulics. I am also knowledgeable about state building codes, safety, and other regulatory guidelines.

My expertise encompasses multisite facilities oversight, staff supervision, project management, and vendor relations. Examples of relevant accomplishments include reduction in annual maintenance costs and improved functional capabilities while consistently delivering quality service.

Equally important are my planning, organization, and communication strengths. Despite the challenges that can often be encountered, I have completed projects on time and under budget on a consistent basis. I would welcome a personal interview to discuss the value I would add to your company. I will contact you next week to set up a time we can meet.

Sincerely,

Allen T. Randolph

Enclosure

295

Maintenance Specialist. *Louise Garver, Enfield, Connecticut*

The individual was a retired person who realized that he wanted to get back to work. The writer created this letter, which communicates the person's talent, energy, and skills. He was hired.

Elizabeth Denton
1814 Taylor Drive ~ North Brunswick, NJ 08902
(555) 555-5555 (H) ~ (000) 000-0000 (C) ~ E-mail: lizdent3@msn.com

Date

Name
Company
Address

RE: Maintenance Mechanic

Dear Sir/Madam:

As a professional **Facilities** and **Maintenance Mechanic,** I understand that success depends on several factors. These include timely upkeep of machinery maintenance and repair, supervision of maintenance programs, and monitoring outside contractors. My extensive hands-on experience as a mechanic has allowed me to ensure timely completion of projects and adherence to corporate safety requirements.

Throughout my career I have been promoted and have acquired increasing responsibilities within every position. In my latest position as a Mechanic for Heinz Foods, I had the reputation for excellent machinery knowledge and a keen attention to detail.

Heinz Foods is downsizing the plant in Edison, NJ, and I have accepted a voluntary separation package from the company. I would like to continue my career with a new company offering me new challenges.

Thank you for your consideration. I possess excellent hands-on knowledge as well as supervisory expertise, and I look forward to meeting with you personally so that we may discuss how I may make a positive contribution to your team. I will call in the coming week to explore the possibility of a personal interview.

Very truly yours,

Elizabeth Denton

Enclosure

296

Maintenance Mechanic. *Beverley and Mitchell I. Baskin, Marlboro, New Jersey*

This applicant had been downsized and was looking for a new, challenging position in which she could use her skills as a mechanic. These are mentioned in the first paragraph. See corresponding Resume 22 in Part 3.

Ralph Forte
43–74 Belt Parkway
Brooklyn, NY 00000

Home: (000) 000-0000   Cell: (000) 000-0000

January 11, 2008

New York Post
P.O. Box 4498
New York, NY 00000

Dear Hiring Manager:

In your ad in last Sunday's *Post,* you stated that you needed an experienced elevator mechanic. As you will see when you read my resume, I believe I have the necessary skills and qualifications to excel at this job.

For most of my career, I have been involved in all aspects of elevator installation and maintenance. I have a thorough understanding of all of the requirements necessary for a successful job, and my organizational ability allows me to complete my assignments well within the acceptable time frame.

My present position entails the coordination of equipment and its component parts according to client specifications as outlined on blueprints. I take pride that my work always has passed rigid inspections.

As I am accustomed to preparing logs and reports, paperwork would be no problem. I am considered a good communicator, using this ability to train other personnel and make recommendations to owners/managers to increase efficiency at the installation sites where I have worked. The frequent travel you describe in your ad would not interfere with my personal obligations.

If this position is still available, I would like the opportunity to talk with you in person and discuss how my skills would benefit your company. You may contact me on my cell phone during the workday or at home after 4:30 p.m.

Sincerely,

Ralph Forte

297

Elevator Mechanic.   *Melanie Noonan, West Paterson, New Jersey*

This response to an ad indicates that the experienced applicant is able to perform all aspects of elevator installation and maintenance, including all of the necessary paperwork.

ADAM A. FRANZ

000 Haven Avenue
Stanhope, NJ 00000

E-mail: automaster@speed.net
Mobile: 000-000-0000

[Date]

[Name]
[Title]
[Company Name]
[Company Street Address]
[Town, State, ZIP]

RE: Position title _____ or Job # _____

Dear Mr. / Ms. _____:

As a state-of-the-art Automotive Technician with 20+ years of experience in maintaining and repairing BMW and Mercedes-Benz automobiles, along with demonstrated ability in mentoring and training junior technicians, I am an ideal candidate for the position of Technical Training Instructor.

My communication and interpersonal skills are outstanding, and I am able to simplify concepts so that students can readily arrive at the solution. My experience teaching *Euro-Auto* in the Edison, NJ, school system required that I communicate well to a diverse audience with varying levels of expertise. From the shop floor to the classroom, my students were engaged and motivated by the learning experience.

Throughout my career, I have been recognized by senior management as a technical resource in the industry. Often, I have been called upon to resolve extremely complex technical problems. My success has been measured by attaining consistently outstanding scores on the monthly Customer Service Index. In addition, my frame-off restorations of BMW automobiles and motorcycles are flawless, and I truly delight in teaching others all aspects of automotive work.

Attached is my resume for your review. I am confident that my demonstrated expertise would add value to your firm and contribute to your continuing success.

I can be available for an interview at your convenience. I will e-mail you to set an appointment.

Very truly yours,

Adam A. Franz

Attachment: resume

298

Technical Training Instructor. *Fran Kelley, Waldwick, New Jersey*

This individual was a master mechanic with an impressive list of accomplishments and training. The writer highlighted his years of specialized experience along with his teaching experience.

TOM NEWTON

0000 Whitewood Court • North Brunswick, New Jersey 08902 • 555.555.5555 • newton@gmail.com

QUALITY ASSURANCE PROFESSIONAL
QUALITY CONTROL ~ LABORATORY TECHNICIAN

Date

Name
Company
Address

Re: Quality Assurance Position

Dear Sir or Madam:

Enclosed is my resume for your review. I am confident that my long-term chemical/food experience with various types of manufacturing processes would serve as an asset to your company.

I have 5 years of experience working as a **Quality Assurance Technician** at Northeast Foods, where I performed analytical checks and quality assurance procedures for food and beverage products.

I am considered a quick learner with high concentration skills. In addition, I feel that my interpersonal skills, honesty, and rapport with fellow employees will benefit the company.

Other skills that I have gained though my employment are weighing and blending of batch ingredients according to formula, as well as inventory control. I have always been known for my accuracy and hardworking attitude.

Thank you for your consideration. I look forward to speaking with you personally so that we may discuss my qualifications in greater detail. I will call in two weeks to set up a time that we can talk further.

Sincerely yours,

Tom Newton

Enclosure

299

Quality Assurance Technician. *Beverley and Mitchell I. Baskin, Marlboro, New Jersey*

The applicant was looking for another quality assurance position. Five brief paragraphs tell of his experience, activities, people skills, on-the-job skills, and interest in an interview. See corresponding Resume 23 in Part 3.

Larry Duvall

41 Grayson Way, Indianapolis IN 55555
larry@yahoo.com ■ (555) 555-5555

January 23, 2008

Mrs. Penelope Jackson
Human Resource Manager
Duncan Electric & Gas Company
Corner of Stapleton and Merryman Avenues
Knoxville, Tennessee 55555

Position Desired: ELECTRICAL LINEMAN

Dear Mrs. Jackson:

Since graduating from Mercy County Technical College two years ago, I have worked in the electrical field on a number of emergency and routine projects, including assignments abroad. This experience involves installation, repair and maintenance of transmission and distribution lines and transformers.

Prior experience involves supervising, coordinating and working with considerable responsibility. I believe that many of the personal and work qualities I offer are ones that employers value and have difficulty finding:

Dependability	Flexibility	High Attendance
Work Ethic and Integrity	Dedication	Commitment to Quality and Accuracy

In a global environment that often requires working alongside people with varying temperaments and from various cultures, I'm especially proud to be able to work effectively and efficiently with all kinds of people. My abilities to communicate well with others and to promote team efforts are excellent, and I'm always willing to lend a hand when needed. Leadership experience has taught me patience, diplomacy and tolerance.

I will be calling your office to check on interview scheduling for this position, and I look forward to the opportunity to meet with you to discuss details. If you need additional information, please contact me at the above phone number.

Sincerely,

Larry Duvall

Enclosure: Resume

300

Electrical Lineman. *Beverley Drake, Rochester, Minnesota*

The applicant indicates in turn his experience, worker traits as transferable skills, people skills, and interest in an interview. His transferable worker traits stand out clearly in three columns.

SANDRA BACHUS, CPP

55 Pinehurst Road
Augusta, Ontario A1A 1A1
(555) 666-9999 • bachus@email.com

February 5, 2008

Pauline Ho
Senior Human Resources Manager
SciTech Pharmaceuticals
2345 Industry Circle
Pinehurst, Ontario
B2C 3D4

Re: Senior Component Technician

Dear Mrs. Ho,

"Sandra is considered an expert in her field…and continues to be the 'go-to' person."

With more than 10 years of experience overseeing packaging specifications, artwork, and production for some of the world's largest pharmaceutical firms, I have developed exhaustive expertise in all aspects of the industry—from technical specifications to quality control, production engineering, artwork, labelling, and distribution.

As the current Senior Component Development Specialist with ABC Packaging Inc., I coordinate 20–30 concurrent packaging projects at any given time for the full range of OTC and prescription products. I am very excited at the prospect of joining your team as your new Senior Component Technician as I am now anxious to apply my expertise to new and more challenging scenarios. The qualifications that distinguish me include the following:

✓ **Certified Packaging Professional** (recertified 2007) and **PAC Alumni certification** (2006)
✓ Exhaustive technical knowledge of **packaging components, processes, equipment, and tooling capabilities**
✓ Reputation for identifying opportunities to **improve processes, maximize efficiencies, and reduce costs** based on engineering and production requirements
✓ Skilled in **managing all artwork and creative processes**—familiar with a wide variety of printing processes and alternatives (flexography, gravure, etc.), further encouraging ability to produce top quality every time
✓ Excellent **communication and client/vendor relations** skills, internally and externally

If you are interested in speaking to a highly motivated and skilled professional with a reputation for excellence and continuous improvement, then I would welcome the opportunity to meet to discuss this opportunity in person.

I look forward to meeting with you and will call next week to set an appointment. Thank you for your consideration.

Sincerely,

Sandra Bachus

Encl.

301

Senior Component Technician. *Ross Macpherson, Whitby, Ontario, Canada*

The page border, thick horizontal line, opening testimonial, and bulleted qualifications in boldface helped this candidate stand head and shoulders above other applicants with more traditional letters.

JEFFREY R. SHAW

555 Prescott Road
Greenwich, CT 55555
(Residence) 555-555-5555
(Mobile) 500-500-5000
jrs1966@aol.com

September 30, 2007

T.R. Patel
CEO
TRP Enterprises
555 West Street
New York, NY 55555

Dear Mr. Patel:

The particular value I offer a technology company is my ability to execute a strategic plan across the enterprise and improve financial performance and customer, partner, and employee satisfaction. I have 10 years of direct P&L and operating management responsibility. My experience spans the software reseller, software licensing/management, and computer hardware industries. I possess an in-depth understanding of the enterprise software market and channel sales and marketing. My experience includes turnaround and transition management.

I have delivered revenue and profit results for a billion-dollar company during periods of intense competition and margin erosion. Most notably, I turned around a failing $750 million North American business unit. Holding P&L, operational, and sales and marketing responsibilities, I was able to achieve these outcomes:

- Accelerated growth of revenue and profits by 33% and continued to produce double-digit revenue growth for five consecutive years.
- Led a reengineering program that reduced operating costs by $18 million within 24 months.
- Delivered technology ROI by reengineering a failing SAP implementation.
- Elevated loyalty scores from major Fortune 500 customers from 60% to 95%.
- Earned coveted top scores from the company's top vendors, including Microsoft and IBM.

Being able to both "zoom out" *and* "zoom in" has enabled me to be successful in creating positive transformations in each of my positions. I view the organization and its market environment holistically, identify areas of waste and underperformance, and translate my assessments into powerful, integrated strategic and tactical plans. Because I am *also* able to "zoom in" and actually execute those change plans operationally, I have been able to create a lean, focused, fast-growth organization.

No change, however, can occur at optimal levels without the active participation of the people who put new initiatives into practice. I know how to improve both employee satisfaction and financial performance by establishing a corporate culture of measurement, accountability, and rewards and then motivating personnel to contribute to the full extent of their abilities.

When the company I led as General Manager was sold to Serus Communications, I played a key role in the transition. Now I am pursuing new challenges. I look forward to speaking with you in the near future about the COO position at JR Patel Enterprises. Thank you.

Sincerely,

Jeffrey R. Shaw

Enclosure

302

Chief Operating Officer. *Jean Cummings, Concord, Massachusetts*

This executive had a broad background in technology and was looking for his next position. The writer presented him as a strong achiever, shown by the bulleted statements.

EVEREST KEENE

55 Square Route • Halifax, Nova Scotia B5B 5B5

September 1, 2007

Mr. Rory O'May
Director, Machining Division
Celtic Mining and Manufacturing
555 East Boring Beltway
Halifax, Nova Scotia B0B 0B0

Dear Mr. O'May:

I would like to be your next **machine operator,** a position I saw advertised in the *Halifax Chronicle* on August 30.

The attached resume documents seven years of progressively responsible experience in this field. I presently serve as *Cell Leader* and Set-up Person for Atlantic Engine Parts. There, I established a reputation as a responsible, competent employee who could be relied on to produce work accurately and on time. In fact, I received the Eureka! award for averting a crisis that emerged when my colleagues and I were machining new parts for a major corporate client.

We were working to a tight deadline, and I had the privilege of serving as team leader. In the process of machining a particular part, the machining equipment was being damaged. This occurred because the part had been recently manufactured, and our company had not yet been able to acquire appropriate tools to machine it. I had no choice but to adapt existing technology to meet the demand. I accomplished this by modifying the cutting wheel and making adjustments to the computer program that guided the process.

The project was completed on time with minimal scrap, and our client was satisfied with the result.

In solving this problem, I demonstrated not only technical skill, but leadership, because all members of my team had to understand the modifications in order to mass-produce the part in question. It was a group effort, with the part passing from one machine operator to another in order to successfully complete the process. The team had to work harmoniously under pressure to get the job done. My ability to relate well with my colleagues, understand the high level of stress under which they were operating, and be flexible with them during this project played an important role in ensuring everything went smoothly and the job was completed on time.

I enjoy both the technical and interpersonal aspects of machine work and hope ultimately to acquire a supervisory position. I like this field because I am interested in the development of new and better technologies, and I enjoy the challenges that come with advancement. In fact, this was a major reason for my decision to enter the field. To this end, I have acquired a Certificate in CNC Programming from Sinclair College and completed a number of related technical courses.

My qualifications and experience are documented in the attached resume. I am confident that, on reviewing it, you will agree I have the potential to become a worthy member of your team. I will call to set a convenient time to meet, so that we could discuss how I might best serve Celtic Mining and Manufacturing.

Sincerely yours,

Everest Keene

P.S. I can be reached at (555) 000-0000.

Attachment: resume

303

Machine Operator. *Howard Earle Halpern, Toronto, Ontario, Canada*

The applicant "saved the day" by figuring out how to avoid damage to his employer's equipment. This story highlights the individual's leadership and ability to motivate others under pressure.

ALEXIS M. SMITH
0000 Archway Drive ▪ Charlotte, North Carolina 28888 ▪ (555) 555-5555

April 5, 2008

www.alltel.com/careers

ATTN: Placement Professional

Someone once said, "There are no great companies, just the people who work for them." Sounds as if the person who said this was referring to an organization—like Alltel—that espouses the philosophy of cooperative teamwork.

Your advertisement in *The Charlotte Observer* (April 4) for a Coordinator–Number Administrator certainly seems to describe such an environment, with an opportunity that rewards team performance.

If so, I'd like to become a member!

Throughout my experience with AT&T, I was given opportunities to contribute to resolving customer problems, provide administrative and technical support, and coordinate processes—through both in-house and field staff, as well as customers. Based on my training in the telecommunications industry, I know how to troubleshoot, monitor, and coordinate line problems. I worked in the Technical Department in the Business Center.

Following retirement from AT&T two years ago, I have continued to upgrade my skills, including advanced training in Word, Access, Excel, PowerPoint, and Windows, among others.

I'm confident that I could contribute effectively to the Alltel team. May we schedule a time to discuss our mutual goals?

Thank you for your consideration.

Sincerely,

Alexis M. Smith

304

Coordinator–Number Administrator. *Doug Morrison, Charlotte, North Carolina*

After 30 years of work, this applicant had "retired." Having energy and youthful vigor, however, she wanted to work for a new team—something that she had always been good at and liked doing.

Dear Hiring Manager:

For as long as I can remember, I have had a talent for keeping things well organized and operating efficiently. Post-it Notes, schedules, databases, and Excel spreadsheets are a part of my everyday life. I bring order to clutter and structure to chaos. If you feel that these skills and talents would prove to be advantageous to the Macy's West Visitors Center, then I would like to schedule a time for us to meet.

In addition to strong organizational skills, I offer you

   + More than five years of experience in the travel, hospitality, and tourism industry

   + Strong computer skills with a knack for Internet research and database creation and management

   + A solid work ethic and a commitment to giving whatever it takes to get a job done, right and on time

My professional office skills and strengths are complemented by a positive, can-do attitude; excellent listening skills; and sense of humor. I have built an extensive network in Las Vegas and have assembled a diverse blend of personal and professional references to attest to my abilities.

I hope you will see what a valuable addition I would make to your team of professionals and phone me. I can be reached at 555.555.5555 or 555.555.0000. Thank you for your consideration.

Sincerely,

Kathryn R. Hill

305

Travel Industry Professional. *Norine Dagliano, Hagerstown, Maryland*

This letter was e-mailed in response to a job posted on the employer's Web site. The letter, a brief overview of the candidate's skills, got an immediate reply. An interview occurred the next day.

Karrie MacNeal

0000 West Union Street ▼ Athens, Ohio 45701 ▼ 555.555.5555 ▼ kmacneal@msn.com

February 12, 2008

Ms. Susan Andrews
Human Resources Manager
Flyaway Travel Agency
229 South First Street
Athens, Ohio 45701

Dear Ms. Andrews:

It was with great interest that I read your recent ad in the *Athens Messenger* for a Travel Consultant, and I would like to be considered a serious candidate for this position. My resume is enclosed for your review and consideration.

Simply stated, travel has been my passion for more than 15 years! Even though my educational and career paths have taken me in a different direction up to this point, I have recently decided to follow my heart and pursue a career in the travel industry. Because of my desire to work in travel, I enrolled in the Travel Associate Training Program through Career Quest and will complete it next month.

Throughout my career I have utilized an ability to communicate effectively, both orally and in writing, with people from all walks of life. My counseling skills enable me to identify and respond appropriately to client needs. In addition, the time I spent as a Customer Service Manager allowed me to develop and enhance skills in sales, public speaking, event planning and database management that I believe would also be invaluable in your Travel Consultant position.

With a passion for travel, successful career experience in sales and current industry training, I am confident I would be an asset to your travel agency. Feel free to contact me to set up an interview or to answer any questions you may have regarding my background and experience. If you don't get a chance to call me in two weeks' time, I will follow up with you. I look forward to speaking with you soon.

Sincerely,

Karrie MacNeal

Enclosure

306

Travel Consultant. *Melissa L. Kasler, Athens, Ohio*

The applicant had a strong travel background and wanted to transition from customer-service counseling to travel consulting. The writer focused on travel-related activities and transferable skills.

DESMOND MASSEY

000 Augusta Court • Pinehurst, Ontario A1A 1A1
(555) 666-7777 • dmassey@email.com

March 12, 2008

Pinehurst Transit Commission
Human Resources Department
Placement Services
1111 Batterley Street
Pinehurst, Ontario
A1A 1A1

<u>**Re: Operator / Driver Positions**</u>

Dear Human Resources Manager,

Put simply, I love to drive—and with more than 600,000 safe miles of large-vehicle driving experience, a conscientious and safety-minded driving style, and years of experience providing the highest levels of customer service, I believe I can offer you both the skills and experience you are looking for in a PTC Operator/Driver.

I have been fortunate. My unique career has afforded me the opportunity to drive and transport loads throughout Canada and the U.S. in a variety of vehicles, including 18- and 30-wheel trailers. While most of my positions were in operations and customer service, these frequent driving opportunities represented an aspect of the job that I thoroughly enjoyed, and as I now find myself seeking a career change, I am finally in the position to pursue a long-standing desire to drive for a living.

I encourage you to review the attached resume detailing my qualifications, highlights of which include

- ✓ **Extensive large-vehicle driving experience—CDL License, Class A with Trailer and Air Brake endorsements**
- ✓ **Outstanding customer service skills from 11+ years in sales and account management— personable, friendly, and professional**
- ✓ **Able to work flexible work schedules and nonstandard shifts**

I would welcome the opportunity to meet and discuss in person the value I could add as a PTC Operator/ Driver. I am very enthusiastic about this opportunity and am confident that I have the right combination of skills and experience to exceed your expectations.

Thank you for your consideration, and I look forward to hearing from you soon. I will follow up in two weeks to answer any questions you might have.

Sincerely,

Desmond Massey

Encl.

307

Operator/Driver. *Ross Macpherson, Whitby, Ontario, Canada*

After 15 years in a family business, this candidate wanted to turn his passion for driving into a full-time career. The letter conveyed his love for driving and his qualifications, making him stand out.

Candy P. Palate

888.555.5555 ● E-mail: cpp555555@media.net ● 5555 Any Street ● Easton, MD 21601

Talbot County Office of Tourism
Attn: Ms. Brenda Carnes
11 S. Harrison St.
Easton, MD 21601

Dear Ms. Carnes,

Throughout my work history, I have always taken great pride in my meticulous attention to detail and in my ability to provide outstanding customer service to clients. More than 15 years of work experience in sales and account management instilled within me a desire to take care of clients and coworkers with the same kind of respect and efficiency that I would expect from a business. I will bring this sense of dedication to customers, combined with a strong work ethic to your organization.

As a long-time resident of the Maryland Eastern Shore, combined with more than 15 years of management experience in the travel industry, I believe that I have the right combination of travel skills and marketing experience for consideration as your new Tourism Coordinator. My friend, Rebecca Noble, who works in your office, especially encouraged me to apply for this position.

While managing corporate travel accounts, I took great pride in getting to know my clients and learning of their personal preferences, schedules, business needs, and travel interests. They consistently complimented me on my ability to handle the meticulous details of their business trips and vacations. I know that as your new Tourism Coordinator, I can effectively develop and promote marketing and promotion plans that will attract more visitors to Talbot County.

As the last few years of my work have been spent creating and marketing my own business, I have learned how to take an ordinary food, such as pecans, and create a unique trademarked brand that is now marketed on a regional level. In just under four years, I have single-handedly contracted with more than 126 retailers to carry and promote my product. I have increased my sales volume by 125% each year, with 2007 sales projections exceeding $80,000. That dollar figure accounts for more than 8,000 bags of pecans being sold in 2007.

This position appeals to me because I can use the skills and experience that I already possess and work in a team environment where my strengths will be emphasized. I will prove to you that I can quickly adapt to new situations, will take initiative to effectively learn my job, and even offer fresh ideas to improve the services and structure of your business.

Ms. Carnes, I would welcome the opportunity to discuss additional work-related accomplishments with you during a personal interview in the upcoming weeks. We can discuss how my combination of travel management and entrepreneurial experience will be a perfect fit for the Talbot County Office of Tourism.

Thank you for your time and consideration. I look forward to speaking with you soon.

Sincerely,

Candy P. Palate

308

Tourism Coordinator. *Beth Colley, Crownsville, Maryland*

The individual had significant travel industry experience as a travel agent but had spent the last five years creating and maintaining a business. The writer quantifies sales achievements.

MARLENA M. LONG

55555 E. Caspian Place
Aurora, CO 80015

marlena6@msn.com

Home (303) 000-5555
Cell (720) 555-0000

March 31, 2008

Hiring Manager
Jet Aviation, Inc.
Attn: In-flight Recruiting
5555 Buchtel Avenue
Philadelphia, PA 00000

Dear Jets Aviation Hiring Manager:

If you are looking for an experienced Flight Attendant with excellent abilities to attend to passenger comfort with a personal touch, as well as take care of passengers in emergencies, then I am the professional you are looking for.

I have excelled in my time at Northeast Air. Along the way, I have gained excellent organizational skills, as well as a strong ability to assess and take care of the needs of the passengers. I also have a strong ability to quickly and efficiently prepare for flights.

My flight attendant training has ensured that I can professionally perform effective decision making, skilled passenger handling, passenger-safety briefings, in-flight emergency procedures, post-evacuation considerations, and any type of medical emergency. I have proven these skills several times since completing my training in real emergency situations.

My past employment has given me the ability to "read" passengers and determine how to relate to them and make them feel the most comfortable. I enjoy my work and like to bring a friendly, humorous atmosphere to every flight. I also have a food service background that I frequently use while I work. I am positive that you will come to rely on my knowledge and abilities just as my past employers have.

My experience with Northeast Air has given me strong practical experience as a Flight Attendant. I am now interested in working for a charter flight corporation and show my abilities to provide personalized, first-class service on an individual basis.

The accompanying resume will provide you with the additional details of my accomplishments and skills. I would welcome the opportunity to meet with you and learn how I can make a positive contribution to your corporation.

Thank you for your time and consideration.

Sincerely,

Marlena M. Long

309

Flight Attendant. *Michele Angello, Aurora, Colorado*

The applicant was a commercial flight attendant and wanted to become a charter flight attendant. She learned the name of the hiring manager and personalized the letter before sending it.

TIM CARLETON
5 Ninth Avenue ▶ Winona, MN 55555
Cell Phone 555-555-5555
E-mail timcarl@chosen.com

January 5, 2008

David Sherrill, Regional Director
Mississippi Express
P.O. Box 555
Wabasha, MN 55555

Dear Mr. Sherrill:

I appreciate the time you spent with me yesterday discussing the sales position in the Rochester area and would like to reiterate my interest in the position. Enclosed is a resume reflecting my work history and philosophy.

A manager's and a company's success in the workplace is measured in many ways: productivity of workers ▶ results from managers ▶ job satisfaction ▶ low employee turnover ▶ quality of work, products and services ▶ accountability ▶ respect toward self, company and customers. A rewarding work environment is one in which employees and managers can expand their knowledge, skills and contributions. When an atmosphere of self-pride and company pride prevails, everyone wins—worker, company and customer. Attitudes mean a lot and reflect greatly on the mental image customers carry with them after the sale.

My record has been a good one. I've been able to motivate myself, as well as others, and to generate trust, respect and win-win results. Stability and accomplishment mark my career, as does ongoing learning. The Internet has opened such possibilities that knowledge is limited only by time and interest in using the Net as a tool for research of industry growth and direction, overall business trends, labor statistics, tax changes and sales and marketing ideas.

While interviews and references are the preferred methods of learning more about candidates, at least a sketch of past accomplishments can help in forming a mental image of the person. You will see that general business skills complement the people skills—which is my greatest strength and interest. I truly enjoy working with others and have been exploring possibilities in which my biggest contributions can be not only helping a company meet its goals, but also creating an avenue in which I'm enriching in some way the lives of others or the world we leave behind. Social responsibility is a high priority.

I look forward to hearing from you further to discuss the company's direction, needs and concerns. In the next few days, I will contact you to determine your plans for filling this position and to see if you have questions or need additional information.

Sincerely,

Tim Carleton

Enclosure: Resume

310

Thank-You Letter. *Beverley Drake, Rochester, Minnesota*

After an interview without a resume, the applicant uses this thank-you letter to impress the reader further. The second paragraph expresses the applicant's views on success and a winning work environment.

KEVIN STERLING

000 Third Avenue/3W • New York, NY 10017 • Tel: 555-555-5555 • Fax: 555-555-5555 • kevin_sterling@msn.com

January 10, 2008

Mr. John Green
15 Green Street
New York, NY 10011

Dear Mr. Green:

It has been a while since we spoke at your company's fundraising event last winter.

As you may know, I have been helping a number of organizations with significant challenges as part of their executive team after successfully selling my company, Media XYZ, Inc., in 2007.

Now that the time has come to move on, I was wondering if you could help me identify contacts that I can approach at Fortune 500 technology ventures, where I can combine my technological and general management skills to provide strong, decisive, hands-on leadership, preferably to an operations, professional services, or consulting division. I currently reside in New York City but am open to relocation.

My success with my own company (integrated marketing, servicing Fortune 100 and e-commerce clients) and my consulting projects, as well as during prior employment, lies in my ability to quickly generate results. Never satisfied with the status quo, I developed a keen eye for identifying and capitalizing on market opportunities and am adept at swiftly responding to market changes and customer demands. Even though my track record goes back only ten years, I have demonstrated achievements in

- Managing businesses to turn around performance and achieve full potential
- Analyzing and controlling all aspects of multisite operations to reduce costs and improve profits
- Negotiating favorable domestic and international deals, acquisitions and strategic alliances, and partnerships
- Combining expertise in strategic/tactical marketing and business development
- Creating and introducing cutting-edge technologies and procedures
- Training, motivating, and directing 140+ personnel to improve individual and group effectiveness

Because I value your experience and perspective, I have taken the liberty of enclosing a resume to assist you in evaluating appropriate contacts and suggestions. I would greatly appreciate any ideas, recommendations, or referrals you could offer. Rest assured that I would happily do the same for you if the situation ever arises. I will call you next week to follow up.

Sincerely,

Kevin Sterling

Enclosure

311

Networking Letter. *Ilona Vanderwoude, Riverdale, New York*

This networking letter was for an ex-entrepreneur reentering the workforce. The writer is upfront about his entrepreneurship instead of masking it with titles such as *president* or *managing partner*.

3

P ◆ A ◆ R ◆ T

Best Resume Tips

Best Resume Tips
at a Glance

Best Resume Tips

In a passive job search, you rely on your resume to do most of the work for you. An eye-catching resume that stands out above all the others may be your best shot at getting noticed by a prospective employer. If your resume is only average and looks like most of the others in the pile, the chances are great that you won't be noticed and called for an interview. If you want to be singled out because of your resume, it should be somewhere between spectacular and award-winning.

In an active job search, however, your resume complements your efforts at being known to a prospective employer *before* that person receives it. For this reason, you can rely less on your resume for getting someone's attention. Nevertheless, your resume has an important role in an active job search that may include the following activities:

- Talking to relatives, friends, and other acquaintances to meet people who can hire you before a job is available

- Creating phone scripts to speak with the person who is most likely to hire someone with your background and skills

- Using a schedule to keep track of your appointments and callbacks

- Working at least 25 hours a week to search for a job

When you are this active in searching for a job, the quality of your resume confirms the quality of your efforts to get to know the person who might hire you, as well as your worth to the company whose workforce you want to join. An eye-catching resume makes it easier for you to sell yourself directly to a prospective employer. If your resume is mediocre or conspicuously flawed, it will work against you and may undo all of your good efforts in searching for a job.

The following list offers ideas for making resumes visually impressive. Many of the ideas are for making resumes pleasing to the eye; other ideas are for eliminating common writing mistakes and stylistic weaknesses.

Some of these ideas can be used with any equipment, from a manual typewriter to a computer with desktop publishing software. Other ideas make sense only if you have a computer system with word processing or desktop publishing. Even if you don't have a computer, take some time to read all of the ideas. Then, if you decide to use the services of a professional resume writer, you will be better informed about what the writer can do for you in producing your resume.

Best Resume Writing Strategies

1. **Although many resume books say that you should spell out the name of the state in your address at the top of the resume, consider using the postal abbreviation instead.** The reason is simple: It's an address. Anyone wanting to contact you by mail will probably refer to your name and address on the resume. If they appear there as they should on an envelope, the writer can simply copy the information you supply. If you spell out the name of your state in full, the writer will have to "translate" the name of the state to its postal abbreviation.

    Not everyone knows all the postal abbreviations, and some abbreviations are easily confused. For example, those for Alabama (AL), Alaska (AK), American Samoa (AS), Arizona (AZ), and Arkansas (AR) are easy to mix up. You can prevent confusion and delay simply by using the correct postal abbreviation.

    If you decide to use postal abbreviations in addresses, make certain that you do not add a period after the abbreviations. This applies also to postal abbreviations in the addresses of references, if you provide them.

    Consider, however, not using the state postal abbreviation when you are indicating only the city and state (not the mailing address) of a school you attended or a business where you worked. In these cases, it makes sense to write out the name of the state in full.

2. **Adopt a sensible form for phone numbers in the contact information and then use that form consistently.** Do this in your resume and in all of the documents you use in your job search. Some forms for phone numbers make more sense than others. Compare the following forms:

123-4567	This form is best for a resume circulated locally, within a region where all the phone numbers have the same area code.
(222) 123-4567	This form is best for a resume circulated in areas with different area codes.
222-123-4567	This form suggests that the area code should be dialed in all cases. But that won't be necessary for prospective employers whose area code is 222. Avoid this form.
222/123-4567	This form is illogical and should be avoided also. The slash can mean an alternate option, as in ON/OFF. In a phone number, this meaning of a slash makes little sense.
1 (222) 123-4567	This form is long, and the digit *1* isn't necessary. Almost everyone will know that 1 should be used before the area code to dial a long-distance number.
222.123.4567	This form is becoming popular, particularly with designers.

Note: For resumes directed to prospective employers *outside* the United States, be sure to include the correct international prefixes in all phone numbers so that you and your references can be reached easily by phone.

3.   **Whether your resume begins with an Objective statement or a Professional Goal, make it focused, developed, or unique so that it grabs the reader's attention.** See the Objective statement in Resume 22. If your opening statement fails to do this, the reader might discard the resume without reading further. Whatever opening you use, it is your first opportunity to sell yourself.

4.   **If you can sell yourself better with some other kind of section, consider omitting an Objective statement and putting a Summary of Qualifications, a Profile, or an Areas of Expertise section just after the contact information.** See Resumes 3, 4, 5, 8, 11, and 15.

5.   **A Professional Highlights section placed early in the resume helps to feature important information.** See Resume 15.

6.   **Displaying your qualifications, areas of expertise, skills, or strengths in columns makes them easy to alter if your target job or target industry changes.** See Resumes 16, 22, and 23.

7.   **Spend considerable time determining how to present your skills.** You can present them in various ways, such as Knowledge and Skill Areas (Resume 1), Office Skills (Resume 3), Areas of Expertise (Resume 8), Competencies (Resume 10), Technical Summary (Resume 11), Computer Skills (Resume 14), Professional Highlights (Resume 15), Career Highlights (Resume 20), Relevant Qualifications (Resume 21), Summary of Qualifications (Resume 22), and Professional Strengths (Resume 23).

8.   **In the Experience section or elsewhere, state accomplishments, not just duties or responsibilities.** The reader often already knows duties and responsibilities for a given position. Accomplishments, however, can be attention-getting. The reader probably considers life too short to be bored by lists of duties and responsibilities in a stack of resumes. See Resumes 3 and 17.

9.   **In the Experience section and for each position held, consider explaining responsibilities in a paragraph and using bullets to point to achievements, contributions, or awards.** See Resumes 1 and 17.

10.   **When you indicate achievements, consider italicizing them (Resume 18), quantifying them (Resumes 1, 3, 10, and 17), or providing a separate heading for them (Resume 19).**

11.   **When skills, abilities, qualifications, or responsibilities are varied, group them according to categories for easier comprehension.** See Resumes 17 and 19.

12.   **Include information that explains lesser-known companies.** See Resume 10.

13.   **Group positions to avoid repetition in a description of duties.** See Resume 5.

Best Resume Design and Layout Tips

14. **Use quality paper correctly.** If you use quality watermarked paper for your resume, be sure to use the right side of the paper. To know which side is the right side, hold a blank sheet of paper up to a light source. If you can see a watermark and "read" it, the right side of the paper is facing you. This is the surface for typing or printing. If the watermark is unreadable or if any characters look backward, you are looking at the "underside" of a sheet of paper—the side that should be left blank.

15. **Use adequate "white space."** A sheet of white paper with no words on it is impossible to read. Likewise, a sheet of white paper with words all over it is impossible to read. The goal is to have a comfortable mix of white space and words. If your resume has too many words and not enough white space, the resume looks cluttered. If it has too much white space and too few words, the resume looks skimpy and unimportant. Make certain that adequate white space exists between the main sections. For resumes with a satisfying amount of white space, see Resumes 3, 6, 8, 15, 20, 21, and 22. For resumes with adequate white space even with a small font size, see Resume 2. For white space accomplished through center-alignment, see Resume 14.

16. **Margins in resumes for executives, managers, and other administrators tend to be narrower than margins in other resumes.** See Resume 16. Narrower margins are often used in connection with smaller type to get more information on a one- or two-page resume.

17. **Be consistent in your use of line spacing.** How you handle line spacing can tell the reader how good you are at details and how consistent you are in your use of them. If, near the beginning of your resume, you insert two line spaces (two hard returns in a word-processing program) between two main sections, be sure to put two line spaces between main sections throughout the resume.

18. **Be consistent in your use of horizontal spacing.** If you usually put two character spaces after a period at the end of a sentence, make certain that you use two spaces consistently. The same is true for colons. If you put two spaces after colons, do so consistently.

    Note that an em dash—a dash the width of the letter m—does not require spaces before or after it. No space should go between the P and O of P.O. Box. Only one space is needed between the postal abbreviation of a state and the ZIP code. You should insert a space between the first and second initials of a person's name, as in I. M. Jobseeker (not I.M. Jobseeker). These conventions have become widely adopted in English and business communications. If, however, you use other conventions, be sure to be consistent. In resumes, as in grammar, consistency is more important than conformity.

19. **Make certain that characters, lines, and images contrast well with the paper.** The quality of "ink" depends on the device used to type or print your resume. For a test, send yourself a copy of your resume and see how it makes the trip through the mail. If you use an inkjet or laser printer, check that the characters are sharp and clean, without ink smudges or traces of extra toner. Mail yourself a laser-printed envelope to make sure that it looks good after a trip through the mail. A cover letter with a flaking address does not make a good impression.

20. **Use vertical alignment in stacked text.** Resumes usually contain tabbed or indented text. Make certain that this "stacked" material is aligned vertically. Misalignment can ruin the appearance of a well-written resume. Try to set tabs or indents that control this text throughout a resume instead of having a mix of tab stops in different sections. If you use a word processor, make certain that you understand the difference between tabbed text and indented text, as in the following examples:

Tabbed text:	This text was tabbed over one tab stop before the writer started to write the sentence.
Indented text:	This text was indented once before the writer started to write the sentence.

Note: In a number of word-processing programs, the Indent command is useful for ensuring the correct vertical alignment of proportionally spaced, stacked text. After you use the Indent command, lines of wrapped text are vertically aligned automatically until you terminate the command by pressing Enter.

21. **For the vertical alignment of dates, try left- or right-aligning the dates.** This technique is especially useful in chronological resumes and combination resumes. For several examples of right-aligned dates, look at Resumes 2, 4, and 6.

22. **Use as many pages as you need for portraying your qualifications adequately to a specific interviewer for a particular job.** Try to limit your resume to one page or two pages, but set the upper limit at four pages. No rule about the number of pages makes sense in all cases. The determining factors are a person's qualifications and experiences, the requirements of the job, and the interests and pet peeves of the interviewer. If you know that an interviewer refuses to look at a resume longer than a page, that says it all. You need to deliver a one-page resume if you want to get past the first gate.

    More important than the question of how many pages is the issue of complete pages. A full page sends a better message than a partial page (which says "not enough to fill"). Therefore, one full page is better than 1.25 pages, and two full pages are better than 1.75 pages.

23. **When you have letters of recommendation, use quotations from them as testimonials.** Devoting some space (or even a full column) to the positive opinions of "external authorities" helps make a resume convincing as well as impressive. When placed effectively, such quotations can build respect, add credibility, and personalize a resume. See Resume 4.

24. **Unless you enlist the services of a professional printer or skilled desktop publisher, resist the temptation to use full justification for text.** The price that you pay for a straight right margin is uneven word spacing. Words may appear too close together on some lines and too spread out on others. Although the resume might look like typeset text, you lose readability. Professional resume writers sometimes use full justification effectively for variety.

25. **If you can choose a typeface for your resume, use a serif font for greater readability.** Serif fonts have little lines extending from the tops, bottoms, and ends of the characters. These fonts tend to be easier to read than sans serif (without serif) fonts, especially in low-light conditions. Compare the following font examples:

Serif	Sans Serif
Baskerville	Avant Garde
Courier	Futura
Times New Roman	Helvetica

Words such as *minimum* and *abilities,* which have several consecutive thin letters, are more readable in a serif font than in a sans serif font.

26. **If possible, avoid using monospaced fonts, such as Courier, in which the width of each character is the same.** For example, in a monospaced font the space for the letter *i* is as wide as the space for the letter *m*. Therefore, in Courier type *iiiii* is as wide as *mmmmm*. Courier was a standard of business communications during the 1960s and 1970s. Because of its widespread use, it is now considered "common." It also takes up a lot of space, so you can't pack as much information on a page with Courier type as you can with a proportionally spaced type such as Times New Roman.

27. **Think twice before using all uppercase letters in parts of your resume.** A common misconception is that uppercase letters are easier to read than lowercase letters. Actually, the ascenders and descenders of lowercase letters make them more distinguishable from each other and therefore more recognizable than uppercase letters. For a test, look at a string of uppercase letters and throw them gradually out of focus by squinting. The uppercase letters become a blur sooner than lowercase letters. Professional resume writers, however, may use uppercase letters effectively for emphasis and variety.

28. **Think twice about underlining some words in your resume.** Underlining defeats the purpose of serifs at the bottom of characters by blending with the serifs. In trying to emphasize words, you lose some visual clarity. This is especially true if you use underlining with uppercase letters in centered or side headings.

29. **If you have access to many fonts through word processing or desktop publishing, beware of becoming "font happy" and turning your resume into a font circus.** Frequent font changes can **distract** the reader, AND SO CAN GAUDY DISPLAY TYPE SUCH AS THIS.

30. **To make your resume stand out, consider using a nonstandard format or an unconventional display font in the contact information or in the headings.** See Resumes 2, 12, and 16. What is usually fitting for resumes for some prospective jobs, however, is not always the most appropriate resume strategy for executive positions. Try to match the style of your resume to the target company's "corporate image" if it has one.

31. **Be aware of the value differences of black type.** Some typefaces are light; others are dark. Notice the following lines:

A quick brown fox jumps over the lazy dog.

A quick brown fox jumps over the lazy dog.

Most typefaces fall somewhere between these two. With the variables of height, width, thickness, serifs, angles, curves, spacing, ink color, ink density, boldfacing, and typewriter double-striking, type offers an infinite range of values from light to dark. Try to make your resume more visually interesting by offering stronger contrasts between light type and dark type. Browse through the Exhibit of Resumes at the end of this section and notice the differences in light and dark type.

32. **Use italic characters carefully.** Whenever possible, use italic rather than underlining as an enhancement when you need to call attention to a word or phrase. You might consider using italic for duties or achievements. Think twice, however, about using italic throughout your resume. The reason is that italic (slanted) characters are less readable than normal (vertical) characters. The reader might have to hold the resume at an angle to make an all-italic resume more readable. Such a maneuver can be irritating. Even so, "all italic" may be just the thing to make a particular resume stand out.

33. **Use boldfacing to make different job titles more evident.** See Resumes 4, 8, 10, and 12.

34. **For getting attention, make headings white on black if you use software that has this capability.** Resume 20 displays the candidate's initials as white letters in a dark box.

35. **If you use word processing or desktop publishing and have a suitable printer, use special characters to enhance the look of your resume.** For example, use enhanced quotation marks (" and ") instead of their typewriter equivalents (" and "). Use an em dash (—) instead of two hyphens (--) for a dash. To separate dates, try using an en dash (a dash the width of the letter *n*) instead of a hyphen, as in 2003–2004. If you use "to" rather than an en dash between dates in a range (as in 2002 to 2007), use "to" consistently. Whenever you use an em dash or an en dash, avoid a space before and after the dash.

36. **To call attention to an item in a list, use a bullet (•) or a box (■) rather than a hyphen (-).** Browse through the sample resumes and notice how bullets are used effectively as attention getters.

37. **For variety, try using bullets of a different style, such as diamond (♦) bullets, rather than the usual round or square bullets.** An example with diamonds is Resume 11. For other kinds of bullets, see Resumes 1 (shadowed squares), 5 (filled squares), 8 (decorative arrow tips), and 9 (unfilled circles).

38. **Make a bullet a little smaller than the lowercase letters after it.** Disregard any ascenders or descenders on the letters. Compare the following bullet sizes:

   • Too small   ● Too large   • Better   • Just right

39. **If possible, visually coordinate the resume and the cover letter with the same font, line enhancement, border, or graphic to catch the reader's attention.** See Resume 3 and Cover Letter 16, Resume 7 and Cover Letter 203, Resume 8 and Cover Letter 86, Resume 12 and Cover Letter 148, Resume 18 and Cover Letter 272, Resume 21 and Cover Letter 286, and Resume 22 and Cover Letter 296.

40. **Use a horizontal line or a combination of lines to separate your contact information from the rest of the resume.** See Resumes 6, 8, 12, and 15. Resume 2 uses a series of small, filled squares to simulate a horizontal line.

41. **Use horizontal lines or bars to separate the different sections of the resume and thus make them visible at a glance.** See Resumes 11, 14, and 23. Resume 16 contains shaded bars to distinguish the headings.

42. **For variety in dividing sections of your resume or in presenting contact information, use partial horizontal lines that extend from the left margin to indented or right-aligned text, or from the end of a short line of left-aligned text to the right margin.** See Resume 16. Note that Resume 8 has partial lines that extend from the centered occupation to *both* the left and right margins.

43. **To avoid a cramped one-page resume that has small print, narrow margins, and reduced line spacing, consider using a two-page resume instead.** (Those who insist on one-page resumes will not agree with this tip.)

44. **Use thicker horizontal lines to call attention to a section of the resume.** See Resume 1.

45. **Use vertical lines or bars to spice up your resume.** See Resumes 4 and 5.

46. **Use various kinds of boxes (single line, shadowed, or decorative) to make a page visually more interesting.** See Resumes 4 and 9.

47. **Use a page border to make a page visually more interesting.** See Resume 3. Resume 5 contains a partial page border for visual interest.

48. **Use centered headings to make them easy to read down a page.** See Resumes 9, 13, 14, 15, and 23.

49. **Consider using hanging indentation of section headings to make them stand out.** See Resumes 11, 12, and 21.

50. **Near the top of the first page but below the contact information, place a list of keywords that can easily be scanned for storage in an online resume database.** See Resumes 1, 13, and 16.

Best Resume Writing Style Tips

51. **Check that words or phrases in lists are parallel.** For example, notice the bulleted items in the Relevant Experience section of Resume 1. All the entries contain verbs in the past tense.

52. **Use capital letters correctly.** Resumes usually contain many of the following:

    Names of people, companies, organizations, government agencies, awards, and prizes

    Titles of job positions and publications

    References to academic fields (such as chemistry, English, and mathematics)

    Geographic regions (such as the Midwest, the East, the state of California, Oregon State, and northern Florida)

Because of such words, resumes are minefields for the misuse of uppercase letters. When you don't know whether a word should have an initial capital letter, don't guess. Consult a dictionary, a handbook on style, or some other authoritative source, such as an official Web site. Often a reference librarian can provide the information you need. If so, you are only a phone call away from an accurate answer. Use headline style in headings. That is, capitalize the first letter of the first word, the last word, and all main words. Use lowercase letters for the first letter of articles (*a, an, the*), conjunctions (*and, but, or, nor, for, yet, so*), and prepositions of four or fewer letters (*at, by, on, into,* and so on). Capitalize, however, the first letter of prepositions of five or more letters (*among, across,* and so on). If you use "small caps" as a font enhancement (Format, Font, Small caps in Microsoft Word), create the heading in upper- and lowercase letters and select the heading before you apply the Small caps option.

53. **Check that you have used capital letters and hyphens correctly in computer terms.** If you want to show in a Computer Experience section that you have used certain hardware and software, you may give the opposite impression if you don't use uppercase letters and hyphens correctly. Note the correct use of capitals and hyphens in the following names of hardware, software, and computer companies:

LaserJet	Hewlett-Packard	Photoshop
PageMaker	QuarkXPress	PostScript
Sound Blaster	Microsoft Word	PhotoSmart

The reason that many computer product names have an internal uppercase letter is for the sake of a trademark. A word with unusual spelling or capitalization is trademarkable. When you use the correct forms of these words, you are honoring trademarks and registered trademarks and showing that you are in the know.

54. **Use all uppercase letters for most acronyms.** An *acronym* is a pronounceable word usually formed from the initial letters of the words in a compound term, or sometimes from multiple letters in those words. Note the following examples:

COBOL	COmmon Business-Oriented Language
ERISA	Employee Retirement Income Security Act
FORTRAN	FORmula TRANslator

An acronym such as *radar* (*ra*dio *d*etecting *a*nd *r*anging) has become so common that it is no longer all uppercase. If you think a reader may not know the meaning of an acronym, use the full term.

55. **Be aware that you may need to use a period with some abbreviations.** An *abbreviation* is a word shortened by removing the latter part of the word or by deleting some letters within the word. Here are some examples:

adj. for adjective	*amt.* for amount
adv. for adverb	*dept.* for department

Usually, you can't pronounce an abbreviation as a word. Sometimes, however, an abbreviation is a set of uppercase letters (without periods) that you can pronounce as letters. AFL-CIO, CBS, NFL, and YMCA are examples.

56. **Be sure to spell every word correctly.** A resume with just one misspelling is not impressive and may undermine all the hours you spent putting it together. Worse than that, one misspelling may be what the reader is looking for to screen you out, particularly if you are applying for a position that requires accuracy with words. If you calculate the salary you don't get *times* the number of years you might have worked for that company, that's an expensive misspelling!

You may be able to catch most misspellings with the spelling checker of your word processor. Be wary of spelling checkers, however. They can detect a misspelled word but cannot detect when you have inadvertently used a wrong word (*to* for *too*, for example). Be wary also of letting someone else check your resume. If the other person is not a good speller, you may not get any real help. The best authority is a good, *current* dictionary.

57. **For words that have more than one correct spelling, use the preferred form.** This form is the one that appears first in a dictionary. For example, if you see the entry **trav·el·ing** *or* **trav·el·ling**, the first form (with one *l*) is the preferred spelling. If you make it a practice to use the preferred spelling, you will build consistency in your resumes and cover letters.

58. **Avoid British spellings.** These slip into American usage through books and online articles published in Great Britain. Note the following words:

British Spelling	American Spelling
acknowledgement	acknowledgment
centre	center
judgement	judgment
towards	toward

59. **Avoid hyphenating words with such prefixes as** *co-, micro-, mid-, mini-, multi-, non-, pre-, re-,* **and** *sub-.* Many people think that words with these prefixes should have a hyphen after the prefix, but most of these words should not. The following words are spelled correctly:

coauthor	microcomputer	minicomputer
coworker	midpoint	multicultural
cowriter	midway	multilevel
nondisclosure	prearrange	reenter
nonfunctional	prequalify	subdirectory

Note: If you look in a dictionary for a word with a prefix and can't find the word, look for the prefix itself in the dictionary. You might find there a small-print listing of a number of words that have the prefix.

60. **Be aware that compounds (combinations of words) present special problems for hyphenation.** Writers' handbooks and books on style do not always agree on how compounds should be hyphenated. Many compounds are evolving from *open* compounds (two different words) to *hyphenated* compounds (two words joined by a hyphen) to *closed* compounds (one word). In different dictionaries, you can therefore find the words *copy editor, copy-editor,* and *copyeditor.* No wonder the issue is confusing! Most style books do agree, however, that when some compounds appear as an adjective before a noun, the compound should be hyphenated. When the same compound appears after a noun, hyphenation is unnecessary. Compare the following two sentences:

I scheduled well-attended conferences.

The conferences I scheduled were well attended.

For detailed information about hyphenation, see a recent edition of *The Chicago Manual of Style* (the 15th edition is now current). You should be able to find a copy at a local library.

61. **Be sure to hyphenate so-called** *permanent* **hyphenated compounds.** Usually, you can find these by looking them up in a dictionary. You can spot them easily because they have a "long hyphen" (–) for visibility in the dictionary. Hyphenate these words (with a standard hyphen) wherever they appear, before or after a noun. Here are some examples:

all-important	self-employed
day-to-day	step-by-step
full-blown	time-consuming

Note that the Chicago Manual of Style, 15th Edition, now recommends that these hyphenated compounds should no longer be considered permanent but should be without a hyphen (or hyphens) when they appear after a noun (see Tip 60).

62. **Use the correct form for certain verbs and nouns combined with prepositions.** You may need to consult a dictionary for correct spelling and hyphenation. Compare the following examples:

start up	(verb)
start-up	(noun)
start-up	(adj.)
startup	(noun, computer and Internet industry)
startup	(adj., computer and Internet industry)

63. **Avoid using shortcut words, such as abbreviations like** *thru* **or foreign words like** *via.* Spell out *through* and use *by* for *via*.

64. **Use the right words.** The issue here is correct *usage*, which often means the choice of the right word or phrase from a group of two or more possibilities. The following words and phrases are often used incorrectly:

alternate (adj.)	Refers to an option used every other time. OFF is the alternate option to ON in an ON/OFF switch.
alternative	Refers to an option that can be used at any time. If cake and pie are alternative desserts for dinner, you can have cake three days in a row if you like. The common mistake is to use *alternate* when the correct word is *alternative*.
center around	A common illogical expression. Draw a circle and then try to draw its center around it. You can't. Use *center in* or *center on* as logical alternatives to *center around*.

For information about the correct *usage* of words, consult a usage dictionary or the usage section of a writer's handbook, such as Strunk and White's *Elements of Style*.

65. **Use numbers consistently.** Numbers are often used inconsistently with text. Should you present a number as a numeral or spell out the number as a word? One approach is to spell out numbers *one* through *nine* but present numbers 10 and above as numerals. Different approaches are taught in different schools, colleges, and universities. Use the approach you have learned, but be consistent.

66. **Use (or don't use) the serial comma consistently.** How should you punctuate a series of three or more items? If, for example, you say in your resume that you increased sales by 100 percent, opened two new territories, and trained four new salespersons, the comma before *and* is called the *serial comma*. It is commonly omitted in newspapers, magazine articles, advertisements, and business documents; but it is often used for precision in technical documents or for stylistic reasons in academic text, particularly in the Humanities.

67. **Use semicolons correctly.** Semicolons are useful because they help to distinguish visually the items in a series when the items themselves contain commas. Suppose that you have the following entry in your resume:

> Increased sales by 100 percent, opened two new territories, which were in the Midwest, trained four new salespersons, who were from Georgia, and increased profitability by 250 percent.

The extra commas (before *which* and *who*) throw the main items of the series out of focus. By separating the main items with semicolons, you can bring them back into focus:

> Increased sales by 100 percent; opened two new territories, which were in the Midwest; trained four new salespersons, who were from Georgia; and increased profitability by 250 percent.

Use this kind of high-rise punctuation even if just one item in the series has an internal comma.

68. **Use dashes correctly.** One of the purposes of a dash (an em dash, or long dash) is to introduce a comment or afterthought about preceding information. A colon *anticipates* something to follow, but a dash *looks back* to something already said. Two dashes are sometimes used before and after a related but nonessential remark—such as this—within a sentence. In this case, the dashes are like parentheses, but more formal.

69. **Use apostrophes correctly.** They indicate possession (Tom's, Betty's), the omission of letters in contractions (can't, don't), and some plurals (x's and o's), but they can be tricky with words ending in *s*, possessive plurals, and plural forms of capital letters and numbers. For review or guidance, consult a style guide or a section on style in a dictionary.

70. **Know the difference between *its* and *it's*.** The form *its'* does not exist in English, so you need to know only how *it's* differs from *its*. The possessive form *its* is like *his* and *her* and has no apostrophe. The form *it's* is a contraction of *it is*. The trap is to think that *it's* is a possessive form.

Exhibit of Resumes

This part of the book contains an Exhibit of 23 resumes that accompanied cover letters in the first part of the book. Cross-references let you know readily which cover letter accompanied a particular resume so that you can view the two documents as a package.

Resume writers commonly distinguish between chronological resumes and functional (or skills) resumes. A *chronological resume* is a photo—a snapshot history of what you did and when you did it. A *functional resume* is a painting—an interpretive sketch of what you can do for a future employer. A third kind of resume, known as a *combination resume,* is a mix of recalled history and self-assessment. Besides recollecting "the facts," a combination resume contains self-interpretation and is therefore more like dramatic history than news coverage. A chronological resume and a functional resume are not always that different; often, all that is needed for a functional resume to qualify as a combination resume is the inclusion of dates for some of the positions held.

Instead of making 200 copies of a resume and sending the same document to different prospective employers, you should consider tailoring each resume to a specific job target. Creating multiple versions of a resume may seem difficult, but it is easy to do if you have (or have access to) a personal computer and a laser printer or some other kind of printer that can produce quality output. You will also need word-processing capability. Remember that most professional resume writers have the hardware and software, and they can make your resume look like those in the Exhibit. A local fast-print shop can make your resume look good, but you will probably not get there the kind of advice and service that a professional resume writer provides.

James M. Olson

9803 Clinton Avenue ▪ Houston, TX 77068
(281) 000-0000 ▪ name@msn.com

ACCOUNTANT

Detail-focused, highly ethical accounting professional with a BBA in Accounting and work experience demonstrating consistent achievement of organizational and fiscal objectives and goals. Able to pinpoint discrepancies and errors to prevent continuing and potentially unnecessary cost expenditures. Willing to accept responsibilities beyond immediate job duties and take on special projects at management request. Proficient in Excel, Access, other MS programs, J.D. Edwards, and proprietary software. *Knowledge and skill areas include*

- Audits & Financial Statements
- Accounts Receivable/Payable
- Financial Reconciliations
- General Ledger Accounting
- Record/Systems Automation
- Financial Research Projects
- Strategic & Financial Analysis
- Audit Review Procedures
- Teamwork & Communication

Education

TEXAS UNIVERSITY, Houston, TX
Bachelor of Business Administration (BBA) in Accounting, 2004

Accounting G.P.A.: 3.5/Member, Beta Alpha Psi—for Honors Accounting, Finance, and IT students

Relevant Experience

Accountant, CITY OF NAME, Anywhere, TX   2005–Present

Fully responsible for several core accounting functions within municipality of 200,000 residents, including preparing financial statements and monthly reports/reconciliations, analyzing expense reports, integrating technology to facilitate accounting tasks, and completing special research projects as needed. Assigned significant role in managing finances of WTMPA, organizing large bodies of financial data, and preparing all financial statements for 2005 and 2006 audits. *Selected Accomplishments:*

- **Records Analysis & Error Identification**—Researched, identified, and helped resolve several large discrepancies in receivables and payables, all favorable to City of Name:
    - *$100,000 in A/R account for City of Name's power purchases;*
    - *$20,000 underpayment for A/R in General Fund Account;*
    - *$10,000 excess in A/P for Internal Service funds.*
- **Policy Development**—Played key role in development of new travel policy, with projected elimination of problems previously stalling productivity of accounting and internal audit functions.
- **Financial Analysis**—Compiled analysis of franchise fees subsequently used by Assistant City Manager in evaluating potential effects of pending legislation.
- **Audit Review Compliance**—Prepared cash-flow and financial statements for external auditors on 13 Internal Service and 10 Special Revenue funds, with zero notes from auditors on review documents.
- **Teamwork & Collaboration**—Coordinated project with legal division that revived dormant accounts and ensured proper disposition. Worked with Chief Accountant to construct new reporting model.
- **Technology Improvement**—Changed automatic accounting instruction table in J.D. Edwards system, leading to correction of multiple unnecessary entries and subsequent cost/time savings.

Collection Agent, CITYBANK, Irving, TX   2001–2005

Trained new employees on account software; prepared detailed financial/customer reports for management.

Manager, TANNING SALON, Irving, TX   2000–2001

Managed A/P, A/R, payroll, and other financial functions in addition to general management activities.

Combination. *Daniel J. Dorotik, Jr., Lubbock, Texas*

The area of interest is the Accountant information below the person's name and above the Education section. The horizontal lines work together as a top-and-bottom frame for the area.

THOMAS DORAN 555-555-5555

....

EDUCATION

BA in Advertising; Minor in Marketing ACADEMIA UNIVERSITY, Camary, Texas *Fall 2007*
17 hours Spanish

FOREIGN EXCHANGE PROGRAMS

THE CENTER FOR BILINGUAL MULTICULTURAL STUDIES, Citalynda, Zapata, Mexico *Spring 2006*
Studied Spanish six hours a day, five days a week. Lived with Mexican family and other foreign students, and traveled throughout Mexico learning foreign culture and economics.

- **Volunteered for Niños de la Calle.**

HUSTER HASS SCHOOL, Don Hogg, Holland *Fall 2002*
Studied international marketing and management and organizational management for six months. Also studied Dutch law. Lived in dorm environment and traveled throughout Europe learning foreign culture. Helped organize school functions and gave new-student orientations.

RELEVANT PROJECTS

ADVERTISING COALITION 2003 NATIONAL STUDENT COMPETITION
Selected out of 21 members to serve on creative team of three members. Created a four-year integrated marketing communications plan book for auto dealership, manufacturer of products for the transportation industry. Researched and analyzed industry; wrote creative brief; designed Web page and magazine ads; and targeted portfolio to financial opinion leaders, stock and shareholders, employees, and customers.

- **Won second place at nationals.**

CAMPAIGN BOOK FOR STATE LOTTERY COMMISSION
One of a group of five compiling proposals for awareness campaign for state lottery. Six-member group created 13 advertisements to be presented to lottery commissioner.

WORK EXPERIENCE

Wait Staff, HOME COOKIN' CORNER, Bullnose and Camary, Texas *2005–Present*
Provide standard wait-staff services and balance out cash and tips each day. Transferred from full-time summer job in Bullnose to part-time position in Camary.

- **Requested by regular customers.**

Director, WeeCare After-School Program, WEECARE, Camary, Texas *2003–2005*
Oversaw five staff members who coordinated activities for 80 children ages 5–12. Handled discipline issues with both staff and participants and dealt with collection issues. Facilitated complete program organization and facility readiness.

- **Asked to return to director's position after study abroad.**

Full-time Daycare Counselor, WEECARE, Bullnose, Texas *Summer 2003*
Organized arts and crafts and play activities for children and created projects. Interfaced with parents and handled issues. Acted as mentor to children.

ACTIVITIES

- Member, State Advertising Federation *2006*
- Member and Social Chair, Kuptta Kai Fraternity *2003–Present*
- Volunteer, Challenged Veterans Store *2002*
- Volunteer, Heart Saving Association *2001*

.....

5555 55ᵗʰ Street ▪ Camary, Texas 55555 ▪ tdoran@yahoo.com

Combination. *Edith A. Rische, Lubbock, Texas*

This student had relevant experience both abroad and in academic competition. His goal was foreign advertising, so foreign language and exchange programs are highlighted.

Angela Granato

1234 Pinewood Street
Charleston, SC 00000

(000) 000-0000
agranato@fastmail.com

PROFILE

Customer service professional, skilled in problem solving and responsive to needs of clients, coworkers and management. Poised, resourceful and adaptable to any office environment. Organizational ability to handle multiple priorities and meet deadline schedules. Attentive to detail, with sharp awareness of omissions/ inaccuracies, and prompt to take corrective action. A self-starter and quick study, eager to assume increasing levels of responsibility.

OFFICE SKILLS

Professional phone manner; data entry and word processing; updating/ maintenance of files and records; composition of routine correspondence.

EMPLOYMENT HISTORY

CUSTOMER SERVICE REPRESENTATIVE
Liberty Insurance Corporation, Charleston, SC (2002–2007)

Hired as data entry operator and advanced to customer service position in less than a year. Took over problem desk, which had been inadequately handled by 2 previous employees. Worked closely with underwriters, answering client inquiries by phone or mail. Analyzed complex situations affecting insurance coverage. Recognized opportunities to increase sales and advised clients when coverage was lacking in specific policy areas.

> *Key Accomplishments:* During major restructuring of company resulting in 70% staff reduction, assumed more than triple the normal account responsibility, from 450 to more than 1,500, while still in training. Simultaneously studied for insurance licensing course; passed exam on first try, with score of 95.

APPLICATIONS SCREENER
Marshall & Reiner Insurance Agency, Charlotte, NC (2000–2002)
(Applications processing center for Mutual Surety Corporation)

Screened homeowners' new lines of business applications, verifying coverage against individual state regulations. Filled in whenever needed for switchboard, typing and clerical assignments.

HOMEMAKER/CHILD CARE RESPONSIBILITIES (1993–2000)

SUBROGATION CLERK
Royal Guard Insurance Company, Middleton, SC (1991–1993)

Started as receptionist and promoted shortly thereafter to handle various clerical assignments in Subrogation Department. Prepared paperwork for file with arbitration board. Kept subrogation ledgers up-to-date for auditors' review.

CENSUS TAKER
U.S. Census Bureau, Charleston, SC (1990)

Visited individuals who had not filled out census forms properly. Worked in a multiethnic territory, overcoming language barriers and mistrust. Clarified discrepancies and ensured accuracy and completeness of reported information.

EDUCATION

Carolina State University—65 credits in Business Administration (1989–1991)

American Insurance Academy—Completed 12-week basic course in Property and Casualty, Insurance Law, and Health Insurance (2003)

3

Combination. *Melanie Noonan, West Paterson, New Jersey*

Bold side headings make it easy to see at a glance the resume's main sections. Italic helps the reader spot employers, schools, and the Key Accomplishments paragraph. See Cover Letter 16.

DAVID E. JOHNSON

2345 Mountainview Court
La Crosse, Wisconsin 55555
Home: (608) 652-9090 / Office (608) 383-5252

PROFILE

Dynamic and results-oriented teaching professional with superior interpersonal communication skills and 12+ years of experience in training, coaching, and motivating. Demonstrated capabilities in the following areas:

- Classroom Management
- Curriculum Development
- Parental Participation
- Instructional Materials
- Special Events Management
- Consultative & Group Instruction

TEACHING EXPERIENCE

LA CROSSE SCHOOL DISTRICT — WISCONSIN   2002 to Pres.
Substitute Teacher (Grades 1–8)
Taught a varied curriculum at 8 elementary schools within the district. Specifically requested by faculty to fill in and remembered by students for interesting and creative teaching methods. Experience in team teaching and adapting curriculum for special-needs students.

LA CROSSE EAST HIGH SCHOOL — WISCONSIN   1988 to 1989
Substitute Teacher & Asst. Coach (Grades 9–12)
Taught in all classrooms and served as Assistant Cross-Country and Track Coach for Varsity and JV teams.

LA CRESCENT SCHOOL DISTRICT — MINNESOTA   1986 to 1988
Substitute Teacher (Grades K–12)
Prepared lesson plans and developed units for physical education curriculum.

BUSINESS MANAGEMENT EXPERIENCE

GOLDMAN FOODS — LA CROSSE, WISCONSIN   1999 to Pres.
Store Director   1988 to 1998
Recruited to turn around unprofitable grocery store. Developed "back to basics" approach and built a team environment among 57 employees. Created an effective action plan; delegated responsibilities; and delivered sales growth of 8%, labor reductions of 1½%, and substantial increases in customer counts (+500/week).

EDUCATION

MARQUETTE UNIVERSITY — MILWAUKEE, WISCONSIN   1986
B.S. Education — Physical Education Major (4-year athletic scholarship)

CERTIFICATIONS

Wisconsin 43 Substitute (current)
Wisconsin 530 Physical Education (current)

INTERESTS

Distance running, softball, and soccer

"Mr. Johnson is an excellent role model for students and they do enjoy his classes. He has excellent people skills and his prior background as a manager of people for a food store has helped sharpen his people skills. Your school will be obtaining an excellent instructor who has unlimited potential for the field of teaching."

Joan White,
Interim Principal,
La Crosse East
Middle School

"Mr. Dave Johnson has taught in the area of physical education [and] demonstrated a knowledge and sincere desire [for] working with students at this level. They respect him even though the position of substitute teacher can be rather difficult. [He] has demonstrated an ability to effectively carry out lesson plans and handle discipline, in whatever unit he has been asked to instruct, with professional assurance."

Bill M. Wolfe,
P.E. Dept. Chair,
La Crosse East
Middle School

4

Combination. *Michele J. Haffner, Glendale, Wisconsin*

The applicant was transitioning to teaching after many years as a successful business manager. Strong testimonials offset a lack of teaching experience other than substitute teaching.

GEORGE CRANDALL, EIT

0000 Smith Avenue
Houston, TX 79000

Home: (000) 000-0000
name@lycos.com

Career Profile

ENVIRONMENTAL ENGINEER-IN-TRAINING

- Focused, analytical professional with strong engineering educational background complemented by work experience involving field research and evaluation projects.
- Able to balance creative thinking with logical design ideas; enjoy opportunities to develop solutions that address challenging environmental problems.
- Work effectively in both self-managed and team-based projects; maintain high ethical and quality standards, professional demeanor, and cooperative attitude.
- Use hands-on, detail-oriented approach in completing projects and assignments.

Knowledge & Skill Areas:

Field Research • Report Writing • Experimental Design & Methods • Project Planning Quality Assurance Standards • Research & Development • Environmental Hazards Systems Analysis • Regulatory & Safety Compliance • Engineering Documentation Environmental Sample Analysis • Risk Assessment • Client/Customer Communications

Education

Master of Environmental Engineering, 2005 / GPA: 3.75
Bachelor of Environmental Engineering, 2003 / GPA: 3.30
University, Houston, TX

Selected Upper-Level Coursework:

- Design of Air Pollution Systems
- Solid & Hazardous Waste Treatment
- Environmental Impact Analysis
- Environmental Systems Design
- Design of Wastewater Treatment Plants
- Groundwater Contaminant Transport
- Geoethnical Practices for Waste Disposal
- Environmental Law & Policies

Project Highlights:

- **"Best Bench Scale Demonstration Award"**—Worked with group of 6 students to plan, develop, and present winning bench scale model (addressing water quality issues) at 2 design competitions, 2002 & 2003, at the Waste Energy Research Consortium.
- **"Design of Wastewater Treatment Plants"**—Played key role in design project for treatment plant based on quality assurance and regulatory compliance factors. Delivered well-received presentation to Master-level class upon completion.
- **"Environmental Impact Statement"**—Developed proposal-oriented report detailing most effective, environmentally sound strategies for controlling brushes within region.

Work Experience

Research Associate, 2005–Present
Research Assistant & Laboratory Technician, 2001–2004
Research Assistant, Summer 2004 (Texas National Environmental & Engineering Lab)
University, Houston, TX (2001–Present)

Conduct research, sample collection and analysis, experimental design, and explosives evaluations using high-performance liquid chromatography, and perform other related activities in positions involving field studies and frequent travel to various counties within East Texas region. Report directly to Laboratory Manager; additionally responsible for daily maintenance of weather stations.

- **Bioremediation of Explosives in Vadose Zone**—Conduct explosives contamination studies and evaluations for government agency Pantex to recommend strategies for remediation projects with highest potential for success.
- **Overall Work Performance**—Put forth consistent effort in meeting and exceeding job requirements; worked overtime hours and maintained full-time class schedule throughout employment. Recognized for intelligent, thorough work habits.

Activities

Society of Environmental Professionals—Member, 3 years; Secretary, 1 year
Civil Engineering Honor Society—Chi Epsilon

5

Combination. *Daniel J. Dorotik, Jr., Lubbock, Texas*

Including information about school-related projects is a way to offset a recent graduate's lack of much work experience. See, for example, Project Highlights in the Education section.

SEAN L. STEEPER

17 Woodcliff Road
Westboro, MA 01581

Home: 333-333-3333
slsteeper@hotmail.com

INDUSTRIAL ENGINEER
New Product Design • Manufacturing Process Redesign • Project Management

EDUCATION

University of Massachusetts ~ Amherst, MA
B.S. Industrial Engineering ~ Graduated with Honors ~ May 2006

RELEVANT COURSEWORK

Engineering Design • Systems Engineering • Computer Integrated Manufacturing • Production Systems
Production Engineering • Operations Research • Oral and Visual Communications
Industrial Psychology • Ergonomics • Quality Management

ACADEMIC PROJECTS

- Researched and recommended alternative methods for coating coronary stents for a leading manufacturer of cardiovascular products. Designed and manufactured prototype for spray-coating each stent, as opposed to the current practice of dipping them, which resulted in a 25% reduction in defects.
- Designed a facility and assembly-line layout to optimize production for an electronics products company.
- Generated a comprehensive Safety and Development Plan for a medical devices company.
- Created an ergonomically efficient material-handling trolley.

ENGINEERING EXPERIENCE

ABC Cardiovascular, Amherst, MA   5/05–10/05
Industrial Engineer, Co-op

- Designed, developed, and implemented a unique device for facilitating the movement of coronary stent and catheter products from one workstation to another, resulting in a 20% decrease in scrapped product.
- Revised and simplified the Standard Operating Procedure for a label-printing machine that included detailed, easy-to-follow troubleshooting procedures and digital photographs.
- Analyzed production reports associated with a crimping machine and successfully identified one product that was consistently more prone to defects than others. Recommended machine adjustments to alleviate defects.
- Optimized floor space by rearranging and redesigning four production cells within a tightly constricted space.
- Member of a team to prepare for a critical FDA audit. Ensured machines were fully validated and safety guards were properly and securely in place.

ADDITIONAL EXPERIENCE

Albright Roofing and Painting, Framingham, MA   9/06–Present
Construction Laborer—Contribute to roofing and home painting projects.

Dunmore Plastering, Southboro, MA   Summers 04 and 06
Plasters Foreman—Organized and monitored building materials and inventory levels.

Independently Employed, Amherst, MA   1/02–5/04
Agricultural Contractor—Performed agricultural contract work for farmers.

6

Combination. *Jeanne Knight, Melrose, Massachusetts*

"The focus on Education, Relevant Coursework, Academic Projects, and Engineering Experience nicely positions this new graduate for a full-time position as an Industrial Engineer"—resume writer's note.

Cathy Carter

321 Maple Way ~ Big Lake, IL 00000
555-555-5555 cellular
ccarter@hotmail.com

Summary of Qualifications

- **Sales Professional** and **Certified Fitness Instructor** with strong combination of business knowledge, communication skills, and healthy lifestyle leadership experience.
- Proven ability as a teambuilder, working with groups of all ages to develop goals, create a fun environment, and achieve desired results.
- AFAA certified in Group Fitness, CPR, and AED.
- Computer skills: Word, PowerPoint, Excel, Access, Publisher.

Professional Experience

Big Computer Corporation, Westbrook, IL, February 2005 to Present
Major distributor of technology products for business, government, and consumer markets
Sales Associate
- Consistently meet or exceed sales goals for the development of business in the education market in Florida, Tennessee, and Alabama.
- Develop and maintain business relationships by phone with buying authorities for all sizes of K–12 school systems.
- Completed extensive training in sales methods and product knowledge.

Big Ten School Recreational Sports Center, Smalltown, IL, February 2002 to December 2004
Group Fitness Instructor
- Led large and small groups of all ages in fitness and aerobic activities, teaching effective methods to develop and achieve goals.
- Increased participant levels by promoting new programs offering fun and healthy ways to improve exercise habits.
- Completed extensive training programs in proper exercise techniques.

Giant Amusement Park, Big Lake, IL, Summer 2004
Editor of GAP employee newsletter
- Developed and produced biweekly newsletter distributed to several thousand employees.
- Created a new program featuring employee profiles; arranged and conducted interviews.
- Planned employee events and organized incentive programs.
- Made sales presentations to promote company services to corporate buyers.

Camp Wauconda, Pleasant Valley, MI, Summers 2000 and 2001
Camp Counselor
- Supervised a cabin of 12 girls; taught boating, swimming, and drama; worked with counselors from Spain, Hungary, Poland, and Italy.

Education

Continuous education in fitness techniques and
healthy lifestyle issues through reading, classes, and seminars

Big Ten University, Smalltown, IL
Bachelor of Science in Selling and Sales Management, minor in Spanish, GPA 3.1, December 2004
Member of Gamma Phi Beta Sorority, Crew Team, and Symphony Orchestra
Earned "Optimist Award" three times for community service

Combination. *Christine L. Dennison, Lincolnshire, Illinois*

After college this applicant went into business technology sales, but her heart wasn't in it. The resume and cover letter are for a transition to the fitness industry—her true passion. See Cover Letter 203.

35–12 Cottonboll Drive
Selma, AL 00000

Yasheika Ojimobi

Phone: (000) 000-0000
Pager: (000) 000-0000

Banquet Management Specialist
yasheika@partytime.com

Areas of Expertise

- Hands-on management in any service area
- Experience with start-up establishments
- Daily opening and closing responsibilities
- Supplier selection/negotiation
- Purchasing of food and paper products

- Inventory maintenance
- Food quality and sanitation issues
- Service staffing and supervision
- Portion/waste/cost control
- Payroll and budgeting

Personal and Professional Qualifications

- Commitment to superior customer service
- Excellent attendance record throughout employment
- Resourceful in dealing with food or staff shortages

- Attentive to special dietary needs
- Maintain high morale and low turnover
- Time management/multitasking ability

Employment

Assistant Banquet Manager
ROYAL INN AND CONFERENCE CENTER, Selma, AL   1997 to Present
A 144-room hotel with professional conference facilities, which include 15 meeting rooms, a grand ballroom with capacity for up to 400, and private meeting and banquet space for up to 250; total banquet seating for 750.

- Report to both banquet manager and general hotel manager. Ensure that all details are attended to in the proper setup for weddings, banquets, meetings, and special events.
- Supervise and schedule staff to service 2–6 daily meetings and 2–3 ongoing banquets evenings and weekends.
- Coordinate bar and kitchen operations, expediting the smooth running of banquet and meeting functions.
- Make arrangements for audio/visual requirements for business meetings.
- Act as the manager on call for problems in other areas of the hotel in absence of regular managers. In this capacity, respond to guest dissatisfaction issues; also intervene in crisis situations that could affect safety and comfort of the guests.
- Take charge of catering functions for hotel employee social events twice a year (average attendance of 350), as well as food/snack service for administrative meetings and recognition luncheons.
- Received Hospitality Award in 2005 for exemplary work to produce happy customers.

Banquet Server
ACE TEMPORARY AGENCY, Selma, AL   1996–1997
- Involved in all phases of service at banquets and private parties contracted through this company.
- Was frequently requested at Royal Inn whenever additional staff was required, then hired permanently.

Counter Person and Back-of-House Worker
ANNIE'S DINER, Selma, AL   1994–1996
- Gained practical experience in every area of running a food-service business.

Education

INTERNATIONAL CORRESPONDENCE SCHOOLS, Scranton, PA
- Certificate course in Hotel Restaurant Management   1997

ROYAL INN CAREER DEVELOPMENT PROGRAM
- Introduction to Computers   2001
- Food Service Sanitation Certification   2000
- Core Skills in Food Service Management   1999

8

Combination. *Melanie Noonan, West Paterson, New Jersey*

As was true for the Profile section in the preceding resume, the two-column lists of bulleted items are easily altered to tailor the resume to each targeted company. See Cover Letter 86.

MARIANNE L. PERRAULT

900 East Shelter Road
Oldetown, Rhode Island 09999

Fax: (401) 555-6666
E-mail: marip@foxx.net
Phone: (401) 333-8877

QUALIFICATIONS

- ➤ Proven ability to train, schedule, supervise, and effectively manage 60 employees preparing 1,000 airline passenger meals per day.
- ➤ Competent leader with extensive experience in prioritizing, delegating, and controlling work flow in municipal government and high-volume private-industry work environments.
- ➤ Proficient in effectively organizing, handling, and monitoring a wide variety of tasks.
- ➤ Comfortable with operating Microsoft Office 2007, Windows Vista, Corel, and Internet research on PC and Macintosh platforms.

EXPERIENCE

Food-Air Associates, Inc., Providence, RI
Vice President and Pricing Administrator for family-owned business, 2001–present
- ○ Manage accounts payable/receivable for very profitable, high-volume airline catering kitchen serving American, USAirways, United, Northwest, Southwest, and Delta Air Lines.
- ○ Review and analyze monthly P&L statement generated by accounting firm.
- ○ Establish costs of goods and services; audit and reconcile inventory.
- ○ Negotiate contract terms with major airline clients.
- ○ Hire, train, schedule, and manage up to 60 employees.
- ○ Design and implement quality-assurance measures to maintain high standards and consistent business retention to clients serving a total of 1,000 passenger meals per day.

Oldetown Police, Oldetown, RI
Administrative Assistant to the Chief of Police (part-time), 1999–2001
- ○ Researched, prepared, and wrote grants for municipal benefit.
- ○ Assisted in assembling data for annual police budget submissions to town council.
- ○ Provided accurate, courteous responses to inquiries on police matters of a sensitive nature.

EDUCATION

John Phelps University, Newport, RI
- ○ Master of Science in Business Administration, 2001

Rhode Island University, Providence, RI
- ○ Bachelor of Science in Finance, 1999
- ○ Cecelia H. Belknap Scholar: GPA over 3.85 (four years)

VOLUNTEER

Providence Chamber of Commerce; Oldetown Animal League; Providence GRO-Business Associates; Air-Transportation League; R.I. Fraternal Order of Police

– EXCELLENT REFERENCES FURNISHED UPON REQUEST –

9

Combination. *Edward Turilli, Newport, Rhode Island*

The two boxes make this resume different from most others. The hollow bullets also are not common. Boldfacing and italic make the name, headings, workplaces, jobs, and universities stand out.

Joseph D. Morten

167 Helman Lane • Bridgewater, New Jersey 08807
908.555.5555 (H) • 908.444.4444 (Fax) • jMorten439@aol.com

HUMAN RESOURCES / CORPORATE TRAINING
Supervision ~ Business Management ~ Employee Relations ~ Coaching

Energetic, reliable and adaptable professional with a solid understanding of human resources, business operations and various corporate environments. Proven abilities in creatively identifying methods for improving staff productivity and organizational behavior. Recognized for ability to introduce innovative management techniques into a multicultural workforce.

Results-oriented professional with excellent communication and interpersonal skills. Accurately perform challenging tasks with precision and attention to detail. Excel at organizing and setting up new procedures, troubleshooting and taking adverse situations and making them positive.

Competencies Include

- Human Resources Management
- Operations Management
- Teambuilding / Leadership
- Organizational & Project Management
- Training & Development
- Staffing Requirements
- Problem Resolution
- Employee Scheduling

Professional Experience

Waste Removal, *Plainfield, NJ (August 2002–September 2007)*
CFA Administrator
Waste Removal is the nation's largest full-service waste removal / disposal company
- Maintained and monitored multiple databases for the more than 120 pieces of equipment in the trucking company inventory.
- Generated accurate reports of budgets, repair costs, and personnel scheduling.
- Dramatically improved maintenance shop productivity through close budget monitoring.
- Served as a key link between management and mechanics, utilizing excellent interpersonal and communications skills. Acknowledged for improving the overall flow of information throughout the organization.
- Initiated, planned and managed the implementation of high-turn inventory-management systems and procedures. The new inventory system was credited with improving the productivity of a very high-volume parts operation.
- Assumed a leadership role in the company by completely reorganizing the physical inventory process to ensure greater accuracy and system integrity.
- Managed the successful integration of two new parts operations, turning a possible negative situation into a very positive one.

Easy Video Entertainment, *Colonia, NJ (March 1999–August 2002)*
Store Manager
Retail video rental and sales chain with more than 600 outlets and 5,000 employees worldwide
- Managed all daily store operations including a staff of 5 employees. Responsible for recruitment, hiring, firing, training and scheduling of all staff members.
- Ability to train and motivate staff to maximize productivity and to control costs with hands-on management and close monitoring of store budgets.
- Attained a 25% increase in sales over a 12-month period, leading all 45 stores in the district. The store ranked 40th in overall sales volume of the 600 stores in the company.
- Maintained a consistent Top 20 ranking for sales of high-profit coupon books.
- Used excellent leadership, team-building and communication skills to develop subordinates and encourage cooperation and responsibility. Ensured compliance with corporate HR programs.
- Developed and implemented creative and aggressive promotional techniques that resulted in the store consistently exceeding its sales goals.

Education

BA ~ Psychology, *FAIRLEIGH DICKINSON UNIVERSITY, Madison, NJ*

10

Combination. *Beverley and Mitchell I. Baskin, Marlboro, New Jersey*

The tilde (~), used to separate fields of activity in the profile, is echoed in the Education section at the bottom of the page. Each workplace in boldface is "explained" by a statement in italic.

RICHARD LEVINSON

0000 Preston Avenue ◆ Houston, TX 77000 ◆ (281) 000-0000 ◆ myname@aol.com

Career Target: Software Programmer / Software Engineer

PROFILE

Talented software programmer with BBA degree, strong educational background in programming, and experience using cutting-edge development tools. Articulate and professional communication skills, including formal presentations and technical documentation. Productive in both team-based and self-managed projects; dedicated to maintaining up-to-date industry knowledge and IT skills.

Knowledge & Skill Areas:

- Software Development Lifecycle
- Object-Oriented Programming
- Problem Analysis & Resolution
- Web Site Design & Development

- Requirements Gathering & Analysis
- Technical & End User Documentation
- Software Testing & Troubleshooting
- Project Teamwork & Communications

TECHNICAL SUMMARY

Languages:	Java, C, C++, JSP, ASP, Rational, HTML, SQL, Unified Process
Operating Systems:	Linux, Windows XP/2000/9x
Object-Oriented Design:	UML, Design Patterns

EDUCATION

TEXAS UNIVERSITY, Houston, TX
Bachelor of Business Administration in Computer Science, 2005

- ◆ Earned place on President's List for 3 semesters (4.0 GPA)
- ◆ Member, Golden Key National Honor Society & Honors Fraternity
- ◆ Selected for listing in *Who's Who Among Students in American Universities and Colleges*

Relevant Coursework:

- Software Engineering
- Project Management
- Database Design

- Systems Engineering
- Differential Equations
- Classical / Modern Physics

- Calculus I, II, III
- Logic Circuits
- Systems Analysis

Project Highlights:

- ◆ **Software Engineering**—Served as Design Team Leader and member of Programming group for semester-long project involving development of software for actual implementation within Texas University Recreation Center. Determined requirements, created "look and feel" for user interface, and maintained explicit written documentation.

- ◆ **Systems Engineering**—Teamed with group of 4 in conceptualizing and designing client-server application to interconnect POS and inventory systems for retail outlet, delivering class presentation that highlighted specifications and projected $2 million in cost savings.

COMMUNITY COLLEGE, Houston, Texas
- ◆ 3.96 GPA / Concentration in Computer Science coursework

EXPERIENCE

DATAFRAME CONCEPTS, L.L.C., Houston, TX   2003–Present
Software Developer

- ◆ Worked with small team of developers to brainstorm and implement ideas for shipping/receiving software, representing leading-edge concept within transportation industry.

- ◆ Planned and initiated redesign of existing standalone application, utilizing object-oriented design/programming and Java in creating thin-client GUI for new distributed system.

- ◆ Collaborated with marketing director in strategies to further business growth, including Web site enhancement that drove 65% increase in visitor interest for product offering.

* References and additional information will gladly be provided upon request.

Combination. *Daniel J. Dorotik, Jr., Lubbock, Texas*

The applicant had limited work experience, so the writer emphasized skills and education. To de-emphasize experience, the writer put the Experience section at the bottom of the resume.

Danielle Quinones

danielleq@homenet.com

Current Residence:
515 Abernathy Court
Richland, NJ 00000
(000) 000-0000

After March 1, 2008:
70 Turtleback Trail
San Jose, CA 00000
(000) 000-0000

Seeking position as Administrative Assistant in a busy law firm that requires a self-starter with exceptional organizational ability

Skills

❖ Computer literacy using Microsoft Word, including legal document applications.
❖ Proficiency with machine dictation/transcription and other office technology.
❖ Meticulous in the setup and maintenance of complex legal files, with associated correspondence and billing detail.
❖ Efficient in managing a diary system to meet all scheduled commitments.
❖ Extensive experience in personal injury litigation (including subrogation), with exposure also to real estate, medical malpractice, construction, environmental and matrimonial cases.

Relevant Experience

Feinberg, Radcliffe, Cullen & Martini, LLP, Newark, NJ   *2003–Present*

Legal Administrative Assistant for law firm employing 14 attorneys and 50 support staff.

❖ Hired in floater position for two summers and during college breaks. Self-trained in all aspects of legal secretarial responsibilities, demonstrating strong dedication and interest in the operations of a law office.
❖ In 2005, promoted to full-time position for an associate involved with defense for insurance companies and claimants.
❖ Manage a heavy volume of files, with more than 100 cases open simultaneously; 20–30 of these are nonroutine subrogation matters.
❖ After minimal instruction, entrusted with the preparation of all details of motions, including signing authority attesting to completion of documents.
❖ Anticipate and fulfill lawyers' needs so that all deadlines are met, thereby protecting the firm from incurring costly penalties.

Other Experience

Banner Shoe Stores, Corporate Office, North Orange, NJ   *2000–2003*

Aide to Purchasing Assistant (part-time during school months)

❖ Handled all secretarial and clerical duties for the Purchasing Department.
❖ Responded promptly to calls from 150 stores nationwide for supplies and services needed to properly run their operations.

Education

Creighton Hill University, North Orange, NJ   *1999–2002*

❖ Completed 3 years toward B.A. in Psychology.
❖ Member, Beta Tau Sorority; Alumni Relations Chairperson.
❖ Financed 30% of educational expenses through part-time employment.

12

Combination. *Melanie Noonan, West Paterson, New Jersey*

An unusual font ties together visually the person's name and side headings. Distinctive bullets help to draw the eye down the page. Boldfacing makes the occupations stand out. See Cover Letter 148.

PATRICIA JUHASZ

555 Riddle Avenue • Smithtown, NY 55555 • (888) 999-0000 • Pjuhasz@telcomm.net

Legal Assistant/Paralegal Assistant

Experienced Legal Assistant with excellent office management and client-attorney relation skills seeking an entry-level Paralegal Assistant position where a working knowledge of legal terminology, general law, and legal proceedings, and continuing education in Paralegal Studies will be utilized and expanded. Bring experience working within a Legal Department/Collection Agency environment in the following select areas:

Civil Litigation…Collections…Settlements…Affidavits…Skip Tracing…Attorney Sourcing & Selection…
Bankruptcies…Judgments…Liens…Summons & Complaint…Estate Searches…Statute of Limitations

PROFESSIONAL EXPERIENCE

Legal Assistant, Legal Recoveries, Inc., Lake Grove, NY   2003–present

Joined this Collection Agency's legal department at a time of unit-wide staffing changes. Responsible for managing a high volume of civil litigation case files for major accounts that partially included Century Detection, Credit Union of New York, AB Bank National Association, and St. Mary's Hospital.

- Collaborate extensively with internal departments including collections, medical billing, finance, production, special projects, and clerical to obtain, verify, and process documentation pertaining to the status of more than 50 weekly referred collections cases forwarded to the legal department.
- Carefully source and select nationally based bonded attorneys utilizing the *American Lawyers Quarterly, Commercial Bar Directory, National Directory List,* and *Columbia Directory List;* determine the appropriate choice upon obtainment and review of resumes, copies of insurance policies, and court filing fees.
- Perform estate searches and integrate traditional investigative methods and the DAKCS database system to gather account histories and case-sensitive documentation for attorneys, including
  debtors and guarantors, credit bureau reports, court affidavits, judgments, skip-tracing records, bankruptcy notices, banking statements, proof of statute of limitations, proof of assets, and trial letters.
- Maintain communications with attorneys and clients from point of referral/discovery to trial phase to facilitate and expedite case settlements that historically award clients a minimum of 80% in recovered funds.

EDUCATION

Bachelor of Science in Paralegal Studies, 2003
ST. JOSEPH'S COLLEGE, Brentwood, NY

COMPUTER SKILLS

Windows 2000; WordPerfect and Microsoft Word; DAKCS

EARLIER WORK HISTORY

Administrative Assistant, State Insurance, Patchogue, NY	2002–2003
Office Support Assistant, Financial Association of America, Inc., Islip, NY	2000–2002
Appointment Coordinator, Phlebotomy Services, Huntington, NY	1996–2001
Senior Office Support Assistant, AB National Bank, Hicksville, NY	1991–1996

Professional References Provided on Request

13

Combination. *Ann Baehr, Brentwood, New York*

The focus is on the applicant's most relevant experience. Earlier experience is put near the bottom. Keywords are used to indicate areas of expertise at the end of the profile. The page border is shadowed.

JENNIFER GONZALES

334–30 Kissena Blvd., Flushing, NY 55555 • (555) 222-7777 • JGonzales@lawandorder.net

---

Seeking a position in the field of

Law Enforcement

CITY——STATE——FEDERAL——PRIVATE

➢ Highly motivated, energetic law enforcement student with strong work ethic and professional goals.
➢ Bring five years of experience in office support and retail sales positions while attending college full time.
➢ Bilingual with an articulate fluency in English and Spanish; personable, easygoing communication style.
➢ Meet challenges head on; work well in stressful situations and fast-paced settings.
➢ Analytical with a lot of common sense, intuitive instincts, and ability to think outside of the box.
➢ Maintain excellent research, organization, time-management, and problem-assessment/resolution skills.

Education

Bachelor of Arts, Forensic Psychology—expected August 2007
John Jay College of Criminal Justice, New York, NY
Honors Candidate: Psi Chi Chapter National Honor Society in Psychology

Academically trained in criminalistics and psychology:

Select Courses: Analysis of Criminal Behavior, Concepts of Forensic Science, Abnormal Psychology,
Physical Fitness in Law Enforcement, Criminal Law, Group Dynamics
Select Projects: Crime Scene Observation, Forensic Study of Microscopic Fibers, Fingerprint Analysis

Work Experience

Receptionist, Volvoville, Massapequa, NY	4/01–Present
Payroll Clerk, People's Alliance Federal Credit Union, Hauppauge, NY	4/03–7/03
Sales Associate, Annie Sez, East Northport, NY	2/01–6/01
Senior Sales Associate, Rainbow Shops, Commack/Bay Shore, NY	9/00–2/01

• Provide front-desk representation, clerical support, and customer service for Volvo and subsidiary, Land Rover, directing customer traffic with a proven ability to maintain open lines of communication.

• Managed more than 50 business payroll accounts utilizing cross-trained experience in teller and payroll services.

• Prepared and uploaded weekly exempt/non-exempt payroll data into network system for clients to download.

• Completed mandatory training that included a film study on a mock robbery to learn observation techniques.

• Held increasingly responsible sales positions, achieving recognition for over-quota floor sales and cashier management skills, and manager-requests to return during school breaks based on performance and reliability.

• Provided excellence in customer service while assisting in all areas of inventory and display merchandising.

Computer Skills

Windows XP/Me; Microsoft Word, LexisNexis, PsychInfo, Criminal Justice Abstracts,
InfoTrak Health, Sociological Abstracts, Internet Research

14

Combination. *Ann Baehr, Brentwood, New York*

Making explicit four areas of interest—city, state, federal, and private—below the Law Enforcement heading reduced the risk that this graduate would be limited to just one area of interest in her job search.

CAROL A. YOUNG

3 TABBY DRIVE • FLEMINGTON, NJ 08822
OFFICE (908) 237-1883 • FAX (908) 237-2069 • CAA@WORLDCLASSRESUMES.COM

Credentialed résumé writer with a demonstrated commitment to providing superior products and top-notch service

SUMMARY OF QUALIFICATIONS

Independent, self-motivated, and conscientious professional with strong customer focus. Excellent writing skills with extensive experience developing marketing materials, customer communications, and job search documents. Able to draw on diverse experience to understand client needs and develop effective, targeted résumés.

PROFESSIONAL HIGHLIGHTS

- Opened résumé business, coordinating all aspects of start-up, including creating and producing all business communications materials: brochures, business cards, flyers, and the company's Web site.
- Established proven record of accomplishment in writing winning résumés and other job search documents.
- With background that spans the fields of research, development, manufacturing, marketing, technical service, administrative customer service, career development, training, and project management, successfully work with technical, administrative, and executive professionals at all levels.
- Competently draw out key information from clients to effectively market skills and abilities.
- Astute and analytical; always operate with the understanding that knowing and adapting to the audience is the key to effective communication.
- Recognized for leadership and commitment to quality improvement. Strong track record of providing outstanding customer satisfaction.

CERTIFICATION

Certified Professional Résumé Writer, Professional Association of Résumé Writers, 2004

EMPLOYMENT HISTORY

WORLD CLASS RÉSUMÉS, *Owner*, 2003 to Present
RESUME.COM, *Elite Writer*, 2003 to Present
LIBERTY LIFE, *Implementation Consultant*, Voluntary Benefits Group, 2002 to 2003
KAPLAN, *Prep Course Instructor and Tutor*, 2002 to 2004
YORK OIL CORPORATION, *Senior Research Engineer*, Fuels Marketing Support, 1998 to 2002
SPECIALTY CHEMICALS, INC., *Staff Engineer*, Petroleum Catalyst Group, 1993 to 1998

EDUCATION

STATE UNIVERSITY, Master of Education (Counseling Psychology), 1999
CITY COLLEGE, Bachelor of Science (Chemical Engineering), 1993

15

Combination. *Carol A. Altomare, Three Bridges, New Jersey*

Here is the resume writer's own resume. It is included in this Exhibit to give an example of at least one professional resume writer's background. Note her degrees in science and psychology.

Collins Mackey

5th Street • Centereach, NY 55555 • (555) 444-2222

OFFICE MANAGER

Bringing 25+ years of office administration and full-charge bookkeeping experience as follows:

- Accounts Payable/Receivable
- Weekly Payroll
- Credit and Collections
- Statement Billings

- Expense Control
- Account Management
- Account Reconciliation
- Month-end Closings

- Human Resources Management
- Staff Training and Supervision
- Customer Service/Client Relations
- Computerized Processes

PROFESSIONAL EXPERIENCE—*Overview*

Recognized throughout longstanding career for ability to develop, implement, and manage full-charge, computerized bookkeeping functions while overseeing multifaceted office administration procedures

- As Office Manager for August Publications, fully manage company-wide accounting and reporting functions for five subsidiaries, as well as weekly payroll processes for 45 salaried employees.
- Liaison among senior management, employees, and clients to ensure proper lines of communication critical in addressing myriad problems and issues requiring immediate attention and resolve.
- Manage Accounts Payable/Receivable and expense-control procedures, including bank and account reconciliation, cash receipts, disbursements, finance charges, billings, invoicing, purchase order and inventory verification, chargebacks, rebates, and preparation of daily bank deposits.
- Negotiate and enforce collections to recover funds and expedite the clearance on delinquent accounts.
- Collaborate extensively with external auditors, providing in-depth assistance with periodic corporate audits.
- Perform thorough credit analyses, research financial histories, and review account status as a prerequisite to qualifying new accounts, authorizing purchases, and extending/increasing lines of credit of up to $200,000.
- Establish and maintain Human Resources–related employee files reflecting salary increases, deductions, garnishments, benefits, payroll exceptions, and W-2 withholdings, exercising a high level of confidentiality.
- Skilled at interviewing, hiring, training, and evaluating employees in areas of accounting procedures.
- Research account transactions, demonstrating a keen ability to recognize and resolve discrepancies.
- Follow through on timely and accurate month-end closings and financial reporting activities.

WORK CHRONOLOGY

Office Manager	August Publications, Hauppauge, NY	2001–present
Office Manager	Quality Insurance, Huntington, NY	1991–2001
Office Manager	DSG Management Corp., Melville, NY	1988–1990
Controller's Assistant	Georgia Interiors, Farmingdale, NY	1984–1988
Credit/Collections Supervisor	EastTel Sales Corp., New York, NY	1983–1984
Accounts Payable/Receivable Clerk	Syobel Corp., New York, NY	1978–1983

COMPUTER PROFICIENCIES

Windows 2000; MS Word and Excel; WordPerfect; Lotus; Peachtree Accounting

EDUCATION

Bachelor of Arts, Business Management/Accounting, Banes College, 1987

16

Combination. *Ann Baehr, Brentwood, New York*

The writer condenses extensive experience onto one page, using keywords, an Overview section representing many similar positions to avoid repetition, and a compact Work Chronology section.

LAURA D. WENN

899 Lancona Road
Dallas, TX 00000

(555) 555-5555
ldw56@yahoo.com

RETAIL MANAGEMENT PROFESSIONAL

Nine years of retail management experience demonstrating a consistent track record of outstanding sales, merchandising and customer service results. Equally strong qualifications in all areas of fine jewelry department operations: P&L, budgeting, inventory control, training, security and other functions. Effective communicator, leader and problem solver who builds teamwork and possesses the initiative to exceed goals.

EXPERIENCE

LAWRENCE FINE JEWELRY CORPORATION, Seattle, WA (1998–present)
Progressed rapidly from part-time position to manager at several stores, including the following:

Manager—G. Fox, Randolph Mall, Dallas, TX (2004–present)
Manager—G. Fox, Valley Mall, Phoenix, AZ (2000–2004)
Manager—G. Fox, Turner Mall, Tucson, AZ (1999–2000)
Assistant Manager—G. Fox, Forest Mall, San Antonio, TX (1998–1999)

Summary of Responsibilities

Operations Management—Hold profit-and-loss accountability; manage all aspects of day-to-day department performance of stores ranging from $500,000 to $2M in annual sales. Direct sales, inventory control, visual merchandising, housekeeping, security, administration and compliance to company policies/procedures. Managed 2 stores concurrently over 4-month period with highly successful sales results during busy Christmas season.

Staff Supervision & Training—Supervise teams of up to 13 fine-jewelry specialists. Experienced in personnel recruiting, selection, training, developing, scheduling and supervising associates. Motivate staff to achieve performance goals and ensure productive department operations.

Customer Relations & Service—Develop and manage customer relations to maximize service satisfaction, promote goodwill and generate repeat/referral business that contributes to sales growth. Monitor and resolve any service issues.

Selected Achievements

- Increased Randolph store sales from $1.1M to $1.4M (27%) in 2005 and maintained .02% shrinkage—well below company average of 2.1%.
- Increased percent-to-store sales at Valley Mall from 2.8% to 5.2%, surpassing company average of 2.5%. Grew annual sales at Valley Mall from $.8M in 2000 to $1.1M (37%) in 2001, $1.4M (27%) in 2002, $1.7M (21%) in 2003 and $2M (18%) in 2004.
- Selected by Regional Manager to serve as Training Store Manager for the region; recognized for the ability to recruit quality candidates who have successfully advanced within the company.

Awards

- Earned **Branch Manager of the Year** and **Branch of the Year** awards in 2005 in the Southwest Region.
- Twice named **Manager of the Year** out of 50 stores in 2003 and 2001 in the Southwest Region.
- Winner of 3 sales performance awards in 2005: **Goal Achievers, Best Increase in % to Store** and **Best Event Business. Christmas Contest** winner in 2004, exceeding sales goal by 15%.
- Selected runner-up for 3 awards in 2005: **Best in Operations, Best Visual Department** and **Best Buyer Communication.** Ranked #3 in **Christmas Contest** in 2005, exceeding sales goal by 21%.

EDUCATION / PROFESSIONAL DEVELOPMENT

B.A., Retail Management, Valhalla College, Dallas, TX

Completed various company-sponsored training courses in management, personnel recruiting, staff training and development, sales, customer service and related topics.

Combination. *Louise Garver, Enfield, Connecticut*

The applicant was applying for a position with a competitor in Arizona. She had held positions with the same responsibilities at several stores. To eliminate repetition, the writer summarized key duties.

AMANDA JONES

000 Cedar Lane • Old Towne, NJ 00000 • mandy000@aol.com • mobile: 000-000-0000 • home: 000-000-0000

SUMMARY

Highly accomplished Sales Professional with an exceptional ability to establish and maintain rapport with affluent clients in real estate, retail, and service industries. Problem solver, able to execute solutions accurately and swiftly. Detail-oriented with outstanding follow-up skills.

PROFESSIONAL EXPERIENCE

EAST COAST REALTORS, Old Towne, NJ ....1992– PRESENT

SALES ASSOCIATE

Sell residential properties from entry level to luxury homes valued at $1 million+ to a highly affluent client base in northern NJ. Clients include physicians, attorneys, CEOs, and other executives. Consistently closed 12–14 high-value transactions annually.

- First year in the position, generated $3 million in sales, receiving company *Rising Star Award*.
- Awarded *Silver Achievement Award (Million Dollar Sales Club)* by NJ Association of Realtors— produced $5 million in sales 3 consecutive years.
- Recipient of 2006 Leadership Team Award ($5 million+ in sales in one year).
- Achieved Highest Closed Dollar Volume in Buyer Sales & Total Production—2005.
- Attained Highest Closed Units in Buyer Sales—2004.
- Achieved membership in *Million Dollar Sales Club* each year.
- Consistently attained monthly top 10% ranking in sales out of 560 full-time associates.

PRESTIGIOUS HOME, Old Towne, NJ 1990–1992

SALES ASSOCIATE

Designed and sold custom window treatments, accessories, and home furnishings to affluent clients.

INTERNATIONAL ADVANTAGES, INC., Washington, DC...1981–1988

EXECUTIVE / PERSONAL ASSISTANT

Provided administrative support to foreign investors and local executives. Served as the representative for international royalty in real estate investments, leisure activities, and financial and insurance transactions. Interacted with property managers and tenants, oversaw lease agreements, and handled all finances including purchase of luxury products such as automobiles and furnishing of multiple residences.

- Oversaw all aspects of management of 6-story office building in Washington, D.C.
- Leased luxury leisure properties in San Diego, CA: Hired staff, procured liability policies including those for weapon-bearing security personnel, handled airport customs, and managed all entertainment and recreation needs.
- Managed highly confidential communications among banks, foreign investors, various dignitaries, heads of state, and celebrities.

EDUCATION

BA—Health Science   UNIVERSITY OF SOUTHERN CALIFORNIA—San Jose, CA

COMMUNITY INVOLVEMENT

REGIONAL REPRESENTATIVE   Brentwood Academy, Brentwood, CA
PAST MEMBER   Junior League of Morris County, NJ

18

Combination. *Fran Kelley, Waldwick, New Jersey*

Because this applicant had some consistent wins in sales, she wanted to transition to pharmaceutical sales. The writer plays up family background—a family of physicians. See Cover Letter 272.

BAXTER A. LEEDS

45 Kaiwan Street   Taipei, Taiwan   555-05050505   bestoys@xix5.net

PROFESSIONAL GOAL

Opportunity in the toy manufacturing industry where experience in creative product development, team leadership, and mass production will contribute to business growth and success in the USA and Asia.

PROFESSIONAL PROFILE

- Successful background in the toy industry with a leading manufacturer in both the USA and Asia.
- Highly creative in design, construction, and production of seasonal, novelty, and licensed products.
- Broad understanding of living and working in Asia; knowledge of customs, beliefs, and culture.
- Dedicated commitment to quality products, expense control, and customer satisfaction.
- Valued by colleagues for work ethic, team leadership, creativity, and open-mindedness.

EXPERIENCE

BESTOYS, INC.—Taipei, Taiwan   **1997–Present**
Creative Director
USA-based toy company with manufacturing operations in Taiwan.

Creative Product Development
- Manage product aesthetic and function during product engineering and development process.
- Conceptualize in 3D with mechanical ability to develop pattern, starting with minimal item definition.
- Strong knowledge of model-building techniques and experience with all relevant materials.
- Collaborate with company's CEO and Asian Division President on product development initiatives.

Management/Team Leadership
- Direct 100-member Taiwan prototype staff in all phases of the prototyping/manufacturing process.
- Independently supervise work, coping with fluctuating work loads while maintaining accuracy to product design without missing deadlines.
- Effective interpersonal skills and a respect for people of all backgrounds and nationalities.
- Communicate via e-mail with USA product management on daily item needs and changes.

Manufacturing for Mass Production/Licensed Products
- Skilled in meeting mass production costs, scheduling, and engineering specifications.
- Work directly with BesToys' Asian engineering staff and production vendor engineering on item construction to meet aesthetic, function, schedule, and item cost.
- Manufacture a vast number of products including boys', girls', spring, seasonal, novelty, and licensed products for extremely successful brand names.
- Effectively complete a large volume of licensed goods for sale/distribution in various world markets.

Key Contributions

- Opened a new prototype facility in Taiwan to meet increased corporate demands, maximize output of sales samples, and reduce prototyping costs.
- Utilize a management style of empowerment, support, and assertiveness in meeting deadlines.
- Monitor and control USA designs built in Taiwan to ensure highest quality standards.

EDUCATION

BFA with Honors
Marketing and Advertising Design—Santa Rosa Fine Arts Academy, Santa Rosa, California, 1997

Combination. *Billie Ruth Sucher, Urbandale, Iowa*

The applicant brought the writer "vast pages of information about his background." The writer organized and categorized this information into keyword/skills areas to showcase his experience.

Gregg S. Lane

Ph.: (555) 555-5555
Fax: (800) 000-0000

129 Avenida del Sol, Apt. 136
Northview, CA 99999
www.spirit.com
soul2@gsl.com

Author ▪ *Producer* ▪ *Inspirational Speaker*

FCC-Certified Cable-Access Producer:

➢ Well-versed in FCC rules and regulations.
➢ Proficient in problem solving, with ability to quickly adapt to the unexpected.
➢ Experienced in preparing run sheets ▪ editing ▪ writing ▪ program planning and coordinating ▪ managing logistics and personnel ▪ virtually all aspects of production.
➢ Effective communicator who interacts well with people from a wide range of social and cultural backgrounds.
➢ Able to tackle issues by producing programs that are relevant, informative, and stimulating.

CAREER HIGHLIGHTS	▪ **Host, Writer, and Executive Producer—***The Spirited Soul* Cable Television Broadcast—Weekly 30-minute teaching program applying philosophy and phenomenology to inspire awareness and appreciation for the spiritual presence in our daily lives. *Originally aired 1995–1999; updated and revived Feb 2007.* Multicultural demographic for both programs: Casitas Heights, Westview, Norwood, Thousand Hills, San Lopez, West/South Marina.	2007
	▪ **Host, Writer, and Executive Producer—***The Spirited Soul* Radio Broadcast Station KTYM—30-minute teaching program with presentations derived from philosophical and spiritual works. Audience demographic: Culturally diverse, encompassing Casitas Heights, Westview, Norwood, Thousand Hills, West Marina.	1995 to 1999
	▪ **Founded Spiritual Essence—A nonprofit outreach program.**	1995
	▪ **Host and Producer—***Computer Awareness* Cable Television Broadcast—Weekly 30-minute show that focused on desktop publishing and related technology. Featured guests who were experts in the field.	1995

EDUCATION	▪ State University—Loma Pointe, CA
	  – *Bachelor of Arts in Communications Studies—2004*
	    Emphasis on Speech and Broadcast Communications, Rhetoric, Advanced Phenomenology
	  – Enrolled in Master's Program—Communications Studies major
	
	▪ Central College—Central City, CA
	  – *Broadcasting—1993*	

PROFESSIONAL AFFILIATIONS	Member—Elite Communications Association Member—Nationwide Communication Association	
PUBLICATIONS	Lane, Gregg S.: *Heritage Unveiled,* Second Edition. Lane Pub. Co. 210 p. Copyright 1996. Lane, Gregg S.: *Modern Predictions.* Jolie Enterprises. 54 p. Copyright 1993. Lane, Gregg S.: *Heritage Unveiled.* Lane Pub. Co. 144 p. Copyright 1975.	

20

Combination. *Gail Taylor, Torrance, California*

The bold script type for the applicant's name and roles captures attention first. The gray box and gray horizontal line are almost as eye-catching. Next, special tip bullets direct the reader's eyes down the page.

ROY NASH

4900 Boulevard, Carson City, NV 00000   Rnash@aol.com   (000) 000-0000

FOCUS
To acquire field experience necessary to become an alcohol and drug rehabilitation counselor.

RELEVANT QUALIFICATIONS

➢ Former alcohol and drug abuser now in recovery, having completed a rigorous rehabilitation program without any recidivism for more than 3 years.
➢ Avid supporter of others experiencing the nightmare of addiction; keenly sensitive to their feelings and needs to enable joining with clients in early stages of interaction.
➢ Confident facilitator; relate comfortably with diverse cultural and socio-economic populations in didactic sessions with groups of from 12 to more than 40.
➢ Observant of clients' behaviors, with documentation of improvements or lack thereof, to assist authorities in planning appropriate actions upon their release from the 28-day program.

EDUCATION

St. Jude's College, Reno, NV
➢ Graduate of the Recovery Assistance Program Training (RAPT), 2004.
➢ Completed 270 educational hours toward CADC certification. Curriculum included Addiction and Its Effects, The Recovery Process, Family Counseling, Individual Counseling, and Group Counseling.

➢ Passed written exam given by the International Certification Reciprocating Consortium (ICRC), 2004.

PROFESSIONAL EXPERIENCE

Counselor-in-Training at Straight and Narrow, a psycho-social 12-step rehabilitative agency in Carson City, NV (2004 to present).
➢ Conduct 1½-hour didactic sessions to groups that include mentally ill chemical abusers (MICA), focusing on their recovery.
➢ Assist with the new client intake process, assessing and prioritizing service requirements.
➢ Orient prospective clients to the rehabilitative setting and the programs available to them.
➢ Facilitate the adjustment of introductory groups daily, providing them with support and encouragement to stay with the program.
➢ Schedule clients for art therapy and daily recreation and coordinate their other activities.
➢ Ease clients' transition into didactic sessions by introducing deep-breathing and relaxation techniques as a part of daily meditation preliminaries.

PREVIOUS EMPLOYMENT

Bartender, Happy Days Bar & Grill, Reno, NV (1993-2003)
Server, Bartolucci's Ristorante, Reno, NV (1991-1993)

VOLUNTEER ACTIVITIES

➢ Initiated support group in Carson City for parents of drug-addicted/alcohol-dependent children and adolescents, working closely with the police department and D.A.R.E. program.

21

Combination. *Melanie Noonan, West Paterson, New Jersey*

As in Resume 12, a strong font ties together the person's name and side headings. Distinctive bullets draw the eye down the page. Boldfacing makes the occupations stand out. See Cover Letter 286.

Elizabeth Denton

1814 Taylor Drive ~ North Brunswick, NJ 08902
(732) 821-7227 (H) ~ (732) 406-1927 (C) ~ E-mail: lizdent3@msn.com

Objective

To continue my career as a Maintenance Professional using my experience in various facets of manufacturing operations.

Summary of Qualifications

Broad-based responsibilities in the following areas:

- Project Management
- Maintenance Supervision
- Budget Management
- Problem Solving
- Electrical Maintenance
- Hydraulic Maintenance
- Quality Assurance Technician
- Chemical Batch Control
- Forklift Maintenance

Profile

Strengths include excellent communications with all levels of personnel...known as a results-oriented professional with attention to detail and accuracy.

Enjoy performing multiple tasks/projects while keeping an eye on bottom-line profits for the company.

Experience

HEINZ FOODS, Edison, NJ   **1999–2007**

Mechanic   **2001–2007**
- Performed preventive maintenance and repair of equipment and facility grounds for this food and beverage manufacturing operation with 7 manufacturing lines.
- Responsible for machine ownership during product changes, including maintenance and process adjustments.
- Recommended process machinery improvement projects of all sizes, some in excess of $1 million.
- Familiarity with conveyors, bottle cleaners, labelers, packers, palletizers, and filling machines.
- Led the team to eliminate iodine spray on fillers during sterilization.
- Thorough knowledge of mechanical, electrical, hydraulic, and plumbing systems for process equipment as well as for the building and grounds.

Maintenance Group Leader   **1999–2001**
- Extensive knowledge of the processes and equipment in the food, beverage, bottling, and packaging industry.
- Served as a forklift technician and driver on a computerized forklift.
- Performed quality assurance procedures on batches during the mixing and bottling process.
- Thorough knowledge of procedures and techniques used for shipping and receiving, and materials handling.

Continued

22

Combination. *Beverley and Mitchell I. Baskin, Marlboro, New Jersey*

A double-line page border ties together visually the two pages of this resume. Left-aligned, bold side headings make the main sections evident throughout. In the Summary of Qualifications, the three-column list of bulleted responsibility areas is useful for tailoring the resume to

Elizabeth Denton

(732) 821-7227 (H) ~ E-mail: lizdent3@msn.com

NORTH BRUNSWICK TOWNSHIP, North Brunswick, NJ   **1993–1998**
School Bus Driver
- Responsible for driving children that were handicapped or had other special needs.

RIDER STUDENT TRANSPORTATION, New Brunswick, NJ   **1991–1993**
School Bus Driver
- Responsible for driving children to and from school along routine routes.

METROPOLITAN LIMOUSINE, East Brunswick, NJ   **1986–1991**
Owner
- Managed all internal functions of the company, including hiring drivers, dispatching drivers to jobs, billing, and ensuring that the vehicles were maintained properly.

Computers

Knowledge of Microsoft Word and Excel, Lotus 1-2-3, e-mail, and the Internet.

Special Training/Licenses

CDL Class B with passenger endorsement

Boat Operators License

Forklift License

PMMI Basic Hydraulic and Pneumatic Components

PMMI Basic Mechanical Components

PMMI Basic Electrical Components

Community Service

Coached North Brunswick Youth Soccer team to 8 consecutive winning seasons.

Hobbies include woodworking, crafting, gardening, and computers.

---

different job targets. That is, you can easily replace one or more items in the list with new items of particular interest to a different employer without altering the resume's formatting. See Cover Letter 296.

TOM NEWTON

1511 Whitewood Court • North Brunswick, New Jersey 08902 • 732.297.8846

QUALITY ASSURANCE PROFESSIONAL
QUALITY CONTROL ~ LABORATORY TECHNICIAN

Top-performing manufacturing professional with an outstanding reputation for enforcing stringent safety and quality protocols. Acknowledged as an expert troubleshooter, able to visualize desired outcomes, design strategic action plans, and follow through during the manufacturing process.

Professional strengths include

- Equipment Calibration
- Lab Solutions Preparation
- Manufacturing Processes
- Troubleshooting/Problem Solving
- Leadership/Supervision

- Analytical Skills
- Juice Batch-Making
- Productivity Improvements
- Production Processes & Standards
- Quality Improvement/Assurance

- Precision Measurements
- Product Analysis/Inspection
- Micro Plating
- RTCIS Product Releases
- Chemical Operations

BUSINESS EXPERIENCE

NORTHEAST FOODS, Dayton, NJ   2001–2007
Quality Assurance Technician

- Monitored and analyzed quality control for food and beverage manufacturing operation.
- Extensive knowledge of quality control issues and processes for juice-making production.
- Conducted laboratory experiments and preventative maintenance work.
- Selected, weighed, and blended ingredients according to formula for the batch-making of a juice drink.
- Performed analytical checks and quality assurance processes for food and beverage products.
- Implemented new ideas and techniques, resulting in improved quality control methodologies and procedures.
- Knowledge of *BOC/GMP* and safe operating practices within the manufacturing environment.
- Utilized *Micro Plating* expertise with micro-bacterial samples to develop new processes for quality assurance.
- Calibrated analytical and laboratory technical equipment such as refractometers, viscometers, balances, and autoclaves.
- Utilized strong troubleshooting and analytical skills to improve the production processes.
- Instituted laboratory solutions for manufacturing processes; utilized packaging equipment knowledge to improve operational functionality.

NATIONAL DISTRIBUTION CENTERS, Dayton, NJ   1995–2001
Building Maintenance Technician

- Responsible for daily maintenance and upkeep of warehouse equipment, the facility, and the building grounds. Performed painting and repairs, and ensured the security of the warehouse.
- Assisted the operational people with inventory control.

EDUCATION
AA ~ Chemistry ~ Middlesex County College ~ Edison, NJ

23

Combination. *Beverley and Mitchell I. Baskin, Marlboro, New Jersey*

Horizontal lines separate visually the main sections, which have centered headings. As in the preceding resume, the three-column bulleted list is easily tailored to different job targets. See Cover Letter 299.

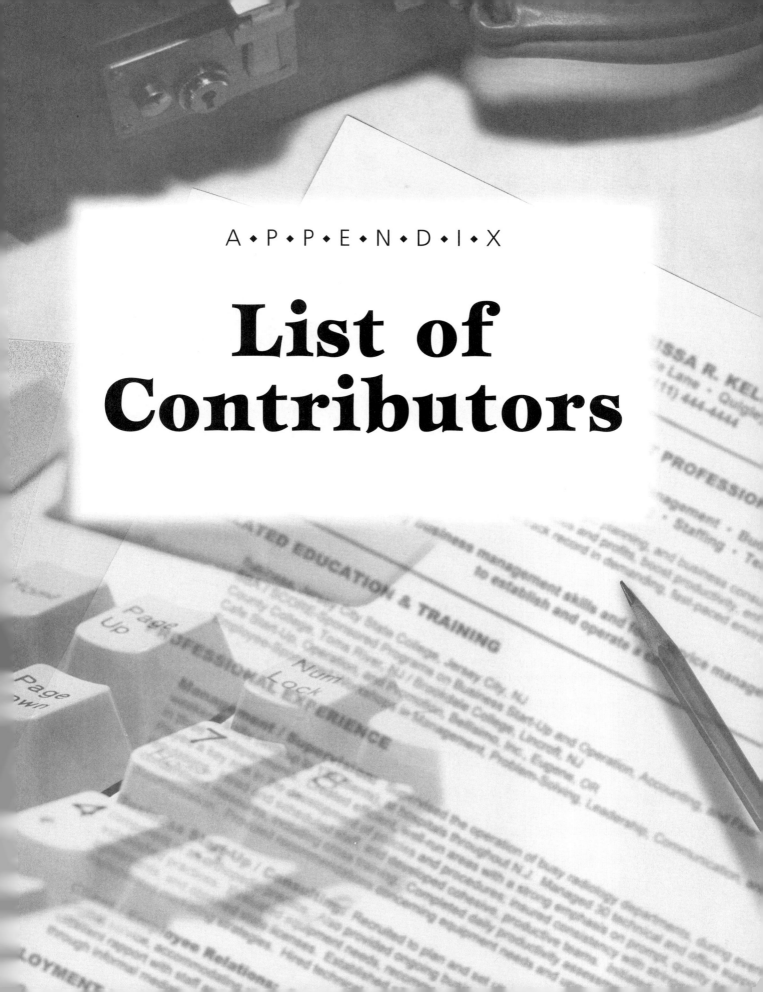

A · P · P · E · N · D · I · X

List of Contributors

List of Contributors

The following professional writers contributed the cover letters and resumes in this book. To include here the names of these writers and information about their business is to acknowledge with appreciation their voluntary submissions and their insights about the cover letters and resumes. Cover letter and resume numbers after a writer's contact information are the *numbers of the writer's cover letters and resumes* included in the Gallery, not page numbers.

Australia

New South Wales

Sydney

Jennifer Rushton
Keraijen
Level 14, 309 Kent St.
Sydney, NSW, 2000 Australia
Phone: 61 02 9994 8050
Mobile: 61 0414 981 062
E-mail: info@keraijen.com.au
Web site: www.keraijen.com.au
Member: AORCP, CDI, CMI
Certification: CARW, CEIC, CRW
Cover letters: 83, 163, 259

Queensland

Victoria Point West

Beverley Neil
d'Scriptive Words
P.O. Box 3281
Victoria Point West, QLD, 4165 Australia
Phone: 61 7 3820 8051
Fax: 61 7 3820 8052
E-mail: d_scriptive@powerup.com.au
Member: AORCP, CDI
Certification: CERW
Cover letters: 22, 89, 204, 270

Victoria

Hallum

Annemarie Cross
Advanced Employment Concepts/AEC Office Services
P.O. Box 91
Hallam, VIC, 3803 Australia
Phone: 1300 137 576 (Toll-free within Australia) and
   61 3 9708 6930 (International)
E-mail: info@annemariecross.com
Web site: www.annemariecross.com
Member: CDI, CMI, PARW/CC
Certification: CEIP, CPRW, CRW, CCM, CECC, CWPP, CERW
Cover letters: 59, 124

Melbourne

Gayle Howard
Top Margin Résumés Online
P.O. Box 74
Chirnside Park, Melbourne, VIC, 3116 Australia
Phone: 61 3 9726 6694
Fax: 61 3 9726 5316
E-mail: getinterviews@topmargin.com
Web site: www.topmargin.com
Member: ASA, CDI, CMI, PARW/CC
Certification: CPRW, CRW, CCM, CERW
Cover letters: 106, 233

Canada

Ontario

Toronto

Howard Earle Halpern
Résu-Card
167 Pannahill Rd.
Toronto, Ontario
Canada M3H 4N6
Phone: (416) 410-7247
Toll-free: (877) 866-5454
E-mail: halpern@sympatico.ca
Web site: www.NoBlock.com
Member: PARW/CC
Certification: CPRW
Cover letters: 17, 66, 142, 303

Whitby

Ross Macpherson
Career Quest
131 Kirby Crescent
Whitby, Ontario
Canada L1N 7C7
Phone: (905) 438-8548
Toll-free: (877) 426-8548
Fax: (905) 438-4096
E-mail:
   ross@yourcareerquest.com
Web site:
   www.yourcareerquest.com
Member: ACPI, CMI, PARW/CC
Certification: MA, CPRW, CJST,
   CEIP, JCTC
Cover letters: 3, 15, 134, 162,
   178, 210, 242, 301, 307

United States

Alabama

Montgomery

Don Orlando
The McLean Group
640 S. McDonough St.
Montgomery, AL 36104
Phone: (334) 264-2020
Fax: (334) 264-9227
E-mail:
   yourcareercoach@aol.com
Member: CMI, PARW/CC,
   Phoenix Career Group
Certification: MBA, CPRW,
   JCTC, CCM, CCMC
Cover letters: 21, 24, 63, 100,
   116, 146, 170, 199, 243, 244,
   261

California

Campbell

Georgia Adamson
*A Successful Career / Adept
   Business Services*
180 W. Rincon Ave.
Campbell, CA 95008-2824
Phone: (408) 866-6859
Fax: (408) 866-8915
E-mail: success@
   ablu/eribbonresume.com
Web sites: www.
   ABlueRibbonResume.com
   and
   www.ASuccessfulCareer.com
Member: CMI, NRWA,
   PARW/CC
Certification: CCMC, CCM,
   CEIP, CPRW, JCTC
Cover letters: 14, 42, 65, 99, 126,
   256, 265

Los Angeles

Alyssa Pera
Legal Authority
605 Birch Blvd.
Los Angeles, CA 90014
Toll-free: (800) 283-3860
Fax: (213) 895-7306
E-mail:
   alyssa@legalauthority.com
Web site:
   www.legalauthority.com
Member: PARW/CC
Certification: CPRW
Cover letters: 151, 153, 154, 156

Torrance

Gail Taylor
A Hire Power Résumé
21213-B Hawthorne Blvd. #5224
Torrance, CA 90503
Phone: (310) 793-4122
Fax: (310) 793-7481
E-mail: hirepwr@yahoo.com
Certification: CEIP, CPRW
Resume: 20

Valencia

Myriam-Rose Kohn
JEDA Enterprises
27201 Tourney Rd., Ste. 201
Valencia, CA 91355-1857
Phone: (661) 253-0801
Toll-free: (800) 600-JEDA
Fax: (661) 253-0744
E-mail: myriam-rose@
   jedaenterprises.com
Web site:
   www.jedaenterprises.com
Member: CMI, NRWA,
   PARW/CC
Certification: CPRW, CEIP,
   IJCTC, CCM, CCMC
Cover letters: 35, 77, 167, 245

Valley Glen

Vivian VanLier
*Advantage Resume & Career
   Services*
6701 Murietta Ave.
Valley Glen, CA 91405
Phone: (818) 994-6655
Fax: (818) 994-6620
E-mail: vvanlier@aol.com,
   Vivian@
   CuttingEdgeResumes.com,
   and VivianVanLier@
   CareerCoach4U.com
Web site: www.
   CuttingEdgeResumes.com
Member: CMI, NRWA
Certification: CPRW, JCTC,
   CEIP, CCMC, CPRC
Cover letters: 122, 209

Colorado

Arvada

Tracy Laswell Williams
CAREER-Magic.com
P.O. Box 74-6142
Arvada, CO 80006-6142
Phone: (303) 424-5451
Toll-free: (888) 384-1744
Fax: (303) 424-1700
E-mail: tracy@career-magic.com
Web site:
   www.CAREER-Magic.com
Member: PARW/CC
Certification: JCTC, CPRW
Cover letters: 123, 275, 276

Aurora

Michele Angello
Corbel Communications
19866 E. Dickenson Pl.
Aurora, CO 80013
Phone: (303) 537-3592
Fax: (303) 537-3542
E-mail: corbelcomm1@aol.com
Web site: www.corbelonline.com
Member: PARW/CC
Certification: CPRW
Cover letters: 11, 150, 181, 309

Louisville

Roberta F. Gamza
Career Ink
Louisville, CO 80027
Phone: (303) 955-3065
Fax: (303) 955-3065
E-mail: roberta@careerink.com
Web site: www.careerink.com
Member: CDI, CMI, NRWA
Certification: CEIP, JCTC, CJST
Cover letters: 5, 111, 129, 238

Connecticut

Durham

Jan Melnik
Absolute Advantage
P.O. Box 718
Durham, CT 06422
Phone: (860) 349-0256
Fax: (860) 349-1343
E-mail: CompSPJan@aol.com
Web site: www.janmelnik.com
Member: CMI, PARW/CC
Certification: MRW, CCM, CPRW
Cover letters: 64, 196

Enfield

Louise Garver
Career Directions, LLC
115 Elm St., Ste. 203
Enfield, CT 06082
Phone: (860) 623-9476
Toll-free: (888) 222-3731
Fax: (860) 623-9473
E-mail: careerpro@cox.net
Web site:
    www.resumeimpact.com
Member: ACA, ACPI, CMI,
    CPADN, NCDA, NRWA,
    PARW/CC
Certification: MA, JCTC, CMP,
    CPRW, MCDP, CEIP
Cover letters: 18, 32, 45, 67, 76,
    79, 80, 105, 110, 135, 166, 191,
    208, 234, 237, 290, 295
Resume: 17

Florida

Tampa

Gail Frank
*Frankly Speaking: Resumes That
    Work!*
10409 Greendale Dr.
Tampa, FL 33626
Phone: (813) 926-1353
Fax: (813) 926-1092
E-mail:
    gailfrank@post.harvard.edu
Web site:
    www.callfranklyspeaking.com
Member: ASTD, CDI, CMI,
    NRWA, PARW/CCSHRM
Certification: NCRW, CPRW,
    JCTC, CEIP, MA
Cover letters: 58, 81, 82, 184,
    187, 190, 212, 236

Valrico

Cindy Kraft
Executive Essentials
P.O. Box 336
Valrico, FL 33595
Phone: (813) 655-0658
Fax: (813) 354-3483
E-mail: careermaster@
    exec-essentials.com
Web site:
    www.exec-essentials.com
Member: AACC, CMI, Coachville,
    IACC
Certification: CCMC, CCM,
    JCTC, CPRW
Cover letters: 1, 62, 73, 230

Georgia

Macon

Lea J. Clark
Lea Clark & Associates
4521 Dorset Dr.
Macon, GA 31206
Phone: (478) 781-4107
Fax: (478) 781-6960
E-mail: writer@prowriter.us
Web site: http://prowriter.us/
Member: CDI, Who's Who in
    Executives and Professionals
Certification: CRW, BIT
Cover letters: 29, 37, 40, 117,
    143, 274

Idaho

Boise

Denette D. Jones
Jones Career Specialties
4702 Gage St.
Boise, ID 83706
Phone: (208) 331-0561
Fax: (208) 361-0122
E-mail: ddjones@
    jonescareerspecialties.com
Web site: www.
    jonescareerspecialties.com
Member: CDI, CMI, NRWA
Cover letters: 84, 193, 202, 231

Illinois

Elk Grove Village

Joellyn Wittenstein-Schwerdlin
*A-1 Quality Résumés & Career
    Services*
1819 Oriole Dr.
Elk Grove Village, IL 60007
Phone: (847) 285-1145
Fax: (847) 285-1838
E-mail: Joellyn@interaccess.com
Web site: www.prwra.com/
    a-1resumes
Member: CDI
Certification: CPRW, JCTC
Cover letter: 285

Lincolnshire

Christine L. Dennison
Dennison Career Services
Lincolnshire, IL 60069
Phone: (847) 405-9775
E-mail:
   chris@thejobsearchcoach.com
Web site:
   www.thejobsearchcoach.com
Member: PARW/CC, Greater
   Lincolnshire Chamber of
   Commerce
Certification: CPC
Cover letter: 253
Resume: 7

Schaumburg

Steven Provenzano
A-Advanced Résumé Service, Inc.
850 E. Higgins Rd., #125-Y
Schaumburg, IL 60173-4788
Phone: (630) 289-1999
E-mail: advresumes@aol.com
Web site: TopSecretResumes.com
Member: PARW/CC
Certification: CPRW
Cover letters: 10, 127

Waukegan

Eva Locke
Workforce Development
415 Washington St., Ste. 104
Waukegan, IL 60085
Phone: (847) 249-2200, ext. 110
Fax: (847) 249-2214
E-mail: elocke@co.lake.il.us
Web site: www.co.lake.il.us/
   workforce
Member: CDI
Cover letters: 91, 95, 138, 213,
   225

Iowa

Urbandale

Billie Ruth Sucher
Billie Sucher & Associates
7177 Hickman Rd., Ste. 10
Urbandale, IA 50322
Phone: (515) 276-0061
Fax: (515) 334-8076
E-mail: betwnjobs@aol.com
Web site: www.billiesucher.com/
Member: CMI, SHRM
Certification: MS, CTMS, CTSB
Cover letter: 258
Resume: 19

Maryland

Crownsville

Beth Colley
Chesapeake Resume Writing Service
P.O. Box 117
Crownsville, MD 21032
Phone: (410) 533-2457
E-mail: resume@chesres.com
Web site: www.chesres.com
Member: NRWA, PARW/CC
Certification: CFJST, CPRW
Cover letters: 113, 252, 282, 308

Hagerstown

Norine Dagliano
ekm Inspirations
14 N. Potomac St., Ste. 200
Hagerstown, MD 21740
Phone: (301) 766-2032
Fax: (301) 745-5700
E-mail: ndagliano@yahoo.com
Web site:
   www.ekminspirations.com
Member: CMI, PARW/CC
Certification: CPRW
Cover letters: 25, 26, 182, 305

Massachusetts

Concord

Jean Cummings
A Resume For Today
123 Minot Rd.
Concord, MA 01742
Phone: (978) 371-9266
Toll-free: (800) 324-1699
Fax: (978) 964-0529
E-mail:
   jc@AResumeForToday.com
Web site:
   www.AResumeForToday.com
Member: CMI, PARW/CC
Certification: MAT, CPRW,
   CEIP
Cover letters: 39, 70, 147, 165,
   224, 251, 302

Melrose

Jeanne Knight
Career and Job Search Coach
P.O. Box 828
Melrose, MA 02176
Phone: (617) 968-7747
E-mail: jeanne@careerdesigns.biz
Web site: www.careerdesigns.biz
Member: CMI, NRWA
Certification: JCTC
Cover letter: 61
Resume: 6

Needham

Wendy Gelberg
21 Hawthorn Ave.
Needham, MA 02492
Phone: (781) 444-0778
Fax: (781) 444-2778
E-mail: wgelberg@aol.com
Member: CMI, NRWA, Career
   Planning & Adult Development
   Network
Certification: CPRW, IJCTC
Cover letters: 9, 97, 119

Springfield

Ellen Mulqueen
A FutureLink
Member: CDI, CMI, NRWA
Certification: MA, CRW, CERW,
   CECC
Cover letters: 28, 247

Michigan

Flint

Janet L. Beckstrom
Word Crafter
1717 Montclair Ave.
Flint, MI 48503-2074
Phone: (810) 232-9257
Fax: (810) 232-9257
Toll-free: (800) 351-9818
E-mail: wordcrafter@voyager.net
Member: CMI, PARW/CC
Certification: CPRW
Cover letters: 8, 13, 38, 46, 68, 78,
   194, 197, 215, 223

Trenton

Maria E. Hebda
Career Solutions, LLC
Trenton, MI 48183
Phone: (734) 676-9170
Fax: (734) 676-9487
E-mail:
   mhebda@writingresumes.com
Web site:
   www.WritingResumes.com
Member: CDI, CMI, NRWA,
   PARW/CC
Certification: CCMC, CPRW
Cover letters: 27, 74, 176, 288

Minnesota

Rochester

Beverley Drake
CareerVision Resume & Job
Search Systems
1816 Baihly Hills Dr. SW
Rochester, MN 55902
Phone: (507) 252-9825
E-mail:
careerexpertise@aol.com
Member: CMI, PARW/CC
Certification: CEIP, IJCTC,
CPRW
Cover letters: 87, 90, 112, 137,
241, 300, 310

Missouri

Kansas City

Gina Taylor
Gina Taylor & Associates
A-1 Advantage Career Services
1111 W. 77th Terrace
Kansas City, MO 64114
Phone: (816) 523-9100 and
(913) 341-5500
Fax: (816) 523-6566
E-mail:
ginaresume@sbcglobal.net
Web site: www.ginataylor.com
Member: CMI, PARW/CC
Certification: CPRW
Cover letters: 6, 164, 239

St. Louis

Sally McIntosh
Advantage Resumes
11611 Misty Moss Ct.
St. Louis, MO 63146
Phone: (314) 434-7599
Fax: (866) 728-9323
E-mail: sally@reswriter.com
Web site: www.reswriter.com
Member: CMI, NRWA
Certification: NCRW, JCTC
Cover letter: 12

New Jersey

Edison

Patricia Traina-Duckers
Prism Writing Services, LLC
P.O. Box 595
Edison, NJ 08818-0595
Phone: (732) 239-8533
Fax: (732) 906-5636
E-mail: sales@
prismwritingservices.com
Web site: www.
PrismWritingServices.com
Member: CDI, NRWA,
PARW/CC
Certification: CPRW, CRW, CEIP
Cover letter: 217

Flemington Area

Carol A. Altomare
World Class Résumés
P.O. Box 483
Three Bridges, NJ 08887-0483
Phone: (908) 237-1883
Fax: (908) 237-2069
E-mail:
caa@worldclassresumes.com
Web site:
www.worldclassresumes.com
Member: PARW/CC
Certification: CPRW
Cover letters: 2, 34
Resume: 15

Iselin

See Marlboro.

Mahwah

Igor Shpudejko
Career Focus
23 Parsons Ct.
Mahwah, NJ 07430
Phone: (201) 825-2865
Fax: (201) 825-7711
E-mail: Ishpudejko@aol.com
Web site:
www.CareerInFocus.com
Member: CMI, PARW/CC
Certification: CPRW, JCTC,
MBA, BSIE
Cover letters: 4, 72

Marlboro

Beverley and Mitchell I. Baskin
BBCS Counseling Services
6 Alberta Dr.
Marlboro, NJ 07746
(Offices also in Iselin, NJ, and
Princeton, NJ)
Toll-free: (800) 300-4079
Fax: (732) 972-8846
E-mail: bbcs@att.net and
info@bbcscounseling.com
Web site:
www.baskincareer.com and
www.job-research.com
Member: NRWA, NCDA,
NECA, MACCA, AMHCA
Certification: Ed.S., MA, LPC,
NCCC, MCC, CPRW
Cover letters: 108, 132, 155,
296, 299
Resumes: 10, 22, 23

Princeton

See Marlboro.

Waldwick

Fran Kelley
The Resume Works
P.O. Box 262
Waldwick, NJ 07463
Phone: (201) 670-9643
Toll-free: (800) 551-6150
Fax: (201) 251-2885
E-mail:
FranKelley@optonline.net
Web site: www.careermuse.com
Member: CMI, NRWA,
PARW/CC
Certification: CPRW, SPHR,
JCTC
Cover letters: 272, 298
Resume: 18

West Paterson

Melanie Noonan
Peripheral Pro, LLC
560 Lackawanna Ave.
West Paterson, NJ 07424
Phone: (973) 785-3011
Fax: (973) 256-6285
E-mail: PeriPro1@aol.com
Member: NRWA, PARW/CC
Certification: CPS
Cover letters: 16, 86, 148, 157,
200, 201, 207, 218, 220, 255,
286, 297
Resumes: 3, 8, 12, 21

New York

Altamont

John Femia
Custom Résumé & Writing Service
1690 Township Rd.
Altamont, NY 12009
Phone: (518) 872-1305
Fax: (518) 872-1305
E-mail: customresume1@aol.com
Member: PARW/CC
Certification: CPRW
Cover letter: 43

Brentwood

Ann Baehr
Best Resumes
122 Sheridan St.
Brentwood, NY 11717
Phone: (631) 435-1879
Fax: (631) 435-3655
E-mail:
    resumesbest@earthlink.net
Web site:
    www.ebestresumes.com
Member: CMI, NRWA
Certification: CPRW
Cover letters: 60, 114, 149, 195,
    240, 248, 287
Resumes: 13, 14, 16

Hauppauge

Donna M. Farrise
Dynamic Resumes of Long Island,
    Inc.
300 Motor Pkwy., Ste. 200
Hauppauge, NY 11788
Phone: (631) 951-4120
Toll-free: (800) 528-6796 and
    (800) 951-5191
Fax: (631) 952-1817
E-mail:
    donna@dynamicresumes.com
Web site:
    www.dynamicresumes.com
Member: CMI, NRWA,
    PARW/CC
Certification: JCTC
Cover letters: 96, 115, 145, 283,
    284

Medford

Deborah Wile Dib
Advantage Resumes of New York
Executive Power Coach
77 Buffalo Ave.
Medford, NY 11763
Phone: (631) 475-8513
Fax: (501) 421-7790
E-mail: deborah.dib@
    advantageresumes.com
Web sites:
    www.advantageresumes.com
    and
    www.executivepowercoach.com
Member: CDI, CMI, NRWA,
    PARW/CC, NAFE
Certification: CCM, CCMC,
    NCRW, CPRW, CEIP, JCTC
Cover letters: 19, 48, 118, 160

Mount Morris

Salome A. Farraro
Careers TOO
3123 Moyer Rd.
Mount Morris, NY 14510
Phone: (585) 658-2480
Toll-free: (877) 436-9378
Fax: (585) 658-2480
E-mail:
    sfarraro@careers-too.com and
    srttoo@frontiernet.net
Web site: www.careers-too.com
Member: PARW/CC
Certification: CPRW
Cover letters: 94, 189, 271, 292

Poughkeepsie

Kristin M. Coleman
Custom Career Services
44 Hillcrest Dr.
Poughkeepsie, NY 12603
Phone: (845) 452-8274
Fax: (845) 452-7789
E-mail:
    kristincoleman44@yahoo.com
Member: CMI
Cover letters: 50, 85, 206, 280

Riverdale

Ilona Vanderwoude
Career Branches
P.O. Box 330
Riverdale, NY 10471
Phone: (718) 884-2213
Fax: (646) 349-2218
E-mail:
    ilona@careerbranches.com
Web site:
    www.CareerBranches.com
Member: CDI, CMI, Coachville
Certification: CCMC, CPRW,
    CJST, CEIP
Cover letters: 198, 264, 311

Rochester

Arnold G. Boldt
Arnold-Smith Associates
625 Panorama Trail, Bldg. One,
    Ste. 120C
Rochester, NY 14625
Phone: (585) 383-0350
Fax: (585) 387-0516
E-mail: Arnie@ResumeSOS.com
Web site: www.ResumeSOS.com
Member: CDI, CMI, NRWA,
    PARW/CC
Certification: CPRW, JCTC
Cover letters: 144, 211

Smithtown

Linda Matias
CareerStrides
34 E. Main St., #276
Smithtown, NY 11787
Phone: (631) 382-2425
Fax: (631) 382-2425
E-mail:
    careerstrides@bigfoot.com
Web site: www.careerstrides.com
Member: NRWA
Certification: CEIP, JCTC
Cover letter: 51

Staten Island

La-Dana R. Jenkins
LRJ Consulting Services
200 Pierce St.
Staten Island, NY 10304
Phone and fax: (718) 448-5825
E-mail: info@lrjconsulting.net
Web site: www.lrjconsulting.net
Member: NRWA, NCDA
Cover letters: 159, 171

North Carolina
Charlotte

Doug Morrison
Career Power
2915 Providence Rd., Ste. 250-B
Charlotte, NC 28211
Phone: (704) 365-0773
E-mail: dmpwresume@aol.com
Web site:
    www.careerpowerresume.com
Member: CDI, CMI, PARW/CC
Certification: CPRW
Cover letters: 7, 98, 120, 263,
    273, 304

Ohio
Athens

Melissa L. Kasler
Resume Impressions
One N. Lancaster
Athens, OH 45701
Phone: (740) 592-3993
Toll-free: (800) 516-0334
Fax: (740) 592-1352
E-mail: resume@frognet.net
Web site:
    www.resumeimpressions.com
Member: PARW/CC
Certification: CPRW
Cover letters: 49, 56, 293, 306

Columbus

Janice Worthington
    (With Jason and Jeremy
    Worthington)
Worthington Career Services
6636 Belleshire Street
Columbus, OH 43229-1510
Phone: (614) 890-1645
Toll-free: (877) 9RESUME
    (973-7863)
Fax: (614) 523-3400
E-mail: Janice@
    WorthingtonResumes.com
Web site:
    www.worthingtoncareers.com
Member: CDI, CMI, PARW/CC
Cover letter: 174

Findlay

Sharon Pierce-Williams, M.Ed.
The Résumé.Doc
609 Lincolnshire Lane
Findlay, OH 45840
Phone: (419) 422-0228
Fax: (419) 425-1185
E-mail:
    Sharon@TheResumeDoc.com
Web site:
    www.TheResumeDoc.com
Member: CMI, PARW/CC,
    Findlay-Hancock County
    Chamber of Commerce
Certification: CPRW
Cover letter: 36

Huber Heights

Teena Rose
Resume to Referral
7211 Taylorsville Rd., Office
    208
Huber Heights, OH 45424
Phone: (937) 236-1360
Fax: (937) 236-1351
E-mail:
    admin@resumetoreferral.com
Web site:
    www.resumebycprw.com
Member: CMI
Certification: CPRW, CEIP, CCM
Cover letter: 140

Oregon
Portland

Rosie Bixel
A Personal Scribe
4800 SW Macadam Ave., Ste.
    105
Portland, OR 97239
Phone: (503) 254-8682
Fax: (503) 255-3012
E-mail: aps@bhhgroup.com
Web site:
    www.apersonalscribe.com/
    page7.html
Member: CDI
Cover letters: 20, 75, 216, 249,
    277, 281, 294

Jennifer Rydell
Simplify Your Life Career
    Services
6327-C SW Capitol Hwy. PMB
    243
Portland, OR 97239-1937
Phone: (503) 977-1955
Fax: (503) 245-4212
E-mail: jennifer@
    simplifyyourliferesumes.com
Web site: www.
    simplifyyourliferesumes.com
Member: NRWA, PARW/CC
Certification: CPRW, NCRW,
    CCM
Cover letters: 33, 57, 130, 192

Pennsylvania
Media

Karen Conway
Premier Resumes
1008 N. Providence Rd.
Media, PA 19063
Phone: (610) 566-8422
Toll-free: (866) 241-5300
Fax: (610) 566-3047
E-mail: premresume@aol.com
Member: PARW/CC
Certification: CPRW, CEIP
Cover letters: 53, 104, 107, 161,
    205, 260

Sharon

Jane Roqueplot
JaneCo's Sensible Solutions
194 N. Oakland Ave.
Sharon, PA 16146
Phone: (724) 342-0100
Toll-free: (888) 526-3267
Fax: (724) 346-5263
E-mail: info@janecos.com
Web site: www.janecos.com
Member: CDI, CMI, NRWA,
    PARW/CC, AJST, NCDA
Certification: CBC, CECC
Cover letters: 23, 103, 109, 152,
    180, 219, 228, 229

Rhode Island

Newport

Edward Turilli
North Kingstown, RI, and
 Bonita Springs, FL
Phone: (401) 268-3020
E-mail: edtur@cox.net
Web site: www.resumes4-u.com
Member: CMI, PARW/CC,
 NCDA, NACE, RICC
Certification: MA
Cover letters: 47, 52, 88, 92, 93,
 214, 221, 235, 266, 289
Resume: 9

Texas

Lubbock

Daniel J. Dorotik, Jr.
100PercentResumes
9803 Clinton Ave.
Lubbock, TX 79424
Phone: (806) 783-9900
Fax: (214) 722-1510
E-mail:
 dan@100percentresumes.com
Web site:
 www.100percentresumes.com
Member: CMI
Certification: NCRW
Cover letters: 41, 102, 128, 139,
 141, 169, 172, 183, 222, 226,
 246, 267, 278, 279, 291
Resumes: 1, 5, 11

Edith A. Rische
Write Away Resume
5908 73rd St.
Lubbock, TX 79424-1920
Phone: (806) 798-0881
Fax: (806) 798-3213
E-mail: erische@door.net
Web site:
 www.writeawayresume.com
Member: NRWA
Certification: NCRW, JCTC
Cover letters: 54, 55, 69, 101,
 121, 131, 175, 262, 269
Resume: 2

Victoria

MeLisa Rogers
Ultimate Career
270 Liveoak Lane
Victoria, TX 77905
Phone: (361) 575-6100
Toll-free: (866) 573-7863
Fax: (361) 574-8830
E-mail:
 success@ultimatecareer.biz
Web site:
 www.ultimatecareer.biz
Member: PARW/CC, SHRM,
 ASTD
Certification: MS HRD, CPRW
Cover letters: 30, 31, 125, 185

Virginia

Reston

Helen Oliff
Principal, Turning Point
2307 Freetown Ct., #12C
Reston, VA 20191
Phone: (703) 716-0077
Fax: (703) 995-0706
E-mail:
 helen@turningpointnow.com
Web site:
 www.turningpointnow.com
Member: CMI
Certification: CPRW, CFRWC,
 ECI
Cover letters: 44, 71, 133, 136,
 179, 186, 232, 250

Washington

Bellingham

Janice M. Shepherd
Write On Career Keys
Top of Alabama Hill
Bellingham, WA 98226-4260
Phone: (360) 738-7958
Fax: (360) 738-1189
E-mail: Janice@
 WriteOnCareerKeys.com
Web site:
 www.WriteOnCareerKeys.com
Member: CMI, PARW/CC
Certification: CPRW, JCTC,
 CEIP
Cover letter: 168

Seattle

Alice Hanson
Aim Resumes
Member: CMI, NRWA,
 PARW/CC, PSCDA, NRWA
Certification: CPRW
Cover letter: 173

Wisconsin

Glendale

Michele J. Haffner
Advanced Résumé Services
1314 W. Paradise Ct.
Glendale, WI 53209
Toll-free: (877) 247-1677
Fax: (414) 247-1808
E-mail:
 info@resumeservices.com
Web site:
 www.resumeservices.com
Member: PARW/CC, Coachville
Certification: CPRW, JCTC
Cover letters: 158, 227, 254
Resume: 4

Three Lakes

Susan Guarneri
Guarneri Associates
6670 Crystal Lake Road
Three Lakes, WI 54562
Phone: (866) 881-4055
Fax: (715) 546-8039
E-mail: Resumagic@AOL.com
Web site:
 www.resume-magic.com
Member: CDI, CMI, PARW/CC
Certification: CPRW, CEIP,
 NCCC, CCMC, IJCTC
Cover letters: 177, 188, 268

Professional Organizations, Certifications, and Finding a Resume Writer or Career Coach

The following sections contain contact information for various career-related organizations and certification programs.

Resume Writers' Organizations

To contact the resume writers' organizations, see the following information:

Career Directors International (CDI)
(Formerly Professional Résumé Writing and Research Association)
Phone: (321) 752-0442
Toll-free: (888) 867-7972
E-mail: info@careerdirectors.com
Web site: www.careerdirectors.com

Career Masters Institute
119 Old Stable Rd.
Lynchburg, VA 24503
Phone: (434) 386-3100
Fax: (434) 386-3200
E-mail: wendyenelow@cminstitute.com
Web site: www.cminstitute.com

National Résumé Writers' Association
P.O. Box 184
Nesconset, NY 11767
Toll-free: (888) NRWA-444
E-mail: AdminManager@nrwaweb.com
Web site: www.nrwaweb.com

Professional Association of Résumé Writers and Career Coaches
1388 Brightwaters Blvd., NE
St. Petersburg, FL 33704
Toll-free: (800) 822-7279
Fax: (727) 894-1277
E-mail: PARWCCHQ@aol.com
Web site: www.parw.com

Federal Job Search and Resumes

For information on the certification programs for Certified Federal Job Search Trainer (CFJST) or Certified Federal Resume Writer & Coach (CFRWC), contact the following:

Ten Steps to a Federal Job™
The Resume Place, Inc.
89 Mellor Ave.
Baltimore, MD 21228
Phone: (410) 744-4324
Fax: (410) 744-0112
E-mail: kathryn@resume-place.com
Web sites: www.resume-place.com and www.tensteps.com

Finding a Resume Writer or Career Coach

For additional online resources regarding certified career professionals, visit the following Web sites:
www.CertifiedResumeWriters.com
www.CertifiedCareerCoaches.com

Occupation Index

Note: The following entries are, in most cases, target positions for the job seekers. (If the target position is not stated clearly, the current or most recent position is listed here.) The numbers are cover letter numbers in the "Gallery," not page numbers.

Resumes Index

Note: The following occupations represent the current or most recent position of the job seekers. The numbers are resume numbers in the "Exhibit of Resumes," not page numbers.

Gallery of Best Resumes, Fourth Edition

A Collection of Quality Resumes by
Professional Resume Writers

David F. Noble, Ph.D.

Sample nearly 200 great resumes with an expansive range of styles, formats, occupations, and situations. Arranged in easy-to-find groups and written by professional resume writers. Get the author's best resume tips on design, layout, writing style, and mistakes to avoid.

ISBN 978-1-59357-365-2 / Order Code LP-J3652 / **$18.95**

Gallery of Best Resumes for People Without a Four-Year Degree, Third Edition

A Collection of Quality Resumes by
Professional Resume Writers

David F. Noble, Ph.D.

Sample more than 200 great resumes with an expansive range of styles, formats, occupations, and situations. Arranged in easy-to-find groups and written by professional resume writers. You also get the author's best resume tips on design, layout, writing style, and mistakes to avoid.

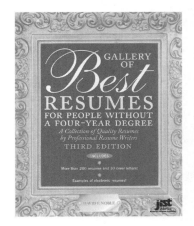

ISBN 978-1-59357-068-2 / Order Code LP-J0686 / **$18.95**

Résumé Magic, Third Edition

Trade Secrets of a Professional Résumé Writer

Susan Britton Whitcomb

Hundreds of winning résumés for every profession and situation, from blue-collar to senior management as well as "before-and-after" transformations. Follow the steps to write, format, and distribute résumés for maximum impact. Includes information on designing Internet-savvy résumés and more than 250 questions to help you identify your contributions to past and present employers.

ISBN 978-1-59357-311-9 / Order Code LP-J3111 / **$18.95**

Visit our Web site at www.jist.com • Call 1-800-648-JIST or Fax 1-800-JIST-FAX

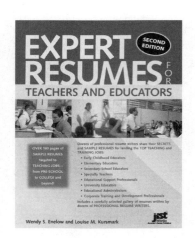

Video training courses are available on the subjects of these books in the James Martin ADVANCED TECHNOLOGY LIBRARY from Deltak Inc., East/West Technological Center, 1751 West Diehl Road, Naperville, Ill. 60566 (Tel: 312-369-3000).

VIDEOTEX	PRINCIPLES OF DISTRIBUTED PROCESSING	INTRODUCTION TO TELEPROCESSING	TELEMATIC SOCIETY
DESIGN OF MAN–COMPUTER DIALOGUES	COMPUTER NETWORKS AND DISTRIBUTED PROCESSING	INTRODUCTION TO COMPUTER NETWORKS	TELE-COMMUNICATIONS AND THE COMPUTER (second edition)
PROGRAMMING REAL-TIME OMPUTER SYSTEMS	DESIGN AND STRATEGY FOR DISTRIBUTED PROCESSING	TELEPROCESSING NETWORK ORGANIZATION	COMMUNICATIONS SATELLITE SYSTEMS
DESIGN OF REAL-TIME OMPUTER SYSTEMS	DISTRIBUTED FILE AND DATA-BASE DESIGN	SYSTEMS ANALYSIS FOR DATA TRANSMISSION	FUTURE DEVELOPMENTS IN TELE-COMMUNICATIONS (second edition)

| Books On | Books On | Books On | Books On |

ACTION DIAGRAMS

A ——————— BOOK

ACTION
Clearly
Program

DIAGRAMS
Structured
Design

JAMES MARTIN

CARMA McCLURE

PRENTICE-HALL, INC. Englewood Cliffs, New Jersey 07632

Library of Congress Cataloging in Publication Data

MARTIN, JAMES (date)
  Action diagrams.

  Bibliography: p.
  Includes index.
  1. Structured programming.   I. McClure, Carma L.
II.   Title.
QA76.6.M3612 1985   001.64′2   85-3579
ISBN 0-13-003302-2

Editorial/production supervision: *Kathryn Gollin Marshak*
Jacket design: *Whitman Studios, Inc.*
Manufacturing buyer: *Gordon Osbourne*

Action Diagrams: Clearly Structured Program Design
James Martin and Carma McClure

© 1985 by James Martin and Carma McClure

Printed in the United States of America

10 9 8 7 6 5 4 3 2 1

ISBN   0-13-003302-2   01

PRENTICE-HALL INTERNATIONAL (UK) LIMITED *London*
PRENTICE-HALL OF AUSTRALIA PTY. LIMITED, *Sydney*
PRENTICE-HALL CANADA INC., *Toronto*
PRENTICE-HALL HISPANOAMERICANA, S.A., *Mexico*
PRENTICE-HALL OF INDIA PRIVATE LIMITED, *New Delhi*
PRENTICE-HALL OF JAPAN, INC., *Tokyo*
PRENTICE-HALL OF SOUTHEAST ASIA PTE. LTD., *Singapore*
EDITORA PRENTICE-HALL DO BRASIL, LTDA., *Rio de Janeiro*
WHITEHALL BOOKS LIMITED, *Wellington, New Zealand*

TO
CORINTHIA
AND
SARAH

CONTENTS

PREFACE

Action diagrams provide a technique that is designed to be as *user friendly* as possible for creating system structures and programs. These diagrams can be used by end users as well as systems analysts and programmers to design program logic. Because they represent program logic in a simple, easy-to-understand graphic format, they help end users understand complex logic and get it right. Action diagrams can be used to represent both high-level overviews of systems and detailed program logic. There is no need to switch diagramming techniques midstream in the design process as has been the case with earlier structured design methods. Being a top-to-bottom design tool, action diagrams support functional decomposition step by step all the way down to program code level.

Action diagrams can be used to represent the program logic for fourth-generation-language programs (and, of course, for third-generation-language programs). Although fourth-generation languages such as FOCUS, NOMAD, RAMIS, MANTIS IDEAL, and NATURAL can greatly simplify programs, fourth-generation-language programs can become subtly complex and error-ridden. Often, there are mistakes made in the use of loops, selection structures, and case structures. For this reason, it is highly desirable first to sketch out the logic of a fourth-generation-language program with action diagrams. This can help to make errors more apparent.

Action diagrams can be *data-base oriented*. Besides being able to represent all the basic *structured* control constructs—sequence, selection, case, repetition—they can also represent data-base actions. The action diagram user can draw simple data accesses—CREATE, READ, UPDATE, DELETE—performed against one instance of one record type and compound data accesses—SORT, SELECT, SEARCH, JOIN, and the like—performed against multiple instances of one or multiple record types. Most of the data-base actions in traditional data processing are simple, but as relational data bases and nonprocedural fourth-generation languages spread, compound data-base actions will become more common.

Action diagrams can be drawn manually, but much benefit derives from using an automated action diagram editor. It can help bring the power of the computer to bear on the difficult task of program design.

This book describes action diagrams. It defines the components of action diagrams and gives many examples of them. The book describes an action diagram editor for personal computers.

The concepts and techniques presented in this book are simple but powerful. They are applicable to large and small systems and programs on large and small computers. Regardless of the computer environment or the program size, the objective of action diagramming is the same: to create correct programs that are easy to maintain.

As computers continue to drop in cost, more and more end users will try their hand at writing software programs. Many have no help other than programming-language manuals. They learn the techniques of program design and coding by trial and error. As a result, they often write incorrect, unstructured programs that are never properly verified and are impossible to maintain.

To expect programs to be correct and complete without thinking out the problem before writing code is as ridiculous as building a skyscraper with plans no more rigorous than those for a garden shed. All but the simplest programs need to be designed before they are coded. All computer users need a design method that is straightforward and simple to use. Action diagrams meet this need.

If either of us were a DP executive managing a large army of analysts and programmers, we would dictate that they all use action diagrams with common action diagramming software, because then they would all speak the same clear, well-structured language. End-users involved with computing would similarly be taught to use action diagrams for specifying systems. They would understand each other's designs and be able to maintain them. A high degree of clarity would be imposed upon their thinking, and they would obtain results faster.

James Martin

Carma McClure

ACTION DIAGRAMS

1 DIAGRAMS AND CLEAR THINKING

MAKING A MESS One of the problems with computing is that it is so easy to make a mess.

Even seemingly simple designs quickly grow messy. Unless we use clean, well-structured design techniques, we can easily make mistakes. When programs grow large, we sometimes have difficulty understanding our own code. If we have difficulty with *our own* code, it is much worse attempting to understand *someone else's* code. The maintenance of systems is expensive and error-prone because of this difficulty.

A LANGUAGE FOR CLEAR THINKING Complex structures and logic can be made much easier to understand if good diagrams are used. It is said that a diagram is worth a thousand words; but in describing program structures, a thousand words can be thoroughly confusing, whereas a good diagram can reveal the structure with immediate clarity. Good diagrams are a language for clear thinking.

Since the earliest days of computing, diagrams have played an important role in representing systems and developing programs. However, the types of diagrams used have changed. In fact, we can trace the evolution of programming methodologies by noting the changes in diagramming techniques.

In the 1950s and 1960s, flowcharts were used to plan out detailed and complicated program logic. In the 1970s, structured techniques became widespread, and with these, structured diagramming techniques such as structure charts were used.

Diagramming techniques are still evolving. When we examine techniques in common use today, we see that many of them have serious deficiencies. Flowcharts have fallen out of favor because they can give neither a high-level nor a structured view of a program. Some of the early structured diagramming

1

techniques need to be replaced because they cannot represent all the basic structured control constructs, such as sequence, selection, and repetition. Because of this, they are not good tools for the automation of programming or the creation of programs with a computer "workbench" environment.

TRENDS THAT AFFECT DIAGRAMMING

Today there are several important trends that affect our requirements for diagramming techniques:

- End users are becoming involved to an increasing extent in creating their own systems. A variety of end-user languages are in use for this. Diagrams that are easy to teach to end users (as opposed to DP professionals) are needed.

- The slowness of DP design and programming has become a major concern. Large improvements are needed in the productivity of system building. These will be achieved by giving systems analysts, programmers, and end users computerized tools. Diagramming techniques that are efficient with these tools are needed.

- Fourth-generation languages are coming into widespread use because results are obtained with them more quickly than with languages such as COBOL or PL/I. Diagramming techniques that link directly to fourth-generation languages are needed.

- Perhaps the most important change in the job of systems analysts and programmers is the use of computer-aided design (CAD). Designs, often involving complex logic and data structures, are created, used, and modified at the screen of a computer. The computer provides as much help as possible in creating the design, verifying it to eliminate errors, and generating executable code from it. Diagramming techniques will be a vital part of the CAD software.

- Maintenance (the modification of previously written code) is becoming an increasing problem, not only because of its cost, but also because it is preventing systems from being changed when they should be changed. This inability to change critical systems can do severe financial harm to corporations. Clear, well-structured diagrams that can be changed on a computer screen should be linked to all code to aid in the maintenance of that code.

ACTION DIAGRAMS

Action diagrams were created with these concerns in mind. They are simple and clear. They appear so obvious in their structure that people tend to ask, "Why weren't they invented twenty years ago?" We believe that they are the simplest and best method of drawing the structures of structured programs.

Experimentation with end users was done as the diagramming technique evolved. Non-DP professionals learn the diagrams quickly and find them easy to use.

Action diagrams are easy to edit on the screen of a personal computer.

Unlike other diagrams in common use, action diagrams can represent a high-level overview of a system and progressively decompose it until executable code is reached.

Unlike most types of diagrams in common use, action diagrams can represent all of the basic constructs of structured programming.

Action diagrams work well with fourth-generation languages. If the authors of this book were teaching a sound fourth-generation language to end users, they would start by teaching action diagrams and the control structures they represent, then fit the code of the language to the action diagrams. The material in this book ought to be basic training in information centers.

With an action diagram editor, programs can be created quickly with far fewer errors than in conventional programming. The programs can be understood and changed easily.

END-USER INVOLVEMENT

It is essential to involve end users in the software development process. Some analysts and programmers prefer to work in isolation without end-user interference or discussion. This is dangerous because it is likely to result in software that does not meet user needs.

Increasingly, some end users are developing their own software with user-friendly fourth-generation languages. Where users do not write their own programs, they should sketch their needs and work hand in hand with an analyst (perhaps from an information center) who develops the software for them. User-driven computing is a vitally important trend for enabling users to get their problems solved with computers.

Diagramming techniques are an essential part of any basic course on computing. As end users become more involved with system design and fourth-generation languages, they should be taught diagramming techniques. We suggest that they be taught action diagrams because these have been designed to be user friendly, easy to learn, easy to use, tailored for use with fourth-generation languages, and easy to manipulate on a personal computer.

BENEFITS OF CLEAR DIAGRAMS

A standard computerized way of representing system and program design enhances team communication and enables management controls. Action diagrams combine graphic and narrative notations to increase understanding. Graphics are especially useful because they tend to be less ambiguous than a narrative description. Also, because they tend to be more concise, graphics can be drawn in much less time than it would take to write a narrative document containing the same amount of information.

When a program is modified, clear diagrams are an essential aid to maintenance. They make it possible for a new programmer to understand how an existing program works and to design changes to that program. When a change is made, it often affects other parts of the program. Clear diagrams of the program structure help maintenance programmers understand the consequential effects of changes they make.

When looking for program bugs, clear diagrams are a highly valuable tool for understanding how the program works and tracking down what might be wrong.

Architects, surveyors, and designers of machine parts have *formal* diagramming techniques that they must follow. Systems analysts and program designers have even a greater need for clear diagrams because their tasks are more complex and because the work of different people must interlock in intricate ways. In the past, however, there has been less formality in programming. This has made systems much more difficult to maintain and change.

For small, one-person projects, an action diagram editor running on a personal computer helps to clarify and speed up design and programming. For large projects, standards are needed for communication among many developers. The larger the project, the greater the need for precision in diagramming. It is impossible for the members of a large project to understand in detail the work of others. Instead, each team member should be familiar with an overview of the system and see where his component fits into it. He should be able to develop his component with as little ongoing interchange with the rest of the team as possible if he has clear, precisely defined and diagrammed interfaces with the work of the others. When one programmer changes his design, it should affect the designs of other programmers as little as possible. To achieve this requires formalized techniques for representing the system design. Action diagrams meet this need.

Certain other types of diagrams are useful for conceptualizing other aspects of complex systems design. As discussed in Chapter 9, these other diagrams, if drawn with appropriate standards, can be *automatically* converted to action diagrams and then to code, on the screen of a personal computer.

LANGUAGES CHANGE OUR THINKING PROCESSES   Philosophers have often described how the language we use for thinking affects what we are capable of thinking. When the world had only Roman numerals, ordinary people could not multiply or divide. When Arabic numbers became widely used, the capability to multiply and divide spread. Diagrams for drawing computer processes are a form of language. With them we can express more complex processes than we can by using English. The designer thinks in diagrams, conceptualizes systems with the aid of diagrams, and refines his design by manipulating the diagrams. The form of a diagram has a direct effect on this process. If the diagram cannot express repetition, sequence, selection, conditions, data-base operations, or parallelism (as is true with some popular types of diagrams for systems analysis), this, like Roman numerals, tends to limit the thinking processes of the designer or user.

A skilled system designer should be fluent with several diagram types that help conceptualize different aspects of systems. Different types of diagrams of processes for which program code will be created should be *automatically* convertible to action diagrams.

The authors have discussed the many types of diagrams in use and have compared action diagrams with alternate techniques in their book *Diagramming Techniques for Analysts and Programmers* [1].

It is desirable for a corporation to standardize diagramming techniques and make this a basic part of its program and system documentation. Having such a corporate standard aids communication among designers and programmers and helps end users to achieve better communication with DP. Without such a corporate standard, maintenance of programs will be unnecessarily difficult. Today the diagramming standard should be the basis of diagramming software. This speeds up the design process, aids communication among designers, and enforces correct use of the standard technique.

We believe that action diagrams should be an essential component of such a standard [2].

REFERENCES

1. James Martin and Carma McClure, *Diagramming Techniques for Analysts and Programmers* (Englewood Cliffs, NJ: Prentice-Hall, Inc., 1985).

2. James Martin, *Recommended Diagramming Standards for Computing,* Savant Research Report (Carnforth, Lancs., England: Savant, 1984).

2 ACTION DIAGRAM BRACKETS

If we were going to build a one-room mud hut, we would not need to do much planning before construction. Only a few materials and tools would be needed. The construction process would involve a few simple steps done by one person. If a mistake was made or a change was necessary, the hut would be easy to modify or rebuild.

At the other extreme, if we were going to build a skyscraper, we would need a detailed architectural plan. Creating this plan would be our first step since no professional builder would attempt such a project without a sound plan. Otherwise, how would we determine what building materials were needed, how many workers to hire, or what jobs to assign to them? If the plan were incomplete or incorrect, the cost to change the building or to modify the construction schedule could cause serious financial problems, possible unsafe conditions, and expensive legal consequences.

Building a single-family house falls somewhere in the middle. An experienced builder could probably construct it without a blueprint, but in most cases this would be inefficient and sometimes foolhardy. By skipping the design phase, the builder could begin actual construction sooner. However, the whole project might take longer to complete. Without a sound design, the house could be of poorer quality because its structure and construction materials would be chosen on the basis of availability rather than quality considerations. Also, because the buyer would not have been given an opportunity to review the plan and perhaps modify his requirements before construction began, he might be less satisfied with the outcome. He might demand many costly changes that would greatly reduce the builder's profit.

We can draw a strong analogy between constructing a building and constructing computer programs. It is as important to design a program as it is to design a building.

DESIGNING WITH   Diagrams are the language of design. Appropriate
ACTION DIAGRAMS   diagrams offer a concise, unambiguous way of de-
                        scribing a program or system of programs. The
choice of diagramming technique has had a major effect on the efficiency of the
designer and the quality of his design [1].

Action diagrams provide a natural way to draw a high-level overview of a
program structure as well as a detailed view of the program logic. They employ
the lessons of structured programs to make the design as clean and well built as
possible. They build on the diagramming techniques of the past, discarding what
has been shown to be ineffective but keeping the constructs that support structured programming. All the basic concepts of a well-structured program, such
as modularization, hierarchical organization, functional decomposition, and
structured control constructs, have been included in action diagrams. Regardless
of whether an end user or a professional programmer is creating a program, the
objective should be a structured program. Structured programs are easier to
build, test, debug, and maintain.

BRACKETS   The basic building block of an action diagram is a
                        bracket:

A bracket encloses a set of actions. An action can be a high-level function,
a procedure, an operation, a program, a program subroutine, or, dropping down
into detail, an individual line of program code.

The following bracket shows high-level functions:

```
┌─ SERVICE A POLICY
│
│     APPORTION REMITTANCE
│     ENDORSE POLICY
│     ASSIGN POLICY
└─    ALLOCATE BONUS
```

The following bracket shows operations that a program must carry out:

```
ADD NEW SUBSCRIBER RECORD
CREATE BILL
CREATE AUDIT RECORD
UPDATE INVENTORY FILE
--- --- --- ---
--- --- --- ---
--- --- --- ---
```

The following bracket shows program code:

```
TOTAL = TOTAL + NEWSUM

MOVE FIELD_EE TO FIELD_EEE

MOVE FIELD_FF TO FIELD_FFF

MOVE SPACES TO FILLER_A, FILLER_B

WRITE FILE_2_RECORD

MOVE 0 TO TOTAL

PERFORM NEW_PAGE
```

A simple control rule applies to the bracket:

You enter it at the top, do the things in it in a top-to-bottom sequence, and exit at the bottom.

Inside the bracket there may be other brackets. Many brackets may be nested. The nesting shows the hierarchical structure of a program. Figure 2.1 shows the representation of a hierarchical structure with brackets.

As can be seen from the examples, the brackets are used both for high-level design or analysis and for detailed programming.

CONDITIONS

Some brackets are executed conditionally. A condition is written at the top of the bracket. If the condition is satisfied, the contents of the bracket are executed:

```
IF CUSTOMER CREDIT IS BAD

    REJECT ORDER

    CREATE SALES NOTIFICATION
```

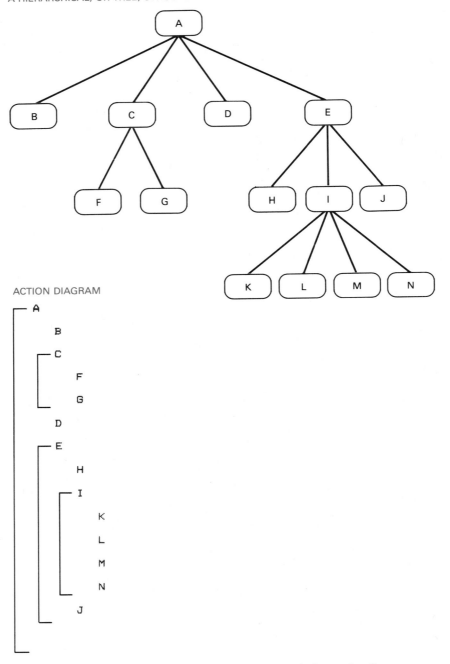

Figure 2.1   A hierarchical tree structure and the equivalent action diagram.

```
┌── IF CODE = 2 THEN

│       PART1 = X + 2YN

│       PART2 = Z

│       PART3 = X * ((3**D)/(-3))

│       A = PART1 + PART2 + PART3
└──
```

```
┌── WHEN SMOKE IS DETECTED

│       SOUND FIRE ALARM

│       CLOSE ROOM DOOR

│       TELEPHONE RECEPTION DESK

│       DO NOT PANIC
└──
```

Condition structures often have two parts, one saying what happens if the condition is true and one saying what happens if it is false:

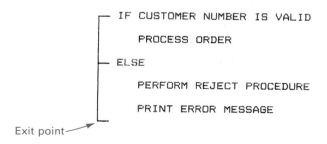

```
┌── IF CUSTOMER NUMBER IS VALID

│       PROCESS ORDER

├── ELSE

│       PERFORM REJECT PROCEDURE

│       PRINT ERROR MESSAGE
└──►
```

Exit point

Here a split bracket is used and the actions in either one part or the other part are executed, depending on the result of testing the condition. Both sets of actions end at a common point (the exit point of the bracket) to continue execution with the next sequential action. This is illustrated in Fig. 2.2.

Condition test

```
┌── IF ERRORS

│       SET INVALID INDICATOR ◄─────── True part

├── ELSE

│       SET VALID INDICATOR ◄─────── False part
└──
```

When the condition structure is used, a condition is tested. If the condition is true, the true part is executed. If the condition is false, the false part is executed. Both parts join at a common exit point, where execution continues.

```
┌── IF INVALID INDICATOR IS SET

│       WRITE ERROR MESSAGE
└──
```

An abbreviated form of the condition structure has only a true part. If the condition is false, execution continues with the next sequential action following the selection structure.

Figure 2.2   The condition structure is used to make the execution of a set of actions dependent on a particular condition.

CASE STRUCTURE

Sometimes there are many mutually exclusive conditions, shown by a bracket divided several times:

```
┌── WHEN KEY = "1"
│     ---- ---- ---- ----

├── WHEN KEY = "2"
│     ---- ---- ---- ----

├── WHEN KEY = "3"
│     ---- ---- ---- ----

├── WHEN KEY = "4"
│     ---- ---- ---- ----
│     ---- ---- ---- ----

├── ELSE
│     ---- ---- ---- ----
│     ---- ---- ---- ----
└──
```

This type of structure is sometimes called a *case structure*. The conditions are tested one after another until a true condition is found. The actions associated with this true condition are executed, and control jumps to the end of the structure, skipping all of the remaining condition tests. Only one of the sets of actions in a case structure is executed.

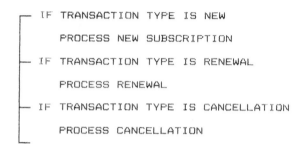

Figure 2.3 Mutually exclusive conditions are represented by a divided bracket on the action diagram. At most, only one of these conditions will be true each time this structure is executed.

Figure 2.3 shows a case structure. Figure 2.4 illustrates nested brackets that show the structure of a process, and one bracket is a case structure. Figure 2.5 shows the difference in drawing mutually exclusive conditions and conditions that are not mutually exclusive.

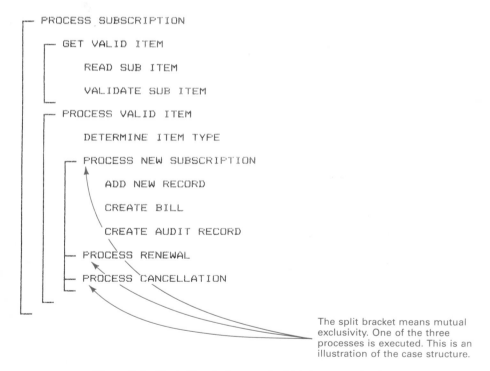

Figure 2.4   Nested brackets, one of which is a case structure.

Mutually exclusive conditions are drawn on one multipart bracket (a case structure)

```
┌─ IF  COLOR  IS  GREEN
│     ---- ---- ---- ----
│     ---- ---- ---- ----
├─ IF  COLOR  IS  RED
│     ---- ---- ----
│     ---- ---- ---- ----
└─
```

Non—mutually exclusive conditions are drawn on separate brackets

```
┌─ IF  COLOR  IS  GREEN
│     ---- ---- ---- ----
│     ---- ---- ---- ----
└─
┌─ IF  EARS  ARE  FURRY
│     ---- ---- ----
│     ---- ---- ---- ----
└─
```

Figure 2.5   The difference between mutually exclusive and non-mutually exclusive conditions.

REPETITION

Often a computer needs to repeat a set of actions; that is to execute a loop. The repetition bracket has a double bar at the top and a thicker vertical line:

The actions inside this bracket may be executed more than once. A statement that controls the execution may be written at the top of the bracket:

If the bracket represents program code, the END instruction that terminates the loop is written at the bottom of the bracket:

```
DO J = 1 TO 9, 16 TO 20
----- ----- ----- -----
----- ----- ----- -----
----- ----- ----- -----
----- ----- ----- -----
END
```

The double line at the top of a repetition bracket looks like a "repeat" in a musical notation:

DO WHILE

A condition that controls execution of the repetition structure can be written at the top of the bracket, as for the conditional structure. Figure 2.6 illustrates this form of repetition bracket, which is called the *DO WHILE* construct:

```
DO while . . .
----- ----- ----- -----
----- ----- ----- -----
----- ----- ----- -----
END
```

The DO WHILE construct works as follows: First, the WHILE condition is tested. If the condition is false, the actions inside the bracket are skipped and execution continues with the next sequential action following the bracket. If the condition is true, the set of actions inside the bracket is sequentially executed; then the condition is again tested. The loop is repeatedly executed until the condition becomes false. If this never happens, the program "loops infinitely." On the other hand, if the condition is initially false, the actions inside the bracket are not executed at all.

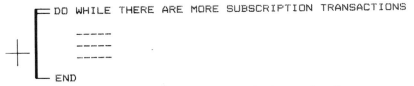

Example of a DO WHILE construct representation in an action diagram

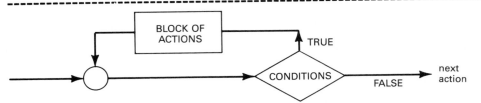

Description of the DO WHILE construct: A loop termination condition is tested. If the condition is false, the loop is terminated and execution continues with the next sequential action. If the condition is true, a block of actions is executed and the condition is tested again. Note that if the condition is initially false, the loop will *not* be executed at all.

Figure 2.6 The DO WHILE construct used to create a repetition structure (program loop).

DO UNTIL

Another form of the repetition structure is the *DO UNTIL* construct. Here the UNTIL control condition is placed at the tail of the bracket:

```
┌─ DO  ---- ---- ---- ----
│      ---- ---- ---- ----
│      ---- ---- ---- ----
│   UNTIL . . .
└─  END
```

Figure 2.7 illustrates the DO UNTIL construct, which works as follows: First, the actions inside the bracket are executed sequentially. Then the UNTIL condition is tested. If the condition is true, the loop is terminated and program execution continues with the next action following the bracket. If the condition is false, the set of actions inside the bracket is executed again; then the condition test is repeated. If the DO UNTIL condition never becomes true, the DO UNTIL construct will execute "infinitely." If the DO UNTIL condition is initially true, the actions inside the bracket will be executed once before execution continues with the next action following the DO UNTIL bracket.

Example of a DO UNTIL construct representation in an action diagram

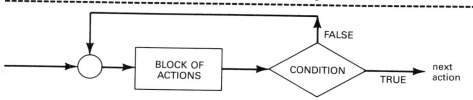

Description of the DO UNTIL construct: A block of actions is executed. Then a loop termination condition is tested. If the condition is true, the loop is terminated and execution continues with the next sequential action following the DO UNTIL construct. If the condition is false, the action block is executed again. Note that the DO UNTIL construct is always executed at least once.

Figure 2.7 The DO UNTIL construct used to create a repetition structure (program loop).

When many people first start to program, they make mistakes with the point at which they test a loop. Sometimes the test should be made before the actions of the loop are performed, and sometimes the test should be made after. This difference can be made clear on brackets by drawing the test either at the top or at the bottom of the bracket:

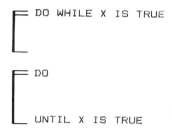

(The lower positioning of the UNTIL cannot be done with certain languages where syntax requires it at the start of the loop.)

SETS OF DATA   Sometimes a procedure needs to be executed on all of the items in a set of items. For example, it might be applied to all transactions or all records in a file (see top of page 19).

```
─* /* Executable Section */
  ┌─ switch (adtab[curline].action){

  ┌─ case ACT_JUNK:
  ┌─ case ACT_CASE:
  ┌─ case ACT_EXIT:
       itfrst = curline;
       itnext = curline + 1;
       break;

  ┌─ case ACT_BEGL:
  ┌─ case ACT_BEGB:
       adlevel = 1;
       itfrst = curline;
     ┌─ for (itnext = curline+1; itnext <= numadtab & adlevel >0; itnext++){

          ┌─ switch (adtab[itnext].action) {
          ┌─ case ACT_BEGL:
          ┌─ case ACT_BEGB:
               adlevel++;
               break;
          ┌─ case ACT_END:
               adlevel--;
                 }
               }
     ┌─ if (adlevel > 0)
          aborts ("ad: ? no matching end ??");

        break;

  ┌─ default:
       itfirst = numadtab;
       itnext = numadtab;
       beep();
         }
     itdel = itnext - itfirst;
  ┌─ for (itab = itfirst; itab < numadtab; itab++) {
       adtab[itab].action = adtab[itab+itdel].action;
       adtab[itab].count  = adtab[itab+itdel].count;
       adtab[itab].text   = adtab[itab+itdel].text;
         }
     numadtab -= itdel;
  ┌─ if (curline > numadtab)
       curline = numadtab;

     showbuffer ();
```

Figure 2.8 Nested brackets, two of which are case structures and two of which are repetition brackets. This is part of a program written in the language C.

```
  ┌─ FOR ALL TRANSACTIONS
  │    ──── ──── ──── ──── ────
  │    ──── ──── ──── ──── ────
  │    ──── ──── ──── ──── ────
  │
  └─
```

Action diagrams have been used with fourth-generation languages such as NOMAD, MANTIS, FOCUS, RAMIS, and IDEAL. They are a good tool for teaching end users to work with these languages. Some of these languages have a FOR construct with a WHERE clause to qualify the FOR. For example:

```
  ┌─ FOR EACH TRANSACTION WHERE CUSTOMER # > 5000
  │    ──── ──── ──── ──── ────
  │    ──── ──── ──── ──── ────
  │    ──── ──── ──── ──── ────
  │
  └─
```

Figure 2.8 has nested brackets with repetitions, showing a part of a program coded in the language C.

THE ESCAPE STRUCTURE

Certain conditions that require skipping over some of the program logic may occur. They may cause the termination of the bracket in which the condition occurs, or they may cause the termination of multiple brackets. Terminations are drawn with a horizontal arrow to the left through one or more brackets, as follows:

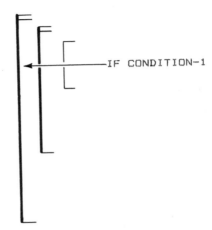

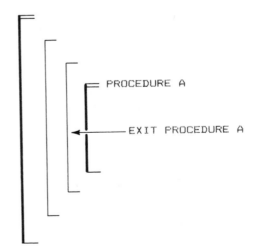

Sometimes a termination exits from a particular bracket but not all of the brackets in a nest of brackets. Thus an EXIT instruction may cause control to pass to the end of PROCEDURE A:

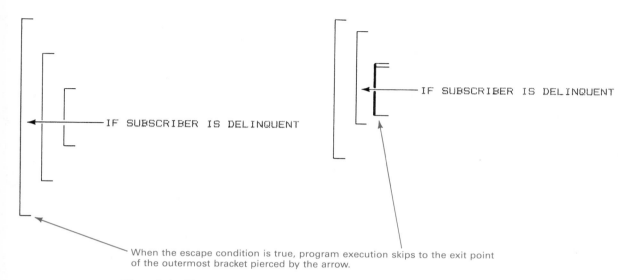

When the escape condition is true, program execution skips to the exit point of the outermost bracket pierced by the arrow.

Figure 2.9 The escape structure in an action diagram.

Figure 2.9 illustrates the escape structure. Notice that the escape condition is written to the right of the horizontal escape arrow. If the escape condition is true, program execution jumps to the exit point of the bracket. If the escape condition is false, program execution continues with the next sequential action following the escape structure. When brackets are nested, the escape arrow can be drawn through multiple levels, causing program execution to jump to the exit point of the outermost bracket through which the arrow has been drawn.

It is important to note that an escape structure allows only a forward skip to the exit point of a bracket. This restriction keeps the structure simple and does not allow action diagrams to degenerate into unstructured "spaghetti" logic.

An escape is different from a GOTO instruction. It represents an orderly closedown of the brackets escaped from. Some fourth-generation languages have an escape construct and no GOTO instruction. The escape command has names such as EXIT, QUIT, BREAK, etc.

GOTO

When a language has a well-implemented *escape,* there is no need for GOTO instructions. However, some languages have GOTO instructions and no escape. Using good structured design the GOTO would be employed to emulate an escape. Any attempt to branch to a distant part of the program should be avoided.

It has been suggested, nevertheless, that a GOTO should be included in the action diagram vocabulary. This can be done by using a dashed arrow to replace the solid escape arrow, thus:

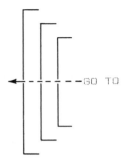

In the interests of structured design we have not included this contract in our recommended list of action diagram features.

NEXT ITERATION   In a repetition bracket a *next-iteration* construct is useful. With this, control skips the remaining instructions in a repetition bracket and goes to the next iteration of the loop. A next iteration construct (abbreviated "NEXT") is drawn as follows:

The arrow does not break through the bracket as with an escape construct.

EASY-TO-READ FORMAT   A program drawn with brackets is easy to understand and change. Glancing ahead, Fig. 6.11 shows a complex segment of code written in a language the reader may not know, the CCITT standards organization's language, CHILL, for programming telephone exchanges and network software. Even without knowing the language, the reader should be able to follow the structure of the program.

An action diagram editor can automatically put the control words of a chosen language onto the brackets that are drawn (see Fig. 2.10). The language control words, shown in red, appear on the screen when the designer selects the diagram constructs required.

CONCURRENCY   For the first four decades of computing, almost all computers performed their operations sequentially. A major difference between the fourth and fifth generations of computers is likely to be that a fifth-generation machine will have multiple processors and will execute operations in parallel where this is possible.

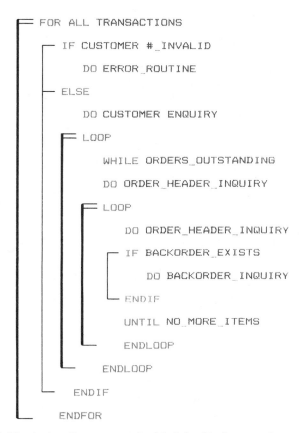

```
  ┌─ FOR ALL TRANSACTIONS
  │    ┌─ IF CUSTOMER #_INVALID
  │    │       DO ERROR_ROUTINE
  │    ├─ ELSE
  │    │       DO CUSTOMER ENQUIRY
  │    │    ┌─ LOOP
  │    │    │       WHILE ORDERS_OUTSTANDING
  │    │    │       DO ORDER_HEADER_INQUIRY
  │    │    │    ┌─ LOOP
  │    │    │    │       DO ORDER_HEADER_INQUIRY
  │    │    │    │    ┌─ IF BACKORDER_EXISTS
  │    │    │    │    │       DO BACKORDER_INQUIRY
  │    │    │    │    └─ ENDIF
  │    │    │    │       UNTIL NO_MORE_ITEMS
  │    │    │    └─     ENDLOOP
  │    │    └─     ENDLOOP
  │    └─     ENDIF
  └─     ENDFOR
```

Figure 2.10 Action diagrams can be labeled with the control statement of fourth-generation language and are an excellent way to teach such languages. This example uses statements from the language IDEAL from ADR [2]. The red words are control words of the language.

At the time of writing, a large uniprocessor mainframe that executes 10 mips (millions of instructions per second) costs about \$500,000. A 32-bit microcompuier chip executing 1 mips costs about \$50. This startling difference in cost has caused research organizations everywhere to ask, "How could a mainframe be constructed from many microcomputers that operate in parallel?" Even if parallelism resulted in substantial inefficiency, a highly parallel computer could be much more cost effective than a high-speed uniprocessor.

It is difficult to take advantage of parallel architectures when using computer languages that are essentially sequential, as almost all computer languages have been. There has been little success in writing COBOL or FORTRAN compilers for parallel computers. Relatively recently, new languages that can exploit parallel hardware architectures have emerged. Some are data-base or knowledge-base languages where searches, joins, or other relational operations can exploit concurrent machine operations. Some are programming languages that can specify concurrent actions. Some are specification languages that indicate that certain actions can occur concurrently.

Where parallel processing is possible, we need a construct on our diagrams that indicates that specified activities can happen concurrently.

The language OCCAM is a tight programming language that can express concurrency [3,4]. It is used for writing programs for multimicroprocessor configurations, or transputer systems. To control the order of execution of processes, OCCAM uses three fundamental mechanisms in addition to the conventional WHILE and IF constructions:

- SEQ   indicates that operations are carried out in sequence
- ALT   indicates that one and only one operation is carried out of several alternate operations
- PAR   indicates that operations can be carried out in parallel

SEQ and ALT are represented in the brackets discussed earlier; ALT is a case structure. PAR requires a new diagramming construct. We will indicate that brackets can be executed concurrently by linking them with a semicircular arc:

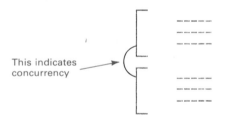

The reader might think of the arc as being a *C* for *concurrency*.

The basic constructs SEQ, ALT and PAR are, then, drawn as follows:

PAR:

Whereas OCCAM is designed for machine programming at a low level, the HOS specification language is designed for systems analysts who begin with a high-level overview of the systems they are designing [5,6]. This specification language has three forms of decomposition: JOIN, OR, and INCLUDE. These again express sequence, alternates, and concurrency. Where they are binary decompositions, they can be drawn as follows:

In some cases the concurrency symbol is on one bracket or block only, indicating that this bracket or block relates to parallel activities. This one subroutine may initialize and use a parallel array of processors. In OCCAM, for example, we may have the following:

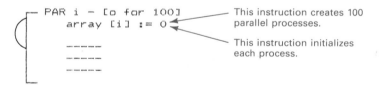

Although the other types of constructs in this book have been extensively used in practice, the concurrency indicator has not as yet because of the essential serial nature of today's programming. Concurrency will be vitally important in future system design.

ADVANTAGES

In addition to being user-friendly and easy to learn to use, action diagrams have been designed for both quick manual manipulation and computerized manipulation. Users and analysts can draw rough sketches on paper or argue at a blackboard using action diagrams. Also, they can build complex diagrams at a computer screen, using the computer to validate, edit, and store the diagrams, possibly linking them to a dictionary, data-base model, or the like. The tool acts rather like a word processor for diagramming, making it easy for users to modify their diagrams. Unlike a word processor, it can perform complex validation and cross-checking on the diagram.

The capability of being automatable is one of the most important distinctions between action diagrams and other diagramming techniques. Earlier diagramming techniques were all intended for use with a plastic template and manual documentation methods. As we change from the era of design with plastic templates to design at the screen of a personal computer (often linked to a mainframe), we need diagramming techniques that are appropriate.

When systems are developed with manual techniques, countless mistakes are made: inputs and outputs that do not correlate, open loops, hanging ENDs, mistakes in data modeling, specifications that are full of errors, ambiguities, and inconsistencies. Because of the numerous details involved, these mistakes are tedious and difficult to find. Correcting them often causes other mistakes. As we use computer-aided design, we would like the computer to perform any checks that are possible on our design while we create the design at a screen. We would like it to fill in any details that it can, with the aid of a dictionary, subroutine library, and knowledge of how a language syntax fits the structures we draw.

Action diagrams, unlike many earlier types of diagrams, can represent all the structures of structured programming: sequence, conditions, case structures, repetition, and so on. They enable us to design a complex structure in an easy-to-understand diagrammatic fashion and have a computer fit the commands of a particular programming language to our structure.

As we will see later, other ways of conceptualizing and validating complex processes can be converted automatically to action diagrams.

An important characteristic of action diagrams is their obvious meaning. They have been designed to be as easy to understand as possible. They avoid the use of abstract symbols that are easily forgotten or hard to learn. We believe that they provide the easiest way to teach end users the concepts of structured design and programming, and as such they should be part of a basic training course in information centers.

Action diagrams were designed to offer the following advantages:

- They are quick and easy to draw and to change.

- They are good for manual sketching and computerized checking.

- They are easy to teach to end users and encourage end users to extend their capability into examination of design or detailed process logic. They are therefore designed as an information center tool.

- They can be drawn on printed or normal paper, making them appropriate for cheap printers and personal computers.

- They can represent all the basic control constructs of structured programming.
- They are data-base-oriented.
- They are fourth-generation-language-oriented.
- They are designed for computerized cross-checking.

BOX 2.1   Components of an action diagram

Brackets

The bracket encloses a set of actions to be performed. It may represent an organizational unit, a process, a subroutine, or a block of code.

BILLING PROCESS

A title may or may not be written at the top of the bracket.

Sequence

action 1

action 2

action 3

One or more actions may be included within a bracket. The actions are listed one after another and are executed in the order in which they are listed.

Selection

IF ERRORS

SET INVALID INDICATOR

ELSE

SET VALID INDICATOR

When the selection (condition) structure is used, a condition is tested; then, depending on whether the test is true or false, one of two alternative sets of actions is executed.

IF ERRORS

PRINT ERROR MESSAGE

An abbreviated form of the selection structure has only a true part.

(Continued)

BOX 2.1 *(Continued)*

Case Structure

```
┌─── IF NEW SUBSCRIPTION
│
│    PROCESS NEW SUBSCRIPTION
│
├─── IF RENEWAL SUBSCRIPTION
│
│    PROCESS RENEWAL
│
├─── IF CANCELLATION SUBSCRIPTION
│
│    PROCESS CANCELLATION
└───
```

A partitioned bracket shows a case structure or mutually exclusive conditions. Only one partition of a partitioned bracket is executed.

Repetition

```
╔═══
║
║   ── ── ──
║
║   ── ── ──
║
║   ── ── ──
║
╚═══
```

A double bar at the top of a bracket indicates that the actions inside the bracket may be executed more than once (i.e., it indicates a program loop structure).

```
╔═══ DO WHILE N > 0
║
║
║
╚═══
```

Conditions controlling the DO WHILE construct are written at the top of the bracket to show that the condition is tested before the actions inside the bracket are executed. The loop stops when the condition becomes false.

```
╔═══ DO
║
║
║
╚═══ UNTIL N = 0
```

Conditions controlling the DO UNTIL construct are written at the bottom of the bracket to show that the condition is tested after the actions inside the bracket are executed. The loop stops when the condition becomes true.

BOX 2.1   *(Continued)*

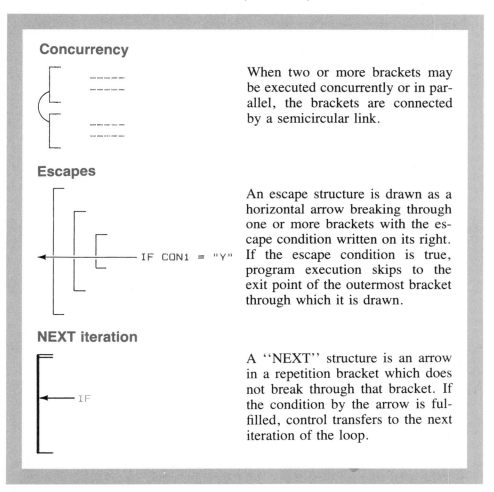

Concurrency

When two or more brackets may be executed concurrently or in parallel, the brackets are connected by a semicircular link.

Escapes

IF CON1 = "Y"

An escape structure is drawn as a horizontal arrow breaking through one or more brackets with the escape condition written on its right. If the escape condition is true, program execution skips to the exit point of the outermost bracket through which it is drawn.

NEXT iteration

IF

A "NEXT" structure is an arrow in a repetition bracket which does not break through that bracket. If the condition by the arrow is fulfilled, control transfers to the next iteration of the loop.

SUMMARY   Box 2.1 summarizes the components of an action diagram that were discussed in this chapter. In the next chapter, we will discuss more components found in action diagrams.

EXERCISES

1. What is the control rule for brackets?
2. Draw the action diagram for the following program logic:

   Send compiler software to the Northern region.

   Send graphics software to the Southern region.

   Send report generator software to the Eastern region.

   Send word processor software to the Midwestern region.

   Send graphics and report generator software to the Western region.

3. Draw the action diagram structure representing concurrent or parallel processes.
4. Use an action diagram DO WHILE construct to represent the following program logic:

   Examine the inventory amount of each of the 76 product types to determine which products have an inventory level of less than 25.

5. Explain the difference between the DO WHILE and DO UNTIL constructs.

REFERENCES

1. James Martin and Carma McClure, *Diagramming Techniques for Analysts and Programmers* (Englewood Cliffs, NJ: Prentice-Hall, Inc., 1985.)

2. IDEAL manuals are available from ARD, Inc., Route 206 and Orchard, CN-8, Princeton, NJ 08540.

3. OCCAM manuals are available from INMOS Corp., P.O. Box 16000, Colorado Springs, CO 80935. Tel.: (303) 630-4000.

4. Richard Taylor and Pete Wilson, "Process-Oriented Language Meets Demands of Distributed Processing," *Electronics,* Nov. 30, 1982.

5. Manuals on USE.IT, which is a tool employing the HOS specification language, are available from Higher Order Software Inc., Cambridge, MA. Tel.: (617) 661-8900.

6. James Martin, *Systems Design from Provably Correct Constructs* (Englewood Cliffs, NJ: Prentice-Hall, Inc., 1985).

3 SUCCESSIVELY DETAILED DECOMPOSITION

Designers tend to build their designs in stages, clarifying the detail as they go. Their action diagrams tend to grow a step at a time.

GROWTH OF A DESIGN   Let us suppose that we want to design a device for waking us up in the morning with music and coffee.
The designer first breaks down the wake-up procedure into three basic operations, each of which occurs at a given clock time. (The times are in seconds.)

```
--- WAKEUP PROCEDURE

    --- WHEN CLOCK_TIME = ALARM_TIME - 150

         HEAT WATER

    --- WHEN CLOCK-TIME = ALARM_TIME - 130

         MAKE BEVERAGE

    --- WHEN CLOCK-TIME = ALARM_TIME

         SWITCH AUDIO CHANNEL TO MUSIC
```

The machine ought to give a choice of beverages. Its user selects one of several choices before going to bed. The designer expands MAKE-BEVERAGE into a case structure to show this:

```
┌─ WAKEUP PROCEDURE
│
│  ┌─ WHEN CLOCK_TIME = ALARM_TIME - 150
│  │
│  │    HEAT WATER
│  └─
│  ┌─ WHEN CLOCK_TIME = ALARM_TIME - 130
│  │
│  │  ┌─ IF SELECTION = 1
│  │  │
│  │  │    MAKE TEA WITH MILK
│  │  ├─ IF SELECTION = 2
│  │  │
│  │  │    MAKE TEA WITHOUT MILK
│  │  ├─ IF SELECTION = 3
│  │  │
│  │  │    MAKE COFFEE WITH CREAM
│  │  ├─ IF SELECTION = 4
│  │  │
│  │  │    MAKE COFFEE WITHOUT CREAM
│  │  └─
│  ┌─ WHEN CLOCK_TIME = ALARM-TIME
│  │
│  │    SWITCH AUDIO CHANNEL TO MUSIC
│  └─
└─
```

There should be a fifth choice: no beverage. If this is the choice, the water should not be heated:

```
┌─ WHEN CLOCK_TIME = ALARM_TIME - 150
│
│  ┌─ IF SELECTION NOT = 5
│  │
│  │    HEAT WATER
│  └─
└─
```

The sleeper might not get out of bed when the music plays, so after 120 seconds the machine is to interrupt the music and announce in a loud voice that it is past wake-up time. The designer expands the bottom bracket to show this:

```
┌─ WHEN CLOCK_TIME = ALARM_TIME
│     SWITCH AUDIO CHANNEL TO MUSIC
│     SET TIMER = 0
│     WAIT
│  ┌─ WHEN TIMER = 120
│  │     SWITCH AUDIO CHANNEL TO SPEECH
│  │     SPEAK "IT IS PAST YOUR WAKE-UP TIME.  THE TIME IS"
│  │     SPEAK CLOCK_TIME
│  │     SWITCH AUDIO CHANNEL TO MUSIC
│  └─
└─
```

Perhaps the speaking routine needs to be repeated a number of times. And if the sleeper does not indicate to the machine that he is awake, he gets a stronger form of wake-up. The designer amends the design as follows:

```
WHEN CLOCK_TIME = ALARM_TIME
    SWITCH AUDIO CHANNEL TO MUSIC
    COUNT = 0

DO 4 TIMES
    ADD 1 TO COUNT
    SET TIMER = 0
    WAIT

        IF ALARM IS SWITCHED OFF
        IF BEVERAGE IS REMOVED
        WHEN TIMER = 120
            IF COUNT < 4
                SWITCH AUDIO CHANNEL TO SPEECH
                SPEAK "IT IS PAST YOUR WAKE-UP TIME.   THE TIME IS"
                SPEAK CLOCK_TIME
                SWITCH AUDIO CHANNEL TO MUSIC
            ELSE
                SWITCH AUDIO CHANNEL TO SIREN


    IF ALARM IS SWITCHED OFF OR BEVERAGE IS REMOVED
        SWITCH AUDIO CHANNEL TO MUSIC
```

Figure 3.1 shows the overall design.

Most systems are more complicated than this wake-up machine example, but they are usually designed in a similar way. The designer creates an overview of what is wanted and steadily fills in detail. He invents and clarifies the design as he goes.

FUNCTIONAL DECOMPOSITION

The technique of designing a system or program in steps that gradually define more and more detail is called *functional decomposition*.

Functional decomposition is a step-by-step process that begins with the most general functional view of what is to be done, breaks this view down into subfunctions, and then repeats the process until all subfunctions are simple enough to be easily understood and small enough to be easily implemented into program code.

Functional decomposition is the basic design technique used by structured methodologies. This method of systematically dividing a program into smaller

```
WAKEUP PROCEDURE
    WHEN CLOCK_TIME = ALARM_TIME - 150
        IF SELECTION NOT = 5
            HEAT WATER

    WHEN CLOCK_TIME = ALARM_TIME - 130
        IF SELECTION = 1
            MAKE TEA WITH MILK
        IF SELECTION = 2
            MAKE TEA WITHOUT MILK
        IF SELECTION = 3
            MAKE COFFEE WITH CREAM
        IF SELECTION = 4
            MAKE COFFEE WITHOUT CREAM

    WHEN CLOCK_TIME = ALARM_TIME
        SWITCH AUDIO CHANNEL TO MUSIC
        COUNT = 0

        DO 4 TIMES
            ADD 1 TO COUNT
            SET TIMER = 0
            WAIT


←─────────────IF ALARM IS SWTICHED OFF
←─────────────IF BEVERAGE IS REMOVED
            WHEN TIMER = 120
                IF COUNT <4
                    SWITCH AUDIO CHANNEL TO SPEECH
                    SPEAK "IT IS PAST YOUR WAKE-UP TIME.   THE TIME IS
                    SPEAK CLOCK_TIME
                    SWITCH AUDIO CHANNEL TO MUSIC
                ELSE
                    SWITCH AUDIO CHANNEL TO SIREN


        IF ALARM IS SWITCHED OFF OR BEVERAGE IS REMOVED
            SWITCH AUDIO CHANNEL TO MUSIC
```

Figure 3.1   An action diagram showing the components of a morning wake-up device.

and smaller pieces is a powerful and essential tool for dealing with complexity that involves many interrelated pieces. It is a way of obtaining a simple, clear view of what is to be done from a tightly interwoven mass of details.

Action diagrams support functional decomposition by representing the design at each level of detail. Action diagrams can be extended all the way from the highest-level overview to working program code.

As the design progresses from its high-level overview to programmable detail, it changes constantly as the designer brings the design into sharper focus and invents the details. Because of this constant change, the designer needs a computerized tool that allows him to sketch his design and successively refine it.

The tool that he uses should be able to represent the high-level overview and the detail with the same diagramming technique so that he can extend his thoughts naturally from his early ideas to his later, polished, code-level design. The designer needs to be able to move naturally between the high levels and low levels of the design.

A problem with the diagramming techniques of the 1970s (most of which are still in use) was that the methods of representing the initial high-level design could not be extended down to the detailed design. The designer had to switch techniques in midstream as he progressed from early design to detailed design. He used techniques such as HIPO diagrams, data-flow diagrams, and structure charts for high-level design. But these could not represent conditions, case structures, repetition, data-base actions, and sometimes not even sequence, so the designer switched to techniques such as pseudocode, structured English, and Nassi-Shneiderman diagrams for detailed design. As he switched from one type of representation to another, he did so manually and usually made mistakes.

Action diagrams are intended to avoid this. They go all the way from basic, initial overview to detailed code structure.

ULTIMATE DECOMPOSITION

The process of extending functional decomposition all the way until executable code is reached is called *ultimate decomposition*.

The designer works at a computer screen starting with an overview diagram. He edits and adjusts the diagram and successively fills in detail until he has working code that can be tested interpretively.

As we will see later, the process of ultimate decomposition should often be linked to a data dictionary and data models built with sound data-base planning and design.

It is much easier to build systems with fourth-generation languages than it is with COBOL or PL/I. With COBOL and PL/I, many systems analysts create specifications that are then programmed by a separate programming team. This limits the design feedback that should occur as the system is being built. With fourth-generation languages, the designer usually finishes the job himself, taking

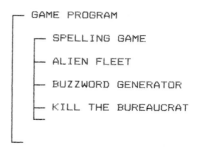

Figure 3.2   The highest-level action diagram for a game program.

his design into executable code and usually making many adjustments as he does so. In Chapter 6, we discuss the use of fourth-generation languages. Fourth-generation languages encourage that ultimate decomposition be done by one designer.

Figures 3.2 to 3.5 illustrate ultimate decomposition using the language MANTIS [1], a popular fourth-generation language.

Figure 3.2 shows the highest-level diagram of a game program. It defines four game choices: Spelling Game, Alien Fleet, Buzzword Generator, and Kill the Bureaucrat. Figure 3.3 shows an expansion of this diagram that begins to define the program logic for the game Buzzword Generator.

Figure 3.4 further decomposes the logic. The inner bracket is a repetition structure that executes 22 times. It is inside a bracket that is terminated by the operator pressing the ESC (escape) key. The last statement in this bracket is

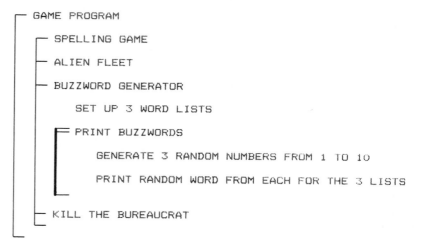

Figure 3.3   An action diagram that begins to define the program logic for the Buzzword Generator game. It is an expansion of the action diagram shown in Fig. 3.2.

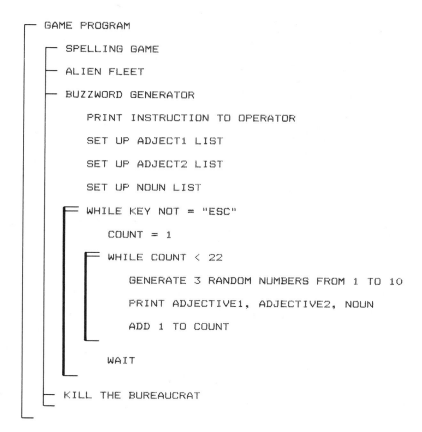

Figure 3.4   A further expansion of the Buzzword Generator game that was defined in the action diagram in Fig. 3.2.

WAIT, indicating that the system will wait after executing the remainder of the bracket until the operator presses the ESC key. This gives the operator as much time as he wants to read the printout.

Figure 3.5 expands the Buzzword Generator bracket into executable code. The commands of the language are now attached to the brackets of the action diagram. Making the brackets language-specific can be done automatically by the software for building the action diagram.

TITLES VERSUS CODE STRUCTURE   At the higher levels of the design process, action diagram brackets represent the names of processes and subprocesses. As the designer descends into program-level detail, the brackets become program constructs; the program-construct brackets may be labeled with appropriate control words. These may

```
ENTER BUZZWORD GENERATOR

    CLEAR
    SHOW "I WILL GENERATE A SCREEN FULL OF 'BUZZ PHRASES' EVERY "
    "TIME YOU HIT 'ENTER'.  WHEN YOU WANT TO STOP, HIT 'ESC'

    TEXT ADJECTIVE1 (10,16), ADJECTIVE2 (10,16), NOUN (10,16)

    ADJECTIVE1 (1) = "INTEGRATED", "TOTAL", "SYSTEMATIZED", "PARALLEL",
        "FUNCTIONAL", "RESPONSIVE", "OPTIONAL", "SYNCHRONIZED",
        "COMPATIBLE", BALANCED"

    ADJECTIVE2 (1) = "MANAGEMENT", "ORGANIZATIONAL", "MONITORED",
        "RECIPROCAL", "DIGITAL", "LOGISTICAL", "TRANSITIONAL",
        "INCREMENTAL", "THIRD GENERATION", "POLICY"

    NOUN(1) = "OPTION", "FLEXIBILITY", "CAPABILITY", "MOBILITY",
        "PROGRAMMING", "CONCEPT", "TIME PHASE", "PROJECTION",
        "HARDWARE", "CONTINGENCY"


    SEED

WHILE KEY NOT = "ESC"
    COUNT = 1

    WHILE COUNT < 22
        A=INT(RND(10)+1)
        B=INT(RND(10)+1)
        C=INT(RND(10)+1)

        SHOW ADJECTIVE1(A)+" "+ADJECTIVE2(B)+" "+NOUN(C)

        COUNT = COUNT+1

        END

        WAIT
        END

    CHAIN "GAMES_MENU"
EXIT
```

Figure 3.5 An expansion of the action diagram of Fig. 3.4 into program code. This is an executable program in the fourth-generation language MANTIS [1]. Successive decomposition of a diagram until it becomes executable code is called *ultimate decomposition.*

be the control words of a particular programming language, or they may be language-independent words.

    To show the difference between title brackets and program brackets, title brackets may have an asterisk at the top of the bracket and may have a dotted vertical line, thus:

```
┌─* GAME PROGRAM
│
└─

┌─* GAME PROGRAM
│   ┌─* SPELLING GAME
│   ├─* ALIEN FLEET
│   ├─* BUZZ GENERATOR
│   │ PRINT INSTRUCTIONS TO USE
│   │ DO MORE THINGS
│   ├─* KILL THE BUREAUCRAT
│   └─
│
└─
```

Title brackets may be drawn with dotted lines and the program brackets with solid lines. The title brackets may be single, repetition, IF-ELSE, or case brackets. The designer may use a mix of title brackets and program brackets such that by displaying the title brackets only, he sees an overview structure of his design.

He may also use comments to clarify his design. A comment line starts with an asterisk. The software may be instructed to display or to hide the comments.

HIERARCHICAL ORDERING

Hierarchical ordering is part of the concept of functional decomposition. The design method of dividing program functions into subfunctions results in a hierarchical (or tree-like) program structure. General program functions are placed at the upper levels of the hierarchy, while more detailed functions are placed at the lower levels of the hierarchy. This tree-like program structure makes the program much easier to understand because the program can be built and understood level by level, and each new level adds more detailed program logic.

The concept of hierarchical ordering is used in many natural systems as well as in business organizations. Hierarchical organization makes it possible to handle control, delegation, and communication problems that can arise in complex systems involving many parts. In the same way, hierarchical organization can help solve complexity problems in large software programs and systems.

One of the fundamental differences between structured and unstructured programs is that structured programs are always hierarchically structured. In a sequentially structured program, one program function (module) is executed after another. When the last function in the sequence has been executed, program execution stops. Spaghetti-like *branches* are used among the code segments. A sequential structure works well only for small programs containing a few modules. For larger programs, a hierarchical structure is needed to help make the program manageable. A hierarchical structure allows us to remove upper levels and still have usable lower levels that can become building blocks for a variation of a system or the base of new systems. This is a powerful mechanism for creating programs that are easy to change and easy to understand.

TREE-STRUCTURE CHARTS   Various forms of structure charts (tree-structure charts) are used to show the hierarchical structure of a structured program. Figure 3.6 is an example of a structure chart for processing an account. Each box on the chart represents one program module. Logically, a module is one problem-related function that the program performs, such as CALCULATE FINANCE CHARGE or PRINT NOTICE. The module name is written inside the box:

> CALCULATE
> FINANCE
> CHARGE

Modules performing high-level functions are placed at the upper levels of the hierarchy, while modules performing low-level, detailed functions appear at lower levels. Looking down the hierarchy, the modules of each successive level contain functions that further define functions performed at the preceding level. For example, the function PROCESS STANDARD TRANSACTION is composed of three subfunctions: CALCULATE FINANCE CHARGE, UPDATE TRANSACTION RECORD, and UPDATE ACCOUNT BALANCE.

CONTROL RELATIONSHIPS   An arrow drawn between two modules at successive levels in the structure chart hierarchy means that program control is passed from one module to the second in the direction of the arrow. We say that the first module *invokes* or *calls* the second module. For example, in Fig. 3.6, module PROCESS STANDARD TRANSACTION invokes module CALCULATE FINANCE CHARGE. After module CALCULATE FINANCE CHARGE finishes executing, control is returned to PROCESS STANDARD TRANSACTION. Returning control to the invoking module is an important difference between structured and unstructured programs and is a major reason why structured programs are easier to understand. The control rules for a structured program have been standardized and are simple. They are listed in Box 3.1.

FORMS OF TREE STRUCTURE   A structure chart as shown in Fig. 3.6 is one way to draw a tree structure. There are various other ways to draw tree structures to show hierarchical organization. An equivalent tree-structure chart is shown in Fig. 3.7. The difference is that this is a left-to-right tree rather than a top-to-bottom tree. A left-to-right tree is read from the left to the right; higher levels of the hierarchy are to the left and lower levels to the right. Within a level, the chart is read from the top down. One advantage of left-to-right trees is that they spread out vertically rather than horizontally and can be more easily printed on a computer printer.

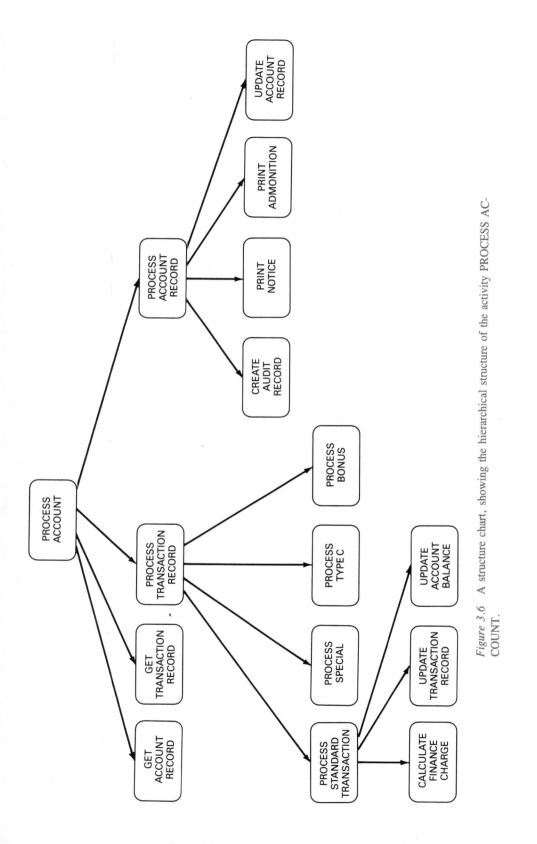

Figure 3.6 A structure chart, showing the hierarchical structure of the activity PROCESS AC-COUNT.

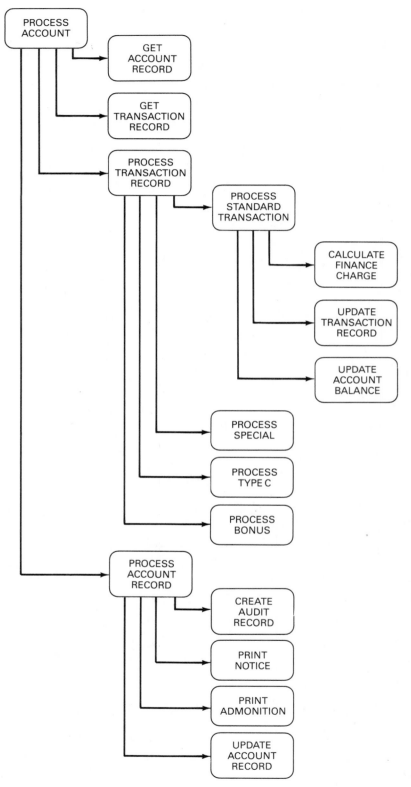

Figure 3.7 The diagram in Fig. 3.6, drawn in a left-to-right format.

BOX 3.1   Control Rules for a Structured Program

- There is one and only one module at the top of the hierarchy. This is where control originates when the program begins executing. This module is called the *root*.

- From the root, control is passed down the hierarchy level by level to the other program modules. Control is always passed back to the invoking module. Therefore, when the program finishes executing, control returns to the root.

Note: Structure charts and action diagrams have additional constructs to show how data and control signals are passed between functions. This is discussed in the following chapter.

LEFT-TO-RIGHT TREES   Action diagrams are tree-structure charts. Because they are hierarchical, they can show the structure of structured programs. They are left-to-right trees. Figure 3.8 shows the same information as Figures 3.6 and 3.7.

Figure 3.8 is simple to draw. The designer draws few lines. The result is closer to actual code. Since we must eventually convert our diagrams into code,

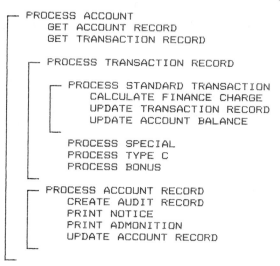

```
┌── PROCESS ACCOUNT
│      GET ACCOUNT RECORD
│      GET TRANSACTION RECORD
│
│   ┌── PROCESS TRANSACTION RECORD
│   │
│   │  ┌── PROCESS STANDARD TRANSACTION
│   │  │      CALCULATE FINANCE CHARGE
│   │  │      UPDATE TRANSACTION RECORD
│   │  │      UPDATE ACCOUNT BALANCE
│   │  │
│   │  │   PROCESS SPECIAL
│   │  │   PROCESS TYPE C
│   │  │   PROCESS BONUS
│   │  └──
│   │── PROCESS ACCOUNT RECORD
│   │      CREATE AUDIT RECORD
│   │      PRINT NOTICE
│   │      PRINT ADMONITION
│   │      UPDATE ACCOUNT RECORD
│   └──
└──
```

Figure 3.8   Figure 3.7 redrawn in an action diagram format.

a simple conversion that minimizes the change in format helps minimize the likelihood of making mistakes.

**MISSING
INFORMATION**
Unfortunately, structure charts as commonly drawn have important information missing. There are certain facts we ought to know about the functions in Fig. 3.6, 3.7, or 3.8 that these diagrams do not tell us:

1. When performing PROCESS ACCOUNT we do GET ACCOUNT RECORD *once* but do GET TRANSACTION RECORD and PROCESS TRANSACTION RECORD *many times*.

2. We do not perform PROCESS ACCOUNT RECORD for every account. We only do it if the account is active.

3. There is a problem with the functions invoked by PROCESS TRANSACTION RECORD. There are three types of transactions: standard transaction, special, and type C. We select *one* of the three blocks PROCESS STANDARD TRANSACTION, PROCESS SPECIAL, and PROCESS TYPE C; however, we *always* invoke PROCESS BONUS.

4. Of the four functions invoked by PROCESS ACCOUNT RECORD, we *always* do CREATE AUDIT RECORD and UPDATE ACCOUNT RECORD but do *either* PRINT NOTICE *or* PRINT ADMONITION.

Repetition, conditions, and mutually exclusive selection need to be shown on the structure chart, otherwise the structure chart is misleading.

Figure 3.9 redraws Fig. 3.8, adding the missing information:

1. GET TRANSACTION RECORD and PROCESS TRANSACTION RECORD are shown inside a repetition bracket.

2. PROCESS ACCOUNT RECORD is inside a condition bracket: IF ACCOUNT ACTIVE.

3. A case-structure bracket is drawn for PROCESS STANDARD TRANSACTION, PROCESS SPECIAL, and PROCESS TYPE C. PROCESS BONUS is outside of this case structure.

4. An IF-ELSE bracket contains PRINT NOTICE and PRINT ADMONITION.

The structure that the designer wanted to show in Fig. 3.6 is better represented in Fig. 3.9.

NESTING
Structured programs have control constructs nested one inside another. This is an application of hierarchical ordering.

When the constructs are nested several levels deep, it becomes difficult to understand the program structure. Diagrams help make nested structures easier

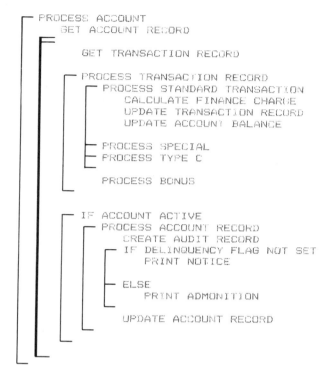

Figure 3.9   The action diagram of Fig. 3.8 with repetition, condition, and case brackets showing important structural information.

to understand by providing a graphic picture of the levels. By looking at the diagram, it is easy to see the entry point and exit point of each construct and exactly how they fit into one another.

The brackets of action diagrams show nesting clearly. Inside brackets there may be other brackets. Many brackets may be nested. Figure 3.10 shows nested IFs. The brackets help identify each matching pair of IFs and ELSEs so we can check that the logic is correct. Figure 3.11 shows an IF structure nested inside a two-level nested DO WHILE structure. Again, the brackets of the action diagram help us see the logical structure more clearly.

PROCEDURES

Often subroutines or subprocedures are drawn on an action diagram. They may be drawn as a round-cornered box with the name of the subprocedure inside the box:

BACKORDER
PROCEDURE

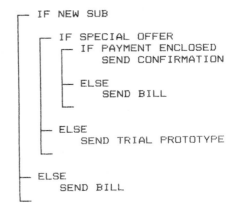

Figure 3.10   An action diagram showing a three-level nested IF structure.

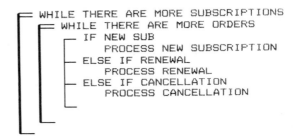

Figure 3.11   An action diagram showing an IF structure inside a two-level DO WHILE structure.

It will be exploded into detail showing the actions it contains in another action diagram.

The use of procedure boxes enables the program designer to concentrate on the parts of a procedure with which he is familiar or that he considers the most critical. Another person may fill in the details for the boxes. This enables an elusive or complex program design to be worked out a step at a time.

Procedure boxes make action diagrams a powerful tool for designing procedures at many levels of abstraction. The topmost level of abstraction shows the most simplified view, while the bottommost level gives the finest details of program logic.

Top-down design can be done by first creating a gross structure with procedure boxes, remaining vague about the contents of each box. The gross structure then can be broken down into successive levels of detail. Each explosion of a box adds another degree of detail, which might itself contain actions and boxes.

Figure 3.12 shows a very high level action diagram for a subscription system. It shows that in order to process a subscription, two procedures, GET

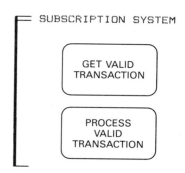

Figure 3.12 A very high level action diagram representing the design of a subscription system. The two procedure boxes GET VALID TRANSACTION and PROCESS VALID TRANSACTION will be exploded to show the program logic they contain in another action diagram.

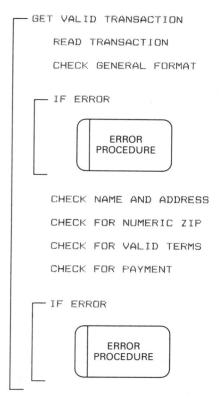

Figure 3.13 An action diagram showing the logic in the procedure GET VALID TRANSACTION from Fig. 3.12.

VALID TRANSACTION and PROCESS VALID TRANSACTION, are needed. Figure 3.13 shows another action diagram for the subscription system. This action diagram explodes the procedure GET VALID TRANSACTION to show its detailed logic.

PROCEDURES NOT YET DESIGNED

In some cases, the designer may wish to specify procedures that are not yet designed. He can represent this as a box with rounded corners and a right edge composed of question marks:

```
         ┌─────────────── ?
         │                ?
         │  ERROR         ?
         │  PROCEDURE     ?
         │                ?
         └───────────────
```

COMMON PROCEDURES

Some procedures appear more than once in an action diagram because they are called (or invoked) from more than one place in the logic. These procedures are called *common procedures*. They are indicated by drawing a vertical line down the left-hand side of the procedure box as shown:

```
         ┌┬─────────────┐
         ││              │
         ││  ERROR       │
         ││  PROCEDURE   │
         └┴─────────────┘
```

CONTRACT AND EXPAND

A very useful feature of an action diagram editor is the ability to contract large action diagrams, hiding much of the detail. The user selects a bracket and says "CONTRACT". The bracket shrinks so that only its top line is seen. Any nested brackets within the contracted bracket disappear. To show the user that information has been hidden, three dots are inserted in front of the text line of the contracted bracket.

In Figure 3.14 the user sets the cursor on a portion of a case structure and says "CONTRACT". The resulting contracted code contains a line beginning with three dots. In Figure 3.15 the user selects this line and says "EX-PAND".

"CONTRACT" may be used multiple times to create hierarchies of contraction. "EXPAND" then reveals lines which themselves can be expanded.

Contracting and expanding permits large programs to be manipulated with ease.

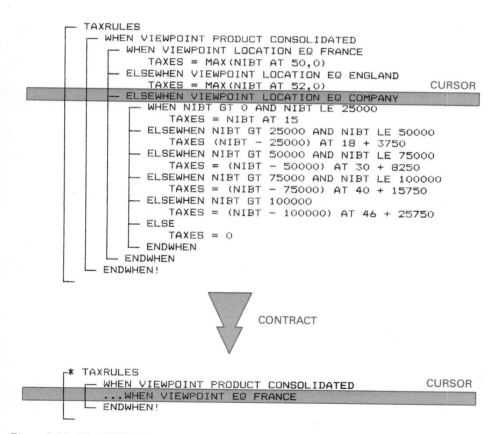

Figure 3.14   The CONTRACT command hides the contents of a bracket. To show that there is hidden information three dots are placed at the start of the contracted bracket.

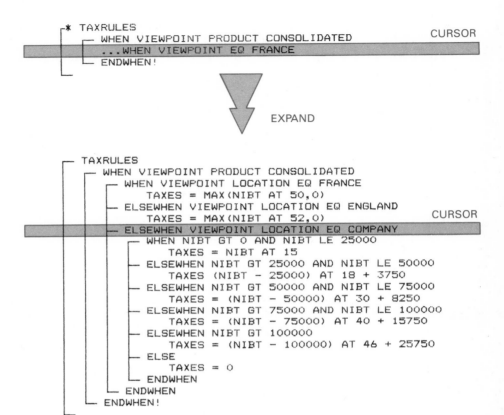

Figure 3.15 The EXPAND command can be applied to lines beginning with three dots. It reveals their hidden contents. This figure and Figure 3.14 show the use of CONTRACT and EXPAND. With these commands large designs can be reduced to summary form. These commands are very useful in practice.

SUMMARY   Box 3.2 summarizes the action diagram components
                        we have discussed in this chapter. In the next chapter, inputs and outputs will be discussed.

BOX 3.2   Components in an action diagram

Hierarchical Organization

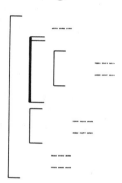

Action diagrams are left-to-right tree-structure charts that show hierarchical organization.

Nesting

Brackets are used to show nesting and hierarchy.

Title Brackets

```
┌─* ERROR ROUTINE
│
│
│
│
│
└
```

A bracket that is merely a title has an asterisk attached to its top bar. The bracket may be dotted.

Contracted Brackets

```
┌ ...DO N = 1 TO 10
└ END


┌─*...OPTIMIZATION ROUTINE
└
```

Three dots preceding a line indicate that actions following that line have been contracted any may be displayed with an EXPAND command when an action diagram editor is employed.

BOX 3.2 *(Continued)*

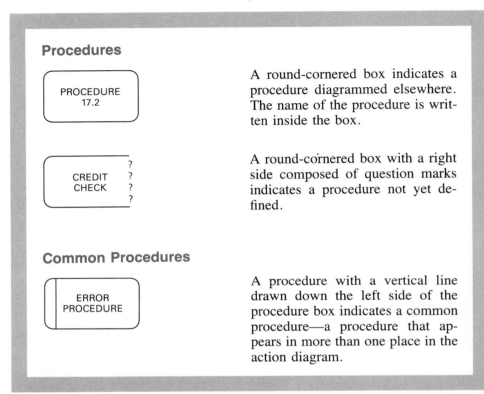

Procedures

PROCEDURE
17.2

A round-cornered box indicates a procedure diagrammed elsewhere. The name of the procedure is written inside the box.

CREDIT   ?
CHECK   ?
              ?

A round-cornered box with a right side composed of question marks indicates a procedure not yet defined.

Common Procedures

ERROR
PROCEDURE

A procedure with a vertical line drawn down the left side of the procedure box indicates a common procedure—a procedure that appears in more than one place in the action diagram.

EXERCISES

1. Describe in your own words the design method called *functional decomposition*.

2. Describe in your own words the term *ultimate decomposition*.

3. Why are structured programs hierarchically ordered?

4. Redraw the following tree-structure chart as a left-to-right tree-structure chart. What advantages does the left-to-right format offer?

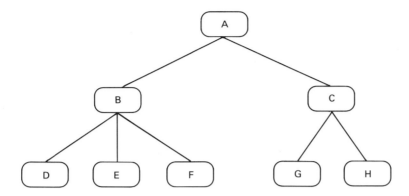

5. Redraw the tree-structure chart in Exercise 4 as an action diagram.

6. The control rules for action diagrams are the same as tree-structure charts. What are they?

7. Draw an action diagram representing the following program logic:

> To process a subscription renewal involves the following: Get the subscriber record for name, address, amount due. For each product ordered, get the product record. Check product availability. If product is not available, process backorder and send confirmation. If only the field-test version is available, send offer to be a beta test site. If product is available, process order, calculate bill, send bill.

REFERENCE

1. The example in Figures 3.2 to 3.5 is adapted from a program in the *Mantis User's Guide,* Cincom Systems, Inc., Cincinnati, OH, 1982.

4 INPUTS AND OUTPUTS

When designing programs, it is useful to show the inputs to and outputs from each module. When one module invokes another module, what data or control flags does it pass to it, and what data or control flags does it receive back?

Showing the inputs and outputs, the designer can use the computer to provide a valuable level of checking to ensure that all the inputs and outputs balance. He also can link his designs to a data dictionary and data model.

To show inputs and outputs to a module, the open bracket (which is quick to draw) is closed into a rectangle. Nested brackets become nested rectangles:

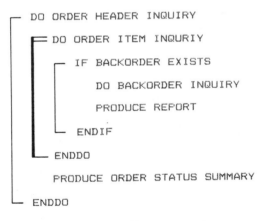

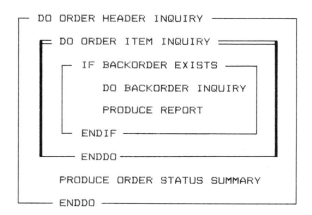

The open brackets may be thought of as a shorthand way of drawing the rectangles. (See Fig. 4.1.)

The data used by a process (the input data) are written at the top right-hand corner. The data that the process creates (the output data) are written at the bottom right-hand corner:

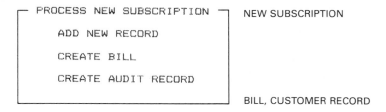

Figure 4.2 shows the above rectangle nested in other rectangles, and the inputs and outputs are shown for each. Figure 4.2 is an expansion of Fig. 4.1. It contains the information on a data-flow diagram that also shows inputs and outputs.

Figure 4.3 shows an action diagram of a recipe for cooking seafood gumbo. The ingredients are shown as inputs in the top right-hand corner of the outer block.

CORRELATION OF INPUTS AND OUTPUTS

When inputs and outputs are shown as in Figures 4.2 and 4.3, it is possible for a computer to check that every input goes into some process and every output comes from some process. The inputs and outputs can be correlated by the action diagram editor while the designer creates the design.

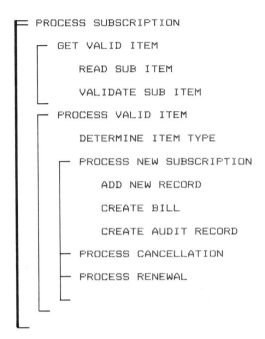

Figure 4.1   A high-level action diagram.

We would like to ask the reader whether the inputs and outputs correlate in the seafood gumbo recipe of Fig. 4.3. In fact they do not. We have made a deliberate mistake. Can you spot it?

Figure 4.4 shows a design for an order-servicing application. VALIDATE CUSTOMER is shown in detail. The blocks below it need further expansion. Do the inputs and outputs correlate correctly? The red arrows on Fig. 4.5 show that they do. This checking can be done by computer.

The design of simple programs does not need automated correlation in inputs and outputs or diagrams like Fig. 4.4 that show the inputs and outputs. In the design of complex specifications, the *automated* correlation of inputs and outputs among program modules is essential if mistakes are to be avoided.

DATA-FLOW   The input/output information on diagrams like Fig.
DIAGRAMS   4.2 is sometimes drawn with data-flow diagrams.
                       Figure 4.6 shows a layered data-flow diagram that
corresponds to Fig. 4.2. As we will see in Chapter 8, if a data-flow diagram is drawn with sufficient rigor, it can be *automatically* converted into an action diagram. Conversely, an action diagram could be automatically converted into a data-flow diagram. Unlike a data-flow diagram, an action diagram can be

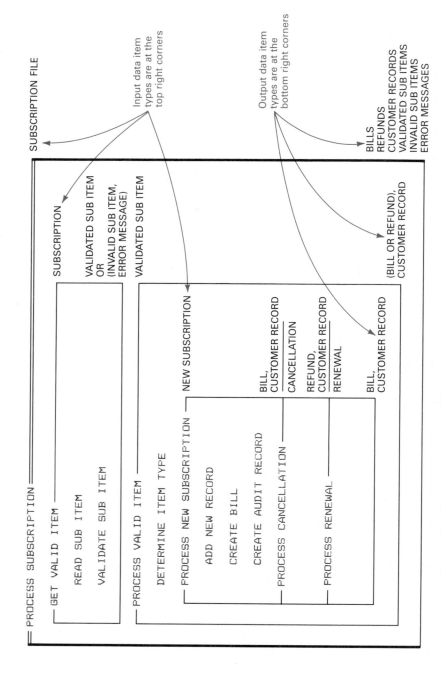

Figure 4.2 The bracket format of Fig. 4.1 is here expanded into the rectangular format used to show the data item types that are input and output to each process. This is designed for computerized cross-checking.

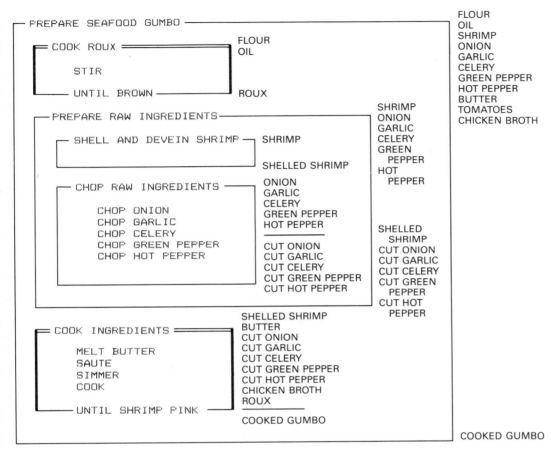

Figure 4.3   An action diagram showing a recipe for making seafood gumbo. The inputs to each module are at the top right-hand corner. The outputs are at the bottom right-hand corner.

extended directly to show the program structure including conditions, case structures, and loop control.

   Some systems analysts draw large data-flow diagrams nested to many layers. Often the data on such diagrams do not correlate correctly. Computer cross-checking can help to make complex specifications more accurate. It is commonly the case that mapping a specification written in English to action diagrams reveals many omissions and errors.

   Particularly important is the linking of the data on action diagrams to the data dictionary and data model used.

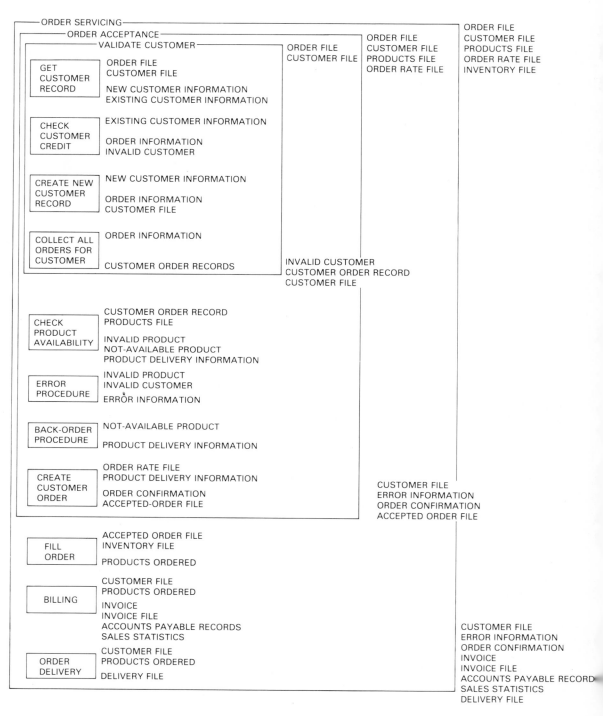

Figure 4.4 An action diagram giving an overview of an order-servicing system, showing inputs and outputs.

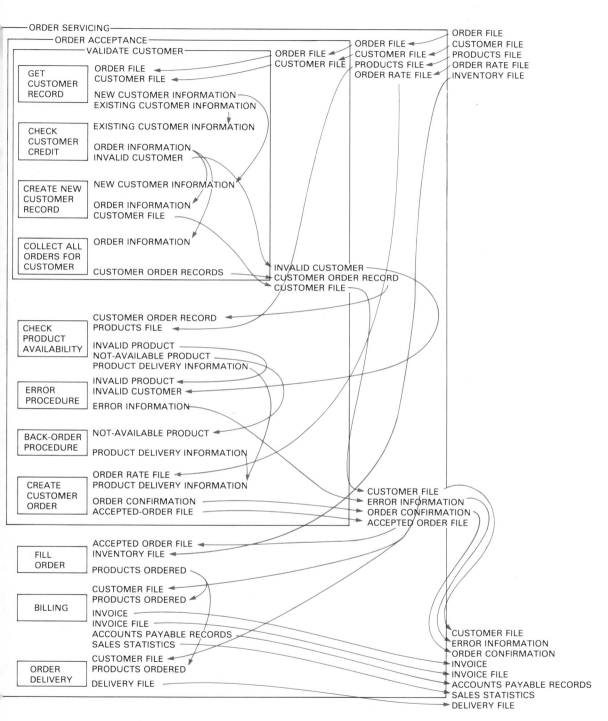

Figure 4.5 Red arrows show correlations of inputs and outputs in Fig. 4.4.

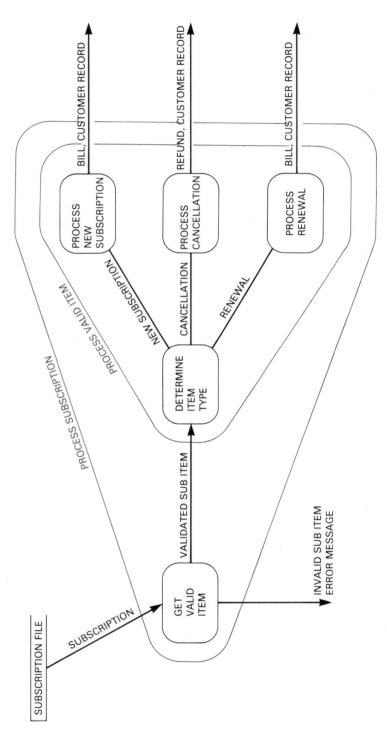

Figure 4.6   A data-flow diagram corresponding to Fig. 4.2.

SUMMARY　　　　Box 4.1 summarizes the action diagram components
　　　　　　　　　　we have discussed in this chapter. In the next chapter, data-base actions will be discussed.

BOX 4.1　Components of an action diagram

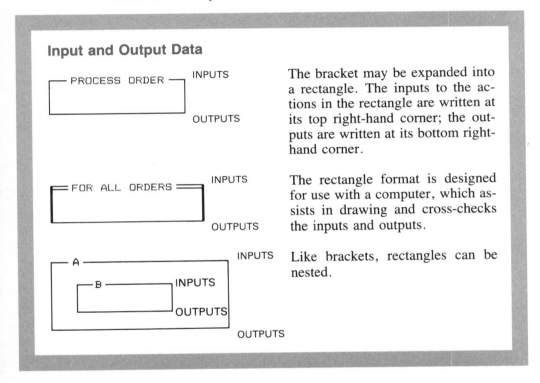

Input and Output Data

PROCESS ORDER — INPUTS ... OUTPUTS	The bracket may be expanded into a rectangle. The inputs to the actions in the rectangle are written at its top right-hand corner; the outputs are written at its bottom right-hand corner.
FOR ALL ORDERS — INPUTS ... OUTPUTS	The rectangle format is designed for use with a computer, which assists in drawing and cross-checks the inputs and outputs.
A ... INPUTS / B INPUTS OUTPUTS ... OUTPUTS	Like brackets, rectangles can be nested.

EXERCISES

1. Extend the action diagram you drew in Exercise 7 of Chapter 3 to include the inputs and outputs for the function PROCESS RENEWAL.

2. Draw an action diagram showing the inputs and outputs for the following recipe for Brandy Bowl Flamer.

1 fifth fruit-flavored brandy

1/2 cup sugar

twist of lemon

4 cups boiling water

Heat first three ingredients, stirring until sugar dissolves. Do not boil. Pour into heated silver bowl, light carefully with a match, and as it burns, slowly stir in boiling water. (Makes 18 cups.)

5 DATA-BASE ACTION DIAGRAMS

Most of the action diagrams drawn for commercial data processing systems relate to data bases or on-line files. A common action on these diagrams is the data-base or file operation. It is desirable that these operations relate to the dictionary and data model employed.

SIMPLE DATA-BASE ACTIONS

We will distinguish between simple and compound data-base actions.

A simple data-base action is an operation applied to *one instance of one record type*. There are four types of simple actions:

- CREATE
- READ
- UPDATE
- DELETE

The memorable acronym CRUD is sometimes used to refer to these and to help remember them.

On an action diagram, a simple data-base action is represented by a rectangular box. The name of the record is written inside the box; the type of action is written on the left side of the box:

READ | SUBSCRIBER

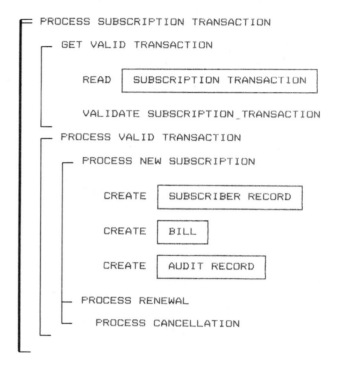

Figure 5.1   An action diagram showing four simple data-base actions.

Figure 5.1 shows an action diagram with several data-base actions.

COMPOUND
DATA-BASE
ACTIONS

A *compound data-base action* also takes a single action against a data base, but the action may use multiple records of the same type and sometimes of more than one type. It may search or sort a logical file. It may be a relational operation that uses an entire relation. It may be a relational operation requiring a join or two or more relations. Fourth-generation languages have instructions for a variety of compound data-base actions. Examples of such instructions are:

- SEARCH
- SORT
- SELECT certain records from a relation or a file
- JOIN two or more relations or files

- PROJECT a relation or file to obtain a subset of it
- DUPLICATE

CREATE, READ, UPDATE, and DELETE may also be used for compound data-base actions. For example, DELETE could be used to delete a whole file.

Most of the data-base actions in traditional data processing are simple data-base actions. As relational data bases and nonprocedural languages spread, *compound* data-base actions will become more common.

A compound data-base action is represented as a double rectangular box. The name of the record is written inside the box; the data-base action is written on the left-hand side of the box:

Often a compound data-base action needs a qualifying statement associated with it to describe how it is performed. For example:

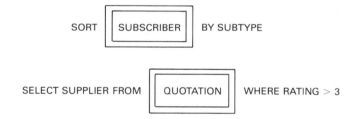

AUTOMATIC NAVIGATION

A compound data-base action may require automatic navigation by the data-base management system. Relational data bases and a few nonrelational ones have this capability. For a data base without automatic navigation, a compiler of a fourth-generation language may generate the required sequence of data accesses.

With a compound data-base action, search parameters or conditions are often an integral part of the action itself. They are written inside a bracket containing the access box.

SIMPLE VERSUS COMPOUND DATA-BASE ACCESSES

There are many procedures that can be done with either simple data-base accesses or compound accesses. If a traditional DBMS is used, the programmer navigates through the data base with simple accesses. If the DBMS or language compiler has automatic navigation, higher-level statements using compound data-base accesses may be employed.

Suppose, for example, that we want to give a $1000 bonus to all employees who are salesmen in the Southeast region. In IBM's data-base language SQL we would write:

```
UPDATE EMPLOYEE
SET SALARY = SALARY + 1000
WHERE JOB = 'SALESMAN'
AND REGION = 'SOUTHEAST'
```

We can diagram this with a compound data-base action as follows:

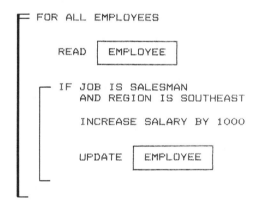

```
UPDATE  | EMPLOYEE |

WHERE JOB IS SALESMAN
AND REGION IS SOUTHEAST
INCREASE SALARY BY 1000
```

With simple actions (no automatic navigation), we can diagram the same procedure as follows:

```
FOR ALL EMPLOYEES

    READ  | EMPLOYEE |

    IF JOB IS SALESMAN
       AND REGION IS SOUTHEAST

       INCREASE SALARY BY 1000

    UPDATE  | EMPLOYEE |
```

RELATIONAL JOINS

A relational join merges two relations (logical files or tables) on the basis of a common field. For example, the EMPLOYEE relation and the REGION relation for a company may look like this:

REGION

REGION-ID	LOCATION	REGION-STATUS	SALES-YTD	
001	NEW YORK	1	198,725	
004	CHICAGO	7	92,615	
006	LA	3	156,230	

EMPLOYEE

SSN	NAME	SALARY	JOB-CODE	LOCATION	
337-48-2713	SMITH	42000	07	CHICAGO	
341-25-3340	JOHNSON	39000	15	LA	
391-62-1167	STRATTON	27000	05	LA	

These relations are combined in such a way that the LOCATION field of the EMPLOYEE relation becomes the same as the LOCATION field of the REGION relation. We can express this with the statement:

REGION.LOCATION = EMPLOYEE.LOCATION

The result is a combined record as follows:

SSN	NAME	SALARY	JOB-CODE	LOCATION	REGION-ID	REGION-STATUS	SALES-YTD
337-48-2713	SMITH	42000	07	CHICAGO	004	7	92,651
341-25-3340	JOHNSON	39000	15	LA	006	3	156,230
391-62-1167	STRATTON	27000	05	LA	006	3	156,230

The data-base system may not combine them in reality but may join the appropriate data in response to the request.

A join is shown on an action diagram by linking the boxes with an access operation applying to the combination:

READ [REGION]===[EMPLOYEE]   REGION. LOCATION = EMPLOYEE.LOCATION

A statement may follow the joined records showing how they are joined. Often this is not necessary because the joined records contain one common field which is the basis for the join. For example, the EMPLOYEE record probably contains the field LOCATION, in which case we can simply show:

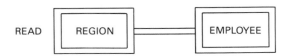

We might, for example, constrain the join operation by asking for employees whose job code is 15, whose salary exceeds $35,000, and whose region status is 3. The result would then be:

SSN	NAME	SALARY
341-25-3340	JOHNSON	39000

From the join of EMPLOYEE and REGION, we might say SELECT SSN, NAME, REGION-STATUS, LOCATION. With the data-base language SQL from IBM, and others, this operation would be expressed as follows:

SELECT SSN, NAME, REGION-STATUS, LOCATION

FROM REGION, EMPLOYEE

WHERE REGION.LOCATION = EMPLOYEE.LOCATION

AND JOB-CODE = 15

AND SALARY > 35000

This can be written on an action diagram as follows:

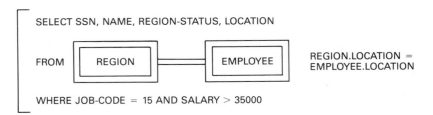

For a simple query such as this, we do not need a diagram representation. The query language itself is clear enough. For a complex operation, we certainly need to diagram the use of compound data actions.

Similarly, a relational join can be represented with either a sequence of single actions or one compound action, as shown in Fig. 5.2. In this example,

Data used in this example

EMPLOYEE

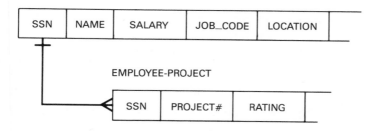

A PROCEDURE FOR GIVING EMPLOYEES AN INCREASE IN SALARY, USING SIMPLE
DATA-BASE ACTIONS:

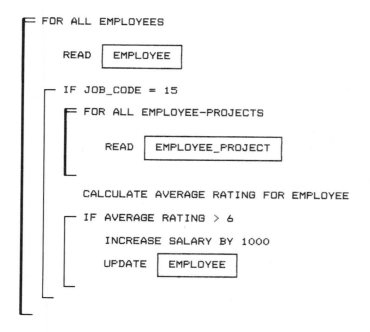

THE SAME PROCEDURE USING A COMPOUND DATA-BASE ACTION:

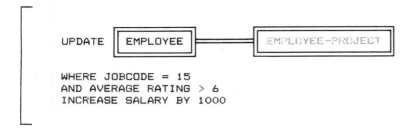

Figure 5.2 Illustration of a procedure that may be done with either three
simple data-base access commands or one compound access command.

there are multiple projects in an EMPLOYEE PROJECT record showing how employees were rated for their work on each project to which they were assigned. They were given a salary raise if their average rating exceeded 6.

THREE-WAY JOINS

In some cases, three-way joins are useful. Suppose an accountant is concerned that accounts receivable are becoming too high. He wants to telephone any branch manager who has six-month-old debt outstanding from a customer. The following record structures exist:

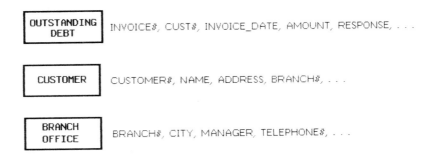

He enters the following query:

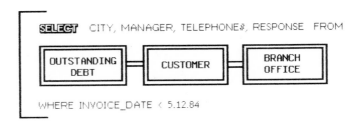

The three-way join is shown in a similar fashion to two-way joins. Figure 5.3 shows this three-way join expressed in the language SQL.

SUMMARY

Box 5.1 summarizes the components of an action diagram that were discussed in this chapter.

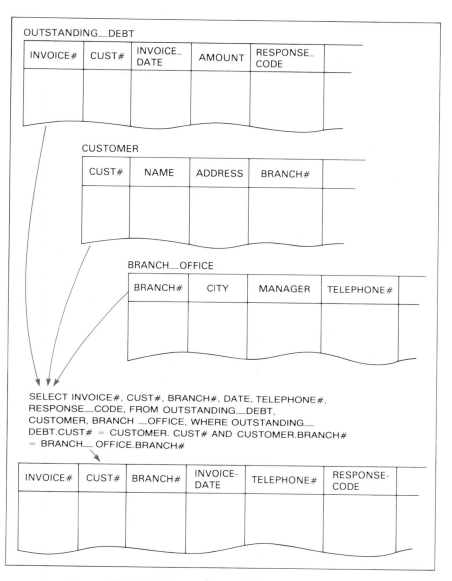

OUTSTANDING__DEBT

INVOICE#	CUST#	INVOICE_ DATE	AMOUNT	RESPONSE_ CODE	

CUSTOMER

CUST#	NAME	ADDRESS	BRANCH#

BRANCH__OFFICE

BRANCH#	CITY	MANAGER	TELEPHONE#	

SELECT INVOICE#, CUST#, BRANCH#, DATE, TELEPHONE#,
RESPONSE__CODE, FROM OUTSTANDING__DEBT,
CUSTOMER, BRANCH __OFFICE, WHERE OUTSTANDING__
DEBT.CUST# = CUSTOMER. CUST# AND CUSTOMER.BRANCH#
= BRANCH__ OFFICE.BRANCH#

INVOICE#	CUST#	BRANCH#	INVOICE- DATE	TELEPHONE#	RESPONSE- CODE	

Figure 5.3 A join between three relations expressed in SQL.

BOX 5.1 Components of an action diagram

THE FOLLOWING RELATE TO DATA-BASE ACTIONS

Simple Data-Base Actions

```
| ------
| ------
|  READ  | SUBSCRIBER |
| ------
| ------
|_
```

A rectangle containing the name of a record type is preceded by the type of simple data-base action: CREATE, READ, UPDATE, or DELETE.

Compound Data-Base Actions

```
| ------
| ------
|  SORT  || SUBSCRIBER ||   BY SUB_NO
|_
```

A double rectangle containing the name of the record type is preceded by a compound data-access action such as SORT, JOIN, PROJECT, or SELECT.

```
|  SELECT SUPPLIER FROM  || QUOTATION ||   WHERE RATING > 6
|_
```

It may be followed by a qualifying statement.

EXERCISES

1. Explain the difference between simple and compound data-base actions. How do we distinguish them on an action diagram?

2. Redraw the action diagram you drew in Exercise 7 of Chapter 3 and extended in Exercise 1 of Chapter 4, this time including the data-base actions.

3. Redraw the following action diagram with compound data-base actions as an equivalent action diagram with simple data-base actions.

```
┌──
│
│
│      UPDATE    ┌┤ SUBSCRIBER ├┐
│                └──────────────┘
│
│      WHERE SUB_TYPE = "SPECIAL"
│      AND REGION = "MIDWEST"
│      DECREASE AMT_DUE BY AMT_DUE * .15
│
└──
```

6 LANGUAGE DIALECTS AND STRUCTURED PROGRAMMING

The brackets of action diagrams can be labeled with the commands of a particular programming language. Alternatively, they can be labeled in a language-independent fashion. Figure 6.1 shows action diagram brackets with language-independent labels. Figure 6.1 represents the basic constructs of structured programming.

The other diagrams in this chapter show action diagrams with the control commands of other languages. A software tool for creating and editing action diagrams can put the commands of a particular language onto the diagrams and can switch from one language to another.

FOURTH-GENERATION LANGUAGES

Particularly important today is the spread of relatively new languages called *fourth-generation languages*. These are sometimes called *high-productivity languages*. Some of them are referred to as *end-user languages*. An objective of these languages is to make programming much quicker and easier than it is with languages such as COBOL or PL/I. Fourth-generation languages use nonprocedural constructs such as report generators, screen formatters, menu generators, dialogue generators, decision tables, screens for specifying data, and screens for specifying rules [1]. They are often coupled to data-base facilities, data dictionaries, and data models. They employ commands such as those on action diagrams to express the flow and structure of programs.

When fourth-generation languages are used, the wording on the action diagram may be the wording that is used in coding programs with the language. Examples of this are as follows, starting after Figure 6.1:

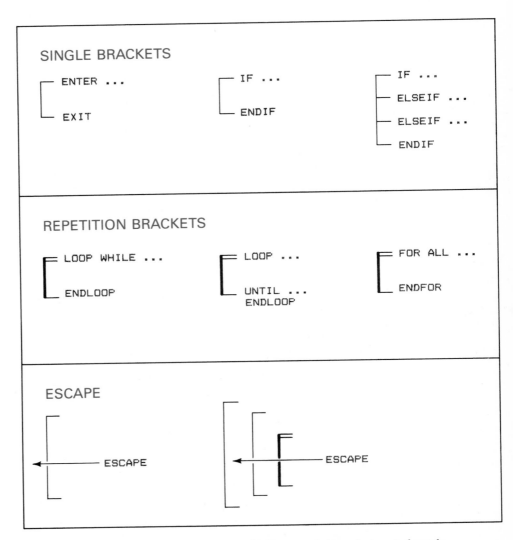

Figure 6.1 Program constructs with language-independent control words.

```
┌─ LOOP WHILE COUNT <25
│
└─ ENDLOOP


┌─ FOR ALL SUBSCRIBERS
│
└─ ENDFOR


┌─ SELECT
│     WHEN SALARY > 25000
│
│     ┌─ IF JOB_CODE = 15
│     │     -----
│     └─ ENDIF
├─ WHEN SALARY > 20000
│
├─ WHEN SALARY > 15000
│
│     ┌─ IF JOB_CODE = 07
│     │
│     │     ┌─ IF REGION = 05
│     │     │
│     │     │     -----
│     │     │
│     │     ├─ ELSE
│     │     │
│     │     │     -----
│     │     │
│     │     └─ ENDIF
│     └─ ENDIF
└─ ENDSELECT


┌─ FOR EACH REGION WHERE SALES_YTD > 1000000
│
└─ ENDFOR


┌─
│   ┌─ DO GRID
│   │   ┌─
│ ◄─┼───┤ IF C1 QUIT GRID
│   │   └─
│   └─ ENDDO
└─
```

Action diagrams are a valuable tool for creating programs with fourth-generation languages. Action diagram brackets with the commands of various fourth-generation languages can be seen in Figures 6.5 to 6.9.

A few fourth-generation languages are ill-structured and incomplete. If the commands of a language are such that a diagram like those in this chapter cannot be filled in, then the language cannot create many of the program constructs needed in a clean, well-structured program. Ill-structured languages are best avoided.

In the design of *new* languages it is desirable that the control structures fit onto action diagram brackets and that designers should be able to build their control structures graphically. The graphic, easy-to-visualize designs should be automatically converted to code structures.

There is much to be said for designing a system in a language-independent fashion, so that the design can be quickly implemented in alternate languages. One language might be used for quick prototyping and another for achieving good machine performance. Language-independent action diagrams serve as the basic documentation for programs and with a computerized tool can be quickly implemented in specific languages.

CONVERSION OF ACTION DIAGRAMS TO CODE   Different computer languages have different commands relating to the constructs drawn on action diagrams. If the action diagram is being edited on a computer screen, a menu of commands can be provided for any particular language. Using the language IDEAL, for example, the designer might select the word LOOP for the top of a repetition bracket, and the software automatically puts ENDLOOP at the bottom of the bracket. The designer might select IF, and the software creates the following bracket:

```
 ┌── IF


 ├── ELSE


 └── ENDIF
```

The user is asked to specify the IF condition.

Structures with the commands for a given language may be generated automatically. The objective is to speed up as much as possible the task of creating error-free code. With different menus of commands for different languages, a designer may switch from one language to another if necessary. This facilitates the adoption of different languages in the future.

ENFORCING CLEANLY STRUCTURED PROGRAMS

A good fourth-generation language should enforce simple, clean, easy-to-understand structures. Earlier languages did not do this. They allowed convoluted code in which it was easy to make errors. Consider, for example, the following PL/I code:

```
IF A = B THEN IF P = Q THEN IF W < 5 THEN B = 1;
   ELSE Q = W;
   ELSE;
ELSE A = 4;
```

Each ELSE clause is associated with the innermost preceding IF clause which does not yet have an ELSE clause. The second ELSE above has no statement with it, merely a semicolon. It is used to balance the second IF so that the statement after the third ELSE relates to the first IF. Confusing!

Drawn with an action diagram it is clearer:

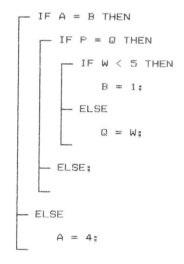

In a modern language, the code is simpler and clearer, and there is less danger of putting punctuation in the wrong place, as the following code written in MANTIS [2] illustrates:

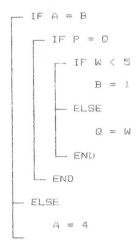

The meaning of control constructs in COBOL can also be confusing. Consider the following example of an actual COBOL coding error, which required several days to detect:

```
IF GRID-SWITCH = 'Y'
   IF ROW-COUNT = 01
      IF TYPE-CODE = 'A'
         PERFORM TITLE-PRINT
      ELSE
         PERFORM SCALE-PROCESS
ELSE
   SET LINE-NO TO +1.
```

According to the indentation, it was the programmer's intention to execute the statement SET LINE-NO TO +1 when the condition GRID-SWITCH = 'Y' is false. When scanning the code, a reader is likely to assume that the indentation correctly represents how the program works. However, this is not the correct interpretation. The COBOL compiler is oblivious to indentation and instead interprets the code according to the ANS COBOL language rule that for nested IF statements, each ELSE is paired with the first preceding IF that is not already paired with an ELSE. Therefore, this ELSE clause will be matched with the condition ROW-COUNT = 01.

If an action diagram editor had been used, this mistake would have been avoided. The editor would automatically set up each IF-ELSE pair as follows:

```
┌── IF GRID-SWITCH = "Y"
│
│    ┌── IF ROW-COUNT = 01
│    │
│    │    ┌── IF TYPE-CODE = "A"
│    │    │
│    │    │       PERFORM TITLE-PRINT
│    │    ├── ELSE
│    │    │
│    │    │       PERFORM SCALE-PROCESS
│    │    └──
│    ├── ELSE
│    │
│    │       NEXT SEQUENCE
│    └──
├── ELSE
│
│       SET LINE-NO TO +1
└──
```

Notice that COBOL has no end boundary marker on its IF structure. Also notice that an empty true or false part is not permitted. Instead, the NEXT SENTENCE clause must be used as a "no-op" instruction. When a COBOL version of the action diagram editor is used, selecting an IF structure provides the following:

```
┌── IF
│
│       NEXT SENTENCE
├── ELSE
│
│       NEXT SENTENCE
└──
```

The user can then add the condition and change the true and false parts appropriately.

Many languages in common use, such as FORTRAN, COBOL, and PL/I, were designed before structured programming was invented. They allow programmers to create confusing structures that are more likely to contain errors than well-structured languages. The use of action diagrams encourages good structuring and makes programs much easier to read and maintain. Figures 6.2 to 6.4 give illustrations of language code represented with action diagrams.

COBOL

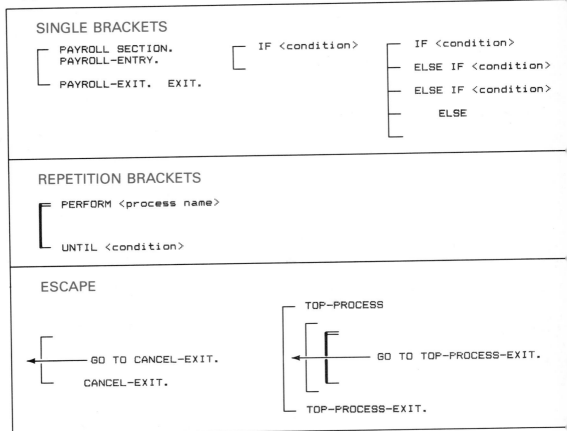

Figure 6.2   Brackets used with COBOL. Notice that COBOL's control constructs are quite limited when compared to more modern languages. For example, there is no end marker on the IF structure, and there is only one version of the loop structure. COBOL offers no DO WHILE.

END-USER COMPUTING

In our view, the best way to program is to use an efficient fourth-generation language and to design the programs with an interactive action-diagram editor that automatically puts the language control commands on the brackets.

The existence of fourth-generation languages that are easy to learn is encouraging many end users to build their own systems. With languages such as NOMAD, FOCUS, RAMIS, SAS, NATURAL, and APPLICATION FACTORY, they sometimes build complex applications. At BankAmerica, about

PL/I

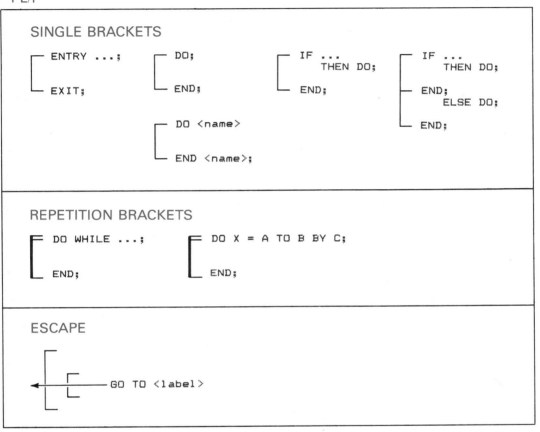

Figure 6.3　Brackets used with PL/I. PL/I is a complex language designed before structured programming was understood. Many old PL/I programs (like COBOL programs) are difficult to maintain because of their convoluted structures.

100,000 systems have been built by end users, mostly using NOMAD2. Many such programs are short, but some are long and complex. Some have over 1000 lines of code (which is equivalent to 10,000 lines of code in COBOL).

The authors have examined a variety of programs written by end users. They are often ill-structured. They are often difficult to understand and very difficult to maintain. Users often make mistakes with incorrect END commands, CASE structures, EXITS, and so on. With complex programs, users can make a mess. When users are taught to draw action diagram brackets and fit the code to them, incorrect structures are infrequent. The code is easy to read, understand, and maintain.

C

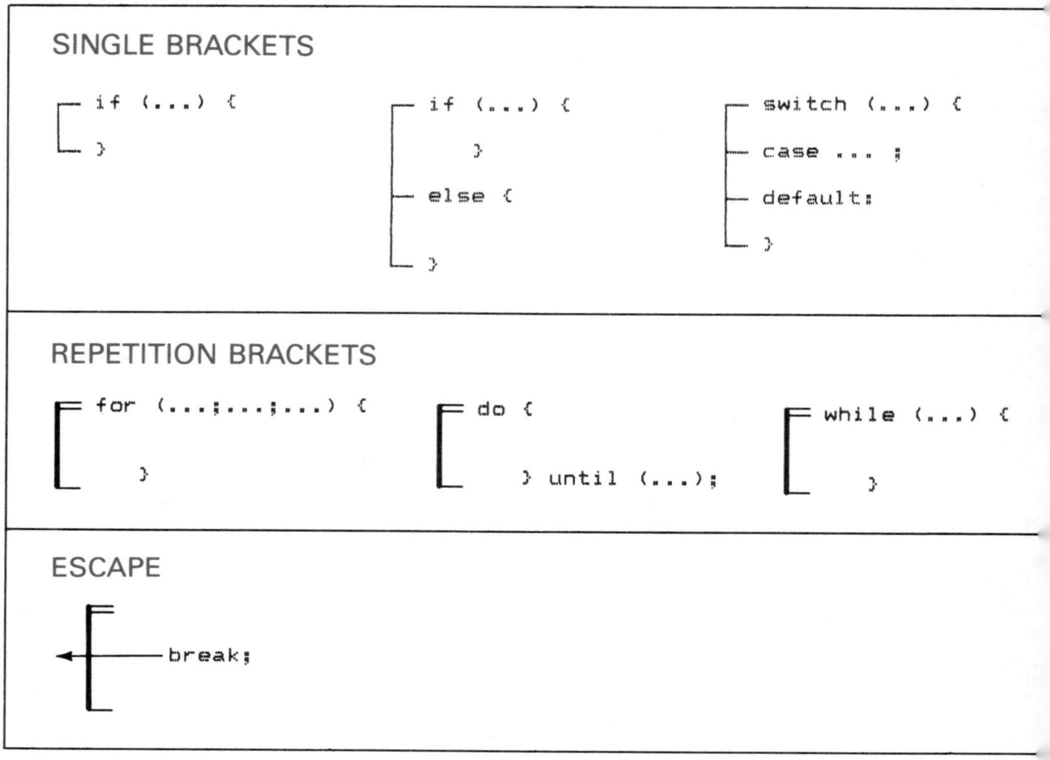

SINGLE BRACKETS

```
┌─ if (...) {              ┌─ if (...) {              ┌─ switch (...) {
└─ }                       │      }                   ├─ case ... ;
                           ├─ else {                  ├─ default:
                           │                          └─ }
                           └─ }
```

REPETITION BRACKETS

```
┌═ for (...;...;...) {     ┌═ do {                    ┌═ while (...) {
│       }                  │      } until (...);      │       }
└                         └                          └
```

ESCAPE

```
┌═
◄──────── break;
└
```

Figure 6.4   Brackets used with C. C is a well-structured language designed for structured programming. There are a separate case construct and three different repetition constructs [3].

An action diagram editor is the key to enabling users to create complex applications that are well structured and easy to maintain.

EXAMPLES OF FOURTH-GENERATION-LANGUAGE CODE

Figures 6.5 to 6.9 give illustrations of fourth-generation-language structures with action diagrams. Figures 6.10 to 6.14 give examples of programs produced with an action diagram editor in various languages.

CHILL

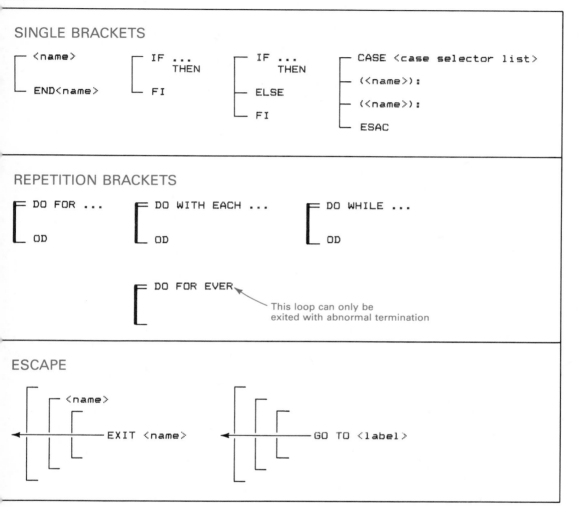

SINGLE BRACKETS

```
┌─ <name>                ┌─ IF ...            ┌─ IF ...            ┌─ CASE <case selector list>
│                        │      THEN          │      THEN          │
│                        │                    │                    ├─ (<name>):
└─ END<name>             └─ FI                ├─ ELSE              │
                                              │                    ├─ (<name>):
                                              └─ FI                │
                                                                   └─ ESAC
```

REPETITION BRACKETS

```
┌═ DO FOR ...            ┌═ DO WITH EACH ...           ┌═ DO WHILE ...
│                        │                             │
└─ OD                    └─ OD                         └─ OD
```

```
┌═ DO FOR EVER
│                        This loop can only be
└                        exited with abnormal termination
```

ESCAPE

```
┌                              ┌
│  ┌─ <name>                   │  ┌
│  │  ┌                        │  │  ┌
◄──┼──┼───── EXIT <name>       ◄──┼──┼──┼──── GO TO <label>
│  │  └                        │  │  │  └
│  └                           │  │  └
└                              │  └
                               └
```

Figure 6.5 Brackets used with CCITT (telecommunications standards organization) high-level language CHILL [4]. This language is designed for programming telephone switching computers and networking software. The IF, CASE, and DO brackets are terminated with these commands spelled backwards: FI, ESAC, OD.

IDEAL

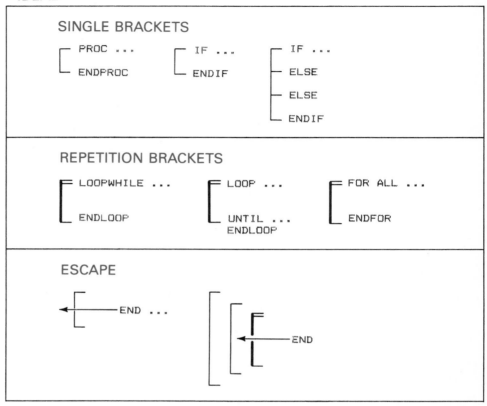

Figure 6.6 Brackets used with the control words from IDEAL [5], a powerful, efficient, fourth-generation language that combines procedural and nonprocedural syntax.

MANTIS

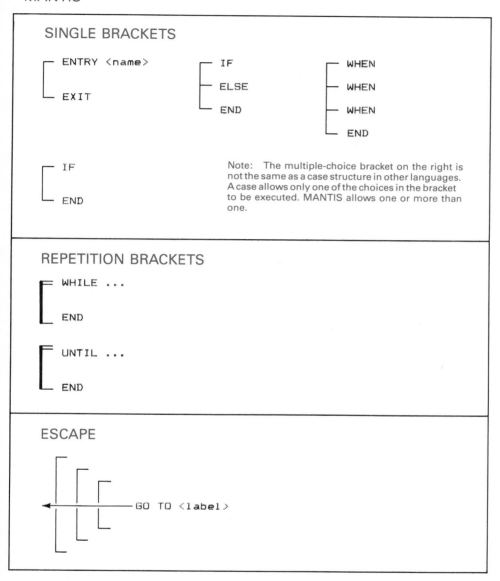

Figure 6.7   Brackets used with MANTIS [2], a simple, efficient, fourth-generation language for DP professionals, which enforces cleanly structured code.

NOMAD

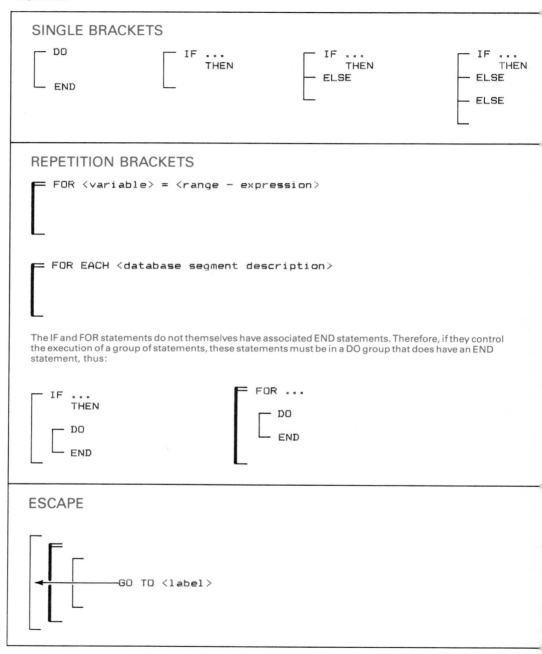

Figure 6.8 Brackets used with NOMAD2 [6], an end-user language which has powerful report-generation and data-base capabilities.

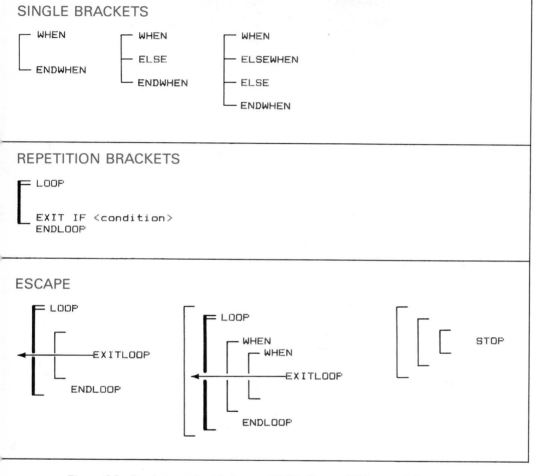

Figure 6.9 Brackets used with System W [7]. System W is a modeling or decision-support language rather than a general-purpose programming language. Most of its use is for analyzing complex data.

```
addel ()

* /* Local Variables */ *****************************************************
    int itab;
    int adlevel;
    int itfrst, itnext, itdel;

* /* Executable Section */ **************************************************
    switch (adtab[curline].action)

    case ACT_JUNK:
    case ACT_CASW:
    case ACT_EXIT:
        itfrst = curline;
        itnext = curline + 1;
        break;

    case ACT_BEGL:
    case ACT_BEGB:
        adlevel = 1;
        itfrst = curline;
        for (itnext = curline+1;
             itnext <= numadtab & adlevel > 0; itnext++)
            switch (adtab[itnext].action)  {
            case ACT_BEGL:
            case ACT_BEGB:
                adlevel++;
                break;
            case ACT_END:
                adlevel--;
            }
        }
        if (adlevel > 0)
            aborts ("ad: ? no matching end ??);

        break;

    default:
        itfrst = numadtab;
        itnext = numadtab;
        beep();
    }
    itdel = itnext - itfrst;
    for (itab = itfrst; itab < numadtab; itab++) {
        adtab[itab].action = adtab[itab+itdel].action;
        adtab[itab].count  = adtab[itab+itdel].count;
        adtab[itab].text   = adtab[itab+itdel].text;
    }
    numadtab -= itdel;
    if (curline > numadtab)
        curline = numadtab;

    showbuffer ();
```

Figure 6.10 Code written in the language C, shown with rectangular brackets.

```
/* Local Variables */ ****************************************************
    int itab;
    int adlevel;
    int itfrst, itnext, itdel;


/* Executable Section */ *************************************************
    switch (adtab[curline].action) {

    case ACT_JUNK:
    case ACT_CASW:
    case ACT_EXIT:
        itfrst = curline;
        itnext = curline + 1;
        break;

    case ACT_BEGL:
    case ACT_BEGB:
        adlevel = 1;
        itfrst = curline;
        for (itnext = curline+1; itnext <= numadtab & adlevel > 0; itnext++)
            switch (adtab[itnext].action) {
            case ACT_BEGL:
            case ACT_BEGB:
                adlevel++;
                break;
            case ACT_END:
                adlevel--;
            }
        }
        if (adlevel > 0)
            aborts ("ad: ? no matching end ??");

        break;

    default:
        itfrst = numadtab;
        itnext = numadtab;
        beep();
    }
    itdel = itnext - itfrst;
    for (itab = itfrst; itab < numadtab; itab++) {
        adtab[itab].action = adtab[itab+itdel].action;
        adtab[itab].count  = adtab[itab+itdel].count;
        adtab[itab].text   = adtab[itab+itdel].text;
    }
    numadtab -= itdel
    if (curline > numadtab)
        curline = numadtab;

    showbuffer ();
```

Figure 6.10   (Continued)

```chill
┌── IF ABS(ABS(NUM(col_2)-NUM(col_1))
│       -ABS(lin-2-lin_1))/=1
│       OR ABS(NUM(col_2)NUM(COL_1))
│           +ABS(lin_2-lin_1)=/3
│       OR arriving.status/=free AND
│       arriving.p.color=starting.p.color
│
│       THEN CAUSE illegal;
│         ((king)(*):
│
└── FI;
        (king),(*):
┌── IF ABS(NUM(col_2)-NUM(col_1)) > 1
│       OR ABS(lin_2-lin1) >1
│       OR lin_2=lin_1 AND col_2=col_1
│       OR arriving.status/=free AND
│           arriving.p.color=starting.p.color
│
│       THEN CAUSE illegal;
└──   FI; /*checking king moving to check not implemented*/
  ESAC;
arriving:=starting;
RETURN;


ok_rook:
   PROC (b board,m move)(BOOL)
┌─ DO WITH m;
│
│  ┌── IF NOT (col_2=col_1 OR lin_1=lin_2_ )
│  │       OR arriving.status/=free AND
│  │       arriving.p.color=starting.p.color
│  │
│  │       THEN RETURN FALSE;
│  └── FI;
│  ┌── IF col_1=col_2
│  │
│  │   ┌── THEN IF lin_1 < lin_2
│  │   │
│  │   │   ┌─ THEN DO FOR 1 :+ lin_1+1 TO lin_2-1;
│  │   │   │  ┌── IF board(1)(col_1).status/=free
│  │   │   │  │      THEN RETURN FALSE;
│  │   │   │  └── FI;
│  │   │   └─ OD;
│  │   │
│  │   │
│  │   └── ELSE
│  │       │
│  │       ┌─ DO FOR 1 := lin_1-1 DOWN TO lin_2 +1
│  │       │  ┌── IF board(1)(col_1).status/free
│  │       │  │      THEN RETURN FALSE;
│  │       │  └── FI;
│  │       └─ OD;
```

Figure 6.11 An action diagram in the CCITT high-level language CHILL [4], showing a portion of a chess-playing program.

```
┌─ ELSE
│
│   ┌─ IF col_2 < col_1
│   │
│   │   ┌─ THEN DO FOR c :+ SUCC(col_1) TO PRED(col_2);
│   │   │   ┌─ IF board(lin_1)(c).status/=free
│   │   │   │     THEN RETURN FALSE
│   │   │   └─ FI;
│   │   ELSE
│   │   ┌─ DO FOR c := SUCC(col_2) DOWN TO PRED(col_1);
│   │   │   ┌─ IF boardlin_1)(c).status/=free
│   │   │   │     THEN RETURN FALSE;
│   │   │   └─ FI;
│   │   └─ OD;
│   └─ FI;
└─ FI;
   RETURN TRUE;
  OD;
END OK_ROOK
```

Figure 6.11   *(Continued)*

```
┌─ TAXRULES
│   ┌─ WHEN VIEWPOINT PRODUCT CONSOLIDATED
│   │   ┌─ WHEN VIEWPOINT LOCATION EQ FRANCE
│   │   │     TAXES = MAX(NIBT AT 50,0)
│   │   ├─ ELSEWHEN VIEWPOINT LOCATION EQ ENGLAND
│   │   │     TAXES = MAX(NIBT AT 52,0)
│   │   ├─ ELSEWHEN VIEWPOINT LOCATION EQ COMPANY
│   │   │   ┌─ WHEN NIBT GT 0 AND NIBT LE 25000
│   │   │   │     TAXES = NIBT AT 15
│   │   │   ├─ ELSEWHEN NIBT GT 25000 AND NIBT LE 50000
│   │   │   │     TAXES (NIBT – 25000) AT 18 + 3750
│   │   │   ├─ ELSEWHEN NIBT GT 50000 AND NIBT LE 75000
│   │   │   │     TAXES = (NIBT – 50000) AT 30 + 8250
│   │   │   ├─ ELSEWHEN NIBT GT 75000 AND NIBT LE 100000
│   │   │   │     TAXES = (NIBT – 75000) AT 40 + 15750
│   │   │   ├─ ELSEWHEN NIBT GT 100000
│   │   │   │     TAXES = (NIBT – 100000) AT 46 + 25750
│   │   │   ├─ ELSE
│   │   │   │     TAXES = 0
│   │   │   └─ ENDWHEN
│   │   └─ ENDWHEN
│   └─ ENDWHEN!
```

Figure 6.12   A set of rules in a financial decision-support application written in System W [7].

```
FOR EACH USER INTERACTION
   ACCEPT
   IF ADD..F EQ "*", THEN
      PERFORM APPEND_SHARE_VR     ;*VRWIOS.INC
      IF RECORD LE 0, THEN
         PERFORM DISPLAY_APPEND_ERROR    ;*SCRFINAL.INC
         NEXT FIRST.FIELD

      SCREEN.CHANGE..F="*"

   IF FUNCTION.TYPE:#WT LL "<ACBO>", THEN
      PERFORM WRITE_VR    ;*VRIOS.INC
      IF RECORD LE 0, THEN
         PERFORM DISPLAY_WRITE_ERROR    ;*SCRFINAL.INC
         NEXT FIRST.FIELD


   IF FUNCTION.TYPE:#WT EQ 'r', THEN
      PERFORM DELETE_VR    ;*VRIOS.INC
      IF RECORD GE 0, THEN
         EXIT SCREEN

      PERFORM DISPLAY_DELETE_ERROR    ;*SCRFINAL.INC
      NEXT FIRST.FIELD
```

Figure 6.13 A subroutine written in Application Factory from Cortex [8].

```
<<ADMIN-PRB>> PROC

    CALL PRBFIND USING PRBMAINT.PR-NO

    IF PR-ARRAY (1) = O
        SET PRBMAINT.ST = "**NO PROBLEMS FOUND**"
        QUIT ADMIN-PRB
    ENDIF
    SET PR-LAST = O
    SET MENU-SELECTION = '3'


    <<NEW-LOOP>> LOOP
        SET NOT-FOUND = FALSE
        SET PRBMAINT.PR-NO = $EDIT(PR-ARRAY (PR-LAST +1),PIC='9999')
        TRANSMIT PRBMAINT
        SELECT FIRST ACTION
            WHEN &ENTER-KERY  ! $PF9 OR $PF21
            SET PRBMAINT.MSG = ' '
            SELECT MENU-SELECTION
                WHEN '3'
                SET PR-LAST = PR-LAST +1
                IF PR-ARRAY (PR-LAST) = O
                    SET PRBMAINT.MSG = 'NO MORE PROBLEMS REMAINING'
                    QUIT ADMIN-PRB
                ENDIF

                          o----------o
                DO   |  UPD-PRB  |
                          o----------o

            WHEN OTHER
                SET PRBMAINT.MSG = 'SELECTION MUST BE IN RANGE.'
            ENDSEL

        WHEN $PF1 ! PF 13

                      o----------o
            DO   |  HELP  |
                      o----------o

        WHEN $PF6 ! $ PF18

            QUIT ADMIN-PRB

        WHEN $PF3 ! PF15
            QUIT RUN

        WHEN OTHER
            SET PRBMAINT.MSG = 'USE PF9/21 TO APPLY OR PF6/18 TO QUIT'
        ENDSEL
    ENDLOOP
ENDPROC
```

Figure 6.14   Code written in the fourth-generation language IDEAL from ADR [5].

EXERCISES

1. Rewrite the following action diagram using the control constructs from the fourth-generation language of your choice.

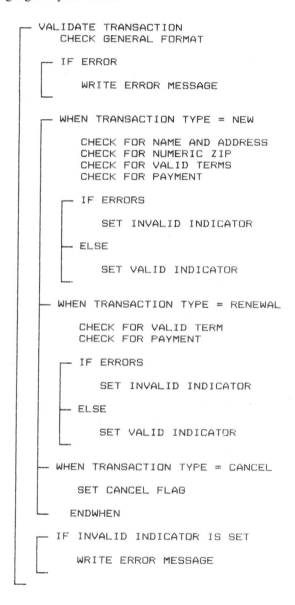

```
── VALIDATE TRANSACTION
       CHECK GENERAL FORMAT

   ── IF ERROR

          WRITE ERROR MESSAGE


   ── WHEN TRANSACTION TYPE = NEW

          CHECK FOR NAME AND ADDRESS
          CHECK FOR NUMERIC ZIP
          CHECK FOR VALID TERMS
          CHECK FOR PAYMENT

      ── IF ERRORS

             SET INVALID INDICATOR

      ── ELSE

             SET VALID INDICATOR


   ── WHEN TRANSACTION TYPE = RENEWAL

          CHECK FOR VALID TERM
          CHECK FOR PAYMENT

      ── IF ERRORS

             SET INVALID INDICATOR

      ── ELSE

             SET VALID INDICATOR


   ── WHEN TRANSACTION TYPE = CANCEL

          SET CANCEL FLAG

   ── ENDWHEN

   ── IF INVALID INDICATOR IS SET

          WRITE ERROR MESSAGE
```

2. Draw an action diagram of the following COBOL code:

```
IF RP-CT = 1
  MOVE Y-COOR TO X-COOR
ELSE IF ROW-CHRYPE = 59 OR 60 OR 62 OR 69
      SUBTRACT 2 FROM Y-COOR
ELSE IF FORMAT-ORIENTATION = 90
      SUBTRACT 4 FROM Y-COOR
ELSE IF FORMAT-ORIENTATION = 0
      IF CHRTPIC-TYPE = 52 OR NOT = STORE-TYPE
        PERFORM CHANGE-TYPE
      ELSE
        NEXT SENTENCE
ELSE
        NEXT SENTENCE
```

3. Draw action diagram brackets around the following Ada code:

```
taskbody CHAN_NEL is
  MESS: MESSAGES;
  begin
    loop
      accept PASS(A: MESSAGES) do
        MESS := A;
      end PASS;
      accept RECEIVE(A: outMESSAGES) do
        A := MESS;
      end RECEIVE;
    endloop
  endCHAN_NEL;
```

REFERENCES

1. James Martin, *Fourth-Generation Languages* (Carnforth, Lancs., England: Savant, 1984).

2. MANTIS manuals are available from Cincom, Inc., 2300 Montana Avenue, Cincinnati, OH 45211.

3. Brian W. Kernighan and Dennis M. Ritchie, *The C Programming Language* (Englewood Cliffs, NJ: Prentice-Hall, Inc., 1978).

4. *CCITT High-Level Language (CHILL)*, Recommendation Z.200 (Geneva: CCITT, 1981).

5. IDEAL manuals are available from ADR, Inc., Route 206 and Orchard, CN-8, Princeton, NJ 08540.

6. NOMAD2 manuals are available from National CSS, Wilton, CT 06896.

7. SYSTEM W manuals are available from Comshare, Inc., Wolverine Tower, 3001 S. State St., P.O. Box 1588, Ann Arbor, MI 48106.

8. Application Factory manuals are available from Cortex Corp., 55 William St., Wellesley, MA 02181.

7 AN ACTION DIAGRAM EDITOR

When creating procedures, an analyst constantly makes modifications to his design, allowing his ideas to take shape. He repeatedly refines his control structures and logic. With action diagrams, he inserts new brackets into existing brackets, adds to case structures, moves or duplicates brackets, and so on. He needs to convert his design into an executable program. To do this quickly, he needs an action diagram editor with which he can build and adjust his design on the screen of a personal computer. The computer can provide much help in checking his design, adding control words to brackets, ensuring that data are used correctly, checking program syntax, and letting him see overviews of the design.

When specifications are written in English, they are usually incomplete and inconsistent. Putting their logic into the form of action diagrams forces the asking of questions that help to make the specifications complete. Figure 7.1 shows a simple example. Here a designer has taken the English description of a part of a specification and written it as an action diagram. There are some question marks. The designer writes, "Don't know what to do here." As he finds out, he keys this into his diagram. He constantly enhances and modifies his design, breaking it down to the code level.

When the designer has code-level detail on his action diagram, he wants to display the overview structure, to display or hide comments. He will display overviews with varying levels of detail.

This chapter describes a personal computer tool for building and editing action diagrams. The tool is called Action Diagrammer™ [1].

WHAT IS ACTION DIAGRAMMER? Action Diagrammer is a software tool for designing systems and programs. It allows analysts, programmers, and end users interactively to create and update action diagrams. It increases the productivity and efficiency of design and programming.

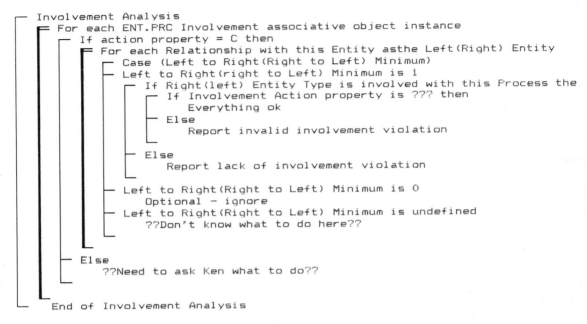

Figure 7.1 A designer has put a segment of a specification written in English into action diagram format. He finds that there are questions to be answered. The logic of specifications should be written in action diagram format to help make them complete and unambiguous.

It can create action diagrams in a particular programming language (often a fourth-generation language) or can create them in a language-independent dialect. Action diagrams created in a language-independent dialect can be converted quickly to any specific language.

Because of the potential changes in choice of fourth-generation language, some DP organizations take the design process as far as possible in a language-independent dialect.

Using Action Diagrammer, a designer may sketch a design at an overview level and successively decompose it until he has executable code. Alternatively, he may build segments of programs and store these for later use. Designers may use both top-down and bottom-up design and link the pieces together. They can store the action diagrams and use them as building blocks in other action diagrams.

The user of the tool can add actions or brackets to the diagrams, change or delete actions, change or delete brackets, nest brackets, and so forth.

Using Action Diagrammer, the analyst or programmer can move or duplicate lines or blocks of code, stretch a bracket to fit around other brackets, remove ("yank") brackets without removing their inner brackets, and otherwise manipulate the action diagram. Many possible moves, stretches, duplicates, yanks, and the like are not valid. The software must catch any attempt to perform an edit operation that is not logically correct.

The text of the action diagrams can be modified with a text editor. The user may tell the software to search for a specified word or pattern of characters. For example, he may tell the software to change the word SUPPLIER to VENDOR everywhere it appears.

The designer can display his design at different levels of detail. He can display an overview structure of a complex program and can edit at the overview level as well as at any other level of detail.

COMMAND MENUS

Action Diagrammer is a menu-driven tool. It uses several levels of menus to list the commands that the user can employ. The menus always appear on the same part of the screen. In addition, the function keys can be used to bypass the menus to go directly to frequently used operations.

The user can select an item from the command menus very quickly with the decisecond response times of a personal computer. The selection may be done in different ways on different systems. If the system has a mouse, the mouse cursor can be used. Arrow keys may be used to move a menu cursor. Or the menu item may be selected by typing. In each level of menu in Fig. 7.2, each menu item starts with a different letter. The user may select the menu item by typing this letter. For example, if "I" is typed, the system knows that the user wants to INSERT something into the action diagram.

When a menu item is followed by periods—for example, INSERT. . .—this indicates that the user has a further menu choice to make before the command can be executed. To help the user understand how to use the tool, whenever he selects a command from the menus, a line appears explaining what that command does.

The red text in Fig. 7.2 shows the line explaining what the menu command does.

The first menu that the user sees contains the following items:

EDIT
LOCATE
SCROLL
ZOOM
COLOR
PRINT
FILE
DEFINE
QUIT
HELP

```
─* Edit
  ┌─* Insert       Insert new action diagramming information
  │    Action        Insert a simple action
  │    Block         Insert a simple block
  │    Title         Insert a title block
  │    Selection     Insert a selection block
  │    Case          Insert a new case into a selection block
  │    Repetition    Insert a repetition block
  │    Exit          Insert an exit
  │    Procedure     Insert a procedure reference
  └    Database      Insert a database action

  ┌─* Bracket      Draw, move, or erase brackets
  │    Draw          Draw a simple block
  │    Case          Draw another case in a selection block
  │    Repetition    Draw a repetition block
  │    Exit          Draw an exit
  │    Move          Move a bracket around existing text
  └    Erase         Erase a bracket, but leave the text

  ┌─* Select     Select part of an action diagram to copy, move, or delete
  │    Beginning    Select the beginning of the part to manipulate
  │    End          Select the end of the part to manipulate
  └    Nothing      Ignore any previously defined beginning and end

  ┌─* Copy    Copy part of an action diagram
  │    Selected     Copy what you selected earlier
  └    Paste        Copy what is in the paste buffer to the current location

  ┌─* Move    Move whatever you selected earlier
  │    Here         Move whatever you selected to the current location
  └    Paste        Move whatever you selected to the paste buffer

  ┌─* Delete     Delete part of an action diagram
  │    Selected     Delete whatever you selected earlier
  │    Block        Delete the enclosing block
  │    Line         Delete the current line
  │    End of Line  Delete from the current character to end of line
  │    Word         Delete the current word
  └    Character    Delete the current character

  ┌─* Replace     Find a character string and replace it with another
  │    All          Replace all occurrences of the specified search string
  │    Next         Replace the next occurrence of the search string
  └    Previous     Replace the previous occurrence of the search string

  ┌─* Locate     Locate and display a specific part of an action diagram
  │    String       Locate and display a specified character strong
  │    Line number  Use a specified relative line number to find a line
  │    Next         Starting here, search forward for a kind of component
  │    Previous     Starting here, search backward for a kind of component
  │    Top          Locate the top of something
  └    Bottom       Locate the bottom of something
```

Figure 7.2 The hierarchy of menu commands used in Action Diagrammer.
What each menu command does is described in red.

104

```
┌─* Scroll    Move around the action diagram
│    Up              Move up a frame or a line
│    Down            Move down a frame or a line
│    Left            Move left to the previous word or character
└    Right           Move right to the next word or character

┌─* Zoom    Display more or less detailed information
│    Contract        Contract a block to show less detail
└    Expand          Expand a block to show more detail

┌─* Color    Choose the colors used for a color monitor
│    Selected        Color whatever is selected
└    All             Color everything of a given type (text, brackets, etc.)

┌─* Print    Make a paper copy of an action diagram

┌─* File    Manipulate action diagram files
│    New             Open a new action diagram file
│    Open            Open an existing action diagram file
│    Include         Add action diagramming information from a specified file
│    Save            Save the latest version of an action diagram with brackets
│    Write           Store action diagramming information into another file
│    Paste           Write the contents of the paste buffer
│    Close           Stop using the current file without recording any changes
└    Directory       Display or change the working directory

┌─* Define    Change Action Diagrammer's defaults
│    Keys            Define special function keys
│    Back-Up         Control the default back-up mechanism
│    Diagramming Control how diagramming is done
│    Typing          Control how typed characters and lines are treated
│    Searching       Describe how to search for character strings
│    Language        Control the language syntax to use
│    Color           Choose the colors used for a color monitor
│    Printer         Describe the default printer
│    Exhibit         Exhibit the current default settings
│    Keys            Exhibit special function keys
└    Settings        Exhibit all of the other current default settings

┌─* Quit    Stop using Action Diagrammer

┌─* Help    Get online documentation
│    Product
│    Action Diagrams
│    Commands
│    More information
└    Keys
```

Figure 7.2   (Continued)

If the user selects EDIT, a second menu appears:

BRACKET
COPY
DELETE
INSERT
MOVE
REPLACE
SELECT

If the user selects INSERT, a third-level menu appears, asking what the user wants to insert:

ACTION
BLOCK
TITLE
SELECTION
CASE
REPETITION
EXIT
PROCEDURE
DATABASE

If the user selects BLOCK, another menu appears asking what type of block:

IF
ELSE
CASE
TITLE
OTHER

The user may enter E for [IF] ELSE, and the following block is inserted:

```
 ┌─── IF


 ├─── ELSE


 └───
```

The user may then add to the IF or ELSE lines, or INSERT ACTION to put one or more lines into the block.

TEXT AND
MENU CURSORS

Action Diagrammer uses a text cursor and a menu cursor. The basic rule for using the tool is as follows:

First select the part of the action diagram you want to work on with the text cursor. Then select what you want to do with the menu cursor.

The text cursor is composed of a cursor bar and a character cursor (illustrated in Fig. 7.3). The user moves the cursor bar up and down to select a position where he wants to insert or delete a bracket or an action line. Within this bar is the character cursor, which can be moved left and right. The character cursor is used for changing a line of text. The user can move the line and character cursors with the cursor control keys:

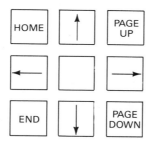

Figure 7.3 shows the character cursor under the S. The user could type characters to change the word SCREEN or to insert another word. If the user wants to insert an IF-ELSE bracket immediately below that line, he selects IN-SERT, ELSE from the menus.

LINE-ORIENTED
AND BRACKET-
ORIENTED EDITOR

The Action Diagrammer thus acts as either a text-oriented editor or a bracket-oriented editor, depending on whether you are working on actions or control constructs.

When you are working with actions, it is a line-oriented editor. You work with one line of action text at a time. When you are working with control constructs, it is a bracket-oriented editor. For example, you may work with one *selection* structure or *loop* structure at a time. Suppose you want to delete an entire IF structure including the IF bracket and its contents. You select the IF structure by marking the beginning and the end of the IF structure. Then select the DE-LETE command. The IF structure bracket and its contents will be deleted. Similarly, brackets, lines, or selected groups of lines can be moved, copied, modified, deleted, or colored.

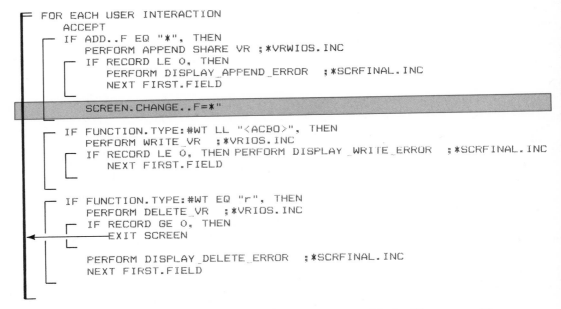

```
┌─ FOR EACH USER INTERACTION
│     ACCEPT
│  ┌─ IF ADD..F EQ "*", THEN
│  │     PERFORM APPEND SHARE VR ;*VRWIOS.INC
│  │  ┌─ IF RECORD LE 0, THEN
│  │  │     PERFORM DISPLAY_APPEND_ERROR   ;*SCRFINAL.INC
│  │  │     NEXT FIRST.FIELD
│  │  └─
│  │     SCREEN.CHANGE..F=*"
│  └─
│  ┌─ IF FUNCTION.TYPE:#WT LL "<ACBO>", THEN
│  │     PERFORM WRITE_VR  ;*VRIOS.INC
│  │  ┌─ IF RECORD LE 0, THEN PERFORM DISPLAY_WRITE_ERROR   ;*SCRFINAL.INC
│  │  │     NEXT FIRST.FIELD
│  │  └─
│  └─
│  ┌─ IF FUNCTION.TYPE:#WT EQ "r", THEN
│  │     PERFORM DELETE_VR  ;*VRIOS.INC
│  │  ┌─ IF RECORD GE 0, THEN
◄──┼──┤     EXIT SCREEN
│  │  └─
│  │     PERFORM DISPLAY_DELETE_ERROR   ;*SCRFINAL.INC
│  │     NEXT FIRST.FIELD
│  └─
└─
```

Figure 7.3   The cursor bar and character cursor of Action Diagrammer. The user may change an entire line of text with the character cursor or insert or change brackets using the cursor bar and menu commands.

COLOR

The designer using a color screen can color the background of selected blocks or groups of actions. He can attach his own meanings to the colors used. Color may be used to enable him to find blocks quickly, to tell him that certain blocks need more work, to highlight special subroutines, or to indicate that someone else should work on a block.

CORTEX ACTION DIAGRAMMER

Another example of an action diagram editor is the CORTEX Action Diagrammer. It has been designed for the development and modification of Builder code, a fourth-generation language from CORTEX [2]. Figure 7.4 is an example of an action diagram in Builder that was generated by the CORTEX Action Diagrammer tool.

REFERENCES

1. The *Action Diagrammer™ User Manual* is available from DDI, Ann Arbor, MI.

2. The CORTEX Action Diagrammer and Syntax Checker Manual is available from CORTEX, Wellesey, MA.

CAD EXAMPLE – AGED ACCOUNTS RECEIVABLE

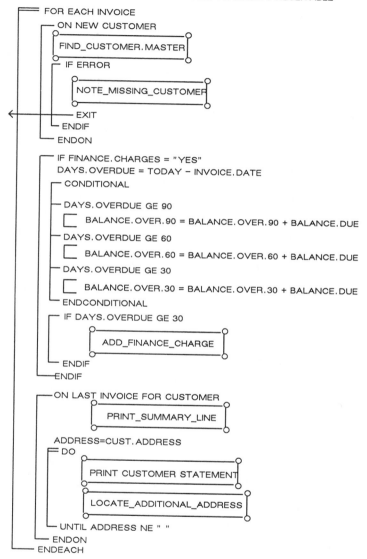

```
╔══ FOR EACH INVOICE
  ┌── ON NEW CUSTOMER
  │  ○───────────────────────────○
  │  │ FIND_CUSTOMER.MASTER       │
  │  ○───────────────────────────○
  │  ┌── IF ERROR
  │  │  ○──────────────────────────○
  │  │  │ NOTE_MISSING_CUSTOMER     │
  │  │  ○──────────────────────────○
  │  ── EXIT
  │  └─ ENDIF
  └── ENDON

  ┌── IF FINANCE.CHARGES = "YES"
  │   DAYS.OVERDUE = TODAY – INVOICE.DATE
  │  ┌── CONDITIONAL
  │  │
  │  ├── DAYS.OVERDUE GE 90
  │  │  ┌─ BALANCE.OVER.90 = BALANCE.OVER.90 + BALANCE.DUE
  │  ├── DAYS.OVERDUE GE 60
  │  │  ┌─ BALANCE.OVER.60 = BALANCE.OVER.60 + BALANCE.DUE
  │  ├── DAYS.OVERDUE GE 30
  │  │  ┌─ BALANCE.OVER.30 = BALANCE.OVER.30 + BALANCE.DUE
  │  └── ENDCONDITIONAL
  │  ┌── IF DAYS.OVERDUE GE 30
  │  │  ○──────────────────────────○
  │  │  │ ADD_FINANCE_CHARGE        │
  │  │  ○──────────────────────────○
  │  └─ ENDIF
  └── ENDIF

  ┌── ON LAST INVOICE FOR CUSTOMER
  │  ○──────────────────────────○
  │  │ PRINT_SUMMARY_LINE        │
  │  ○──────────────────────────○
  │   ADDRESS=CUST.ADDRESS
  │  ╔═ DO
  │  │  ○──────────────────────────○
  │  │  │ PRINT CUSTOMER STATEMENT  │
  │  │  ○──────────────────────────○
  │  │  ○──────────────────────────○
  │  │  │ LOCATE_ADDITIONAL_ADDRESS │
  │  │  ○──────────────────────────○
  │  └─ UNTIL ADDRESS NE " "
  └── ENDON
╚══ ENDEACH
```

Loop through invoice summary records and compute overdue amounts and finance charges.
Print a summary report line and a statement. Include multiple copies to different mailing
addresses requested by some customers.

Figure 7.4 An action diagram in Builder which was generated by the COR-
TEX Action Diagrammer tool [2].

8 USING ACTION DIAGRAMS

USING ACTION DIAGRAMMER

Imagine that your assignment is to develop the subscription system for the Soft-Way Publishing Company. The function of the system is to respond to customers' subscriptions for software applications programs. Soft-Way Publishing Company is one of the oldest and largest software publishing houses. It leases all sorts of software application programs to its subscribers. Lease periods range from three-month special offers to three-year subscriptions. Soft-Way also conducts software-of-the-month clubs.

The subscription system processes three types of transactions: new subscriptions, renewals, and cancellations. Each transaction is first validated. For new subscriptions, a subscriber record is created, and a bill is generated for the total amount due. For renewals, the existing subscriber record is retrieved, the expiration date is updated, and a bill is generated for the total amount due. For cancellations, the subscriber record is flagged for deletion, and a refund is issued when the software is returned.

The structured methodology for building software systems teaches that a top-down functional decomposition method is best. When you build top down, you first build the overall structure and then fill in the details in incremental steps. The structured methodology also teaches that describing a design in diagrams is much easier and more powerful than explaining it in words. Action Diagrammer automates the structured methodology with action diagrams.

This chapter takes you through steps outlined over the next several pages to create a design for the subscription system. Through the design of the subscription system, you will be introduced to many of the action diagram structures.

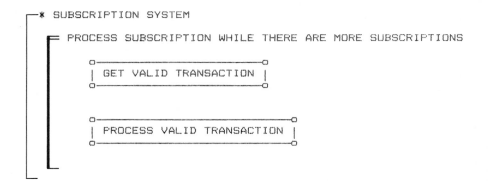

Figure 8.1   An action diagram overview of the subscription system.

A HIGH-LEVEL ACTION DIAGRAM OF THE SUBSCRIPTION SYSTEM

To begin our design of the subscription system, we need to create a high-level diagram describing in very general terms what the subscription system does. Then we can develop our design further by expanding the action diagram to show the detailed logic needed. This program design method, which gradually defines more and more detail, is known as functional decomposition and was discussed in Chapter 3.

Figure 8.1 shows our high-level action diagram. The steps for building it are outlined below:

1. We start with the title bracket labeled SUBSCRIPTION SYSTEM.
2. Next we add a loop that will be executed once for each subscription transaction. The loop is represented by a repetition bracket. In this example, we have chosen the DO WHILE version of the repetition construct.
3. We finish the action diagram by adding two process boxes, GET VALID TRANS-ACTION and PROCESS VALID TRANSACTION. They are executed sequentially in the order shown on the diagram.

There are many possible variations for the design of the subscription system even at this very high level. For example, instead of specifying the two process boxes, we could have defined some detail for each of these processes, as shown in Fig. 8.2.

Here we used a divided bracket to show that PROCESS VALID TRANS-ACTION consists of three mutually exclusive processes: PROCESS NEW SUB-SCRIPTION, PROCESS RENEWAL, and PROCESS CANCELLATION.

When using a top-down design method, we have several choices in how

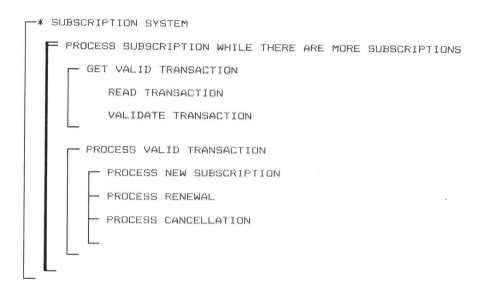

Figure 8.2   An alternative overview action diagram for the subscription system.

to expand the design. For example, we could define in more detail either GET VALID TRANSACTION or PROCESS VALID TRANSACTION. As our next step, we choose to expand the design for GET VALID TRANSACTION. This is shown in Fig. 8.3. The action diagram design steps are as follows:

1. Replace the action READ TRANSACTION with the simple data-base action for accessing the transaction record.

2. Replace the action VALIDATE TRANSACTION with detailed logic. This includes adding a case structure to handle different validation steps depending on the transaction type: new subscription, renewal subscription, or cancellation. The IF structure is added to process error messages when a transaction is invalid. We also added the process ERROR PROCESS for handling errors detected by the validation steps.

Next we define the logic for PROCESS NEW SUBSCRIPTION. This part of the action diagram is shown in Fig. 8.4. It includes several different action diagram structures:

1. Data-base actions for reading the subscriber record, the credit record, and the product record and for updating the order rate record.

2. An escape from the procedure if the credit limit is exceeded with the requested software purchase.

3. A loop structure represented by a DO UNTIL structure. It is executed once for each product ordered by a subscriber.

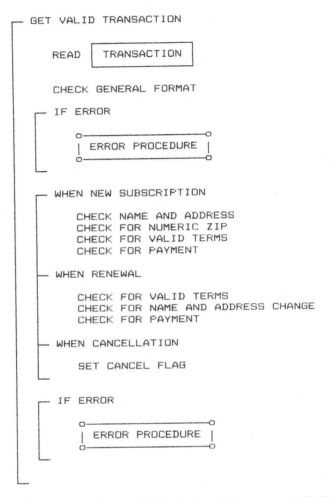

Figure 8.3 An action diagram for the design of the process GET VALID TRANSACTION.

4. An IF structure to process the order if the software is available or to place a back-order if it is not available.

Figure 8.5 shows the action diagram for the PROCESS RENEWAL. This part of the action diagram also includes several different action diagram structures.

1. Simple data-base actions for reading a subscriber record and a product record and for creating a backorder record and a confirmation.

2. A process block for PROCESS ORDER.

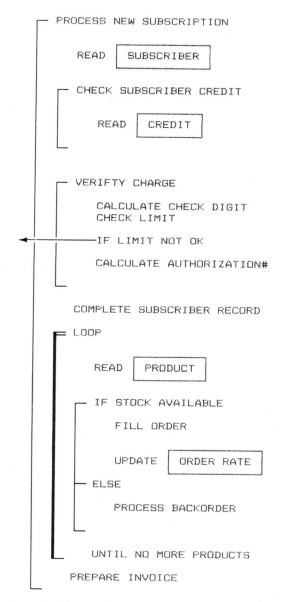

Figure 8.4 An action diagram for the design of the process PROCESS NEW SUBSCRIPTION.

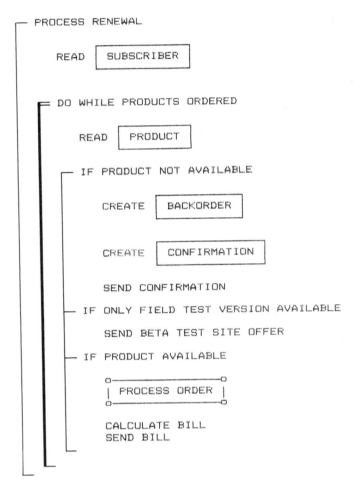

Figure 8.5   An action diagram for the design of the process PROCESS RE-
NEWAL.

3. A DO WHILE repetition structure that is executed once for each product a subscriber
   has ordered.
4. An IF structure to select the logic for backordering, for a field-test version, or for a
   regular product order.
5. An action for calculating a bill, and an action for sending a bill.

Figure 8.6 shows that action diagram for PROCESS CANCELLATION.
It includes simple data-base actions for updating the subscriber record by setting
the cancellation flag and for creating a product return request.

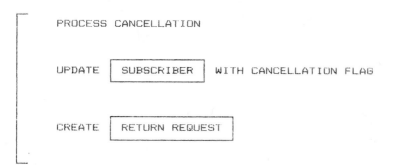

Figure 8.6   An action diagram for the design of the process PROCESS CAN-
CELLATION.

**ULTIMATE
DECOMPOSITION
SUBSCRIPTION
SYSTEM DESIGN**

The action diagram we have produced for the subscription system design is written with language-independent structures. The logic is defined in enough
detail at this point so that it can be easily transformed
into actual programming-language instructions.

9 LINKAGE TO OTHER TYPES OF DIAGRAMS AND DOCUMENTATION

OTHER TYPES OF DIAGRAMS

Good diagramming techniques help people to think clearly about complex design. A poor choice of diagramming method may inhibit thinking; a good choice makes it easier for most people to visualize and create useful designs.

There are many ways to think about the logic of computer systems. Different aspects of design should be tackled with forms of diagrams that help the designer's creativity. To be able to think as clearly as possible about the design of complex systems a designer should be familiar with several diagramming techniques. Useful techniques other than action diagrams are decision trees and tables, dependency or data-flow diagrams, data-model diagrams, and data navigation diagrams. Each of these gives a view of a particular aspect of a system that is important in the appropriate circumstance.

AUTOMATIC DIAGRAM CONVERSION

It is beyond the subject of this book to discuss other forms of diagramming. The authors have done that elsewhere [1]. However, other forms of diagrams that relate to programs should be *automatically* convertible to action diagrams. Figure 9.1 illustrates this. The red arrows represent diagram conversion *by computer*.

If a diagram of a procedure cannot be converted by computer to an action diagram, that diagram lacks the requisite precision. Unfortunately, most of the diagram types that analysts were taught to draw until recently *did* lack precision. They were designed for use with a plastic template. When diagrams are designed for use at a computer screen linked to software for computer-aided programming, we have to be more precise. *In any corporation, a set of standards that enforces precision in DP diagrams is a necessity* [2]. When these standards are used, the diagrams analysts use can be converted at a computer screen

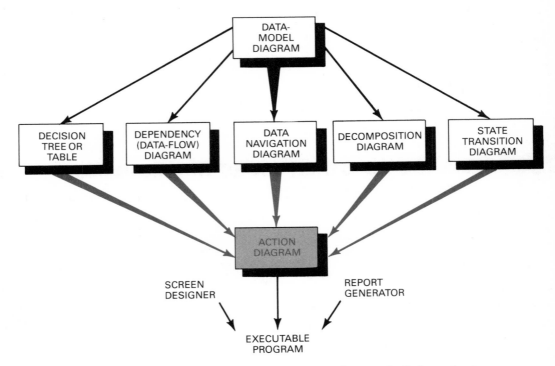

Figure 9.1   Action diagrams can be generated *automatically* from other types of diagrams systems designers use if these diagrams are drawn with appropriate standards [2].

into action diagrams and thence into executable code. The objectives of this computer-aided design (CAD) are to speed up the building of systems, including highly complex systems, and to produce better-quality systems that are easy to change (maintain).

In this chapter we look briefly at other types of diagrams and their automatic conversion to action diagrams.

DECISION TREES   Figure 9.2 shows a decision tree relating to the computing of a derived data item, ORDER.DISCOUNT. The drawing of decision trees clarifies complex decisions such as this. Figure 9.3 shows an action diagram that is derived automatically from the decision tree of Fig. 9.2.

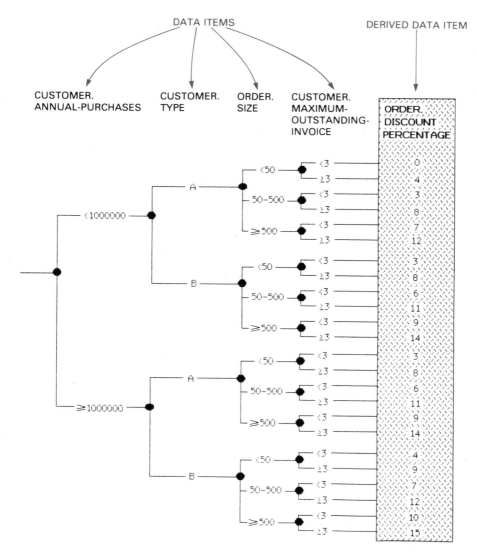

Figure 9.2   A decision tree for computing ORDER.DISCOUNT.

DATA FLOW AND DEPENDENCY DIAGRAMS

A data flow diagram shows activities in round-cornered boxes like those we use on action diagrams:

```
┌─ IF CUSTOMER.ANNUAL-PURCHASES =< 1000000
│   ┌─ IF CUSTOMER.TYPE = A
│   │   ┌─ IF ORDER.SIZE < 50
│   │   │   ┌─ IF CUSTOMER.MAXIMUM_OUTSTANDING_INVOICE =< 3
│   │   │   │    ORDER.DISCOUNT = 0
│   │   │   ├─ ELSE
│   │   │   │    ORDER.DISCOUNT = 4
│   │   │   └─ ENDIF
│   │   ├─ ELSEIF ORDER.SIZE >= 50 AND < 500
│   │   │   ┌─ IF CUSTOMER.MAXIMUM_OUTSTANDING_INVOICE =< 3
│   │   │   │    ORDER.DISCOUNT = 3
│   │   │   ├─ ELSE
│   │   │   │    ORDER.DISCOUNT = 8
│   │   │   └─ ENDIF
│   │   ├─ ELSEIF ORDER.SIZE >= 500
│   │   │   ┌─ IF CUSTOMER.MAXIMUM_OUTSTANDING_INVOICE =< 3
│   │   │   │    ORDER.DISCOUNT = 7
│   │   │   ├─ ELSE
│   │   │   │    ORDER.DISCOUNT = 12
│   │   │   └─ ENDIF
│   │   └─ ENDIF
│   ├─ ELSEIF CUSTOMER.TYPE = B
│   │   ┌─ IF ORDER.SIZE < 50
│   │   │   ┌─ IF CUSTOMER.MAXIMUM_OUTSTANDING_INVOICE =< 3
│   │   │   │    ORDER.DISCOUNT = 3
│   │   │   ├─ ELSE
│   │   │   │    ORDER.DISCOUNT = 8
│   │   │   └─ ENDIF
│   │   ├─ ELSEIF ORDER.SIZE >= 50 AND < 500
│   │   │   ┌─ IF CUSTOMER.MAXIMUM_OUTSTANDING_INVOICE =< 3
│   │   │   │    ORDER.DISCOUNT = 6
│   │   │   ├─ ELSE
│   │   │   │    ORDER.DISCOUNT = 11
│   │   │   └─ ENDIF
│   │   ├─ ELSEIF ORDER.SIZE > 500
│   │   │   ┌─ IF CUSTOMER.MAXIMUM_OUTSTANDING_INVOICE =< 3
│   │   │   │    ORDER.DISCOUNT = 9
│   │   │   ├─ ELSE
│   │   │   │    ORDER.DISCOUNT = 14
│   │   │   └─ ENDIF
│   │   └─ ENDIF
│   └─ ENDIF
```

Figure 9.3 An action diagram equivalent to the decision tree in Fig. 9.2.

```
├─ ELSE
│   ├─ IF CUSTOMER.TYPE = A
│   │   ├─ IF ORDER.SIZE < 50
│   │   │   ├─ IF CUSTOMER.MAXIMUM_OUTSTANDING_INVOICE = < 3
│   │   │   │      ORDER.DISCOUNT = 3
│   │   │   ├─ ELSE
│   │   │   │      ORDER.DISCOUNT = 8
│   │   │   └─ ENDIF
│   │   ├─ ELSEIF ORDER.SIZE >= 50 AND < 500
│   │   │   ├─ IF CUSTOMER.MAXIMUM_OUTSTANDING_INVOICE =< 3
│   │   │   │      ORDER.DISCOUNT = 6
│   │   │   ├─ ELSE
│   │   │   │      ORDER.DISCOUNT = 11
│   │   │   └─ ENDIF
│   │   ├─ ELSEIF ORDER.SIZE > 500
│   │   │   ├─ IF CUSTOMER.MAXIMUM_OUTSTANDING_INVOICE =< 3
│   │   │   │      ORDER.DISCOUNT = 9
│   │   │   ├─ ELSE
│   │   │   │      ORDER.DISCOUNT = 14
│   │   │   └─ ENDIF
│   │   └─ ENDIF
│   ├─ ELSEIF CUSTOMER.TYPE = B
│   │   ├─ IF ORDER.SIZE < 50
│   │   │   ├─ IF CUSTOMER.MAXIMUM_OUTSTANDING_INVOICE =< 3
│   │   │   │      ORDER.DISCOUNT = 4
│   │   │   ├─ ELSE
│   │   │   │      ORDER.DISCOUNT = 9
│   │   │   └─ ENDIF
│   │   ├─ ELSEIF ORDER.SIZE >= 50 AND < 500
│   │   │   ├─ IF CUSTOMER.MAXIMUM_OUTSTANDING_INVOICE =< 3
│   │   │   │      ORDER.DISCOUNT = 7
│   │   │   ├─ ELSE
│   │   │   │      ORDER.DISCOUNT = 12
│   │   │   └─ ENDIF
│   │   ├─ ELSEIF ORDER.SIZE > 500
│   │   │   ├─ IF CUSTOMER.MAXIMUM_OUTSTANDING_INVOICE =< 3
│   │   │   │      ORDER.DISCOUNT = 10
│   │   │   ├─ ELSE
│   │   │   │      ORDER.DISCOUNT = 15
│   │   │   └─ ENDIF
│   │   └─ ENDIF
│   └─ ENDIF
└─ ENDIF
```

Figure 9.3   (Continued)

Sometimes the boxes show high-level processes; sometimes they show detailed procedures that will be program subroutines.

Arrows drawn between boxes represent data flows, as in this example:

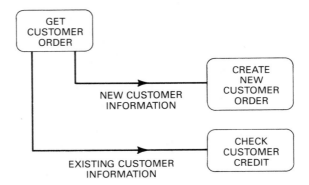

A dependency diagram is similar to a data-flow diagram. The arrow going from process A to process B indicates that process B cannot be executed until process A has been executed. Process B is dependent on process A. The reason for the dependency is often that process A creates data that process B needs. The arrow from process A to process B is labeled with the name of those data.

Figure 9.4 shows a dependency diagram. It is similar to a data flow diagram. If it is created at the screen of a computer, the computer asks the designer questions (or gives him panels to fill in) that enable the machine to have enough information to convert the diagram automatically into an action diagram. Figure 9.5 shows the result.

DATA MODELS

A data model shows how data items (fields) are grouped into logical records and how the logical records relate to one another. Figure 9.6 shows a simple data model.

It indicates that a CUSTOMER record is associated with *zero, one,* or

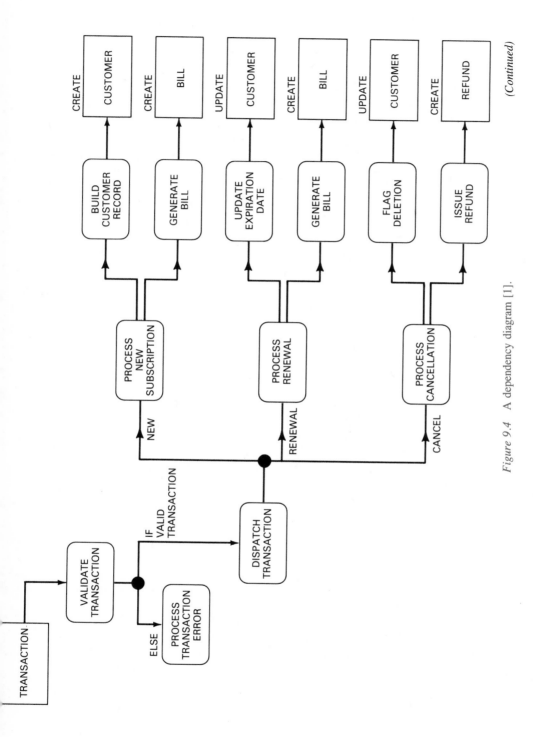

Figure 9.4   A dependency diagram [1].

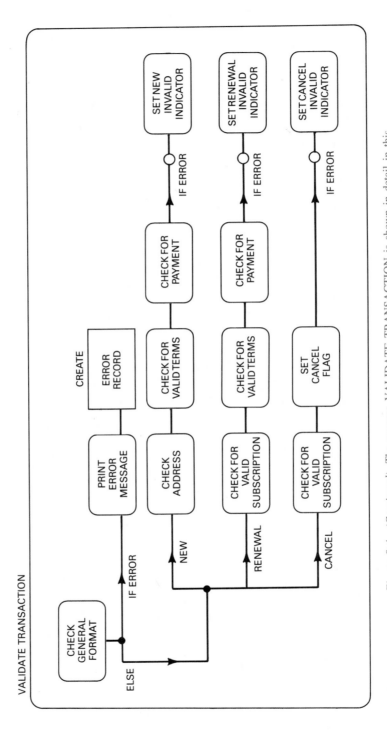

Figure 9.4 (Continued). The process VALIDATE TRANSACTION is shown in detail in this dependency diagram.

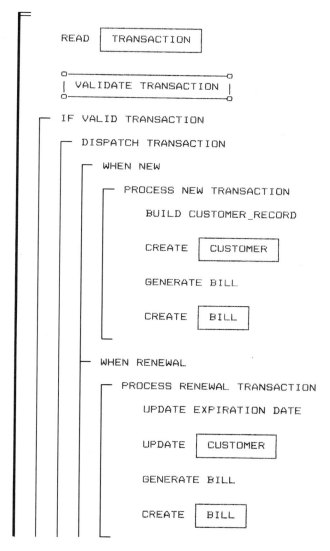

Figure 9.5 An action diagram automatically generated from the dependency diagram shown in Fig. 9.4. *(Continued)*

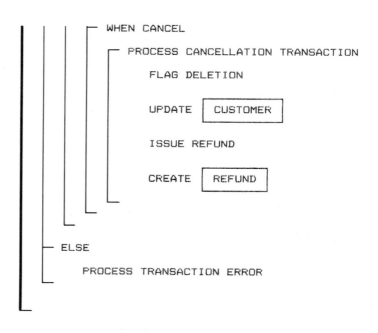

```
        ┌  WHEN CANCEL
        │
        │   ┌  PROCESS CANCELLATION TRANSACTION
        │   │
        │   │     FLAG DELETION
        │   │
        │   │     UPDATE    │ CUSTOMER │
        │   │
        │   │     ISSUE REFUND
        │   │
        │   │     CREATE    │ REFUND │
        │   └
        └

  ┌  ELSE
  │
  │     PROCESS TRANSACTION ERROR
  └
```

```
  ┌  VALIDATE TRANSACTION
  │      CHECK GENERAL FORMAT
  │
  │   ┌  IF ERROR
  │   │      PRINT ERROR MESSAGE
  │   │
  │   │      CREATE    │ ERROR RECORD │
  │   └
  │   ┌  WHEN NEW
  │   │      CHECK ADDRESS
  │   │      CHECK FOR VALID TERMS
  │   │      CHECK FOR PAYMENT
  │   │
  │   │   ┌  IF ERROR
  │   │   │      SET NEW_INVALID_INDICATOR
  │   │   └
  │   ┌  WHEN RENEWAL
  │   │      CHECK FOR VALID SUBSCRIPTION
  │   │      CHECK FOR VALID TERMS
  │   │      CHECK FOR PAYMENT
  │   │
  │   │   ┌  IF ERROR
  │   │   │      SET RENEWAL_INVALID_INDICATOR
  │   │   └
  │   ┌  WHEN CANCEL
  │   │      CHECK FOR VALID SUBSCRIPTION
  │   │      SET CANCEL FLAG
  │   │
  │   │   ┌  IF ERROR
  │   │   │      SET CANCEL_INVALID_INDICATOR
  │   │   └
  └
```

Figure 9.5   (Continued)

many CUSTOMER-ORDER records. A CUSTOMER-ORDER record is associated with *one* CUSTOMER record:

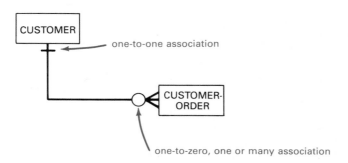

Similar associations apply in Fig. 9.6 to PRODUCT, ORDER-RATE, and the other logical records.

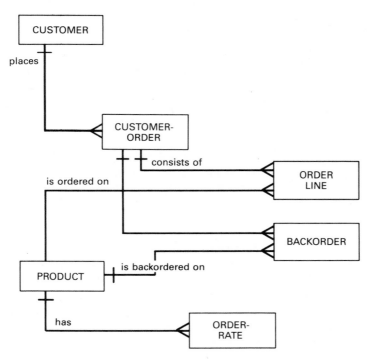

Figure 9.6   A fragment of a data model that an analyst has extracted from a full data model in order to build an application as shown in Figures 9.7 to 9.10.

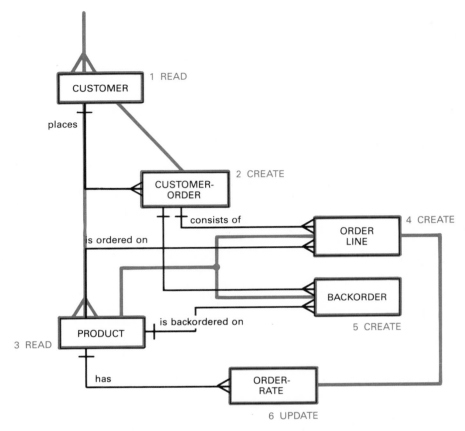

Figure 9.7 A data navigation diagram drawn by hand on top of the data model of Fig. 9.6. It shows the sequence and types of data accesses in a procedure. Figure 9.8 shows a computer-drawn version of the same diagram that can be converted automatically to an action diagram.

DATA NAVIGATION DIAGRAM

A data navigation diagram is shown on top of a data model. The designer selects the record types he is going to use (creating a submodel) and draws a diagram on this data model showing the type and sequence of accesses that a procedure will use. Figure 9.7 shows a hand-drawn navigation diagram drawn on the data model of Fig. 9.6. It indicates that the following data-base actions will take place:

1. Read CUSTOMER record. This is done many times.

2. For each CUSTOMER record read, create a CUSTOMER-ORDER record.

3. For each CUSTOMER record read, read multiple PRODUCT records.

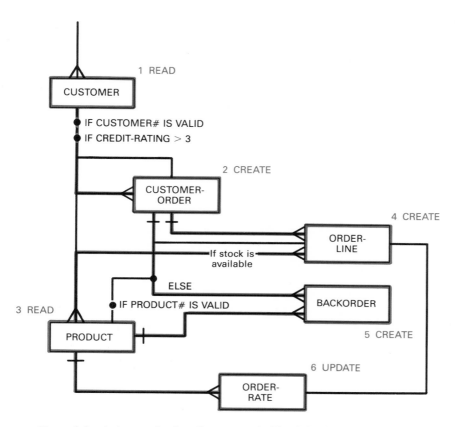

Figure 9.8 A data navigation diagram, as in Fig. 9.7, drawn by computer on top of the data model of Fig. 9.6.

4. For each PRODUCT record read, either create an ORDER-LINE record linked to the CUSTOMER-ORDER record, or . . .

5. Create a BACKORDER record.

6. For each ORDER-LINE record created update an ORDER-RATE record.

When a data navigation diagram is created at a computer screen with the machine drawing the paths and boxes, the machine can ask the designer certain questions. It asks about conditional paths and the criteria that cause an optional path to be taken. Under what circumstances is a BACKORDER record created in Fig. 9.7?

Figure 9.8 shows a machine-drawn navigation diagram, like Fig. 9.7, but with more detail added. Figure 9.8 is sufficiently rigorous to be automatically converted to an action diagram. Figure 9.9 shows the action diagram that is derived automatically from 9.8.

Figure 9.9 is a language-independent diagram. Figure 9.10 shows the ac-

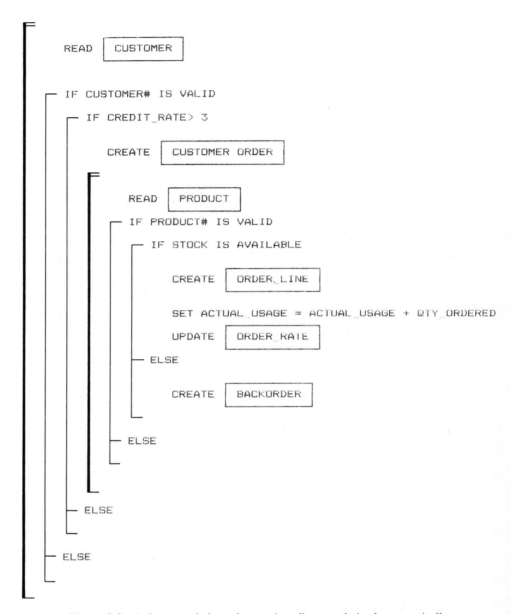

READ   CUSTOMER

IF CUSTOMER# IS VALID

    IF CREDIT_RATE> 3

        CREATE   CUSTOMER ORDER

            READ   PRODUCT

            IF PRODUCT# IS VALID

                IF STOCK IS AVAILABLE

                    CREATE   ORDER_LINE

                    SET ACTUAL_USAGE = ACTUAL_USAGE + QTY_ORDERED
                    UPDATE   ORDER_RATE
                ELSE

                    CREATE   BACKORDER

            ELSE

    ELSE

ELSE

Figure 9.9 A language-independent action diagram derived automatically
from a data navigation diagram.

```
┌─ <<ORDER_ACCEPTANCE >> PROC
│     EACH CUSTOMER
│
│  ┌─ IF CUSTOMER# VALID
│  │
│  │  ┌─ IF CREDIT_RATING >3
│  │  │
│  │  │     WRITE CUSTOMER ORDER
│  │  │     SET ORDER TOTAL
│  │  │
│  │  │  ┌═ LOOP WHILE EACH PRODUCT
│  │  │  │
│  │  │  │  ┌─ IF PRODUCT# VALID
│  │  │  │  │
│  │  │  │  │  ┌─ IF QUANTITY ON HAND > 0
│  │  │  │  │  │
│  │  │  │  │  │     SET LINE_ITEM_PRICE = CATALOG_PRICE
│  │  │  │  │  │     SET LINE_TOTAL = QTY_ORDERED * LINE_ITEM_PRICE
│  │  │  │  │  │     SET ORDER_TOTAL = ORDER_TOTAL + LINE_TOTAL
│  │  │  │  │  │     WRITE ORDER_LINE
│  │  │  │  │  │     EACH ORDER_RATE
│  │  │  │  │  │     SET ACTUAL_USAGE = ACTUAL_USAGE + QTY_ORDERED
│  │  │  │  │  │     WRITE ORDER_RATE
│  │  │  │  │  │
│  │  │  │  │  ┌─ ELSE
│  │  │  │  │  │
│  │  │  │  │  │     WRITE BACKORDER
│  │  │  │  │  │     PRINT BACKORDER NOTICE
│  │  │  │  │  │
│  │  │  │  │  └─ ENDIF
│  │  │  │  │
│  │  │  │  ┌─ ELSE
│  │  │  │  │
│  │  │  │  │     PRINT ERROR MESSAGE
│  │  │  │  │
│  │  │  │  └─ ENDIF
│  │  │  │
│  │  │  └─ ENDLOOP
│  │  │
│  │  │     SET ORDER_TOTAL = ORDER_TOTAL * [1 - DISCOUNT / 100]
│  │  │     SET ORDER_STATUS = 0
│  │  │     WRITE CUSTOMER_ORDER
│  │  │
│  │  ┌─ ELSE
│  │  │
│  │  │     CALL POOR CREDIT
│  │  │
│  │  └─ ENDIF
│  │
│  ┌─ ELSE
│  │
│  │     PRINT REJECT NOTICE
│  │
│  └─ ENDIF
│
└─ ENDPROC
```

Figure 9.10   Executable code for the action diagram of Fig. 9.9 in the fourth-
generation language IDEAL.

tion diagram with the commands of the fourth-generation language IDEAL [3]. The designer has added details of calculation. The code in Fig. 9.10 is an executable program.

RIGOR IN DIAGRAMMING

The point we wish to make with these brief examples is that various types of diagrams for system designers can be converted automatically to action diagrams. Action diagrams as illustrated in Fig. 9.1 are the base type of diagram for creating procedural code.

Various types of diagrams that have been drawn traditionally *cannot* be converted to action diagrams automatically. This indicates that these types of diagrams lack precision. Diagram types of insufficient precision should either be dropped and not taught to any more DP professionals, or else they should be enhanced so that they have enough rigor to be convertible to actual program code or action diagrams.

PROGRAM DOCUMENTATION

Documentation is of vital importance on systems that may require maintenance. DP personnel, and now end users, continually underestimate the need for documentation because they underestimate the need to change programs.

There is a major problem with traditional documentation techniques. Programs are frequently changed, and the programmers who make the change have neither the time nor the inclination to change the documentation accordingly. Consequently, the documentation slips out of phase with the latest version of the program code and eventually becomes useless.

The solution to this dilemma is to use computerized diagrams as the documentation. When changes are made, they should be made at the screen of the diagram editor. Action diagrams are ideal for this. Each programmer making a change works with the action diagrams, and the updates to the diagrams are filed. When high-level diagrams, which convert automatically to action diagrams, are used, a change may be made to the higher-level diagram, an action diagram generated, and previous code pasted into the new diagram with the action diagram editor. Changes to the structure of the action diagram can be automatically reflected into the higher-level diagram, where this is useful. For example, a decision tree or a data navigation diagram may be updated.

The data model and data dictionary need to be managed with sound data administration. A data administrator designs the data to be as stable as possible (again using computerized tools). The various diagramming tools need to be coupled to the dictionary and data model to ensure that correct representations of data are used. The computerized data model and data dictionary are a vital part of the documentation.

Both high-level and detailed-level documentation are needed, depending on the user's purpose. If he is searching for a bug, he needs detailed action diagrams, perhaps with animation showing how control moves through the diagram for tracing purposes. If he wants to determine in which of several programs a function is performed, high-level documentation may be the most helpful.

EXPANDING AND SHRINKING ACTION DIAGRAMS   Action diagrams should have comments added where this can help a person to understand what the program is doing. The action diagram editor should display the comments at the head of an appropriate bracket only when needed. Each comment line starts with an asterisk so that the editor knows which lines are comments.

An action diagram on a computer screen can be expanded or shrunk in various ways. It can be expanded to show comments. It can be shrunk to show only the overview structure of a program. It can be displayed in overview form with comments.

Documentation as well as programs must be maintainable, and the key to maintainable documentation is simplicity. Producing voluminous amounts of detailed program documentation requiring a major update effort each time the program is modified can only compound the maintenance burden. Instead, what is needed is succinct, high-quality documentation that is easily accessible and easily updatable.

Documentation should fit the program. Small, simple programs require less detailed documentation than do large, complex software systems. Programs written, used, and maintained by one individual require less documentation than programs supporting many users and maintained by many different programmers. Programs written in higher-level languages require less documentation than those written in low-level languages.

Good program documentation is a fundamental component in building high-quality software. *Good documentation* is documentation that:

- Enhances the readability and usability of programs employing action diagrams at various levels
- Is easy and inexpensive to produce and update
- Gives a high-level view of a system and its structure
- Provides a blueprint for representing requirements in a design and then for translation of the design into program code
- Links data dictionary, data model, and encyclopedia tools

UTILITY OF DOCUMENTATION   Diagramming techniques should produce both internal and external program documentation. *Internal documentation* is embedded in the program source code or automatically generated as a part of the compilation or assembly process. Program comments and cross-reference listings are common examples of internal documentation.

External documentation is separate from the source code and has traditionally been manually produced. Structure charts, data flow diagrams, and HIPO diagrams are examples of external documentation.

External program documentation has commonly been discarded once the program is developed. It is considered too expensive to keep up-to-date during the remainder of the system life cycle. Maintenance programmers mistrust most external documentation because they know that in practice it is seldom updated. Even the external documentation for a newly released system is unlikely to describe a program accurately.

The solution to this problem is to have one diagramming technique that represents both the overview of a system and the detail. The diagram is edited on a computer screen; when the detail is changed, this is automatically reflected in the overview representation. An action diagram editor does this.

The automatic production and update of diagrammatic documentation is an essential function of computer-aided design.

FUNCTIONS OF STRUCTURED DIAGRAMS

In summary, diagramming techniques thus need to provide the following important functions:

- An aid to clear thinking and problem solving
- Precise and recorded communication among members of the development team, users, and management
- Standardized representation of program architectural structure
- An aid to finding program bugs
- An aid to changing programs (maintenance)
- Fast development (with computer-aided diagramming)
- Enabling end users to review the program design
- Encouraging end users to sketch their needs and even build some of their own software
- Enabling automatic error checking and code generation
- A mechanism for program documentation

Action diagrams have been designed to provide each of these functions.

REFERENCES

1. James Martin and Carma McClure, *Diagramming Techniques for Analysts and Programmers* (Englewood Cliffs, NJ: Prentice-Hall, Inc., 1985).

2. James Martin, *Recommended Diagramming Standards for Computing,* Savant Research Report (Carnforth, Lancs., England: Savant, 1984).

3. IDEAL manuals are available from ADR, Inc., Route 206 and Orchard, CN-8, Princeton, NJ 08540.

APPENDIX:
SUMMARY OF
NOTATION USED IN
ACTION DIAGRAMS

Brackets

The bracket encloses a set of activities that are to be performed. It may represent an organizational unit, a process, a program, a subroutine, or a block of code.

```
─* BILLING RUN
:       ──── ──── ──── ────
:       ──── ──── ──── ────
:       ──── ──── ──── ────
:       ──── ──── ──── ────
```

A title may or may not be written at the top of the bracket. A title bracket has an asterisk on its top bar. It may be drawn as a dotted bracket.

Sequence

```
┌────
│   action 1
│   action 2
│   action 3
└────
```

One or more actions may be included within a bracket.
The actions are listed one after another and are executed in the order in which they are listed.

Conditions

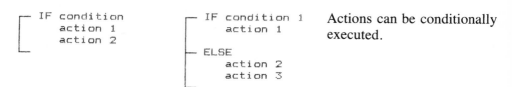

Actions can be conditionally executed.

Conditions controlling the use of a bracket are written by its top bar.

Case Structure

```
    IF KEY = "A"

    IF KEY = "B"

    IF KEY = "C"

    IF KEY = "D"
```

A divided bracket shows a case structure or mutually exclusive conditions. Only one partition of a divided bracket is executed.

Repetition

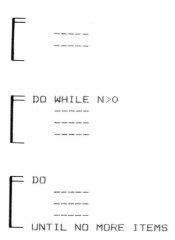

A double bar at the top of a bracket indicates that the contents of the bracket will be executed multiple times (i.e., a loop.)

Conditions controlling a DO WHILE loop are written at the top of the bracket, showing that the condition is tested before the contents of the bracket are executed.

Conditions controlling a DO UNTIL loop are written at the bottom of the bracket, showing that the condition is tested after the contents of the bracket are executed.

Nesting

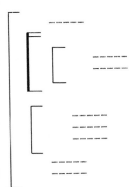

Brackets are nested to show a hierarchy—a form of tree structure.

Conditions can be nested.

```
IF condition-1
   action 1

   IF condition-2
      action 2
```

Rectangle Format

The bracket may be expanded into a rectangle. The inputs to the activities in the rectangle are written at its top left corner; the outputs are written at its bottom right corner.

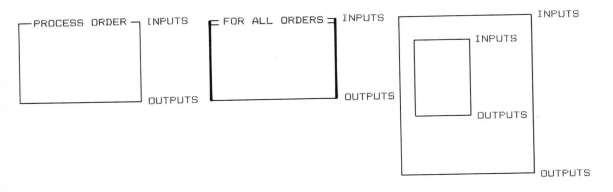

Exits

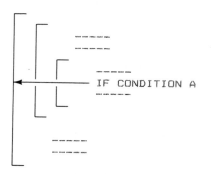

An arrow to the left penetrating one or more brackets indicates that the brackets it passes through are terminated if the condition written by the arrow is satisfied.

Subprocedures

A round-cornered box (or a box with circles at each corner) within a bracket indicates a procedure diagrammed elsewhere.

A round-cornered box with question marks on the right edge indicates a procedure not yet thought out in more detail.

Common Procedures

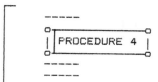

A procedure box with a vertical line drawn through the left side indicates a common procedure—that is, a procedure that appears more than once in the action diagram.

Concurrency

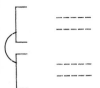

Where brackets may be executed concurrently, they are joined by a semicircular link.

GOTO

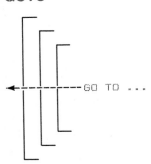

GO TO ...

A dashed arrow, like an escape arrow, is used for a GOTO instruction.
It is recommended that this not be used. Structured design and programming which employs *escape* constructs does not need GOTO constructs.

NEXT Iteration

IF

An arrow to the left which does not penetrate the bracket is used in repetition brackets to terminate the current iteration of a loop and transfer control to the next iteration.

Lines That Can Be Expanded

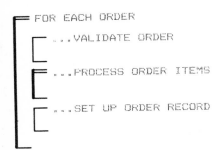

FOR EACH ORDER
...VALIDATE ORDER
...PROCESS ORDER ITEMS
...SET UP ORDER RECORD

Three dots at the start of a line indicate that part of the diagram has been contracted and that it may be expanded with the EXPAND command.

THE FOLLOWING RELATE TO DATA-BASE ACTION DIAGRAMS

Simple Data Action

A rectangle containing the name of a record type or entity type is preceded by a simple data-access action: CREATE, READ, UPDATE, or DELETE.

Compound Data Action

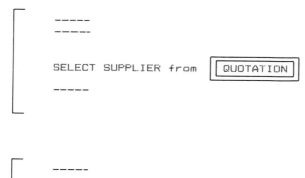

A double rectangle containing the name of a record type or entity type is preceded by a compound data-access action such as SORT, JOIN, PROJECT, or SELECT. Words of a nonprocedural language may accompany the double rectangle.

ANSWERS TO EXERCISES

Chapter 2

1. Enter at the top of the bracket. Execute the actions inside the bracket sequentially. Exit at the bottom of the bracket.

2.
```
    ┌── IF REGION = "NORTHERN"

    │       SEND COMPILER SOFTWARE

    ├── IF REGION = "SOUTHERN"

    │       SEND GRAPHICS SOFTWARE

    ├── IF REGION = "EASTERN"

    │       SEND REPORT GENERATOR SOFTWARE

    ├── IF REGION = "MIDWESTERN"

    │       SEND WORD PROCESSING SOFTWARE

    ├── IF REGION = "WESTERN"

    │       SEND GRAPHICS SOFTWARE AND REPORT GENERATOR SOFTWARE

    └──
```

3.

4.
```
┌─ DOWHILE PRODUCT_TYPE_NO < 77
│  ┌─ IF INVENTORY (PRODUCT_TYPE_NO) < 25
│  │    PRINT PRODUCT_TYPE_NO, INVENTORY
│  └
└
```

5. In the DO WHILE construct, the condition is tested first. If the condition is false, the loop is terminated. In the DO UNTIL construct, the loop is executed first, then the condition is tested. When the condition becomes true, the loop is terminated.

Chapter 3

1. Functional decomposition is a method of designing a system or program in steps, gradually defining more and more detailed program logic. It is a top-down design method.

2. Ultimate decomposition is the final level of functional decomposition where the program design has been extended all the way down to working-code level.

3. A hierarchical program structure makes the program easier to understand and to change because each hierarchical level adds more detailed program functions. Also, the program functions can be separated out and used as building blocks to construct new programs.

4.

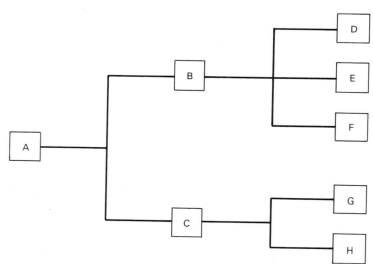

5.

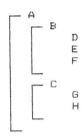

6. There is one and only one module at the top of the hierarchy. Execution begins and ends with this module.
Execution is transferred level by level "down" the hierarchy. Execution always returns to the calling module.

7.

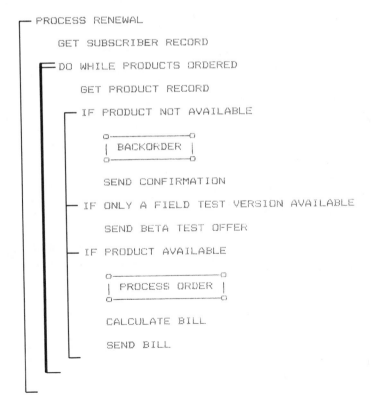

Chapter 4

1.

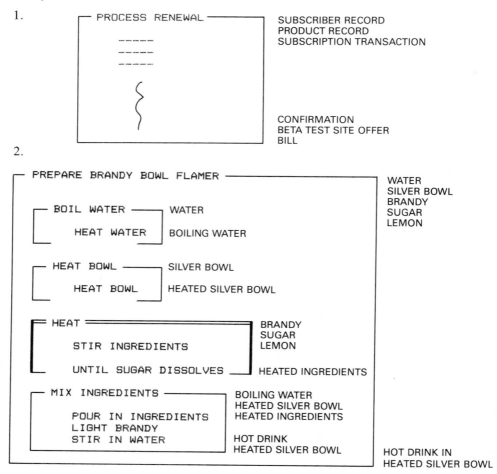

2.

Chapter 5

1. A simple data-base action is an operation applied to one instance of one record type. A compound data-base action is applied to multiple instances of one or multiple data types.

    A simple data-base action is drawn as a rectangular box on the action diagram. The name of the record type is written inside the box, and the type of operation is written to the left of the box.

READ | EMPLOYEE |

A compound data-base action is drawn as a double rectangular box on the action diagram. The name of the record type is written inside the box, and the type of operation written to the left of the box.

2.

```
┌─ PROCESS RENEWAL
│
│     READ  │ SUBSCRIBER RECORD │
│
├═ DO WHILE PRODUCTS ORDERED
│
│       READ  │ PRODUCT RECORD │
│
│    ┌─ IF PRODUCT NOT AVAILABLE
│    │
│    │     o───────────────o
│    │     │ BACKORDER │
│    │     o───────────────o
│    │
│    │     CREATE  │ CONFIRMATION │
│    │
│    ├─ IF FIELD TEST VERSION
│    │
│    │     CREATE  │ BETA TEST OFFER │
│    │
│    ├─ IF PRODUCT AVAILABLE
│    │     o───────────────o
│    │     │ ORDER PROCESS │
│    │     o───────────────o
│    │
│    │     CALCULATE BILL
│    │
│    │     CREATE  │ BILL │
│    └─
└─
```

3.

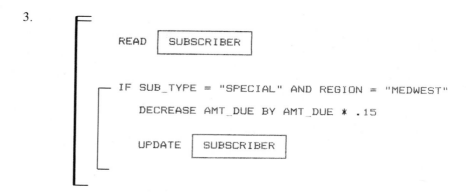

```
READ      SUBSCRIBER

IF SUB_TYPE = "SPECIAL" AND REGION = "MEDWEST"

    DECREASE AMT_DUE BY AMT_DUE * .15

UPDATE     SUBSCRIBER
```

Chapter 6

1. An action diagram written using the control constructs from the fourth-generation
language IDEAL.

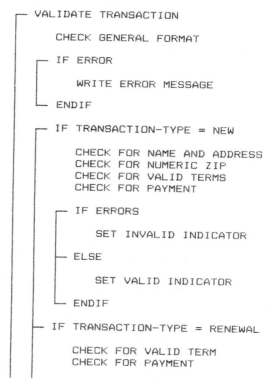

```
VALIDATE TRANSACTION

    CHECK GENERAL FORMAT

    IF ERROR

        WRITE ERROR MESSAGE

    ENDIF

    IF TRANSACTION-TYPE = NEW

        CHECK FOR NAME AND ADDRESS
        CHECK FOR NUMERIC ZIP
        CHECK FOR VALID TERMS
        CHECK FOR PAYMENT

        IF ERRORS

            SET INVALID INDICATOR

        ELSE

            SET VALID INDICATOR

        ENDIF

    IF TRANSACTION-TYPE = RENEWAL

        CHECK FOR VALID TERM
        CHECK FOR PAYMENT
```

```
        ┌── IF ERRORS
        │
        │       SET INVALID INDICATOR
        │
        ├── ELSE
        │
        │       SET VALID INDICATOR
        │
        └── ENDIF
   ├── IF TRANSACTION-TYPE = CANCEL
   │
   │       SET CANCEL FLAG
   │
   └── ENDIF
   ┌── IF INVALID INDICATOR IS SET
   │
   │       WRITE ERROR MESSAGE
   │
   └── ENDIF
```

2.
```
┌── IF RP-CT = 1
│
│       MOVE Y-COOR TO X-COOR
│
├── ELSE IF ROW-CHRYPE = 59 OR 60 OR 62 OR 69
│
│       SUBTRACT 2 FROM Y-COOR
│
├── ELSE IF FORMAT-ORIENTATION = 90
│
│       SUBTRACT 4 FROM Y-COOR
│
├── ELSE IF FORMAT-ORIENTATION = 0
│
│   ┌── IF CHRTPIC-TYPE = 52 OR NOT = STORE-TYPE
│   │
│   │       PERFORM CHANGE-TYPE
│   │
│   ├── ELSE
│   │
│   │       NEXT SENTENCE
│   │
│   └──
│
├── ELSE
│
│       NEXT SENTENCE
│
└──
```

3.

```
taskbody CHAN-NEL is
    MESS:MESSAGES;

  begin

    loop

        accept PASS(A: MESSAGES)
        do

            MESS :=A;

        endPASS;

        accept RECEIVE(A: outMESSAGES)
        do

            A := MESS;

        endRECEIVE;

    endloop;

  endCHAN_NEL;
```

INDEX

YOU'VE GOT THE METHOD.
NOW GET THE TOOL.

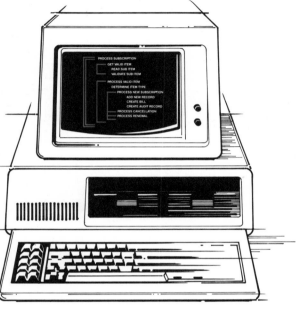

Having read his ideas about diagramming, you can clearly see why James Martin recommends *action diagrams* to best represent structured logic. Now you can get the **Action Diagrammer**™ action diagram editor for your IBM-PC* or compatible. It's the one software tool that helps you realize the productivity gains that action diagrams offer in structured programming. • Encourages clear, effective, structured thinking • Speeds up application development • Improves communication among analysts, programmers, and users • Facilitates top-down design by handling any level of logic, including systems overview and program code • Shifts development to PC's, freeing up mainframe resources and improving response time.

Buy the Action Diagrammer Software for $495

The Action Diagrammer action diagram editor is a complete structured programming tool with simple, easy-to-understand graphics. With Action Diagrammer you can rapidly create and edit action diagrams with clear representation of all structured constructs.

Action Diagrammer is applicable to almost any programming language. It produces hard copy on common IBM-PC graphics printers and on the HP7470A plotter. The software provides ample help messages and on-line documentation. And it comes with a complete, easy-to-follow user's manual.

Or Try It First with Our $25 Demo Diskette

If you're not yet sure that Action Diagrammer is for you, order our demonstration diskette first. It includes all the functions and features of Action Diagrammer and a step-by-step demonstration guide.

The demonstration diskette does limit your use to demonstration-sized diagrams. For real projects, you'll need the full version of Action Diagrammer.

Each demonstration diskette is packaged with a $25 coupon applicable to your purchase of the Action Diagrammer action diagram editor. This gives you full credit for your demonstration purchase.

Two Ways to Order

(1) CALL: 1-800-237-1977, EXT. 1100
Call our toll-free order line between 8:00 AM and 8:00 PM Monday through Friday. Credit card payments only.

(2) MAIL THE SOFTWARE ORDER FORM
Cut out or copy the form below. Complete and mail with your check or credit card information to:

> **Database Design, Inc.**
> **Order Processing Dept. P-100**
> **P.O. Box 1000 • 101 Union Street**
> **Plymouth, MI 48170**

Allow 4 weeks for delivery

*IBM-PC is a trademark of International Business Machines, Inc.

Software Order

QUANTITY	DESCRIPTION	AMOUNT
	ACTION DIAGRAMMER action diagram editor @ $495	
	Demonstration Diskette @ $25	
	4% Sales Tax on shipments to Michigan	
	Shipping & Handling ($2.50 per item)	
	TOTAL	

Shipping Information

NAME _____ TITLE _____

COMPANY _____ PHONE (____) _____

ADDRESS _____ CITY _____ STATE ____ ZIP _____

Payment Method

☐ American Express   ☐ MasterCard   ☐ Visa   ☐ Check enclosed

Card Account Number

Month   Year

Card Expiration Date Required

Customer Signature
(required for credit card orders)

National Account Program

☐ Our organization could use multiple copies of Action Diagrammer. Please send information on quantity discounts for additional copies.

Approximate number of copies _____ .

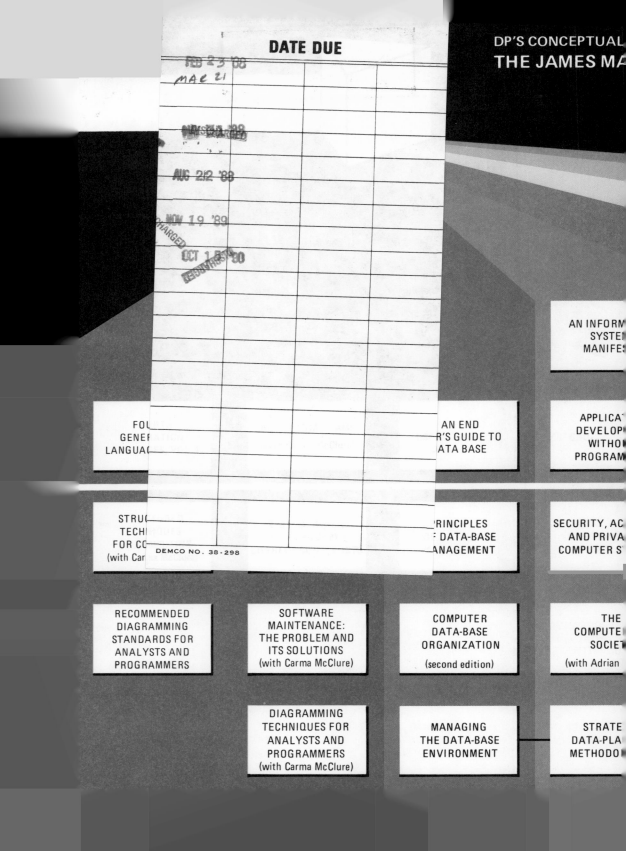

DP'S CONCEPTUAL
THE JAMES MA

AN INFORM
SYSTE
MANIFES

FOU
GENER
LANGUAG

AN END
R'S GUIDE TO
ATA BASE

APPLICA
DEVELOP
WITHO
PROGRAM

STRUC
TECH
FOR CC
(with Car

RINCIPLES
DATA-BASE
ANAGEMENT

SECURITY, AC
AND PRIVA
COMPUTER S

RECOMMENDED
DIAGRAMMING
STANDARDS FOR
ANALYSTS AND
PROGRAMMERS

SOFTWARE
MAINTENANCE:
THE PROBLEM AND
ITS SOLUTIONS
(with Carma McClure)

COMPUTER
DATA-BASE
ORGANIZATION

(second edition)

THE
COMPUTE
SOCIET

(with Adrian

DIAGRAMMING
TECHNIQUES FOR
ANALYSTS AND
PROGRAMMERS
(with Carma McClure)

MANAGING
THE DATA-BASE
ENVIRONMENT

STRATE
DATA-PLA
METHODO